MOTIVATION
AND WORK
BEHAVIOR

Hyun Jung Lee

28/9/95

McGraw-Hill Series in Management

Fred Luthans and Keith Davis, Consulting Editors

Also available from McGraw-Hill

Schaum's Outline Series in Accounting, Business, and Economics

Most outlines include basic theory, definitions, and hundreds of solved problems and supplementary problems with answers.

Titles on the current list include:

Accounting I, 3d edition
Accounting II, 3d edition
Advanced Accounting
Advanced Business Law
Advertising
Bookkeeping and Accounting
Introduction to Business
Business Law
Business Mathematics
Introduction to Business Organization and Management
Business Statistics, 2d edition
College Business Law
Contemporary Mathematics of Finance
Cost Accounting I, 2d edition
Cost Accounting II, 2d edition
Development Economics
Financial Accounting
Intermediate Accounting I, 2d edition
International Economics, 3d edition
Macroeconomic Theory, 2d edition
Managerial Accounting
Managerial Economics
Managerial Finance
Marketing
Mathematics for Economists, 2d edition
Mathematics of Finance
Microeconomic Theory, 3d edition
Money and Banking
Operations Management
Personal Finance
Personal Finance and Consumer Economics
Principles of Economics
Statistics and Econometrics
Tax Accounting

Available at your College Bookstore. A complete listing of Schaum titles may be obtained by writing to: Schaum Division
McGraw-Hill, Inc.
Princeton Road, S-1
Hightstown, NJ 08520

MOTIVATION AND WORK BEHAVIOR

FIFTH EDITION

Richard M. Steers

Graduate School of Management
University of Oregon

Lyman W. Porter

Graduate School of Management
University of California, Irvine

McGRAW-HILL, INC.

New York   St. Louis   San Francisco   Auckland   Bogotá
Caracas   Hamburg   Lisbon   London   Madrid   Mexico   Milan   Montreal
New Delhi   Paris   San Juan   São Paulo   Singapore   Sydney   Tokyo   Toronto

International Edition 1991
Exclusive rights by McGraw-Hill Book Co-Singapore for manufacture and export. This book cannot be re-exported from the country to which it is consigned by McGraw-Hill.

Copyright © 1991, 1987, 1983, 1979, 1975 by McGraw-Hill, Inc. All rights reserved. Except as permitted under the United States Copyright Act of 1976, no part of this publication may be reproduced or distributed in any form or by any means, or stored in a data base or retrieval system, without the prior written permission of the publisher.

567890BJE954

This book was set in Times Roman by the College Composition Unit
in cooperation with Monotype Composition Company.
The editors were Alan Sachs and Dan Alpert;
the production supervisor was Annette Mayeski.
The cover was designed by Karen K. Quigley.
New drawings were done by J&R Services, Inc.

Library of Congress Cataloging-in-Publication Data

Motivation and work behaviour / [compiled by] Richard M. Steers, Lyman
   W. Porter. – 5th ed.
      p.   cm. – (McGraw-Hill series in management)
   Includes index.
   ISBN 0-07-060956-X
   1. Employee motivation.   2. Psychology, Industrial.   I. Steers,
   Richard M.   II. Porter, Lyman W.   III. Series
   HF5549.5.M63M667   1991
   658.3'14–dc20   90-25537

When ordering this title use ISBN 0-07-100948-5

Printed in Singapore

ABOUT THE AUTHORS

Richard M. Steers is the Kazumitsu Shiomi Professor of Management and International Studies in the Graduate School of Management at the University of Oregon. Professor Steers is the author of 16 books and over 60 articles on topics ranging from employee motivation and performance to organizational effectiveness and comparative management. He is past president and fellow of the Academy of Management, as well as a fellow of both the American Psychology Association and the American Psychological Society. He has served on several editorial boards, including *Administrative Science Quarterly*, *Academy of Management Journal*, and *Academy of Management Review*. He holds a Ph.D. from the University of California, Irvine, and has served as a visiting professor at Irvine, Nijenrode School of Business (The Netherlands), and Oxford University (England).

Lyman W. Porter is currently Professor of Management in the Graduate School of Management at the University of California, Irvine, and was formerly dean of that school. Prior to joining UCI in 1967, he served on the faculty of the University of California, Berkeley, and as a visiting professor at Yale University. Professor Porter is a past president of the Academy of Management and in 1983 received that organization's Award for Scholarly Contributions to Management. He has also served as president of the Society of Industrial-Organizational Psychology and in 1989 received the society's Award for Distinguished Scientific Contributions. Professor Porter's major fields of interest are organizational psychology and management. His most recent book (with Lawrence McKibbin) is *Management Education and Development* (McGraw-Hill, 1988), which reports the findings of a nationwide study of business school education and postdegree management development.

CONTENTS

PREFACE

Interest in the topic of motivation in work organizations has risen steadily over the years. Some 40 years ago the level of knowledge and research in the area consisted largely of classic, though singular, efforts to set forth some basic theoretical generalizations based on only fragmentary research data. Beginning in the early 1960s, however, interest in motivational problems of organizations increased significantly. This trend has continued through the 1970s and the 1980s. It is difficult to pick up a current research journal in organizational behavior, industrial psychology, or the general area of management without finding at least one selection dealing with motivational problems at work.

Such intense interest in the field is a healthy sign that increased knowledge will be gained on this important topic. Simultaneously, however, a potential problem exists in ensuring that the various research efforts are somehow integrated and synthesized so that we can maximize our understanding of the main issues involved. This book, through its several editions, is largely the result of our concern for this potential problem. Several major theories of motivation have been advanced and tested during recent years. Moreover, while a great deal has been written concerning the relation of motivational processes to various other important organizational factors (such as job design and group dynamics), this literature also has been largely fragmentary. Our hope in organizing this book, then, is to bring together in one volume the major contemporary theories, research, and applications in the area of motivation and work behavior.

It is our belief that a thorough knowledge of motivation as it affects organizational processes requires several important inputs. First, the reader should gain a general knowledge of what is meant by the concept of motivation, as well as of historical approaches to the study of motivation. Also, the reader needs a fairly comprehensive framework for analyzing the various theories and applications that exist. We have attempted to deal with these matters in Part One of the book. Second, it is our contention that the serious student of motivation must be conversant with the major theories that exist in the field today. These theories, and the research associated with them, are described in Part Two. This part in the fifth edition focuses primarily on reinforcement and cognitive theories, particularly as they relate to the "person-environment interaction" in determining motivation.

We believe that theories alone are of little value unless the student can understand how motivational processes relate to other organizational variables. Such interrelationships are covered in detail in Part Three. In this part, a new section has been added on the cross-cultural context of motivation.

Part Four centers on motivational techniques and approaches that have direct applications to work and employment settings. Finally, Part Five attempts to review and synthesize what has been learned concerning the role of motivation in organizational settings.

Throughout the fifth edition, readings have been extensively updated. Two-thirds (24) of the selections are new in this edition.

The approach taken here is to integrate text materials with selections authored by some of the foremost scholars in the field. The major focus in the text and readings is on a blend of theoretical formulations with practical applications. Thus, the chapters (especially in Parts Three and Four) generally contain some major theoretical propositions, some research evidence relevant to the theories, and some examples of how such models have been or could be applied in existing organizations. Furthermore, each chapter contains a set of questions to stimulate discussion and analysis of the major issues.

This book is designed primarily for students of organizational behavior, industrial psychology, and general management. It also can be useful for managers who wish to gain an increased understanding of problems of work motivation. It is assumed that the reader has had some previous exposure to organizational behavior, perhaps through an introductory course. This volume attempts to build upon such knowledge and to analyze general organizational processes, using the concept of motivation as the basic unit of analysis.

We wish to express our sincere appreciation to all those who have contributed to the realization of this project in its various editions. In particular, our thanks go to Cynthia D. Fisher, University of Baltimore; Susan Jackson, New York University; and Barbara D. Mandell, Springfield College, for their helpful comments and suggestions for this fifth edition. We are also greatly indebted to Angela Tripoli for her valuable assistance in preparing the manuscript for publication. In addition, we want to thank our respective schools, the University of Oregon and the University of California, Irvine, for providing stimulating motivational environments in which to work. Finally, as in the past, a special note of appreciation is due our wives, Sheila and Meredith, for their continuing support and encouragement throughout the various editions of this book.

Richard M. Steers
Lyman W. Porter

PART ONE

INITIAL CONSIDERATIONS

CHAPTER 1

THE ROLE OF MOTIVATION IN ORGANIZATIONS

The topic of motivation at work has received considerable and sustained attention in recent years among both practicing managers and organizational researchers. One has only to ask first-level supervisors what their most taxing work problems are for evidence of the importance of the concept to management. Likewise, one can observe the large number of empirical articles relating to the topic in psychological and management journals for evidence of its importance to researchers. Several factors appear to account for the prominence of this topic as a focal point of interest.

To begin with, managers and organizational researchers cannot avoid a concern with the *behavioral* requirements of an organization. In addition to the necessity to acquire financial and physical resources, every organization needs people in order to function. More specifically, Katz and Kahn (1978) have posited that organizations have three behavioral requirements in this regard: (1) people must be attracted not only to join the organization but also to remain in it; (2) people must perform the tasks for which they are hired, and must do so in a dependable manner; and (3) people must go beyond this dependable role performance and engage in some form of creative, spontaneous, and innovative behavior at work. In other words, for an organization to be effective, according to this reasoning, it must come to grips with the motivational problems of stimulating both the decision to participate and the decision to produce at work.

A second and related reason behind the attention directed toward motivation centers around the pervasive nature of the concept itself. Motivation as a concept represents a highly complex phenomenon that affects, and is affected by, a multitude of factors in the organizational milieu. A comprehensive understanding of the way in which organizations function requires that at least some attention be directed toward the question of why people behave as they do on the job (that is, the determinants of employee work behavior *and* the ramifications of such behavior for an organization). An understanding of the topic of motivation is thus essential in order to comprehend more fully the effects of variations in other factors (such as leadership style, job redesign, and salary systems) as they relate to performance, satisfaction, and so forth.

Third, given the ever-tightening constraints placed on organizations by governmental regulations, increased foreign and domestic competition, citizens' lobbies, and the like, management has had to look for new mechanisms to increase—and in some cases just to maintain—its level of organizational effectiveness and efficiency. Much of the "slack" that organizations could depend upon in the past has disappeared in the face of these new environmental types of constraints. Because of this, management must ensure that it is deriving full potential benefit from those resources—including human resources—that it does have at its disposal. Thus, organizational effectiveness becomes to some degree a question of management's ability to motivate its employees to direct at least a reasonable effort toward the goals of the organization.

A fourth reason can be found in the nature of present and future technology required for production. As technology increases in complexity, machines tend to become necessary *yet insufficient* vehicles of effective and efficient operations. Modern technology can no longer be considered synonymous with the term "automation." Consider the example of the highly technologically based aerospace programs in the United States. While mastery of the technological aspects of engineering is a prerequisite for developing complex projects, a second and equally important ingredient is the ability of organizations to bring together thousands of employees, who often must work at peak capacity to *apply* the technology required for success. In other words, it becomes necessary for an organization to ensure that it has employees who are both capable of using and willing to use the advanced technology to achieve organizational objectives.

Finally, while organizations have for some time viewed their financial and physical resources from a long-term perspective, only recently have they begun seriously to apply this same perspective to their human resources. Many organizations are now beginning to pay increasing attention to developing their employees as future resources (a "talent bank") upon which they can draw as they grow and develop. Evidence for such concern can be seen in the recent growth of management and organization development programs, in the increased popularity of "assessment center" appraisals, in recent attention to personnel planning, and in the emergence of "human resource accounting" systems. More concern is being directed, in addition, toward stimulating employees to enlarge their job skills (through training, job design, job rotation, and so on) at both the blue-collar and the white-collar levels in an effort to ensure a continual reservoir of well-trained and highly motivated people.

In summary, then, there appear to be several reasons why the topic of motivation has been receiving increased attention by both those who study organizations and those who manage them. The old simplistic, prescriptive guidelines concerning "economic man" are simply no longer sufficient as a basis for understanding human behavior at work. New approaches and greater understanding are called for to deal with the complexities of contemporary organizations.

Toward this end, this book will attempt to assist the serious student of motivation to obtain a more comprehensive and empirically based knowledge of motivation at work. This will be done through a combination of explanatory text and readings on current theories, research, and applications in the field. Before discussing some of the more current approaches to motivation, however, some consideration is in order concerning the nature of basic motivational processes. This consideration is followed by a brief history of early psychological and managerial approaches to the topic. Finally, a conceptual framework is presented to aid in the comprehension and evaluation of the various theories and models that follow. Throughout this book, emphasis is placed on the comparative approach; that is, we are primarily concerned with similarities among—and differences between— the various theories and models rather than with the presentation and defense of one particular theory. Moreover, because of the pervasive nature of the topic, we feel that the concept of motivation can best be understood only by considering its role as it affects—and is affected by—other important variables which constitute the work environment. Thus, special emphasis is placed throughout on the study of *relationships* between major variables (for example, motivation as it relates to reward systems, group influences, and job design) rather than on the simple enumeration of facts or theories.

THE NATURE OF MOTIVATION

The term "motivation" was originally derived from the Latin word *movere,* which means "to move." However, this one word is obviously an inadequate definition for our purposes here. What is needed is a description which sufficiently covers the various aspects inherent in the process by which human behavior is activated. A brief selection of representative definitions indicates how the term has been used:

> . . . the contemporary (immediate) influences on the direction, vigor, and persistence of action. (Atkinson, 1964)
> . . . how behavior gets started, is energized, is sustained, is directed, is stopped, and what kind of subjective reaction is present in the organism while all this is going on. (Jones, 1955)
> . . . a process governing choice made by persons or lower organisms among alternative forms of voluntary activity. (Vroom, 1964)
> . . . motivation has to do with a set of independent/dependent variable relationships that explain the direction, amplitude, and persistence of an individual's behavior, holding constant the effects of aptitude, skill, and understanding of the task, and the constraints operating in the environment. (Campbell & Pritchard, 1976)

These definitions appear generally to have three common denominators which may be said to characterize the phenomenon of motivation. That is, when we dis-

cuss motivation, we are primarily concerned with (1) what energizes human behavior, (2) what directs or channels such behavior, and (3) how this behavior is
maintained or sustained. Each of these three components represents an important
factor in our understanding of human behavior at work. First, this conceptualization points to energetic forces within individuals that *drive* them to behave in
certain ways and to environmental forces that often trigger these drives. Second,
there is the notion of goal orientation on the part of individuals; their behavior is
directed *toward* something. Third, this way of viewing motivation contains a *systems orientation*; that is, it considers those forces in the individuals and in their
surrounding environments that feed back to the individuals either to reinforce
the intensity of their drive and the direction of their energy or to dissuade
them from their course of action and redirect their efforts. These three components of motivation appear again and again in the theories and research that
follow.

THE MOTIVATIONAL PROCESS: BASIC CONSIDERATIONS

Building upon this definition, we can now diagram a *general* model of the motivational process. While such a model is an oversimplification of far more complex relationships, it should serve here to represent schematically the major sets
of variables involved in the process. Later, we can add to this model to depict
how additional factors may affect human behavior at work.

The basic building blocks of a generalized model of motivation are (1) needs or
expectations, (2) behavior, (3) goals, and (4) some form of feedback. The interaction of these variables is shown in Exhibit 1. Basically, this model posits that
individuals possess in varying strengths a multitude of needs, desires, and expectations. For example, they may have a high need for affiliation, a strong desire for
additional income, or an expectation that increased effort on the job would lead
to a promotion. These "activators" are generally characterized by two phenomena. First, the emergence of such a need, desire, or expectation generally creates
a state of disequilibrium within the individuals which they will try to reduce;
hence, the energetic component of our definition above. Second, the presence of
such needs, desires, or expectations is generally associated with an anticipation
or belief that certain actions will lead to the reduction of this disequilibrium;
hence, the goal-orientation component of our definition.

EXHIBIT 1
A generalized model of the basic motivation process.
(After Dunnette & Kirchner, 1965.)

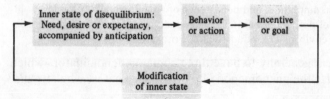

In theory, the following is presumed to be the chain of events: On the basis of some combination of this desire to reduce the internal state of disequilibrium and the anticipation or belief that certain actions should serve this purpose, individuals act or behave in a certain manner that they believe will lead to the desired goal. The initiation of this action then sets up a series of cues, either within the individuals or from their external environment, which feed information back to the individuals concerning the impact of their behavior. Such cues may lead them to modify (or cease) their present behavior, or they may reassure them that their present course of action is correct.

An example should clarify this process. Individuals who have a strong desire to be with others (that is, have a high "need for affiliation") may attempt to increase their interactions with those around them (behavior) in the hope of gaining their friendship and support (goal). On the basis of these interactions, they may eventually reach a point where they feel they have enough friends and may then direct their energies toward other goals. Or, conversely, they may receive consistent negative feedback that informs them that their behavior is not successful for goal attainment, and they may then decide to modify such behavior. In either case, we can see the important moderating effect of feedback on subsequent behavior and goals.

The general model of the motivational process appears fairly simple and straightforward. Such is not the case, however. Several complexities exist which tend to complicate the theoretical simplicity. Dunnette and Kirchner (1965) and others have identified four such complications. First, motives can really only be *inferred*; they cannot be seen. Thus, when we observe individuals putting in a great deal of overtime, we really do not know whether they are doing it because of the extra income they receive or simply because they enjoy their work. In fact, at least five reasons have been identified for why it is difficult to infer motives from observed behavior: (1) any single act may express several motives; (2) motives may appear in disguised forms; (3) several motives may be expressed through similar or identical acts; (4) similar motives may be expressed in different behavior; and (5) cultural and personal variations may significantly moderate the modes of expression of certain motives (Hilgard & Atkinson, 1967).

A second complication of the model centers around the dynamic nature of motives. Any individual at any one time usually has a host of needs, desires, and expectations. Not only do these motives change but they may also be in conflict with each other. A desire to put in extra hours at the office to "get ahead" may be in direct conflict with a desire to spend more time with one's family. Thus, given the changing nature of an individual's particular set of motives, and given their often conflicting nature, it becomes exceedingly difficult to observe or measure them with much certainty.

Third, considerable differences can exist among individuals concerning the manner in which they select certain motives over others and the intensity with which they pursue such motives. A salesperson who has a strong need for achievement may in large measure satisfy this need by one big sale and then turn his or her attention to other needs or desires. A second salesperson, however, may be spurred on by such a sale to increase his or her achievement motive and to try for an even bigger sale in the near future. Or, as found by Atkinson and Reitman (1956), a high need for achievement may be related to performance only when certain other needs (such as need for affiliation) were not aroused. In other words, it is important to realize that individual differences exist among employees which can significantly affect what they desire and how they pursue such desires.

A final complication of the model is the impact of goal attainment on subsequent motives and behavior. The intensity of certain motives (such as hunger, thirst, sex) is generally considerably reduced upon gratification. When this happens, other motives come to the forefront as primary motivating factors. However, the attainment of certain other goals may lead to an *increase* in the intensity of some motives. For example, as Herzberg, Mausner, and Snyderman (1959) and others have argued, giving a person a pay raise does not long "satisfy" the desire for more money; in fact, it may even heighten this desire. Similarly, promoting an employee to a new and more challenging job may intensify the drive to work harder in anticipation of the *next* promotion. Thus, while the gratification of certain needs, desires, and expectations may at times lead individuals to shift their focus of attention toward different motives, at other times such gratification can serve to increase the strength of the motive.

In conclusion, it must be remembered that the above description of motivational processes represents a very general model of human behavior. As will be seen in the following chapters, considerable research has been done in an attempt to more rigorously define the nature of the relationships between the major variables in this process, particularly as they relate to behavior in the work situation. We have reviewed this general model in an effort to provide a basic framework for the understanding and analysis of the more specific theories that follow. However, before proceeding with these theories, we shall first review very briefly some early psychological approaches to motivation and then follow our review with a discussion of some traditional management approaches to motivating employees.

PSYCHOLOGICAL APPROACHES TO MOTIVATION

Most psychological theories of motivation, both early and contemporary, have their roots—at least to some extent—in the principle of *hedonism*. This principle, briefly defined, states that individuals tend to seek pleasure and avoid pain. Hedonism assumes a certain degree of conscious behavior on the part of individuals whereby they make intentional decisions or choices concerning future actions. In theory, people rationally consider the behavioral alternatives available to them and act to maximize positive results and to minimize negative results. The concept of hedonism dates back to the early Greek philosophers; it later reemerged as a popular explanation of behavior in the eighteenth and nineteenth centuries, as seen in the works of such philosophers as Locke, Bentham, Mill, and Helvetius. Bentham even went so far as to coin the term "hedonic calculus" in 1789 to describe the process by which individuals calculate the pros and cons of various acts of behavior.

Toward the end of the nineteenth century, motivation theory began moving from the realm of philosophy toward the more empirically based science of psychology. As consideration of this important topic grew, it became apparent to those who attempted to use the philosophically based concept of hedonism that several serious problems existed. Vroom explained this dilemma as follows:

> There was in the doctrine no clear-cut specification of the type of events which were pleasurable or painful, or even how these events could be determined for a particular individual; nor did it make clear how persons acquired their conceptions of ways of attaining pleasure and pain, or how the source of pleasure and pain might be modified by experience. In short the hedonistic assumption has no empirical content and was untestable. Any form of behavior could be explained, after the fact, by postulating particular sources of pleasure or pain, but no form of behavior could be predicted in advance. (1964, p. 10)

In an effort to fill this void, several theories of motivation began evolving which attempted to formulate empirically verifiable relationships among sets of variables which could be used to predict behavior. The earliest such theory centered on the concept of instinct.

Instinct Theories

While not rejecting the notion of hedonism, psychologists like James, Freud, and McDougall argued that a more comprehensive explanation of behavior was necessary than simply assuming a rational person pursuing his or her own best interest. In short, they posited that two additional variables were crucial to our understanding of behavior: instinct and unconscious motivation.

Instead of seeing behavior as being highly rational, these theorists saw much of it as resulting from instinct. McDougall, writing in 1908, defined an instinct as "an inherited or innate psychophysical disposition which determines its possessor to perceive, or pay attention to, objects of a certain class, to experience an emotional excitement of a particular quality upon perceiving such an object, and to act in regard to it in a particular manner, or at least, to experience an impulse to such an action." However, while McDougall saw instinct as purposive and goal-directed, other instinct theorists, like James, defined the concept more in terms of blind and mechanical action. James (1890) included in his list of instincts the following: locomotion, curiosity, sociability, love, fear, jealousy, and sympathy. Each person was thought by James and McDougall to have such instincts in greater or lesser degree and these instincts were thought to be the prime determinants of behavior. In other words, individuals were seen as possessing automatic *predispositions* to behave in certain ways, depending on internal and external cues.

The second major concept associated with instinct theories is that of unconscious motivation. While the notion of unconscious motivation is implicit in the writings of James, it was Freud (1915) who most ardently advocated the existence of such a phenomenon. On the basis of his clinical observations, Freud argued that the most potent behavioral tendencies were not necessarily those that individuals *consciously* determined would be in their best interests. Individuals were

not always aware of all their desires and needs. Rather, such unconscious phenomena as dreams, slips of the tongue ("Freudian slips"), and neurotic symptoms were seen by Freud as manifestations of the hedonistic principle on an
unconscious level. Thus, a major factor in human motivation was seen here as
resulting from forces unknown even to the individual.

The instinct theory of motivation was fairly widely accepted during the first
quarter of this century. Then, beginning in the early 1920s, it came under increasing attack on several grounds (Hilgard & Atkinson, 1967; Morgan & King, 1966).
First, there was the disturbing fact that the list of instincts continued to grow,
reaching nearly six thousand in number. The sheer length of such a list seriously
jeopardized any attempt at parsimony in the explanation of motivation. Second,
the contention that individuals varied greatly in the strengths or intensities of
their motivational dispositions was becoming increasingly accepted among psychologists, adding a further complication to the ability of instinct theory to explain behavior fully. Third, some researchers found that at times there may be
little relation between the strengths of certain motives and subsequent behavior.
Fourth, some psychologists came to question whether the unconscious motives
as described by Freud were really instinctive or whether they were *learned* behavior. In fact, this fourth criticism formed the basis of the second "school" of
motivation theorists, who later became known as "drive" theorists.

Drive and Reinforcement Theories

Researchers who have been associated with drive theory typically base their
work on the influence that learning has on subsequent behavior. Thus, such theories have a historical component, which led Allport (1954) to refer to them as
"hedonism of the past"; that is, drive theories generally assume that decisions
concerning present behavior are based in large part on the consequences, or rewards, of past behavior. Where past actions led to positive consequences, individuals would tend to repeat such actions; where past actions led to negative consequences or punishment, individuals would tend to avoid repeating them. This
position was first elaborated by Thorndike in his "law of effect." Basing his
"law" on experimental observations of animal behavior, Thorndike posited:

> Of several responses made to the same situation, those which are accompanied or
> closely followed by satisfaction to the animal will, other things being equal, be more
> firmly connected with the situation, so that when it recurs, they will be more likely to
> occur; those which are accompanied or closely followed by discomfort to the animal
> will, other things being equal, have their connections with that situation weakened, so
> that when it recurs, they will be less likely to occur. The greater the satisfaction or
> discomfort, the greater is the strengthening or weakening of the bond. (1911, p. 244)

While this law of effect did not explain why some actions were pleasurable or
satisfying and others were not, it did go a long way toward setting forth an empirically verifiable theory of motivation. Past learning and previous "stimulus-
response" connections were viewed as the major causal variables of behavior.

The term "drive" was first introduced by Woodworth (1918) to describe the reservoir of energy that impels an organism to behave in certain ways. While Woodworth intended the term to mean a general supply of energy within an organism, others soon modified this definition to refer to a host of specific energizers (such as hunger, thirst, sex) toward or away from certain goals. With the introduction of the concept of drive, it now became possible for psychologists to predict in advance—at least in theory—not only what goals an individual would strive toward but also the strength of the motivation toward such goals. Thus, it became feasible for researchers to attempt to test the theory in a fairly rigorous fashion, a task that was virtually impossible for the earlier theories of hedonism and instinct.

A major theoretical advance in drive theory came from the work of Cannon in the early 1930s. Cannon (1939) introduced the concept of "homeostasis" to describe a state of disequilibrium within an organism which existed whenever internal conditions deviated from their normal state. When such disequilibrium occurred (as when an organism felt hunger), the organism was motivated by internal drives to reduce the disequilibrium and to return to its normal state. Inherent in Cannon's notion was the idea that organisms exist in a dynamic environment and that the determining motives for behavior constantly change, depending upon where the disequilibrium exists within the system. Thus, certain drives, or motives, may move to the forefront and then, once satisfied, retreat while other drives become paramount. This concept can be seen to a large extent in the later work of Maslow (see Chapter 2).

The first comprehensive—and experimentally specific—elaboration of drive theory was put forth by Hull. In his major work *Principles of Behavior,* published in 1943, Hull set down a specific equation to explain an organism's "impetus to respond": Effort = Drive × Habit. "Drive" was defined by Hull as an energizing influence which determined the intensity of behavior, and which theoretically increased along with the level of deprivation. "Habit" was seen as the strength of relationship between past stimulus and response (S-R). Hull hypothesized that habit strength depended not only upon the closeness of the S-R event to reinforcement but also upon the magnitude and number of such reinforcements. Thus, Hull's concept of habit draws very heavily upon Thorndike's "law of effect." Hull argued that the resulting effort, or motivational force, was a *multiplicative* function of these two central variables.

If we apply Hull's theory to an organization setting, we can use the following example to clarify how drive theory would be used to predict behavior. A person who has been out of work for some time (high deprivation level) would generally have a strong need or desire to seek some means to support himself or herself (goal). If, on the basis of *previous* experience, this person draws a close association between the securing of income and the act of taking a job, we would expect him or her to search ardently for employment. Thus, the motivation to seek employment would be seen, according to this theory, as a multiplicative function of the intensity of the need for money (drive) and the strength of the feeling that work has been associated with the receipt of money in the past (habit).

Later, in response to empirical evidence which was inconsistent with the theory, Hull (1952) modified his position somewhat. Instead of positing that behavior was wholly a function of antecedent conditions (such as past experiences), he added an incentive variable to his equation. His later formulation thus read: Effort = Drive × Habit × Incentive. This incentive factor, added in large measure in response to the attack by the cognitive theorists (see below), was defined in terms of anticipatory reactions to future goals. It was thus hypothesized that one factor in the motivation equation was the size of, or attraction to, future potential rewards. As the size of the reward varied, so too would the motivation to seek such a reward. This major revision by Hull (as amplified by Spence, 1956) brought drive theory into fairly close agreement with the third major category of motivational theories, the cognitive theories. However, while cognitive theories have generally been applied to humans, including humans at work, drive theory research has continued by and large to study animal behavior in the laboratory.

Just as drive theory draws upon Thorndike's "law of effect," so do modern reinforcement approaches (e.g., Skinner, 1953). The difference is that the former theory emphasizes an internal state (i.e., drive) as a necessary variable to take into account, while reinforcement theory does not. Rather, the reinforcement model places total emphasis on the *consequences* of behavior. Behavior initiated by the individual (for whatever reason) that produces an effect or consequence is called *operant* behavior (i.e., the individual has "operated" on the environment), and the theory deals with the contingent relationships between this operant behavior and the pattern of consequences. It ignores the inner state of the individual and concentrates solely on what happens to a person when he or she takes some action. Thus, strictly speaking, reinforcement theory is not a theory of motivation because it does not concern itself with what energizes or initiates behavior. Nevertheless, since a reinforcement approach provides a powerful means of analysis of what controls behavior (its direction and maintenance), it is typically considered in discussions of motivation and will be given prominent attention later in this book (Chapters 3 and 4).

Cognitive Theories

The third major line of development in psychological approaches to motivation is the cognitive theories. Whereas drive theories viewed behavior largely as a function of what happened in the past, cognitive theories saw motivation as a sort of "hedonism of the future." The basic tenet of this theory is that a major determinant of human behavior is the beliefs, expectations, and anticipations individuals have concerning future events. Behavior is thus seen as purposeful and goal-directed, and based on conscious intentions.

Two of the most prominent early researchers in this field were Edward Tolman and Kurt Lewin. While Tolman studied animal behavior and Lewin human behavior, both took the position that organisms make conscious decisions concerning future behavior on the basis of cues from their environment. Such a theory is largely *ahistorical* in nature, as opposed to the historical notion inherent in drive theory. Tolman (1932) argued, for example, that learning resulted more from changes in beliefs about the environment than from changes in the strengths of past habits. Cognitive theorists did not entirely reject the concept that past events may be important for present behavior, however. Lewin (1938), whose work is characterized by an ahistorical approach, noted that historical and ahistorical approaches were in some ways complementary. Past occurrences could have an impact on present behavior to the extent that they modified present conditions. For example, the past experience of a child who burned a finger on a hot stove may very likely carry over into the present to influence behavior. In general, however, the cognitive theorists posit that it is the "events of the day" that largely influence behavior; past events are important only to the extent that they affect present and future beliefs and expectations.

In general, cognitive theories, or expectancy/valence theories (also called "instrumentality" theories) as they later became known (see Chapter 4), view motivational force as a multiplicative function of two key variables: expectancies and valences. "Expectancies" were seen by Lewin (1938) and Tolman (1959) as beliefs individuals had that particular actions on their part would lead to certain outcomes. "Valence" denoted the amount of positive or negative value placed on the outcomes by an individual. Individuals were viewed as engaging in some form of choice behavior where they first determined the potential outcomes of various acts of behavior and the value they attached to each of these outcomes. Tolman (1959) refers to this as a "belief-value matrix." Next, individuals selected that mode of behavior which maximized their potential benefits. When put into equation form, such a formulation reads: Effort = Expectancy × Valence.

This conceptualization of the motivational process differs from drive theory in several respects. First, as has already been mentioned, while drive theory emphasizes past stimulus-response connections in the determination of present behavior, expectancy/valence theory stresses anticipation of response-outcome connections.

Second, as pointed out by Atkinson (1964), a difference exists between the two theories with regard to what is activated by a drive (in drive theory) or expectation (in expectancy/valence theory). In drive theory, the magnitude of the goal is seen as a source of *general* excitement; that is, it represents a nonselective influence on performance. In expectancy/valence theory, on the other hand, *positively* valent outcomes are seen as acting *selectively* to stimulate particular forms of behavior that should lead to these outcomes.

Third, a subtle difference exists concerning the nature in which outcomes and rewards acquire their positive or negative connotations. The difference has been described by Porter and Lawler as follows:

> For drive theory, this has traditionally come about through their ability to reduce the tension associated with the deprivation of certain physiologically based drives. It also states that some outcomes acquire their rewarding or adverse properties through their association with primary reinforcers. Outcomes that gain their values this way are typically referred to as secondary reinforcers. Expectancy theory has been much less explicit on this point. However, expectancy theorists seem typically to have included more than just physiological factors as determinants of valence. For example, needs for esteem, recognition, and self-actualization have been talked about by expectancy the-

ory with explaining performance. Drive theory, on the other hand, has focused largely on learning rather than performance and has not found it necessary to deal with motives like self-actualization in order to explain this learning. (1968, p. 11)

However, while several differences can thus be found between drive theories and cognitive theories. Atkinson (1964) has emphasized that the two approaches actually share many of the same concepts. Both stress the importance of some form of goal orientation; that is, both posit the existence of some reward or outcome that is desired and sought. Moreover, both theories include the notion of a learned connection between central variables; drive theory posits a learned stimulus-response association, while cognitive theories see a learned association between behavior and outcome.

Just as there has been an evolutionary process in psychological theories of motivation, so too have there been major developments and trends in the way managers in work organizations approach motivation in the work situation. With these general psychological theories in mind, we shall now shift our attention to the workplace and review some of these early managerial approaches to motivating employees. It will be noted in the discussion below that, although psychological and managerial models of motivation developed, roughly, during the same period, there are few signs of any cross-fertilization of ideas until relatively recently.

MANAGERIAL APPROACHES TO MOTIVATION

Despite the fact that large-scale, complex organizations have existed for several hundred years, managerial attention to the role of motivation in such organizations is a most recent phenomenon. Before the industrial revolution, the major form of "motivation" took the form of fear of punishment—physical, financial, or social. However, as manufacturing processes became more complex, large-scale factories emerged which destroyed many of the social and exchange relationships which had existed under the "home industries," or "putting-out," system of small manufacturing. These traditional patterns of behavior between workers and their "patron" were replaced by the more sterile and tenuous relationship between employees and their company. Thus, the industrial revolution was a revolution not only in a production sense but also in a social sense.

The genesis of this *social* revolution can be traced to several factors. First, the increased capital investment necessary for factory operation required a high degree of efficiency in order to maintain an adequate return on investment. This meant that an organization had to have an efficient work force. Second, and somewhat relatedly, the sheer size of these new operations increased the degree of impersonalization in superior-subordinate relationships, necessitating new forms of supervising people. Third, and partly as a justification of the new depersonalized factory system, the concept of social Darwinism came into vogue. In brief, this philosophy argued that no person held responsibility for other people and that naturally superior people were destined to rise in society, while naturally inferior ones would eventually be selected out of it. In other words, it was "every man for himself" in the workplace.

These new social forces brought about the need for a fairly well defined *philosophy* of management. Many of the more intrinsic motivational factors of the home industry system were replaced by more extrinsic factors. Workers—or, more specifically, "good" workers—were seen as pursuing their own best economic self-interests. The end result of this new approach in management was what has been termed the "traditional" model of motivation.

Traditional Model

This model is best characterized by the writings of Frederick W. Taylor (1911) and his associates in the scientific management school. Far from being exploitative in intent, these writers viewed scientific management as an economic boon to the worker as well as to management. Taylor saw the problem of inefficient production as a problem primarily with management, not workers. It was management's responsibility to find suitable people for a job and then to train them in the most efficient methods for their work. The workers having been thus well trained, management's next responsibility was to install a wage incentive system whereby workers could maximize their income by doing exactly what management told them to do and doing it as rapidly as possible. Thus, in theory, scientific management represented a joint venture of management and workers to the mutual benefit of both. If production problems arose, they could be solved either by altering the technology of the job or by modifying the wage incentive program.

This approach to motivation rested on several very basic contemporary assumptions about the nature of human beings. Specifically, workers were viewed as being typically lazy, often dishonest, aimless, dull, and, most of all, mercenary. To get them into the factories and to keep them there, an organization had to pay a "decent" wage, thus outbidding alternative forms of livelihood (e.g., farming). To get workers to produce, tasks were to be simple and repetitive, output controls were to be externally set, and workers were to be paid bonuses for beating their quotas. The manager's major task was thus seen as closely supervising workers to ensure that they met their production quotas and adhered to company rules. In short, the underlying motivational assumption of the traditional model was that, for a price, workers would tolerate the routinized, highly fractionated jobs of the factory. These assumptions and expectations, along with their implied managerial strategies, are summarized in Exhibit 2.

As this model became increasingly applied in organizations, several problems began to arise. To begin with, managers, in their quest for profits, began modifying the basic system. While jobs were made more and more routine and specialized (and "efficient" from a mass-production standpoint), management began putting severe constraints on the incentive system, thereby limiting worker income. Soon, workers discovered that, although their output was increasing, their wages were not (at least not proportionately). Simultaneously, fear of job security arose. As factories became more "efficient," fewer workers were needed to do the job and layoffs and terminations became commonplace. Workers responded to the situation through elaborate and covert methods of restriction of output in an attempt to optimize their incomes, while at the same time protecting

EXHIBIT 2
GENERAL PATTERNS OF MANAGERIAL APPROACHES TO MOTIVATION

Traditional model	Human relations model	Human resources model
Assumptions		
1 Work is inherently distasteful to most people. 2 What they do is less important than what they earn for doing it. 3 Few want or can handle work which requires creativity, self-direction, or self-control.	1 People want to feel useful and important. 2 People desire to belong and to be recognized as individuals. 3 These needs are more important than money in motivating people to work.	1 Work is not inherently distasteful. People want to contribute to meaningful goals which they have helped establish. 2 Most people can exercise far more creative, responsible self-direction and self-control than their present jobs demand.
Policies		
1 The manager's basic task is to closely supervise and control subordinates. 2 He or she must break tasks down into simple, repetitive, easily learned operations. 3 He or she must establish detailed work routines and procedures, and enforce these firmly but fairly.	1 The manager's basic task is to make each worker feel useful and important. 2 He or she should keep subordinates informed and listen to their objections to his or her plans. 3 The manager should allow subordinates to exercise some self-direction and self-control on routine matters.	1 The manager's basic task is to make use of "untapped" human resources. 2 He or she must create an environment in which all members may contribute to the limits of their ability. 3 He or she must encourage full participation on important matters, continually broadening subordinate self-direction and control.
Expectations		
1 People can tolerate work if the pay is decent and the boss is fair. 2 If tasks are simple enough and people are closely controlled, they will produce up to standard.	1 Sharing information with subordinates and involving them in routine decisions will satisfy their basic needs to belong and to feel important. 2 Satisfying these needs will improve morale and reduce resistance to formal authority—subordinates will "willingly cooperate."	1 Expanding subordinate influence, self-direction, and self-control will lead to direct improvements in operating efficiency. 2 Work satisfaction may improve as a "by-product" of subordinates making full use of their resources.

Source: After Miles, Porter, & Craft, 1966.

their jobs. Unionism began to rise, and the unparalleled growth and efficiency that had occurred under scientific management began to subside.

In an effort to overcome such problems, some organizations began to reexamine the simplicity of their motivational assumptions about employees and to look for new methods to increase production and maintain a steady work force. It should be pointed out, however, that the primary economic assumption of the traditional model was not eliminated in the newer approaches and that it remains a central concept of many motivational approaches today. Recent studies among both managers and workers indicate that money is a primary motivational force and that many workers will, in fact, select jobs more on the basis of salary prospects than job content. (See Chapter 11.) However, newer approaches have tended to view the role of money in more complex terms as it affects motivational force. Moreover, these newer theories argue that additional factors are also important inputs into the decision to produce. One such revisionist approach to motivation at work is the "human relations" model.

Human Relations Model

Beginning in the late 1920s, initial efforts were begun to discover why the traditional model was inadequate for motivating people. The earliest such work, carried out by Mayo (1933, 1945) and Roethlisberger and Dickson (1939), pointed the way to what was to become the human relations school of management by arguing that it was necessary to consider the "whole person" on the job. These researchers posited that the increased routinization of tasks brought about by the industrial revolution had served to drastically reduce the possibilities of finding satisfaction in the task itself. It was believed that, because of this change, workers began seeking satisfaction elsewhere (such as from their coworkers). On the basis of this early research, some managers began replacing many of the traditional assumptions with a new set of propositions concerning the nature of human beings (see Exhibit 2). Bendix (1956, p. 294) best summarized this evolution in managerial thinking by noting that the "failure to treat workers as human beings came to be regarded as the cause of low morale, poor craftsmanship, unresponsiveness, and confusion."

The new assumptions concerning the "best" method of motivating workers were characterized by a strong social emphasis. It was argued here that management had a responsibility to make employees *feel* useful and important on the job, to provide recognition, and generally to facilitate the satisfaction of workers' social needs. Attention was shifted away from the study of worker-machine relations and toward a more thorough understanding of interpersonal and group relations at work. Behavioral research into factors affecting motivation began in earnest, and morale surveys came into vogue in an attempt to measure and maintain job satisfaction. The basic ingredient that typically was *not* changed was the nature of the required tasks on the job.

The motivational strategies which emerged from such assumptions were several. First, as noted above, management felt it had a new responsibility to make workers feel important. Second, many organizations attempted to open up vertical communication channels so employees would know more about the organization and would have greater opportunity to have their opinions heard by management. Company newsletters emerged as one source of downward communication; employee "gripe sections" were begun as one source of upward communication. Third, workers were increasingly allowed to make routine decisions concerning their own jobs. Finally, as managers began to realize the existence of informal groups with their own norms and role prescriptions, greater attention was paid to employing *group* incentive systems. Underlying all four of these developments was the presumed necessity of viewing motivation as largely a social process. Supervisory training programs began emphasizing the idea that a supervisor's role was no longer simply that of a taskmaker. In addition, supervisors had to be understanding and sympathetic to the needs and desires of their subordinates. However, as pointed out by Miles (1965), the basic goal of management under this strategy remained much the same as it had been under the traditional model; that is, both strategies aimed at securing employee compliance with managerial authority.

Human Resources Models

More recently, the assumptions of the human relations model have been challenged, not only for being an oversimplified and incomplete statement of human behavior at work, but also for being as manipulative as the traditional model. These later models have been proposed under various titles, including McGregor's (1960) "Theory Y," Likert's (1967) "System 4," Schein's (1972) "Complex Man," and Miles' (1965) "Human Resources" model. We shall adopt the latter term here as being more descriptive of the underlying philosophy inherent in these newer approaches.

Human resources models generally view humans as being motivated by a complex set of interrelated factors (such as money, need for affiliation, need for achievement, desire for meaningful work). It is assumed that different employees often seek quite different goals in a job and have a diversity of talent to offer. Under this conceptualization, employees are looked upon as reservoirs of potential talent and management's responsibility is to learn how best to tap such resources.

Inherent in such a philosophy are several fairly basic assumptions about the nature of people. First, it is assumed that people want to contribute on the job. In this sense, employees are viewed as being somewhat "premotivated" to perform. In fact, the more people become involved in their work, the more meaningful the job can often become. Second, it is assumed that work does not necessarily have to be distasteful. Many of the current efforts at job enrichment and job redesign are aimed at increasing the potential meaningfulness of work by adding greater amounts of task variety, autonomy, responsibility, and so on. Third, it is argued that employees are quite capable of making significant and rational decisions affecting their work and that allowing greater latitude in employee decision making is actually in the best interests of the organization. Finally, it is assumed that this increased self-control and direction allowed on the job, plus the completion of more meaningful tasks, can in large measure determine the level of satisfaction on the job. In other words, it is generally assumed that good and meaningful performance leads to job satisfaction and not the reverse, as is assumed in the human relations model.

Certain implied managerial strategies follow naturally from this set of assumptions. In general, this approach would hold that it is management's responsibility to first understand the complex nature of motivational patterns. On the basis of such knowledge, management should attempt to determine how best to use the potential resources available to it through its work force. It should assist employees in meeting some of their own *personal* goals within the organizational context. Moreover, such a philosophy implies a greater degree of participation by employees in relevant decision-making activities, as well as increased autonomy over task accomplishment. Thus, in contrast to the traditional and human relations models, management's task is seen not so much as one of manipulating employees to accept managerial authority as it is of setting up conditions so that employees can meet their own goals at the same time as meeting the organization's goals.

In conclusion, it should be pointed out that the human resources approach to motivation has only lately begun to receive concentrated attention. Many organizations have attempted to implement one or more aspects of it, but full-scale adoptions of such models, including the multitude of strategic implications for managers, are still relatively rare. In fact, when one looks across organizations, it becomes readily apparent that all three models have their advocates, and empirical evidence supportive of a given approach can be offered in defense of one's preferred strategy. In recent years, in fact, the notion of a multiple strategy— using all three approaches at one time or another depending upon the nature of the organization, its technology, its people, and its goals and priorities—has come to be labeled a "contingency approach" to management. In effect, a contingency perspective allows one to dispense with the unlikely assumption that a single approach will be equally effective under any and all circumstances, and rather substitutes an emphasis on diagnosis of the situation to determine which approach will be more useful and appropriate under the *particular* circumstances.

A FRAMEWORK FOR ANALYSIS

Before proceeding to a consideration of some of the more highly developed or widely accepted contemporary theories of motivation, we should place this complex topic within some meaningful conceptual framework. Such a framework would serve as a vehicle not only for organizing our thoughts concerning human behavior at work but also for evaluating the ability of each of the theories that follows to deal adequately with all the factors in the work situation. In other words, it should provide a useful beginning for later analyses by pointing to several important factors to look for in the theoretical approaches that follow.

The conceptual model we wish to pose here (after Porter & Miles, 1974) consists of two parts. First, it assumes that motivation is a complex phenomenon that can best be understood within a multivariate framework: that is, *several* important—and quite often distinct—factors must be taken into account when explaining motivational processes. Second, the model proposed here argues that these motivationally relevant factors must be viewed within a systems framework; we must concern ourselves with interrelationships and interactive effects among the various factors. It is our belief, then, that a full comprehension of the intricacies of human behavior at work requires the student of motivation to consider both parts of this equation: a multivariate conceptual approach and an integrating systems framework. Let us briefly examine each part of this proposed framework for analysis.

Multivariate Conceptual Approach

If motivation is concerned with those factors which energize, direct, and sustain human behavior, it would appear that a comprehensive theory of motivation at work must address itself to at least three important sets of variables which constitute the work situation. First, some consideration must be given to the characteristics of the individual; second, some thought should be directed toward the behavioral implications of the required job tasks; and third, some concern should be shown for the impact of the larger organizational environment. These three sets of variables, along with examples of each, are depicted in Exhibit 3.

Characteristics of the Individual   The natural starting point for discussing any theory of motivation is the nature of the individual. We are concerned with what the employee *brings to* the work situation. Considerable research (see, for example, Atkinson, 1964; Vroom, 1964) has demonstrated that differences in individuals can at times account for a good deal of the variance in effort and performance on a job. Thus, when we examine the factors constituting the motivational force equation, we must ask how large an input is made by these variations within people themselves. At least three major categories of individual difference characteristics have been shown to affect the motivational process: interests, attitudes, and needs.

EXHIBIT 3
VARIABLES AFFECTING THE MOTIVATIONAL PROCESS IN ORGANIZATIONAL SETTINGS

I. Individual characteristics	II. Job characteristics (examples)	III. Work environment characteristics
1 Interests	Types of intrinsic rewards	1 Immediate work environment
2 Attitudes		• Peers
	Degree of autonomy	• Supervisor(s)
• Toward self		
• Toward job	Amount of direct	2 Organizational actions
• Toward aspects of the work situation	performance feedback	• Reward practices
		• Systemwide rewards
	Degree of variety in tasks	• Individual rewards
3 Needs		• Organizational climate
• Security		
• Social		
• Achievement		

Note: These lists are not intended to be exhaustive, but are meant to indicate some of the more important variables influencing employee motivation.
Source: After Porter & Miles, 1974.

"Interests" refers to the direction of one's attention. It appears likely that the nature of an employee's interest would affect both the manner and the extent to which external stimuli (like money) would affect behavior. Consider the example of two people working side by side on the same job and earning identical salaries. Person A is highly interested in the work; person B is not. In this example, person A can be seen as "self-motivated" to some degree because he or she is pursuing a central interest (his or her work), and we would expect this person to derive considerable satisfaction from the activity. If person A were offered a pay raise to take a less interesting job, he or she would be faced with making a decision on whether to keep the more interesting job or to earn more money, and it is not inconceivable that the intrinsic rewards of the present job would be motivation enough *not* to accept the transfer. Person B, however, who is not interested in the work, has no such conflict of choice in our simplified example; there is no motivation to stay on the present job and the added income of the new job could be a strong incentive for change. Some empirical research exists in support of our hypothetical example. Several studies have shown that an employee's motivation to participate (stay on the job) is to a large extent determined by the degree of fit between his or her vocational interests and the realities of the job. Thus, interests may be considered one factor that individuals generally bring to the organization that, at least to some extent, can affect how they behave at work.

In addition to interests, employees' attitudes or beliefs may also play an important role in their motivation to perform. Individuals who are very dissatisfied with their jobs, or with their supervisor, or any number of other things, may have little desire to put forth much effort. Several theories of motivation have encompassed the notion of attitudes as they relate to performance behavior at work. For example, Korman (1970, 1971) has proposed a theory of motivation centering around one's attitudes about oneself (that is, one's self-image). This theory posits that individuals attempt to behave in a fashion consistent with their own self-image. If employees see themselves as failures on the job, they will not put forth much effort and their resulting performance will probably be poor. Such action will then reinforce the negative self-image. Two important points can be made here. First, various attitudes (in this case, attitudes about oneself) can play an important role in motivational force to perform. Second, in this example, there is a specific implied managerial strategy to improve employee effort: the manager should attempt to modify the employees' self-image. If the employees in our example were proud to work for the XYZ Company and if they saw themselves as effective contributors to the company's goals, they would, in theory, be more likely to perform at a higher level.

The individual characteristic that has received the most widespread attention in terms of motivation theory and research is the concept of "needs." A need may be defined as an internal state of disequilibrium which causes individuals to pursue certain courses of action in an effort to regain internal equilibrium. For example, individuals who have a high need for achievement might be motivated to engage in competitive acts with others so they can "win," thereby satisfying this need. The theories of Maslow and of McClelland and Atkinson use this concept of need as the basic unit of analysis. While further discussion of these types of theories is reserved for the following chapter, suffice it to say that variations in human needs can be significant factors in the determination of effort and performance.

Characteristics of the Job   A second set of variables to be considered when viewing the motivational process involves those factors relating to the attributes of an individual's job. We are concerned here with what an employee *does* at work. Factors such as the variety of activities required to do the job, the significance of the tasks, and the type of feedback one receives as a consequence of performing the job all have a role to play in motivation. Later in the book (Chapter 10) a model developed by Hackman and Oldham (1976) will be presented that attempts to provide a theoretical explanation of how these types of job-related variables interact to affect motivation and performance. Other parts of that chapter will provide additional evidence on the role that job design changes and employee involvement can play in determining employee behavior. In effect, whether jobs are designed well or poorly (from either the organization's or the employee's point of view), they are crucial in their impact on the motivational process in the work setting.

Characteristics of the Work Environment   The final set of variables under our analytical framework that appears to be relevant to the motivational process is concerned with the nature of the organizational, or work, environment. Work environment factors can be divided for our purposes into two major categories: those associated with the immediate work environment (the work group), and those associated with the larger problem of organizationwide actions. Both categories, however, focus primarily on *what happens to* the employee at work.

As indicated in Exhibit 3, there are at least two major factors in the immediate work environment that can affect work behavior. The first is the quality of peer-group interactions. Research dating from the Hawthorne studies (Roethlisberger & Dickson, 1939) indicates that peer-group influence can significantly influence an employee's effort. Such influence can occur at both ends of the productivity continuum: peers can exert pressure on "laggards" to contribute their fair share of output, or they can act to curb the high productivity of the "rate-buster." These considerations are discussed in Chapter 5. Similarly, supervisory or leadership style can influence effort and performance under certain circumstances. Immediate supervisors can play an important role in motivation because of their control over desired rewards (such as bonuses, raises, feedback) and because of their central role in the structuring of work activities. In other words, supervisors have considerable influence over the ability or freedom of employees to pursue their own personal goals on the job.

The second major category of work environment variables—organizationwide actions—are concerned with several factors which are common throughout the organization and are largely determined by the organization itself. Such factors would include both systemwide rewards (like fringe benefits) and individual rewards (such as overall salary system and allocation of status). Moreover, the emergent organizational climate that pervades the work environment would also fall into this category. Factors such as openness of communication, perceived relative emphasis on rewards versus punishment, degree of interdepartmental cooperation, and so forth, may at times influence individuals' decisions to produce on the job.

Interactive Effects

The foregoing discussion makes it apparent that a multitude of variables throughout the organizational milieu can be important inputs into the motivational force equation. Such a conclusion forces us to take a broad perspective when we attempt to understand or explain why employees behave as they do at work. However, this simple enumeration of motivationally relevant factors fails to recognize how these variables may interact with one another within a systems type of framework to determine work behavior. In other words, the second half of our conceptual framework stresses the fact that we must consider motivational models from a dynamic perspective. For example, an individual may have a strong desire to perform well on the job, but he or she may lack a clear understanding of his or her proper role. The employee may thus waste or misdirect effort and thereby fail to receive expected rewards. Similarly, an employee may truly want to perform at a high level, but simply lack the necessary ability for good performance on his or her particular job. The important point here is that, when viewing various approaches to motivation, it becomes clear that one must be aware of the interactive or "system" dynamics between major sets of variables that may influence resulting effort and performance.

Each of the theories of work motivation that will be considered in the following chapters has focused on *at least* one of these three major factors: the individual, the job, or the organizational environment. Several of the theories have included more than one factor. Moreover, some of the more highly developed models have placed such variables within a systems framework and have studied the interactive effects between the major sets of variables. Hopefully, the framework for analysis presented here will aid in understanding the pervasive nature of motivation and in evaluating the adequacy of each of the major theories to explain human behavior at work.

A note of caution is in order, however. When evaluating the theories and the research evidence that follow, the student of motivation must determine whether it is helpful to try to find the "one best way" to motivate individuals in the work situation or whether different approaches may be more or less relevant, depending upon the uses for which the theory is employed. That is, as with theories of management in general, both practicing managers and organizational researchers must decide whether they want to search for an ultimate universal theory of motivation which can be applied in all types of situations, or whether they want to adopt a contingency approach and select that theory which appears most pertinent to the specific problem at hand. In this connection, it is well to keep in mind that many of the theories, concepts, and approaches that will be discussed throughout the book are in fact complementary to one another, and therefore the search for understanding and for practical application is as much one of trying to seek out integration as it is one of making choices.

PLAN OF THE BOOK

This book is divided into five parts. Part One has consisted of the introductory materials presented in this chapter. In Part Two, we will systematically examine current theories focusing on employee motivation. The three chapters making up Part Two are divided into theories that focus on the role of the person in motivation, theories that emphasize the environmental determinants of motivation and, finally, theories that stress the interrelationship between people and their environments as these factors jointly influence motivation and performance.

On the basis of this review of current theories, in Part Three we look at several central issues in work motivation. Included here are such topics as social influences, job attitudes, absenteeism and turnover, and cross-cultural considerations as each relates to motivation. This is followed, in Part Four, by a discussion of several of the more common techniques on motivation. Included here are the topics of goal-setting, work design, reward systems, and communication and feedback techniques. Such techniques are commonly used by managers interested in increasing employee motivation levels through changes in either organization design, management practices, or both. Finally, Part Five presents an integrative summary, including some concluding observations and implications for management.

In all, we present 36 articles on various aspects of employee motivation, written by some of the most respected researchers in the field. Some of these articles are more theoretical, while others are more applied. Some argue in support of one particular theory or technique, while others suggest more eclectic approaches. Taken together, however, these articles should provide a comprehensive portrait of the dynamics of employee motivation in the contemporary world of work.

REFERENCES

Allport, G. W. The historical background of modern social psychology. In G. Lindzey (Ed.), *Handbook of social psychology*. Cambridge, Mass.: Addison-Wesley, 1954.

Atkinson, J. W. *An introduction to motivation*. Princeton, N.J.: Van Nostrand, 1964.

Atkinson, J. W., & Reitman, W. R. Performance as a function of motive strength and expectancy of goal attainment. *Journal of Abnormal Social Psychology*. 1956, **53,** 361–366.

Bendix, R. *Work and authority in industry*. New York: Wiley, 1956.

Campbell, J. P., & Pritchard, R. D. Motivation theory in industrial and organizational psychology. In M. D. Dunnette (Ed.), *Handbook of industrial and organizational psychology*. Chicago: Rand McNally, 1976.

Cannon, W. B. *The wisdom of the body*. New York: Norton, 1939.

Cofer, C. N., & Appley, M. H. *Motivation: Theory and research*. New York: Wiley, 1964.

Dunnette, M. D., & Kirchner, W. K. *Psychology applied to industry.* New York: Appleton-Century-Crofts, 1965.

Freud, S. The unconscious. In *Collected papers of Sigmund Freud,* Vol. IV (J. Rivière, Trans.). London: Hogarth, 1949. (First published in 1915.)

Hackman, J. R., & Oldham, G. R. Motivation through the design of work: Test of a theory. *Organizational Behavior and Human Performance,* 1976, **16,** 250–279.

Herzberg, F. Mausner, B., & Snyderman, B. B. *The motivation to work.* New York: Wiley, 1959.

Hilgard, E. R., & Atkinson, R. C. *Introduction to psychology.* New York: Harcourt, Brace & World, 1967.

Hull, C. L. *Principles of behavior.* New York: Appleton-Century-Crofts, 1943.

Hull, C. L. *A behavior system: An introduction to behavior theory concerning the individual organism.* New Haven, Conn.: Yale University Press, 1952.

James, W. *The principles of psychology,* Vols. I and II. New York: Henry Holt, 1890.

Jones, M. R. (Ed). *Nebraska symposium on motivation.* Lincoln: University of Nebraska Press, 1955.

Katz, D., & Kahn, R. *The social psychology of organizations.* New York: Wiley, 1978.

Korman, A. K. Toward an hypothesis of work behavior. *Journal of Applied Psychology,* 1970, **54,** 31–41.

Korman, A. K. Expectancies as determinants of performance. *Journal of Applied Psychology,* 1971, **55,** 218–222.

Lewin, K. *The conceptual representation and the measurement of psychological forces.* Durham, N.C.: Duke University Press, 1938.

Likert, R. *The human organization.* New York: McGraw-Hill, 1967.

March, J. G., & Simon, H. A. *Organizations.* New York: Wiley, 1958.

Mayo, E. *The human problems of an industrial civilization.* New York: Macmillan, 1933.

Mayo, E. *The social problems of an industrial civilization.* Cambridge, Mass.: Harvard University Press, 1945.

McDougall, W. *An introduction to social psychology.* London: Methuen, 1908.

McGregor, D. *The human side of enterprise.* New York: McGraw-Hill, 1960.

Miles, R. E. Human relations or human resources? *Harvard Business Review,* 1965, **43**(4), 148–163.

Miles, R. E., Porter, L. W., & Craft, J. A. Leadership attitudes among public health officials. *American Journal of Public Health,* 1966, **56,** 1990–2005.

Morgan, C. T., & King, R. A. *Introduction to psychology.* New York: McGraw-Hill, 1966.

Opsahl, R. L., & Dunnette, M. D. The role of financial compensation in industrial motivation. *Psychological Bulletin,* 1966, **66,** 94–118.

Porter, L. W., & Lawler, E. E., III. *Managerial attitudes and performance.* Homewood, Ill.: Irwin, 1968.

Porter, L. W., & Miles, R. E. Motivation and management. In J. W. McGuire (Ed.), *Contemporary management: Issues and viewpoints.* Englewood Cliffs, N.J.: Prentice-Hall, 1974.

Roethlisberger, F., & Dickson, W. J. *Management and the worker.* Cambridge, Mass.: Harvard University Press, 1939.

Schein, E. *Organizational psychology.* Englewood Cliffs, N.J.: Prentice-Hall, 1972.

Skinner, B. F. *Science and human behavior.* New York: Macmillan, 1953.

Spence, K. W. *Behavior theory and conditioning.* New Haven, Conn.: Yale University Press, 1956.

Taylor, F. W. *Scientific management.* New York: Harper, 1911.

Thorndike, E. L. *Animal intelligence: Experimental studies*. New York: Macmillan, 1911.

Tolman, E. C. *Purposive behavior in animals and men*. New York: Appleton-Century-Crofts, 1932.

Tolman, E. C. Principles of purposive behavior. In S. Koch (Ed.), *Psychology: A study of a science,* Vol. 2. New York: McGraw-Hill, 1959.

Vroom, V. H. *Work and motivation*. New York: Wiley, 1964.

Woodworth, R. S. *Dynamic psychology*. New York: Columbia University Press, 1918.

QUESTIONS FOR DISCUSSION

1 Exactly what is meant by the term "motivation"?

2 Describe the basic motivational process.

3 What similarities are there in the development of psychological theories of motivation compared with the development of managerial theories? What differences?

4 What are the basic differences between drive or reinforcement models of motivation and cognitive models? Which approach seems more applicable to motivation in work settings?

5 What is the real difference between the human resources model and the earlier human relations model?

6 What value is there from a managerial standpoint in taking a comprehensive approach to motivational problems, as suggested in this chapter?

7 Why do many people casually equate motivation with performance? Can you think of situations where the two variables would be virtually equivalent?

PART **TWO**

THEORETICAL
APPROACHES
TO MOTIVATION

THE "PERSON" IN MOTIVATION

As we emphasized in Chapter 1 (and as outlined in Exhibit 3 of that chapter), "a comprehensive theory of motivation at work must address itself to at least three important sets of variables which constitute the work situation"—the characteristics of the individual, the job, and the work environment—and their interaction. Since most motivational theories have concentrated on the first (the individual) and third (the environment) categories of these factors and their interaction, Part Two of this book focuses on them. Detailed consideration of the other major variable, the job, will be reserved for Chapter 10, "Work Design."

Here in Chapter 2, we cover the "person" in motivation, that is, what the individual *brings to* the work situation. Primarily, this means that the focal point will be the concept of human *needs* because this is the characteristic that has received the most attention from motivational theorists. Individuals' needs—"internal states of disequilibrium"—are a critical determinant of *what* people want from the environment. Therefore, theories of human needs have been termed "content theories" of motivation, as distinct from "process theories," which attempt to answer questions of *how* motivation operates. In short, need theories help explain motivational differences among individuals when they encounter similar work conditions and circumstances.

In the first selection in this chapter, Cherrington briefly reviews the historical background of need theories, then discusses in detail two of the most prominent—and, certainly, influential—of these types of theories: Maslow's need hierarchy and McClelland's learned needs. As Cherrington points out, Maslow's need hierarchy theory has proved to be exceptionally difficult to test in any comprehensive and scientific manner. Nevertheless, it has served as a useful framework for many managers in organizational settings to think about how individual employees may differ in what they want to attain from work. The notion of some sort of a hierarchy of needs—even if the categories and ordering of needs are not necessarily as Maslow postulates—provides a potentially helpful way to understand at least some aspects of human motivation. Later refinements of Maslow's theory, such as Alderfer's ERG theory (as described in Cherrington's article), have provided additional insights as to how the needs hierarchy concept may be useful in analyzing motivation in work settings.

The Cherrington selection also discusses another needs theory that has received wide attention: McClelland's learned needs. McClelland and his colleagues have placed particular emphasis on the fact that individuals can—and do—acquire "behavioral predispositions" (i.e., learned needs) by virtue of their particular interactions with their environment. Once acquired, such needs can, according to McClelland, have a significant and persisting impact on a person's behavior. In other words, the fact that a need is "learned" does not make it weak or uninfluential in motivation. In contrast to Maslow, McClelland's theoretical approach does not concern itself with any ordering or hierarchy among needs, but instead concentrates on how learned needs are acquired, how they can be changed, and, especially, how they affect an individual's behavior. The most frequently studied of these learned needs—the need for achievement—is obviously directly relevant for motivation in work situations, and thus it is important to understand how it is developed and how it operates. Indeed, given today's intensely competitive business climate worldwide, one can speculate about how the typical level of need for achievement among individuals across various nations and cultures may be affecting the relative economic success of different countries.

The second article in this chapter, by Deci and Ryan, provides a detailed explanation of the concept of "intrinsic motivation." As defined by these authors, "intrinsic motivation is based on the innate, organismic needs for competence and self-determination." This definition highlights the idea that any consideration of intrinsic motivation fundamentally involves a consideration of needs—in this case, the two particular needs of competence and self-determination. The senior author of this selection, Deci, has been a pioneer in studies that attempt to separate the operation of intrinsic motivation from that of extrinsic, or environmentally determined, motivation. The issue is not that extrinsic motivation does not exist or is not powerful. Rather, the issue for Deci is what is the impact of intrinsic motivation *irrespective* of factors external to the individual. Therefore, for our purposes in this chapter, the focus, as with need theories, is on what the person *brings to* the work situation independently of what happens subsequently in that situation. For Deci and Ryan, the central core of intrinsic motivation is the individual's "capacity to choose and to have those choices, rather than [external factors], be the determinants of one's actions." Thus, intrinsic motivation is inferred "when a person does [an] activity in the absence of a reward contingency or control." To the extent that such behavior occurs, it implies that any complete understanding of behavior in organizational and work settings must take into account the nature of intrinsic *as well as* extrinsic motivation.

Need Theories of Motivation

David J. Cherrington

Content theories of motivation describe the psychological constructs within individuals that energize and sustain behavior. In other words, content theories examine the specific things inside individuals that motivate them.

EARLY THEORIES OF MOTIVATION

The most prominent historical views of human nature were based on the assumption that people are essentially rational beings with conscious desires and capacities to fulfill these desires. These ideas were central to the thinking of ancient philosophers such as Aristotle and Plato, medieval philosophers like Thomas Aquinas, and more recent philosophers such as Descartes, Hobbes, and Spinoza.

For many years the idea of a person's "will" played a large role in explaining human behavior. Will was considered to be one of the faculties of the mind, similar to thought and feelings. "Strong-willed" and "will-power" are current concepts derived from the early idea that people can consciously determine how they are going to behave. The implication of this idea is that to get people to change their behavior, you have to convince them to change their will, as expressed in this proverb: "A man convinced against his will is of the same opinion still." Since people had the capacity to control their own will, they were responsible for their actions.[1] In spite of all that was written about it, however, the concept of will was never very adequate for explaining human behavior. The failure of the will to assist in predicting and describing behavior finally gave way to other conceptualizations of motivation.

Hedonism

An important construct in many early philosophical writings was hedonism, or hedonistic calculus. The ancient Greek philosophers used this principle as the core concept to explain what motivated human behavior. It served as a philosophical foundation for several centuries and was especially popular in the eighteenth and nineteenth centuries among such philosophers as John Locke, Jeremy Bentham, and John Stuart Mill.[2]

Basically, the principle of hedonism states that individuals seek pleasure and avoid pain—they pursue things that bring comfort and satisfaction and avoid things that bring pain and discomfort. Hedonism was a very simple principle that focused specifically on physical gratification and pain.

The basic principle of hedonism is still found in many of our current theories of motivation; however, it is far too simplistic to adequately explain the complexity

From D. J. Cherrington, *Organizational behavior*. Needham Heights, Mass.: Allyn & Bacon, 1989. All rights reserved.

of human behavior. Hedonism fails to explain why people engage in activities that are physically unpleasant. For example, this simple principle cannot explain why the early Puritans rejected physical comforts and intentionally pursued an ascetic life of arduous physical toil.

Instinct Theory

Another early explanation for behavior was based on a theory of instincts. According to Charles Darwin's theory of evolution, certain intelligent actions were inherited. The simplest of these were reflexes such as the sucking reflex of newborn infants. More complex behaviors, which were also more variable and adapted by individuals to the circumstances, were called instincts. Darwin believed instincts arose through natural selection and were necessary for survival.

Around the turn of the century, several psychologists used instincts as part of their theories of motivation, especially William James, William McDougall, and Sigmund Freud. James defined an instinct as the ability to perform an action without the foresight of knowing what the act would produce and without having previously learned how to perform it. Instincts were natural, unlearned behaviors, and James believed that an important difference between humans and other mammals was that humans possessed a great many more instincts than other mammals.[3] McDougall claimed that instincts were inherited, purposive, goal-seeking tendencies which explained how individuals perceived objects and were aroused to take action regarding them. In 1908, McDougall published a list of twelve instincts: flight, repulsion, curiosity, cognacity, self-abasement, self-assertion, parenting, reproduction, hunger, gregariousness, acquisitiveness, and constructiveness.[4] Freud's writings were largely centered around two instincts, aggression and sex, although toward the end of his career when he was suffering from cancer of the mouth, he also wrote extensively about the death instinct.[5]

During the first quarter of this century, instincts were used extensively to explain behavior. In the 1920s, however, instincts were discredited for two reasons. First, the list of instincts became both unwieldy and unreasonable. The list of instincts totalled nearly 6,000, including an "instinct to avoid eating apples in one's own orchard." The most significant attack against instincts, however, came from a group of behaviorists and cultural anthropologists who began to show that these behaviors were learned rather than inherited. Today, instincts are no longer used to explain behavior except for some animal behaviors, a few innate responses of newborn infants, and such actions as the knee-jerk response to taping the patella tendon, blinking in response to tapping the eyebrow, and head turning in response to touching the cheek. However, these actions are generally called reflex responses rather than instincts.

Needs

After instincts were discredited, explanations for behavior shifted to the notion of needs. A need was defined as an internal state of disequilibrium or deficiency which has the capacity to energize or trigger a behavioral response. The cause of

EXHIBIT 1
Relationship between needs and motivated behavior.

the deficiency could be physiological, such as hunger; psychological, such as a need for power; or sociological, such as a need for social interaction. The presence of a need motivates an individual to action to restore a state of equilibrium, as shown in Exhibit 1. A basic assumption of all need theories is that when need deficiencies exist, individuals are motivated to action to satisfy them.

One of the earliest theories of needs was the manifest need theory proposed by Henry A. Murray.[6] Murray believed that needs are mostly learned rather than inherited and are activated by cues from the external environment. For example, an employee who has a high need for affiliation will pursue that need by associating with others only when the environmental conditions are appropriate. Only then would the need be *manifest*. When the need was not cued, the need was said to be *latent* or not activated.

Murray identified a wide range of needs that people supposedly acquire to one degree or another through interaction with their environment. Murray first developed a list of fifteen needs that were classified as viscerogenic (primary) and psychogenic (secondary). The needs for food, water, sex, urination, defecation, and lactation, all associated with physiological functioning, are examples of Murray's viscerogenic needs. Murray's psychogenic needs include abasement, achievement, affiliation, aggression, autonomy, deference, dominance, and power.

Murray's need categories attempted to focus on specific, relatively narrow need-related issues and a separate need was created for almost every human behavior. Murray's list of needs was not derived from empirical research but from his personal observations and clinical experience. Periodically he added additional needs to his list, and the length of the list increased with his career.

MASLOW'S NEED HIERARCHY

Abraham Maslow was a clinical psychologist whose theory of motivation was part of a larger theory of human behavior. Maslow was a humanist who was deeply concerned about the dignity and worth of individuals. He frequently talked of the differences between healthy and unhealthy individuals, and believed that individuals had a positive capacity to improve the quality of their lives. His theories of behavior emerged from his clinical experiences as he attempted to sift and integrate the ideas of other leading psychologists.[7]

Hierarchy of Needs

Based on his experience as a counselor, Maslow formulated a theory that explained human behavior in terms of a hierarchy of five general needs. He believed everyone possessed a common set of five universal needs that were ordered in a hierarchy of importance from the lowest-level basic needs through the highest-order needs.

1 *Physiological needs.* Physiological needs were the most basic needs in Maslow's hierarchy and included needs that must be satisfied for the person to survive, including food, water, oxygen, sleep, sex, and sensory satisfaction.

2 *Safety and security needs.* If the physiological needs are relatively satisfied, Maslow claimed that safety and security needs would emerge. These needs include a desire for security, stability, dependency, protection, freedom from fear and anxiety, and a need for structure, order, and law. Threats of physical harm, assault, tyranny, or wild animals prevent individuals from satisfying their safety needs and cause them to focus their energies almost exclusively on eliminating these threats.

3 *Social needs.* Originally Maslow referred to this need as the need for belongingness and love. Social needs include the need for emotional love, friendship, and affectionate relationships with people in general, but especially a spouse, children, and friends. Individuals who are unable to satisfy this need will feel pangs of loneliness, ostracism, and rejection.

4 *Ego and esteem.* The need for ego and esteem includes the desire for self-respect, self-esteem, and for the esteem of others, and may be focused either internally or externally. When focused internally, the esteem needs include a desire for strength, achievement, adequacy, mastery, confidence, independence, and freedom. When focused externally this need consists of a desire for reputation or prestige, status, fame and glory, dominance, recognition, attention, importance, dignity, and appreciation.

5 *Self-actualization.* The highest need in Maslow's hierarchy was for self-actualization, which refers to the needs for self-realization, continuous self-development, and the process of becoming all that a person is capable of becoming.

According to Maslow, these five needs are arranged in a hierarchy of importance which he called *prepotency*. Higher-level needs are not important and are not manifest until lower-level needs are satisfied. Once lower-level needs are satisfied, needs at the next highest level emerge and influence behavior. The levels of the need hierarchy are not rigidly separated but overlap to some extent. Thus, it is possible for a higher-level need to emerge before a lower-level need is completely satisfied. In fact, Maslow estimated that average working adults have satisfied about 85 percent of their physiological needs, 70 percent of their safety needs, 50 percent of their social needs, 40 percent of their self-esteem needs, and

EXHIBIT 2
APPLYING MASLOW'S NEED HIERARCHY

Need levels	General rewards	Organizational factors
1 Physiological	Food, water, sex, sleep	a Pay b Pleasant working conditions c Cafeteria
2 Safety	Safety, security, stability, protection	a Safe working conditions b Company benefits c Job security
3 Social	Love, affection, belongingness	a Cohesive work group b Friendly supervision c Professional associations
4 Esteem	Self-esteem, self-respect, prestige, status	a Social recognition b Job title c High status job d Feedback from the job itself
5 Self-actualization	Growth, advancement, creativity	a Challenging job b Opportunities for creativity c Achievement in work d Advancement in the organization

10 percent of their self-actualization needs. Although Maslow never collected data to support these estimates, numerous studies have found that lower-level needs are more satisfied than higher-level needs.[8]

Maslow's theory has been widely adopted by organizations and is frequently used as the foundation for organizational development programs such as participative management, job enrichment, and quality of work-life projects. According to his theory, an organization must use a variety of factors to motivate behavior since individuals will be at different levels of the need hierarchy. A list of the general rewards and organizational factors used to satisfy different needs is illustrated in Exhibit 2.

In Maslow's need hierarchy the effects of money are not clear. The needs most directly related to money are physiological and security needs since money contributes significantly to securing a comfortable and safe environment. Money is usually considered relatively unimportant for satisfying higher-level needs, and the general belief is that most American workers are mainly concerned about higher-level needs. Therefore, according to Maslow's need hierarchy, money is not considered an effective motivator.

Self-Actualization

One of Maslow's unique contributions to motivation theory was his description of self-actualization. Self-actualization refers to the process of developing our true potential as individuals to the fullest extent, and expressing our skills, talents, and emotions in the most personally fulfilling manner. Self-actualization is a process, not an end state—individuals do not become self-actualized in the sense

EXHIBIT 3
CHARACTERISTICS OF SELF-ACTUALIZING PEOPLE

1 Superior perception of reality
2 Increased acceptance of self, of others, and of nature
3 Increased spontaneity
4 Increased in problem-centering
5 Increased detachment and desire for privacy
6 Increased autonomy and resistance to restrictive cultural norms
7 Greater freshness of appreciation and richness of emotional reaction
8 Greater frequency of peak experiences
9 Increased identification with the human race
10 Improved interpersonal relations
11 More democratic values and character structure
12 Greatly increased creativity
13 A carefully designed system of values

that they have finally reached an ultimate goal. Instead they are continually in the process of becoming more and more of what they are uniquely capable of becoming.

In his later writings Maslow suggested that the need for self-actualization could not be gratified or satiated like the other needs. Instead, the need for self-actualization tends to increase in potency as individuals engage in self-actualizing behaviors. Thus, self-actualization is an ongoing process of becoming that is intensified and sustained as people achieve self-fulfillment.

How self-actualization is manifest varies greatly from person to person. Maslow believed that individuals possess a genetic potential that serves as a blueprint to describe what they are uniquely capable of becoming. In one individual the process of self-actualization might take the form of becoming an ideal mother, while other individuals could express the same need athletically, musically, artistically, or administratively. Self-actualization does not demand that individuals excel as the best in the world, but only as the best they can possibly be. For example, individuals expressing their self-actualization through athletics do not have to be world-class athletes to develop and enjoy their athletic talents. Fulfillment can also be derived from achieving their own personal best performances. Although Maslow said self-actualization could not be defined precisely, he attempted to describe some of the characteristics manifested by individuals who he thought were advanced in the process of self-actualization. These characteristics are shown in Exhibit 3.

Alderfer's ERG Theory

Maslow's research supporting his theory was largely limited to analyzing the biographies of self-actualizing people and his own clinical experiences. Maslow acknowledged the fact that the research supporting his theory was weak and inadequate, and expressed the hope that more research would ultimately be directed toward confirming and refining his theory. He noted, however, that neither animal nor human laboratory studies could possibly examine the full range of human needs in an acceptable way.[9]

The most popular refinement of Maslow's theory is one proposed by Clayton Alderfer. Based on a series of studies, Alderfer condensed Maslow's need hierarchy from five needs to just three, which he referred to as the ERG theory.[10]

1 *Existence needs.* The existence needs refer to all forms of material and physiological factors necessary to sustain human existence. This need encompassed Maslow's physiological and safety needs.

2 *Relatedness needs.* These needs include all socially oriented needs which include Maslow's social needs and parts of the safety and esteem needs.

3 *Growth needs.* Growth needs are those related to the development of human potential which includes Maslow's self-actualization plus the internally-based portion of self-esteem needs.

Alderfer agreed with Maslow that individuals tended to move up the hierarchy as they satisfied lower-level needs. However, Alderfer did not believe that one level of needs had to be satisfied before the next level need would emerge. All of the needs could be simultaneously active for a given individual. Studies examining the ERG theory using bank employees, nurses, and life insurance personnel seem to suggest that Maslow's theory can be condensed from five needs to three, and that all three needs can be simultaneously active in motivating behavior.

Research on the Need Hierarchy Theory

Maslow's theory has generated several research studies in organizational settings. One study, for example, found that managers in higher organizational levels place greater emphasis on self-actualization needs and are generally more able to satisfy their growth needs than lower-level managers.[11] These results were interpreted to support Maslow's theory, since higher-level managers tend to have more challenging, autonomous jobs where it is possible to pursue growth needs, while lower-level managers tend to have more routine jobs, making it more difficult to satisfy these needs.

Support for Maslow's theory has also come from the observations of those who have traveled in foreign countries and studied the effects of economic conditions on cultural development. Cultural arts and creative expression are found much more frequently in countries where the basic survival needs are largely satisfied. Higher-level expressions of self-esteem and self-actualization are not found as frequently in poorer countries where the majority of people are struggling for survival.

Although some evidence seems to support Maslow's theory, an extensive review of the research findings on the need hierarchy concept concluded with an interesting paradox: the theory is widely accepted but there is little research evidence to support it.[12] This extensive review examined three propositions of

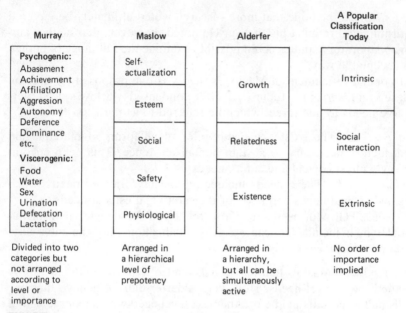

Murray	Maslow	Alderfer	A Popular Classification Today
Psychogenic: Abasement Achievement Affiliation Aggression Autonomy Deference Dominance etc. **Viscerogenic:** Food Water Sex Urination Defecation Lactation	Self-actualization Esteem Social Safety Physiological	Growth Relatedness Existence	Intrinsic Social interaction Extrinsic
Divided into two categories but not arranged according to level or importance	Arranged in a hierarchical level of prepotency	Arranged in a hierarchy, but all can be simultaneously active	No order of importance implied

EXHIBIT 4
Comparison of need theories. (From David J. Cherrington, *Personnel management.* Dubuque, Iowa: Wm. C. Brown Company Publishers, 1983, p. 255.)

Maslow's model: (1) the existence of the hierarchy itself, (2) the proposition that an unfulfilled need leads individuals to focus exclusively on that need, and (3) the proposition that gratification of one need activates the next higher need.

Seventeen studies were reviewed to examine the first issue, and the results indicated that there was no clear evidence showing that human needs are classified into five distinct categories, or that these categories are structured in any special hierarchy. Most of these studies instead condensed the needs to just two categories—deficiency and growth needs. The deficiency needs, also called lower-order needs, refer to physiological, safety, and social needs. The growth needs, also called higher-order needs, are comprised of the needs for self-esteem and self-actualization. Occasionally, needs are also categorized into extrinsic, interactive, and intrinsic needs. Extrinsic needs are associated with biological comforts and physical rewards; interactive needs refer to the desire for social approval, affiliation, and companionship; and intrinsic needs concern the yearnings for self-development, confidence, mastery, and challenge. These needs categories help to explain the nature of rewards and how they influence behavior. A comparison of these need theories is presented in Exhibit 4.

The second proposition, that unfulfilled needs lead individuals to focus exclusively on them, produced mixed results. Some studies supported this proposition while others failed to support it. The third proposition, that lower-level needs must be filled before higher-level needs are activated, was also not supported. Apparently higher-level needs can influence behavior even when lower-level needs are largely unfulfilled. Indeed, a review of some of the greatest artistic and cultural contributions in society showed that they were produced by people whose lower-level needs were seriously deficient.[13]

Although it lacks empirical support, Maslow's need hierarchy continues to be a very popular theory of motivation. His description of self-actualizing people and his enduring belief in the developmental potential of people provide a useful model of personal development that is consistent with what Maslow hoped to achieve by his theory. Maslow's theory was not intended as a model for predicting individual behavior, but as a model describing the potential of a fully functioning human being.

McCLELLAND'S LEARNED NEEDS

Another well-known need theory is the learned needs theory developed by David McClelland and his associates. McClelland's theory is closely associated with learning theory since he believed that needs were learned or acquired by the kinds of events people experienced in their culture. These learned needs represented behavioral predispositions that influence the way individuals perceive situations and motivate them to pursue a particular goal. Individuals who acquire a particular need behave differently from those who do not possess it. McClelland and his associates, particularly John Atkinson, investigated three of Murray's needs: achievement, affiliation, and power. In the literature these three needs are abbreviated "nAch," "nAff," and "nPow."[14]

The Need for Achievement—nAch

The most thorough series of studies conducted by McClelland and his associates concerned the need for achievement. They defined the need for achievement as behavior directed toward competition with a standard of excellence.

McClelland's first step in studying the need for achievement was to develop a method for measuring achievement. Rather than simply infer achievement from an individual's behavior or a self-report questionnaire, McClelland and his associates developed a projective test called the Thematic Apperception Test (TAT). This test consists of showing individuals a series of pictures and asking them to write a story about each picture. Their scores are calculated by counting how many times they referred to achievement-oriented ideas in their stories. McClelland believed that analyzing these fantasies is the best way to measure the strength of their needs. Individuals with a high need for achievement write stories about people who are striving to accomplish a particular goal and think about how to do it. On the other hand, individuals who write stories that center on social interactions and being with others, have a high need for affiliation, while stories about dominating, controlling, and influencing others indicate a high need for power.

Through his research McClelland identified three characteristics of high-need achievers.

1 High-need achievers have a strong desire to assume personal responsibility for performing a task or finding a solution to a problem. Consequently, they tend to work alone rather than with others. If the task requires the presence of others, they tend to choose coworkers based upon their competence rather than their friendship.

2 High-need achievers tend to set moderately difficult goals and take calculated risks. Consequently, in a ring-toss game where children tossed rings at a peg at any distance they chose, high-need achievers chose an intermediate distance where the probability of success was moderate, while low-need achievers chose either high or low probabilities of success by standing extremely close or very far away from the peg.

3 High-need achievers have a strong desire for performance feedback. These individuals want to know how well they have done, and they are anxious to receive feedback regardless of whether they have succeeded or failed.

In his research on the need for achievement, McClelland found that money did not have a very strong motivating effect on high-need achievers; they were already highly motivated. In a laboratory study, for example, high-need achievers performed very well with or without financial incentives.[15] Low-need achievers did not perform well without financial incentives, but when they were offered money for their work, they performed noticeably better. This study does not mean that money is unimportant to high-need achievers. Instead, to them, money is a form of feedback and recognition. When high-need achievers succeed, they look to monetary rewards as evidence of their success.

High-need achievers are characterized by their single-minded preoccupation with task accomplishment. Consequently, the need for achievement is an important motive in organizations because many managerial and entrepreneurial positions require such a single-minded preoccupation in order for the individual to be successful. McClelland believed that a high need for achievement was essential to entrepreneurial success. In a series of rather unique and interesting studies McClelland examined the need for achievement among managers in a number of current societies to show that a high need for achievement was correlated with managerial success and economic activity. By examining the literature of earlier civilizations, McClelland was also able to show that the rise and fall of economic activity within the civilization was correlated with the rise and fall of the achievement motive.

This line of research is perhaps best illustrated by a study of the need for achievement in England between 1500 and 1850 A.D. To measure the achievement orientation of the English culture, the literature written at various points during this period was analyzed. The need for achievement was measured by counting the number of achievement themes per 100 lines of literature. The measure of economic activity came from historical records showing the tons of coal exported from England. The results show that the rise and fall of economic activity followed the rise and fall of the need for achievement by about 50 years.[16]

McClelland concluded from his research that the need for achievement, like other personality characteristics, is apparently learned at an early age and largely influenced by child-rearing practices and other influences of parents. Children tend to have a fairly high need for achievement if they have been raised by parents who have fairly strict expectations about right and wrong behavior, who provide clear feedback on the effectiveness of their performance and who help their children accept a personal responsibility for their actions.[17]

McClelland argued that economic development and national prosperity were closely related to the need for achievement and recommended that U.S. foreign aid programs to poorer countries focus on raising the need for achievement rather than on providing financial aid. He argued that the achievement motive could be taught and described the kinds of training needed to raise the need for achievement. The training focused on four objectives. First, managers were encouraged to set personal goals and keep a record of their performance. Second, they were taught the language of achievement—to think, talk, and act like people with a high achievement motive. Third, managers were given cognitive or intellectual support—they were taught why the achievement motive was important to success. Fourth, they were provided with group support—a group of budding entrepreneurs met periodically to share success stories. In short, the managers were taught how to think and behave as entrepreneurs with a high achievement motive. Their new success-oriented behavior was reinforced verbally, intellectually, and through peer group influences.

Following this model, McClelland conducted a training program for fifty-two business executives in Hyderabad, India. Six to ten months after the course, many executives had doubled their natural rate of entrepreneurial activity. These findings have important implications for efforts to assist underdeveloped nations because they suggest that beyond giving economic aid lies a greater need to instill the achievement motive in the population.[18]

The Need for Affiliation—nAff

The need for affiliation is defined as a desire to establish and maintain friendly and warm relations with other individuals. In many ways the need for affiliation is similar to Maslow's social needs. Individuals with a high need for affiliation possess these characteristics.

1 They have a strong desire for approval and reassurance from others.
2 They have a tendency to conform to the wishes and norms of others when they are pressured by people whose friendships they value.
3 They have a sincere interest in the feelings of others.

Individuals with a high need for affiliation seek opportunities at work to satisfy this need. Therefore, individuals with a high nAff prefer to work with others rather than to work alone, and they tend to have good attendance records. Evidence also indicates that individuals with a high nAff tend to perform better in situations where personal support and approval are tied to performance.[19]

The implications for organizations of the need for affiliation are fairly straightforward. To the extent that managers can create a cooperative, supportive work environment where positive feedback is tied to task performance, individuals with a high nAff tend to be more productive. The explanation for this is rather simple. By working hard in such an environment, individuals with high nAff can satisfy their affiliation needs. On the other hand, individuals who have a low need for affiliation should be placed in positions allowing them to work fairly independently, since they prefer to work alone.

The Need for Power—nPow

The need for power has been studied extensively by McClelland and others.[20] This need is defined as the need to control others, to influence their behavior, and to be responsible for them. Some psychologists have argued that the need for power is the major goal of all human activity. These people view human development as the process by which people learn to exert control over the forces that exert power over them. According to this view, the ultimate satisfaction comes from being able to control environmental forces, including other people.

Individuals who possess a high need for power are characterized by:

1 A desire to influence and direct somebody else.
2 A desire to exercise control over others.
3 A concern for maintaining leader-follower relations.

Individuals with a high need for power tend to make more suggestions, offer their opinions and evaluations more frequently, and attempt to bring others around to their way of thinking. They also tend to seek positions of leadership in group activities, and their behavior within a group, either as leader or member, is described as verbally fluent, talkative, and sometimes argumentative.

In his research on the need for power, McClelland describes "two faces of power." The need for power can take the form of *personal power*, in which individuals strive for dominance almost for the sake of dominance, or *social power* in which individuals are more concerned with the problems of the organization and what can be done to facilitate goal attainment. Individuals with a high need for personal power tend to behave like conquistadores or tribal chiefs who inspire their subordinates to heroic performance, but they want their subordinates to be accountable to the leader, not to the organization. Individuals with a high need for social power, however, satisfy their power needs by working with the group to formulate and achieve group goals. This method of satisfying power needs is oriented toward achieving organizational effectiveness rather than satisfying a self-serving egotism.[21]

McClelland has recently argued that the need for social power is the most important determinant of managerial success. Although a high need for achievement may be necessary for entrepreneurial activity, most managerial positions in today's corporate world require managers who have a strong need for social power. Successful managers also need to have a relatively high need for achievement, but achievement is not as important for corporate managers in large corporations as it is for entrepreneurs.

Although individuals with a high need for social power tend to be more effective managers, McClelland provides some evidence suggesting that these individuals pay a fairly high price for their success in terms of their own personal health. McClelland measured the need for power among a group of Harvard graduates and followed their careers over a twenty-year period. He found that 58 percent of those rated high in nPow either had high blood pressure or had died of heart failure.[22]

NOTES

1 William James, *Principles of Psychology,* 2 vols. (1890), republished in *The Great Books* collection, vol. 53 (Chicago: Encyclopaedia Britannica, 1952), Chap. 26.

2 John Locke, *An Essay Concerning Human Understanding,* Book II (1689), Chaps. 7, 10, and 11, in *The Great Books,* vol. 35 (Chicago: Encyclopaedia Britannica, 1952); John Stuart Mill, *On Liberty* (1859), *Utilitarianism* (1863), in *The Great Books,* vol. 43 (Chicago: Encyclopaedia Britannica, 1952).

3 William James, *Principles of Psychology,* Chap. 24.

4 William McDougall, *An Introduction to Social Psychology* (London: Methuen Publishers, 1908).

5 Sigmund Freud, *Beyond the Pleasure Principle* (1920), trans. C. J. M. Hubback (London: Hogarth Press, 1930); *Civilization and Its Discontents* (1929) trans. Joan Rivière (London: Hogarth Press, 1930).

6 Henry A. Murray, *Explorations in Personality* (New York: Harper & Row, 1954, 1970).

7 Abraham H. Maslow, *Motivation and Personality* (New York: Harper & Row, 1954).

8 Abraham H. Maslow, "A Theory of Human Motivation," *Psychological Review,* vol. 1 (1943), pp. 370–396.

9 Abraham H. Maslow, *Toward a Theory of Being* (New York: Van Nostrand Reinhold, 1968).

10 Clayton P. Alderfer, "An Empirical Test of a New Theory of Human Needs," *Organizational Behavior and Human Performance,* vol. 4 (1969), pp. 142–175.

11 Lyman W. Porter, "A Study of Perceived Need Satisfactions in Bottom and Middle Management Jobs," *Journal of Applied Psychology,* vol. 45 (1961), pp. 1–10; Lyman W. Porter, "Job Attitudes in Management: I. Perceived Deficiencies in Need Fulfillment as a Function of Job Level," *Journal of Applied Psychology,* vol. 46 (1962), pp. 375–384.

12 M. A. Wahba and L. G. Bridwell, "Maslow Reconsidered: A Review of Research on the Need Hierarchy Theory," *Organizational Behavior and Human Performance,* vol. 15 (1976), pp. 212–240.

13 Salvatore Maddi, *Theories of Personality, A Comparative Analysis,* rev. ed. (Homewood, Ill.: The Dorsey Press, 1972).

14 David C. McClelland, "Toward a Theory of Motive Acquisition," *American Psychologist,* vol. 20 (1965), pp. 321–333.

15 J. W. Atkinson and W. R. Reitman, "Performance as a Function of Motive Strength and Expectancy of Goal-Attainment," *Journal of Abnormal Social Psychology,* vol. 53 (1956), pp. 361–366.

16 David C. McClelland, *The Achieving Society* (New York: The Free Press, 1961).

17 David C. McClelland, "Achievement Motivation Can Be Developed," *Harvard Business Review* (November–December 1965), pp. 6–24.

18 David C. McClelland, "Business Drive and National Achievement," *Harvard Business Review,* vol. 40 (July 1962), pp. 99–112.

19 Reviewed by Kae H. Chung, *Motivational Theories and Practices* (Columbus, Ohio: Grid, Inc., 1977), pp. 47–48.

20 David C. McClelland, "The Two Faces of Power," *Journal of International Affairs,* vol. 24, no. 1 (1970), pp. 29–47; Jeffrey Pfeffer, *Power in Organizations* (Marshfield, Mass.: Pitman Pub., 1981).
21 David C. McClelland, "The Two Faces of Power," *Journal of International Affairs,* vol. 24 (1970), pp. 29–47.
22 David C. McClelland, "Power Is the Great Motivation," *Harvard Business Review,* vol. 54, no. 2 (1976), pp. 100–110.

Intrinsic Motivation and Self-Determination in Human Behavior

Edward L. Deci

Richard M. Ryan

NEEDS AND AFFECTS

Other theorists have conceptualized intrinsic motivation in terms of generalized needs and affects that are psychological rather than physiological in nature. This approach, which was evident in the early writings of McDougall (1908), Engle (1904), and Woodworth (1918), has gained widespread acceptance in the last decade. Currently, it is being used in the formulation and interpretation of a great deal of empirical research and in the theoretical integration of findings and perspectives from many areas of psychology. In essence, the central concerns being dealt with relate to the human needs for free and effective interactions with the environment and to the feelings of interest and enjoyment that are integrally involved with these needs.

The Need for Competence

Woodworth (1918, 1958), in his behavior-primacy theory, proposed that behavior is generally aimed at producing an effect on the environment. This behavior is ongoing and primary, so drives such as hunger must break into its flow of activity in order to achieve satisfaction. In motivational terms, this implies a need for having an effect, for being effective in one's interactions with the environment. Prior to Woodworth, McDougall (1908) had proposed a curiosity instinct that is closely related to an effectance need, yet the idea of effectance is able to encompass a greater array of phenomena than a curiosity instinct. Curiosity is implicit in effectance.

White (1959), in the landmark paper mentioned earlier in this chapter, formally proposed a need for effectance as a basic motivational propensity that energizes a wide range of non-drive-based behaviors. There is, he suggested, inherent sat-

From E. L. Deci and R. M. Ryan, *Intrinsic motivation and self-determination in human behavior.* New York: Plenum Press, 1985.

isfaction in exercising and extending one's capabilities. White referred to the energy behind this activity as *effectance motivation* and to the corresponding affect as the feeling of *efficacy*. He used the term *competence* to connote the structures through which effectance motivation operates. Competence is the accumulated results of one's interactions with the environment, of one's exploration, learning, and adaptation. In the broad, biological sense, competence refers to the capacity for effective interactions with the environment that ensure the organism's maintenance. Because the capacity is called competence, the motivational counterpart is often called competence motivation as well as effectance motivation. Some writers, such as Kagan (1972), use the term mastery motivation.

The development of competencies—walking, talking, manipulating abstract symbols, or formulating a story—are in part maturational, according to White, yet they are in large measure learned, and the learning is motivated. The need for competence provides the energy for this learning. Effectance motivation is broader in its scope than learning, however. Whereas the biological aim of competence motivation is survival of the organism, the experiential aim is the feeling of competence that results from effective action. Thus, for example, children seem to exercise their newly acquired competencies simply to experience the sense of satisfaction that they provide. In time, of course, the children move on to new undertakings, for the old ones become repetitious, and thus less interesting. Stated differently, the reward for competency-motivated behavior is the inherent feeling of competence that results from effective functioning, yet the motivation is such that the feelings seem to result only when there is some continual stretching of one's capacities. With each new acquisition of a skill there is some room for playful exercising of that skill, but boredom soon sets in when one merely exercises the same skill over and over.

Whereas drives tend to operate cyclically in that once satisfied they do not reemerge for some number of hours or days, effectance motivation is persistent and is always available to occupy "the spare waking time between episodes of homeostatic crisis" (White, 1959, p. 321). In other words, effectance motivation is not intense and immediate like thirst or fear, but rather is an ongoing process that is periodically interrupted by tissue needs, though of course there are times when a hungry, cold, or pained person will stick to an intrinsically motivated activity in spite of the tissue needs. Like Berlyne, White located the source of this non-drive-based energy in the central nervous system of the organism.

Deci (1975) suggested that the need for competence leads people to seek and conquer challenges that are optimal for their capacities, and that competence acquisition results from interacting with stimuli that are challenging. A study by Danner and Lonky (1981) provided support for this contention by showing that when children were free to select the activities they would work on, they selected ones that were just beyond their current level of competence.

Harter (1978) took the position that White's generalized need for effectance was too broad and should be broken into components. She suggested three components—preference for challenge, curiosity, and independent mastery—and then used these three components to develop three subscales in her intrinsic versus extrinsic motivation scale for children (Harter, 1981). Although it may be useful to conceptualize components of intrinsic motivation for purposes of measuring individual differences, we assert that it is necessary to maintain the generalized conception for purposes of greater theoretical integration.

Interest-Excitemer.t and Flow

Another important strand of the current perspective on intrinsic motivation is represented by theories that focus on affects and emotions as either initiators or concomitants of intrinsically motivated behavior. As previously noted these relatively invariant qualities associated with intrinsic motivation include interest, enjoyment, and direct involvement with one's environment. Affective theories place these features at the core of their explanation of intrinsic motivation.

Izard (1977) proposed that there are 10 different human emotions; that each is involved in the motivation of behavior; and that each has a unique experiential component. Among these emotions, interest-excitement is said to be the basis of intrinsically motivated behavior, and joy is said to play a relevant though secondary role. Interest is involved whenever one orients toward an object, and it plays an important role in the amplification and direction of attention. Interest-excitement can therefore activate many types of investigatory or manipulative behaviors, particularly under conditions of novelty and freedom from other pressing demands of drives or emotions. Because interest can amplify other emotions it also plays a regulatory role with regard to a variety of experiences and behaviors. Izard (1977) thus recognized the centrality of interest-excitement in the adaptation, development, and coordination of human behavior, and even labeled interest the fundamental motivator.

Csikszentmihalyi (1975) placed greater emphasis on enjoyment. For him, intrinsically motivated activities are ones characterized by enjoyment, those for which the reward is the ongoing experience of enjoying the activity. He uses the term *autotelic* to refer to the fact that the goal of intrinsically motivated behaviors is indeed their inherent experiential aspects. Csikszentmihalyi proposed that true enjoyment accompanies the experience of *flow*, that peculiar, dynamic, wholistic sensation of total involvement with the activity itself. In the state of flow, action and experience seem to move smoothly from one moment to the next, and there seems to be no clear distinction between the person and the activity. Flow involves a "loss of ego" and an experienced unity with one's surroundings.

Csikszentmihalyi's research suggests that flow states emerge under some specifiable conditions. Most important among these is optimal challenge. When one engages an optimally challenging activity with respect to one's capacities there is maximal possibility for task-involved enjoyment or flow. Activities that are below one's optimal challenge (i.e., activities that are too easy) lead to boredom, and activities that greatly exceed one's current capacities generate anxiety and disrupt flow. Thus the perspective offered by Csikszentmihalyi also implicates the competence theories previously discussed, indicating that people will be intrinsically motivated under conditions of optimal challenge.

In sum, interest and excitement are central emotions that accompany intrinsic motivation, and the concept of flow represents a descriptive dimension that may signify some of the purer instances of intrinsic motivation. When highly intrinsically motivated, organisms will be extremely interested in what they are doing and experience a sense of flow.

The Need for Self-Determination

The previous approaches have highlighted the significance of competence and interest in intrinsically motivated behavior. However, many non-intrinsically motivated behaviors may be competence-oriented, and some may even be characterized by interest. To be truly intrinsically motivated, a person must also feel free from pressures, such as rewards or contingencies. Thus, we suggest, intrinsic motivation will be operative when action is experienced as autonomous, and it is unlikely to function under conditions where controls or reinforcements are the experienced cause of action.

Because self-determination or freedom from control is necessary for intrinsic motivation to be operative, several theorists have posited that intrinsically motivated activity is based in the need for self-determination. DeCharms (1968) for example, proposed that intrinsically motivated behaviors result from a desire to experience personal causation.

> Man's primary motivational propensity is to be effective in producing changes in his environment. Man strives to be a causal agent, to be the primary locus of causation for, or the origin of, his behavior; he strives for personal causation. (deCharms, 1968, p. 269)

According to deCharms, this basic desire to be in control of one's fate is a contributing factor in all motivated behavior, though it is the central force only for intrinsically motivated behavior.

In further discussing the notion of intrinsic motivation, deCharms used Heider's (1958) concept of perceived locus of causality:

> Whenever a person experiences himself to be the locus of causality for his own behavior . . . he will consider himself to be intrinsically motivated. Conversely, when a person perceives the locus of causality to be external to himself . . . he will consider himself to be extrinsically motivated. (deCharms, 1968, p. 328)

The postulate of a basic motivational propensity for self-determination is, of course, closely related to the postulate of a need for effectance. Angyal (1941), for example, suggested that human development can be characterized in terms of movement toward greater autonomy and that this movement depends in part on the continual acquisition of a variety of competencies. To be self-determining one must have the skills to manage various elements of one's environment. Otherwise, one is likely to be controlled by them.

Recent work on the psychology of control has indicated that people have a need to experience control over their environment or their outcomes. Although the need to control is not the same as the need for self-determination, evidence in support of the former is relevant to the latter. One set of studies focused on people's apparent desire or need to control the environment by showing that people believe they have more control than they actually do, particularly in situations where controllability cues are present (Langer, 1975). People, it seems, have such a strong desire for control that they may even project it into situations where they do not actually have it.

A more direct test of the hypothesis that people have a need for control was done by Schorr and Rodin (1984), who created experimental conditions in which people's intentional performance on one task would determine whether they, or others, would be in control of a future task. The researchers found, first, that subjects did display behavior which signified a need for control, and second, that to some extent the need for control was "for its own sake" rather than for increasing the likelihood of gaining preferred outcomes. It does appear, then, that people have a need to control aspects of their environment.

In reviewing research on control, Deci (1980) suggested that the intrinsic need that was operative for subjects in the various control studies was not a need to control the environment, but rather a need to be self-determining, that is, to have a choice. It is true, he said, that the need for self-determination is often manifest as a need to control the environment, so the previously cited research represents partial support for the need for self-determination, but there are very important differences between the concepts of control and self-determination. Control refers to there being a contingency between one's behavior and the outcomes one receives, whereas self-determination refers to the experience of freedom in initiating one's behavior. A person has control when his or her behaviors reliably yield intended outcomes, but this does not ensure self-determination, for the person can, in the words of deCharms (1968), become a "pawn" to those outcomes. In those cases the person's behavior would be determined by the outcomes rather than by choices, even though the person would be said to have control. It is true that a person needs control over outcomes to be self-determined in attaining them, but the need is for self-determination rather than for control *per se*. Further, we assert that people do not always want control of outcomes; indeed, they often prefer to have others take control. What they want is *choice* about whether to be in control. Thus, using the concept of a need for self-determination (i.e., of choice) rather than a need for control allows for the explanation of the fact that people need to feel free from dependence on outcomes over which they have control, and that people sometimes prefer not to control outcomes.

Support for the conception that the need for self-determination is basic to intrinsic motivation comes in part from research that confirms that the opportunity to be self-determining enhances intrinsic motivation, and that denial of the opportunity to be self-determining undermines it. Further support comes from the work of Brehm (1966), who showed that when people perceive their freedom to be threatened, they experience reactance, which is a motivation to restore the threatened freedom. With prolonged denial of freedom, Wortman and Brehm (1975) suggested, the reactance motivation will tend to diminish and people will fall into amotivation: they will feel helpless and their effectiveness will be impaired.

A wide range of evidence supports the view that the need for self-determination is an important motivator that is involved with intrinsic motivation and is closely intertwined with the need for competence. We conceptualize intrinsic motivation in terms of the needs for competence and self-determination. The two needs are closely related, but we refer to both to emphasize their mutual importance. Whereas White (1959) made competence the backbone of intrinsic motivation, it is important to emphasize that it is not the need for competence alone that underlies intrinsic motivation; it is the need for self-determined competence.

INTRINSIC MOTIVATION CONCEPTUALIZED

Human beings engage in a substantial amount of intrinsically motivated behavior, so theories of motivation must be able to explain behaviors that are motivated by "rewards that do not reduce tissue needs" (Eisenberger, 1972). This requires an adequate conception of intrinsic motivation and a general theory of motivation that includes intrinsic as well as other types of motivation. The conceptualizations of intrinsic motivation that have been proposed are summarized in Table 1. We saw that the attempts to integrate intrinsically motivated phenomena into Hullian drive theory and Freudian instinct theory proved inadequate. As Koch (1956) had pre-

TABLE 1
SUMMARY OF VARIOUS CONCEPTUALIZATIONS OF INTRINSIC MOTIVATION ALONG WITH THE PRIMARY PROPONENTS OF EACH APPROACH

Approach	Proponents
Drive naming	
Exploratory drive	Montgomery, 1954
Avoid boredom	Myers & Miller, 1954
Manipulation drive	Harlow, 1953
Sensory drive	Isaac, 1962
Visual exploration	Butler, 1953
Physiological arousal	
Optimal arousal	Hebb, 1955; Leuba, 1955; Fiske & Maddi, 1961
Psychological incongruity	
Dissonance reduction	Festinger, 1957
Uncertainty reduction	Kagan, 1972; Lanzetta, 1971
Discrepancy from adaptation	McClelland et al., 1953
Optimal incongruity	Dember & Earl, 1957; Hunt, 1965
Optimal arousal potential	Berlyne, 1971
Psychoanalytic	
Instinct to master	Hendrick, 1942
Anxiety reduction	Fenichel, 1945
Ego energy	Hartmann, 1958; White, 1963
Competence and self-determination	
Effectance	Harter, 1978; White, 1959
Self-determination	Angyal, 1941
Personal causation	deCharms, 1968
Competence and self-determination	Deci & Ryan (this volume)
Emotions	
Interest-excitement	Izard, 1977
Enjoyment and flow	Csikszentmihalyi, 1975

dicted, it was necessary to posit the existence of a fundamentally different motivational source. At the physiological level this was done by arousal theories; at the psychological level it was done by incongruity theories and by theories that focus on the needs for competence and self-determination, or the emotions of interest and enjoyment. Drawing on these various works, we now offer a definition of intrinsic motivation.

Intrinsic motivation is based in the innate, organismic needs for competence and self-determination. It energizes a wide variety of behaviors and psychological processes for which the primary rewards are the experiences of effectance and autonomy. Intrinsic needs differ from primary drives in that they are not based in tissue deficits and they do not operate cyclically, that is, breaking into awareness, pushing to be satisfied, and then when satisfied, receding into quiescence. Like drives, however, intrinsic needs are innate to the human organism and function as an important energizer of behavior. Furthermore, intrinsic motivation may interact with drives in the sense of either amplifying or attenuating drives and of affecting the way in which people satisfy their drives.

The intrinsic needs for competence and self-determination motivate an ongoing process of seeking and attempting to conquer optimal challenges. When people are free from the intrusion of drives and emotions, they seek situations that interest them and require the use of their creativity and resourcefulness. They seek challenges that are suited to their competencies, that are neither too easy nor too difficult. When they find optimal challenges, people work to conquer them, and they do so persistently. In short, the needs for competence and self-determination keep people involved in ongoing cycles of seeking and conquering optimal challenges.

A challenge is something that requires stretching one's abilities, trying something new. One way to conceptualize challenge is in terms of an incongruity between one's internal structures and aspects of the external world. Thus, to seek an optimal challenge is to seek an optimal incongruity. People seek incongruities in order to reduce them and to incorporate the discrepant elements into their existing structures. Intrinsically motivated behavior, behavior motivated by the needs for competence and self-determination, therefore can be seen to involve an ongoing process of seeking and reducing optimal incongruities.

Emotions are integrally related to intrinsic motivation. The emotion of interest plays an important directive role in intrinsically motivated behavior in that people naturally approach activities that interest them. Interest is, to a large extent, a function of optimal challenge, though there are other factors that also influence people's developing interests. The emotions of enjoyment and excitement accompanying the experiences of competence and autonomy represent the rewards for intrinsically motivated behavior. These rewards are not properly called reinforcements, of course, because they neither reduce a tissue deficit (Hull, 1943) nor are operationally separate from the activity itself (Skinner, 1953).

When people are intrinsically motivated, they experience interest and enjoyment, they feel competent and self-determining, they perceive the locus of causality for their behavior to be internal, and in some instances they experience flow. The antithesis of interest and flow is pressure and tension. Insofar as people are pressuring themselves, feeling anxious, and working with great urgency, we can be sure that there is at least some extrinsic motivation involved. Their self-esteem may be on the line, they may have deadlines, or some material reward may be involved.

In addition to the psychological definition, we need operational definitions for research purposes. First, we infer intrinsic motivation for an activity when a person does the activity in the absence of a reward contingency or control. This has been the basis of the so-called free-choice measure of intrinsic motivation that has been widely used in the experimental research that will be reviewed throughout this book. Like all operational definitions it is not perfectly correlated with the psychological definition, so it requires the use of some perspective in its application. A simplistic use of the operational definition, without proper judgment, has led to some confusing experimental findings. When applying this operational definition, it is useful to note subjects' affective reactions. For example, Ryan (1982) found that when subjects were ego-involved in an activity, when their self-esteem depended on their doing well, they experienced pressure and tension. If one observed subjects' feeling pressured and tense, even if they were behaving in the absence of any apparent "external" reward, one might suspect that there was some other motivational dynamic involved, and one would properly look deeper to understand the processes rather than naively infer intrinsic motivation.

Second, we sometimes look at the quality of performance or of outcomes as indicators of intrinsic motivation. Because intrinsic motivation has been associated with greater creativity (Amabile, 1983), flexibility (McGraw & McCullers, 1979), and spontaneity (Koestner, Ryan, Bernieri, & Holt, 1984), the presence of those characteristics can signify intrinsic motivation.

Finally, we use questionnaire measures of intrinsic motivation. For example, because intrinsic motivation involves interest and enjoyment, assessing subjects' interest and enjoyment allows us to infer intrinsic motivation. Higher levels of perceived competence and self-determination also imply intrinsic motivation and can be useful measures, particularly when used in conjunction with other measures. Again, with this operational definition it is important to employ perspective. For example, if subjects were rewarded and then asked how much they enjoyed the experience, they may say "very much." But did they enjoy the activity, or did they enjoy getting the reward? The former is relevant to intrinsic motivation; the latter is not.

SELF-DETERMINATION: A BRIEF HISTORY

The empirical exploration of intrinsic motivation has held importance for psychological theory because it has explicated the functioning of a class of behaviors that had not been well handled by drive or reinforcement theories. The study of intrinsic motivation has required the assumption that people are active organisms working to master their internal and external environments, and it has led to an examination of the importance of self-determination in a wide range of human behaviors and experiences. In fact it has led to the realization that self-determination is important in the development and exercise of extrinsic and intrinsic motivation. Consequently we shall attempt to show how the use of the concept of self-determination permits a more refined and elaborated conception of extrinsic motivation. In essence, extrinsic motivation refers to behavior where the reason for doing it is something other than an interest in the activity itself. Such behavior may, however, to a greater or lesser extent, be something the person feels pressured to do versus genuinely wants to do. Extrinsically motivated behaviors may range from being determined largely by controls to being determined more by choices based on one's own values and desires. In the latter case, they would be more self-determined.

Concepts related to self-determination have appeared in a variety of empirical and nonempirical psychological writings. Fundamentally, self-determination is an issue of choice and therefore necessitates a theory built on concepts such as volition, intentionality, or will. James (1890) was the first psychologist to discuss the importance of volition and in so doing to present a theory of will. However, since psychology became dominated by nonvolitional theories during the first half of the present century, these concepts were ruled out of consideration.

Around the middle of the century two important developments occurred that began to set the stage for self-determination to be considered. First, several theories posited fundamental tendencies for the developmental movement from heteronomy toward autonomy in the determination of behavior. And, second, the cognitive movement shifted attention from associative bonds to decisions as the central concept in the directionality of behavior.

Maslow (1943, 1955), for example, outlined a theory of motivation utilizing a concept that he, like Goldstein (1939), called *self-actualization*. All individuals, Maslow said, seek to actualize their unique potentials, to become all that they are capable of and to be autonomous in their functioning. A similar point was made by Rogers (1963), who argued that life activity can be understood in terms of the actualizing tendency, which is the organisms' propensity to maintain and enhance itself. Although not the same as self-determination, the concept of self-actualization emphasizes the importance of choice and other self-related constructs.

Loevinger (1976), in her theory of ego development, used a structural perspective and outlined the stages through which one moves in the developmental progression toward more unified, autonomous functioning. Shapiro (1981), also working in the psychoanalytic tradition, discussed autonomy in terms of the flexibility of psychological structures. Focusing primarily on the rigid structures that interfere with autonomy, Shapiro highlighted the notion of autonomy and its importance for understanding qualities of the ego's adaptation.

Lewin (1951), who, along with Tolman (1932), was extremely influential in bringing about the cognitive movement in psychology, argued forcefully in support of intentionality and will as important motivational constructs. This led to the formulation of expectancy theories of motivation that explored the determinants of behavioral decision making and to the empirical study of control that explored the importance of control over one's outcomes. Both of these developments within the cognitive movement were based on the assumption that behavior is a function of one's expectations about future outcomes, so the issue of whether or not one has control over outcomes is extremely important. Consequently, numerous researchers have studied the effects of one's beliefs about whether one has control on a wide variety of dependent variables.

Many of the studies have focused on the positive effects of enhanced perceived control over outcomes. For example, studies by Glass and Singer (1972) and by Miller (1980) demonstrated that when people believe they have or can gain control over aversive events in their environment, they perform more effectively than when they believe they cannot. Rodin, Solomon, and Metcalf (1978) and Langer and Saegert (1977) found that people with greater perceived control reported experiencing crowded spaces as less aversive than did people with less perceived control.

A related set of studies has demonstrated the negative effects of lack of perceived control over one's outcomes. Pennebaker, Burnam, Schaeffer, and Harper (1977), for example, reported that the lack of perceived control led to more reported physical symptoms, such as headaches. Seligman and his colleagues (Hiroto, 1974; Hiroto & Seligman, 1975; Seligman, 1968, 1975) have demonstrated repeatedly that lack of perceived control over outcomes leads to helplessness, in which case people display increased emotionality and impaired learning and performance.

Other studies have related control directly to health and well-being. For example, Schulz (1976) found that a sample of institutionalized aged people who were given greater opportunity to control outcomes was rated by staff members as becoming more psychologically healthy; showed evidence of being less physically ill; and had a lower mortality rate than a matched control group. Langer and Rodin (1976) reported similar results in a different institution for the aged. Follow-ups of these two studies (Schulz & Hanusa, 1978; Rodin & Langer, 1977) led to the important conclusion that long-term positive effects on people's well-being require that the people learn to accept greater personal responsibility for attaining their desired outcomes.

In general, then, considerable research suggests that greater perceived control over one's outcomes tend to be associated with a variety of positive effects, though some studies have shown that there are conditions within which perceived control can have negative consequences (e.g., Averill, 1973; Fegley, 1984).

As we mentioned earlier, the concepts of self-determination and control are not the same, though they are related. To be self-determining with respect to outcomes, people must have control over those outcomes, and not being able to control outcomes—which precludes self-determination—will have negative consequences, as the studies previously reviewed have shown. But having control does not ensure self-determination. If people feel pressured to attain certain outcomes or if they feel pressured to exercise control, they are not self-determined. Self-determination means that people experience choice. It will be in evidence either when they choose to exercise control and are free with respect to what outcomes they attain, or when they choose to give up the control. In either case, we predict positive effects. However, when people experience having to be in control or having to attain particular outcomes (i.e., when they are not being self-determining), the effects will be negative, just as they are when people cannot gain control.

Cognitive theories set the stage for the study of self-determination. By introducing the concepts of behavioral decision making (i.e., intentionality) and control over outcomes, they allowed self-determination theorists such as deCharms (1968) and Deci (1980) to point out that only some intended behaviors (namely, those with an internal perceived locus of causality) are self-determined, and that having control over outcomes does not ensure self-determination.

SELF-DETERMINATION CONCEPTUALIZED

Self-determination is a quality of human functioning that involves the experience of choice, in other words, the experience of an internal perceived locus of causality. It is integral to intrinsically motivated behavior and is also in evidence in some extrinsically motivated behaviors. Stated differently, self-determination is the capacity to choose and to have those choices, rather than reinforcement contingencies, drives, or any other forces or pressures, be the determinants of one's actions. But self-determination is more than a *capacity*; it is also a *need*. We have posited a basic, innate propensity to be self-determining that leads organisms to engage in interesting behaviors, which typically has the benefit of developing competencies, and of working toward a flexible accommodation with the social environment. This tendency toward adequate accommodation in the service of one's self-determination is central to the development of extrinsic motivation.

The psychological hallmark of self-determination is flexibility in managing the interaction of oneself and the environment. When self-determined, one acts out of choice rather than obligation or coercion, and those choices are based on an awareness of one's organismic needs and a flexible interpretation of external events. Self-determination often involves controlling one's environment or one's outcomes, but it may also involve choosing to give up control.

Although we define self-determination as a quality of human functioning, we also emphasize that it can be either supported or hindered by environmental forces, so we study it in part by exploring environmental influences. Further, we often speak of the opportunity to be self-determining, implying that when the environment supports self-determination, the person will be more self-determining. Technically, of course, we can only define self-determination with respect to the person's actual functioning.

Self-determination has also been operationalized for research purposes. Thus far this has been done with questionnaire measures, though it could be done with behavioral measures as well. In either case, we would look for evidence of persistence in the absence of immediate extrinsic contingencies and for a minimum of pressure, tension, and anxiety.

REFERENCES

Amabile, T. M. *The social psychology of creativity.* New York: Springer-Verlag, 1983.
Angyal, A. *Foundations for a science of personality.* New York: Commonwealth Fund, 1941.

Averill, J. R. Personal control over aversive stimuli and its relationship to stress. *Psychological Bulletin*, 1973, *80*, 286–303.

Berlyne, D. E. What next? Concluding summary. In H. I. Day, D. E. Berlyne, & D. E. Hunt (Eds.), *Intrinsic motivation: A new direction in education*. Toronto: Holt, Rinehart & Winston of Canada, 1971.

Butler, R. A. Discrimination learning by rhesus monkeys to visual exploration motivation. *Journal of Comparative and Physiological Psychology*, 1953, *46*, 95–98.

Csikszentmihalyi, M. *Beyond boredom and anxiety*. San Francisco: Jossey-Bass, 1975.

Danner, F. W., & Lonky, E. A cognitive-developmental approach to the effects of rewards on intrinsic motivation. *Child Development*, 1981, *52*, 1043–1052.

deCharms, R. *Personal causation: The internal affective determinants of behavior*. New York: Academic Press, 1968.

Deci, E. L. *Intrinsic motivation*. New York: Plenum Press, 1975.

Deci, E. L. *The psychology of self-determination*. Lexington, Mass.: D. C. Heath (Lexington Books), 1980.

Dember, W. N., & Earl, R. W. Analysis of exploratory, manipulatory, and curiosity behaviors. *Psychological Review*, 1957, *64*, 91–96.

Eisenberger, R. Explanation of rewards that do not reduce tissue needs. *Psychological Bulletin*, 1972, *77*, 319–339.

Engle, J. S. *Analytic interest psychology and synthetic philosophy*. Baltimore, Md.: King Brothers, 1904.

Fegley, B. J. *The effects of contingent versus noncontingent instruction on children's responses to selected radiologic procedures*. Unpublished doctoral dissertation, University of Rochester, 1984.

Fenichel, O. *The psychoanalytic theory of neurosis*. New York: Norton, 1945.

Festinger, L. *A theory of cognitive dissonance*. Evanston, Ill.: Row, Peterson, 1957.

Fiske, D. W., & Maddi, S. R. *Functions of varied experience*. Homewood, Ill.: Dorsey, 1961.

Glass, D. C., & Singer, J. E. *Urban stress: Experiments on noise and social stressors*. New York: Academic Press, 1972.

Goldstein, K. *The organism*. New York: American Book Co., 1939.

Harlow, H. F. Motivation as a factor in the acquisition of new responses. In *Current theory and research on motivation*. Lincoln: University of Nebraska Press, 1953.

Harter, S. Effectance motivation reconsidered: Toward a developmental model. *Human Development*, 1978, *1*, 34–64.

Harter, S. A new self-report scale of intrinsic versus extrinsic orientation in the classroom: Motivational and informational components. *Developmental Psychology*, 1981, *17*, 300–312.

Hartmann, H. *Ego psychology and the problem of adaptation*. New York: International Universities Press, 1958. (Originally published, 1939.)

Hebb, D. O. Drives and the c.n.s. (conceptual nervous system). *Psychological Review*, 1955, *62*, 243–254.

Heider, F. *The psychology of interpersonal relations*. New York: Wiley, 1958.

Hendrick, I. Instinct and the ego during infancy. *Psychoanalytic Quarterly*, 1942, *11*, 33–58.

Hiroto, D. S. Locus of control and learned helplessness. *Journal of Experimental Psychology*, 1974, *102*, 187–193.

Hiroto, D. S., & Seligman, M. E. P. Generality of learned helplessness in man. *Journal of Personality and Social Psychology*, 1975, *31*, 311–327.

Hull, C. L. *Principles of behavior: An introduction to behavior theory.* New York: Appleton-Century-Crofts, 1943.

Hunt, J. McV. Intrinsic motivation and its role in psychological development. In D. Levine (Ed.), *Nebraska symposium on motivation* (Vol. 13). Lincoln, NB: University of Nebraska Press, 1965.

Isaac, W. Evidence for a sensory drive in monkeys. *Psychological Reports,* 1962, *11,* 175–181.

Izard, C. *Human emotions.* New York: Plenum Press, 1977.

James, W. *The principles of psychology.* New York: Holt, 1890.

Kagan, J. Motives and development. *Journal of Personality and Social Psychology,* 1972, *22,* 51–66.

Koch, S. Behavior as "intrinsically" regulated: Work notes toward a pre-theory of phenomena called "motivational." In M. R. Jones (Ed.), *Nebraska symposium on motivation* (Vol. 4). Lincoln: University of Nebraska Press, 1956.

Koestner, R., Ryan, R. M., Bernieri, F., & Holt, K. Setting limits on children's behavior: The differential effects of controlling versus informational styles on intrinsic motivation and creativity. *Journal of Personality,* 1984, *52,* 233–248.

Langer, E. J. The illusion of control. *Journal of Personality and Social Psychology,* 1975, *32,* 311–328.

Langer, E. J., & Rodin, J. The effects of choice and personal responsibility for the aged: A field experiment in an institutional setting. *Journal of Personality and Social Psychology,* 1976, *34,* 191–198.

Langer, E., & Saegert, S. Crowding and cognitive control. *Journal of Personality and Social Psychology,* 1977, *35,* 175–182.

Lanzetta, J. T. The motivational properties of uncertainty. In H. I. Day, D. E. Berlyne, & D. E Hunt (Eds.), *Intrinsic motivation: A new direction in education.* Toronto: Holt, Rinehart & Winston of Canada, 1971.

Leuba, C. Toward some integration of learning theories: The concept of optimal stimulation. *Psychological Reports,* 1955, *1,* 27–33.

Lewin, K. Intention, will, and need. In D. Rapaport (Ed.), *Organization and pathology of thought.* New York: Columbia University Press, 1951.

Loevinger, J. *Ego development.* San Francisco: Jossey-Bass, 1976.

Maslow, A. H. A theory of human motivation. *Psychological Review,* 1943, *50,* 370–396.

Maslow, A. H. Deficiency motivation and growth motivation. In M. R. Jones (Ed.), *Nebraska symposium on motivation* (Vol. 3). Lincoln: University of Nebraska Press, 1955.

McClelland, D. C., Atkinson, J. W., Clark, R. W., & Lowell, E. L. *The achievement motive.* New York: Appleton-Century-Crofts, 1953.

McDougall, W. *Social psychology.* New York: Luce & Co., 1908.

McGraw, K. O., & McCullers, J. C. Evidence of a detrimental effect of extrinsic incentives on breaking a mental set. *Journal of Experimental Social Psychology,* 1979, *15,* 285–294.

Miller, S. M. Why having control reduces stress: If I can stop the roller coaster, I don't want to get off. In J. Garber & M. E. P. Seligman (Eds.), *Human helplessness.* New York: Academic Press, 1980.

Montgomery, K. C. The role of exploratory drive in learning. *Journal of Comparative and Physiological Psychology,* 1954, *47,* 60–64.

Myers, A. K., & Miller, N. E. Failure to find a learned drive based on hunger: Evidence for learning motivated by "exploration." *Journal of Comparative and Physiological Psychology,* 1954, *47,* 428–436.

Pennebaker, J. W., Burnam, M. A., Schaeffer, M. A., & Harper, D. C. Lack of control as a determinant of perceived physical symptoms. *Journal of Personality and Social Psychology*, 1977, *35*, 167–174.

Rodin, J., & Langer, E. J. Long-term effects of a control-relevant intervention with the institutionalized aged. *Journal of Personality and Social Psychology*, 1977, *35*, 897–902.

Rodin, J., Solomon, S. K., & Metcalf, J. The role of control in mediating perceptions of density. *Journal of Personality and Social Psychology*, 1978, *36*, 988–999.

Rogers, C. The actualizing tendency in relation to "motives" and to consciousness. In M. R. Jones (Ed.), *Nebraska symposium on motivation* (Vol. 11). Lincoln: University of Nebraska Press, 1963.

Ryan, R. M. Control and information in the intrapersonal sphere: An extension of cognitive evaluation theory. *Journal of Personality and Social Psychology*, 1982, *43*, 450–461.

Schorr, D., & Rodin, J. Motivation to control one's environment in individuals with obsessive-compulsive, depressive, and normal personality traits. *Journal of Personality and Social Psychology*, 1984, *46*, 1148–1161.

Schulz, R. Effects of control and predictability on the physical and psychological well-being of the institutionalized aged. *Journal of Personality and Social Psychology*, 1976, *33*, 563–573.

Schulz, R., & Hanusa, B. H. Long-term effects of control and predictability-enhancing interventions: Findings and ethical issues. *Journal of Personality and Social Psychology*, 1978, *36*, 1194–1201.

Seligman, M. E. P. Chronic fear produced by unpredictable electric shock. *Journal of Comparative and Physiological Psychology*, 1968, *66*, 402–411.

Seligman, M. E. P. *Helplessness: On depression, development, and death*. San Francisco: Freeman, 1975.

Skinner, B. F. *Science and human behavior*. New York: Macmillan, 1953.

Tolman, E. C. *Purposive behavior in animals and men*. New York: Century, 1932.

White, R. W. Motivation reconsidered: The concept of competence. *Psychological Review*, 1959, *66*, 297–333.

White, R. W. *Ego and reality in psychoanalytic theory* (Psychological Issues Series, Monograph No. 11). New York: International Universities Press, 1963.

Woodworth, R. S. *Dynamic psychology*. New York: Columbia University Press, 1918.

Woodworth, R. S. *Dynamics of behavior*. New York: Holt, 1958.

Wortman, C. B., & Brehm, J. W. Responses to uncontrollable outcomes: An integration of reactance theory and the learned helplessness model. In L. Berkowitz (Ed.), *Advances in experimental social psychology*, (Vol. 8). New York: Academic Press, 1975.

QUESTIONS FOR DISCUSSION

1 Why do you think Maslow's theory of motivation has been so popular among both managers and organizational researchers?

2 Considering the disconfirming research evidence on Maslow's theory, what aspects of Maslow's hierarchy of needs would you consider useful to the practicing manager?

3 If needs are activated by the environment, what complications does this suggest for the design of jobs and organizations?

4 As a manager, how would you utilize the knowledge that an employee of yours has a high need for achievement (*nAch*)?

5 If high *nAch* people tend to be superior performers, why not simply increase organizational performance by hiring only high *nAch* employees?

6 Researchers have found that a person with a high need for achievement may simultaneously have a low need for affiliation. What are the implications of this type of finding?

7 McClelland argues that the best manager is one who has a high need for power. Under what circumstances might it be more beneficial to have a manager with high *nAch*, and high *nAff*?

8 How does intrinsic motivation differ from extrinsic motivation? How is intrinsic motivation distinct from Maslow's lower-order drives/needs?

9 What well-intentioned actions taken by managers can inadvertently undermine the intrinsic motivation of employees?

10 What types of jobs would be most appropriate for someone with a high need for self-determination?

CHAPTER **3**

THE "ENVIRONMENT" IN MOTIVATION

In this chapter we turn our attention to theoretical approaches that emphasize the role of environmental consequences—that is, the response of the environment—in shaping the behavior of individuals. This category of theory has been termed "reinforcement theory" because such environmental consequences are hypothesized to increase (and thus to reinforce) or decrease the tendency of a person to respond in the same way when confronted with similar circumstances in the future. This basic approach to understanding motivated behavior was pioneered in the 1930s by the psychologist B. F. Skinner. Skinner's work through the years, as well as the subsequent research of many others, demonstrated the powerful effects of environmental consequences (whether positive or negative) on behavior, particularly when those consequences are arranged or delivered in some sort of organized and systematic fashion. Strictly speaking, Skinner did not use the concept of motivation because he thought it superfluous when explaining the effects of different schedules or patterns of reinforcement. Nevertheless, this type of approach is usually considered by organizational scholars to be highly pertinent to understanding motivation.

In considering the two selections by Hamner and Komaki that follow, remember that although the focus in this chapter is on the environment, it is the environment responding to the behavior of the individual. Thus, in a larger sense, reinforcement theory deals with the person-environment interaction (the subject of the next chapter), but the primary emphasis is on how the environment can be "constructed" or modified to bring about particular types of effects on a person's behavior. The basic principles of this approach are outlined in the first article by Hamner, who also goes on to discuss its relevance for the management of organizations as well as to identify some of the ethical and other concerns that have been raised about this particular approach. Not surprisingly, the so-called operant conditioning (Skinner's term, which is explained in Hamner's article) techniques that are generated by this way of viewing behavior have been extremely controversial when applied to humans—as compared to, say, pigeons or other similar laboratory animals on which the principles were originally developed. It is highly appropriate, therefore, for the reader to keep these kinds of issues in the forefront when considering applications of the reinforcement approach.

The second article, written especially for this book by Komaki and her colleagues, focuses directly on such applications in work and organizational settings. For some time there has been strong interest in applications of reinforcement theory in the everyday work environment. Komaki's article, based on research studies carried out over the past 20 years, highlights the issues and problems involved in such practical implementations of the theory. As the article demonstrates, the theory has been used to improve performance in a wide variety of work situations, on a wide set of behaviors, and with a wide range of consequences. Of particular interest, and representing a unique contribution of the article, is the latter section that explores the issue of how reinforcement theory can help us better understand from a motivational perspective why people do what they do.

Reinforcement Theory and Contingency Management in Organizational Settings

W. Clay Hamner

Traditionally management has been defined as the process of getting things done through other people. The succinctness of this definition is misleading in that, while it may be easy to say *what* a manager does, it is difficult to describe the determinants of behavior, i.e., to tell *how* the behavior of the manager influences the behavior of the employee toward accomplishment of a task. Human behavior in organizational settings has always been a phenomenon of interest and concern. However, it has only been in recent years that a concerted effort has been made by social scientists to describe the principles of reinforcement and their implications for describing the determinants of behavior as they relate to the theory and practice of management (e.g., see Nord, 1969; Wiard, 1972; Whyte, 1972; Jablonsky and DeVries, 1972; Hersey and Blanchard, 1972; and Behling, Schriesheim, and Tolliver, in press).[1]

Organizational leaders must resort to environmental changes as a means of influencing behavior. Reinforcement principles are the most useful method for this purpose because they indicate to the leader how he might proceed in designing or modifying the work environment in order to effect specific changes in behavior (Scott and Cummings, 1973). A reinforcement approach to management does not consist of a bag of tricks to be applied indiscriminately for the purpose of coercing unwilling people (Michael and Meyerson, 1962). Unfortunately, many people who think of Skinnerian applications (Skinner, 1969) in the field of management and personnel think of manipulation and adverse control over employees. Increased knowledge available today of the positive aspects of conditioning as applied to worker performance should help to dispel these notions.

The purpose of this paper is to describe the determinants of behavior as seen from a reinforcement theory point of view, and to describe how the management of the contingencies of reinforcement in organizational settings is a key to successful management. Hopefully, this paper will enable the manager to understand how his behavior affects the behavior of his subordinates and to see that in most cases the failure or success of the worker at the performance of a task is a direct function of the manager's own behavior. Since a large portion of the manager's time is spent in the process of modifying behavior patterns and shaping them so that they will be more goal oriented, it is appropriate that this paper begin by describing the processes and principles that govern behavior.

LEARNING AS A PREREQUISITE FOR BEHAVIOR

Learning is such a common phenomenon that we tend to fail to recognize its occurrence. Nevertheless, one of the major premises of reinforcement theory is that

From H. L. Tosi and W. C. Hamner (Eds.), *Organizational behavior and management: A contingency approach*. Chicago: St. Clair Press, 1974. © 1974, St. Clair Press. Reprinted by permission of John Wiley & Sons, Inc.

all behavior is learned—a worker's skill, a supervisor's attitude and a secretary's manners. The importance of learning in organizational settings is asserted by Costello and Zalkind when they conclude:

> Every aspect of human behavior is responsive to learning experiences. Knowledge, language, and skills, of course; but also attitudes, value systems, and personality characteristics. All the individual's activities in the organization—his loyalties, awareness of organizational goals, job performance, even his safety record have been learned in the largest sense of that term. (1963, p. 205)

There seems to be general agreement among social scientists that learning can be defined as *a relatively permanent change in behavior potentiality that results from reinforced practice or experience*. Note that this definition states that there is change in behavior potentiality and not necessarily in behavior itself. The reason for this distinction rests on the fact that we can observe other people responding to their environments, see the consequences which accrue to them, and be vicariously conditioned. For example, a boy can watch his older sister burn her hand on a hot stove and "learn" that pain is the result of touching a hot stove. This definition therefore allows us to account for "no-trial" learning. Bandura (1969) describes this as imitative learning and says that while behavior can be *acquired* by observing, reading, or other vicarious methods, "*performance* of observationally learned responses will depend to a great extent upon the nature of the reinforcing consequences to the model or to the observer" (p. 128).

Luthans (1973, p. 362) says that we need to consider the following points when we define the learning process:

1 Learning involves a change, though not necessarily an improvement, in behavior. Learning generally has the connotation of improved performance, but under this definition bad habits, prejudices, stereotypes, and work restrictions are learned.

2 The change in behavior must be relatively permanent in order to be considered learning. This qualification rules out behavioral changes resulting from fatigue or temporary adaptations as learning.

3 Some form of practice or experience is necessary for learning to occur.

4 Finally, practice or experience must be reinforced in order for learning to occur. If reinforcement does not accompany the practice or experience, the behavior will eventually disappear.

From this discussion, we can conclude that learning is the acquisition of knowledge, and performance is the translation of knowledge into practice. The primary effect of reinforcement is to strengthen and intensify certain aspects of ensuing behavior. Behavior that has become highly differentiated (shaped) can be understood and accounted for only in terms of the history of reinforcement of that behavior (Morse, 1966). Reinforcement generates a reproducible behavior process in time. A response occurs and is followed by a reinforcer, and further responses occur with a characteristic temporal patterning. When a response is reinforced it subsequently occurs more frequently than before it was reinforced.

Reinforcement may be assumed to have a characteristic and reproducible effect on a particular behavior, and usually it will enhance and intensify that behavior (Skinner, 1938; 1953).

TWO BASIC LEARNING PROCESSES

Before discussing in any detail exactly how the general laws or principles of reinforcement can be used to predict and influence behavior, we must differentiate between two types of behavior. One kind is known as *voluntary* or *operant* behavior, and the other is known as *reflex* or *respondent* behavior. Respondent behavior takes in all responses of human beings that are *elicited* by special stimulus changes in the environment. An example would be when a person turns a light on in a dark room (stimulus change), his eyes contract (respondent behavior).

Operant behavior includes an even greater amount of human activity. It takes in all the responses of a person that may at some time be said to have an effect upon or do something to the person's outside world (Keller, 1969). Operant behavior *operates* on this world either directly or indirectly. For example, when a person presses the up button at the elevator entrance to "call" the elevator, he is operating on his environment.

The process of learning or acquiring reflex behavior is different from the processes of learning or acquiring voluntary behavior. The two basic and distinct learning processes are known as *classical conditioning* and *operant conditioning*. It is from studying these two learning processes that much of our knowledge of individual behavior has emerged.

Classical Conditioning[2]

Pavlov (1902) noticed, while studying the automatic reflexes associated with digestion, that his laboratory dog salivated (unconditioned response) not only when food (unconditioned stimulus) was placed in the dog's mouth, but also when other stimuli were presented before food was placed in the dog's mouth. In other words, by presenting a neutral stimulus (ringing of a bell) every time food was presented to the dog, Pavlov was able to get the dog to salivate to the bell alone.

A stimulus which is not a part of a reflex relationship (the bell in Pavlov's experiment) becomes a *conditioned stimulus* for the response by repeated, temporal pairing with an *unconditioned* stimulus (food) which already elicits the response. This new relationship is known as a conditioned reflex, and the pairing procedure is known as classical conditioning.

While it is important to understand that reflex behavior is conditioned by a different process than is voluntary behavior, classical conditioning principles are of little use to the practicing manager. Most of the behavior that is of interest to society does not fit in the paradigm of reflex behavior (Michael and Meyerson, 1962). Nevertheless, the ability to generalize from one stimulus setting to another is very important in human learning and problem solving, and for this reason, knowledge of the classical conditioning process is important.

Operant Conditioning[3]

The basic distinction between classical and operant conditioning procedures is in terms of the *consequences* of the conditioned response. In classical conditioning, the sequence of events is independent of the subject's behavior. In operant conditioning, consequences (rewards and punishments) are made to occur as a consequence of the subject's response or failure to respond. The distinction between these two methods is shown in Figure 1.

In Figure 1, we see that classical conditioning involves a three stage process. In the diagram, let *S* refer to *stimulus* and *R* to *response*. We see that in stage 1, the unconditioned stimulus (food) elicits an unconditioned response (salivation). In stage 2, a neutral stimulus (bell) elicits no known response. However, in stage 3, after the ringing of the bell is repeatedly paired with the presence of food, the bell alone becomes a conditioned stimulus and elicits a conditioned response (salivation). The subject has no control over the unconditioned or conditioned response, but is "at the mercy" of his environment and his past conditioning history.

Note, however, that for voluntary behavior, the consequence is dependent on the behavior of the individual in a given stimulus setting. Such behavior can be said to "operate" (Skinner, 1969) on the environment, in contrast to behavior which is "respondent" to prior eliciting stimuli (Michael and Meyerson, 1962). Reinforcement is not given every time the stimulus is presented, but is *only* given when the correct response is made. For example, if an employee taking a work break puts a penny (R) in the soft drink machine (S), nothing happens (consequence). However, if he puts a quarter (R) in the machine (S), he gets the soft drink (consequence). In other words, the employee's behavior is *instrumental* in determining the consequences which accrue to him.

The interrelationships between the three components of (1) *stimulus* or environment, (2) *response* or performance, and (3) consequences or *reinforcements* are known as the *contingencies* of reinforcement. Skinner (1969) says "The class

FIGURE 1
Classical vs. operant conditioning.

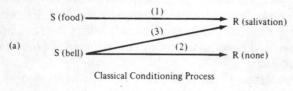

Classical Conditioning Process

— — — — — — — (S = stimulus, R = responses, arrow = leads to) — — — — — — —

Operant Conditioning Process

of responses upon which a reinforcer is *contingent* is called an operant, to suggest the action on the environment followed by reinforcements (p. 7).'' Operant conditioning presupposes that human beings explore their environment and act upon it. This behavior, randomly emitted at first, can be constructed as an operant by making a reinforcement contingent on a response. Any stimulus present when an operant is reinforced acquires control in the sense that the rate of response for that individual will be higher when it is present. "Such a stimulus does not act as a *goal*; it does not elicit the response (as was the case in classical conditioning of reflex behavior)[4] in the sense of forcing it to occur. It is simply an essential aspect of the occasion upon which response is made and reinforced (Skinner, 1969, p. 7).''

Therefore, an adequate formulation of the interaction between an individual and his environment must always specify three things: (1) the occasion upon which a response occurs, (2) the response itself and (3) the reinforcing consequences. Skinner holds that the consequences determine the likelihood that a given operant will be performed in the future. Thus to change behavior, the consequences of the behavior must be changed, i.e., the contingencies must be rearranged (the ways in which the consequences are related to the behavior) (Behling, *et al.,* in press). For Skinner, this behavior generated by a given set of contingencies can be accounted for without appealing to hypothetical inner states (e.g., awareness or expectancies). "If a conspicuous stimulus does not have an effect, it is not because the organism has not attended to it or because some central gatekeeper has screened it out, but because the stimulus plays no important role in the prevailing contingencies (Skinner, 1969, p. 8).''

Arrangement of the Contingencies of Reinforcement

In order to *understand* and *interpret* behavior, we must look at the interrelationship among the components of the contingencies of behavior. If one expects to influence behavior, he must also be able to manipulate the consequences of the behavior (Skinner, 1969). Haire (1964) reports the importance of being able to manipulate the consequences when he says,

> Indeed, whether he is conscious of it or not, the superior is bound to be constantly shaping the behavior of his subordinates by the way in which he utilizes the rewards that are at his disposal, and he will inevitably modify the behavior patterns of his work group thereby. For this reason, it is important to see as clearly as possible what is going on, so that the changes can be planned and chosen in advance, rather than simply accepted after the fact.

After appropriate reinforcers that have sufficient incentive value to maintain stable responsiveness have been chosen, the contingencies between specific performances and reinforcing stimuli must be arranged (Bandura, 1969). Employers intuitively use rewards in their attempt to modify and influence behavior, but their efforts often produce limited results because the methods are used improperly, inconsistently, or inefficiently. In many instances considerable rewards are bestowed upon the workers, but they are not made conditional or contingent on the behavior the manager wishes to promote. Also, "long delays often intervene between the occurrence of the desired behavior and its intended consequences; special privileges, activities, and rewards are generally furnished according to fixed time schedules rather than performance requirements; and in many cases, positive reinforcers are inadvertently made contingent upon the wrong type of behavior" (Bandura, 1969, pp. 229–230).

One of the primary reasons that managers fail to "motivate" workers to perform in the desired manner is due to a lack of understanding of the power of the contingencies of reinforcement over the employee and of the manager's role in arranging these contingencies. The laws or principles for arranging the contingencies are not hard to understand, and if students of behavior grasp them firmly, they are powerful managerial tools which can be used to increase supervisory effectiveness.

As we have said, operant conditioning is the process by which behavior is modified by manipulation of the contingencies of the behavior. To understand how this works, we will first look at various *types* (arrangements) of contingencies, and then at various *schedules* of the contingencies available. Rachlin (1970) described the four basic ways available to the manager of arranging the contingencies—*positive reinforcement, avoidance learning, extinction,* and *punishment.* The difference among these types of contingencies depends on the consequence which results from the behavioral act. Positive reinforcement and avoidance learning are methods of strengthening *desired* behavior, and extinction and punishment are methods of weakening *undesired* behavior.

Positive Reinforcement "A positive reinforcer is a stimulus which, when added to a situation, strengthens the probability of an operant response (Skinner, 1953, p. 73)." The reason it strengthens the response is explained by Thorndike's (1911) Law of Effect. This law states simply that behavior which appears to lead to a positive consequence tends to be repeated, while behavior which appears to lead to a negative consequence tends not to be repeated. A positive consequence is called a reward.

Reinforcers, either positive or negative, are classified as either: (1) unconditioned or primary reinforcers, or (2) conditioned or secondary reinforcers. Primary reinforcers such as food, water, and sex are of biological importance in that they are innately rewarding and have effects which are independent of past experiences. Secondary reinforcers such as job advancement, praise, recognition, and money derive their effects from a consistent pairing with other reinforcers (i.e., they are conditioned). Secondary reinforcement, therefore, depends on the individual and his past reinforcement history. What is rewarding to one person may not be rewarding to another. Managers should look for a reward system which has maximal reinforcing consequences to the group he is supervising.

Regardless of whether the positive reinforcer is primary or secondary in nature, once it has been determined that the consequence has reward value to the worker, it can be used to increase the worker's performance. So the *first step* in the successful application of reinforcement procedures is to select reinforcers that are sufficiently powerful and durable to "maintain responsiveness while complex patterns of behavior are being established and strengthened'' (Bandura, 1969, p. 225).

The *second step* is to design the contingencies in such a way that the reinforcing events are made contingent upon the desired behavior. This is the rule of reinforcement which is most often violated. Rewards must result from performance, and the greater the degree of performance by an employee, the greater should be his reward. Money as a reinforcer will be discussed later, but it should be noted that money is not the only reward available. In fact, for unionized employees, the supervisor has virtually no way to tie money to performance. Nevertheless, other forms of rewards, such as recognition, promotion and job assignments, can be made contingent on good performance. Unless a manager is willing to discriminate between employees based on their level of performance, the effectiveness of his power over the employee is nil.

The arrangement of positive reinforcement contingencies can be pictured as follows:

$$\text{Stimulus} \rightarrow \text{Desired response} \rightarrow \text{Positive consequences}$$
$$(S \rightarrow R \rightarrow R^+)$$

The stimulus is the work environment which leads to a response (some level of performance). If this response leads to positive consequences, then the probability of that response being emitted again increases (Law of Effect). Now, if the behavior is undesired, then the supervisor is conditioning or teaching the employee that undesired behavior will lead to a desired reward. It is important therefore that the reward administered be equal to the performance input of the employee. Homans (1950) labels this as the rule of distributive justice and stated that this reciprocal norm applies in both formal (work) and informal (friendship) relationships. In other words, the employee *exchanges* his services for the rewards of the organization. In order to maintain desired performance, it is important that the manager design the reward system so that the level of reward administered is proportionately contingent on the level of performance emitted.

The *third step* is to design the contingencies in such a way that a reliable procedure for eliciting or inducing the desired response patterns is established; otherwise, if they never occur there will be few opportunities to influence the desired behavior through contingent management. If the behavior that a manager wishes to strengthen is already present, and occurs with some frequency, then contingent applications of incentives can, from the outset, increase and maintain the desired performance patterns at a high level. However, as Bandura (1969) states, "When the initial level of the desired behavior is extremely low, if the criterion for reinforcement is initially set too high, most, if not all, of the person's responses go unrewarded, so that his efforts are gradually extinguished and his motivation diminished (p. 232)."

The nature of the learning process is such that acquiring the new response patterns can be easily established. The principle of operant conditioning says that an operant followed by a positive reinforcement is more likely to occur under similar conditions in the future. Through the process of *generalization,* the more nearly alike the new situation or stimulus is to the original one, the more the old behavior is likely to be emitted in the new environment. For example, if you contract with an electrician to rewire your house, he is able to bring with him enough old behavioral patterns which he generalized to this unfamiliar, but similar, stimulus setting (the house) in order to accomplish the task. He has learned through his past reinforcement history that, when in a new environment, one way to speed up the correct behavior needed to obtain reward is to generalize from similar settings with which he has had experience. Perhaps one reason an employer wants a person with work experience is because the probability of that person emitting the correct behavior is greater and thus the job of managing that person simplified.

Just as generalization is the ability to react to similarities in the environment, *discrimination* is the ability to react to differences in a new environmental setting. Usually when an employee moves from one environment (a job, a city, an office) to another he finds that only certain dimensions of the stimulus conditions change. While all of the responses of the employee in this new setting will not be correct, by skilled use of the procedures of reinforcement currently being discussed, we can bring about the more precise type of stimulus control called discrimination. When we purchase a new car, we do not have to relearn how to drive a car (generalizable stimulus). Instead we need only learn the differences in the new car and the old car so that we can respond to these differences in order to get reinforced. This procedure is called *discrimination training*. "If in the presence of a stimulus a response is reinforced, and in the absence of this stimulus it is extinguished, the stimulus will control the probability of the response in high degree. Such a stimulus is called a *discriminative stimulus* (Michael and Meyerson, 1962)."

The development of effective discriminative repertoires is important for dealing with many different people on an interpersonal basis. Effective training techniques will allow the supervisor to develop the necessary discriminative repertoires in his new employees (e.g., see Bass and Vaughan, 1966, *Training in Industry: The Management of Learning*).

Using the principles of generalization and discrimination in a well-designed training program allows the manager to accomplish the third goal of eliciting or inducing the desired response patterns. Training is a method of *shaping* desired behavior so that it can be conditioned to come under the control of the reinforcement stimuli. Shaping behavior is necessary when the response to be learned is not currently in the individual's repertoire and when it is a fairly complex behavior. In shaping, we teach a desired response by reinforcing the series of successive steps which lead to the final response. This method is essentially the one your parents used when they first taught you to drive. You were first taught how to adjust the seat and mirror, fasten the seat belt, turn on the lights and windshield wipers, and then how to start the engine. Each time you successfully completed each stage you were positively reinforced by some comment. You then were allowed to practice driving on back roads and in empty lots. By focusing on one of these aspects at a time and reinforcing proper responses, your parents were able to shape your driving behavior until you reached the final stage of being able to drive. After your behavior was shaped, driving other cars or driving in new territories was accomplished successfully by the process of generalization and discrimination. This same process is used with a management trainee who is rotated from department to department for a period of time until he has "learned the ropes." After his managerial behavior has been minimally shaped, he is transferred to a managerial position where, using the principles of generalization and discrimination, he is able to adjust to the contingencies of the work environment.

Avoidance Learning   The second type of contingency arrangement available to the manager is called escape, or avoidance learning. Just as with positive reinforcement, this is a method of strengthening desired behavior. A contingency arrangement in which an individual's performance can terminate an already noxious stimulus is called *escape* learning. When behavior can prevent the onset of a noxious stimulus the procedure is called *avoidance learning.* In both cases, the result is the development and maintenance of the desired operant behavior (Michael and Meyerson, 1962).

An example of this kind of control can be easily found in a work environment. Punctuality of employees is often maintained by avoidance learning. The noxious stimulus is the criticism by the shop steward or office manager for being late. In order to avoid criticism other employees make a special effort to come to work on time. A supervisor begins criticizing a worker for "goofing off." Other workers may intensify their efforts to escape the criticism of the supervisor.

The arrangement of an escape reinforcement contingency can be diagrammed as follows:

$$\text{Noxious stimulus} \rightarrow \text{Desired response} \rightarrow \text{Removal of noxious stimulus}$$
$$(S^- \rightarrow R \nrightarrow S^-)$$

The distinction between the process of strengthening behavior by means of positive reinforcement techniques and avoidance learning techniques should be noted carefully. In one case, the individual works hard to gain the consequences from the environment which result from good work, and in the second case, the individual works hard to avoid the noxious aspects of the environment itself. In both cases the same behavior is strengthened.

While Skinner (1953) recognizes that avoidance learning techniques can be used to condition desired behavior, he does not advocate their use. Instead a Skinnerian approach to operant conditioning is primarily based on the principles of positive reinforcement.

Extinction   While positive reinforcement and avoidance learning techniques can be used by managers to strengthen desired behavior, extinction and punishment techniques are methods available to managers for reducing undesired behavior. When positive reinforcement for a learned or previously conditioned response is withheld, individuals will continue to exhibit that behavior for an extended period of time. Under repeated nonreinforcement, the behavior decreases and eventually disappears. This decline in response rate as a result of nonrewarded repetition of a task is defined as *extinction.*

The diagram of the arrangement of the contingency of extinction can be shown as follows:

(1) Stimulus → Response → Positive consequences
    $(S \rightarrow R \rightarrow R^+)$

(2) Stimulus→Response→Withholding of positive consequences
    $(S \rightarrow R \nrightarrow R^+)$

(3) Stimulus → Withholding of response
    $(S \nrightarrow R)$

The behavior which was previously reinforced because (a) it was desired or (b) by poor reinforcement practices is no longer desired. To extinguish this behavior in a naturally recurring situation, response patterns sustained by positive reinforcement (stage 1) are frequently eliminated (stage 3) by discontinuing the rewards (stage 2) that ordinarily produce the behavior. This method when combined with a positive reinforcement method is the procedure of behavior modification recommended by Skinner (1953). It leads to the least negative side effects and when the two methods are used together, it allows the employee to get the rewards he desires and allows the organization to eliminate the undesired behavior.

Punishment A second method of reducing the frequency of undesired behavior is through the use of punishment. Punishment is the most controversial method of behavior modification, and most of the ethical questions about operant methods of control center around this technique. "One of the principal objections to aversive control stems from the widespread belief that internal, and often unconscious, forces are the major determinant of behavior. From this perspective, punishment may temporarily suppress certain expressions, but the underlying impulses retain their strength and press continuously for discharge through alternative actions (Bandura, 1969, p. 292)." While Skinner (1953) discounts the internal state hypothesis, he recommends that extinction rather than punishment be used to decrease the probability of the occurrence of a particular behavior.

Punishment is defined as presenting an aversive or noxious consequence contingent upon a response, or removing a positive consequence contingent upon a response. Based on the Law of Effect, as rewards strengthen behavior, punishment weakens it. This process can be shown as follows:

(1) Stimulus → Undesired behavior → Noxious consequence or withholding of
    $(S \rightarrow R \rightarrow R^-)$ positive consequence
    $(\quad$ or $\nrightarrow R^+)$

(2) Stimulus → Undesired behavior
    $(S \nrightarrow R)$

Notice carefully the difference in the withholding of rewards in the punishment process and the withholding of rewards in the extinction process. In the extinction process, we withhold rewards for behavior that has previously been administered the rewards because the behavior was desired. In punishment, we withhold a reward because the behavior is undesired, has never been associated with the reward before, and is in fact a noxious consequence. For example, if your young son began imitating an older neighborhood boy's use of profanity and you thought it was "cute," you might reinforce the behavior by laughing or by calling public attention to it. Soon, the son learns one way to get the recognition he craves is to use profanity—even though he may have no concept of its meaning. As the child reaches an accountable age, you decide that his use of profanity is no longer as cute as it once was. To stop the behavior you can do one of three things: (1) You can withhold the previous recognition you gave the child by ignoring him (extinction), (2) You can give the child a spanking (punishment by noxious consequence), or (3) You can withhold his allowance or refuse to let him watch television (punishment by withholding of positive consequences not previously connected with the act.)

It should be noted that method 2 and perhaps method 3 would be considered cruel because of the parent's own inconsistencies. Punishment should rarely be used to extinguish behavior that has previously been reinforced if the person administering the punishment is the same person who previously reinforced the behavior. However, had the parent failed to extinguish the use of profanity prior to sending the child out in society (e.g., school, church), it is possible that the society may punish the child for behavior that the parent is reinforcing or at least tolerating. It is often argued therefore that the failure to use punishment early in the life of a child for socially unacceptable behavior (e.g., stealing, driving at excessive speeds, poor table manners) is more cruel than the punishment itself, simply because the society will withhold rewards or administer aversive consequences for the behavior which the parents should have extinguished.

The use of aversive control is frequently questioned on the assumption that it produces undesirable by-products. In many cases this concern is warranted. Bandura (1969) states that it depends on the circumstances and on the past reinforcement history of the reinforcement agent and the reinforcement target as to whether punishment or extinction should be used. He says:

> Many of the unfavorable effects, however, that are sometimes associated with punishment are not necessarily inherent in the methods themselves but result from the faulty manner in which they are applied. A great deal of human behavior is, in fact, modified and closely regulated by natural aversive contingencies without any ill effects. On the basis of negative consequences people learn to avoid or to protect themselves against hazardous falls, flaming or scalding objects, deafening sounds, and other hurtful stimuli. . . . In instances where certain activities can have injurious effects, aversive contingencies *must* be socially arranged to ensure survival. Punishment is rarely indicated for ineffectiveness or deleterious side effects when used, for example, to teach young children not to insert metal objects into electrical outlets, not to cross busy thoroughfares. . . . Certain types of negative sanctions, if applied considerately, can

likewise aid in eliminating self-defeating and socially detrimental behavior without creating any special problems. (p. 294)

Rules for Using Operant Conditioning Techniques   Several rules concerning the arrangement of the contingencies of reinforcement should be discussed. While these rules have common sense appeal, the research findings indicate that these rules are often violated by managers when they design control systems.

Rule 1. Don't reward all people the same. In other words, differentiate the rewards based on performance as compared to some defined objective or standard. We know that people compare their own performance to that of their peers to determine how well they are doing ("Social Comparison Theory," Festinger, 1954) and they compare their rewards to the rewards of their peers ("Equity Theory," Adams, 1965) in order to determine how to evaluate their rewards. While some managers seem to think that the fairest system of compensation is one where everyone in the same job classification gets the same pay, employees want differentiation so that they know their importance to the organization. Based on social comparison and equity theory assumptions, it can be argued that managers who reward all people the same are encouraging, at best, only average performance. Behavior of high performance workers is being extinguished (ignored) while the behavior of average performance and poor performance workers is being strengthened by positive reinforcement.

Rule 2. Failure to respond has reinforcing consequences. Managers who find the job of differentiating between workers so unpleasant that they fail to respond must recognize that failure to respond modifies behavior. "Indeed, whether he is conscious of it or not, the superior is bound to be constantly shaping the behavior of his subordinates by the way in which he utilizes the rewards that are at his disposal, and he will inevitably modify the behavior of his work group (Haire, 1964)." Managers must be careful that they examine the performance consequence of their non-action as well as their action.

Rule 3. Be sure to tell a person what he can do to get reinforced. By making clear the contingencies of reinforcement to the worker, a manager may be actually increasing the individual freedom of the worker. The employee who has a standard against which to measure his job will have a built-in feedback system which allows him to make judgments about his own work. The awarding of the reinforcement in an organization where the worker's goal is specified will be associated with the performance of the worker and not based on the biases of the supervisor. The assumption is that the supervisor rates the employee accurately (see Scott and Hamner, 1973a) and that he then reinforces the employee based on his ratings (see Scott and Hamner, 1973b). If the supervisor fails to rate accurately or administer rewards based on performance, then the stated goals for the worker will lose stimulus control, and the worker will be forced to search for the "true" contingencies, i.e., what behavior should he perform in order to get rewarded (e.g., ingratiation? loyalty? positive attitude?).

Rule 4. Be sure to tell a person what he is doing wrong. As a general rule, very few people find the act of failing rewarding. One assumption of behavior therefore is that a worker wants to be rewarded in a positive manner. A supervisor should never use extinction or punishment as a sole method for modifying behavior, but if used judiciously in conjunction with other techniques designed to promote more effective response options (Rule 3) such combined procedures can hasten the change process. If the supervisor fails to specify why a reward is being withheld, the employee may associate it with past desired behavior instead of the undesired behavior that the supervisor is trying to extinguish. The supervisor then extinguishes good performance while having no effect on the undesired behavior.

Rules 3 and 4, when used in combination, should allow the manager to control behavior in the best interest of reaching organizational goals. At the same time they should give the employee the clarity he needs to see that his own behavior and not the behavior of the supervisor controls his outcomes.

Rule 5. Don't punish in front of others. The reason for this rule is quite simple. The punishment (e.g., reprimand) should be enough to extinguish the undesired behavior. By administering the punishment in front of the work group, the worker is doubly punished in the sense that he is also put out of face (Goffman, 1959). This additional punishment may lead to negative side-effects in three ways. First, the worker whose self-image is damaged may feel that he must retaliate in order to protect himself. Therefore, the supervisor has actually increased undesired responses. Secondly, the work group may misunderstand the reason for the punishment and through "avoidance learning" may modify their own behavior in ways not intended by the supervisor. Third, the work group is also being punished in the sense that observing a member of their team being reprimanded has noxious or aversive properties for most people. This may result in a decrease in the performance of the total work group.

Rule 6. Make the consequences equal to the behavior. In other words be fair. Don't cheat the worker out of his just rewards. If he is a good worker, tell him. Many supervisors find it very difficult to praise an employee. Others find it very difficult to counsel an employee about what he is doing wrong. When a manager fails to use these reinforcement tools, he is actually reducing his effectiveness. When a worker is overrewarded he may feel guilty (Adams, 1965) and based on the principles of reinforcement, the worker's current level of performance is being conditioned. If his performance level is less than others who get the same reward, he has no reason to increase his output. When a worker is underrewarded, he becomes angry with the system (Adams, 1965). His behavior is being extinguished and the company may be forcing the good employee (underrewarded) to seek employment elsewhere while encouraging the poor employee (overrewarded) to stay.

An Argument for Positive Reinforcement

Most workers enter the work place willingly if not eagerly. They have a sense of right and wrong and have been thoroughly conditioned by their parents and by society. By the time they reach adulthood, it can be assumed that they are mature. For these reasons, it is argued here as well as by others (Skinner, 1953; Wiard, 1972), that the only tool needed for worker motivation is the presence or absence of positive reinforcement. In other words, managers do not, as a general rule, need to use avoidance learning or punishment techniques in order to control behavior.

Whyte (1972) says "positive reinforcers generally are more effective than negative reinforcers in the production and maintenance of behavior" (p. 67). Wiard (1972) points out, "There may be cases where the use of punishment has resulted in improved performance, but they are few and far between. The pitfalls of punishment can be encountered with any indirect approach" (p. 16). However, a positive reinforcement program is geared toward the desired results. It emphasizes what needs to be done, rather than what should not be done. A positive reinforcement program is result oriented, rather than process oriented. A well designed program encourages individual growth and freedom, whereas negative approach (avoidance learning and punishment) encourages immaturity in the individual and therefore eventually in the organization itself.

The reason organizations are ineffective according to Skinner (1969) is because they insist on using avoidance learning or punishment techniques, and because they fail to use a positive reinforcement program in an effective manner. He says:

> The contingencies of positive reinforcement arranged by governmental and religious agencies are primitive, and the agencies continue to lean heavily on the puritanical solution. Economic reinforcement might seem to represent an environmental solution, but it is badly programmed and the results are unsatisfactory for both the employer (since not much is done) and the employee (since work is still work). Education and the management of retardates and psychotics are still largely aversive. In short, as we have seen, the most powerful forces bearing on human behavior are not being effectively used. . . . Men are happy in an environment in which active, productive, and creative behavior is reinforced in effective ways. (pp. 63–64)

Schedules of Positive Reinforcement

The previous discussion was primarily concerned with methods of arranging the contingencies of reinforcement in order to modify behavior. Two major points were discussed. First, some type of reinforcement is necessary in order to produce a change in behavior. Second, a combined program of positive reinforcement and extinction are more effective for use in organizations than are programs using punishment and/or avoidance learning techniques. The previous discussion thus tells what causes behavior and why it is important information for the manager, but it does not discuss the several important issues dealing with the scheduling or administering of positive reinforcement.

According to Costello and Zalkind (1963), "The speed with which learning takes place and also how lasting its effects will be is determined by the timing of reinforcement" (p. 193). In other words, the effectiveness varies as a function of the schedule of its administration. A reinforcement schedule is a more-or-less formal specification of the occurrence of a reinforcer in relation to the behavioral sequence to be conditioned, and effectiveness of the reinforcer depends as much upon its scheduling as upon any of its other features (magnitude, quality and degree of association with the behavioral act) (Adam and Scott, 1971).

There are many conceivable arrangements of a positive reinforcement schedule which managers can use to reward workers (Ferster and Skinner, 1957). Aldis (1961) identifies two basic types of schedules which have the most promise concerning possible worker motivation. These schedules are *continuous* and *partial reinforcement* schedules.

Continuous Reinforcement Schedule Under this schedule, every time the correct operant is emitted by the worker, it is followed by a reinforcer. With this schedule, behavior increases very rapidly but when the reinforcer is removed (extinction) performance decreases rapidly. For this reason it is not recommended for use by the manager over a long period of time. It is also difficult or impossible for a manager to reward the employee continuously for emitting desired behavior. Therefore a manager should generally consider using one or more of the partial reinforcement schedules when he administers both financial and nonfinancial rewards.

Partial Reinforcement Schedules Partial reinforcement, where reinforcement does not occur after every correct operant, leads to slower learning but stronger retention of a response than total or continuous reinforcement. "In other words, *learning is more permanent when we reward correct behavior only part of the time*" (Bass and Vaughan, 1966, p. 20). This factor is extremely relevant to the observed strong resistance to changes in attitudes, values, norms, and the like.

Ferster and Skinner (1957) have described four types of partial reinforcement schedules for operant learning situations. They are:

1 Fixed Interval Schedule Under this schedule a reinforcer is administered only when the desired response occurs after the passage of a specified period of time since the previous reinforcement. Thus a worker paid on a weekly basis would receive a full pay check every Friday, assuming that the worker was performing minimally acceptable behavior. This method offers the least motivation for hard work among employees (Aldis, 1961). The kind of behavior often observed with fixed interval schedules is a pause after reinforcement and then an increase in rate of responding until a high rate of performance occurs just as the interval is about to end. Suppose the plant manager visits the shipping department each day at approximately 10:00 A.M. This fixed schedule of supervisory recognition will probably cause performance to be at its highest just prior to the plant manager's visit and then performance will probably steadily decline thereafter and not reach its peak again until the next morning's visit.

2 Variable Interval Schedule Under this schedule, reinforcement is administered at some variable interval of time around some average. This schedule is not recommended for use with a pay plan (Aldis, 1961), but it is an ideal method to use for administering praise, promotions, and supervisory visits. Since the reinforcers are dispensed unpredictably, variable schedules generate higher rates of response and more stable and consistent performance (Bandura, 1969). Suppose our plant manager visits the shipping department on an *average* of once a day but at randomly selected time intervals, i.e., twice on Monday, once on Tuesday, not on Wednesday, not on Thursday, and twice on Friday, all at different times during the day. Performance will be higher and have less fluctuation than under the fixed interval schedule.

3 Fixed Ratio Schedule Here a reward is delivered only when a fixed number of desired responses take place. This is essentially the piece-work schedule for pay. The response level here is significantly higher than that obtained under any of the interval (or time-based) schedules.

4 Variable Ratio Schedule Under this schedule, a reward is delivered only after a number of desired responses with the number of desired responses changing from the occurrence of one reinforcer to the next, around an average. Thus a person working on a 15 to 1 variable ratio schedule might receive reinforcement after ten responses, then twenty responses, then fifteen responses, etc., to an average of one reinforcer per fifteen responses. Gambling is an example of a variable ratio reward schedule. Research evidence reveals that of all the variations in scheduling procedures available, this is the most powerful in sustaining behavior (Jablonsky and DeVries, 1972). In industry, this plan would be impossible to use as the only plan for scheduling reinforcement. However, Aldis (1961) suggests how this method could be used to supplement other monetary reward schedules:

> Take the annual Christmas bonus as an example. In many instances, this "surprise" gift has become nothing more than a ritualized annual salary supplement which everybody expects. Therefore, its incentive-building value is largely lost. Now suppose that the total bonus were distributed at irregular intervals throughout the year and in small sums dependent upon the amount of work done. Wouldn't the workers find their urge to work increased? (p. 63)

An important point to remember is that to be effective a schedule should always include the specification of a contingency between the behavior desired and the occurrence of a reinforcer. In many cases it may be necessary to use each of the various schedules for administering rewards—for example, base pay of a fixed interval schedule, promotions and raises on a variable interval schedule, recognition of above average performance with a piece-rate plan (fixed ratio) and supplementary bonuses on a variable ratio schedule. The effect of each of the types of reinforcement schedules and the various methods of arranging reinforcement contingencies on worker performance is summarized in Table 1.

The necessity for arranging appropriate reinforcement contingencies is dramatically illustrated by several studies in which rewards were shifted from a response-contingent (ratio) to a time-contingent basis (interval). During the period in which rewards were made conditional upon occurrence of the desired behavior, the appropriate response patterns were exhibited at a consistently high level. When the same rewards were given based on time and independent of the worker's behavior, there was a marked drop in the desired behavior. The reinstatement of the performance-contingent reward schedule promptly restored the high level of responsiveness (Lovaas, Berberich, Perloff, and Schaeffer, 1966; Baer, Paterson, and Sherman, 1967). Similar declines in performance were obtained when workers were provided rewards in advance without performance requirements (Ayllon and Azrin, 1965; Bandura and Perloff, 1967).

TABLE 1
OPERANT CONDITIONING SUMMARY

Arrangement of reinforcement contingencies	Schedule of reinforcement contingencies	Effect on behavior when applied to the individual	Effect on behavior when removed from the individual
	Continuous reinforcement	Fastest method to establish a new behavior	Fastest method to extinguish a new behavior
	Partial reinforcement	Slowest method to establish a new behavior	Slowest method to extinguish a new behavior
	Variable partial reinforcement	More consistent response frequencies	Slower extinction rate
	Fixed partial reinforcement	Less consistent response frequencies	Faster extinction rate
Positive reinforcement Avoidance reinforcement		Increased frequency over preconditioning level	Return to preconditioning level
Punishment Extinction		Decreased frequency over preconditioning level	Return to preconditioning level

Source: Adapted from Behling et al., reprinted with permission of the author from "Present Theories and New Directions in Theories of Work Effort," *Journal Supplement and Abstract Service* of the American Psychological Corporation.

Aldis (1961) encourages businessmen to recognize the importance of a positive reinforcement program. He also says that experimentation with various schedules of positive reinforcement is the key to reducing job boredom and increasing worker satisfaction. He concludes:

> Most of us fully realize that a large proportion of all workers hold jobs that are boring and repetitive and that these employees are motivated to work not by positive rewards but by various oblique forms of threat. . . . The challenge is to motivate men by positive rewards rather than by negative punishment or threats of punishments. . . . Businessmen should recognize how much their conventional wage and salary systems essentially rely on negative reinforcement.
>
> Thus the promise of newer methods of wage payments which rely on more immediate rewards, on piece-rate pay, and greater randomization does not lie only in the increase in productivity that might follow. The greater promise is that such experiments may lead to happier workers as well. (p. 63)

MANAGEMENT AND THE DISSEMINATION OF KNOWLEDGE

Previously we defined *learning* as the acquisition of knowledge (by the process of operant conditioning), and performance as the translation of knowledge into behavior (depending on the consequences). It can be argued therefore that what managers do is disseminate knowledge to those they manage in order to gain the desired level of performance. The question that remains to be answered is "What is knowledge, i.e., what information should one disseminate to control behavior?"

There are two types of knowledge according to Skinner (1969). *Private knowledge* (Polanyi, 1960; Bridgeman, 1959) is knowledge established through experience with the contingencies of reinforcement. Skinner says, "The world which establishes contingencies of reinforcement of the sort studied in an operant analysis is presumably 'what knowledge is about.' A person comes to know that world and how to behave in it in the sense that he acquires behavior which satisfies the contingencies it maintains" (1969, p. 156). The behavior which results from private knowledge is called *contingency-shaped* behavior. This is the knowledge which one must possess in order to perform correctly in order to get rewarded. This knowledge does not assume any awareness on the part of the person but is based entirely on the person's past reinforcement history. A person can "know how" to play golf, for example, as indicated by a series of low scores—yet it is an entirely different thing to be able to tell others how to play golf. A machine operator may be an excellent employee, but make a poor foreman. One reason may be that, while he possesses private knowledge about his job, he is unable to verbalize the contingencies to other people.

Public knowledge, then, is the ability to derive rules from the contingencies, in the form of injunctions or descriptions which specify occasions, responses, and consequences (Skinner, 1969, p. 160). The behavior which results from public knowledge is called *rule-governed* behavior.

The reason the possession of public knowledge is important to the manager is simple. The employee looks to the manager for information about what behavior is required, how to perform the desired behavior, and what the consequences of the desired behavior will be. Before a manager can give correct answers to these questions, he must understand the true contingencies himself, since his business is not in doing, but in telling others how to do. The point is to be able to analyze the contingencies of reinforcement found in the organization and "to formulate rules or laws which make it unnecessary to be exposed to them in order to behave appropriately" (Skinner, 1969, p. 166).

After living in a large city for a long time, a person is able to go from Point A to Point B with little trouble. The knowledge of how to get around in the city was shaped by the past history with the environment. This behavior is an example of contingency-shaped behavior. If a stranger arrives in the same city and desires to go from Point A to Point B he too will have little trouble. He will look at a map of the city, and follow the path specified by the map. This behavior is an example of rule-governed behavior. Whether or not a person will continue to follow the map (rule) in the future is dependent on the consequences of following the map in the past. If the rule specified the correct contingencies, he probably will continue to use the map, but if a person found the map to be in error, then he will probably look to other sources of information (e.g., asking someone with private knowledge). The same thing happens in industry. If a manager is correct in the specification of the rules, i.e., the new worker follows the rules and receives a reward, then the worker will probably follow the other rules specified by the manager. If the manager specifies incorrect rules, then the worker may look to his peers or to other sources for information (e.g., the union steward) and specification of rules which describe behavior that will be rewarded.

There are two kinds of rules the manager can specify to the employee. A command or *mand* is a rule that specifies behavior and consequences of the behavior, where the consequences are arranged by the person giving the command. The specified or implied consequences for failure to act are usually aversive in nature and the judgment of the correctness of the behavior is made by the person given the command. A foreman who tells the worker to be on time for work is giving the worker a command. The implied consequence is that if the employee fails to report on time, the foreman will take action.

Advice and warnings are called *tacts* and involve rules which specify the reinforcements contingent on prior stimulations from rules, or laws. They specify the same contingencies which would directly shape behavior (private knowledge). The specifications of the tact speeds up the conditioning process. If a secretary tells her boss he should take an umbrella when he goes to lunch she is describing a tact. She has no control over the consequences (getting wet) of the behavior (not carrying the umbrella). Instead it is determined by the environment itself (weather). Skinner (1969) says:

> *Go west, young man* is an example of advice (tacting) when the behavior it specifies will be reinforced by certain consequences which do not result from action taken by the advisor. We tend to follow advice because previous behavior in response to similar verbal stimuli has been reinforced. Go west, young man is a command when some consequences of the specified action are arranged by the commander—say, the aversive consequences arranged by an official charged with relocating the inhabitants of a region. When maxims, rules, and laws are advice, the governed behavior is reinforced by consequences which might have shaped the same behavior directly in the absence of the maxims, rules, and laws. When they are commands, they are effective only because special reinforcements have been made contingent upon them. (p. 148)

While a manager must possess public knowledge as well as private knowledge in order to accomplish his task of "getting things done through other people" in keeping with a plea for positive reinforcement and unbiased reward systems, tacting is the method of rule specification recommended. Skinner (1969) recommends that by specifying the contingencies in such a way that the consequences are positive in nature and failure to respond is met with the withholding of a reward rather than by aversive stimuli, "the 'mand' may be replaced by a 'tact' describing conditions under which specific behavior on the part of the listener will be reinforced (p. 158)." Instead of saying "Give me that report" say "I need the report." "The craftsman begins by ordering his apprentice to behave in a given way; but he may later achieve the same effect simply by describing the relation between what the apprentice does and the consequences" (Skinner, 1969, p. 158). Thus, the technique which managers use to direct the employee can make a lot of difference in the acceptance of the rule by the employee. A mand operates from an avoidance learning base while a tact operates from a positive reinforcement base. A tact is more impersonal and gives the employee freedom in that it does not "enjoin anyone to behave in a given way, it simply describes the contingencies under which certain kinds of behavior will have certain kinds of consequences" (Skinner, 1969, p. 158).

CONTROVERSIES SURROUNDING AN OPERANT APPROACH TO MANAGEMENT

The reinforcement approach to the study and control of human behavior has met with resistance and criticism, primarily through a lack of understanding of its recommended uses and limitations. Goodman (1964) said, "Learning theory has two simple points to make and does so with talmudic ingenuity, variability, intricacy, and insistence. They are reinforcement and extinction. What has to be left out . . . is thought."

While the criticisms would be too numerous to mention here, an attempt will be made to examine three of the major controversies surrounding an operant approach to the management of people in organizational settings.

1 *The application of operant conditioning techniques ignores the individuality of man.* Ashby (1967) said "now the chief weakness of programmed instruction is that it rewards rote learning, and worse than that—it rewards only those responses which are in agreement with the programme." Proponents of an operant approach to contingency management recognize that a poorly designed program can lead to rigidity in behavior. This is one of the major reasons that they recommend a program of reinforcement, which best fits the group or individuals being supervised. It is untrue, however, that behaviorists ignore the individuality of man. Each man is unique based on his past reinforcement history. When personnel psychologists build sophisticated selection models to predict future performance, they are actually trying to identify those applicants who will perform well under the contingencies of that particular organization. That does not mean that a person rejected cannot be motivated, but only that the current reward system of that organization is better suited for another applicant.[5]

In other words, the problem a manager faces is not to design contingencies that will be liked by all men, "but a way of life which will be liked by those who live it" (Skinner, 1969, p. 4). As Hersey and Blanchard (1972) point out, "Positive reinforcement is anything that is rewarding to the individual being reinforced. Reinforcement, therefore, depends on the individual (p. 22)." What is reinforcing to one may not be reinforcing to someone else based on the person's past history of satiation, deprivation and conditioning operations. A manager can do two things to ensure that the contingencies of reinforcement are designed to support the individuality of the worker. First, as noted earlier he can strive to hire the worker who desires the rewards offered by the firm; i.e., can the person be happy or satisfied with this firm? Second, if it seems that the contingencies are ineffective, the manager can change the contingencies by using a democratic process—letting the employees design their own reward structure within the limits set by the organization. "Democracy is an effort to solve the problem by letting the people design the contingencies under which they are to live or—to put it another way—by insisting that the designer himself live under the contingencies he designs" (Skinner, 1969, p. 43).

In summary, therefore, it can be concluded that a voluntary society, where man has freedom to move from one organization to another, operant methods of control should not ignore the individuality of man. Instead man should seek work where his individuality can best be appreciated and industries should select employees who can best be motivated by the contingencies available to them. It should be noted, however, that through the unethical application of conditioning principles, some employers may exploit workers. The overall evidence would seem to indicate that this is not due to the weakness in behavioral theory, but due to the weakness of man himself.

2 *The application of operant conditioning techniques restricts freedom of choice.*

> Discussion of the moral implications of behavioral control almost always emphasizes the Machiavellian role of change agents and the self-protective maneuvers of controllers. . . . The tendency to exaggerate the powers of behavioral control by psychological methods alone, irrespective of willing cooperation by the client, and the failure to recognize the reciprocal nature of interpersonal control obscure both the ethical issues and the nature of the social influence processes. (Bandura, 1969, p. 85)

Kelman (1965) noted that the primary criterion that one might apply in judging the ethical implications of social influence approaches is the degree to which they promote freedom of choice. If individualism is to be guaranteed, it must be tempered by a sense of social obligation by the individual and by the organization.

Bandura (1969) noted that a person is considered free insofar as he can partly influence future events by managing his own behavior. A person in a voluntary society can within limits exert some control over the variables that govern his own choices. Skinner (1969) noted that "Men are happy in an environment in which active, productive, and creative behavior is reinforced in effective ways" (p. 64). One method of effectively reinforcing behavior is by allowing the employee some determination in the design of the reinforcement contingencies. Another method is to design self-control reinforcement systems in which individuals regulate their own activities (Ferster, Nurenberger and Levitt, 1962; Harris, 1969).

While it cannot be denied that reinforcers which are "all too abundant and powerful" (Skinner, 1966) can restrict freedom of choice, it is not true that a behavioral or Skinnerian approach is against freedom of choice; the opposite is true. As Bandura noted, "Contrary to common belief, behavioral approaches not only support a humanistic morality, but because of their relative effectiveness in establishing self-determination these methods hold much greater promise than traditional procedures for enhancement of behavioral freedom and fulfillment of human capabilities" (p. 88).

3 *Operant theory, through its advocacy of an external reward system, ignores the fact that individuals can be motivated by the job itself.* Deci (1971, 1972) among others (Likert, 1967; Vroom and Deci, 1970) criticizes behaviorists for advocating a system of employee motivation that only utilizes externally mediated rewards, i.e., rewards such as money and praise administered by someone other than the employee himself. In so doing, according to Deci, management is attempting to control the employee's behavior so he will do what he is told. The limitations of this method of worker motivation, for Deci, is that it only satisfies man's "lower-order" needs (Maslow, 1943) and does not take into account man's "higher-order" needs for self-esteem and self-actualization. Deci states, "It follows that there are many important motivators of human behavior which are not under the direct control of managers and, therefore, cannot be contingently administered in a system of piece-rate payments" (1972, p. 218).

Deci recommends that we should move away from a method of external control, and toward a system where individuals can be motivated by the job itself. He says that this approach will allow managers to focus on higher-order needs where the rewards are mediated by the person himself (intrinsically motivated). To motivate employees intrinsically, tasks should be designed which are interesting, creative and resourceful, and workers should have some say in decisions which concern them "so they will feel like causal agents in the activities which they engage in" (Deci, 1972, p. 219). Deci concludes his argument against a contingency approach to management by saying:

> . . . It is possible to pay workers and still have them intrinsically motivated. Hence the writer favors the prescription that we concentrate on structuring situations and jobs to arouse intrinsic motivation, rather than trying to structure piece-rate and other contingency payment schemes. Workers would be intrinsically motivated and would seek to satisfy their higher-order needs through effective performance. The noncontingent payments (or salaries) would help to satisfy the workers and keep them on the job, especially if the pay were equitable (Adams, 1965; Pritchard, 1969). (1972, p. 227)

Deci levels criticism at a positive reinforcement contingency approach on the basis of four issues: (1) advocating that external rewards be administered by someone else, (2) ignoring the importance of the task environment, (3) ignoring the importance of internal rewards, and (4) advocating a contingent payment plan. Deci makes two errors, from a reinforcement theory point of view, when he advocates noncontingent equitable pay plans. First, equity theory (Adams, 1965) assumes that rewards are based on performance. If they weren't, then the pay would be equal, not equitable. Second, and more crucial, is Deci's assumption that a pay plan can be noncontingent. Bandura notes that "all behavior is inevitably controlled, and the operation of psychological laws cannot be suspended by romantic conceptions of human behavior, any more than indignant rejection of the law of gravity as antihumanistic can stop people from falling" (1969, p. 85). Homme and Tosti (1965) made the point that, "either one manages the contingencies or they get managed by accident. Either way there will be contingencies, and they will have their effect" (p. 16). In other words, if managers instituted a pay plan that was "noncontingent," they would in fact be rewarding poor performance and extinguishing good performance (see Rules 1, 2, and 6).

The assertion that a contingency approach advocates that the rewards always be administered by someone else is false. Skinner specifically (1969, p. 158) recommends that manding behavior be replaced by tacting methods for achieving the same effect. Skinner suggested that one safeguard against exploitation is to make sure that the design of the contingencies never controls. In addition to recommending that the contingencies be so designed that they are controlled by the environment (tacting), operant theories have advocated self-control processes in which individuals regulate their own behavior by arranging appropriate contingencies for themselves (Ferster, Nurenberger and Levitt, 1962). Bandura (1969) concluded that:

> The selection of well-defined objectives, both intermediate and ultimate, is an essential aspect of any self-directed program of change. The goals that individuals choose for themselves must be specified in sufficiently detailed behavioral terms to provide adequate guidance for the actions that must be taken daily to attain desired outcomes. . . . Individuals can, therefore, utilize objective records of behavioral changes as an additional source of reinforcement for their self-controlling behavior. (p. 255)

Studies which have explored the effect of self-reinforcement on performance have shown that systems which allowed workers to keep a record of their own output to use as a continuous feedback system and for reinforcement purposes helped the workers to increase their performance (Kolb, Winter and Berlew, 1968; Fox, 1966). Michigan Bell Telephone company and the Emery Air Freight Corporation are two of several firms which are currently using self-reinforcement programs in order to increase worker motivation and performance. Both programs have been immensely successful (see *Business Week,* December 18, 1971, and December 2, 1972).

It should be noted that even though the individual is determining his own reward in the self-feedback program, the reinforcers are both externally (money, recognition, praise) and internally (self-feedback) mediated. According to Skinner (1957) and Bem (1967) the self-report feedback is a "tract" or description of an internal feeling state. In both cases, the rewards must be contingent on performance for effective control of the behavior to take place.

Deci's recommendation that jobs should be designed so that they are interesting, creative, and resourceful is wholeheartedly supported by proponents of a positive reinforcement program. Skinner (1969) warns managers that too much dependency on force and a poorly designed monetary reward system may actually reduce performance, while designing the task so that it is automatically reinforcing can have positive effects on performance. Skinner says:

> The behavior of an employee is important to the employer, who gains when the employee works industriously and carefully. How is he to be induced to do so? The standard answer was once physical force: men worked to avoid punishment or death. The by-products were troublesome, however, and economics is perhaps the first field in which an explicit change was made to positive reinforcement. Most men now work, as we say, 'for money.'
>
> Money is not a natural reinforcer; it must be conditioned as such. Delayed reinforcement, as in a weekly wage, raises a special problem. No one works on Monday morning because he is reinforced by a paycheck on Friday afternoon. The employee who is paid by the week works during the week to avoid losing the standard of living which depends on a weekly system. Rate of work is determined by the supervisor (with or without the pacing stimuli of a production line), and special aversive contingencies maintain quality. The pattern is therefore still aversive. It has often been pointed out that the

attitude of the production-line worker toward his work differs conspicuously from that of the craftsman, who is envied by workers and industrial managers alike. One explanation is that the craftsman is reinforced by more than monetary consequences, but another important difference is that when a craftsman spends a week completing a given set object, each of the parts produced during the week is likely to be automatically reinforcing because of its place in the complete object. (p. 18)

Skinner (1969) also agrees with Deci that the piece-rate may actually reduce performance in that it is so powerful it is most often misused, and "it is generally opposed by those concerned with the welfare of the worker (and by workers themselves when, for example, they set daily quotas)" (p. 19).

It appears therefore, that critics of operant conditioning methods misunderstand the recommendations of behaviorists in the area of worker motivation. Operant theory does advocate interesting job design and self-reinforcement feedback systems, where possible. It does not advocate force or try to control the employee's behavior by making the employee "do what he is told." It is not against humanistic morality; rather it advocates that workers be rewarded on their performance and not on their needs alone.

While other controversies about operant conditioning could be reviewed, the examination of these three issues should give the reader a flavor of the criticisms which surround the use of a contingency approach to behavioral control.

ETHICAL IMPLICATIONS FOR WORKER CONTROL

The deliberate use of positive and negative reinforcers often gives rise to ethical concern about harmful effects which may result from such practices. Poorly designed reward structures can interfere with the development of spontaneity and creativity. Reinforcement systems which are deceptive and manipulative are an insult to the integrity of man. The employee should be a willing party to the influence attempt, with both parties benefiting from the relationship.

The question of whether man should try to control human behavior is covered in a classic paper by Rogers and Skinner (1956). The central issue discussed was one of personal values. Rogers contends that "values" emerge from the individual's "freedom of choice," a realm unavailable to science. Skinner, in rebuttal, points out that the scientific view of man does not allow for such exceptions, and that choice and the resulting values are, like all behavior, a function of man's biology and his environment. Since biology and environment lie within the realm of science, "choice" and "value" must be accessible to scientific inquiry. Skinner and Rogers are both concerned with abuse of the power held by scientists, but Skinner is optimistic that good judgment will continue to prevail. Krasner (1964) agrees with Skinner that we should apply scientific means to control behavior, but warns that behavioral control can be horribly misused unless we are constantly alert to what is taking place in society.

Probably few managers deliberately misuse their power to control behavior. Managers should realize that the mismanagement of the contingencies of reinforcement is actually self-defeating. Workers will no longer allow themselves to be pushed around, but instead will insist that the work environment be designed in such a way that they have a chance at a better life. The effective use of a positive reinforcing program is one of the most critical challenges facing modern management.

The first step in the ethical use of behavioral control in organizations is the understanding by managers of the determinants of behavior. Since reinforcement is the single most important concept in the learning process, managers must learn how to design effective reinforcement programs that will encourage creative, productive, satisfied employees. This paper has attempted to outline the knowledge available for this endeavor.

NOTES

1 The author is indebted to Professor William E. Scott, Jr., Graduate School of Business, Indiana University for sharing with him his Skinnerian philosophy.
2 Classical conditioning is also known as respondent conditioning and Pavlovian conditioning.
3 Operant conditioning is also known as instrumental conditioning and Skinnerian conditioning.
4 Parentheses added.
5 This is true because the criterion variable is some measure of performance, and performance is directly tied to the reinforcement consequences for the current employees used to derive the selection model.

REFERENCES

Adams, E. E., and Scott, W. E., The application of behavioral conditioning procedures to the problems of quality control, *Academy of Management Journal,* 1971, **14,** 175–193.

Adams, J. S., Inequity in social exchange, in L. Berkowitz (ed.), *Advances in Experimental Psychology,* Academic Press, 1965, 157–189.

Aldis, O., Of pigeons and men, *Harvard Business Review,* 1961, **39,** 59–63.

Ayllon, T., and Azrin, N. H., The measurement and reinforcement of behavior of psychotics, *Journal of the Experimental Analysis of Behavior,* 1965, **8,** 357–383.

Ashby, Sir Eric, Can education be machine made?, *New Scientist,* February 2, 1967.

Baer, D. M., Peterson, R. F., and Sherman, J. A., The development of imitation by reinforcing behavioral similarity to a model, *Journal of the Experimental Analysis of Behavior,* 1967, **10,** 405–416.

Bandura, A., and Perloff, B., The efficacy of self-monitoring reinforcement systems, *Journal of Personality and Social Psychology,* 1967, **7,** 111–116.

Bandura, A., *Principles of Behavior Modification,* Holt, Rinehart and Winston, Inc., New York, 1969.

Bass, B. M., and Vaughan, J. A., *Training in Industry: The Management of Learning,* Wadsworth Publishing Company, Belmont, Calif., 1966.

Behling, O., Schriesheim, C., and Tolliver, J., Present theories and new directions in theories of work effort, *Journal Supplement Abstract Service* of the American Psychological Corporation, in press.

Bem, D. J., Self-perception: An alternative interpretation of cognitive dissonance phenomena, *Psychological Review,* 1967, **74,** 184–200.

Bridgeman, D. W., *The Way Things Are,* Harvard Press, Cambridge, Mass., 1959.

Costello, T. W., and Zalkind, S. S., *Psychology in Administration,* Prentice-Hall, Inc., Englewood Cliffs, N.J., 1963.

Deci, E. L., The effects of externally mediated rewards on intrinsic motivation, *Journal of Personality and Social Psychology,* 1971, **18,** 105–115.

Deci, E. L., The effects of contingent and noncontingent rewards and controls on intrinsic motivation, *Organizational Behavior and Human Performance,* 1972, **8,** 217–229.

Festinger, L., A theory of social comparison processes, *Human Relations,* 1954, **7,** 117–140.

Ferster, C. B., and Skinner, B. F., *Schedules of Reinforcement,* Appleton-Century-Crofts, New York, 1957.

Ferster, C. B., Nurenberger, J. I., and Levitt, E. B., The control of eating. *Journal of Mathematics,* 1962, **1,** 87–109.

Fox, L., The use of efficient study habits, In R. Ulrich, T. Stachnik, and J. Mabry (eds.), *Control of Human Behavior,* Scott, Foresman, Glenview, Ill., 1966, 85–93.

Goffman, E., *The Presentation of Self in Everyday Life,* Doubleday, New York, 1959.

Goodman, Paul, *Compulsory Mis-education,* Horizon Press, New York, 1964.

Haire, Mason, *Psychology in Management,* 2nd ed., McGraw-Hill, New York, 1964.

Harris, M. B., A self-directed program for weight control: A pilot study, *Journal of Abnormal Psychology,* 1969, **74,** 263–270.

Henry, Jules, Review of human behavior: An inventory of scientific findings by Bernard Berelson and Gary A. Steiner, *Scientific American,* July, 1964.

Hersey, P., and Blanchard, K. H., The management of change: Part 2, *Training and Development Journal,* February, 1972, 20–24.

Hilgard, E. R., *Theories of Learning,* 2nd ed., Appleton-Century-Crofts, New York, 1956.

Homme, L. E., and Tosti, D. T., Contingency management and motivation, *Journal of the National Society for Programmed Instruction,* 1965, **4,** 14–16.

Jablonsky, S., and DeVries, D., Operant conditioning principles extrapolated to the theory of management, *Organizational Behavior and Human Performance,* 1972, **7,** 340–358.

Keller, F. S., *Learning: Reinforcement Theory,* Random House, New York, 1969.

Kelman, H. C., Manipulation of human behavior: An ethical dilemma for the social scientist, *Journal of Social Issues,* 1965, **21,** 31–46.

Kolb, D. A., Winter, S. K., and Berlew, D. E., Self-directed change: Two studies, *Journal of Applied Behavioral Science,* 1968, **4,** 453–471.

Krasner, L., Behavior control and social responsibility, *American Psychologist,* 1964, **17,** 199–204.

Likert, R., *New Patterns of Management,* McGraw-Hill, New York, 1961.

Lovaas, O. I., Berberich, J. P., Perloff, B. F., and Schaeffer, B., Acquisition of imitative speech for schizophrenic children, *Science,* 1966, **151,** 705–707.

Luthans, F., *Organizational Behavior,* McGraw-Hill, New York, 1973.

Maslow, A. H., A theory of human motivation, *Psychological Review,* 1943, **50,** 370–396.

McGregor, D., *The Human Side of Enterprise,* New York, McGraw-Hill, 1960.

Michael, J., and Meyerson, L., A behavioral approach to counseling and guidance, *Harvard Educational Review,* 1962, **32,** 382–402.

Morse, W. H., Intermittent reinforcement, in W. K. Honig (ed.), *Operant Behavior,* Appleton-Century-Crofts, New York, 1966.

New tool: Reinforcement for good work, *Business Week,* December, 18, 1971, 68–69.

Nord, W. R., Beyond the teaching machine: The neglected area of operant conditioning in the theory and practice of management, *Organizational Behavior and Human Performance,* 1969, 375–401.

Pavlov, I. P., *The Work of the Digestive Glands* (translated by W. H. Thompson), Charles Griffin, London, 1902.

Polanyi, M., *Personal Knowledge,* University of Chicago Press, 1960.

Rachlin, H., *Modern Behaviorism,* W. H. Freeman and Co., New York, 1970.

Rogers, Carl R., and Skinner, B. F., Some issues concerning the control of human behavior: A symposium, *Science,* 1956, **124,** 1057–1066.

Scott, W. E., and Cummings, L. L., *Readings in Organizational Behavior and Human Performance,* Revised Edition, Irwin, Homewood, Ill., 1973.

Scott, W. E., and Hamner, W. Clay, The effects of order and variance in performance on supervisory ratings of workers, Paper presented at the *45th Annual Meeting,* Midwestern Psychological Association, Chicago, 1973.

Scott, W. E., and Hamner, W. Clay, The effect of order and variance in performance on the rewards given workers by supervisory personnel, mimeograph, Indiana University, 1973.

Scott, W. E., Activation theory and task design. *Organizational Behavior and Human Performance,* 1966, **1,** 3–30.

Skinner, B. F., *The Behavior of Organisms,* New York, Appleton-Century, 1938.

Skinner, B. F., *Walden Two,* New York, The Macmillan Company, 1948.

Skinner, B. F., Are theories of learning necessary? *Psychological Review,* 1950, **57,** 193–216.

Skinner, B. F., *Science and Human Behavior,* New York, The Macmillan Company, 1953.

Skinner, B. F., Freedom and the control of men, *American Scholar,* 1956, **25,** 47–65.

Skinner, B. F., Some issues concerning the control of human behavior, *Science,* 1956, **124,** 1056–1066.

Skinner, B. F., *Verbal Behavior,* New York, Appleton-Century-Crofts, 1957.

Skinner, B. F., Behaviorism at fifty, *Science,* 1963a, **134,** 566–602.

Skinner, B. F., Operant behavior, *American Psychologist,* 1963b, **18,** 503–515.

Skinner, B. F., *Contingencies of Reinforcement,* Appleton-Century-Crofts, New York, 1969.

Skinner, B. F., *Beyond Freedom and Dignity,* Alfred A. Knopf, New York, 1971.

Thorndike, E. L., *Animal Intelligence,* Macmillan, New York, 1911.

Vroom, V. H., and Deci, E. L., An overview of work motivation. In V. H. Vroom and E. L. Deci (eds.), *Management and Motivation,* Penguin Press, Baltimore, 1970, 9–19.

Wiard, H., Why manage behavior? A case for positive reinforcement, *Human Resource Management,* Summer, 1972, 15–20.

Where Skinner's theories work, *Business Week,* December, 1972, 64–65.

Whyte, W. F., Skinnerian theory in organizations, *Psychology Today,* April, 1972, 67–68, 96, 98, 100.

Motivational Implications of Reinforcement Theory

Judith L. Komaki
Timothy Coombs
Stephen Schepman

Two decades ago in the heady, idealistic times of the late 1960s, reports began streaming in that illustrated the application of reinforcement theory, a motivational theory emphasizing the consequences of performance. When consequences—such as feedback and recognition—were judiciously rearranged, dramatic improvements

This paper was written especially for this volume. A special note of thanks to Terry Coombs for her delightful gift with words.

occurred in clinical, educational, and work settings. Children who were thought to be autistic and destined to spend the remainder of their lives in institutions began to communicate and to help themselves when they were reinforced for successive approximations to desired behaviors.[1] First-graders in a disadvantaged neighborhood learned skills critical to further achievement.[2] When dockworkers at Emery Air Freight were recognized for their efforts and received feedback, they worked more efficiently.[3] Even Army recruits in boot camp met the rigorous standards of their superiors when a token economy program was used.[4] Given these indications of the positive impact of reinforcement theory, industrial/ organizational psychologists began discussing the promise of an innovative approach to motivation.[5-8]

Twenty years later, legitimate questions have been raised, particularly where adults in complex organizations are concerned, as to whether or not the reinforcement approach has lived up to its promise. In the first section of this article we review how it has been used in the past two decades to *promote* performance. We survey over 50 studies, all of them meticulously controlled. We outline the major findings as well as the people, the places, and the duration of the studies. We describe the types of reinforcers that have been used and the range of target behaviors.

The next section of the article discusses how reinforcement theory can lead to a better *understanding* of why people in organizations do seemingly perplexing things. We discuss how employees who do an outstanding job are inadvertently punished and why professors who genuinely believe in the importance of education sometimes neglect their teaching. The chapter ends with a forecast of what is likely to occur in the next two decades.

First, let us talk about reinforcement theory: what it hopes to do, what it is, and how it is typically used in work settings.

REINFORCEMENT THEORY IN APPLIED SETTINGS

Aims

The importance of motivating workers to maintain their performance over extended periods is eloquently portrayed by Isak Dinesen.[9] Responsible for a coffee plantation near Nairobi, she describes how workers must do many things over and over—setting plants in regular rows of holes, 600 trees to the acre; and how they must coordinate among themselves, first hulling, then grading and sorting the coffee, and then packing the coffee in sacks, 12 to a ton. These tasks are not unimportant. They must be done day in and day out, season after season, in just the right way. Motivating workers to sustain their performance is a formidable challenge that continues to elude practitioners and scholars alike.[10,11] Reinforcement theory, referred to as operant conditioning theory, behavior modification, or applied behavior analysis, identifies ways of helping persons like Dinesen secure the continued cooperation of workers.[12-14] Of the three aspects of motivation—initiating, directing, and maintaining performance[15,16]—reinforcement theory is particularly suited to maintaining performance on an ongoing basis.

Reflecting the visionary values of the late 1960s, reinforcement theorists hope to make a difference. When they work in applied settings, they aim to enhance behaviors of importance in a meaningful way. The studies, for example, aim at ensuring that mental health staff consistently implement residents' programs[17] and that policy board members learn how to work together to solve problems.[18] In fact, three spokespersons have gone on record, voicing their hope that "better application . . . will lead to a better state of society."[19]

Features

Reinforcement theory has two features which distinguish it from other motivation theories: its emphasis on the consequences of performance, and its techniques for assessing performance and evaluating effectiveness.

Focus on Performance Consequences The consequences of our performance—the feedback we receive, the comments we hear—are thought to make a powerful impact on what we do from day to day. When frequent, contingent, positive consequences have been arranged to follow performance, substantial and meaningful improvements have occurred in literally thousands of experiments conducted on animals at all levels of the phylogenetic scale, including humans.[20–23] In fact, one of the major tenets of reinforcement theory is that behavior is a function of its consequences.

A distinction is made between consequences which occur *after* the behavior of interest and antecedents which occur *before* the behavior. When bosses do something which occurs after subordinate's behavior, for example, these actions are called consequences. Because the providing of feedback, recognition, and incentives typically follow subordinate performance, they would generally be categorized as consequences. When a packaging supervisor grins, thrusts out his hand for a quick congratulatory shake, and says to workers: "Good running last night. 537 cases," his actions and his statement are considered consequences.[24] On the other hand, when bosses do something *before* the occurrence of a subordinate's particular behavior, these actions are called antecedents. Because the providing of training, the setting of goals, and the communication of company policy typically precede subordinate performance, they would generally be categorized as antecedents. When Hector in the *Iliad* "sprang from his chariot clad in his suit of armour, and went about among the host brandishing his two spears, exhorting the men to fight and raising the terrible cry of battle,"[25] his exhortations were antecedent to the event.

How do consequences differ from antecedents? Consequences function in a motivational role, increasing or decreasing the probability of behaviors recurring, whereas antecedents serve in an educational or cuing role, clarifying expectations for performance, specifying the relationship between behavior and its consequences, and/or signaling occasions in which consequences are likely to be provided. For example, even though antecedents were provided (e.g., workers were exhorted to perform safely, they were provided information about proper safety procedures, and rules were posted), workers did not change their safety practices.[26] Only when consequences (in the form of feedback) were delivered did they consistently perform safely on the job. This study is consistent with other studies, which show that antecedents alone do not result in substantial improvements over an extended period in ongoing work settings.[27-29] Thus, antecedents are not considered sufficient to act as the sole motivating force. Consequences are critical. In fact, close examination of studies successful in sustaining performance, whether they are positive reinforcement studies or even Japanese management cases,[30] shows that they include at least one consequence.

Emphasis on Rigorous Evaluation Another noteworthy feature of reinforcement theory is its emphasis on evidence of a particular sort, that is, on empirical data.[31] No number of expert opinions substitutes for evidence that A actually changed and that B was truly responsible for A.

The development of fair and accurate ways of obtaining information about workers' performance has been a priority for reinforcement theorists. Referred to as *applied operant measures,*[32-35] these differ from traditional methods in two ways. First, they directly sample workers' performance, rather than rely on self-reports or indirect measures. For example, when assessing the service provided to customers, reinforcement theorists look at what the salesperson actually said to the customer rather than at "helpfulness" scores on rating scales or at sales volume or customer traffic, which are typically affected by many extraneous factors of which sales performance is only one tiny aspect. Similarly, when measuring safety, the focus is on the practices of workers on the job rather than on their reports of safety awareness or on accident statistics.

Secondly, the test of interrater reliability plays a critical role during three stages of the measurement process:

1 *During the developmental stage.* Two observers independently record and then calculate a percentage agreement score (number of agreements divided by number of agreements and disagreements). Revisions continue until agreement is reached on the scoring of virtually all checklist items all the time. When this criterion is achieved, then and only then are the terms considered objectively defined.

2 *In the training of observers.* Trainees are not considered trained until they can pass the test of interrater reliability.

3 *During the formal data collection.* Checks are made regularly to see whether observers have become stricter or more lenient than they were when they were trained. In short, when reinforcement theorists measure performance in applied settings, they directly sample what workers do and/or produce and they rely on the test of interrater reliability.

These applied operant measures form the foundation for the providing of consequences that are related to performance.

This empirical emphasis also makes imperative the rigorous evaluation of the effectiveness of programs. Reinforcement theorists want to know if the relationship between A and B is a result of happenstance or cause and effect. To evaluate with confidence requires the use of a particular type of research design, referred to as an *internally valid design*. Two families of designs are considered internally valid: (1) the traditional control-group designs such as the pretest-posttest control group design[36] and (2) the within-group designs such as the reversal and the multiple-baseline designs.[37,38]

Within-group designs, commonly used by reinforcement theorists, have the advantage of allowing one to draw cause-and-effect conclusions with assurance. At the same time, they do not require the random assignment of subjects to either treatment and control group, as the control-group design does. Rarely is it possible in the wrapping and makeup departments of a bakery, for example, to randomly assign workers so that two new groups are formed, one of which is treated and one of which is not treated. With within-group designs, each group serves as its own control. In the reversal design, for example, there are at least three phases: (1) a baseline phase, during which performance is measured before introducing any program, (2) an intervention phase, during which the program is introduced, while continuing to measure performance, and (3) a reversal phase, during which the treatment is discontinued or altered. The group's performance is assessed during baseline, intervention, and reversal phases. When performance improves during the intervention stage and "reverses" back to baseline during the reversal stage, it is possible to rule out the possibility that other factors such as technological innovations or practice were responsible and say with assurance that the program was responsible for the changes.

Another type of within-group design, the multiple-baseline design, is also used when evaluating the effectiveness of programs. A multiple-baseline design was used to assess the impact of a reinforcement program in two departments of a wholesale bakery (described in the next section). A versatile design, the multiple-baseline design can be used with intact groups (e.g., Crenshaw, Baldwin Hills branches), with individual workers, and with different behaviors (e.g., smiling, talking to customers). Perhaps not surprisingly, the reversal and multiple-baseline designs are used in many reinforcement studies.

Four-Step Process

A positive reinforcement program typically includes four steps: specifying desired performance, measuring workers' progress, judiciously rearranging consequences, and evaluating the effectiveness of the program. To get an idea of how this process typically works, let us take an example of a program carried out by the first author and two students at Georgia Tech.[39] Injuries had jumped sharply at a wholesale bakery, and management was naturally alarmed. To encourage employees to maintain safe practices, management introduced a four-step positive-reinforcement program that was very different from the usual approach of posting signs and admonishing workers to be careful.

1 *Specify desired behavior.* First, desired work practices were defined. To establish what workers should do to avoid having similar accidents in the future, verbs such as "turn off" and "release," rather than adjectives such as "careful" and "conscientious," were encouraged. A list of definitions was generated (e.g.,

"Walk around conveyer belt," "Look toward knife being sharpened"). To ensure that the definitions were objective, each definition had to meet the test of interrater reliability. When the criterion of 90 percent or better was achieved, then and only then were the terms considered objectively defined.

2 *Measure desired performance.* Observers, trained until they passed the test of interrater reliability, went to the work site and recorded the percent of incidents performed in a safe or unsafe manner. The observations were made frequently, four times a week on average. Checks on interrater reliability were conducted regularly.

3 *Provide frequent, contingent, positive consequences.* The consequence for safe practices was feedback. The department's safety scores were presented on a graph so that workers could see at a glance how their group had done and how this compared to their previous record. The graph was posted publicly in the work area, thus fostering a healthy competition between departments. When workers asked, they were also told what they had done correctly and incorrectly.

4 *Evaluate effectiveness on the job.* To assess whether or not the program was effective, a within-group research design—the multiple-baseline design across groups—was used. The two groups were the wrapping and makeup departments. Data were collected in both groups. The program was introduced in a staggered manner: after 5½ weeks in the wrapping department and after 13½ weeks in the makeup department.

The results: From performing safely 70 percent and 78 percent of the time, employees in the two departments substantially improved their safety performance to 96 percent and 99 percent, respectively. Within a year, the number of lost-time injuries dropped from 53 to 10. Although this is only one of a series of examples, it shows the four steps involved in sustaining the motivation of workers.

The next section surveys the reinforcement studies that have been conducted in work settings over the past 20 years.

USING REINFORCEMENT THEORY TO PROMOTE PERFORMANCE

Reinforcement theory has been found to work with a variety of target behaviors, for extended durations, with a range of subjects and settings, and using a variety of different consequences. A recent review shows that at least 51 well-controlled studies have been reported, addressing whether or not positive reinforcement results in improvements of performance on the job.[40] Of the 51 studies, 47 resulted in substantial improvements in performance, for a success rate of 92.2 percent of the studies. The positive results are consistent with previous reviews of the literature.[41–46]

With a Variety of Target Behaviors

The studies, as a group, show broad generality. The target areas ranged from soliciting suggestions from mental health employees for solving common problems[47] to encouraging field salespersons to keep in touch with the home office.[48]

Productivity improvements have been reported in both the quantity and the quality of the work. Increases were obtained in the amount of time resource room teachers actually spent instructing pupils[49] and the percentage of pages that staff correctly types.[50]

Among the most popular target areas has been that of increasing *attendance and punctuality*. Approximately 20 studies have examined one or both of these topics.[51] Attending work on time is critical in organizations which rely on having a certain number of qualified workers present before running equipment or assembly lines. In some industries, the absenteeism rate can run as high as 10 to 20 percent of the work force on any given day, with costs estimated in the billions of dollars each year.[52] Thus, the decline in absenteeism from 3.01 percent to 2.4 percent at a unionized manufacturing and distribution center was significant both statistically and financially.[53]

In addition to these traditional areas, *safety and health*—an area of concern to both management and workers—has been the topic of over a dozen studies. Workers showed improvements in safety practices,[26,39] as well as other performance areas (housekeeping,[54] hazards,[55] and earplug usage[56]), thus lessening the chance of incurring a disabling injury. Working together, employees in a fiberglass-reinforced plastics plant were also able to reduce their exposure to likely carcinogenic substances such as styrene and to enhance their chances of remaining healthy.[57]

A critical area for consumers, the *quality of service,* has been a regular subject of interest. Tellers in banks[58] and salespersons in department stores[59,60] upgraded their interactions with customers. Besides approaching customers more quickly, salespersons learned to assess customers' needs and then to provide relevant information.

With a Wide Range of Subjects and Settings

The settings of the studies ranged from real-estate offices to the U.S. Marine Corps.[61,62] Approximately half of the studies were conducted in the private sector, in manufacturing or service industries. The other half took place in the public sector, in social service agencies or in institutional or educational settings. The locations included the United States, as well as Scandinavia[54] and the Middle East.[56,58]

Among the subjects were bus drivers[63] and baseball players.[64] White- (e.g., supervisors), pink- (e.g., real estate agents), and blue-collar (e.g., factory workers) workers were represented. Sample sizes included the staff of 12 residential units in a psychiatric hospital[65] and over 1000 miners.[66]

With a Range of Different Types of Consequences

At least five different classes of consequences were used. Because all of the classes are not in everyday parlance, they are described in more detail.

1 *Organizational.* Indigenous to work settings, organizational consequences include promotions, pay raises, and special training opportunities. In a regional transportation authority, benefits such as free gasoline and free monthly passes on the bus system were offered to workers as an incentive for reducing accidents.[63]

2 *Generalized.* Generalized reinforcers derive their potency from the fact that they can be exchanged for backup reinforcers. Examples of generalized reinforcers include cash, frequent flyer coupons, and trading stamps. Trading stamps were given to miners who had not suffered a lost-time injury during the month.[66] Backup reinforcers include choices such as what, where, and with whom you work. The opportunity to select a clerical assignment was used as a backup reinforcer in a job training center for trainees who had earned coupons.[67]

3 *Activity.* Another class of consequences, derived from the Premack principle, is referred to as an activity consequence.[68] Basically, the Premack principle states that any activity which workers engage in more regularly than another activity can be used as a positive reinforcer. A novel application of the Premack principle took place in a sales organization.[69] When it was found that the callers liked to make renewal calls, rather than new service calls, the opportunity to sell five renewal contracts was made contingent upon one new service contract sale. When callers could only make renewal calls after making a service sale, they substantially increased new service sales.

4 *Social.* Typically expressed by individuals, social consequences include commendations, compliments, criticism, reviews, and recognition for a job well done. For example, winning teams were "personally congratulated by the director of operations."[63] In another example, hospital supervisors made comments to staff members, such as, "I'm pleased to see you interacting with clients, but I'm sure Mary [the client] is even more pleased."[70]

5 *Informational.* Informational consequences, as the label suggests, are ones in which information is provided about a person's performance. The information can be conveyed a variety of different ways. For example, feedback notes were passed on to supervisors to encourage the completion of accident reports; the number of total items that had been included, as well as any increases in completeness over prior submissions were mentioned.[71] In other studies, graphs of baseline and intervention levels of workers' performance were used.[26,39,54,55,59,62] The information itself can also vary. In the area of safety, the information provided included the percentage of incidents performed safely by the group,[26,39] the frequency of hazards,[55] the percentage of correct housekeeping practices,[54] and audiograms at the beginning and at the end of workers' shifts, showing the temporary hearing losses that occurred when earplugs were not worn.[72]

Consequences are often used in combination. Lessening the perennial procrastination associated with long-range, relatively unstructured projects—such as completing master's theses—was the aim of one study.[73] Realizing how easy it is to let more immediately pressing activities disrupt progress, the authors set up a system of weekly deadlines, monitoring, and a host of consequences. To help maintain a steady rate of work, they used social, informational, and organizational consequences. For the organizational consequences, the authors incorporate their evaluations of a student's progress on his or her master's thesis in the letters of recommendation they sent out for the student.

For Extended Durations

Each of the 51 studies was conducted in the field over a considerable amount of time. In fact, the median length of time that an intervention lasted was not 1, not 2, but 8 weeks. Illustrating the potential longevity of any positive reinforcement program, a token economy program was successful in reducing accidents for 11 years in one mine in Arizona and for 12 years in another mine in Wyoming.[66]

The next section takes a different perspective and describes how reinforcement theory can be used to explain workers' actions.

USING REINFORCEMENT THEORY TO UNDERSTAND WHY PEOPLE DO WHAT THEY DO

Have you ever wondered why normally long-sighted individuals end up taking short-term solutions? By analyzing the consequences for performance, you can gain insight into why workers do the sometimes perplexing things they do. The following principles, all involving performance consequences, aid in our understanding: (1) positive reinforcement, (2) negative reinforcement, (3) punishment by application, (4) punishment by withdrawal, and (5) extinction.[74] The first two principles, positive reinforcement and negative reinforcement, help explain why some behaviors are inadvertently strengthened. The last three principles explain why some behaviors are mistakenly weakened.

How Undesired Behaviors Are Mistakenly Reinforced

Rewarding A While Hoping For B   The principle of positive reinforcement can be used to promote either desired *or* undesired behavior. Its placement is critical. In an article aptly titled "On the Folly of Rewarding A, While Hoping For B," Kerr gives examples of how organizations "hope for" employee efforts in such areas as cooperation, creativity, and long-term strategic planning, while formally rewarding none of these.[75] Organizations "hope" that managers will be willing to incur huge start-up costs for programs that will potentially yield fruit in 60 months, while these same organizations promote persons who show bottom-line results in 60 days. Charting this example in Table 1, we can see a case of positive reinforcement inappropriately applied. The consequences, the rewards of promotion and additional staff, are positive. Unfortunately, the behavior they follow is

TABLE 1
POSITIVE REINFORCEMENT AT WORK

Behavior	Consequence	Principle
Efforts to change profit picture in 60 days	Followed by positive reinforcers: promotion to vice president, additional staff	Positive reinforcement
Staff procrastinates until 2 months before deadline	Followed by positive reinforcers: extra personnel hired, workload lightened, bonus paid for effort extended	Positive reinforcement

the one favoring the short-term strategy. Thus, these positive reinforcers inadvertently encourage an undesired perspective. By looking at the consequences accruing to the individual, it helps us to understand how "rational" it is to sacrifice long-term growth despite the exhortations of the CEO who continually stresses strategic planning for the future.

Another example is presented in Table 1. The company's tenth anniversary is 6 months away. The public relations staff knows they need to produce a report describing the company's history and its current activities. The staff believes that the project will take very little time. Two months before the anniversary celebration, the public relations staff begins to gather information and finds that the report is far more complicated than originally expected. Because the deadline must be met, the staff is permitted to hire temporary staff at company expense and set all other work aside. When the report is finally completed in a frenzy of activity, the staff are given a bonus for working so hard to meet the deadline. Seeing how the staff was inappropriately reinforced for their procrastination, it becomes easier to understand why they might procrastinate on future projects.

Take a moment now to analyze a situation you are faced with every day, the instruction you receive. What are the consequences for your professors for the desired behavior of teaching? What are the consequences for publishing? Do you think that your professors will devote the necessary time it takes to prepare lectures and examinations when they are promoted for the length of their publication records?

Negative Reinforcement at Work The principle of negative reinforcement, like positive reinforcement, also helps to explain why behavior is strengthened. Negative reinforcement, unlike positive reinforcement, involves escaping from or avoiding negative consequences such as nagging or litigation.

The case of a unionized production shop having a promotion-by-seniority policy is portrayed in Table 2. Though the boss firmly believes that there is an exemplary candidate who merits a promotion, she recommends for that promotion a person with a merely adequate record. The reason: the latter happens to be higher in seniority and the boss thus avoids complaints of favoritism or bias. In the past, such grievances have taken hours in litigation. By recommending the senior candidate, the boss has avoided exposing herself to unnecessary problems. Analyzing this situation from the point of view of negative reinforcement helps explain why the boss ends up recommending for promotion the person with a less than exemplary record.

TABLE 2
NEGATIVE REINFORCEMENT AT WORK

Behavior	Consequence	Principle
Boss recommends for promotion individual with adequate record, who is highest in seniority	Avoids complaints of favoritism and a grievance being filed with union	Negative reinforcement

How Desired Behaviors Are Inadvertently Discouraged

We have seen how two principles—positive and negative reinforcement—aid us in understanding why some behaviors are strengthened. Now, let us look at how three principles—punishment by application, punishment by removal, and extinction—help explain why workers get discouraged from doing the very things they are being encouraged to do.

Punishment by Application The most typical reason why workers fail to do what they are expected to do is that they are punished for doing as desired.[76] The inherent punishment involved in pioneering new areas helps to explain why some engineers shun such endeavors (Table 3). As a necessary part of forging these new frontiers, engineers are presented with negative consequence after negative consequence. They are frustrated by time-consuming, seemingly fruitless literature searches. They work with concepts which are, as yet, incomprehensible to their peers, whose companionship they therefore lack. And because they are pioneering new fields, they must spend inordinate amounts of time in research and setup before having anything to show for their efforts. As a result of all of these negative consequences being applied (hence, the term "punishment by application"), it is no wonder that some eventually forgo their pioneering efforts and return to more tried-and-true research topics.

Here is another example of punishment by application: In a delightful, well-written book on analyzing performance problems, Mager and Pipe describe how one of them was called in to solve an "attitude problem" on the part of physicians who were resisting the using of computers to place prescriptions.[76] An analysis of the situation revealed that there were many negative consequences attached to using the computer. The environs of the terminals were crowded, noisy, and busy, with no room to work. Moreover, the terminals were placed so as to make their use fairly uncomfortable for those who wear bifocals. Not surprisingly, physicians were less than enthusiastic about using the computers when the result was inconvenient, slightly embarrassing and, for some, even mildly painful. When these negative consequences were changed, their "attitude problem" disappeared and the physicians began using the computers regularly.

TABLE 3
PUNISHMENT BY APPLICATION

Behavior	Consequence	Principle
Engineers pioneering new areas	Endure frustrating, time-consuming literature searches	Punishment by application
	Have trouble communicating with peers	
	Have problems demonstrating accomplishments	

TABLE 4
PUNISHMENT BY REMOVAL

Behavior	Consequence	Principle
Administrator comes in under budget	Gets positive reinforcer withdrawn, i.e., budget slashed for next fiscal year	Punishment by removal

What would you predict? Employees at Emery Air Freight were supposed to fill out damage forms about packages damaged during shipment. The paperwork was time-consuming, airline representatives were likely to give them flak, and it took time away from other priorities that the company was striving toward. For a description of how the employees actually reacted, refer to the article, "At Emery Air Freight."[77]

Punishment by Removal   The principle of punishment by removal, which involves the withdrawal of a positive reinforcer following a person's behavior, also helps explain why some behaviors are weakened. For example, an administrator of a government-sponsored program is extremely careful of funds and displays outstanding efficiency to end the fiscal year under budget (Table 4). The government "rewards" this efficiency by cutting the following year's budget. It is small wonder that next year the administrator's efficiency tends to weaken.

Another example of punishment by removal: Tom Wolfe, in the book *The Right Stuff*,[78] refers to the reluctance of the young fighter pilots to admit when they had maneuvered themselves into a bad corner they couldn't get out of. Such an admission triggered a complex and very public chain of events at the field: all other incoming flights were held up, fire trucks trundled out to the runway, and the bureaucracy geared up to investigate. Perhaps most importantly, the pilot's peers started to question whether the pilot had "the right stuff." As Table 5 shows, the desired behavior (that of responsibly admitting to a problem) is weakened by (1) the certainty that such an admission will cause a great deal of trouble for the pilot (punishment by application) and (2) the loss of that most important conviction on the part of the pilot's peers (punishment by removal).

TABLE 5
PUNISHMENT BY APPLICATION AND REMOVAL

Behavior	Consequence	Principle
Fighter pilot declaring emergency	Complex and public set of events is triggered: flights held up, fire trucks sent out, paperwork flow starts	Punishment by application
	Gets positive reinforcer withdrawn, e.g., peers don't think pilot has "right stuff"	Punishment by removal

TABLE 6
EXTINCTION AT WORK

Behavior	Consequence	Principle
Workers perform safely	Few positive reinforcers, e.g., little management recognition, few coworker comments	Extinction

It should be noted that reinforcement theorists do *not* recommend punishment procedures as a way of changing behavior. Instead, as we trust is illustrated here, these weakening procedures can best be used to analyze why people don't do what they are supposed to do. Based on this better understanding, we can then devise ways to positively reinforce the performance that is desired.

Extinction   The principle of extinction—that is, stopping or not delivering positive reinforcers—also explains why workers don't always do what it seems they should. In the area of occupational safety, for example, it is frequently perplexing that workers continue to perform unsafely despite compelling arguments to perform otherwise. To understand why, it is helpful to raise questions about the consequences of performing safely. An analysis of the performance consequences, as shown in Table 6, helps explain why workers persist in acting unsafely, despite cogent reasons for conducting themselves in a safe manner. When one closely examines what happens when workers perform as desired, one finds relatively few positive consequences occur when workers perform safely. Coworkers rarely comment. Management recognition is rare. The fact that there are few, if any, positive reinforcers delivered for performing as desired illustrates the principle of extinction.

Further analysis of situations involving safety reveals that even when workers are performing safely, an accident may occur; for example, a truck lid flies up, and through no fault of the worker, he ends up with a broken nose. Thus, there is some chance for a punishing consequence such as an accident to occur. On the other hand, when one examines what happens when workers perform in an undesired manner, one finds a lack of punishment. The "natural" consequence of performing unsafely, having an accident, is typically, albeit fortunately, missing; studies have shown that workers can perform unsafely literally hundreds of times without incurring an accident. As you can see by examining the consequences of performance, one can better understand why workers perform the way they do, despite cogent reasons to the contrary.

Using All the Principles to Analyze a Situation

To see how the principles, as a group, can be used to better understand a given situation, let us turn to a final example. The management of a manufacturing engineering group was particularly interested in upgrading the quality of the work so as to reduce the lag time, that is, the time it took from gear design to tooling. One of the authors and a class of graduate students looked in depth at the con-

TABLE 7
HOW THE PRINCIPLES OF BEHAVIOR CAN BE USED IN TANDEM

Consequence	Principle
Workers doing quality work	
Pay and raises not contingent on performance; promotions rare; little management recognition; few peer comments; little, if any, task feedback	Extinction
Being asked to check peers' work	Punishment by application
Avoid having the shop return the design work	Negative reinforcement
Workers doing poor-quality work	
Infrequent reprimands; few peer comments	Lack of punishment by application
Pay and raises still forthcoming; no loss of friends on job	Lack of punishment by removal
Avoid being asked to check	Negative reinforcement

sequences for producing high-quality work. Table 7 describes what we found. In the first place, pay raises and promotions were not awarded on the basis of merit. Instead, the same percentage raise was given to each worker. Few opportunities existed for promotions of any kind. Employees received little or no overt feedback from either peers or management. What the exceptional employees received was extra work. Those who were most capable were assigned the unpleasant task of checking on the design work of their peers. These checkers, however, discovered that they need not critique the work of their peers. They could simply OK the work and pass it on to the shop where prototypes were built from the designs. If the design work was shoddy, the shop returned it to the designer, thereby avoiding the problem of peer criticism. Having failed to "catch" the design problems, the checkers were not again asked to critique the work of the others, thus lightening their workload and keeping their friends.

As you can see, this example illustrates how workers are sometimes inadvertently reinforced for undesired behavior. At the same time, this example shows how employees are sometimes punished for desired behavior and how desired performance is extinguished. By using the strengthening principles—positive and negative reinforcement—and the weakening principles—punishment by application and removal and extinction—to analyze situations, we can better understand why people do what they do.

LOOKING AHEAD

What does the future hold? As we move into the twenty-first century with its changing demographic and organizational forces, three developments are forecast.[79,80]

Shoring Up and Shifting Content

our first prediction is that reinforcement theory will be employed to fully utilize the fewer number of young people entering the job market and to upgrade the level of literacy and basic skills of entry-level workers. We also predict that it will be employed in manufacturing as well as the rapidly expanding service sector, and in jobs involving routine assembly work as well as those requiring the troubleshooting of computerized equipment. The same four-step process of specifying desired performance, measuring performance, rearranging consequences, and evaluating effectiveness will be used. What will be different is that a shift will occur in the content of workers' performance so that more studies will focus on troubleshooting and service-related behaviors.[58-60]

Expanding Upward

With the nature of organizations themselves changing as they rebound from mergers and downsizing, we predict that reinforcement theory can be used beneficially at the upper echelons of organizations. The idea that reinforcement principles can be used to satisfy the demand for savvy and successful leaders has been suggested.[81-83] Recently, a model of effective supervision has been developed, based on reinforcement theory.[84] Two categories in particular are identified as being key in motivating others: monitoring and providing consequences.[85,86] Effective managers are much more likely than so-so managers to monitor, that is, to examine the work and observe workers in action. They do not leave this fact finding to chance. The data also show that effective managers provide consequences. They let workers know how they are doing. They compliment workers in a casual, off-the-cuff fashion. Reinforcement theory can be used to bolster how leaders interact with their subordinates, and thus improve the functioning of organizations as a whole.

Helping Workers to Help Themselves

Lastly, we predict that workers will learn to use reinforcement theory to design their own motivational programs. The idea of self-management is well established in clinical settings.[87-88] The idea has been broached by industrial/organizational psychologists,[89-92] but, with few exceptions,[93-95] it has not been extensively applied in work settings. Recently, however, a study in a unionized state government agency illustrates how workers can successfully learn to help themselves improve their own attendance.[96] First, the employees specified what they wished to attain; they set attendance goals and, just as important, they identified ways of overcoming obstacles preventing them from coming to work. Then, they kept track of their attendance and how they coped. Lastly, they identified and delivered consequences for attaining or failing to attain the goals they had set. The results showed that employees substantially improved their attendance at work. Furthermore, they raised their confidence in their ability to control their own behavior.

Thus, from the heady, idealistic era of the late 1960s to the changing demographics of the twenty-first century, we can see how reinforcement theory has been and can be beneficially employed. In the past two decades, reinforcement theory has been used to promote a wide variety of behaviors with diverse populations in different work settings. It has also yielded valuable insights into why workers behave as they do. Reinforcement theory holds considerable promise for addressing the challenges of the twenty-first century.

NOTES

1 Lovaas, O. I. (1966). A program for the establishment of speech in psychotic children. In J. K. Wing (Ed.), *Early childhood autism*. London: Pergamon.

2 Becker, W. C., Madsen, C. H. Jr., Arnold, C. R., & Thomas D. R. (1967). The contingent use of teacher attention and praise in reducing classroom behavior problems. *The Journal of Special Education, 1*(3), 287–307.

3 Where Skinner's theories work. (1972, December), *Business Week*, pp. 64–65.

4 Datel, W. E., & Legters, L. J. (1970, June). *The psychology of the army recruit*. Paper presented at the meeting of the American Medical Association, Chicago.

5 Hamner, W. C. (1974). Reinforcement theory and contingency management in organizational settings. In H. L. Tosi & W. C. Hamner (Eds.), *Organizational behavior and management: A contingency approach*. Chicago: St. Clair Press.

6 Nord, W. R. (1969). Beyond the teaching machine: The neglected area of operant conditioning in the theory and practice of management. *Organizational Behavior and Human Performance, 4*, 375–401.

7 Porter, L. W. (1973). Turning work into nonwork: The rewarding environment. In M. D. Dunnette (Ed.), *Work and nonwork in the year 2001*, pp. 113–133. Belmont, Calif.: Wadsworth.

8 Whyte, W. F. (1972). Skinnerian theory in organizations. *Psychology Today*, April, pp. 67–68, 96, 98, 100.

9 Dinesen, I. (1937). *Out of Africa*. New York: Vintage.

10 Campbell, J. P., & Pritchard, R. D. (1976). Motivation theory in industrial organizational psychology. In M. D. Dunnette (Ed.), *Handbook of industrial and organizational psychology* (pp. 63–130). New York: Wiley.

11 Mitchell, T. R. (1982). Motivation: New directions for theory, research, and practice. *Academy of Management Review, 7*, 80–88.

12 Kazdin, A. E. (1989). *Behavior modification in applied settings* (4th ed.). Pacific Grove, Calif.: Brooks/Cole.

13 Skinner, B. F. (1974). *About behaviorism*. New York: Vintage.

14 Stolz, S. B., Wienckowski, L. A., & Brown, B. S. (1975, November). Behavior modification: A perspective on critical issues. *American Psychologist*, 1027–1048.

15 Cofer, C. N., & Appley, M. H. (1964). *Motivation: Theory and research*. New York: Wiley.

16 Steers, R. M., & Porter, L. W. (1987). *Motivation and work behavior* (4th ed.). New York: McGraw-Hill.

17 Pommer, D. A., & Streedbeck, D. (1974). Motivating staff performance in an operant learning program for children. *Journal of Applied Behavior Analysis, 7*, 217–221.

18 Briscoe, R. V., Hoffman, D. B., & Bailey, J. S. (1975). Behavioral community psychology: Training a community board to problem solve. *Journal of Applied Behavior Analysis, 8*, 157–168.

19 Baer, D. M., Wolf, M. M., & Risley, T. R. (1968). Some current dimensions of applied behavior analysis. *Journal of Applied Behavior Analysis,* **1,** 91–97.

20 Honig, W. K. (1966). *Operant behavior: Areas of research and application.* New York: Appleton-Century-Crofts.

21 Ulrich, R., Stachnik, T., & Mabry, J. (Eds.) (1966). *Control of human behavior* (Vol. 1). Glenview, Ill.: Scott, Foresman.

22 Ulrich, R., Stachnik, T., & Mabry, J. (Eds.) (1970). *Control of human behavior* (Vol. 2). Glenview, Ill.: Scott, Foresman.

23 Ulrich, R., Stachnik, T., & Mabry, J. (Eds.) (1974). *Control of human behavior: Behavior modification in the workplace* (Vol. 3). Glenview, Ill.: Scott, Foresman.

24 Gellerman, S. W. (1976, March–April). Supervision: Substance and style. *Harvard Business Review,* 89–99.

25 Homer (1952). The Iliad of Homer (Book 5, Verse 493). In R. M. Hutchins (Ed.), *Great books of the Western world.* Chicago: Encyclopedia Britannica.

26 Komaki, J., Heinzmann, A. T., & Lawson, L. (1980). Effect of training and feedback: component analysis of a behavioral safety program. *Journal of Applied Psychology,* **65,** 261–270.

27 Geller, E. S., Eason, S. L., Phillips, J. A., & Pierson, M. D. (1980). Interventions to improve sanitation during food preparation. *Journal of Organizational Behavior Management,* **2,**(3), Summer.

28 Kreitner, R., & Golab, M. (1978). Increasing the rate of salesperson telephone calls with a monetary refund. *Journal of Organizational Behavior Management,* **1,** 192–195.

29 Quilitch, H. R. (1975). A comparison of three staff-management procedures. *Journal of Applied Behavior Analysis,* **8,** 59–66.

30 Schonberger, R. J. (1982). *Japanese manufacturing techniques: Nine hidden lessons in simplicity.* New York: The Free Press.

31 Whaley, D. L., & Surratt, S. L. (1967). *Attitudes of science: A program for a student-centered seminar* (3rd ed.). Kalamazoo, Mich.: Behaviordela.

32 Bellack, A. S., & Hersen, M. (1988). *Behavioral assessment: A practical handbook.* New York: Pergamon.

33 Ciminero, A. R., Calhoun, K. S., & Adams, H. E. (1977). *Handbook of behavioral assessment.* New York: Wiley.

34 Komaki, J., Collins, R. L., & Thoene, T. J. F. (1980). Behavioral measurement in business, industry, and government. *Behavioral Assessment,* **2,** 103–123.

35 Nelson, R. O., & Hayes, S. C. (1986). *Conceptual foundations of behavioral assessment.* New York: Guilford.

36 Campbell, D. T., & Stanley, J. C. (1963). Experimental and quasiexperimental designs for research. In N. L. Gage (Ed.), *Handbook of research on teaching.* Chicago: Rand McNally.

37 Kazdin, A. E. (1982). *Single case research designs: Methods for clinical and applied settings.* New York: Oxford University Press.

38 Komaki, J., & Jensen, M. (1986). Within-group designs: An alternative to traditional control group designs. In M. F. Cataldo & T. J. Coates (Eds.), *Health & industry* (pp. 86–138). New York: Wiley.

39 Komaki, J. L., Barwick, K. D., & Scott, L. R. (1978). A behavioral approach to occupational safety: Pinpointing and reinforcing safety performance in a food manufacturing plant. *Journal of Applied Psychology,* **63,** 434–445.

40 Komaki, J. L., Coombs, T., & Schepman, S. (1990). *A review of two decades of the operant conditioning literature in business and industry.* Manuscript in preparation. Purdue University, Department of Psychological Science, West Lafayette, IN.

41 Andrasik, F. (1979). Organizational behavior modification in business settings: A methodological and content review. *Journal of Organizational Behavior Management,* **2,**(2), 85–102.

42 Babb, H. W., & Kopp, D. G. (1978). Applications of behavior modification in organizations: A review and a critique. *Academy of Management Review,* **3,** 281–292.

43 Hopkins, B. L., & Sears, J. (1982). Managing behavior for productivity. In L. W. Frederiksen (Ed.), *Handbook of organizational behavior management.* New York: Wiley.

44 Merwin, G. A., Jr., Thomason, J. A., & Sanford, E. E. (1989). A methodology and content review of organizational behavior management in the private sector: 1978–1986. *Journal of Organizational Behavior Management,* **10**(1), 39–57.

45 O'Hara, K., Johnson, C. M., & Beehr, T. A. (1985). Organizational behavior management in the private sector: A review of empirical research and recommendations for further investigation. *Academy of Management Review,* **10,** 848–864.

46 Schneier, C. E. (1974). Behavior modification in management: A review and a critique. *Academy of Management Journal,* **17,** 528–548.

47 Quilitch, H. R. (1978). Using a simple feedback procedure to reinforce the submission of written suggestions by mental health employees. *Journal of Organizational Behavior Management,* **1**(2), 155–163.

48 Kreitner, R., & Golab, M. (1978). Increasing the rate of salesperson telephone calls with a monetary refund. *Journal of Organizational Behavior Management,* **1**(3), 192–195.

49 Maher, C. A. (1982). Improving teacher instructional behavior: Evaluation of a time management training program. *Journal of Organizational Behavior Management,* **4**(3/4), 27–36.

50 Nordstrom, R., Hall, R. V., Lorenzi, P., & Delquadri,J. (1988). Organizational behavior modification in the public sector: Three field experiments. *Journal of Organizational Behavior Management,* **9**(2), 91–112.

51 Hermann, J. A., DeMontes, A. I., Dominguez, B., Montes, F., & Hopkins, B. L. (1973). Effects of bonuses for punctuality on the tardiness of industrial workers. *Journal of Applied Behavior Analysis,* **6,** 563–570.

52 Steers, R. M., & Rhodes, S. R. (1978). Major influences on employee attendance: A process model. *Journal of Applied Psychology,* **63,** 391–407.

53 Pedalino, E., & Gamboa, V. U. (1974). Behavior modifications and absenteeism: Intervention in one industrial setting. *Journal of Applied Psychology,* **59,** 694–698.

54 Nasanen, M., & Saari, J. (1987). The effects of positive feedback on housekeeping and accidents at a shipyard. *Journal of Occupational Accidents,* **8,** 237–250.

55 Sulzer-Azaroff, B., & De Santamaria, M. C. (1980). Industrial safety hazard reduction through performance feedback. *Journal of Applied Behavior Analysis,* **13,** 287–295.

56 Zohar, D., & Fussfeld, N. (1981). Modifying earplug wearing behavior by behavior modification techniques. An empirical evaluation. *Journal of Organizational Behavior Management,* **3**(2), 41–52.

57 Hopkins, B. L., Conard, R. J., & Smith, M. J. (1986). Effective and reliable behavioral control technology. *American Industrial Hygiene Association Journal,* December.

58 Elizur, D. (1987). Effect of feedback on verbal and non-verbal courtesy in a bank setting. *Applied Psychology: An International Review,* **36,** 147–156.

59 Komaki, J. L., Collins, R. L., & Temlock, S. (1987). An alternative performance measurement approach: Applied operant measurement in the service sector [Special Issue]. *Applied Psychology: An International Review,* **36**(1), 71–89.

60 Luthans, F., Paul, R., & Taylor, L. (1985). The impact of contingent reinforcement on retail salespersons' performance behaviors: A replicated field experiment. *Journal of Organizational Behavior Management,* 7(1/2), 25–35.

61 Anderson, D. C., Crowell, C. R., Sponsel, S. S., Clarke, M., & Brence, J. (1982). Behavior management in the public accommodations industry: A three-project demonstration. *Journal of Organizational Behavior Management,* 4(1/2), 33–66.

62 Komaki, J., & Collins, R. L. (1982). Motivation of preventive maintenance performance. In R. M. O'Brien, A. M. Dickinson, & M. Rosow (Eds.), *Industrial behavior modification: A learning-based approach to business management* (pp. 243–265). New York: Pergamon.

63 Haynes, R. S., Pine, R. C., & Fitch, H. G. (1982). Reducing accident rates with organizational behavior modification. *Academy of Management Journal,* 25, 407–416.

64 Heward, W. L. (1978). Operant conditioning of a .300 hitter? The effects of reinforcement on the offensive efficiency of a barnstorming baseball team. *Behavior Modification,* 2, 25–40.

65 Prue, D. M., Krapfl, J. E., Noah, J. C., Cannon, S., & Maley, R. F. (1980). Managing the treatment activities of state hospital staff. *Journal of Organizational Behavior Management,* 2(3), 165–181.

66 Fox, D. K., Hopkins, B. L., & Anger, W. K. (1987). The long-term effects of a token economy on safety performance in open-pit mining. *Journal of Applied Behavior Analysis* 20, 215–224.

67 Deluga, R. J., & Andrews, H. M. (1985–1986). A case study investigating the effects of a low-cost intervention to reduce three attendance behavior problems in a clerical training program. *Journal of Organizational Behavior Management,* 7(3/4), 115–124.

68 Premack, D. (1965). Reinforcement theory. In D. Levine (Ed.), *Nebraska symposium on motivation.* Lincoln: University of Nebraska Press.

69 Gupton, T., & LeBow, M. D. (1971). Behavior management in a large industrial firm. *Behavior Therapy,* 2, 78–82.

70 Brown, K. M., Willis, B. S., & Reid, D. H. (1981). Differential effects of supervisor verbal feedback and feedback plus approval on institutional staff performance. *Journal of Organizational Behavior Management,* 3(1), 57–68.

71 Fox, C. J., & Sulzer-Azaroff, B. (1987). Increasing completion of accident reports. *Journal of Safety Research,* 18, 65–71.

72 Zohar, D., Cohen, A., & Azar, N. (1980). Promoting increased use of ear protectors in noise through information feedback, *Human Factors,* 22(1), 69–79.

73 Dillon, M. J., Kent, H. M., & Malott, R. W. (1980). A supervisory system for accomplishing long-range projects: An application to master's thesis research. *Journal of Organizational Behavior Management,* 2(3), 213–228.

74 Miller, L. K. (1980). *Principles of everyday behavior analysis* (2nd ed). Belmont, Calif.: Wadsworth.

75 Kerr, S. (1975). On the folly of rewarding A, while hoping for B. *Academy of Management Journal,* 18, 769–782.

76 Mager, R. F., & Pipe, P. (1984). *Analyzing performance problems: You really oughta wanna* (2nd ed). Belmont, Calif.: Lake.

77 "At Emery Air Freight: Positive reinforcement boosts performance." (1973) *Organizational Dynamics,* 1(3), 41–50.

78 Wolfe, T. (1979). *The right stuff.* New York: Bantam.

79 Offermann, L. R., & Gowing, M. K. (1990). Organizations of the future: Changes and challenges. *American Psychologist,* 45(2), 95–108.

80 Katzell, R. A., & Thompson, D. E. (1990). Work motivation: Theory and practice. *American Psychologist,* **45**(2), 144–153.
81 Luthans, F., Hodgetts, R. M., & Rosenkrantz, S. A. (1988). *Real managers.* Cambridge, Mass.: Ballinger.
82 Scott, W. E., Jr., & Podsakoff, P. M. (1985). *Behavioral principles in the practice of management.* New York: Wiley.
83 Sims, H. P. (1977). The leader as a manager of reinforcement contingencies: An empirical example and a model. In J. G. Hunt & L. L. Larson (Eds.), *Leadership: The cutting edge* (pp. 121–137). Carbondale, Ill.: Southern Illinois University Press.
84 Komaki, J. L., & Desselles, M. (in press). *Leadership from an operant perspective: Making it work.* Boston: Hyman & Unwin.
85 Komaki, J. L. (1986). Toward effective supervision: An operant analysis and comparison of managers at work. *Journal of Applied Psychology,* **71**, 270–279.
86 Komaki, J. L., Desselles, M. L., & Bowman, E. D. (1989). Definitely not a breeze: Extending an operant model of effective supervision to teams. *Journal of Applied Psychology,* **74**, 522–529.
87 Meichenbaum, D. H. (1973). Cognitive factors in behavior modification: Modifying what clients say to themselves. *Annual Review of Behavior Therapy Theory & Practice,* **1**, 416–431.
88 Thoresen, C. E., & Mahoney, M. J. (1974). *Behavior self-control.* New York: Holt, Rinehart & Winston.
89 Blood, M. R. (1978). Organizational control of performance through self rewarding. In B. T. King, S. Streufert, & F. E. Fiedler (Eds.), *Managerial control and organizational democracy.* Washington, D.C.: Winston & Sons.
90 Manz, C. C., & Sims, H. P., Jr. (1980). Self-management as a substitute for leadership: A social learning theory perspective. *Academy of Management Review,* **5**, 361–367.
91 Wexley, K. N. (1984). Personnel training. *Annual Review of Psychology,* **35**, 519–551.
92 Brief, A. P., & Hollenbeck, J. R. (1985). An exploratory study of self-regulating activities and their effects on job performance. *Journal of Occupational Behaviour,* **6**, 197–208.
93 Gaetani, J. J., Johnson, C. M., & Austin, J. T. (1983). Self-management by an owner of a small business: Reduction of tardiness. *Journal of Organizational Behavior Management,* **5**(1), 31–39.
94 Lamal, P. A., & Benfield, A. (1978). The effect of self-monitoring on job tardiness and percentage of time spent working. *Journal of Organizational Behavior Management,* **1**(2), 142–149.
95 Luthans, F., & Davis, T. R. V. (1979, Summer). Behavioral self-management: The missing link in managerial effectiveness. *Organizational Dynamics,* pp. 42–60.
96 Frayne, C. A, & Latham, G. P. (1987). Application of social learning theory to employee self-management of attendance. *Journal of Applied Psychology,* **72**, 387–392.

QUESTIONS FOR DISCUSSION

1 Why do operant conditioning principles stress the necessity of avoiding negative feedback?
2 From a managerial standpoint, what is really new and innovative about operant conditioning?
3 What potential drawbacks exist when you attempt to use operant conditioning at work?
4 Would operant conditioning tend to work better among blue- or white-collar employees? Why?

5 Would the general principles of operant conditioning be as applicable to solving the problems of turnover or absenteeism as they would to solving those of performance? Why or why not? Cite examples to illustrate your answer.
6 Why does a variable ratio reward schedule tend to be the most effective in sustaining behavior? How can this type of schedule be used in organizations? Give examples.
7 How can the principles of reinforcement theory be used to explain why employees avoid performing the very activities which they are encouraged by their superiors to perform?

4

THE "PERSON-ENVIRONMENT INTERACTION" IN MOTIVATION

Ultimately, the question of motivation comes down to the complex interactions between the "push" forces within the person and the "pull" forces originating from the environment. Therefore, most of the theorizing in the last 20 years or so about motivation in work settings has been directed toward understanding the nature of these interactions. Furthermore, almost all of these theoretical approaches have involved a strong emphasis on *cognition*. As noted in Chapter 1, such cognitively based theories generally assume that individuals engage in some form of conscious behavior relating to the performance of tasks. People are seen as being reasoning, thinking individuals who often consider the *anticipated* consequences of their actions at work. Thus, cognitive theories attempt to develop models concerning the thought processes people go through as they decide to participate (i.e., accept employment with an organization and continue to work for it) and perform in the workplace.

In this chapter, we consider three types of cognitive theories: (1) equity theory; (2) expectancy theory (also called valence-instrumentality-expectancy theory, or VIE theory for short); and (3) social learning theory. The reader will want to focus on how these three cognitively based approaches compare with one another and also especially on how they compare with the need theories and reinforcement approaches that were discussed in the previous chapters. The fundamental question that has not been fully answered by research to date is this: To what extent are these various theories in general agreement and more or less consistent with each other, and to what extent are they in direct or partial conflict in their attempts to explain and predict behavior?

This chapter begins with an examination of a theory—equity theory—that was originally developed in the 1960s. The first article, by Mowday, describes the basic formulation of this theory, which is grounded in social exchange processes, and summarizes a considerable body of research related to the theory. The emphasis of equity theory on social comparison aspects of interactions or "exchanges" among people make it relevant to many aspects of behavior in work situations, especially those involving the effects of compensation on individuals' levels of motivation for task performance.

Although there have not been many recent advances in the development of equity theory in the last decade or so, the theory nevertheless has led to some interesting and relatively new (in terms of concerted research attention) issues. One such issue is that of procedural justice in the workplace, which is explored in the second article in this chapter, by Cropanzano and Folger. These authors highlight the distinction between two types of justice: *distributive* justice, which is at the heart of equity theory and which deals with the differing amounts of rewards (or punishments) "distributed" to different individuals; and *procedural* justice, which focuses on *how* decisions to distribute particular rewards or punishments are made. As Cropanzano and Folger emphasize, distributive justice is concerned with "ends," whereas procedural justice is concerned with "means." Thus, strictly speaking, procedural justice is not a component of equity theory but rather a logical extension of it in terms of understanding the motivated behavior of individuals. In light of society's increasing attention to procedural due process—especially in the employment situation—a focus on procedural justice would seem to be particularly relevant in today's world of work.

The third article in this chapter, by Pinder, provides a comprehensive overview of expectancy theory, with particular emphasis on the three concepts—valence, instrumentality, and expectancy—that constitute the essence of this way of looking at motivation. The article demonstrates why expectancy theory is a prime example of what organizational scholars refer to as a *process* theory, as distinct from a content theory, of motivation. Expectancy theory is also a good example of a theory that uses person-environment interactions as a basic framework for understanding motivated behavior.

The final two articles in this chapter provide a description and analysis of a highly influential theory that has major implications for thinking about motivation in work settings, namely, social learning theory. This theory has received considerable attention in recent years from the field of psychology, and it seems especially applicable to work situations, since almost all such situations are to some degree, at least, "social." The first article, by Kreitner and Luthans, presents a succinct overview of this theory and shows how it builds both on reinforcement principles and on knowledge about cognitive processes. The theory, as demonstrated in this article, stresses the *reciprocal* interaction of the person, behavior, and the environment. The article concludes with a set of action steps that managers can take to implement an approach consistent with the fundamentals of the theory. The last article, by Wood and Bandura—the latter author being the primary developer of social learning theory—provides additional elaboration of the fundamentals of the theory. The authors emphasize the importance of beliefs in one's own competencies and explain how self-regulation of motivation operates by means of individuals' internal standards or goals and their comparisons of their behavior with those goals. A social learning theory approach to motivation is an appropriate place to end this part of the book, as it serves as a natural—and optimistic—lead-in to Part Three, which covers central issues in motivation at work.

Equity Theory Predictions of Behavior in Organizations

Richard T. Mowday

Employees are seldom passive observers of the events that occur in the workplace. They form impressions of others and the events that affect them and cognitively or behaviorally respond based on their positive or negative evaluations. A great deal of theory and research in the social sciences has been devoted to understanding these evaluative processes. More specifically, research has attempted to uncover the major influences on individual reactions in social situations and the processes through which these reactions are formed. One useful framework for understanding how social interactions in the workplace influence employee reactions to their jobs and participation in the organization is provided by theories of social exchange processes (Adams, 1965; Homans, 1961; Jacques, 1961; Patchen, 1961; Simpson, 1972).

Exchange theories are based on two simple assumptions about human behavior. First, there is an assumed similarity between the process through which individuals evaluate their social relationships and economic transactions in the market. Social relationships can be viewed as exchange processes in which individuals make contributions (investments) for which they expect certain outcomes. Individuals are assumed to have expectations about the outcomes that should result when they contribute their time or resources in interaction with others.

The second assumption concerns the process through which individuals decide whether or not a particular exchange is satisfactory. Most exchange theories assign a central role to social comparison processes in terms of how individuals evaluate exchange relationships. Information gained through interaction with others is used to determine whether an exchange has been advantageous. For example, individuals may compare their outcomes and contributions in an exchange with the outcomes and contributions of the person with whom they are interacting. Where there is relative equality between the outcomes and contributions of both parties to an exchange, satisfaction is likely to result from the interaction.

The popularity of social exchange theories may be attributable to their agreement with commonsense observations about human behavior in social situations. Exchange theories suggest that individuals in social interaction behave in a manner similar to the "economic man" of classical economics. Most theories of motivation assume that individuals are motivated to maximize their rewards and minimize their costs (Vroom, 1964; Walster, Bercheid, & Walster, 1976). The major difference between assumptions made about economic man and social exchange theories is that the latter recognize that individuals exist in environments characterized by limited and imperfect information. The ambiguity present in

This paper was written especially for this volume. Support for the preparation of the manuscript was partially provided by a grant from the Office of Naval Research, Contract No. N00014-76-C-0164, NR 170-812. The assistance of Thom McDade in the early stages of preparing the paper is gratefully acknowledged.

most social situations results in individuals relying heavily on information provided by others to evaluate their actions and those of others (Darley & Darley, 1973). Social interactions therefore play a central role in providing information to individuals on the quality of their relationships with others. Our reliance upon others for valued information, however, may place constraints on how we behave in our interactions with others. In order to maintain our social relationships it may be necessary to conform to certain social norms that prevent us from maximizing our outcomes without regard to the outcome of others.

The purpose of this paper is to examine one prominent theory of social exchange processes: Adams' (1963a, 1965) theory of equity. Although Adams' theory is only one of several exchange theories that have been developed, it deserves special attention for several reasons. First, Adams' theory is perhaps the most rigorously developed statement of how individuals evaluate social exchange relationships. The careful formulation of the theory has led to considerable research interest in testing its specific predictions. The large number of studies available on equity theory provides evidence upon which to evaluate the adequacy of social exchange models. Second, the majority of research on equity theory has investigated employee reactions to compensation in employer-employee exchange relationships. The theory and supporting research are therefore highly relevant to increasing our understanding of behavior in organizational settings.

In the sections that follow, Adams' equity theory will be briefly summarized and the research evidence reviewed. The major empirical and conceptual questions surrounding the theory will then be discussed. Finally, the generalizability of the theory will be considered and suggestions made for applying equity theory to several previously neglected areas of organizational behavior.

EQUITY THEORY

Antecedents of Inequity

The major components of exchange relationships in Adams' theory are inputs and outcomes. Inputs or investments are those things a person contributes to the exchange. In a situation where a person exchanges his or her services for pay, inputs may include previous work experience, education, effort on the job, and training. Outcomes are those things that result from the exchange. In the employment situations, the most important outcome is likely to be pay. In addition, other outcomes such as supervisory treatment, job assignments, fringe benefits, and status symbols may also be considered in evaluating the exchange. To be considered in evaluating exchange relationships, inputs and outcomes must meet two conditions. First, the existence of an input or outcome must be recognized by one or both parties to the exchange. Second, an input or outcome must be considered relevant to the exchange (i.e., have some marginal utility). Unless inputs or outcomes are both recognized and considered relevant, they will not be considered in evaluating an exchange relationship.

Adams suggests that individuals weight their inputs and outcomes by their importance to the individual. Summary evaluation of inputs and outcomes are developed by separately summing the weighted inputs and weighted outcomes. In the summation process, inputs and outcomes are treated as independent even though they may be highly related (e.g., age and previous work experience would be considered as separate inputs). The ratio of an individual's (called "person's") outcomes to inputs is compared to the ratio of outcomes to inputs of another individual or group (called "other"). Other may be a person with whom you are engaged in a direct exchange, another individual engaged in an exchange with a common third party, or person in a previous or anticipated work situation. The selection of comparison others is discussed in more detail below. The important consideration at this point is that person evaluates his or her outcomes and inputs by comparing them with those of others.

Equity is said to exist whenever the ratio of person's outcomes to inputs is equal to the ratio of other's outcomes and inputs.

$$\frac{O_p}{I_p} = \frac{O_o}{I_o}$$

Inequity exists whenever the two ratios are unequal.

$$\frac{O_p}{I_p} < \frac{O_o}{I_o} \quad \text{or} \quad \frac{O_p}{I_p} > \frac{O_o}{I_o}$$

Several important aspects of this definition should be recognized. First, the conditions necessary to produce equity or inequity are based on the individual's perceptions of inputs and outcomes. In behavioral terms, the objective characteristics of the situation are of less importance than the person's perceptions. Second, inequity is a relative phenomenon. Inequity does not necessarily exist if person has high inputs and low outcomes as long as the comparison other has a similar ratio. Employees may therefore exhibit satisfaction on a job that demands a great deal and for which they receive very little if their comparison other is in a similar position. Third, inequity exists when a person is relatively underpaid and relatively overpaid. It is this implication of Adams' theory that has generated the most attention since it suggests that people will react in a counterintuitive fashion when they are overpaid. Research evidence indicates, however, that the threshold for underpayment is lower than that associated with overpayment (Leventhal, Weiss, & Long, 1969). As might be expected, individuals are somewhat more willing to accept overpayment in an exchange relationship than they are to accept underpayment. The relationship between the ratios of outcomes to inputs of person and other might best be considered along a continuum reflecting different degrees of inequity ranging from overpayment on one extreme to underpayment on the other. The midpoint of the continuum represents the point at which the two ratios are equal. Equity is defined as a zone which is asymmetric about the midpoint. The asymmetry reflects the fact that the thresholds for overpayment and underpayment may differ.

One final aspect of Adams' formulation should be mentioned. Walster et al. (1976) have shown that the formula relating to two ratios of person and other is inadequate in situations where inputs might be negative. Following their example, consider the situation where person's inputs have a value of 5 and outcomes are -10 while other's inputs and outcomes are -5 and 10, respectively. Using Adams' formula, these two ratios are equal and thus a condition of equity would be said to exist.

$$\frac{O_p}{I_p} = \frac{-10}{5} = -2 \quad \text{and} \quad \frac{O_o}{I_o} = \frac{10}{-5} = -2$$

Obviously, a situation in which person makes positive inputs but receives negative outcomes is inequitable when compared to another who makes negative inputs but receives positive outcomes. Walster et al. (1976) have proposed an alternative formulation that overcomes this problem. Equity and inequity are defined by the following relationship.

$$\frac{\text{Outcomes}_p - \text{Inputs}_p}{(|\text{Inputs}_p|)_p^k} \quad \text{compared with} \quad \frac{\text{Outcomes}_o - \text{Inputs}_o}{(|\text{Inputs}_o|)_o^k}$$

The reader interested in pursuing this subject further can find a more detailed discussion of this formula and its terms in Walster et al. (1976).

Consequence of Inequity

The motivational aspects of Adams' theory are derived from the hypothesized consequences of perceived inequity. The major postulates of the theory can be summarized simply: (1) perceived inequity creates tension in the individual; (2) the amount of tension is proportional to the magnitude of the inequity; (3) the tension created in the individual will motivate him or her to reduce it; and (4) the strength of the motivation to reduce inequity is proportional to the perceived inequity (Adams, 1965). In others words, the presence of inequity motivates the individual to change the situation through behavioral or cognitive means to return to a condition of equity.

The methods through which individuals reduce inequity are referred to as methods of inequity resolution. Adams describes six alternative methods of restoring equity: (1) altering inputs; (2) altering outcomes; (3) cognitively distorting inputs or outcomes; (4) leaving the field; (5) taking actions designed to change the inputs or outcomes of the comparison other; or (6) changing the comparison other. The choice of a particular method of restoring equity will depend upon the characteristics of the inequitable situation. Adams suggests, however, that the person will attempt to maximize positively valent outcomes and minimize increasingly effortful inputs in restoring equity. In addition, person will resist changing the object of comparison and distorting inputs that are considered central to the self-concept. In general, it is considered easier to distort other's inputs and outcomes than the person's own inputs or outcomes. Finally, leaving the field (e.g., turnover from an organization) as a method of reducing inequity will only be considered in extreme cases of inequity.

RESEARCH ON EQUITY THEORY PREDICTIONS
OF EMPLOYEE REACTIONS TO PAY

Considerable research interest has been generated in testing predictions from Adams' theory. The most recent review of equity theory research summarized the results from over 160 investigations (Adams & Freedman, 1976). Although equity considerations are relevant to a number of different types of social relationships (cf., Walster et al., 1976), most early research focused attention on the employer-employee exchange relationship. These studies were generally laboratory investigations in which subjects were hired to perform relatively simple tasks such as proofreading or interviewing. The simple nature of the tasks suggests that differences found between subjects in the quantity or quality of performance would be attributable to motivation levels rather than differences in skills or abilities. Perceived inequity was induced by either manipulating the subject's perceived qualifications to be hired for the task (qualifications manipulation) or by actual differences in pay rates (manipulation by circumstances).

Predictions from equity theory about employee reactions to pay distinguish between two conditions of inequity (underpayment versus overpayment) and two methods of compensation (hourly versus piece rate). Specific predictions are summarized for each condition in Table 1. The methodology and results of selected studies designed to test these predictions are presented in Table 2. More extensive reviews of this literature can be found in Adams and Freedman (1976), Campbell and Pritchard (1976), Goodman and Friedman (1971), Lawler (1968a), Opsahl and Dunnette (1966), and Pritchard (1969).

A review of the studies summarized in Table 2 suggests general support for equity theory predictions. In the overpayment-hourly condition, a number of studies have provided some support for the prediction that overpaid subjects will produce higher quantity than equitably paid subjects (Adams & Rosenbaum, 1962; Arrowood, 1961; Goodman & Friedman, 1968; Lawler, 1968b; Pritchard, Dunnette, & Jorgenson, 1972; Wiener, 1970). Several studies have either failed to support or provided mixed support for equity theory predictions in this condition, although they often differed from the supporting studies in the manner in which perceived inequity was experimentally manipulated (Anderson & Shelly, 1970; Evans & Simmons, 1969; Friedman & Goodman, 1967; Valenzi & Andrews,

TABLE 1
EQUITY THEORY PREDICTIONS OF EMPLOYEE REACTIONS TO INEQUITABLE PAYMENT

	Underpayment	Overpayment
Hourly payment	Subjects underpaid by the hour produce less or poorer-quality output than equitably paid subjects	Subjects overpaid by the hour produce more or higher-quality output than equitably paid subjects
Piece-rate payment	Subjects underpaid by piece rate will produce a large number of low-quality units in comparison with equitably paid subjects	Subjects overpaid by piece rate will provide fewer units of higher quality than equitably paid subjects

TABLE 2
SUMMARY OF EQUITY THEORY RESEARCH ON EMPLOYEE REACTIONS TO PAY

Study	Equity condition	Method of induction	Task	Dependent variables	Results
Adams (1963b)	Overpayment: hourly and piece rate	Qualifications	Interviewing	Productivity, work quality	Hourly-overpaid subjects produced greater quantity and piece-rate-overpaid subjects produced higher quality and lower quantity than equitably paid subjects.
Adams and Jacobsen (1964)	Overpayment: piece rate	Qualifications	Proofreading	Productivity, work quality	Overpaid subjects produced less quantity of higher quality.
Adams and Rosenbaum (1962)	Overpayment: hourly and piece rate	Qualifications	Interviewing	Productivity	Hourly-overpaid subjects produced more quantity while piece-rate-overpaid subjects produced less quantity.
Anderson and Shelly (1970)	Overpayment: hourly	Qualifications, importance of task	Proofreading	Productivity, work quality	No differences were found between groups
Andrews (1967)	Overpayment and underpayment: piece rate	Circumstances, previous wage experiences	Interviewing Data checking	Productivity, work quality	Overpaid subjects produced higher quality and underpaid subjects produced greater quantity and lower quality.
Arrowood (1961)	Overpayment: hourly	Qualifications, work returned	Interviewing	Productivity	Overpaid subjects had higher productivity.
Evans and Simmons (1969)	Overpayment and underpayment: hourly	Competence, authority	Proofreading	Productivity, work quality	Underpaid subjects produced more of poorer quality in competence condition. No differences found in other conditions.

Study	Payment	Independent variable	Method	Dependent variable	Results
Friedman and Goodman (1967)	Overpayment: hourly	Qualifications	Interviewing	Productivity	Qualifications induction did not affect productivity. When subjects were classified by perceived qualifications, unqualified subjects produced less than qualified subjects.
Goodman and Friedman (1968)	Overpayment and underpayment: hourly	Qualifications, quantity versus quality emphasis	Questionnaire coding	Productivity, work quality	Overpaid subjects produced more than equitably paid subjects. Emphasis on quantity versus quality affected performance.
Goodman and Friedman (1969)	Overpayment: piece rate	Qualifications, quantity versus quality emphasis	Questionnaire scoring	Productivity, work quality	Overpaid subjects increased productivity or work quality, depending upon induction.
Lawler (1968b)	Overpayment: hourly	Qualifications, circumstances	Interviewing	Productivity, work quality	Overpaid (unqualified) subjects produced more of lower quality. Subjects overpaid by circumstances did not differ from equitably paid group.
Lawler, Koplin, Young, and Fadem (1968)	Overpayment: piece rate	Qualifications	Interviewing	Productivity, work quality	Overpaid subjects produced less of higher quality in initial work session. In later sessions, subject's perceived qualifications and productivity increased. The need for money was related to productivity for both groups.
Lawler and O'Gara (1967)	Underpayment: piece rate	Circumstances	Interviewing	Productivity, work quality	Underpaid subjects produced more of lower quality and also perceived their job as more interesting but less important and complex.

TABLE 2
SUMMARY OF EQUITY THEORY RESEARCH ON EMPLOYEE REACTIONS TO PAY (CONTINUED)

Study	Equity condition	Method of induction	Task	Dependent variables	Results
Pritchard, Dunnette, and Jorgenson (1972)	Overpayment and underpayment: hourly and piece rate	Circumstances, actual change in payment	Clerical task	Performance satisfaction	Circumstances induction did not result in performance differences for piece rate, but some support was found for hourly overpay and underpay. Changes in pay rate supported hourly predictions. Some support found for piece-rate-overpayment prediction but not for underpayment.
Valenzi and Andrews (1971)	Overpayment and underpayment: hourly	Circumstances	Clerical task	Productivity, work quality	No significant differences found between conditions. 27 percent of underpaid subjects quit. No other subjects in other conditions quit.
Wiener (1970)	Overpayment: hourly	Qualifications, inputs versus outcomes, ego-oriented versus task-oriented	Word manipulation	Productivity, work quality	Outcome-overpayment subjects produced more. Input-overpaid subjects produced more only on ego-oriented task.
Wood and Lawler (1970)	Overpayment: piece rate	Qualifications	Reading	Amount of time reading, quality	Overpaid subjects produced less, but this could not be attributed to striving for higher quality.

1971). In the overpayment-piece-rate condition, support for the theory has been found by Adams (1963b), Adams and Jacobsen (1964), Adams and Rosenbaum (1962), Andrews (1967), and Goodman and Friedman (1969). Mixed or marginal support for the theory was provided by Lawler, Koplin, Young, and Fadem (1968), and Wood and Lawler (1970). Although fewer studies have examined the underpayment conditions, support for both the hourly and piece-rate predictions have been reported (Andrews, 1967; Evans & Simmons, 1969; Lawler & O'Gara, 1967; Pritchard et al., 1972).

Although the support for Adams' theory appears impressive, several questions concerning the interpretation of the study results need to be considered. Following Vroom (1964), Goodman and Friedman (1971) suggest that the following concepts must be operationalized to provide a complete and unambiguous test of equity theory: (1) person's evaluation of his or her inputs; (2) person's perception of the relevance of the inputs for task performance; (3) person's perception of the experimenter's perception of the inputs; (4) person's perception of other's outcome-input ratio; (5) person's perception of future outcomes; (6) person's perception of the outcomes relative to alternative outcomes (e.g., past outcomes); and (7) relative importance person attaches to using 4, 5, and 6 as comparison objects. Control over these factors is central to ensuring a high degree of internal validity for the results of experimental studies. To the extent these factors may remain uncontrolled, conclusive tests of the theory become very difficult and alternative explanations for the study results can be raised. It should be apparent that many of these factors remain uncontrolled in even the most rigorous laboratory experiment. For example, Goodman and Friedman (1971) point out that the comparison other used by subjects is ambiguous in most studies. To the extent subjects use different comparison others than intended by the experimenter, interpretation of the study results becomes problematic.

A number of writers have been critical of research on equity theory precisely because several alternative explanations may exist for observed differences in the performance of subjects, particularly in the overpayment condition (Campbell & Pritchard, 1976; Goodman & Friedman, 1971; Lawler, 1968a; Pritchard, 1969). Two problems are commonly raised in interpreting the results of research on overpayment inequity, and both have to do with experimental manipulations of perceived inequity. Inequity is commonly induced in subjects by challenging their qualifications for the job. Subjects are led to believe they do not possess the necessary experience or training to qualify for the rate of pay they are to receive. Although seldom verified, it is assumed that this will result in experienced overpayment inequity (i.e., subjects believe they are being paid more than they should receive given their qualifications).

Challenging the qualifications of subjects, however, may also be experienced as threatening their self-esteem or perceived job security. Subjects may therefore work harder to prove to themselves (and to the experimenter) that they are capable of performing the task or to protect their job security. In other words, subjects may perform as predicted by the theory for reasons related to the experimental treatment but not to perceived inequity. Support for these alternative explanations for results of research on overpayment inequity comes from several sources. Andrews and Valenzi (1970) had subjects role-play an overpayment inequity situation in which subject qualifications to perform the task were challenged. When asked to indicate how they would respond in this situation, none of the subjects responded in terms of wage inequity. A majority of subjects, however, responded in terms of their self-image as a worker. In another study, Wiener (1970) found that overpaid subjects produced more than equitably paid subjects only when the task was ego-involving (i.e., task performance was central to the self-concept). Based on this finding, he argued that the performance of subjects in the overpayment condition was more highly attributable to devalued self-esteem brought about by challenges to their qualifications than to feelings of inequity. In studies where perceived inequity has been manipulated by means other than challenging the subject's qualifications (e.g., by actual changes in pay rates), less support is commonly found for equity theory predictions (Evans & Simmons, 1969; Pritchard et al., 1972; Valenzi & Andrews, 1971).

Several writers have seriously questioned the extent to which overpayment in work organizations may lead to perceived inequity. Locke (1976), for example, argues that employees are seldom told they are overpaid or made to feel incompetent to perform their job duties as is the case in laboratory experiments. He argues that employees are more likely to simply adjust their idea of equitable payment to justify what they are getting. This raises the possibility that employees in organizations use their pay rates as a primary source of information about their contributions (e.g., "if the organization is willing to pay this much, I must be making a valuable contribution"). Campbell and Pritchard (1976) also point out that employer-employee exchange relationships are highly impersonal when compared to exchanges between two close friends. Perceived overpayment inequity may be more likely in the latter exchange relationship than in the former. Individuals may react to overpayment inequity only when they believe their actions have led to someone else's being treated unfairly (Campbell & Pritchard, 1976; Walster et al., 1976). From the employee's standpoint in work organizations, there may be little objective evidence that the organization feels it is being treated unfairly.

In summary, predictions from Adams' theory about employee reactions to wage inequities have received some support in the research literature. Research support for the theory appears to be strongest for predictions about underpayment inequity. Although there are fewer studies of underpayment than of overpayment, results of research on underpayment are relatively consistent and subject to fewer alternative explanations. There are both theoretical and empirical grounds for being cautious in generalizing the results of research on overpayment inequity to employee behavior in work organizations. Where such studies have manipulated perceived inequity by challenging subjects' qualifications for the job, observed differences in performance can be explained in ways that have little to do with inequity. Where other methods of inducing overpayment inequity are used, considerably less support is often found for the theory. Predicted differences in productivity and satisfaction due to overpayment inequity are often in the predicted direction but fail to reach acceptable levels of statistical significance.

Conceptual Issues in Equity Theory

In addition to the methodological considerations discussed with respect to research on equity theory, several writers have also raised questions about the conceptual adequacy of the theory (e.g., Weick, 1967). Since theories or models of social processes are ways of making sense out of our environment by simplifying relationships between variables, it should not be surprising that any given theory fails to capture the complexity we know to exist in the real world. Consequently, there are usually a number of limitations that can be pointed out in any given theory, and equity theory is no different from other motivation approaches in this regard. The conceptual issues to be discussed below point to several limitations of the present formulation of equity theory, and they should be viewed as areas in which the theory may be clarified or extended through further research.

Concept of Equity

The concept of equity is most often interpreted in work organizations as a positive association between an employee's effort or performance on the job and the pay he or she receives (Goodman, 1977). In other words, it is believed that employees who contribute more to the organization should receive higher amounts of the rewards the organization has to offer. This belief is often referred to as the "equity norm." Adams (1965) suggests that individual expectations about equity or "fair" correlations between inputs and outcomes are learned during the process of socialization (e.g., in the home or at work) and through comparison with the inputs and outcomes of others. Although few would question the existence of an equity norm governing social relationships, the derivation of this norm and its pervasiveness remain somewhat unclear. In addition, it is important to determine the extent to which the equity norm is defined by an individuals' effort and performance or by other types of contributions they may make to organizations.

Walster et al. (1976) suggest the norm of equity originates in societal attempts to develop methods of allocating rewards that maximize the amount of collective reward. Through evolving ways to "equitably" distribute rewards and costs among its members, groups or organizations can maximize the total rewards available. Groups therefore induce their members to behave equitably and establish reinforcement systems to ensure this norm is followed in social relationships. It should be apparent, however, that groups or society in general frequently deviate from the equity norm in distributing rewards. Social welfare programs and old-age medical assistance, for example, are instances in which resources are distributed on the basis of need rather than an assessment of the individual's contribution to the larger group.

The equity norm appears to be only one of several norms that govern the distribution of rewards in social relationships. An important question concerns what factors influence the extent to which rewards are distributed equitably or allocated on some other basis. In an analysis of reward allocation in small groups, Leventhal (1976) suggests that the particular distribution rule adopted in allocating rewards is related to both the goals of the reward system and characteristics of the allocator. Table 3 contrasts three decision rules that can be used in allo-

TABLE 3
DISTRIBUTION RULES FOR ALLOCATING REWARDS

Distribution rule	Situations where distribution rule is likely to be used	Factors affecting use of distribution rule
Equity/contributions (outcomes should match contributions)	1 Goal is to maximize group productivity. 2 A low degree of cooperation is required for task performance.	1 What receiver is expected to do 2 What others receive 3 Outcomes and contributions of person allocating rewards 4 Task difficulty and perceived ability 5 Personal characteristics of person allocating rewards and person performing
Social responsibility/needs (outcomes distributed on the basis of needs)	1 Allocator of rewards is a close friend of the receiver, feels responsible for the well-being of the receiver, or is successful or feels competent.	1 Perceived legitimacy of needs 2 Origin of need (e.g., beyond control of the individual)
Equality (equal outcomes given to all participants)	1 Goal is to maximize harmony, minimize conflict in group. 2 Task of judging performer's needs or contribution is difficult. 3 Person allocating rewards has a low cognitive capacity. 4 A high degree of cooperation is required for task performance. 5 Allocator anticipates future interactions with low-input member.	1 Sex of person allocating rewards (e.g., females more likely to allocate rewards equally than males) 2 Nature of task

Source: Adapted from Leventhal (1976).

cating rewards (equity, equality, and responsiveness to needs) and the situations where each rule is most likely to be used. The equity norm appears to be most closely associated with the goal of maximizing productivity in a group, while rewards are most likely to be distributed equally when the goal is to minimize group conflict.

Distribution rules represent an important concept in understanding reward systems (Cook, 1975; Goodman, 1977). Distribution rules identify the association between any dimension of evaluation and the levels of outcomes to be distributed. A consideration of distribution rules suggests both that different norms may govern the distribution of rewards in organizations and that different factors may weight more heavily in allocating rewards using any given norm. For example, in organizations where an equity norm is followed, it is common to find that an individual's contribution in terms of seniority is a more important basis for rewards than is actual job performance. Our ability to predict how individuals react to reward systems therefore depends upon identifying the particular norm they believe should be followed and the specific dimension (i.e., input) they feel is most important in allocating rewards. Equity theory often assumes that rewards should be given in relation to a person's contribution and, further, that performance is the most important contribution in the work setting. The accuracy of our predictions of employee reactions to reward systems can be increased, however, by recognizing the existence of several norms governing the distribution of rewards and the differential importance that may be attached to employee inputs.

Choice of a Method of Inequity Resolution

Although the several factors Adams (1965) suggested individuals will take into consideration in choosing among alternative methods of reducing inequity make the theory more testable, they do not allow a totally unequivocal set of predictions to be made from the theory (Wicklund & Brehm, 1976). In any situation, a given method of restoring inequity may satisfy one of these rules while at the same time violating another. Cognitively distorting inputs as a method of reducing inequity, for example, may allow the individual to maximize positively valent outcomes, but at the expense of threatening aspects central to his or her self-concept. When such a conflict occurs, it is difficult to specify how an individual will react to inequity. Opsahl and Dunnette (1966) have pointed out that the inability to predict how individuals will react to inequity makes conclusive tests of the theory problematic. If an overcompensated group fails to respond to inequity by increasing inputs, can this be interpreted as a disconfirmation of the theory or as an instance in which other methods of reducing inequity (e.g., cognitively distorting your own or other's inputs or outcomes) are being used? This ambiguity associated with equity theory appears to result in a situation where almost any result of empirical research can be explained in terms of the theory.

Many of the studies of equity theory have failed to capture the complexity of inequity resolution processes (Adams & Freedman, 1976). It is common in such studies to set up an inequitable situation and determine the extent to which subjects reduce inequity by changing work quantity or quality. In more personal exchange relationships, however, the method of reducing inequity chosen may be sensitive to cues from the other party to the exchange (Adams & Freedman, 1976). For example, in overpayment situations, an organization may suggest employees increase their skills and abilities through further education rather than increasing their effort on the job. Research also suggests that strategies for reducing inequity are dynamic and may change over time. Lawler et al. (1968) found that subjects reduced overpayment-piece-rate inequity by increasing work quality in an initial work session but increased their perceived qualifications to perform the task in subsequent sessions. Cognitively changing perceived inputs (qualifications) may have allowed subjects to reduce the overpayment inequity in a manner that permitted increased quantity of production and thus increased rewards to be received.

The way in which individuals reduce perceived inequity appears to be a complex process. A greater understanding of this process is essential to increasing the accuracy of predictions from equity theory.

Choice of a Comparison Other

One area of recent concern in equity theory is to develop a greater understanding of how individuals choose comparison standards against which to evaluate inputs and outcomes. Adams (1965) suggested that comparison others may be the other party to the exchange or another individual involved in an exchange with the same third party. Until recently, little has been known about the actual comparison standards people use or the process through which alternative comparisons are chosen.

Goodman (1974) differentiated between three classes of referents: (1) others, (2) self-standards, and (3) system referents. Others are people who may be involved in a similar exchange either with the same organization or with some other organization. Self-standards are unique to the individual but different from his or her current ratio of outcomes and inputs; for example, individuals may compare their current ratio against inputs and outcomes associated with an earlier job. System referents are implicit or explicit contractual expectations between an employer and employee. At the time of being hired, an employee may be promised future rewards and this can become a basis for evaluating the exchange. In a study of 217 managers, Goodman (1974) found each of these referents was used in determining the degree of satisfaction with pay. Perhaps his most important finding was that a majority of managers reported using multiple referents in assessing their satisfaction. For example, 28 percent of the managers indicated they compared their present situation against both those of others and self-standards. He also found that higher levels of education were associated with choosing a comparison referent outside the organization.

Based on his research, Goodman (1977) has developed a model of the factors that may influence the selection of comparison person or standard. This model is presented in Figure 1. He postulates that the choice of a referent is a function of both the availability of information about the referent and the relevance or attractiveness of the referent for the comparison. Availability of information about referents is primarily determined by the individual's propensity to search and his or her position in an organization (i.e., access to information). The relevance or attractiveness of a referent is determined jointly by the instrumentality of the referent for satisfying the individual's comparison needs and the number and strength of needs related to a referent. A more detailed discussion of this model can be found in Goodman (1977).

Goodman's (1974, 1977) work represents an important step in increasing our understanding of how social comparison processes are made. If his model is supported by subsequent research, it will provide an important tool for both researchers and managers in determining who or what employees use in making comparisons about their present level of rewards.

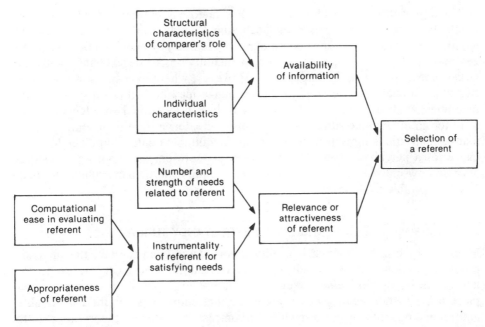

FIGURE 1
Factors influencing the selection of a referent in social comparison processes. (Adapted from Goodman, 1977.)

Individual and Situational Differences in Reactions to Inequity

One area of research on equity theory that has received little attention is the impact of individual and situational differences on employee perceptions and reactions to inequity. The importance of considering individual differences was first demonstrated by Tornow (1971). Recognizing that the classification of something as an input or an outcome is often ambiguous in equity comparisons, he suggested that individuals may have a stable tendency to classify ambiguous job elements as either inputs or outcomes. Using the data collected by Pritchard et al. (1972), he subsequently classified subjects as either input- or outcome-oriented and found this factor had an impact on their reactions to inequity. For example, outcome-oriented individuals were found to be more sensitive to overpayment than were subjects with an input orientation. Individual differences were therefore having an effect on how individuals reacted to perceived inequity. This is an area in which more research is needed to isolate the stable traits of individuals that can affect inequity perceptions. One variable that may be promising is the individual's level of internal/external control (Rotter, 1966). It is possible that individuals who believe events that happen to them are under their control (internals) would have a greater propensity to attempt to reduce perceived inequity than individuals who believe events are largely beyond their control (externals).

The importance of considering situational factors in employee reactions to inequity has already been noted in discussing Campbell and Pritchard's (1976) personal-impersonal exchange continuum. In the overpayment situation, employees may not react strongly to perceived inequity since the exchange with the larger organization is quite impersonal. However, where exchanges are between two close friends, both parties to the exchange may be highly sensitive to any inequities. Walster et al. (1976) have noted that an individual who feels responsible for an inequitable situation may express greater tension than someone who inadvertently finds himself or herself in an inequitable relationship. The locus of cause for a perceived inequity may therefore represent an important consideration in how individuals react to perceived inequity, particularly when the inequity is favorable to themselves.

RELATIONSHIP OF EQUITY THEORY TO EXPECTANCY THEORY

Much of the original interest in equity theory came from the fact that it made predictions about individual behavior that were difficult to incorporate into existing theories of motivation (Weick, 1967). For example, in the overpayment-piece-rate situation equity theory predicted that employees will increase quality and reduce quantity of performance. In contrast, expectancy theory appears to suggest that individuals attempt to maximize the attainment of valued outcomes and that motivation levels should be high whenever attractive outcomes (e.g., pay) are made directly contingent upon performance. Considerable research interest has been generated in trying to test these seemingly competing predictions.

Lawler (1968a) was one of the first to suggest that equity theory and expectancy theory may not be irreconcilable in terms of their predictions. A review of the equity theory literature led Lawler to conclude that the results of studies of the hourly payment condition could be explained equally well by expectancy theory. In the piece-rate conditions, expectancy theory could make the same predictions as equity theory if it was assumed that perceived inequity influenced the valence or attractiveness of rewards. It is possible that increasingly large piece-rate rewards have a decreasing valence for employees and that the amount of reward that has been received influences the valence of additional amounts of the reward. Lawler felt that if perceived equity were explicitly recognized as one of the factors affecting the valence of outcomes, expectancy theory could explain the results of equity theory research. Lawler (1973) and others (Campbell & Pritchard, 1976) have therefore concluded that equity considerations could be subsumed under the more general expectancy theory of motivation.

Although the two theories do not really appear to be in conflict, it is unclear whether this reflects genuine similarity or the ambiguity with which the theories are stated. As noted by Campbell and Pritchard (1976), both theories are somewhat ambiguous and thus it always is possible to come up with some previously unrecognized outcome that will reconcile competing predictions. In addition, the effects of perceived inequity on the valence of outcomes remains to be demonstrated. Although Lawler et al. (1968) found that the need for money correlated more highly with productivity for overpaid subjects than for equitably paid subjects, need for money was not experimentally manipulated and thus the direction of causality is difficult to establish. In addition, a composite measure of need for money was constructed based on measures taken both before and after the manipulation of perceived overpayment. Consequently, the effects of the inequity manipulation on the subject's need for money (an indicator of valence of money) cannot be determined.

In view of the ambiguity surrounding the two theories and the lack of evidence concerning the effects of perceived inequity on the valence of outcomes, it is perhaps premature to conclude that equity theory can be incorporated into expectancy theory. As Adams (1968) has argued, it may be less useful to debate which theory can be incorporated into the other than to identify the conditions in which individual behavior is guided by either equity or expectancy considerations.

CONCLUSIONS AND DIRECTIONS FOR FUTURE RESEARCH

Evaluating the current status of equity theory presents something of a dilemma; depending upon the particular body of literature one examines, very different conclusions can be drawn. On the one hand, researchers interested in organizations have largely moved away from equity theory to other motivation approaches in explaining behavior in the workplace. After a high level of initial research interest, organization researchers appear to have followed the arguments of Lawler (1973) and others that equity theory can be incorporated into expectancy theory. Consequently, research involving applications of equity theory to organizational settings has decreased in recent years. If the current literature in social psychology is examined, on the other hand, a very different picture emerges. Walster et al. (1976) recently introduced a reformulation of Adams' original theory, and it has been heralded as a general theory of social behavior capable of integrating a number of the minitheories (e.g., reinforcement theory, cognitive consistency theory) that currently exist. Berkowitz and Walster (1976, p. xi) go so far as to talk about "a new mood of optimism" emerging in social psychology, at least in part attributable to the promise of equity theory for developing a more comprehensive understanding of social behavior.

Has equity theory largely outlived its usefulness as a theory of motivation in organizations, or is it a theory capable of providing general explanations of behavior in a number of different social settings? This is a difficult question to answer at the present time. However, it appears that equity theory has more to contribute to our understanding of organizational behavior than previous research would suggest. The early emphasis of organizational research on equity theory predictions of employee reactions to pay was perhaps both its greatest strength and weakness. On the positive side, focusing on monetary rewards provided a research setting in which the variables were easily quantifiable and the predictions were relatively unambiguous (or so it seemed at the time). On the negative side, exclusive interest in employee reactions to pay prevented the extension of equity theory to other areas of social relationships in organizations. Adams (1965) was careful to note that equity theory was relevant to any social situations in which exchanges may take place (e.g., between coworkers, between superiors and subordinates, etc.). With the exception of Goodman's (1977) recent work on social comparison process in organizations, the extension of the theory to a broad range of social relationships has been left to social psychologists (see Berkowitz & Walster, 1976). Several areas of behavior in organizations that might profitably be examined in equity theory terms are discussed below.

Previous research on equity theory has largely been concerned with individual reactions to perceived inequity. What appears to have been neglected are the instrumental uses of inequity in interpersonal relationships (Adams & Freedman, 1976). Individuals in organizations, for example, may purposely create perceived inequity in social relationships as a way of improving their situation or achieving certain goals. Supervisors may routinely attempt to convince employees that they are not contributing as much as another employee or at a level expected for the pay they receive. Creating perceptions of overpayment inequity may therefore be viewed as a strategy designed to increase the level of employee performance. Just as routinely, employees may attempt the same strategy, but in reverse. Ingratiation attempts (Wortman & Linsenmeier, 1977) may be viewed as strategies on the part of lower-status employees to increase the outcomes of those in higher level positions. To the extent that those in higher positions perceive an inequity in their social relationships with lower-level employees, they will feel obligated to reciprocate. Research evidence that individuals may create perceived inequity in social relationships as a means of accomplishing certain objectives was presented by Leventhal and Bergman (1969). They found that subjects who were moderately underrewarded attempted to reduce the inequity by taking some of their partner's money when given the opportunity. Subjects who were extremely underrewarded, however, increased the discrepancy between their own rewards and those of their partner by increasing his or her advantage. By intensifying the inequity, subjects may have been following a deliberate strategy designed to convince their partner that a more equitable distribution of rewards was necessary.

Campbell, Dunnette, Lawler, and Weick (1970) have suggested the importance of viewing leadership processes in terms of exchanges between superiors and subordinates. In describing what they call the "unilateral fiction" in leadership research, they point out that managers are most often viewed as initiating the action of others and that superior-subordinate interactions are assumed to end when the manager issues a directive. Relationships between superiors and subordinates in organizations, however, are more accurately characterized by reciprocal-influence processes. A great deal of interaction between managers and employees in organizations may involve bargaining processes in which the terms of an exchange are established to the satisfaction of each party. When the manager issues a directive that is carried out by the employee, it is reasonable to assume that expectations of repayment are formed in the employee. Furthermore, when employees do a favor for the manager it may result in a perceived obligation to reciprocate on the part of the manager. Reciprocal relationships between managers and employees can be described in terms of equity theory; taking such a perspective may increase our understanding of the leadership process.

Equity theory appears to offer a useful approach to understanding a wide variety of social relationships in the workplace. Additional research is needed to extend predictions from the theory beyond simple questions about how employees react to their pay. As Goodman and Friedman (1971) have noted, equity theory predictions about employee performance levels may be one of the less interesting and useful applications of the theory. The effects of perceived inequity on employee performance levels are often slight and of limited time duration. The utility of equity theory may be greatest for increasing our understanding of interpersonal interactions at work (e.g., supervisory-subordinate relationships). In this regard, researchers interested in organizations may want to follow the lead of social psychologists in extending applications of the theory.

REFERENCES

Adams, J. S. Toward an understanding of inequity. *Journal of Abnormal and Social Psychology*, 1963, **67**, 422–436. (a)

Adams, J. S. Wage inequities, productivity and work quality. *Industrial Relations*, 1963, **3**, 9–16. (b)

Adams, J. S., Inequity in social exchange. In L. Berkowitz (Ed.), *Advances in experimental social psychology*. Vol. 2. New York: Academic Press, 1965. Pp. 267–299.

Adams, J. S. Effects of overpayment: Two comments on Lawler's paper. *Journal of Personality and Social Psychology*, 1968, **10**, 315–316.

Adams, J. S., & Freedman, S. Equity theory revisited: Comments and annotated bibliography. In L. Berkowitz & E. Walster (Eds.), *Advances in experimental social psychology*, Vol. 9. New York: Academic Press, 1976. Pp. 43–90.

Adams, J. S., & Jacobsen, P. R. Effects of wage inequities on work quality. *Journal of Applied Psychology*, 1964, **69**, 19–25.

Adams, J. S., & Rosenbaum, W. B. The relationship of worker productivity to cognitive dissonance about wage inequities. *Journal of Applied Psychology*, 1962, **46**, 161–164.

Anderson, B., & Shelly, R. K. Reactions to inequity, II: A replication of the Adams experiment and a theoretical reformulation. *Acta Sociologica*, 1970, **13**, 1–10.

Andrews, I. R. Wage inequity and job performance: An experimental study. *Journal of Applied Psychology*, 1967, **51**, 39–45.

Andrews, I. R., & Valenzi, E. Overpay inequity or self-image as a worker: a critical examination of an experimental induction procedure. *Organizational Behavior and Human Performance*, 1970, **53**, 22–27.

Arrowood, A. J. Some effects on productivity of justified and unjustified levels of reward under public and private conditions. Unpublished doctoral dissertation, University of Minnesota, 1961.

Berkowitz, L., & Walster, E. (Eds.), *Advances in experimental social psychology*, Vol. 9. New York: Academic Press, 1976.

Campbell, J. P., Dunnette, M. D., Lawler, E. E., & Weick, K. E. *Managerial behavior, performance, and effectiveness*. New York: McGraw-Hill, 1970.

Campbell, J., & Pritchard, R. D. Motivation theory in industrial and organizational psychology. In M. Dunnette (Ed.), *Handbook of industrial and organizational psychology*. Chicago: Rand McNally, 1976. Pp. 63–130.

Cook, K. S. Expectations, evaluations and equity. *American Sociological Review*, 1975, **40**, 372–388.

Darley, J. M., & Darley, S. A. *Conformity and deviation*. Morristown, N.J.: General Learning Press, 1973.

Evans, W. M., & Simmons, R. G. Organizational effects of inequitable rewards: Two experiments in status inconsistency. *Administrative Science Quarterly,* 1969, **14,** 224–237.

Friedman, A., & Goodman, P. Wage inequity, self-qualifications, and productivity. *Organizational Behavior and Human Performance,* 1967, **2,** 406–417.

Goodman, P. S. An examination of referents used in the evaluation of pay. *Organizational Behavior and Human Performance,* 1974, **12,** 170–195.

Goodman, P. S. Social comparison processes in organizations, In B. Staw & G. Salancik (Eds.), *New directions in organizational behavior.* Chicago: St. Clair, 1977. Pp. 97–132.

Goodman, P. S., & Friedman, A. An examination of the effect of wage inequity in the hourly condition. *Organizational Behavior and Human Performance,* 1968, **3,** 340–352.

Goodman, P. S., & Friedman, A. An examination of quantity and quality of performance under conditions of overpayment in piece-rate. *Organizational Behavior and Human Performance,* 1969, **4,** 365–374.

Goodman, P. S., & Friedman, A. An examination of Adams' theory of inequity. *Administrative Science Quarterly,* 1971, **16,** 271–288.

Homans, G. C. *Social behavior: Its elementary forms.* New York: Harcourt, Brace & World, 1961.

Jaques, E. *Equitable payment.* New York: Wiley, 1961.

Lawler, E. E. Equity theory as a predictor of productivity and work quality. *Psychological Bulletin,* 1968, **70,** 596–610. (a)

Lawler, E. E. Effects of hourly overpayment on productivity and work quality. *Journal of Personality and Social Psychology,* 1968, **10,** 306–313. (b)

Lawler, E. E. *Motivation in work organizations.* Belmont, Calif.: Brooks/Cole, 1973.

Lawler, E. E., Koplin, C. A., Young, T. F., & Fadem, J. A. Inequity reduction over time and an induced overpayment situation. *Organizational Behavior and Human Performance,* 1968, **3,** 253–268.

Lawler, E. E., & O'Gara, P. W. Effects of inequity produced by underpayment on work output, work quality, and attitudes toward the work. *Journal of Applied Psychology,* 1967, **51,** 403–410.

Leventhal, G. S. Fairness in social relationships. In J. Thibaut, J. Spence, & R. Carson (Eds.), *Contemporary topics in social psychology.* Morristown, N.J.: General Learning Press, 1976.

Leventhal, G. S., & Bergman, J. T. Self-depriving behavior as a response to unprofitable inequity. *Journal of Experimental Social Psychology,* 1969, **5,** 153–171.

Leventhal, G. S., Weiss, T., & Long, G. Equity, reciprocity, and reallocating rewards in the dyad. *Journal of Personality and Social Psychology,* 1969, **13,** 300–305.

Locke, E. A. The nature and causes of job satisfaction. In M. Dunnette (Ed.), *Handbook of industrial and organizational psychology.* Chicago: Rand McNally, 1976. Pp. 1297–1349.

Opsahl, R. L., & Dunnette, M. The role of financial compensation in industrial motivation. *Psychological Bulletin,* 1966, **66,** 94–118.

Patchen, M. *The choice of wage comparisons.* Englewood Cliffs, N.J.: Prentice-Hall, 1961.

Pritchard, R. D. Equity theory: A review and critique. *Organizational Behavior and Human Performance,* 1969, **4,** 176–211.

Pritchard, R. D., Dunnette, M. D., & Jorgenson, D. O. Effects of perceptions of equity and inequity on worker performance and satisfaction. *Journal of Applied Psychology,* 1972, **56,** 75–94.

Rotter, J. B. Generalized expectancies for internal versus external control of reinforcement. *Psychological Monographs,* 1966, **80** (1, Whole No. 609).

Simpson, R. L. *Theories of social exchange*. Morristown, N.J.: General Learning Press, 1972.

Tornow, W. W. The development and application of an input-outcome moderator test on the perception and reduction of inequity. *Organizational Behavior and Human Performance*, 1971, **6**, 614–638.

Valenzi, E. R., & Andrews, I. R. Effect of hourly overpay and underpay inequity when tested with a new induction procedure. *Journal of Applied Psychology*, 1971, **55**, 22–27.

Vroom, V. H. *Work and motivation*. New York: Wiley, 1964.

Walster, E., Bercheid, E., & Walster, G. W. New directions in equity research. In L. Berkowitz & E. Walster (Eds.), *Advances in experimental social psychology*. Vol. 9. New York: Academic Press, 1976. Pp. 1–42.

Weick, K. E. The concept of equity in the perception of pay. *Administrative Science Quarterly*, 1967, **2**, 414–439.

Wicklund, R. A., & Brehm, J. W. *Perspectives on cognitive dissonance*. Hillsdale, N.J.: Lawrence Erlbaum, 1976.

Wiener, Y. The effects of "task-" and "ego-oriented" performance on 2 kinds of over-compensation inequity. *Organizational Behavior and Human Performance*, 1970, **5**, 191–208.

Wood, I., & Lawler, E. E. Effects of piece-rate overpayment on productivity. *Journal of Applied Psychology*, 1970, **54**, 234–238.

Wortman, C. B., & Linsenmeier, J. A. W. Interpersonal attraction and methods of ingratiation in organizational settings. In B. M. Staw & G. R. Salancik (Eds.), *New directions in organizational behavior*. Chicago: St. Clair, 1977. Pp. 133–178.

Procedural Justice and Worker Motivation

Russell Cropanzano
Robert Folger

When people do not receive the rewards to which they feel entitled, they are often motivated to do something about it. The problem comes in specifying which types of actions most employees will take. Some are likely to become angry and work less hard, increase their absenteeism, or even leave their jobs. Others will work even harder in the hope of eventually obtaining what they want. Because not all employees receive what they think they deserve, managers need to know the conditions under which each reaction is likely to occur.

We argue that when employees react to the way they are treated at work, their motivation to respond in one fashion or another cannot be understood adequately without taking into account two separate notions of fairness. Traditionally the organizational science literature has considered only one way of describing what it means to be fairly treated, namely, the notion of distributive justice. That way of

This paper was written especially for this volume.

conceptualizing fairness is illustrated by equity theory (Adams, 1965). According to equity theory, people determine whether they have been treated fairly at work by examining their own payoff ratio of outcomes (e.g., size of a raise) to inputs (e.g., level of performance) and comparing that ratio with the corresponding outcome-input ratio obtained by others such as their coworkers.

A second way of thinking about what it means to be treated fairly—namely, the notion of procedural justice—focuses not on the results of compensation decisions or other administrative decisions that involve allocations of scarce resources among employees (i.e., the payoff ratio of outcomes to inputs), but instead focuses on the fairness of the manner in which the decision-making process is conducted. In other words, the focus shifts from *what* was decided to *how* the decision was made. Someone who says that "the ends do not justify the means," for example, calls attention to the importance of following some general guidelines of fairness with respect to the *process* of making an allocation decision. The implication is that certain procedures are not justified, even though they might produce equitable results.

The way courtroom trials are conducted helps to illustrate the distinction between distributive and procedural justice. Judges, as the persons with administrative authority in a courtroom, are responsible for ensuring that the procedures used to conduct a trial (e.g., procedures regulating how evidence can be presented) have been administered impartially and in accordance with the law. Juries, on the other hand, may be given the responsibility for ensuring that verdicts are in some sense equitable—that is, making the verdict as an outcome fit with the "inputs" or actions of the person on trial. Clearly it is possible for a jury's decision to seem inequitable even though the judge was completely fair and impartial with respect to all rulings regarding the presentation of evidence, as well as with respect to every other matter concerning how the trial was conducted.

In light of the distinction between procedural and distributive justice, it is plausible for a person to have reasons for believing that a (procedurally) fair hearing might result in an (inequitably) unfair verdict; similarly, a fair (equitable) outcome might result from an unfair (procedurally inappropriate or unlawfully conducted) hearing. The point is that the fairness of the end results and the fairness of the determining processes can be evaluated independently of one another. The two types of fairness may, at times, even conflict with one another, for example, when the strict observance of a defendant's procedural rights seems to interfere with obtaining the evidence necessary for determining that person's guilt or innocence.

PROCEDURAL JUSTICE AS A SUPPLEMENT TO EQUITY THEORY

Equity theory (Adams, 1965) says that people assess fairness by first dividing their own outcomes (such as pay or status) by their inputs (such as effort or time), then calculating the corresponding ratio that involves the outcomes and inputs of some referent other. These two quotients are compared. If a person's own ratio is bigger, the person may feel remorse and guilt. If the referent's ratio is larger, the person with the smaller ratio may feel angry and resentful. In both cases the emotions are unpleasant, and the person is motivated to reduce these negative feelings. For example, people can lower their inputs (i.e., work less) or cognitively distort the outcomes of the other person. Indeed, any of the four terms in the equation can be altered, and this can be done by either cognitions or behaviors.

Although equity theory has received broad support, it has also been criticized as not being particularly "useful" (e.g., Locke & Henne, 1986). A major limitation to equity theory's usefulness is the difficulty of specifying what type of action an aggrieved employee will take. Serious consequences for organizations can arise when perceived unfair treatment leads to some form of retaliation by employees. In defining unfair treatment by outcome-input ratios, equity theory provides grounds for predicting that retaliation (e.g., work slowdowns as a way of lowering employee inputs) might accompany underpayment. Unfortunately, the same formula also provides a basis for exactly the opposite prediction: If the inequity is resolved via cognitive adjustment (e.g., perceptually raising own outcomes), then the underpaid employee might well become one of the organization's hardest workers.

Equity theory's failure to resolve these opposing predictions may stem from placing too much emphasis on the results of reward allocations and ignoring the process that led up to them. Similarly, the research done to test equity has focused only on distributive justice issues and has neglected procedural justice issues. Experience suggests that two people may react very differently to the same inequity if they believe different things about how that inequity was created (e.g., if two different decision-making processes were used). As Bies (1987) has argued, for example, employees disadvantaged by a two-tier pay system are likely to respond very differently depending on whether the system is seen as being the only way for a company to stay in business or as a union-busting ploy by management.

Leventhal (1980) lists some possible determinants of procedural justice. For example, procedures should remain consistent across different people and different times. A fair procedure would be one that is based on society's shared ethical standards and takes into account the concerns of everyone involved. Justice also requires that the procedure be free from bias and based on accurate information. Finally, a fair procedure should include some system that allows erroneous decisions to be corrected.

Tyler (1989) has recently found evidence for three aspects of concern about procedural fairness as administered by an authority or decision maker: (1) the extent to which the decision maker exhibits neutrality, (2) the extent to which the intentions of the decision maker can be trusted, and (3) the extent to which the decision maker shows respect for the rights of the parties to a decision (those whom the decision affects). These three types of considerations represent the central features of what it means for decisions to be made in a procedurally fair manner. Note that this perspective emphasizes the importance of the behavior and inferred qualities of the decision maker, as well as the characteristics of the decision-making process.*

---

*Throughout our presentation we use the term "procedures" very broadly to include various aspects of the decision maker's conduct. In particular, we mean the term to be inclusive of procedurally related behavior that may occur even after the decision itself (such as providing explanations), thereby encompassing what some authors (e.g., Bies & Shapiro, 1987) have termed *interactional* fairness judgments pertaining to conduct associated with the implementation of a procedure.

The following sections review in greater detail the advantages of considering procedural justice. In particular we will note the implications of procedural justice for specific predictions about employee attitudes and behavior. Each of these will be considered in turn.

PROCEDURAL JUSTICE AND EMPLOYEE ATTITUDES

Ample evidence attests to the importance of procedural justice, but much of it has been collected outside of the organizational context. For example, Tyler (1984) examined defendants' perceptions of courtroom fairness. In this study, questionnaire items assessed distributive fairness (i.e., whether the verdict was fair) and procedural justice (i.e., whether the procedures were administered impartially). The pattern of results would have been impossible to predict with equity theory. Tyler found that distributive justice was indeed related to outcome satisfaction. The defendants' evaluation of the judicial system, however, was only predicted by the fairness of the procedures. More to the point, if a person was treated in a procedurally fair manner and still received an unfavorable verdict, that person would derogate the verdict (a distributive inequity) but not the court system.

Those results have been replicated by Tyler (1987), who found that perceived legitimacy and support for legal authorities (such as police officers) were predicted by procedural fairness rather than distributive justice. This finding has also been extended into the realm of political behavior. Tyler, Rasinski, and McGraw (1985) found that "trust in national government" was predicted only by the perceived extent of procedural fairness. Finally, Barrett-Howard and Tyler (1986) have shown that procedures are the fundamental determinants of perceived fairness in a wide variety of situations, including the workplace. Findings such as this have caused Lind and Tyler to state that "procedural justice has especially strong effects on attitudes about institutions and authorities, as opposed to attitudes about the specific outcome in question" (1988, p. 179).

In the field of organizational behavior, procedural justice gained prominence by a less direct route. In particular, problems with the equity or distribution factors caused researchers to consider administration and procedural variables. A good example occurs in the work of Dyer and Theriault (1976), who examined Lawler's (1971) model of pay satisfaction. Generally speaking, in the Lawler model pay is a function of two cognitions: the amount to which an employee feels entitled, and the amount he or she actually receives. When the two cognitions are compared, the employee is unhappy if a discrepancy exists. Lawler had noted that this model borrows heavily from equity theory.

Dyer and Theriault pointed out that Lawler had excluded pay administration variables (such as the superior's accuracy in work assessments and the superior's influence over pay decisions). That is, the discrepancy framework has not examined the effects of a fair (or unfair) system of administering organizational rewards. To alleviate this problem, Dyer and Theriault added 12 administration items to their questionnaire. They assessed fairness over three different samples.

Although the absolute level of pay was the best predictor of satisfaction, the procedural administration variables significantly improved the fit of the model for each sample. Weiner (1980) conducted a similar assessment of the Lawler model. Weiner found that by considering pay administration she could predict pay satisfaction, absenteeism, and turnover better than with the distributive justice variables alone.

Similar findings have come from research on performance appraisal satisfaction. Landy, Barnes, and Murphy (1978) mailed a short fairness questionnaire to 711 employees at a large manufacturing firm. They found that five items predicted whether "performance [had] been fairly and accurately evaluated." In descending order these were: the opportunity for the subordinate to express his or her feelings, the existence of a formal appraisal program, the supervisor's knowledge of the subordinate's performance, the existence of action plans to improve performance weaknesses, and the frequency of evaluations. These are all procedural items. Although Landy et al. did not directly assess distributive justice, they did do a follow-up of the managers about a year later (Landy, Barnes-Farrell, & Cleveland, 1980). The results showed that their original findings were not affected by the actual level of the evaluation (i.e., whether the evaluation had been favorable or unfavorable).

A second study on appraisal satisfaction and fairness was conducted by Dipboye and de Pontbriand (1981). The methodology was essentially the same as Landy, Barnes, and Murphy (1978). This time a short survey was mailed to 971 exempt employees at a research and development firm. Dipboye and de Pontbriand found that four of their independent variables were related to the evaluation of both the rater and the rating system. Only one of these (favorability of the appraisal) was a distributive item. The other three (discussion of plans, relevance, opportunity to participate, and goal-setting) were administration variables. Interestingly, the favorability of the appraisal was highly related to the rating of the appraiser but had a smaller relationship to the rating of the system as a whole. That finding, of course, is consistent with the work of Tyler and his colleagues discussed earlier.

Greenberg (1986) had a sample of 217 managers generate statements concerning their most fair and unfair performance evaluations. Using a Q-sort technique, a second subsample of these managers placed the items into seven categories. When these categories were factor-analyzed, Greenberg found that only two factors emerged. Five of the categories loaded on a procedural factor, and two loaded on a distributive factor. Greenberg reported no significant differences between the two factors. Together they accounted for 94.7 percent of the variance. He cautioned future researchers not to neglect either dimension at the expense of the other.

Greenberg's warning is especially important in light of the legal and political findings reviewed above. It could be that distributive and procedural justice exert their influence on different attitudes. In particular, distribution predicts satisfaction with the outcome received, whereas procedural justice influences the evaluation of the organization. Such a pattern would certainly be consistent with the work of Tyler and his colleagues. Unfortunately, except for Dipboye and de Pontbriand's study (which found supportive results) none of the organizational studies were set up to examine this issue in detail. Specifically, there was either a limited number of criterion variables (outcome satisfaction and commitment were not both included), independent variables (adequate measures of both types of justice were absent), or both.

Recently, a more extensive series of studies has examined the effects of procedural justice in the workplace. These studies yielded highly consistent results. The first of these examined employee attitudes in a company's head office (Konovsky, Folger, & Cropanzano, 1987). Stepwise regression analysis showed that procedural factors influenced organizational commitment, whereas distributive factors predicted satisfaction with pay. These findings were extended in a second study by Folger and Konovsky (1989). The authors examined employee responses to pay raise decisions. Causal analyses showed that once again procedural justice accounted for more variance in attitudes about the organization and its authorities (i.e., trust-in-supervision and organizational commitment), whereas distributive justice was a better predictor of pay satisfaction. Finally, in the most extensive project to date, Martin (1987) assessed the pay satisfaction of 1685 workers at a financial services company. Martin stated that "both distributive and procedural justice determined satisfaction, while organizational commitment was determined by perceptions of procedural fairness" (p. ix).

There are significant implications regarding these findings about the relationship between procedural justice and employees' attitudes toward the organization and its authorities, especially because such attitudes may be related to important employee behaviors. Bateman and Organ (1983) found that satisfaction with supervision had a strong relationship with good "citizenship" behavior, for example, which included such things as dependability, keeping the work space clean, avoiding waste, and taking time to train new workers. Similarly, committed employees are less likely to leave the organization (Mowday, Porter, & Steers, 1982) and more likely to engage in voluntary prosocial behavior (O'Reilly & Chatman, 1986). Given these findings, the role of procedural justice in increasing the individual's evaluation of the organization takes on added significance. If employees can be guaranteed fair procedural treatment, they are less likely to leave and more likely to become loyal organizational members. Further, besides the ethical and moral reasons for justice, fair procedures can often be implemented in a relatively inexpensive manner. Recall from our review that when individuals perceived a fair allocation of rewards, they were satisfied with the institution even in the face of negative outcomes (e.g., Folger & Konovsky, 1989).

One limitation of the above studies is that they operationalize distributive and procedural justice as competing constructs. That is, both are measured and the amount of variance each accounts for is assessed. On this basis one is considered "more" or "less" important for predicting a given phenomenon. We have already mentioned Greenberg's (1986) warning against this approach, and it bears repeating here. Recent research has shown that outcomes and allocations work together to create a sense of injustice. A full understanding of fairness cannot be achieved by examining the two constructs separately. Rather, one needs to consider the interaction between outcomes and procedures.

A TWO-COMPONENT MODEL OF JUSTICE

Perceptions of injustice or unfair treatment can be broken down into two components (e.g., Cropanzano & Folger, 1989; Folger, 1987). One component involves a person's perception of having received an inequitable or negative outcome—for example, a low raise based on a poor performance rating. This component is the domain traditionally addressed by equity theory. The second component involves perceptions of the events leading up to and accompanying the unfavorable outcome. Such perceptions influence how an individual assesses procedural fairness. If the events associated with the allocation are just, it is more difficult to question the outcomes that have resulted. For example, it is more difficult to press a claim of unfair treatment if the poor performance rating stemmed from the supervisor's having conducted a rating process generally regarded as fair and impartial. There should still be a desire to do something about the low rating, but there should be less motivation to retaliate in some fashion against the supervisor or the organization.

The two-component approach assumes that the perception of an unfair or negative outcome (the distributive component) energizes behavior. Simply put, when people receive outcomes they do not want, they are motivated to do something. Some of the things a person might be motivated to do under such circumstances can be called "destructive" because of the harmful effects on other people, their property, or their sources of livelihood. Employees seeking to rectify perceived injustice by working less, by quitting, or by going on strike, for example, are threatening their employers' profits. Obviously employers are likely to regard other actions as examples of "constructive" motivation, such as when an employee redoubles his or her efforts in order to prove that a low performance rating unfairly characterized his or her ability.

According to this two-component approach, the motivational route an employee will travel—in other words, whether in a constructive or destructive direction—is predicted to be determined by the perceived fairness of the procedures. Specifically, if the procedures are fair then the system under which the employee works is also assumed to be fair. Hence, the negative outcome will be addressed constructively. Conversely, if the system is determined to be unfair, then the worker is expected to retaliate by using destructive tactics. Thus a two-component approach suggests that although the distribution of outcomes provides an energizing or motivational force, procedures determine the direction in which behavior will travel (i.e., whether action will be taken *against* an employer or the agents of employers such as supervisors and managers).

This line of reasoning implies that both components are crucial for influencing perceptions of injustice. Folger and Martin (1986) have described such an approach by saying that before someone will take action against another person in the name of rectifying unfair treatment, two types of questions must be answered affirmatively. One question considers whether more favorable outcomes were possible: Would outcomes have been better under some other set of conditions? This is the distributive component. Can the individual imagine a reasonable and positive alternative outcome? If so, then behavior is energized.

A second type of question addresses interpersonal behavior (other people's actions, such as the steps taken by a supervisor in appraising performance) and asks whether those in authority followed appropriate norms of conduct: Should a different decision-making process have been used? This is the procedural component. If the answer to this second question is yes, then the potential for hostile (destructive) attitudes and behaviors will be increased. If the answer is no, then the experience of injustice will be reduced and perhaps eliminated; certainly there will be less of a tendency for someone to "blame the system," and hence actions taken against the organization are diminished.

It is important to note that if the individual perceives the procedures to be fair, then even if the distribution is inequitable, he or she will be less inclined to take destructive actions against those in authority. This fair-process effect (Folger, Rosenfield, Grove, & Corkran, 1979) has been widely documented (see reviews by Folger & Greenberg, 1985; and Lind & Tyler, 1988). It should also be noted that dual-component formulations are fairly recent, however, and many parameters and implications have not yet been subjected to rigorous examination. Having issued that caveat, we turn to examining the existing empirical evidence.

Three sections comprise the discussion that follows. In the first, we examine the case where the allocation is favorable but the procedures are unfair. In the second, attention shifts to the situation where outcomes are inequitable but the procedures are perceived as fair. Finally, we review the negative reactions that occur when both the distribution and administration rules are unjust. Within each of these sections the reader should be attentive to three sets of dependent variables: attitudinal effects, individual behavioral effects, and collective action.

Fair Distribution with Unfair Procedures

To date the research seems to indicate that people are not concerned with procedural fairness following a fair distribution. If their outcome is positive (Greenberg, 1987) or if a favorable alternative is unimaginable (Cropanzano & Folger, 1989), then subjects are not upset about inequity. The clearest example of this can be found in Greenberg (1987). In this study people achieved either high, moderate, or low outcomes because of fair or unfair procedure. In the fair procedure condition, Greenberg paid subjects for high performance; the unfair procedure was to use the room in which subjects had worked as the basis for their pay (a completely arbitrary decision).

Greenberg found that even when it worked to their advantage, people were able to clearly recognize an unfair administration rule. However, individuals did not become upset about this procedure until a negative outcome took place. Specifically, Greenberg had subjects rate the unfairness of procedures and the extent to which this unfairness concerned them. He found that paying subjects based on the room in which they worked was always rated as unfair. However, subjects did not report concern about this outcome until it caused them to earn less money. Further, although the unfair treatment caused subjects to like the experimenter less, they tended to voice complaints only when a low outcome was paired with an unfair procedure.

As a dual-component model would predict, it seems that the motivating "kick" of a low outcome is an important stimulus to action. Whereas by itself an inequitable allocation does not predict the direction a response will take, this study indicates that alone a procedural injustice is sometimes unlikely to provoke any action at all. This finding is consistent with the work of Cropanzano and Folger (1989), who found that low levels of resentment were reported in a situation similar to the one described above. Although further evidence is required to clarify the extent of this effect, for now it appears that when the outcome is positive and the procedures are negative, people will note the injustice without becoming particularly upset. They know the rules are unjust, and they do not like the person responsible for them (i.e., the experimenter). They seem relatively unmotivated, however, to take any action to alleviate the problem.

Presumably these findings could be qualified. For example, if a person expects to interact with the system again, that person should be concerned with procedures. Such increased concern would be reasonable; although procedural unfairness might not cause much of a negative effect in the short run (and may even result in a short-term increase in one's own outcomes), a fundamentally unfair set of procedural practices does represent an ever-present threat of unfair outcomes over the long run. On the other hand, if the procedural unfairness is both stable and advantageous (e.g., tending to favor one sex or race), then perhaps the favored person will continue to ignore it. That this prediction has yet to be tested is unfortunate, because the case of repeated interactions would be most applicable to the workplace.

Altruism, social consciousness, and humanitarian interests could also lead people to express concern about others who are victims of unjust procedures. This may be particularly true if the wronged individual is a friend or similar other. In such a case, unfair procedural rules could be motivating even for the person not directly affected. Once again, more research is needed to clarify this point. However, even given these potential moderators, at present it seems safe to state that a procedural injustice that hurts no one will not be very motivating.

Unfair Distribution with Fair Procedures

The findings reviewed above stand in marked contrast to what occurs when an inequitable distribution is assigned by a fair administrative procedure. In that case people may express some dissatisfaction with their outcomes (e.g., Greenberg, 1987), but they tend not to report much unfairness and not to express much resentment (Cropanzano & Folger, 1989). In fact, Cropanzano and Folger found some evidence that when a negative outcome was assigned by fair procedures, subjects became angry at themselves rather than angry at an experimenter. These findings are consistent with the field studies reviewed earlier. For example, recall that Folger and Konovsky (1989) found that low wages were related to pay satisfaction but not to organizational commitment or the evaluation of the company's authorities.

The evidence also indicates that just administration rules curb behavioral retaliation. In the Greenberg (1987) and Folger and Martin (1986) studies, subjects did not attempt to report the experimenter's behavior unless there was a procedural injustice. Even after the loss of a desired reward, individuals did not tend to retaliate so long as the allocation rules were fair. Other researchers have found similar results (Taylor, Moghaddam, Gamble, & Zellerer, 1987): After being denied membership in a high-status group, participants tended to avoid collective action if the reasons for the refusal were perceived as just. The Taylor et al. study offers additional evidence for a two-component approach. Subjects were allowed to work on the task a second time and reapply for group membership. When a negative outcome occurred under a fair procedure condition, individual performance increased significantly. Participants simply worked harder. When a negative outcome was followed by an unfair procedure, Taylor et al. found that performance dropped.

Taylor et al. is the first experiment to take performance measures. As a result, their findings need to be replicated and extended. It is likely that various situational factors may limit the generalizability of this study. For example, the unfair procedure used in this experiment may have offered little likelihood of future success. Therefore, procedures may influence performance by changing reward contingencies. Even given this limitation, the situation was hardly an unusual one. Consider, for example, possible charges of sex discrimination with respect to procedures. When promotion decisions will be made by an all-male group, then suspected procedural unfairness might lower the performance of females.

Unfair Distribution with Unfair Procedures

Once an inequitable outcome is paired with an unfair decision rule, the typically negative things associated with injustice began to occur. Even though people may tolerate poor procedures following a positive outcome, they respond vigorously after a negative one. For example, Cropanzano and Folger (1989) had subjects fail to achieve a desired reward as a result of working on a difficult task. Even though the objective outcome was always negative, they found that if subjects were allowed to select the task for themselves, they reported low levels of resentment (this is the poor-outcome, fair-procedure case mentioned above). When a free choice was not granted, however, subjects reported high levels of resentment, low levels of a willingness to be understanding, and a sense of having been treated unfairly within the experiment.

Greenberg (1987) and Folger and Martin (1986) gave individuals the opportunity to report an unfair experimenter to the human subjects committee. Both studies found that subjects only expressed an intent to report the injustice if both an unfair outcome and an unfair procedure were simultaneously present. Lacking either of these components, the individuals were unlikely to take action against the experimenter.

In a more extensive study, Taylor et al. (1987) gave individuals the opportunity to organize against a group that had denied them membership for either fair or unfair reasons. Alternatively, subjects could apply for membership a second time. Performance measures were taken following the unfair treatment. These authors found that when both the outcomes and the procedures were negative, workers did indeed become motivated, but not to work harder. Performance dropped significantly following the dual injustice. Instead, subjects expressed an intent to organize into a group and take action against the individuals who had wronged them. This activity did not take place when the procedures were fair— even when subjects failed to attain membership in the desired organization.

Collective action, it would seem, can be a prominent response used to correct a procedural injustice that has caused poor outcomes. There are probably at least two reasons for this. First, a distributive inequity tends to involve more individualized and idiosyncratic perceptions, such as those regarding which inputs are relevant and what the respective contributions of various group members are. Because the relative values of both outcomes and inputs are "in the eye of the beholder," judgments about distributive justice present difficulties with respect to mustering collective support. A procedural injustice, on the other hand, is more likely to involve the treatment of a substantial number of organization members (e.g., a companywide policy). Hence, since many people may be affected simultaneously, collective action should be facilitated.

A second reason why procedural injustices trigger collective action can be found in the work of Tyler (1987), Folger and Konovsky (1989), and others. Procedural injustice lowers the evaluation of the entire organization. It undermines loyalty to both the institution and to its appointed representatives. To move against an organization requires the strength found in numbers. On the other hand, by itself a distributive inequity has a more localized effect on outcome satisfaction. Addressing a distributive inequity, as a matter of individualized dissatisfaction, is less apt to require a large group.

CONCLUSION

The incorporation of procedural justice into organizational research has been a recent innovation. Thus far, it seems to have been a productive one. Field studies have shown that outcomes and procedures exert their influence on different employee attitudes. The amount that people receive affects outcome satisfaction, whereas procedures (and the related actions of authorities) affect organizational commitment. More recently, a two-component model of injustice has been proposed. One component is a distributive inequity that energizes behavior. Although people can recognize an unfair decision-making process, they may not be motivated to change it until a negative outcome occurs. The second component is a procedural injustice that directs the individual's response in a specific direction. If administrative conduct and procedures are just, people are predicted to work within the system (e.g., increase performance). If procedures are implemented in an unfair manner, however, employees lower their commitment and take retaliatory action (e.g., lower performance). Most evidence so far has been supportive, but a great deal more research is needed.

In a work of finite resources people cannot have all of the things they want. Although organizations should strive for the best allocations possible, some perceptions of unfavorable outcomes are inevitable. The existence of fair procedures may be a more realistic goal. If procedures are just, then the negative consequences of unfavorable outcomes are less likely. Procedural fairness should motivate employees away from activities viewed by management as being destructive and should motivate employees toward activities seen as being more constructive.

REFERENCES

Adams, J. S. (1965). Inequity in social exchange. In L. Berkowitz (Ed.), *Advances in experimental social psychology* (Vol. 2). New York: Academic Press.

Barrett-Howard, E., & Tyler, T. R. (1986). Procedural justice as a criterion in allocation decisions. *Journal of Personality and Social Psychology, 50,* 296–305.

Bateman, T. S., & Organ, D. W. (1983). Job satisfaction and the Good Soldier: The relationships between affect and employee "citizenship." *Academy of Management Journal, 26,* 163–169.

Bies, R. J., & Shapiro, D. (1987). Interactional fairness judgments: The influence of causal accounts. *Social Justice Research, 1,* 199–218.

Bies, R. J. (1987). The predicament of injustice: The management of moral outrage. In L. L. Cummings & B. M. Staw (Eds.), *Research in organizational behavior* (Vol. 9). Greenwich, Conn.: JAI Press.

Cropanzano, R., & Folger, R. (1989). Referent cognitions and task decision autonomy: Beyond equity theory. *Journal of Applied Psychology, 74,* 293-299.

Dipboye, R. L., & de Pontbriand, R. (1981). Correlates of employee reactions to performance appraisals and appraisal systems. *Journal of Applied Psychology, 66,* 248–251.

Dyer, L., & Theriault, R. (1976). The determinants of pay satisfaction. *Journal of Applied Psychology, 61,* 596–604.

Folger, R. (1987). Reformulating the preconditions of resentment: A referent cognitions model. In J. C. Masters & W. P. Smith (Eds.), *Social comparison, social justice, and relative deprivation* (pp. 183–215). Hillsdale, N.J.: Lawrence Erlbaum Associates.

Folger, R., & Greenberg, J. (1985). Procedural justice: An interpretive analysis of personnel systems. In K. Rowland & G. Ferris (Eds.), *Research in personnel and human resources management* (Vol. 3). Greenwich, Conn.: JAI Press.

Folger, R., & Konovsky, M. A. (1989). Effect of procedural and distributive justice on reactions to pay raise decisions. *Academy of Management Journal, 32,* 115–130.

Folger, R., & Martin, C. (1986). Relative deprivation and referent cognitions: Distributive and procedural justice effects. *Journal of Experimental Social Psychology, 22,* 531–546.

Folger, R., Rosenfield, D., Grove, J., & Corkran, L. (1979). Effects of "voice" and peer opinions on responses to inequity. *Journal of Personality and Social Psychology, 37,* 2253-2261.

Greenberg, J. (1986). Determinants of perceived fairness of performance evaluations. *Journal of Applied Psychology, 71,* 340–342.

Greenberg, J. (1987). Reactions to procedural injustice in payment distributions: Do the means justify the ends? *Journal of Applied Psychology, 72,* 55–61.

Konovsky, M. A., Folger, R., & Cropanzano, R. (1987). Relative effects of procedural and distributive justice on employee attitudes. *Representative Research in Social Psychology, 17,* 15–24.

Landy, F. J., Barnes, J. L., & Murphy, K. R. (1978). Correlates of perceived fairness and accuracy of performance evaluation. *Journal of Applied Psychology, 63*, 751–754.

Landy, F. J., Barnes-Farrell, J. L., & Cleveland, J. N. (1980). Perceived fairness and accuracy of performance evaluation: A follow-up. *Journal of Applied Psychology, 65*, 355–356.

Lawler, E. E. (1971). *Pay and organizational effectiveness: A psychological view.* New York: McGraw-Hill.

Leventhal, G. S. (1980). What should be done with equity theory? In R. J. Gergen, M. S. Greenberg, & R. H. Willis (Eds.), *Social exchange: Advances in theory and research* (pp. 27–55). New York: Plenum Press.

Lind, E. A., & Tyler, T. R. (1988). *The social psychology of procedural justice.* New York: Plenum Press.

Locke, E. A., & Henne, D. (1986). Work motivation theories. In C. L. Cooper & I. Robertson (Eds.), *International review of industrial and organizational psychology: 1986* (pp. 1–35). New York: Wiley.

Martin, C. L. (1987). *Distributive and procedural justice effects on satisfaction and commitment.* Unpublished doctoral dissertation, Georgia Institute of Technology, Athens, Georgia.

Mowday, R., Porter, L., & Steers, R. (1982). *Organizational linkages: The psychology of commitment, absenteeism, and turnover.* New York: Academic Press.

O'Reilly, C., & Chatman, J. (1986). Organizational commitment, and psychological attachment: The effects of compliance, identification, and internalization on prosocial behavior. *Journal of Applied Psychology, 71*, 492–499.

Taylor, D. M., Moghaddam, F. M., Gamble, I., & Zellerer, E. (1987). Disadvantaged group responses to perceived inequity: From passive acceptance to collective action. *Journal of Social Psychology, 127*(3), 259–272.

Tyler, T. R. (1984). The role of perceived injustice in defendants' evaluations of their courtroom experience. *Law and Society Review, 18*, 51–74.

Tyler, T. R. (1987). Conditions leading to value-expressive effects in judgments of procedural justice: A test of four models. *Journal of Personality and Social Psychology, 42*, 333–344.

Tyler, T. R. (1989). The psychology of procedural justice: A test of the group-value model. *Journal of Personality and Social Psychology, 57*, 830–838.

Tyler, T. R. (1990). *Why people obey the law: Procedural justice, legitimacy, and compliance.* New Haven, Conn.: Yale University Press.

Tyler, T. R., Rasinski, K., & McGraw, K. M. (1985). The influence of perceived injustice on the endorsement of political leaders. *Journal of Applied Social Psychology, 15*, 700–725.

Weiner, N. (1980). Determinants and behavioral consequences of pay satisfaction: A comparison of two models. *Personnel Psychology, 33*, 741–757.

Valence-Instrumentality-Expectancy Theory

Craig C. Pinder

Probably the most popular theory of work motivation among organizational scientists in recent years has been that which is referred to as Valence-Instrumentality-Expencancy Theory or Expectancy Theory (Locke, 1975). Actually, there are a variety of theories included under these general titles, although the similarities among them are more important than are the differences. Each of these theories has its modern roots in Vroom's (1964) book on work motivation, although earlier theory in psychology relating to general human motivation quite clearly predates Vroom's interpretation for organizational science (e.g., Atkinson, 1958; Davidson, Suppes, and Siegel, 1957; Lewin, 1938; Peak, 1955; Rotter, 1955; Tolman, 1959), and an early study by Georgopoulos, Mohoney, and Jones (1957) demonstrated the relevance of the theory for work behavior.

Since Vroom's book was published, there have been a number of variations and revisions of his basic concepts, although most of the theoretical work has been vastly superior to the numerous empirical attempts to test the theory in all of its various forms. In fact, it can be defensibly argued that, in spite of the numerous studies conducted since 1964 that have ostensibly sought to test versions of the theory, very little is known about its validity. This is because, as has been the case with so much research on employee motivation, studies directed at VIE Theory have been fraught with serious flaws—flaws which make it almost impossible to conclude whether the theory, in any of its forms, holds any scientific merit (Arnold, 1981; Campbell and Pritchard, 1976; Locke, 1975; Pinder, 1977). Nevertheless, let's take a look at the theory in its most basic form—that proposed by Vroom (1964) for application to work settings.

VROOM'S ORIGINAL THEORY

Vroom's theory assumes that " . . . the choices made by a person among alternative courses of action are lawfully related to psychological events occurring contemporaneously with the behavior" (1964, pp. 14–15). In other words, people's behavior results from conscious choices among alternatives, and these choices (behaviors) are systematically related to psychological processes, particularly perception and the formation of beliefs and attitudes. The purpose of the choices, generally, is to maximize pleasure and minimize pain. Like Equity Theory then, VIE Theory assumes that people base their acts on perceptions and beliefs, although we need not anticipate any one-to-one relationships between particular beliefs and specific behaviors (such as job behaviors).

To understand why Vroom's theory and those which have followed it are re-

Excerpted from Chapter 7 of C. C. Pinder, *Work motivation*. Glenview, Ill.: Scott, Foresman, 1984. Reprinted by permission.

ferred to as *VIE Theory,* we must examine the three key mental components that are seen as instigating and directing behavior. Referred to as Valence, Instrumentality, and Expectancy, each of these components is, in fact, a *belief.*

The Concept of Valence

VIE theory assumes that people hold preferences among various outcomes or states of nature. For example, the reader probably prefers, other things equal, a higher rate of pay for a particular job over a lower rate of pay. Here, pay level is the *outcome* in question, and the preference for high pay over low pay reflects the strength of the reader's basic underlying need state. Likewise, some people hold preferences among different types of outcomes (as opposed to greater or lesser amounts of a particular outcome). For example, many employees would seem to prefer an opportunity to work with other people, even if the only jobs featuring high levels of social interaction entail less comfortable surroundings, lower pay, or some other trade-off. The point is that people have more or less well-defined preferences for the outcomes they derive from their actions.

Vroom uses the term *valence* to refer to the affective (emotional) orientations people hold with regard to outcomes. An outcome is said to be positively valent for an individual if she would prefer having it to not having it. For example, we would say that a promotion is positively valent for an employee who would rather be promoted than not be promoted. Likewise, we say that an outcome which a person would prefer to avoid has negative valence for her, or simply that it is negatively valent. For example, fatigue, stress, and layoffs are three outcomes that are usually negatively valent among employees. Finally, it is sometimes the case that an employee is indifferent toward certain outcomes; it such cases, the outcome is said to hold zero valence for that individual.

The most important feature of people's valences concerning work-related outcomes is that they refer to the level of satisfaction the person *expects* to receive from them, *not from the real value the person actually derives from them.* So, for example, the reader may be enrolled in a program of business management because she expects that the outcomes to follow (an education and a diploma, among others) will be of value to her when she is finished. It may be the case, however, that when the student graduates there will be little or no market demand for the services she has to offer the world of business and administration, so the degree may have little real value. The point here is that people attribute either positive or negative preferences (or indifference) to outcomes according to the satisfaction or dissatisfaction they *expect* to receive from them. It is often the case that the true value of an outcome (such as a diploma) is either greater or lesser than the valence (expected value) that outcome once held for the individual who was motivated to either pursue it or avoid it. As a final example, consider the individual who fears being fired, but learns after actually being dismissed from a job that she is healthier, happier, and better off financially in the new job she acquired after having been terminated by her former employer. In this case, being fired was a negatively valent outcome before it occurred, but eventually turned out to be of positive value after it occurred.

Performance as an Outcome Of the many outcomes tʰat follow an employee's work effort, one of the most important, of course, is the level of performance that is accomplished. In fact, for the sake of understanding Vroom's theory, the strength of the connection in the mind of the employee between his effort and the performance level he achieves is very important, as we will see shortly. Further, the degree to which the employee believes that his performance will be connected to other outcomes (such as pay, for example) is also critical. The point here is that work effort results in a variety of outcomes, some of them directly, others indirectly. The level of job performance is the most important outcome for understanding work motivation from a VIE Theory perspective. So, *V* stands for valence—the expected levels of satisfaction and/or dissatisfaction brought by work-related outcomes.

The Concept of Instrumentality

We have just stated that outcomes carry valences for people. But what determines the valence of a particular outcome for an employee? For example, we noted that performance level is an important outcome of a person's work effort, but what determines the valence associated with a given level of performance? For Vroom, the answer is that a given level of performance is positively valent if the employee believes that it will lead to other outcomes, which are called *second-level outcomes*. In other words, if an employee believes . . . that a high level of performance is *instrumental* for the acquisition of other outcomes that he expects will be gratifying (such as a promotion, for example), and/or if he believes that a high performance level will be instrumental for avoiding other outcomes that he wishes to avoid (such as being fired), then that employee will place a high valence upon performing the job well.

Consider the meaning of the adjective *instrumental*. The author's typewriter at the present time is instrumental in the preparation of this book. It contributes to the job; it helps. Something is said to be instrumental if iᵗ is believed to lead to something else, if it helps achieve or attain something else. Hence, studying is commonly seen by students as instrumental for passing exams. In turn, passing exams is often *believed* instrumental for the acquisition of diplomas, which, in turn, are *believed* to be instrumental for landing jobs in tight labor market conditions.

Vroom (1964) suggests that we consider instrumentality as a probability belief linking one outcome (performance level) to other outcomes, ranging from 1.0 (meaning that the attainment of the second outcome is certain if the first outcome is achieved), through zero (meaning that there is no likely relationship between the attainment of the first outcome and the attainment of the second), to −1.0 (meaning that the attainment of the second outcome is certain without the first and that it is impossible with it). For example, bonus pay that is distributed at random would lead to employee instrumentality perceptions linking bonus pay to performance equal to zero. ("Performance and pay have no connection around here!") On the other hand, commission pay schemes which tie pay directly to performance, and only to performance, are designed to make employees perceive that performance is positively instrumental for the acquisition of money. Finally, an employee who has been threatened with dismissal for being drunk on the job may be told by his supervisor, in effect, that lack of sobriety at work is negatively instrumental for continued employment, or alternatively, that further imbibing will be positively instrumental for termination. (The notion of negative instrumentalities makes Vroom's original formulation of VIE Theory somewhat more difficult and cumbersome than it might otherwise be, so subsequent versions of the theory have avoided using it, choosing instead to speak only of positive instrumentalities.)

Consider the case of an employee who perceives that high performance will *not* lead to things he desires, but that it will be more instrumental for attaining outcomes to which he attributes negative valences. High performance will not be positively valent for such a person, so we would not expect to see him striving to perform well. As a further example, an employee might perceive that taking a job as a traveling salesman will be instrumental for attaining a number of outcomes, some of which he expects will be positive, some of which he believes will be negative. On the positively valent side, meeting new people and seeing the countryside may be appealing to him, because he expects that these outcomes will be instrumental for satisfying his relatedness and growth needs, while the possible threat to his family life may be aversive to him, the popularly acknowledged exploits to traveling salesmen notwithstanding!

In short, the *I* in VIE Theory stands for instrumentality—an outcome is positively valent if the person believes that it holds high instrumentality for the acquisition of positively valent consequences (goals or other outcomes), and the avoidance of negatively valent outcomes. But in order for an outcome to be positively valent, the outcomes to which the person believes it is connected must themselves, in turn, be seen as positively valent. If an employee anticipates that high levels of performance will lead primarily to things he dislikes, then high performance will not be positively valent to him. Likewise, if the individual perceives that high performance is generally rewarded with things he desires, he will place high valence on high performance and—other things being equal—he will strive for high performance. Of course, the valence of such second-level-outcomes is determined by the nature of the person's most salient needs and values.

Already, the reader should be able to distill a few implications for the design of reward systems in organizations: if management wants high performance levels, it must tie positively valent outcomes to high performance *and be sure that employees understand the connection*. Likewise, low performance must be seen as connected to consequences that are of either zero or negative valence.

The Concept of Expectancy

The third major component of VIE Theory is referred to as *expectancy*. Expectancy is the strength of a person's belief about whether a particular outcome is possible. The author, for example, would place very little expectancy on the prospect of becoming an astronaut. The reasons are, of course, personal, but the point is that he doesn't believe that any amount of trying on his part will see him aboard the space shuttle! If a person believes that he can achieve an outcome, he will be more motivated to try for it, assuming that other things are equal (the other things, of course, consist of the person's beliefs about the valence of the outcome, which, in turn, is determined by the person's beliefs about the odds that the outcome will be instrumental for acquiring and avoiding those things he either wishes to acquire or avoid, respectively).

Vroom (1964) spoke of expectancy beliefs as *action-outcome* associations held in the minds of individuals, and suggested that we think of them in probability terms ranging from zero (in the case where the person's subjective probability of attaining an outcome is psychologically zero—"I can't do it") through to 1.0, indicating that the person has no doubt about his capacity to attain the outcome. In practice, of course, people's estimates tend to range between these two extremes.

There are a variety of factors that contribute to an employee's expectancy perceptions about various levels of job performance. For example, his level of confidence in his skills for the task at hand, the degree of help he expects to receive from his supervisor and subordinates, the quality of the materials and equipment available, the availability of pertinent information and control over sufficient budget, are common examples of factors that can influence a person's expectancy beliefs about being able to achieve a particular level of performance. Previous success experiences at a task and a generally high level of self-esteem also strengthen expectancy beliefs (Lawler, 1973). The point is that an employee's subjective estimate of the odds that he can achieve a given level of performance is determined by a variety of factors, both within his own control and beyond it.

The Concept of Force

Vroom (1964) suggests that a person's beliefs about expectancies, instrumentalities, and valences interact psychologically to create a motivational force to act in those ways that seem most likely to bring pleasure or to avoid pain. "Behavior on the part of a person is assumed to be the result of a field of forces each of which has a direction and magnitude" (p. 18). Vroom likens his concept of force to a variety of other metaphorical concepts, including things such as *performance vectors* and *behavior potential*. We can think of the force as representing the strength of a person's *intention* to act in a certain way. For example, if a person elects to strive for a particular level of job performance, we might say that the person's beliefs cause the greatest amount of force to be directed toward that level, or that he intends to strive for that level rather than for other levels.

Symbolically, Vroom (1964, p. 18) summarizes his own theory as follows:

$$F_i = f \sum_{i=1}^{n}(E_{ij}V_j) \quad \text{and} \quad V_j = f\left[\sum_{j=1}^{n}I_{jk}V_k\right]$$

where F_i = the psychological force to perform an act (i) (such as strive for a particular level of performance)

E_{ij} = the strength of the expectancy that the act will be followed by the outcome j

V_j = the valence for the individual of outcome j

I_{jk} = instrumentality of outcome j for attaining second-level outcome k

V_k = valence of second-level outcome k

or, in his words:

> The force on a person to perform an act is a monotonically increasing function of the algebraic sum of the products of the valences of all outcomes and the strength of his expectancies that the act will be followed by the attainment of these outcomes.

So people choose from among the alternative acts the one(s) corresponding to the strongest positive (or weakest negative) force. People attempt to maximize their overall best interest, using the information available to them and their evaluations of this information. *In the context of work motivation, this means that people select to pursue that level of performance that they believe will maximize their overall best interest (or subjective expected utility).*

Notice from the formula above that there will be little or no motivational force operating on an individual to act in a certain manner if any of three conditions hold: (1) if the person does not believe that she can successfully behave that way (that is, if her expectancy of attaining the outcome is effectively zero); (2) if she believes that there will be no positively valent outcomes associated with behaving in that manner; (3) if she believes the act will result in a sufficient number of outcomes that are negatively valent to her.

The Choice of a Performance Level   When we think of the levels of job performance that an employee might strive for as the outcome of interest, Vroom's theory suggests that the individual will consider the valences, instrumentalities, and expectancies associated with each level of the entire spectrum of performance levels and will elect to pursue the level that generates the greatest positive force (or lowest negative force) for him. If the person sees more good outcomes than bad ones associated with performing at a high level, he will strive to perform at that level. On the other hand, if a lower level of performance results in the greatest degree of psychological force, we can anticipate that he will settle for such a level. The implication is that low motivation levels result from employee choices to perform at low levels, and that these choices, in turn, are the result of beliefs concerning the valences, instrumentalities, and expectancies held in the mind of the employee.

REFINEMENTS TO THE THEORY

Since the publication of Vroom's book in 1964, there has been a considerable amount of both theoretical and empirical attention paid to expectancy-type models of work motivation. Aside from attempting to test the validity of the theory in its simple form, most of these efforts have sought to study the characteristics of people and organizations that influence valence, instrumentality, and expectancy beliefs, or to examine the types of conditions within which VIE-type predictions of work motivation can be expected to apply. A complete discussion of these refinements could easily constitute an entire book—well beyond our present purposes. The reader who is interested in pursuing major theoretic advances in VIE Theory is referred to the following sources: Campbell, Dunnette, Lawler, and Weick, 1970; Dachler and Mobley, 1973; Feldman, Reitz, and Hiterman, 1976; Graen, 1969; House, Shapiro, and Wahba, 1974; Kopelman, 1977; Kopelman and Thompson, 1976; Lawler, 1971, 1973; Naylor, Pritchard, and Ilgen, 1980; Porter and Lawler, 1968; Reinharth and Wahba, 1976; Staw, 1977; and Zedeck, 1977. Thorough reviews of the *research evidence* pertaining to VIE Theory are provided by Heneman and Schwab, (1972), Mitchell and Biglan (1971), and Campbell and Pritchard (1976).

For the purpose of the present discussion, only one of the many theoretical advancements of VIE Theory will be presented, followed by a brief summary of the validity of the theory and a number of difficulties that have been encountered in determining its validity. Finally, we will conclude with a discussion of the major implications of VIE Theory for the practice of management. So, to begin, let's take a look at one of the most important modifications and extensions offered to Vroom's work—the model offered by Porter and Lawler (1968).

The Porter/Lawler Model

Vroom's (1964) statement of VIE Theory left a number of questions unanswered. Perhaps the most important of these concerned the origins of valence, instrumentality, and expectancy beliefs, and the nature of the relationship, if any, between employee attitudes toward work and job performance. Porter and Lawler (1968) developed a theoretic model and then tested it, using a sample of managers, and revised it to explore these issues. The revised statement of their model is provided in schematic form in Figure 1.

In a nutshell, their theory suggests the following. *Employee effort* is jointly determined by two key factors: the *value* placed on certain outcomes by the individual, and the *degree to which the person believes that his effort will lead to the attainment of these rewards.* As predicted by Vroom, Porter and Lawler found that these two factors interact to determine effort level; in other words, they found that people must both positively value outcomes and believe that these outcomes result from their effort for any further effort to be forthcoming.

However, effort may or may not result in *job performance,* which they defined as the accomplishment of those tasks that comprise a person's job. The reason? The level of *ability* the person has to do his job, and his *role clarity,* the degree of clarity of the understanding the person has concerning just what his job consists of. Thus, a person may be highly motivated (putting out a lot of effort), but that effort will not necessarily result in what can be considered performance, unless he has both the ability to perform the job as well as a clear understanding of the ways in which it is appropriate to direct that effort. The student reader is probably familiar with at least one colleague who has high motivation to learn and succeed in university, but who lacks either the ability or the *savoir faire* needed

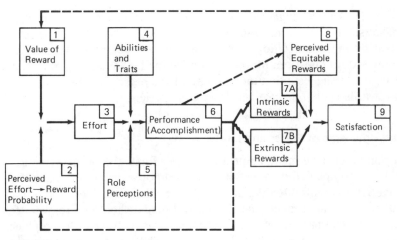

FIGURE 1
The revised Porter/Lawler model.

to direct his energy into what can be considered performance in the academic context: learning and self-development. In short, all three ingredients are needed to some degree, and if any of them is absent, performance cannot result.

Next, what is the relationship between performance (at whatever level is accomplished) and *job satisfaction?* As reflected in Figure 1, Porter and Lawler argue that performance and satisfaction may or may not be related to one another, depending upon a number of factors. First, they note that it is not always the case that performance results in rewards in organizations. Further, they recognize that there are at least two types of rewards potentially available from performance: intrinsic and extrinsic. Porter and Lawler recognize that intrinsic rewards can be much more closely connected with good performance than extrinsic rewards, because the former result (almost automatically) from performance itself, whereas the latter depend upon outside sources (both to recognize that performance has been attained and to administer rewards accordingly).

Porter and Lawler suggest that the level of performance a person believes she has attained will influence the level of rewards that she believes will be *equitable.* So, if an employee believes that her efforts have resulted in a high degree of performance, she will expect a greater level of reward than would be the case if she believes that her performance is not as high. As a result, a particular reward, if any is forthcoming, will be assessed in terms of its level of equity in the mind of the employee, rather than in terms of its absolute level. We sometimes hear statements such as "That pay increase was an insult, considering all I do for this company," reflecting Porter and Lawler's belief that it is not the absolute amount of reward that follows performance which determines whether it is satisfying; rather, the amount, however large or small, must be seen by the employee as equitable in order for it to be satisfying.

Satisfaction was defined in Porter and Lawler's research as " . . . the extent to which rewards actually received meet or exceed the perceived equitable level of rewards'' (p. 31). And, as suggested by the feedback loop at the top of Figure 1, the level of satisfaction or dissatisfaction experienced by the person as a result of his treatment by the organization helps determine the value he places in the future on the rewards in question. Moreover, notice the feedback loop at the bottom of the diagram. It suggests that the strength of the person's belief that effort will result in rewards is also determined through experience.

Comments and Criticisms of Porter and Lawler

A number of points must be made about this model. First, the primary focus of the research that accompanied its development was upon *pay* and the role of pay in employee motivation. Although the authors limited their consideration of outcomes other than pay, they argued that the general model should be relevant for consequences other than pay. In addition, since pay was the focus, the emphasis was upon positive consequences only rather than upon both positive and negative consequences (such as fatigue, demotions, or various forms of punishment).

Secondly, Porter and Lawler tested the propositions they derived from their model *cross-sectionally* (rather than over time), and using only managers from the extreme ends of the distributions on the important variables in that model, excluding those individuals who fell near the middle in each case. This is a common practice in research, but one that causes overestimates of the validity of the model being tested (Taylor and Griess, 1976). Additionally, they measured job satisfaction using a technique that is also commonly used, but one which has subsequently been shown to be inappropriate, probably reducing the apparent validity of the model (Johns, 1981).

A third point is that although their model posits the importance of ability as an interactive factor with motivation as a determinant of job performance, Porter and Lawler's *own research* did not pay much attention to examining the specific role of ability. However, other researchers have addressed this issue, and the results seem to suggest that while ability has an important influence on performance, it may not *interact* with motivation in the manner believed by Vroom (1964) and Porter and Lawler (cf. Terborg, 1977).

Fourthly, while Porter and Lawler use the term *value* rather than *valence*, it seems clear that they had the same concept in mind as Vroom. The reader is reminded again of the importance of distinguishing between valence and value when considering motivation from a VIE Theory perspective: it is the anticipated value (valence) of an outcome that is crucial in determining effort, not actual value, per se.

Another point has to do with the way the connection between effort and rewards was conceptualized and measured. Current theories recognize that employee beliefs about the strength of the connection between effort and reward distribution can usefully be broken down into two components: (1) the strength of the belief that a person's effort will result in job performance; and (2) the strength of the person's belief that performance, if achieved, will eventuate into rewards. Porter and Lawler acknowledge the prospect for breaking this overall cognition down into its component parts, and subsequent work by Lawler (1973) and others maintains this distinction.

Performance and Satisfaction (Again) A major contribution of the Porter-Lawler model consists of the implications it holds for the issue concerning the relationship between performance and satisfaction. Consider the diagram in Figure 1. According to the theory, will satisfaction and performance be related to one another? If so, when? The figure suggests that these two factors may or may not be related to one another, but that when they are, the order of causality is far from simple.

First, how might satisfaction be a contributing determinant of performance levels? A number of conditions must hold.

1 That satisfaction must leave the person desirous of attaining more of the same outcome(s). Satisfied needs tend to lose their capacity to motivate behavior, although growth need satisfaction seems to increase the strength of these needs.

2 Even if the reward maintains its valence, effort will result only if the person believes that effort results in the attainment of the reward (which, as we have discussed, is not always the case).

3 In order for the individual's effort to result in performance, the person must have the ability to perform, as well as have a clear idea concerning how to try to perform—where to direct his effort.

4 The performance must result in rewards, and these rewards must be perceived as equitable, for the reasons discussed earlier.

In short, in order for satisfaction to be a contributing cause of performance, as was believed during the days of the human relations movement (and as is still commonly believed by managers and people on the street), all of the foregoing individual and organizational conditions must apply. Rather complicated, to say the least.

Can performance be a cause of satisfaction? The model implies that it can. First, as already noted, high performance can be an immediate cause of intrinsic satisfaction, assuming that job provides sufficient challenge to appeal to growth needs. Secondly, however, performance can contribute to extrinsic satisfaction if at least three conditions hold:

1 Desired rewards must be tied to that performance (as opposed to being tied to chance or other factors).

2 The person must perceive the connection between his performance and the rewards he receives.

3 The person must believe that the rewards he receives for his performance are equitable.

Again, not a very simple relationship, but Porter and Lawler's model helps explain why the relationships observed between performance and satisfaction have traditionally been so low, although, in their research, the two factors were found to be more strongly connected than is usually the case.

In conclusion, Porter and Lawler have provided a useful elaboration of the fundamental concepts of VIE Theory as presented only a few years earlier by Vroom. The dynamic features of their model (as reflected in the feedback loops) indicate the ongoing nature of the motivation process, and sheds some light on why some employees are more productive than others, why some employees are more satisfied with their work than others, and when we can expect to find a relationship between employee attitudes and performance.

THE VALIDITY OF VIE THEORY

In spite of the fact that there have been innumerable tests of the scientific validity of VIE Theory, only recently have researchers begun to perform studies that can be considered fair or appropriate, given the claims made by the theory itself. In fact, Campbell and Pritchard (1976) have identified at least twelve common problems in the many studies conducted to that time.

The Between/Within Issue

Probably the most important of these problems has had to do with testing the theory as if it were intended to make behavioral and attitudinal predictions *across* individuals, as opposed to *within* individuals (Arnold, 1981; Kopelman, 1977; Mitchell, 1974). In other words, the theory is intended to make predictions about which behavioral alternatives an individual will choose from among those that confront him. The theory states that the alternative which is perceived to maximize the individual's overall expected utility and satisfaction will be the one selected. On the other hand, a major proportion of the investigations reported to date have ignored or violated this assumption by computing expected levels of motivational force (or effort) for a number of people using those peoples' scores on VIE factors, and then correlating these predicted scores, across individuals, with ratings on some other form of score representing actual behavior or attitudes.

To illustrate more completely, suppose we were to compute expected effort scores for a sample of twenty people, using the information these people provide us through interviews or questionnaires. We would calculate these scores using some form of $E(\Sigma VI)$ formula. Then suppose we rank ordered these people on the basis of the magnitude of this overall predicted effort level. Next, we gather supervisory ratings of the actual typical effort levels of these same people and rank order them again, this time on the basis of their supervisory ratings. Finally, assume we correlate these *actual* effort scores with our predicted effort scores, attempting to determine whether the people with the highest predicted scores tended to have the highest supervisory ratings, and whether those with the lowest predicted scores also had the lowest ratings.

The approach just described is referred to as a between-individual one, for apparent reasons. This has been the methodology which has been erroneously used so many times, and the results generated from this type of research design have appeared not to support the theory, because, in fact, there has tended not to be very strong relationships between predicted effort and rated effort, when the data were compiled in this fashion. Accordingly, researchers have concluded that, by and large, the theory is only moderately valid.

Consider the mistake being made in studies conducted this way. The theory merely purports to make predictions concerning *single* individuals, one at a time, about the decision alternatives each of them will select. So, for example, Parker and Dyer (1976) were able to make better than chance predictions about the decisions reached by naval officers as to whether or not to retire voluntarily. Likewise, Arnold (1981) made predictions supportive of the theory concerning the choices of jobs made by undergraduate students; Matsui, Kagawa, Nagamatsu, and Ohtsuka (1977) predicted which of six insurance policies agents would prefer to sell; while Nebeker and Mitchell (1974) and Matsui and Ohtsuka (1978) predicted the leadership styles of supervisors in different settings and in different cultures.*

What is wrong with the between-individual approach for testing the theory? It does not take into account differences between people in ability, the difficulty of the jobs they perform, differences in the level of rewards they receive for their work, and various other things. The difference between these two approaches is subtle when first considered, but incredibly significant for the conclusions one reaches about the validity of the theory. Moreover, the between-individuals approach assumes that people who hold identical valence, instrumentality, and expectancy beliefs will respond identically to instruments designed to assess these constructs. Clearly, this assumption is dubious (Mitchell, 1974). As noted by Atkinson (1964) and Kopelman (1977), the last person in a family to arrive at the dinner table is not necessarily the least hungry! So, to conclude that the theory is not very valid on the basis of research that utilizes an across (or between) individuals approach hardly seems fair.

Other Research Difficulties

In addition to the between/within problem just described, there have been a variety of other typical mistakes made by researchers interested in VIE Theory (Campbell and Pritchard, 1976). A complete discussion of these is beyond our present purpose, but brief mention can be made of a few:

1 The use of incorrect mathematical procedures for testing the interaction effects between effort and ability posited by the theory (see Arnold, 1981 for a way of dealing with this problem).

2 The use of supervisory ratings of *performance* as the criterion against which predictions of employee force is compared. The use of performance rather than effort has occurred because of the difficulty of assessing the latter. But since the theory purports to predict effort, and because effort is only one determinant of performance, the results of these studies have been negatively biased against the theory.

3 Low validity and reliability of valence, instrumentality, and expectancy

---

*The interested student reader may wish to read of a study in which the researchers utilized a VIE model to predict the academic effort and performance of a sample of college students, employing a statistical technique to control for the between/within person problem (Mitchell and Nebeker, 1973).

measures (see de Leo and Pritchard, 1974). The effect of these problems has been to cause underestimates of the validity of the theory.

4 The use of cross-sectional research designs, in spite of the fact that the theory speaks of changes, at one point in time, of V, I, and E perceptions being predictive of changes of effort at some subsequent point in time (see Mayes, 1978a for a discussion of this problem and Lawler and Suttle, 1973 and Kopelman, 1979 for attempts to get around it).

5 Assuming that the valence, instrumentality, and expectancy beliefs people hold are independent of one another, then multiplying these scores algebraically. It may be that these three beliefs are not in fact independent of one another, such that people may place higher valence upon outcomes that are believed more difficult to attain. Multiplication assumes independence.

6 Assuming that people are, in fact, as rational as the theory would suggest, for all aspects of their behavior, when, in fact, we know that people have limited cognitive capacities and that much of human behavior is habitual and subconscious (Locke, 1975; Mayes, 1978b; Staw, 1977; Simon, 1957).

Conclusion

The self-correcting cycle of research activity has raised questions about these and other common problems in the research on VIE Theory, and the more recent studies have taken many of them into account. As a result, it appears that VIE Theory may be a more valid representation of work-related attitudes and behaviors than has been concluded by many authors who have surveyed studies that were fraught with the problems identified above. In short, we conclude that the situation for VIE Theory may be similar to that for Maslow's need hierarchy theory, Equity Theory, and maybe even Herzberg's two-factor theory: although there have been many studies conducted with the intention of testing its validity, only recently have there been many appropriately-conducted studies, leaving us with grounds for optimism that the theory is a reasonably valid model of the causes of work behavior.

IMPLICATIONS OF VIE THEORY FOR MANAGEMENT

Beliefs about work (or about life in general) are based on the individual's perceptions of the surrounding environment, and these perceptions are influenced by information stored in the person's memory. It is assumed here that valence, instrumentality, and expectancy beliefs are established and influenced in the same manner as are other beliefs. Therefore, it also follows that because beliefs may not be valid or accurate, the person's behavior may not seem appropriate to observers. And it also follows that because these three beliefs are merely beliefs (as opposed to intentions), they may not result in behavior at all, or at least, they may not result in any specifically predictable behaviors. They should, however, influence an individual's *intentions* to act certain ways. Accordingly, a number of implications follow from VIE Theory for any supervisor who wishes to try to "motivate" his staff.

Expectancy-Related Factors

First, in order to generate positive expectancy forces, the supervisor must assign his personnel to jobs for which they are trained, and which they are capable of performing. This requires that the supervisor understand the skills, strengths, and weaknesses of each of his subordinates, as well as the nature of the skill requirements of the jobs to which he is assigning them. If people are assigned to tasks that they are not capable of performing, according to VIE Theory, their expectancy perceptions will be low, and we will not expect to see them trying to perform.

Consider how difficult it is, in practice, for supervisors completely to appreciate the skill requirements of the jobs their employees must perform, and to recognize that it is the level of skills of the *employees* vis à vis the jobs, not their own skill levels, that matter. Jobs often change with time and as incumbents come and go, making it difficult to keep track of what they require. In addition, supervisors who have performed some or all of the jobs under their purview may forget how difficult these jobs are to newcomers, so they may either overestimate or underestimate the difficulty level of jobs for any of these reasons. Finally, it is important to recognize that employees' skills and abilities change over time, both as a result of formal training and education, as well as from the natural consequences of maturation and simple work experiences.

But adequate skill levels are not sufficient to assure positive expectancy perceptions. In addition, the employee must *believe* that the other circumstances surrounding his effort are favorable and conducive to his success. For example, the supervisor must be sure that machinery and equipment are in good repair, and that the employee's own staff, if any, are trained and capable of being of assistance. Likewise, there must be sufficient budget to make successful performance possible. In short, the job must be capable of being performed by an employee if we are to expect the employee to try to perform it, and—more importantly—the person must perceive that it is so. But countless practical factors can combine to make it very difficult for any supervisor to accurately estimate the expectancy beliefs held by particular employees about specific jobs; accordingly, they make it difficult for supervisors to fully implement the implications that follow from the expectancy component of VIE Theory.

Of particular importance for supervisors is the structuring of the expectancy beliefs of newcomers to a work setting (Hall, 1976). Managers often take a "sink or swim" approach with new employees, assigning them work duties that are too difficult, given their relative lack of familiarity with the rules, procedures, and the myriad other circumstances that must be understood in order to make work efforts successful. An alternative approach is to under-challenge newcomers, requiring them to work through a tedious series of trivial jobs before being given any real challenge. Recent college graduates often complain of this treatment upon landing their first jobs after graduating, and, as a result, turnover among recent graduates is usually very high (Mobley, 1982). A third approach, the desired one, is to strike a balance using a combination of achievement-oriented, supportive, and directive leadership styles (as defined in the previous section), attempting to make the newcomer's initial experiences challenging and successful. Success experiences are necessary for developing strong expectancy beliefs, and for maintaining a positive self-concept about one's work—a feeling of competence, self-determination, and high self-esteem (cf. Deci, 1975; Hall, 1976; Korman, 1970, 1976).

Instrumentality-Related Factors

In order to operationalize the concepts of instrumentality and valence, supervisors must make sure that positively valent rewards are associated with good job performance, *and that their employees perceive this connection.* In practice, this also is difficult for a number of reasons. Most supervisors have a limited stock of rewards available to them for distribution to their subordinates. Company policies with regard to pay and benefits are usually restrictive, for the good reasons of control and the maintenance of equity. Further, union contracts are generally quite clear about the bases of reward distribution and often require that pay and other rewards be based on seniority rather than merit, further restricting the capacity of individual supervisors always to know who their meritorious employees are. This problem is especially common among managerial, professional, and technical personnel, in whose jobs good performance is normally very hard to measure, even when someone tries diligently to do so. As a result of these and other practical difficulties, implementing the instrumentality implications of VIE is often (perhaps usually) very difficult.

Valence-Related Factors

Where does the notion of valence fit into practice? VIE Theory would prescribe that those rewards which are distributed for good performance should be the types of things that employees desire. All that we know from common sense, as well as that which we have learned from research into human needs, tells us that different people have different need profiles at different times, so it follows that different outcomes will be rewarding for different people at different times. Hence, even the same outcome (such as a job transfer to another city) may be positively valent for some people, while being negatively valent for others. And to the extent that satisfied needs tend to lose their capacity to motivate behavior, we can expect certain organizationally-distributed rewards to be satisfying and perhaps motivating for a particular individual in some circumstances, but not so in other circumstances. Hence, older employees often have no desire to meet and befriend new employees on the job: their relatedness needs are already well met and secured by interactions with old friends and acquaintances. In short, implementing VIE, with regard to providing valent outcomes for work, can be very difficult in practice.

Individual Organizations

One leading authority has discussed the importance of attempting to reward individuals with outcomes that are best suited to their individual needs (Lawler, 1973, 1976). His suggestions entail comprehensive analyses of both the employees and the jobs in organizations, followed by the careful assignment of people to those jobs in which they will find outcomes they desire, *especially as a consequence of good performance*.

A notable attempt to structure rewards on a more-or-less individualized basis can be found in the concept of *cafeteria-style* compensation plans (Lawler, 1966; Nealy, 1963; Schuster, 1969). The general design of these plans is for the individual employee to be allotted a fixed dollar sum of compensation that she can distribute according to her own preferences across a variety of forms of compensation, including salary, and any of a number of fringe benefits, deferred earnings, stock options, and the like.

Cafeteria-style plans have not, however, been widely adopted; in large measure because of a number of practical considerations that were discussed above (Belcher, 1974). For example, these plans tend to make payroll accounting procedures more complicated and more expensive to administer (Hettenhouse, 1971). In addition, there seems to be some belief on the part of management groups that employees should be required to invest their earnings in at least some amount of protection from insecurity (such as long-term disability and health insurance), whether they desire to do so or not. Another problem concerns the fact that many group life and health insurance plans are priced according to the number of persons in an organization who subscribe to them. Therefore, any sort of compensation system that allows some people to opt out of a group plan may result in higher premiums for those who opt into group coverage, thereby discouraging the individual decisions to opt out. Yet another difficulty that can arise from cafeteria-style plans results when employees elect to take all or most of their compensation in the form of cash, thereby threatening the relationship of internal equity between job level and pay level in the eyes of the employees involved. Finally, Belcher (1974) suggests that some of the negative reactions to cafeteria plans arise from a fear that if compensation were completely individualized, the infinite number of combinations and blends that are possible would be completely unmanageable, but that it should be possible to offset this fear by arranging a limited number of combinations from which individuals may choose. It may be, according to Belcher, that it is not necessary to *totally* individualize compensation plans. In fact, a study by Mahoney (1964) supports this view.

Another problem usually encountered by managerial attempts to individualize employee rewards in a fashion consistent with VIE Theory concerns the difficulty of accurately determining the actual *needs* of individual employees. . . . Managers simply may not be able to accurately determine the needs of their employees, so they must rely on techniques such as attitude surveys and one-on-one discussions to learn about employee *values*.

The distinction between needs and values may appear academic, but it is more than that. Rewards may be satisfying, according to Locke (1976), as long as they correspond with employee values and are not inconsistent with employee needs. But when employee values deviate from needs (meaning that people desire things that are not actually conducive to their best interests), organizational reward systems aimed at fulfilling employee values may not be at all beneficial, for either the individuals involved or for the organization as a whole. So, for example, certain employees may indicate that they desire greater responsibility and decision making power in their jobs. This stated preference reflects first a value—something the individuals *believe* will be good for themselves. In many cases, this value, if attained, will in fact satisfy needs—in this case, greater responsibility may be instrumental for fulfilling growth needs. In other cases, however, employees find that greater responsibility on their jobs is burdensome, stressful, and very frustrating: not everybody benefits from having responsible jobs.

The point of all this is that attempts to structure organizational reward systems in accordance with VIE Theory require that managers determine, somehow, what their subordinates want, and that they then proceed to tie job performance to the distribution of those outcomes. As noted above, systematic attempts to do this are frequently undertaken with the aid of employee attitude surveys; therefore VIE Theory may serve to guide the construction of such surveys, as we will see.

The Content of Employee Surveys

While a complete discussion of the design and use of employee attitude surveys is beyond our present purpose, VIE Theory clearly has a number of implications for this process. Specifically, rather than including only questions dealing with employee attitudes (as is commonly the case), greater benefit can be gained from seeking insight into the nature of employee beliefs, particularly beliefs about whether people feel it is typically possible to convert effort into performance, and whether rewards are seen as being tied to performance and as being equitable (Lawler, 1967b). In addition, more can be learned from enquiring *why* employees hold high or low expectancy and instrumentality beliefs, as well as why they believe the distribution of rewards is seen as inequitable, should that be the case.

The reader who is interested in greater detail about the construction of employee surveys is referred to recent books by Nadler (1977) and Dunham and Smith (1979). Detail concerning the administration of surveys in organizational settings is provided by Williams, Seybolt, and Pinder (1975).

Summary

The point here is that even those managers and supervisors who understand VIE Theory, and who are capable of distilling practical implications from it for application on their jobs, are usually severely handicapped by countless practical features of organizations, work groups, union contracts, standard practices and policies, history, and precedents. More importantly however, we must remember that even if managers are able to structure work settings and reward distribution systems so as to comply with the implications of VIE Theory, they will not be successful unless their policies and practices result in beliefs and perceptions, on the part of employees, which are consistent with high performance levels. For example, employees might not realize that rewards are, in fact, distributed in accordance with merit, even if that is actually the case. Likewise, employees may underestimate their chances of succeeding at a task, because they are not aware of the help that is available to them at the time. According to VIE Theory, it is beliefs that ultimately determine employee behavior, so unless managerial practices translate into beliefs that are favorable toward high job performance, beliefs will not result in employee intentions to perform well.

To conclude, VIE Theory offers a number of elegant implications for managerial practices aimed at generating and sustaining high levels of employee motivation. But putting these implications into practice can be difficult, because managers are often quite limited in the degree of control they have over the practical factors that must be manipulated in order to totally determine their employees' expectancy, valence, and instrumentality beliefs, and thereby influencing their intentions to perform well.

REFERENCES

Arnold, H. J. A test of the validity of the multiplicative hypothesis of expectancy- valence theories of work motivation. *Academy of Management Journal,* 1981, *24,* 128–141.

Atkinson, J. W. Towards experimental analysis of human motivation in terms of motives, expectancies, and incentives. In J. W. Atkinson (Ed.) *Motives in fantasy, action, and society.* Princeton: Van Nostrand, 1958.

Atkinson, J. W. *An introduction to motivation.* Princeton, N.J.: Van Nostrand, 1964.

Belcher, D. *Compensation administration.* Englewood Cliffs, N.J.: Prentice-Hall, 1974.

Campbell, J. P., Dunnette, M. D., Lawler III, E. E. and Weick, K. E. *Managerial behavior, performance and effectiveness.* N.Y.: McGraw-Hill, 1970.

Campbell, J. P. & Pritchard, R. D. Motivation theory in industrial and organizational psychology. In M. D. Dunnette (Ed.) *Handbook for industrial and organizational psychology.* Chicago: Rand McNally, 1976.

Dachler, H. P. & Mobley, W. Construct validation of an instrumentality-expectancy-task-goal model of work motivation: Some theoretical boundary conditions. *Journal of Applied Psychology,* 1973, *58,* 397–418.

Davidson, D., Suppes, P. & Siegel, S. *Decision making: An experimental approach.* Stanford: Stanford University Press, 1957.

Deci, E. L. *Intrinsic motivation.* N.Y.: Plenum Press, 1975.

deLeo, P. J. & Pritchard, R. D. An examination of some methodological problems in testing expectancy-valence models with survey techniques. *Organizational Behavior and Human Performance,* 1974, *12,* 143–148.

Dessler, G. & Valenzi, E. R. Initiation of structure and subordinate satisfaction: A path analysis test of Path-Goal Theory. *Academy of Management Journal,* 1977, *20,* 251–260.

Downey, H. K., Sheridan, J. E. & Slocum, J. W. The Path-Goal Theory of leadership: A longitudinal analysis. *Organizational Behavior and Human Performance,* 1976, *16,* 156–176.

Dunham, R. B. & Smith, F. J. *Organizational surveys: An internal assessment of organizational health.* Glenview, Ill.: Scott, Foresman and Co., 1979.

Evans, M. G. The effects of supervisory behavior on the path-goal relationship. *Organizational Behavior and Human Performance,* 1970, *5,* 277–298.

Evans, M. G. Extensions of a path-goal theory of motivation. *Journal of Applied Psychology.*

Faltermayer, E. Who will do the dirty work tomorrow? *Fortune,* 1974, *89*(1), 132–138.

Feldman, J. M., Reitz, H. J. & Hiterman, R. J. Alternatives to optimization in expectancy theory. *Journal of Applied Psychology,* 1976, *61,* 712–720.

Georgopoulos, B. C., Mahoney, G. M. & Jones, N. W. A path-goal approach to productivity. *Journal of Applied Psychology,* 1957, *41,* 345–353.

Graen, G. Instrumentality theory of work motivation: Some experimental results and suggested modifications. *Journal of Applied Psychology Monograph,* 1969, *53,* No. 2, Part 2.

Greene, C. N. Questions of causation in the path-goal theory of leadership. *Academy of Management Journal,* 1979, *22,* 22–41.

Hall, D. T. *Careers in organizations.* Pacific Palisades, Calif.: Goodyear, 1976.

Heneman, H. G. III & Schwab, D. P. Evaluation of research on expectancy theory predictions of employee performance. *Psychological Bulletin,* 1972 *78*(1), 1–9.

Hettenhouse, G. W. Compensation cafeteria for top executives. *Harvard Business Review,* 1971, *49*(5), 113–119.

House, R. J. A path-goal theory of leadership. *Administrative Science Quarterly,* 1971, *16,* 321–338.

House, R. J. & Dessler, G. The path-goal theory of leadership: Some post hoc and a priori tests. In J. G. Hunt (Ed.) *Contingency approaches to leadership.* Carbondale, Ill.: Southern Illinois University Press, 1974.

House, R. J. & Mitchell, T. R. Path-goal theory of leadership, *Journal of Contemporary Business,* 1974, *3,* 81–98.

House, R. J., Shapiro, H. J., & Wahba, M. A. Expectancy theory as a predictor of work behavior and attitude: A reevaluation of empirical evidence. *Decision Sciences,* 1974, *5,* 481–506.

Johns, G. Difference score measures of organizational behavior variables: A critique. *Organizational Behavior and Human Performance,* 1981, *27,* 443–463.

Kopelman, R. E. Across-individual, within-individual and return on effort versions of expectancy theory. *Decision Sciences,* 1977, *8,* 651–662.

Kopelman, R. E. A causal correlational test of the Porter and Lawler framework. *Human Relations,* 1979, *32,* 545–556.

Kopelman, R. E. & Thompson, P. H. Boundary conditions for expectancy theory predictions of work motivation and job performance. *Academy of Management Journal,* 1976, *19,* 237–258.

Korman, A. K. Toward a hypothesis of work behavior. *Journal of Applied Psychology,* 1970, *54,* 31–41.

Korman, A. K. Hypothesis of work behavior revisited and an extension. *Academy of Management Review,* 1976, *1,* 50–63.

Lawler, E. E. The mythology of management compensation. *California Management Review,* 1966, *9,* 11–22.

Lawler, E. E. Attitude surveys and job performance. *Personnel Administration,* 1967b, *30*(5), 3–5, 22–24.

Lawler, E. E. *Pay and organization effectiveness: A psychological view.* New York: McGraw-Hill, 1971.

Lawler, E. E. *Motivation in work organizations.* Monterey: California: Brooks/Cole, 1973.

Lawler, E. E. Individualizing Organizations: A Needed Emphasis in Organizational Psychology. In H. Meltzer and F. R. Wickert (Eds.) *Humanizing organizational behavior.* Springfield, Ill.: Charles C. Thomas, 1976.

Lawler, E. E. & Suttle, J. L. Expectancy theory and job behavior. *Organizational Behavior and Human Performance,* 1973, *9,* 482–503.

Lewin, K. The conceptual representation of the measurement of psychological forces. *Contributions to Psychological Theory,* Durham, N.C.: Duke University Press, 1938, 1, No. 4.

Locke, E. A. The Nature and Causes of Job Satisfaction. In M. D. Dunnette (Ed.) *Handbook of industrial and organizational psychology.* Chicago: Rand McNally, 1976.

Locke, E. A. Personnel attitudes and motivation. *Annual Review of Psychology,* 1975, *26,* 457–480.

Mahoney, T. A. Compensation preferences of managers. *Industrial Relations*, 1964, *3*, 135–144.

Matsui, T., Kagawa, M., Nagamatsu, J. & Ohtsuka, Y. Validity of expectancy theory as a within-personal behavioral choice model for sales activities. *Journal of Applied Psychology*, 1977, *62*, 764–767.

Matsui, T. And Ohtsuka, Y. Within-person expectancy theory predictions of supervisory consideration and structure behavior. *Journal of Applied Psychology*, 1978, *63*, 128–131.

Mayes, B. T. Incorporating time-lag effects into the expectancy model of motivation: A reformulation of the model. *Academy of Management Review*, 1978a, *3*, 374–379.

Mayes, B. T. Some boundary conditions in the application of motivation models. *Academy of Management Review*, 1978b, *3*, 51–58.

Mitchell, T. R. Expectancy models of satisfaction, occupational preference and effort: A theoretical, methodological and empirical appraisal. *Psychological Bulletin*, 1974, *81*, 1053–1077.

Mitchell, T. R. & Biglan, A. Instrumentality theories: Current uses in psychology. *Psychological Bulletin*, 1971, *76*, 432–454.

Mitchell, T. R. & Nebeker, D. M. Expectancy theory predictions of academic effort and performance. *Journal of Applied Psychology*, 1973, *57*, 61–67.

Mobley, W. H. *Employee turnover: Causes, consequences, and control*. Reading, Mass.: Addison-Wesley, 1982.

Nadler, D. A. *Feedback and organization development: Using data-based methods*. Reading, Mass.: Addison-Wesley, 1977.

Naylor, J. D., Pritchard, R. D., & Ilgen, D. R. *A theory of behavior in organizations*. New York: Academic Press, 1980.

Nealey, S. M. Pay and benefit preference. *Industrial Relations*, 1963, *3*, 17–28.

Nebeker, D. M. & Mitchell, T. R. Leader behavior: An expectancy theory approach. *Organizational Behavior and Human Performance*, 1974, *11*, 355–367.

Parker, D. F. & Dyer, L. Expectancy theory as a within person behavioral choice model: An empirical test of some conceptual and methodological refinements. *Organizational Behavior and Human Performance*, 1976, *17*, 97–117.

Peak, H. Attitude and motivation. In M. R. Jones (Ed.) *Nebraska Symposium on Motivation*. Lincoln: University of Nebraska Press, 1955.

Pinder, C. C. Concerning the application of human motivation theories in organizational settings. *Academy of Management Review*, 1977, *2*, 384–397.

Porter, L. W. & Lawler, E. E. *Managerial Attitudes and Performance*. Homewood, Illinois: Dorsey Press, 1968.

Reinharth, L. & Wahba, M. A. A test of alternative models of expectancy theory. *Human Relations*, 1976, *29*, 257–272.

Rotter, J. B. The Role of the Psychological Situation in Determining the Direction of Human Behavior. In M. R. Jones (Ed.) *Nebraska Symposium on Motivation*, Lincoln: University of Nebraska Press, 1955.

Schriesheim, C. A. & DeNisi, A. S. Task dimensions as moderators of the effects of instrumental leadership: A two-sample replicated test of path-goal leadership theory. *Journal of Applied Psychology*, 1981, *66*, 589–597.

Schriesheim, C. & Von Glinow, M. A. The path-goal theory of leadership: A theoretical and empirical analysis. *Academy of Management Journal*, 1977, 398–405.

Schriesheim, J. F. & Schriesheim, C. A. A test of the path-goal theory of leadership and some suggested directions for future research. *Personnel Psychology*, 1980, *33*, 349–370.

Schuster, J. R. Another look at compensation preferences. *Industrial Management Review*, 1969, *10*, 1–18.

Simon, H. A. *Administrative behavior*. (2nd ed.) New York: Macmillan, 1957.

Staw, B. M. Motivation in Organizations: Toward Synthesis and Redirection. In B. M. Staw and G. R. Salancik (Eds.) *New directions in organizational behavior*. Chicago: St. Clair Press, 1977.

Taylor, E. K. & Griess, T. The missing middle in validation research. *Personnel Psychology*, 1976, *29*, 5–11.

Terborg, J. R. Validation and extension of an individual differences model of work performance. *Organizational Behavior and Human Performance*, 1977, *18*, 188–216.

Tolman, E. C. Principles of Purposive Behavior. In S. Koch (Ed.) *Psychology: A Study of a Science*. Vol. 2. New York: McGraw-Hill, 1959.

Vroom, V. H. *Work and motivation*. New York: Wiley, 1964.

Walter, G. A. & Marks, S. E. *Experiential learning and change*. New York: Wiley, 1981.

Williams, L. K., Seybolt, J. W., & Pinder, C. C. On administering questionnaires in organizational settings. *Personnel Psychology*, 1975, *28*, 93–103.

Zedeck, S. An information processing model and approach to the study of motivation. *Organizational Behavior and Human Performance*, 1977, *18*, 47–77.

A Social Learning Approach to Behavioral Management: Radical Behaviorists "Mellowing Out"

Robert Kreitner
Fred Luthans

We are said to be living in an age of synthesis, a time when emphasis has shifted from analyzing isolated details to studying the whole picture. Although we have learned a great deal by taking things apart and analyzing them, much remains to be understood about complex interrelations in phenomena such as the human body, organizations, and ecosystems; for example, it is difficult to fully appreciate a day at the beach by staring at a single grain of sand. There comes a time in every discipline when essential pieces of information need to be synthesized into meaningful wholes. Many areas of management have already moved in this direction: strategic planning, manufacturing-resources planning, and career planning are some examples. Unfortunately, human resources management lags in this regard; a bits-and-pieces approach and conflicting models are still commonplace in this field.

An overview of the conceptual development of organizational behavior quickly reveals that analysis has been emphasized to the near exclusion of synthesis. As indicated on the right-hand pendulum of Exhibit 1, traditional motivation theories have

Reprinted by permission of the publisher, from *Organizational Dynamics*, Autumn 1984. Copyright © 1984 American Management Association, New York. All rights reserved.

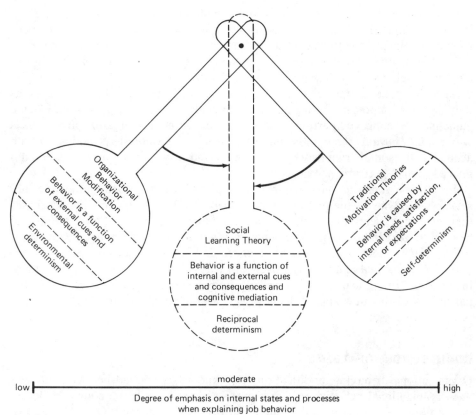

EXHIBIT 1
Conceptual pendulum of organizational behavior.

long been preoccupied with a host of complex internal causes of behavior such as needs, satisfaction, and expectations. Then, about a decade ago, we suggested a significantly different model of organizational behavior carrying the label *organizational behavior modification* (O.B. Mod.). This alternative perspective was anchored in B. F. Skinner's technology of operant conditioning and his underlying philosophy of radical behaviorism. The original conceptualization of O.B. Mod. was to make specific, on-the-job behavior occur more or less often by systematically managing *antecedent conditions* (that serve to cue the target behavior) and/or by managing *contingent consequences* that serve to encourage or discourage repetition of the target behavior. Unlike the then popular motivation theories that dealt with unobservable internal states, the external O.B. Mod. approach suggested that managers should focus on actual behavior and on factors in the environment that controlled behavior.

Both the internal and external theories of organizational behavior have made contributions to understanding and managing employees. Those who wish to manage employee behavior need to consider relevant cognitive processes such as expectations and attributions in addition to such internal states as needs and satisfaction. Similarly, behavior and its environmental cues and consequences should be considered. But because internal and external theorists alike have focused too much on analysis and not enough on synthesis, a realistic picture of employee behavior still has not emerged. Neither the internal nor the external perspective, taken alone, gives a complete picture of why employees behave as they do; more important from a managerial standpoint, neither provides adequate guidelines for improved performance at all levels of modern organizations. This is why *social learning theory,* the middle position in Exhibit 1, provides both an academically sound framework for research and a practical framework for improved human performance at work.

In taking a social learning perspective, we are not abandoning objective, observable behavior as the primary unit of analysis. However, cognitive processes that result in expectations, self-evaluative standards, and causal attributions will be used to explain how employee behavior is acquired and maintained. Covert (or internal) cues, behavior, and consequences all play an important role. It is our hope that the social learning approach will lead to a comprehensive understanding and better practical control of today's human resources. Before exploring the particulars of this new approach, however, a brief review of the O.B. Mod. approach is necessary.

CONTRIBUTIONS OF O.B. MOD.

Organizational behavior modification (also known as applied behavior analysis and organizational behavior management) seems to have had a considerable impact on human resources management during the past decade. O.B. Mod.'s primary contributions are (1) emphasis on observable employee behavior; (2) recognition of the impact that contingent consequences have on performance; (3) recognition that positive reinforcement is more effective than punishment when managing employees; and (4) a demonstrated, causal effect on the bottom-line performance of employees working in a wide variety of organizations.

Behavior Is the Key

By making instances of *behavior* the primary units of analysis, O.B. Mod. has encouraged human resources managers to deal with something they can see, record, and later use to measure progress. Managing behavior is much more useful than dealing with inferred internal states, when the aim is to improve the quantity and quality of work. For instance, which of the following managers has a better chance of affecting job performance: manager A, who says, "Joe has a bad attitude; he better shape up or ship out!" or manager B, who says, "Joe has failed to use the new computerized work station for six different tasks this week"? By pinpointing a specific behavior problem, manager B has the comparative advantage. This behavioral orientation is gaining popularity in other areas as well. For example, behaviorally anchored rating scales (BARS) are recommended for performance appraisal.

Consequences Influence Behavior

The basic premise of O.B. Mod. has been that behavior is a function of its consequences. For managers preoccupied with cognition (internal processes connected with needs, valences, or expectations), the notion of focusing on contingent environmental consequences to explain behavior is quite foreign. Yet everyday experience confirms the influence of contingent consequences. For example, busy executives give difficult assignments to their best people because they want quick results. These overworked middle managers soon learn that being a go-getter doesn't pay off, so they cut back. A manager familiar with the relationship between consequences and behavior would realize that the assignment of extra work is punishing rather than reinforcing and may bring about a decline in performance.

Behavior that is reinforced either positively (something desirable is presented) or negatively (something undesirable is withdrawn) tends to be repeated. On the other hand, behavior that is ignored or punished (something undesirable is presented, or something of value is withdrawn) tends to be replaced by behavior that pays off. As the previous example of the go-getter illustrates, the haphazard management of behavioral consequences can detract from rather than improve job performance and goal attainment.

Taking a Positive Approach

How can we improve employees' performance as well as enhance their dignity and feeling of self-worth? O.B. Mod.'s method is to increase desirable behaviors (those that contribute to goal attainment) with positive reinforcement instead of decreasing undesirable behaviors (those that diminish goal attainment) with punishment. Positive reinforcement, a term rarely heard in executive boardrooms and management circles a decade ago, has become a widely known technique. Popular books like *In Search of Excellence* and *The One Minute Manager,* which extol the virtues of positive reinforcement, have been labeled mandatory reading by enlightened executives.

Desirable and undesirable behavior (for example, being prompt versus being tardy) are reciprocal sides of the same coin; only one side can show at a time. The manager who positively reinforces desirable behaviors among employees eventually achieves the same performance improvement that the punitive manager seeks, but without the erosion of trust and goodwill and without any attendant fear, suspicion, and revenge.

One does not have to go far to uncover horror stories about punitive managers. For instance, a field sales representative recently told us how his manager had tried to "motivate" people by making the low seller for the month take home a live goat for a weekend. The implication was that the laggard was "goat of the month," and the hope was that the unfortunate employee, embarrassed by questions from neighbors and relatives, would be bullied into improved performance. Of course, the manager's punitive approach precipitated mistrust and turnover but failed to improve sales. Taking on O.B. Mod. approach, the sales representative convinced his boss to institute a pilot program of positive reinforcement (a small cash bonus) for a specific behavior (calling the office three times a day).

Significant positive results were achieved immediately. A desirable side-effect was that people felt better about themselves, their boss, and the company.

Impact on Performance Behaviors

Unlike most approaches to human resources management, O.B. Mod. has been demonstrated to have a *causal* impact on the performance behaviors of employees in a wide variety of organizations. Starting with the widely publicized Emery Air Fright experience, there have been a growing number of reported successful applications of O.B. Mod. Some of these reports are based on anecdotal or testimonial evidence—for example, the Emery Air Freight experience and most of the applications described in the recent *Handbook of Organizational Behavior Management*—but sophisticated research also shows the impact of O.B. Mod. in areas such as employee productivity, absenteeism, tardiness, safety, and sales.

Along with a number of colleagues, we focused our own research in the past ten years on the application of O.B. Mod. in manufacturing plants (small, medium, and large), retail stores, and hospitals as well as on a number of individual managers using self-management at every level in many kinds of organizations. Using such experimental designs as control groups, reversal, and multiple base lines, we found that O.B. Mod. had a dramatic, positive impact on the quantity and quality of output in manufacturing plants, on the sales performance and absence from the work station of department store clerks, and on a host of hospital performance measures, both medical (procedures accomplished, patient throughput, retake rates, posting or filing errors) and nonmedical areas (average time to repair, product waste, time to admit, and systems log-on time).

Experimental research studies have shown that executives using self-management techniques can deliberately alter their own behaviors in the areas of notifying someone when leaving the office, depending upon the boss to make decisions, spending time on the phone, filling out daily expense forms, writing a plan, following a plan, reducing stress, processing paperwork, and meeting deadlines. It has been amply demonstrated that O.B. Mod. does improve performance at different levels and in different types of organizations.

LIMITATIONS OF THE O.B. MOD. MODEL

Although the O.B. Mod. model produces positive results, it does have two limitations: (1) it excludes important cognitive processes; and (2) it does not treat the influence of antecedents on behavior. The first limitation much more than the second has led critics to call O.B. Mod. mechanistic and to question its long-term value as a realistic approach to human resources management.

Exclusion of Cognitive Processes

According to Skinner, the search for inner causes of behavior merely distracts one from identifying the environmental factors that are actually responsible for directing, shaping, and altering behavior. On the other hand, cognitive theorists insist that any theory of human behavior is deficient if it does not take into account a person's unique ability to remember, anticipate, and symbolize. After all, they argue, we are not empty-headed automatons blindly reacting to environmental stimulation. We perceive, judge, and choose; hence any approach to behavioral management should take these cognitive processes into account.

Ignored Antecedents of Behavior

Unlike the first limitation, the second limitation has been pinpointed by O.B. Mod. advocates. They note that environmental consequences have been emphasized to the near exclusion of antecedents or cues. In the original formulation of O.B. Mod., we used the three-term contingency, A → B → C (antecedent leads to behavior leads to consequence) to assist the manager in analyzing employee behavior. The antecedent in this model serves as a cue prompting the person to behave in a given way. Yet the behavior is still a function of its contingent consequence. But antecedents cue specific behavior through their association with contingent consequences. When walking down the hall at work, for example, we stop to chat with those who say things that please us and avoid those who are unpleasant. All things considered, antecedents deserve much more attention because they exercise potent *feedforward* control over a great deal of employee behavior. Extending O.B. Mod. with social learning theory overcomes these limitations of our model.

SOCIAL LEARNING THEORY

When Albert Bandura, Stanford's noted behavioral psychologist, was conducting his pioneering experiments on vicarious learning, he became convinced that cognitive functioning must not be overlooked in explaining complex human behavior. He observed that mental cues and memory aids help people learn and retain behavior more efficiently than trial-and-error shaping. This challenged operant conditioning as well as radical behaviorism. A practical example of Bandura's position is the salesperson who relies on a mental image of an apple to remember Applegate, the name of a prospective client. In Bandura's view, this way of learning is more efficient than rote memorization of clients' names in a structured training session. But, unlike the radical cognitive theorists, Bandura gives a great deal of weight to the impact of environmental cues and consequences on actual behavior. Bandura and others such as Michael Mahoney, Donald Meichenbaum, and Walter Mischel have formulated social learning theory, a theory of behavior that takes into account intrapersonal and environmental determinants.

The notion that behavior is a function of both personal and environmental factors appeared in original formulations of the social psychology of Kurt Lewin and others. Today's social learning theorists, however, stress that behavior itself (ignored by traditional social psychologists) as well as cognitive processes and environmental factors are *reciprocal determinants*. This describes a dynamic relationship in which the person neither mechanistically reacts to environmental forces nor exercises unrestricted free will. In the social learning approach, people

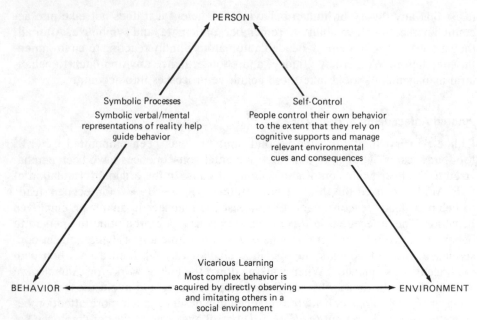

PERSON

Symbolic Processes
Symbolic verbal/mental
representations of reality help
guide behavior

Self-Control
People control their own behavior
to the extent that they rely on
cognitive supports and manage
relevant environmental
cues and consequences

Vicarious Learning
Most complex behavior is
BEHAVIOR ◄──── acquired by directly observing ────► ENVIRONMENT
and imitating others in a
social environment

EXHIBIT 2
A basic model of social learning theory.

influence their environment, which in turn influences the way they think and behave. Exhibit 2 is a summary model of the dimensions and relationships of social
learning theory (SLT).

Definition of Social Learning

Social learning refers to the fact that we acquire much of our behavior by observing and imitating others within a social context. This is not a one-way flow of
influence. According to social learning theory, people's behavior and environment influence each other. For example, at a societal level we are held accountable for obeying unpopular laws until we elect officials who will repeal or amend
them (the military draft), practice civil disobedience in order to influence legisla-
tors to change laws (Civil Rights Movement), or rise up in revolt (the Boston Tea
Party). Inherent in this complex social equation is the reciprocal influence of our
behavior, our cognitive processes, and our social environment. Sometimes individual behavior prevails; at other times the environment prevails. Meanwhile,
people perceive, judge, choose, and exercise a measure of self-control.

For modern managers who are disenchanted with traditional behavioral theories, Bandura's portrayal of SLT is particularly helpful because it improves on
popular work motivation theories and extends operant learning theory. Although
traditional work motivation theories (like Abraham Maslow's needs hierarchy) do
address the employee's need for social interaction, they fail to explain the nature

of that interaction. SLT improves upon the traditional theories by assigning a prominent role to vicarious or observational learning. Similarly, SLT extends the operant model of learning—what we have called the external approach—by explaining how the individual processes environment stimuli. This helps us understand why similar employees in similar situations often behave quite differently; the operant model is limited in its ability to explain such variations.

SLT also is quite different from work-motivation and operant-conditioning theories because it gives attention to three important processes: vicarious learning or modeling, symbolism, and self-control. By understanding the roles these three processes play in the reciprocal triangle illustrated in Exhibit 2, managers can begin to appreciate how social learning theory integrates the internal and external approaches in a way that translates into improved techniques for managing human resources.

Effectiveness of Modeling

Vicarious learning and observational learning are alternative labels for the modeling process of acquiring new behavior within the SLT framework. When compared with tedious operant shaping whereby someone is systematically reinforced for approximating a desired behavior (a machine operator is complimented by the supervisor for getting progressively closer to tolerance), modeling is much more efficient. Complex behavior can be learned quickly through this process. In fact, organizational participants, especially in the executive and managerial ranks, probably acquire far more behavior by observing and imitating behavior models than by trial-and-error shaping. Research shows that people tend to imitate models with whom they personally identify (consider the use of outdated training films). Moreover, modeled behavior that pays off with a desired consequence tends to be readily imitated (consider a "do-as-I-say, not-as-I-do" management style). There is also evidence that modeling is valuable in teaching sales techniques and other skills that were traditionally believed to be intuitive or to stem from years of experience.

Use of Symbolism

According to SLT, verbal and mental symbolism helps people to organize and store convenient representations of reality. For instance, the mnemonic phrase "red—right—returning" has reminded generations of sailors that vessels returning to port from sea should keep the red buoys on their right-hand side to avoid running aground. Furthermore, it is more efficient and in some cases safer to imagine solutions to problems and to anticipate consequences to actions than to experience everything firsthand. For today's harried executives, imagining the consequences of a stressful and unhealthy life style and taking appropriate preventive steps is certainly a better solution than experiencing a heart attack. Values, goals, beliefs, and rules are convenient symbolic guideposts for appropriate behavior. With this information, executives are challenged to systematically and proactively manage their own and others' symbolic coding and processing rather than simply to leave matters to reaction and chance.

Role of Self-Control

According to SLT, people can control their own behavior if they can cue it, support it, and reward or punish it. In other words, to the extent that we can manage our environment and cognitive processes, we can manage our own behavior. For example, an overweight manager who is tempted to eat a between-meal snack might think of how nice a new, smaller outfit would look and feel. And eliminating all snacks from the immediate work area or offering only low-calorie ones would be a helpful way of altering the environment. Eventually, when the weight goal is reached, purchasing and enjoying the new outfit will be very rewarding.

Beyond the O.B. Mod. Model

As stated earlier, the original model for O.B. Mod. utilized the A $\rightarrow$ B $\rightarrow$ C contingency. In this operant paradigm, environmental antecedents (A) were said to cue behaviors (B) that were then followed by positive or negative contingent consequences (C) in the environment. Then, according to the law of effect, a supportive, positive environment increased the frequency and magnitude of behavior whereas unsupportive, negative consequences discouraged behavior. In this model we characterized effective behavioral management as the appropriate arrangement of supportive environmental antecedents and consequences.

Now, by merging the time-honored, cognitive situation-organism-behavior contingency ((S-O-B) with the operant A-B-C contingency, we have derived an S $\leftrightarrow$ O $\leftrightarrow$ B $\leftrightarrow$ C model. This expanded model for O.B. Mod. (shown in Exhibit 3) clearly reflects the influence of social learning theory because of the interaction among the situation, organism, behavior, and consequence components. A one-way linear flow of influence lacks the dynamic interaction emphasized by SLT. It is important to recognize that even in this expanded model, overt behavior remains the primary unit of analysis, but the mediating effects of cognition along with covert cues, behavior, and consequences are now taken into consideration.

In Exhibit 3, three cognitive mediating processes are listed under the Organism portion of our expanded O.B. Mod. model. These are goal acceptance/rejection, expectations, and causal attributions. Because each of them serves as a highly personalized gatekeeper that determines which cues and consequences will prompt which particular behavior, and because they were not part of the original O.B. Mod. model, we will examine them closely.

Goal Acceptance/Rejection Goals and goal setting have been a central feature of management theory and practice since Peter Drucker coined the term "management by objectives" (MBO) 30 years ago. Researchers like Edwin Locke have proved time and again that people who have goals or objectives (preferably difficult and measurable ones) consistently outperform those who have no goals and those who are instructed to do their best. Nevertheless, conflicting research findings on goal setting still crop up, and MBO is known as both a failure and a success. From a behavioral perspective, a major stumbling block for MBO programs may be goal rejection at the individual level. An imposed goal, no matter how well conceived, is the property of the organization until the individual personally adopts it. To date, the

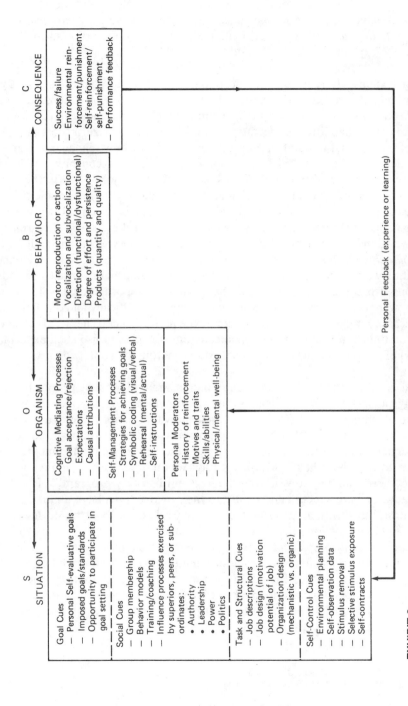

EXHIBIT 3

Expanded model for organizational behavior modification (S-O-B-C model). (From Fred Luthans & Robert Kreitner, *Organizational Behavior Modification and Beyond: An Operant and Social Learning Approach*, Glenview, Ill.: Scott, Foresman, 1985.)

173

most popular prescription for encouraging members of an organization to accept its goals is to have them help set the goals. Therefore we have included *opportunity to participate in goal setting* as a goal cue under the situation portion of the S-O-B-C model (the expanded O.B. Mod. model).

Expectations   Largely due to the popularity of Victor Vroom's and Lyman Porter and Edward Lawler's expectancy models of work motivation, the concept of expectations is fairly well established in the behavioral-management literature. In terms of probabilities, expectations vary from a low of zero (no chance) to a high of one (virtual certainty). Expectations influence how managers behave and make decisions (e.g., "Will I get a bonus this year so I can buy a new car?" "How will the new electronic office system affect my job?" "Will the new director of personnel significantly change our staffing or training policies?").

Expectancy motivation theorists carefully distinguish between effort-performance expectations and performance-reward expectations. Taking a social learning perspective, Bandura has labeled the former type *efficacy* expectations and the latter type *outcome* expectations. For example, salespeople have high efficacy expectations if they firmly believe that they are capable of closing an important sale and high outcome expectations if they believe that closing an important deal will lead to desired rewards like pay raises or promotions. Thus, high efficacy and outcome expectations are prerequisites for effective employee performance. The S-O-B-C model is intended to help managers to systematically understand and use such expectancies instead of considering them out of context or ignoring them altogether.

Causal Attributions   It is becoming increasingly clear that people have self-serving cause-and-effect models in their heads which greatly affect the way they behave. Common experience and research show that people tend to attribute successes to their ability ("I solved the problem with the new data processing program") and/or effort ("I worked hard to get the new system implemented") and failures to their bad luck ("Murphy's Law was in operation") and/or task difficulty ("there's no way to work out the bugs in this crazy program"). People who generally attribute success and failure to their own actions have an *internal* locus of control; those with an *external* locus of control generally attribute success and failure to factors beyond their control. Of course, differing attributions will affect how employees interpret and respond to cues. For example, a training film demonstrating how to use a microcomputer would probably be imitated more readily by a person who believes that ability is the key to success than by one who believes that success depends upon luck. Like goal acceptance/rejection and expectations, causal attributions are subtle but powerful cognitive gatekeepers that facilitate or hamper S-O-B-C reciprocation.

NEW O.B. MOD. TECHNIQUES FOR IMPROVING PERFORMANCE AT WORK

The insights gained from social learning theory and the S-O-B-C model will be used to examine some specific, new O.B. Mod. techniques for improving performance at work: feedforward control, feedback control, and self-management. Although elements of self-management could be subsumed under feedforward and feedback control, self-management deserves separate attention because it is a cornerstone of the social learning extension of O.B. Mod.

Feedforward Control and Management of Employee Behavior

Managers have two ways to turn plans into action: (1) they can wait for problems to arise and then try to correct them (a reactive approach); or (2) they can anticipate problems and take preventive action (a proactive approach). *Feedback* control is the term commonly applied to the first approach; the second approach can be labeled *feedforward* control. Feedforward control is acknowledged to be the better approach because it encourages managers to act in anticipation of rather than in response to a problem. Feedforward control makes it easier to prevent grievances, equipment breakdowns, and defects in goods or services. In the expanded O.B. Mod. approach, managers can exercise feedforward control over employee performance by systematically managing goal cues, social cues, and task and structural cues (see *Situation* in Exhibit 3). A supportive situation will increase the chances that the job will be done right the first time.

Goal Cues Employees with challenging and measurable goals tend to outperform those without goals. Social learning theorists have pointed out that a personal goal serves not only as a target for performance but also as a basis for assessing progress. Unfortunately, personal goals and organizational goals in complex organizations are often at odds with one another. This means that organizations must impose at least some goals on employees. Consequently, participation in goal setting is important because it increases the chances of goal acceptance. Managers and executives should encourage their people to set their own performance goals and accept imposed goals by having them participate. If these personal or participative goals are measurable in behavioral terms, they will serve as the focal point for the entire S-O-B-C process.

Social Cues Because members of organizations acquire much of their behavior by observing others (social learning), managers can ensure that these people are exposed to constructive rather than destructive behavior models. Transferring a potentially productive employee away from the influence of troublemakers is an obvious way of rearranging the social cues. More formal feedforward control of employee performance can be achieved by incorporating modeling into training programs. Training programs based on observation of behavior models, structured practice of specific behaviors, and positive reinforcement for successful imitation have proved much more effective than lectures or discussions.

Every manager is a powerful behavior model for subordinates, regardless of his or her intentions or desires. "Do-as-I-say, not-as-I-do" managers need to learn the truth of the American Indian lament: "What you do speaks so loudly that I cannot hear what you say." Executives and managers influence subordinates when they exercise authority, leadership, and power. A manager who smokes while leaning against a no-smoking sign but tries to enforce smoking policies loses credibility. High-level Japanese managers who roll up their sleeves and pitch in when necessary understand the value of a "do-as-I-do" approach.

Task and Structural Cues A healthy measure of feedforward control can be exercised by making sure that employees have a clear idea of what is expected of them. In addition to measurable objectives, clear and concise job descriptions can get employees headed in the right direction. Beyond that, the motivating potential of the work itself can be enhanced through progressive job design. As researchers have pointed out in recent years, meaningful jobs that offer a sense of personal responsibility and knowledge of results tend to cue better performance than do fragmented, boring, and repetitious jobs. Moreover, as it has been forcefully pointed out by the best-selling book, *In Search of Excellence,* employees who desire creative latitude will respond more favorably to fluid and flexible organic structure than to rigid, bureaucratic, mechanistic structures.

Maintaining and Improving Behavior through Feedback Control

The influence of social learning in the expanded O.B. Mod. model is clearly evident in the preceding discussion of feedforward control. Social learning places much emphasis on situational cues. These cues prompt desirable behavior by enhancing goal acceptance, raising efficacy and outcome expectations, and personalizing causal attributions. On the other hand, feedback control reflects the influence of Skinner's operant conditioning, which emphasizes that behavior is a function of its consequences. Feedback control of employee behavior involves the systematic management of consequences.

Four primary sources of consequences are listed in the consequence portion of Exhibit 3. Success, positive reinforcement from relevant others, self-reinforcement, and constructive performance feedback all strengthen behavior. Similarly, behaviors that fail or that are punished or ignored by relevant others, self-punished, or followed by negative or inadequate feedback on performance are weakened. Managers are challenged to arrange, within an S-O-B-C framework, a supportive consequence climate for productive behavior. Good intentions are insufficient, and productive behavior that is ignored or not rewarded eventually gives way to counterproductive behavior that has more immediate payoffs for the individual. Kenneth Blanchard and Spencer Johnson, in *The One Minute Manager,* underscore positive reinforcement in managing behavior when they say, "catch employees doing something *right.*" This is feedback control through positive reinforcement.

The Use of Self-Management

A unique contribution of social learning theory is its emphasis on self-management. This bottom-up approach stands in marked contrast to our conventional, top-down theories of management. Managing has traditionally been conceptualized and practiced as something a superior *does to* an organization, a group, or a subordinate. The attention that leadership theories have received throughout the years clearly shows the entrenchment of this top-down bias. Even the so-called democratic or participative leadership styles fail to break out of the top-down rut because they imply that management *lets* subordinates participate only if and when it is convenient.

The S-O-B-C model is an alternative: it includes a system of cues, cognitive processes, and consequences that help people manage their own behavior. We believe that self-management is the most efficient form of management because it precludes the need for costly, close supervision. With this in mind, let's take a close look at the ways that managers can use self-control cues, self-management processes, and self-reinforcement/self-punishment.

Self-Control Cues   Members of organizations can do a number of things to create a physical/social environment that cues their own desirable behavior and discourages unwanted behavior. This *environmental planning* can take the form of one or a combination of the following techniques.

1 *Self-observation data.* By observing and recording how often a target behavior occurs, a participant can accomplish two things: (1) obtain an objective measurement of the behavior, and (2) formulate a self-management plan. For example, a manager who is always "putting out fires" and never seems to get anything done might find it instructive to keep track of interruptions by unscheduled phone calls. Hard data would permit an objective assessment of the problem and provide a rationale for schedule adjustments.

2 *Stimulus removal.* This self-management technique involves the removal of cues that prompt unwanted behavior. For instance, an engineer who is given to daydreaming may find it helpful to remove pictures of family members or favorite vacation spots and other distracting stimuli from the work area.

3 *Selective stimulus exposure.* Instead of eliminating a disruptive cue from the environment, one can fall back on selective exposure. A manager who is disrupted by unscheduled visits because of an unrestricted open-door policy, for example, might trim the open-door period to a stated hour in the morning and in the afternoon. Similarly, disruptive phone calls can be channeled through a secretary or an answering device.

4 *Self-contracts.* A self-contract is an if-then deal with oneself. For instance, an executive might hold off working on a preferred project until a less preferred one is completed. Self-contracts and personal goal setting go hand in hand.

Self-Management Processes   From a social learning perspective of O.B. Mod. there are four cognitive processes that can facilitate self-management.

1 *Strategies for achieving goals.* Goal setting is a recognized prerequisite of effective management, but strategies and action plans need to be formulated if goals are to become reality. Managers at all levels can enhance their self-management skills by systematically considering strategies and formulating action plans aimed at accomplishing their self-improvement goals.

2 *Symbolic coding.* Visual and verbal codes can help people remember things of importance. A mental image of a newspaper picture showing someone injured, for example, could serve as a reminder to take out additional employee accident insurance. As a verbal code phrase, like "Monday/Fun day" might remind a manager who is driving home on Friday to file a budget request on Monday.

3 *Rehearsal.* Whether covert or overt, rehearsal of desired behavior prepares managers to deal with unfamiliar situations. It is no accident that successful salespeople anticipate customer questions or complaints and mentally rehearse replies. Practice, both in one's thoughts and in reality, is a cornerstone of successful selling and other crucial management skills (dealing with problem employees, or selling middle managers on a new idea).

4 *Self-instruction.* Cognitive supports in the form of self-instruction can help managers do the right thing at the right time. Many stress-management programs encourage executives to use self-instruction that prompts them to relax, slow down, do one thing at a time, and stick to priorities.

Self-Reinforcement/Self-Punishment

Both covert and overt behaviors need positive consequences if they are to be sustained and strengthened. When combined with the techniques just discussed, self-granted rewards can lead to self-improvement. But as failed dieters and smokers can attest, there are short-run as well as long-run influences on self-reinforcement. For the overeater, the immediate gratification of eating has more influence over behavior than the promise of a new wardrobe. The same sort of dilemma plagues procrastinators. Consequently, one needs to weave a powerful web of cues, cognitive supports, and internal and external consequences to win the tug-of-war with status-quo payoffs. Primarily because it is so easy to avoid, self-punishment tends to be ineffectual. As with managing the behavior of others, positive instead of negative consequences are recommended for effective self-management.

CONCLUSION

Social learning theory is practical. It provides a framework for *understanding* and *controlling* human resources in today's organizations. This framework includes internal processes as well as the behavior and the antecedent or consequent environmental contingencies. To date, behavioral theories have suffered from an imbalance, and managers have had to rely on disjointed theories and techniques: need theory, job design, expectancy theory, goal setting, operant theory, and positive reinforcement. Now, with social learning theory, we finally have a *balanced* and *systematic* way of understanding employee behavior as well as a set of proven and potentially powerful techniques for controlling employee behavior and self-behavior for the purpose of improved performance.

American organizations are still among the most productive in the world largely because of our technology. Organizations in the Far East and even in Western Europe have made substantial gains in many industries largely because they are better than we are at human resources management. In the United States the difference between good and excellent organizations can be largely attributed to how people are managed.

A social learning approach and its accompanying techniques may provide the basis for increasing the productivity of our human resources and thus may provide the impetus for getting us back on track as the industrial leader of the world. For example, modeling can have a revolutionary impact on training at all levels. More objective behavior-based rather than trait-based performance evaluations can be used to revamp the appraisal systems currently under fire. But the real key to improvements may be found in new ways managers and executives look at and actually manage the "front end" (antecedents) and the "back end" (consequences) of their people's performances.

On the front end, managers have traditionally done a good job on task and structural cues. (See Exhibit 3.) Considerable time and energy have been devoted to job descriptions, job design (including quality-of-work-life), and organization design and development. But the goal cues, the social cues, and the self-control cues identified in Exhibit 3 have been largely ignored. Goal setting and participation are practical goal cues; quality circles and team-oriented and group-oriented leadership styles are practical social cues; and screening techniques, data display boards, and self-goals/self-contracts are practical self-control cues.

These new approaches to front-end management, according to social learning theory, provide the setting in which productive behaviors can occur. Once the behaviors are elicited by these cues, however, there must be contingent consequences that sustain and increase the resulting productive behaviors. In other words, the contingent reward systems of the organization and of individual managers are critical to the performance of the people in the organization.

The answer to back-end management is not necessarily in more exotic profit-sharing or bonus plans, but instead may be found in contingent performance-feedback systems that are objective, immediate, positive, and visual; supervisor/manager attention and recognition; and, ultimately, deliberate self-rewards manifested as a sense of accomplishment and the feelings that go with a job well done.

Social Cognitive Theory of Organizational Management

Robert Wood
Albert Bandura

Many theories have been proposed over the years to explain human psychosocial functioning. They differ in the conceptions of human nature they adopt and in what they regard as the basic determinants and mechanisms of human motivation and action. Human behavior often has been explained in terms of one-sided determinism. In such models of unidirectional causation, behavior is depicted as being shaped and controlled either by environmental influences or by internal dispositions. Social cog-

From *Academy of Management Review*, 1989, **14**(3), 361–383. Adapted by permission.

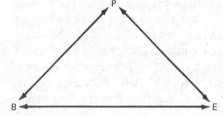

FIGURE 1
Schematization of the relations among behavior (B), cognitive and other personal factors (P), and the external environment (E).

nitive theory explains psychosocial functioning in terms of triadic reciprocal causation (Bandura, 1986). In this model of reciprocal determinism, behavior, cognitive, and other personal factors and environmental events operate as interacting determinants that influence each other bidirectionally (see Figure 1). Reciprocality does not mean that the different sources of influences are of equal strength. Nor do the reciprocal influences occur simultaneously. It takes time for a causal factor to exert its influence and to activate reciprocal influences. Because of the bidirectionality of influence, people are both products and producers of their environment.

This article focuses on how personal factors contribute to this dynamic transaction in the management of organizations. In the analysis of the personal determinants in this interactional causal structure, social cognitive theory accords a central role to cognitive, vicarious, self-regulatory, and self-reflective processes. Three aspects of social cognitive theory are especially relevant to the organizational field (Bandura, 1988d): the development of people's cognitive, social, and behavioral competencies through mastery modeling, the cultivation of people's beliefs in their capabilities so that they will use their talents effectively, and the enhancement of people's motivation through goal systems.

DEVELOPMENT OF COMPETENCIES THROUGH MASTERY MODELING

Psychological theories traditionally have emphasized learning through the effects of one's actions. If knowledge and skills could be acquired only through direct experience, the process of human development would be greatly retarded, not to mention exceedingly tedious, costly, and hazardous. Fortunately, people can expand their knowledge and skills on the basis of information conveyed by modeling influences. Indeed, virtually all learning phenomena resulting from direct experience can occur vicariously by observing people's behavior and the consequences of it (Bandura, 1986; Rosenthal & Zimmerman, 1978).

Mechanisms Governing Modeling

Observational learning is governed by four component processes. *Attentional processes* determine what people selectively observe in the profusion of modeling influences and what information they extract from ongoing modeled activities. People cannot be much influenced by observed accomplishments if they do not remember them. A second major subfunction governing observational learning concerns cognitive *representational processes*. Retention involves an active process of transforming and restructuring information about events in the form of rules and conceptions. Retention is greatly aided when people symbolically transform the modeled information into memory codes and mentally rehearse the coded information.

In the third subfunction in modeling—*behavioral production processes*—symbolic conceptions are translated into appropriate courses of action. This is achieved through a conception-matching process, in which people's centrally guided patterns of behavior are enacted and the adequacy of their actions is compared against their conceptual model (Carroll & Bandura, 1987). Individuals then modify their behavior on the basis of the comparative information in order to achieve close correspondence between their conceptions and their action. The richer the repertoire and subskills that people possess, the easier it is to integrate these skills in the production of new behavior patterns.

The fourth subfunction in modeling concerns *motivational processes*. Social cognitive theory distinguishes between acquisition and performance because people do not do everything they learn. Performance of observationally learned behavior is influenced by three major types of incentive motivators—*direct, vicarious,* and *self-produced*. People are most likely to adopt modeled strategies if the strategies produce valued outcomes, rather than unrewarding or punishing effects. The observed cost and benefits that are accrued to others influence observers' adoption of modeled patterns in much the same way as do directly experienced consequences. People are motivated by the successes of others who are similar to themselves, but they are discouraged from pursuing behaviors that they have seen often result in adverse consequences. Personal standards of conduct provide a further source of motivation. The self-evaluations people generate about their own behavior regulate which observationally learned activities they are most likely to pursue. They express what they find self-satisfying and reject what they disapprove of.

Modeling is not merely a process of behavioral mimicry. People may adopt functional patterns of behavior, which constitute proven skills and established customs, in essentially the same form as they are exemplified. However, for many activities, subskills must be improvised to suit changing circumstances. Modeling influences also convey rules for generative and innovative behavior. In this form of abstract modeling, observers extract the rules governing the specific judgments or actions exhibited by others. Once they learn the rules, they can use them to judge events and to generate courses of action that go beyond what they have seen or heard. Much human learning is aimed at developing cognitive skills on how to acquire and use knowledge for different purposes. Observational learning of thinking skills is greatly facilitated if models verbalize their thought processes in conjunction with their action strategies (Bandura, 1986; Meichenbaum, 1984).

Guided Mastery Modeling

Mastery modeling has been widely used with good results to develop intellectual, social, and behavioral competencies (Bandura, 1986, 1988d). The method that produces the best results includes three major elements. First, the appropriate skills are modeled to convey the basic competencies. Effective modeling teaches people general rules and strategies for dealing with different situations, rather than specific responses. People need to learn how the rules can be widely applied and adjusted to fit changing conditions. Modeling influences must be designed to build self-assurance in one's capabilities as well as to convey skills. The impact that modeling has on beliefs about one's capabilities is greatly increased by one's perceived similarity to the models.

The second aspect involves guided skill mastery. After individuals understand the new skills, they need guidance and opportunities to perfect them. Initially, they test their newly acquired skills in simulated situations in which they need not fear making mistakes or appearing inadequate. This is best achieved by role-playing, in which they practice handling the types of situations they must manage in their work environment and they receive instructive feedback. The feedback that is most informative and helps to achieve the greatest improvements is based on corrective modeling.

Modeling and guided performance under simulated conditions are well suited for creating competencies, but it is unlikely that the new skills will be used for long, unless they prove useful when they are put into practice in work situations. The third aspect of mastery modeling is a transfer program aimed at providing self-direct success. People must experience sufficient success when using what they have learned in order to believe both in themselves and the value of the new ways. This is best achieved by a transfer program, in which newly acquired skills are first tried on the job in situations that are likely to produce good results. As individuals gain skill and confidence in handling easier situations, they gradually take on more difficult problems. If they do not gain sufficient success to convince themselves of their new effectiveness, they will apply the new skills weakly and inconsistently, and they will rapidly abandon their newly acquired skills when they either fail to get quick results or experience difficulties.

Mastery modeling programs have been successfully applied to help supervisors develop competencies. Mastery modeling produces lasting improvements in supervisors' skills (Latham & Saari, 1979). Simply explaining to supervisors the rules and giving them strategies on how to handle problems on the job without using modeling and guided practice does not improve their supervisory competencies. To enhance competencies, people need instructive modeling, guided practice with corrective feedback, and help in transferring new skills to everyday situations. Porras and his colleagues have shown that mastery modeling affects the morale and productivity of organizations as well as supervisors' skills (Porras et al., 1982). Supervisors who had the benefit of the modeling program improved and maintained their supervisory problem-solving skills, as rated by their employees. The plant in which the modeling program was applied had a lower absentee rate, lower turnover of employees, and a higher level of productivity in follow-up assessments.

SELF-EFFICACY REGULATORY MECHANISM

In social cognitive theory (Bandura, 1986, 1988a), self-regulation of motivation and performance attainments is governed by several self-regulatory mechanisms that operate together. One of the mechanisms that occupies a central role in this regulatory process works through people's beliefs in their personal efficacy. Perceived self-efficacy concerns people's beliefs in their capabilities to mobilize the motivation, cognitive resources, and courses of action needed to exercise control over events in their lives. There is a difference between possessing skills and being able to use them well and consistently under difficult circumstances. To be successful, one not only must possess the required skills, but also a resilient self-belief in one's capabilities to exercise control over events to accomplish desired goals. People with the same skills may, therefore, perform poorly, adequately, or extraordinarily, depending on whether their self-beliefs of efficacy enhance or impair their motivation and problem-solving efforts.

Sources of Self-Efficacy Beliefs

People's beliefs about their efficacy can be instilled and strengthened in four principal ways. The most effective way individuals develop a strong sense of efficacy is through *mastery experiences*. Performance successes strengthen self-beliefs of capability. Failures create self-doubts. However, if people experience only easy successes, they come to expect quick results and are easily discouraged by failure. To gain a resilient sense of efficacy, people must have experience in overcoming obstacles through perseverant effort. Some setbacks and difficulties in human pursuits serve a useful purpose in teaching that success usually requires sustained effort. After people become assured of their capabilities through repeated successes, they can manage setbacks and failures without being adversely affected by them.

The second way to strengthen self-beliefs is through *modeling*. Proficient models build self-beliefs of capability by conveying to observers effective strategies for managing different situations. Modeling also affects self-efficacy beliefs through a social comparison process. People partly judge their capabilities in comparison with others. Seeing similar others succeed by sustained effort raises observers' beliefs about their own capabilities, whereas observing similar others fail despite high effort lowers observers' judgments of their own capabilities and undermines their efforts.

Social persuasion is a third way of increasing people's beliefs that they possess the capabilities to achieve what they seek. If people receive realistic encouragements, they will be more likely to exert greater effort and to become successful than if they are troubled by self-doubts. However, if their beliefs of personal efficacy are raised to unrealistic levels, they run the risk of failures that undermine their perceptions of personal efficacy. Successful motivators and efficacy builders do more than convey positive appraisals. In addition to raising people's beliefs in their capabilities, they assign tasks to them in ways that bring success and avoid placing them prematurely in situations in which they are likely to fail. To ensure progress in personal development, success should be measured in terms of self-improvement, rather than through triumphs over others.

People also rely partly on judgments of their *physiological states* when they assess their capabilities. They read their emotional arousal and tension as signs of vulnerability to poor performance. In activities involving strength and stamina, people judge their fatigue, aches, and pains as signs of physical incapability. The fourth way of modifying self-beliefs of efficacy is for people to enhance their physical status, to reduce their stress levels, or to alter their dysfunctional construals of somatic information.

Diverse Effects of Self-Efficacy Beliefs

People's beliefs in their efficacy can affect their psychological well-being and performance through several intervening processes (Bandura, in press-a). People can exert some influence over their lives through the environments they select and the environments they create. One's judgments of personal efficacy affect one's choice of activities and environments. People tend to avoid activities and situations they believe will exceed their coping capabilities, but they readily undertake challenging activities and pick social environments they judge themselves capable of managing. The social influences in the selected environments can set the direction of personal development through the competencies, values, and interests these influences promote. This process is well illustrated in research on the impact that perceived self-efficacy has on choice of career paths. The stronger the people's self-beliefs of efficacy, the more career options they consider to be possible and the better they prepare themselves educationally for different occupational pursuits (Betz & Hackett, 1986; Lent & Hackett, 1987; Miura, 1987). People often restrict their career options because they believe they lack the necessary capabilities, although they have the actual ability. This self-limitation arises more from self-doubts, rather than from inability. Women are especially prone to limit their interests and range of career options through the self-beliefs that they lack the necessary capabilities for occupations that are traditionally dominated by men, even when they do not differ from men in actual ability.

People's self-beliefs of efficacy also determine their level of motivation, which is reflected in how much effort they will exert and how long they will persevere. The stronger the belief in their capabilities, the greater and more persistent are their efforts (Bandura, 1988a). When faced with difficulties, people who have self-doubts about their capabilities slacken their efforts or abort their attempts prematurely and quickly settle for mediocre solutions. Those who have a strong belief in their capabilities exert greater effort to master the challenge (Bandura & Cervone, 1983, 1986; Cervone & Peake, 1986; Jacobs, Prentice-Dunn, & Rogers, 1984; Weinberg, Gould, & Jackson, 1979). Strong perseverance usually pays off in performance accomplishments. Studies of manufacturing industries indicate that the impact that training programs have on the acceptance of production goals and level of productivity is partly mediated by changes in employee's self-beliefs of efficacy (Earley, 1986).

People's self-beliefs of efficacy affect how much stress and depression they experience in threatening or taxing situations, as well as their level of motivation. People who believe they can exercise control over potential threats do not conjure up apprehensive cognitions and, therefore, are not perturbed by them. But those who believe they cannot manage potential difficulties experience high levels of stress. They tend to dwell on their deficiencies and view many aspects of their environment as threatening (Ozer & Bandura, 1989). Disbelief in one's capabilities to attain valued goals that affect one's sense of self-worth or to secure things that bring satisfaction to one's life also creates depression (Bandura, 1988a; Holahan & Holahan, 1987a, b; Kanfer & Zeiss, 1983). Through inefficacious thought, such people distress and depress themselves and constrain and impair their level of functioning (Bandura, 1988b, 1988c; Lazarus & Folkman, 1984; Meichenbaum, 1977; Sarason, 1975).

Self-beliefs of efficacy also affect thought patterns that may be self-aiding or self-hindering. These cognitive effects take various forms. Much human behavior is regulated by forethought in the form of cognized goals. Personal goal setting is influenced by one's self-appraisal of capabilities. The stronger the perceived self-efficacy, the higher the goals people set for themselves and the firmer are their commitments to these goals (Bandura & Cervone, 1986; Locke, Frederick, Lee, & Bobko, 1984; Taylor, Locke, Lee, & Gist, 1984). Many activities involve analytic judgments that enable people to predict and control events in probabilistic environments. Strong belief in one's problem-solving capabilities fosters efficient analytic thinking. And finally, people's perceptions of their efficacy influence the types of anticipatory scenarios they construct and reiterate. Highly self-efficacious individuals visualize success scenarios that provide positive guides for performance, whereas those who judge themselves as inefficacious are more inclined to visualize failure scenarios, which undermine performance. One's perceived self-efficacy and cognitive simulation affect each other bidirectionally. People's high sense of efficacy fosters cognitive constructions of effective actions, and people's cognitive reiteration of efficacious courses of action strengthens their self-beliefs of efficacy (Bandura & Adams, 1977; Kazdin, 1979).

The sociocognitive benefits of a sense of personal efficacy do not arise simply from the incantation of capability. Saying something is so should not be confused with believing it. Self-efficacy beliefs are the product of a process of self-persuasion that relies on diverse sources of efficacy information that must be selected, weighted, and integrated (Bandura, 1986). If people's self-efficacy beliefs are firmly established, they remain resilient to adversity. In contrast, individuals with weakly held self-beliefs are highly vulnerable to change, and negative experiences readily reinstate their disbelief in their capabilities.

SELF-REGULATION OF MOTIVATION AND ACTION THROUGH GOAL SYSTEMS

Social cognitive theory also emphasizes human capacities for self-direction and self-motivation (Bandura, 1988a). The self-regulation of motivation and action operates partly through people's internal standards and their evaluations of their own behavior. People seek self-satisfactions from fulfilling valued goals, and they are motivated by discontent with substandard performances. Thus, discrepancies between behavior and personal standards generate self-reactive influences, which serve as motivators and guides for action designed to achieve desired results. Through self-evaluative reactions, people keep their conduct in line with their personal standards.

Hierarchical Dual Control Mechanism

Many theories of motivation and self-regulation are founded on a negative feedback control model (Carver & Scheier, 1981; Kanfer, 1977; Lord & Hanges,

1987). This type of system functions as a motivator and regulator of action through a discrepancy reduction mechanism. Perceived discrepancy between performance and an internal standard triggers action to reduce the incongruity. In negative feedback control, if the performance matches the standard, the person does nothing. A regulatory process in which matching a standard occasions inactivity does not characterize human self-motivation. Such a feedback control system would produce circular action that leads nowhere. In fact, people transcend feedback loops by setting new challenges for themselves.

Human self-motivation relies on *discrepancy production* as well as on *discrepancy reduction*. It requires both *active control* and *reactive control* (Bandura, 1988a; in press-b). People initially motivate themselves through active control by first setting valued standards that create a state of disequilibrium and then by mobilizing their effort on the basis of what it would take to accomplish what they seek. Feedback control comes into play in one's subsequent adjustments of effort to achieve desired results. After people attain the standards they have been pursuing, they generally set higher standards for themselves. Their adoption of further challenges creates new motivating discrepancies to be mastered. Thus, self-motivation involves a dual control mechanism that operates through discrepancy production, which is followed by discrepancy reduction.

Diverse Effects of Goals

Many of the activities that people perform are aimed at obtaining future outcomes. Therefore, they must create guides and motivators in the present for activities that lead to outcomes in the future. This is achieved by adopting goals and evaluating one's progress in relation to those goals. Goals can improve individuals' psychological well-being and accomplishments in several ways. First, goals have strong motivational effects. Goals provide a sense of purpose and direction, and they raise and sustain the level of effort needed to reach them. When people are unclear about what they are trying to accomplish, their motivation is low and their efforts are poorly directed. Investigations of varied domains of functioning under both laboratory and naturalistic conditions provide substantial converging evidence that explicit, challenging goals enhance and sustain people's motivation (Latham & Lee, 1986; Locke, Shaw, Saari, & Latham, 1981; Mento, Steel, & Karren, 1987).

Goals not only guide and motivate performance, they also help to build people's beliefs in their capabilities. Without standards against which to measure their performances, people have little basis either for judging how they are doing or for evaluating their capabilities. Subgoals serve this purpose well (Bandura & Schunk, 1981). Success in attaining challenging subgoals increases people's self-beliefs in their capabilities. Accomplishing challenging goals also creates self-satisfaction and increases one's interest in what one is doing. The closer the attainments match valued goals, the greater are the positive self-reactions (Bandura & Cervone, 1986; Locke, Cartledge, & Knerr, 1970). Goals have these beneficial effects when they serve as challenges, rather than as onerous dictates.

The beneficial effects of goals are partly determined by how far into the future they are set. Short-term, or proximal, goals raise one's effort and direct what one does during the short run. Distant goals are too far removed in time to be effective self-motivators. Usually, there are too many competing influences in everyday life for distant aims to exert much control over one's current behavior. Motivation is best regulated by long-range goals that set the course for one's endeavors combined with a series of attainable subgoals that guides and sustains the efforts along the way (Bandura & Schunk, 1981; Bandura & Simon, 1977; Morgan, 1985). Making complex tasks manageable by breaking them down into a series of subgoals also helps to reduce one's self-demoralization through high aspiration. A person's accomplishment may indicate significant progress when evaluated against a proximal subgoal, but it may appear disappointing if compared against long-range lofty aspirations. People can be making good progress but deriving little sense of accomplishment because of the wide disparity between current standing and distal aspiration.

Recent research into the effects that goals have on complex decision making has shown that challenging goals lead people to use more effort in the development of strategies (Earley, Wojnaroski, & Prest, 1987). However, challenging goals also may lead to suboptimal cognitive processing (Huber, 1985) and the selection of less effective strategies (Earley, Connolly, & Ekegren, in press). Managerial goals that are difficult to attain increase the likelihood of failure and one's vulnerability to self-debilitating modes of thought.

Self-Influence Governing Cognitive Motivation

Motivation based on personal standards or goals involves a cognitive comparison process. By making self-satisfaction conditional on matching adopted goals, people give direction to their actions and create self-incentives to help them persist in their effort until their performances match their goals. The motivational effects do not stem from the goals themselves, but rather from people responding evaluatively to their own behavior. Their goals specify the conditional requirements for positive self-evaluation.

Activation of self-evaluation processes through internal comparison requires both comparative factors—a personal standard and knowledge of the level of one's own performance. Neither performance knowledge without goals, nor goals without performance knowledge has any lasting motivational impact (Bandura & Cervone, 1983; Becker, 1978; Strang, Lawrence, & Fowler, 1978). However, the combined influence of goals and performance feedback heightens motivation.

Cognitive motivation based on goal intentions is mediated by three types of self-influences: affective self-evaluation, perceived self-efficacy for goal attainment, and adjustment of personal standards. As already noted, goals motivate by enlisting self-evaluative involvement in the activity, and perceived self-efficacy determines whether discrepancies between standards and attainments are motivating or discouraging. The goals people set for themselves at the outset of an endeavor are likely to change, depending on the pattern and level of progress they are making (Campion & Lord, 1982). Individuals may maintain their original goal, they may lower their sights, or they may adopt an even more challenging goal. Thus, the third constituent, self-influence in the ongoing regulation of motivation, concerns the readjustment of one's goals in light of one's attainments. Taken together, these self-reactive influences account for a major share of the variation in motivation under different goal structures (Bandura & Cervone, 1983, 1986).

Concluding Remarks

The value of psychological theory is judged not only by its explanatory and predictive power, but also by its operational power to improve human functioning. Social cognitive theory provides a conceptual framework for clarifying the psychological mechanisms through which social-structural factors are linked to organizational performance. Within the model of triadic reciprocal causation, both personal and organizational factors operate through a bidirectionality of influence. Many conceptual systems are dressed up in appealing terminology, but they remain prescriptively ambiguous on how to effect psychosocial changes. Social cognitive theory provides explicit guidelines about how to equip people with the competencies, the self-regulatory capabilities, and the resilient sense of efficacy that will enable them to enhance both their well-being and their accomplishments.

REFERENCES

Bandura, A. (1986) *Social foundations of thought and action: A social cognitive theory.* Englewood Cliffs, NJ: Prentice-Hall.

Bandura, A. (1988a) Self-regulation of motivation and action through goal systems. In V. Hamilton, G. H. Bower, & N. H. Frijda (Eds.), *Cognitive perspectives on emotion and motivation* (pp. 37–61). Dordrecht, Netherlands: Kluwer Academic Publishers.

Bandura, A. (1988b) Perceived self-efficacy: Exercise of control through self-belief. In J. P. Dauwalder, M. Perrez, & V. Hobi (Eds.), *Annual series of European research in behavior therapy* (Vol. 2, pp. 27–59). Lisse, Netherlands: Swets & Zeitlinger.

Bandura, A. (1988c) Self-efficacy conception of anxiety. *Anxiety Research,* 1, 77–98.

Bandura, A. (1988d) Organizational applications of social cognitive theory. *Australian Journal of Management,* 13, 137–164.

Bandura, A. (in press-a) Reflections on nonability determinants of competence. In J. Kolligan, Jr., & R. J. Sternberg (Eds.), *Competence considered: Perceptions of competence and incompetence across the lifespan.* New Haven, CT: Yale University Press.

Bandura, A. (in press-b) Human agency in social cognitive theory. *American Psychologist.*

Bandura, A., & Adams, N. E. (1977) Analysis of self-efficacy theory of behavioral change. *Cognitive Therapy and Research,* 1, 287–308.

Bandura, A., & Cervone, D. (1983) Self-evaluative and self-efficacy mechanisms governing the motivational effects of goal systems. *Journal of Personality and Social Psychology,* 45, 1017–1028.

Bandura, A., & Cervone, D. (1986) Differential engagement of self-reactive influences in cognitive motivation. *Organizational Behavior and Human Decision Processes,* 38, 92–113.

Bandura, A., & Schunk, D. H. (1981) Cultivating competence, self-efficacy and intrinsic interest through proximal self-motivation. *Journal of Personality and Social Psychology,* 41, 586–598.

Bandura, A., & Simon, K. M. (1977) The role of proximal intentions in self-regulation of refractory behavior. *Cognitive Therapy and Research,* 1, 177–193.

Becker, L. J. (1978) Joint effect of feedback and goal setting on performance: A field study of residential energy conservation. *Journal of Applied Psychology,* 63, 428–433.

Betz, N. E., & Hackett, G. (1986) Applications of self-efficacy theory to understanding career choice behavior. *Journal of Social and Clinical Psychology,* 4, 279–289.

Campion, M. A., & Lord, R. G. (1982). A control systems conceptualization of the goal-setting and changing process. *Organizational Behavior and Human Performance,* 30, 265–287.

Carroll, W. R., & Bandura, A. (1987) Translating cognition into action: The role of visual guidance in observational learning. *Journal of Motor Behavior,* 19, 385–398.

Carver, C. S., & Scheier, M. F. (1981) *Attention and self-regulation: A control-theory approach to human behavior.* New York: Springer-Verlag.

Cervone, D., & Peake, P. K. (1986) Anchoring, efficacy, and action: The influence of judgmental heuristics on self-efficacy judgments and behavior. *Journal of Personality and Social Psychology,* 50, 492–501.

Earley, P. C. (1986) Supervisors and shop stewards as sources of contextual information in goal setting: A comparison of the United States with England. *Journal of Applied Psychology,* 71, 111–117.

Earley, P. C., Connolly, T., & Ekegren, C. (in press) Goals, strategy development and task performance: Some limits on the efficacy of goal-setting. *Journal of Applied Psychology.*

Earley, P. C., Wojnaroski, P., & Prest, W. (1987) Task planning and energy expended: Exploration of how goals affect performance. *Journal of Applied Psychology,* 72, 107–114.

Holahan, C. K., & Holahan, C. J. (1987a) Self-efficacy, social support, and depression in aging: A longitudinal analysis. *Journal of Gerontology,* 42, 65–68.

Holahan, C. K., & Holahan, C. J. (1987b) Life stress, hassles, and self-efficacy in aging: A replication and extension. *Journal of Applied Social Psychology,* 17, 574–592.

Huber, V. L. (1985) Effects of task difficulty, goal-setting and strategy on performance of a heuristic task. *Journal of Applied Psychology,* 70, 492–504.

Jacobs, B., Prentice-Dunn, S., & Rogers, R. W. (1984) Understanding persistence: An interface of control theory and self-efficacy theory. *Basic and Applied Social Psychology,* 5, 333–347.

Kanfer, F. H. (1977) The many faces of self-control, or behavior modification changes its focus. In R. B. Stuart (Ed.), *Behavioral self-management* (pp. 1–48). New York: Brunner/Mazel.

Kanfer, R., & Zeiss, A. M. (1983) Depression, interpersonal standard-setting, and judgments of self-efficacy. *Journal of Abnormal Psychology,* 92, 319–329.

Kazdin, A. E. (1979) Imagery elaboration and self-efficacy in the covert modeling treatment of unassertive behavior. *Journal of Consulting and Clinical Psychology,* 47, 725–733.

Latham, G. P., & Lee, T. W. (1986) Goal setting. In E. A. Locke (Ed.), *Generalizing from laboratory to field settings* (pp. 101–117). Lexington, MA: Heath.

Latham, G. P., & Saari, L. M. (1979) Application of social learning theory to training supervisors through behavioral modeling. *Journal of Applied Psychology,* 64, 239–246.

Lazarus, R. S., & Folkman, S. (1984) *Stress, appraisal, and coping.* New York: Springer.

Lent, R. W., & Hackett, G. (1987) Career self-efficacy: Empirical status and future directions. *Journal of Vocational Behavior,* 30, 347–382.

Locke, E. A., Cartledge, N., & Knerr, C. S. (1970) Studies of the relationships between satisfaction, goal setting, and performance. *Organizational Behavior and Human Performance, 5,* 135–158.

Locke, E. A., Frederick, E., Lee, C., & Bobko, P. (1984) Effect of self-efficacy, goals, and task strategies on task performance. *Journal of Applied Psychology, 69,* 241–251.

Locke, E. A., Shaw, K. N., Saari, L. M., & Latham, G. P. (1981) Goal setting and task performance: 1969–1980. *Psychological Bulletin, 90,* 125–152.

Lord, R. G., & Hanges, P. J. (1987) A control system model of organizational motivation: Theoretical development and applied implications. *Behavioral Science, 32,* 161–178.

Meichenbaum, D. H. (1977) *Cognitive-behavior modification: An integrative approach.* New York: Plenum Press.

Meichenbaum, D. (1984) Teaching thinking: A cognitive-behavioral perspective. In R. Glaser, S. Chipman, & J. Segal (Eds.), *Thinking and learning skills* (Vol. 2): *Research and open questions* (pp. 407–426). Hillsdale, NJ: Erlbaum.

Mento, A. J., Steel, R. P., & Karren, R. J. (1987) A meta-analytic study of the effects of goal setting on task performance: 1966–1984. *Organizational Behavior and Human Decision Processes, 39,* 52–83.

Miura, I. T. (1987) The relationship of computer self-efficacy expectations to computer interest and course enrollment in college. *Sex Roles, 16,* 303–311.

Morgan, M. (1985) Self-monitoring of attained subgoals in private study. *Journal of Educational Psychology, 77,* 623–630.

Ozer, E., & Bandura, A. (1989) *Mechanisms governing empowerment effects: A self-efficacy analysis.* Manuscript submitted for publication.

Porras, J. I., Hargis, K., Patterson, K. J., Maxfield, D. G., Roberts, N., & Bies, R. J. (1982) Modeling-based organizational development: A longitudinal assessment. *Journal of Applied Behavioral Science, 18,* 433–446.

Rosenthal, T. L., & Zimmerman, B. J. (1978) *Social learning and cognition.* New York: Academic Press.

Sarason, I. G. (1975) Anxiety and self-preoccupation. In I. G. Sarason & D. C. Spielberger (Eds.), *Stress and anxiety* (Vol. 2, pp. 27–44). Washington, DC: Hemisphere.

Strang, H. R., Lawrence, E. C., & Fowler, P. C. (1978) Effects of assigned goal level and knowledge of results on arithmetic computation: Laboratory study. *Journal of Applied Psychology, 63,* 446–450.

Taylor, M. S., Locke, E. A., Lee, C., & Gist, M. E. (1984) Type A behavior and faculty research productivity: What are the mechanisms? *Organizational Behavior and Human Performance, 34,* 402–418.

Weinberg, R. S., Gould, D., & Jackson, A. (1979). Expectations and performance: An empirical test of Bandura's self-efficacy theory. *Journal of Sport Psychology, 1,* 320–331.

QUESTIONS FOR DISCUSSION

1 What boundary conditions would you propose as the limitations within which expectancy (VIE) theory is an effective model of motivation?

2 How might predictions about behavior made from social learning theory differ from predictions arising from B = f(P,E)?

3 Using expectancy theory, outline ways in which a manager might directly affect each component of the model.

4 How would you compare expectancy theories with need theories of motivation?

5 Some managerial behaviors are well planned, and others may be merely the by-products of personal style or habit. What incidental managerial behaviors might affect valence, instrumentality, and expectancy calculations by subordinates?

6 What implications does the Porter and Lawler definition of satisfaction ("a derivative variable") have for determining rewards?

7 How would your evaluate the research evidence in support of equity theory?

8 Why do you think equity theory has been largely ignored by many managers and writers working in the field of organizational behavior?

9 What can line managers learn from equity theory that could help them improve their supervisory abilities? What can they learn from the procedural justice research in particular?

10 How do the prescriptions for effective managerial behavior which follow from equity theory differ from those derived from Murray's needs theory?

11 Suggest some new applications for equity theory in work organizations in addition to those in the area of pay.

12 What influence can self-efficacy beliefs have on an individual's motivation and performance?

13 How do those with high self-efficacy beliefs tend to differ from those with low self-efficacy beliefs in their reactions to negative feedback?

14 Social learning theory suggests that behavior may be maintained through direct reinforcement and punishment or through a person's observation (or modeling) of the reinforcing or punishing outcomes of other people's behavior. How might the effects of these two methods (direct and indirect) differ?

15 Compare and contrast expectancy theory with the "cognitive processes" and "self-control processes" of social learning theory.

16 Consider a case in which two employees are passed over for a promotion. Using the concepts of procedural and distributive justice, explain why the two employees might have entirely different reactions—one works even harder, while the other decreases effort.

THREE

CENTRAL ISSUES IN MOTIVATION AT WORK

CHAPTER 5

SOCIAL INFLUENCES
ON MOTIVATION

Dating from the early work of Allport (1924), Mayo (1933), and Roethlisberger and Dickson (1939), a considerable body of research data has accumulated on the effects of the social aspects of an employee's work environment on motivation and behavior. In this chapter we first will consider group processes and their impacts; then we will examine the crucial process of organizational socialization. This discussion should serve to emphasize the fact that individuals seldom work in isolation and that they are continuously and often strongly affected by the social forces that exist in both the immediate and the larger organizational setting.

Defining precisely what constitutes a "group" is no easy task. The boundaries of group membership tend to be rather permeable, with new members joining and old ones leaving at a fairly consistent rate. Moreover, members of one group are generally also members of several additional groups, thereby dividing their time and loyalties. Because of problems such as these, we tend to discuss and define groups more in terms of processes than in terms of specific members and their personal characteristics. Thus, a typical definition of a group would include the notion of a collectivity of people who share a set of norms (or common viewpoints), who generally have differentiated roles, and who jointly pursue common goals. While it is not possible to specify the "required" size of such a collectivity, the number usually averages between four and seven.

Groups form for a variety of reasons. Some groups result simply from proximity. The day-to-day interactions with one's immediate coworkers tend to facilitate group formation. Other groups form for economic reasons. For example, where bonuses are paid to workers on the basis of *group* productivity, an incentive exists to band together for mutual gain. Still other groups form as the result of various social-psychological forces. Such groups can satisfy employees' social needs for interaction, reinforce feelings of self-worth, and provide emotional sup-port in times of stress. Whatever the reason for their formation, they can be a potent factor in the determination of both individual job effort and individual job satisfaction.

Primarily as a result of the Hawthorne studies (Roethlisberger & Dickson, 1939) and the later research they stimulated, we have developed a fairly clear pic-ture of some of the more common characteristics of a group. To begin with, as mentioned above, there are generally rather detailed norms, or shared beliefs, that are held by the group members and that guide their behavior. In addition, various members often have specific duties, or role prescriptions, for which they are responsible. Groups usually have acknowledged control procedures, such as ostracism, to minimize behavior deviating from their norms. They also develop their own systems or patterns of communications, which often include special or technical words (jargon). They tend to have an informal leader whose responsi-bility it is to enforce the norms and assure goal attainment. Finally, groups pro-vide a useful source of support for their members. Employees who find little sat-isfaction in a dull, repetitive job may refrain from quitting because they really enjoy their coworkers, who provide comfort, support, and satisfaction on an otherwise meaningless job. Moreover, groups also provide support in a different sense where the group intends to regulate its rate of output. If one member re-stricts output, a very real possibility exists that he or she will be punished or even terminated by the organization. However, if all group members restrict output in unison, there is much less chance of "retribution" by the company.

From a motivational standpoint, perhaps the most important group process is the tendency toward conformity (Asch, 1958; Sherif, 1936). One of the basic pre-requisites for continued group membership is adherence to group standards, norms, and so forth. Once a work group has determined an acceptable rate of output, for example, it tends to punish or reject members whose output is above ("rate-busters") or below ("goldbricks") this rate. If a company offers individual incentives for increased output but the group decides the new rate of output is too high (perhaps out of fear of working themselves out of a job), the group will exert force on its members not to increase output, despite the potential short-run mon-etary gain. On the other hand, however, if group support can be won for the new rate of output, conformity could then lead to increased output. The application of this latter example can be seen in such programs as the Lincoln Electric and the Scanlon plans, where workers have a significant voice in the determination of production rates and in the introduction of new production techniques. Under such plans, participation in program formulation *and* in the rewards from the new techniques appears to lead to group acceptance of the innovations, resulting in increased output.

In summary, then, research indicates that groups often serve useful functions for their members and must be taken into account as potential moderator vari-ables in any program designed by the organization to increase employee effort and performance. It is important to recognize that from an organization's per-spective, or the perspective of an individual manager, groups are neither "good" nor "bad" per se. From a motivational standpoint, groups have the potential to either facilitate or inhibit performance of their individual members. What kind of effect a particular group will have on its members will depend on a number of factors in the work situation in which the group operates. In any event, it is necessary to keep in mind that since most of us who work in organizations are social in nature, groups can exert very powerful influence. It is also necessary to note that the effects of a group on its members can change over time. Therefore, while a group may have had a negative impact on its members' performance or attitudes in the past, this does not imply that this must be the case in the future. Group effects can change direction, given a change in the influences from outside of a group as well as changes that may take place internally. Thus, the direction of the motivational impact a group can have on a set of individuals potentially can be altered in either a more positive or a more negative direction.

In the first reading in this chapter, Porter, Lawler, and Hackman review several mechanisms by which groups influence individual employees to produce (or not to produce). Included in this discussion is a consideration of how managers may try to change the work environment so that group processes are more compatible with organizational goals. The second article, by Sussmann and Vecchio, highlights the importance of social influence attempts as a major set of factors determining the motivation of individuals in work settings. A conceptual framework is provided, along with suggested hypotheses based on this way of viewing the motivational process. The reader will want to compare the ideas presented in this article with the social learning approach described by Kreitner and Luthans in Chapter 4. In the next article, Feldman examines how group norms develop and the role they have in influencing the motivation and behavior of group members. Again, like the preceding articles, this selection serves to emphasize the decidedly social nature of motivation in organizational circumstances.

The fourth article, by Krackhardt and Porter, addresses an interesting question of social influence on motivation: What effect does turnover—the act of leaving an organization—by certain individuals have on the attitudes of those who remain in that organization? Utilizing a grouplike work situation and focusing on friendship relationships among employees, the empirical study reported in this article collected data at two different points in time at three fast-food restaurants and examined the impact of social networks on the satisfaction and commitment of the "stayers." Contrary to what might be assumed, the closer an employee who remained was to someone who left, the *more* positive became the attitude of that person toward the job and the organization. The study thus demonstrated that there was, in fact, significant social influence operating in the aftermath of this type of event—employee turnover—that occurs so often in the workplace.

The final article in this chapter presents an analysis by a prominent organizational scholar, O'Reilly, on the effects of the broad *organizational* context, specifically, the "culture" of organizations (in business firms, the "corporate culture"), on motivation and commitment. In this article, the role of norms existing at the organizational level—as distinct from just the group level—is a central feature of O'Reilly's analysis.

REFERENCES

Allport, F. H. *Social psychology*. Boston: Houghton Mifflin, 1924.

Asch, S. E. The effects of group pressure upon the modifications and distortion of judgments. In E. E. Maccoby, T. E. Newcomb, & E. L. Hartley (Eds.), *Readings in social psychology*. New York: Holt, 1958. (First published in 1939.)

Mayo, E. *The human problems of an industrial civilization*. New York: Macmillan, 1933.

Roethlisberger, F. J., & Dickson, W. J. *Management and the worker*. Cambridge, Mass.: Harvard University Press, 1939.

Sherif, M. *The psychology of social norms*. New York: Harper, 1936.

Ways Groups Influence
Individual Work Effectiveness

Lyman W. Porter
Edward E. Lawler III
J. Richard Hackman

To analyze the diversity of group and social influences on individual work effectiveness, it may be useful to examine group effects separately on each of four summary classes of variables that have been shown to influence employee work behavior. These four classes of variables are:

1 The job-relevant knowledge and skills of the individual
2 The level of psychological arousal the individual experiences while working
3 The performance strategies the individual uses during his work
4 The level of effort the individual exerts in doing his work

Below, we shall examine the ways in which work groups influence each of these four major influences on individual performance.

GROUP INFLUENCES BY AFFECTING
MEMBER KNOWLEDGE AND SKILLS

Performance on many tasks and jobs in organizations is strongly affected by the job-relevant knowledge and skills of the individuals who do the work. Thus, even if an employee has both high commitment toward accomplishing a particular piece of work and well-formed strategy about how to go about it, the implementation of that plan can be constrained or terminated if he does not know how to carry it out, or if he knows how but is incapable of doing so. While ability is relevant to the performance of jobs at all levels in an organization, its impact probably is somewhat reduced for lower-level jobs. The reason is that such jobs often are not demanding of high skill levels. Further, to the extent that organizational selection, placement, and promotion practices are adequate, *all* jobs should tend to be occupied by individuals who possess the skills requisite for adequate performance.

Discussion in the previous chapter focused on how groups can improve the job-relevant knowledge and skills of an individual through direct instruction, feedback, and model provision. For jobs in which knowledge and skill are important determiners of performance effectiveness, then, groups can be of help. Nevertheless, the impact of groups on member performance effectiveness by improving member knowledge and skill probably is one of the lesser influences groups can have—both because employees on many jobs tend already to have many or all of the skills needed to perform them effectively and because there are other

Slightly revised from L. W. Porter, E. E. Lawler, & R. J. Hackman, *Behavior in organizations*. New York: McGraw-Hill, 1975, pp. 411–422. Used by permission.

sources for improving skills which may be more useful and more potent than the work group, such as formal job training programs and self-study programs.

GROUP INFLUENCES BY AFFECTING MEMBER AROUSAL LEVEL

A group can substantially influence the level of psychological arousal experienced by a member—through the mere pressure of the other group members and by those others sending the individual messages which are directly arousal-enhancing or arousal-depressing. The conditions under which such group-promoted changes in arousal level will lead to increased performance effectiveness, however, very much depend upon the type of task being worked on (Zajonc, 1965).

In this case, the critical characteristics of the job have to do with whether the initially *dominant task responses* of the individual are likely to be correct or incorrect. Since the individual's output of such responses is facilitated when he is in an aroused state, arousal should improve performance effectiveness on well-learned tasks (so-called performance tasks) in which the dominant response is correct and needs merely to be executed by the performer. By the same token, arousal should impair effectiveness for new or unfamiliar tasks (learning tasks) in which the dominant response is likely to be incorrect.

It has sometimes been argued that the *mere* presence of others should heighten the arousal of individuals sufficiently for the predicted performance effects to be obtained. However, the evidence now seems to indicate that the *mere* presence of others may not result in significant increases in arousal. Instead, only when the other group members are—or are seen as being—in a potentially evaluative relationship vis-à-vis the performer are the predictions confirmed (cf. Zajonc & Sales, 1966; Cottrell et al., 1968; Hency & Glass, 1968).

Groups can, of course, increase member arousal in ways other than taking an evaluative stance toward the individual. Strongly positive, encouraging statements also should increase arousal in some performance situations—for example, by helping the individual become personally highly committed to the group goal, and making sure he realizes that he is a very important part of the team responsible for reaching that goal. What must be kept in mind, however, is that such devices represent a double-edged sword: while they may facilitate effective performance for well-learned tasks, they may have the opposite effect for new and unfamiliar tasks.

What, then, can be said about the effects on performance of group members when their presence (and interaction) serves to *decrease* the level of arousal of the group member—as, for example, when individuals coalesce into groups under conditions of high stress? When the other members of the group are a source of support, comfort, or acceptance to the individual (and serve to decrease his arousal level), it would be predicted that performance effectiveness would follow a pattern exactly opposite to that described above: the group would impair effectiveness for familiar or well-learned performance tasks (because arousal helps on these tasks and arousal is being lowered) and facilitate effectiveness for unfamiliar or complicated learning tasks (because in this case arousal is harmful, and it is being lowered).

The relationships predicted above are summarized in Figure 1. As the group becomes increasingly threatening, evaluative, or strongly encouraging, effectiveness should increase for performance tasks and decrease for learning tasks. When the group is experienced as increasingly supportive, comforting, or unconditionally accepting, effectiveness should decrease for performance tasks and increase for learning tasks. And when no meaningful relationship at all is experienced by the individual between himself and the group, performance should not be affected. While some of the predictions have been tested and confirmed in small group experimental settings, others await research.

Even that research which has focused on these relationships has not been designed or conducted in actual organizational settings, and the findings must be generalized with caution. It is clear, however, that individuals in organizations do use their group memberships as a means of achieving more comfortable levels of arousal. Individuals in high-pressure managerial jobs, for example, often find that they need to gather around themselves a few trusted associates who can and do provide reassurance and continuing acceptance when the going gets especially tough. This, presumably, should help reduce the manager's level of arousal and thereby increase the likelihood that he will be able to come up with *new and original* ways of perceiving and dealing with his immediate problem. If the theory is correct, however, this practice should not facilitate performance of the more "routine" (i.e., well-learned) parts of his job.

FIGURE 1
Individual performance effectiveness as a function of type of task and experienced relationship to the group.

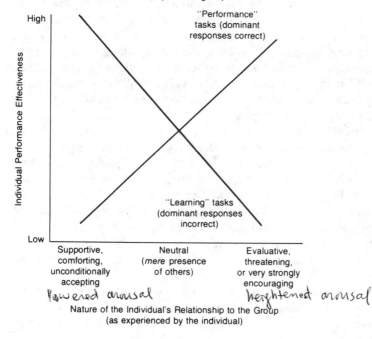

Nature of the Individual's Relationship to the Group
(as experienced by the individual)

It is well known that overly routine jobs can decrease a worker's level of arousal to such an extent that his performance effectiveness is impaired. It seems quite possible, therefore, that the social environment of workers on such jobs can be designed so as to compensate partially for the deadening effects of the job itself and thereby lead to an increment in performance on well-learned tasks.

Finally, the supervisor probably has a more powerful effect on level of arousal of a worker than any other single individual in his immediate social environment. By close supervision (which usually results in the worker's feeling more or less constantly evaluated) supervisors can and do increase the level of arousal experienced by workers. While this may, for routine jobs, have some potential for improving performance effectiveness, it also is quite likely that the worker's negative reactions to being closely supervised ultimately will result in his attention being diverted from the job itself and focused instead on ways he can either get out from "under the gun" of the supervisor or somehow get back at the supervisor to punish him for his unwanted close supervision.

GROUP INFLUENCES BY AFFECTING LEVEL OF MEMBER EFFORT AND MEMBER PERFORMANCE STRATEGIES

The level of effort a person exerts in doing his work and the performance strategies he follows are treated together here because both variables are largely under the performer's *voluntary* control.

Direct versus Indirect Influences on Effort and Strategy

We have used a general "expectancy theory" approach to analyze those aspects of a person's behavior in organizations which are under his voluntary control. From this perspective a person's choices about his effort and work strategy can be viewed as hinging largely upon (1) his *expectations* regarding the likely consequences of his choices and (2) the degree to which he *values* those expected consequences. Following this approach, it becomes clear that the group can have both a direct and an indirect effect on the level of effort a group member exerts at his job and on his choices about performance strategy.

The *direct* impact of the group on effort and strategy, of course, is simply the enforcement by the group of its own norms regarding what is an "appropriate" level of effort to expend on the job and what is the "proper" performance strategy. We previously discussed in some detail how groups use their control of discretionary stimuli to enforce group norms, and thereby affect such voluntary behaviors. Thus, if the group has established a norm about the level of member effort or the strategies members should use in going about their work, the group can control individual behavior merely by making sure that individual members realize that their receipt of valued group-controlled rewards is contingent upon their behaving in accord with the norm.

The *indirect* impact of the group on the effort and performance strategies of the individual involves the group's control of information regarding the state of the organizational environment outside the boundaries of the group. Regardless of any norms the group itself may have about effort or strategy, it also can communicate to the group member "what leads to what" in the broader organization, and thereby affect the individual's *own* choices about his behavior.

For example, it may be the case in a given organization, that hard work (i.e., high effort) tends to lead to quick promotions and higher pay; the group can influence the effort of the individual by helping him realize this objective state of affairs. Similarly, by providing individual members with information about what performance strategies are effective in the organization, the group can indirectly affect the strategy choices made by the person. Whether high quality of output or large quantities of output are more likely to lead to organizational rewards, for example, is information that the group can provide the individual with to assist him in making his own choices about work strategy.

Moreover, groups can affect the *personal preferences and values* of individual members—although such influences tend to occur relatively slowly and over a long period of time. When such changes do occur, the level of desire (or the valence) individuals have for various outcomes available in the organizational setting will change as well. And as the kinds of outcomes valued by the individual change, his behavior also will change to increase the degree to which the newly valued outcomes are obtained at work. The long-term result can be substantial revision of the choices made by the individual about the effort he will expend and the performance strategies he will use at work.

It should be noted, however, that such indirect influences on a member's effort and performance strategy will be most potent early in the individual's tenure in the organization when he has not yet had a chance to develop through experience his own personal "map" of the organization. When the individual becomes less dependent upon the group for data about "what leads to what" and "what's good" in the organization, the group may have to revert to direct norm enforcement to maintain control of the work behavior of individual members.

In summary, the group can and does have a strong impact on both the level of effort exerted by its members and the strategies members use in carrying out their work. This impact is realized both directly (i.e., by enforcement of group norms) and indirectly (i.e., by affecting the beliefs and values of the members). When the direct and indirect influences of a group are congruent—which is often the case—the potency of the group's efforts on its members can be quite strong. For example, if at the same time that a group is enforcing its *own* norm of, say, moderately low production, it also is providing a group member with data regarding the presumably *objective* negative consequences of hard work in the particular organization, the group member will experience two partially independent and mutually reinforcing influences aimed at keeping his rate of production down.

Effort, Strategy, and Performance Effectiveness

What, then, are the circumstances under which groups can improve the work *effectiveness* of their members through influences on individual choices about the level of effort and about strategy? Again, the answer depends upon the nature of the job. Unless a job is structured so that effort level or performance strategy actually can make a real difference in work effectiveness, group influences on effort or strategy will be irrelevant to how well individual members perform.

Strategy: In general, groups should be able to facilitate member work effectiveness by influencing strategy choices more for complex jobs than for simple, straightforward, or routine ones. The reason is that on simple jobs, strategy choices usually cannot make much of a difference in effectiveness; instead, how well one does is determined almost entirely by how hard one works. On jobs characterized by high variety and autonomy, on the other hand, the work strategy used by the individual usually is of considerable importance in determining work effectiveness. By helping an individual develop and implement an appropriate work strategy—of where and how to put in his effort—the group should be able to substantially facilitate his effectiveness.

Effort: In the great majority of organizational settings, most jobs are structured such that the harder one works, the more effective his performance is likely to be. Thus, group influences on the effort expended by members on their jobs are both very pervasive and very potent determiners of individual work effectiveness. There are, nevertheless, some exceptions to this generalization; the success of a complicated brain operation, for example, is less likely to depend upon effort expended that it is upon the strategies used and the job-relevant knowledge and skills of the surgeon.

When neither effort or strategy or both are in fact important in determining performance effectiveness, the individual has substantial personal control over how well he does in his work. In such cases, the degree to which the group facilitates (rather than hinders) individual effectiveness will depend jointly upon (1) the degree to which the group has accurate information regarding the task and organizational contingencies which are operative in that situation and makes such information available to the individual and (2) the degree to which the norms of the group are congruent with those contingencies and reinforce them.

Participation

One management practice which in theory should contribute positively to meeting both of the above conditions is the use of group participation in making decisions about work practices. Participation has been widely advocated as a management technique, both on ideological grounds and as a direct means of increasing work effectiveness. And, in fact, some studies have shown that participation can lead to higher work effectiveness (e.g., Coch & French, 1948; Lawler & Hackman, 1969). In the present framework, participation should contribute to increased work effectiveness in two different ways.

1 Participation can increase the amount and the accuracy of information workers have about work practices and the environmental contingencies associated with them. In one study (Lawler & Hackman, 1969), for example, some groups themselves designed new reward systems keyed on coming to work regularly (a

task clearly affected by employee effort—i.e., trying to get to work every day). These groups responded both more quickly and more positively to the new pay plans than did groups which had technically identical plans imposed upon them by company management. One reason suggested by the authors to account for this finding was that the participative groups simply may have understood their plans better and had fewer uncertainties and worries about what the rewards were (and were not) for coming to work regularly.

2 Participation can increase the degree to which group members feel they "own" their work practices—and therefore the likelihood that the group will develop a norm of support for those practices. In the participative groups in the study cited above, for example, the nature of the work-related communication among members changed from initial "shared warnings" about management and "things management proposes" to helping members (especially new members) come to understand and believe in "our plan." In other words, as group members come to experience the work or work practices *as under their own control or ownership*, it becomes more likely that informal group norms supportive of effective behavior vis-à-vis those practices will develop. Such norms provide a striking contrast to the "group protective" norms which often emerge when control is perceived to be exclusively and unilaterally under management control.

We can see, then, that group participative techniques can be quite facilitative of individual work effectiveness—but only under certain conditions:

1 The topic of participation must be relevant to the work itself. There is no reason to believe that participation involving task-irrelevant issues (e.g., preparing for the Red Cross Bloodmobile visit to the plant) will have facilitative effects on work productivity. While such participation may indeed help increase the cohesiveness of the work group, it clearly will not help group members gain information or develop norms which are facilitative of high work effectiveness. Indeed, such task-irrelevant participation may serve to direct the attention and motivation of group members *away from* work issues and thereby even lower productivity (cf. French, Israel, & As, 1960).

2 The objective task and environmental contingencies in the work setting must actually be supportive of more effective performance. That is, if through participation group members learn more about what leads to what in the organization, then it is increasingly important that there be real and meaningful positive outcomes which result from effective performance. If, for example, group members gain a quite complete and accurate impression through participation that "hard work around here pays off only in backaches," then increased effort as a consequence of participation is most unlikely. If, on the other hand, participation results in a new and better understanding that hard work can lead to increased pay, enhanced opportunities for advancement, and the chance to feel a sense of personal and group accomplishment, then increased effort should be the result.

3 Finally, the work must be such that increased effort (or a different and better work strategy) objectively can lead to higher work effectiveness. If it is true—as argued here—that the main benefits of group participation are (1) increased un-

derstanding of work practices and the organizational environment and (2) increased experienced "ownership" by the group of the work and work practices, then participation should increase productivity only when the *objective determinants of productivity are under the voluntary control of the worker*. There is little reason to expect, therefore, that participation should have a substantial facilitative effect on productivity when work outcomes are mainly determined by the level of skill of the worker and/or by his arousal level (rather than effort expended or work strategy used) or when outcomes are controlled by objective factors in the environment over which the worker can have little or no control (e.g., the rate or amount of work which is arriving at the employee's station).

IMPLICATIONS FOR DIAGNOSIS AND CHANGE

This section has focused on ways that the group can influence the performance effectiveness of individual group members. While it has been maintained throughout that the group has a substantial impact on such performance effectiveness, it has been emphasized that the nature and extent of this impact centrally depends upon the characteristics of the work being done.

To diagnose and change the direction or extent of social influences on individual performance in an organization, then, the following three steps might be taken.

1 An analysis of the task or job would be made to determine which of the four classes of variables (i.e., skills, arousal, strategies, effort) objectively affect measured performance effectiveness. This might be done by posing this analytical question: "If skills (or arousal, or effort, or strategies) were brought to bear on the work differently than is presently the case, would a corresponding difference in work effectiveness be likely to be observed as a consequence?" By scrutinizing each of the four classes of variables in this way, it usually is possible to identify which specific variables are objectively important to consider for the job. In many cases, of course, more than one class of variables will turn out to be of importance.

2 After one or more "target" classes of variables have been identified, the work group itself would be examined to unearth any ways in which the group was blocking effective individual performance. It might be determined, for example, that certain group norms were impeding the expression and use of various skills which individuals potentially could bring to bear on their work. Or it might turn out that the social environment of the worker created conditions which were excessively (or insufficiently) arousing for optimal performance on the task at hand. For effort and strategy, which are under the voluntary control of the worker, there are two major possibilities to examine: (a) that norms are enforced in the group which coerce individuals to behave in ineffective ways or (b) that the group provides information to the individual members about task and environmental contingencies in an insufficient or distorted fashion, resulting in their making choices about their work behavior which interfere with task effectiveness.

3 Finally, it would be useful to assess the group and the broader social environment to determine if there are ways that the "people resources" in the situation could be more fully utilized in the interest of increased work effectiveness. That is, rather than focusing solely on ways the group may be blocking or impeding performance effectiveness, attention should be given as well to any unrealized *potential* which resides in the group. It could turn out, for example, that some group members would be of great help to others in increasing the level of individual task-relevant skills, but these individuals have never been asked for help. Alternatively, it might be that the group could be assisted in finding new and better ways of ensuring that each group member has available accurate and current information about those tasks and environmental contingencies which determine the outcomes of various work behaviors.

The point is that the people who surround an individual at work can facilitate as well as hinder his performance effectiveness—and that any serious attempt to diagnose the social environment in the interest of improving work performance should explicitly address unrealized possibilities for enhancing performance as well as issues for which remedial action may be required.

When particular organizational changes will be called for on the basis of such a diagnosis—or what techniques should be used to realize these changes—will, of course, largely depend upon the particular characteristics of the organization and of the resources which are available there. The major emphasis of this section has been that there is *not* any single universally useful type of change or means of change—and that, instead, intervention should always be based on a thorough diagnosis of the existing social, organizational, and task environment. Perhaps especially intriguing in this regard is the prospect of developing techniques of social intervention which will help groups see the need for (and develop the capability of) making such interventions *on their own* in the interest of increasing the work effectiveness of the group as a whole.

REFERENCES

Coch, L., & French, J. R. P., Jr., Overcoming resistance to change. *Human Relations,* 1948, **1,** 512–532.

Cottrell, N. B., Wack, D. L., Sekerak, F. J., & Rittle, R. H. Social facilitation of dominant responses by the presence of an audience and the mere presence of others. *Journal of Personality and Social Psychology,* 1968, **9,** 245–250.

French, J. R. P., Jr., Israel, J., & As, D. An experiment on participation in a Norwegian factory. *Human Relations,* 1960, **19,** 3–19.

Hency, T., & Glass, D. C. Evaluation apprehension and the social facilitation of dominant and subordinate responses. *Journal of Personality and Social Psychology,* 1968, **10,** 446–454.

Lawler, E. E., & Hackman, J. R. The impact of employee participation in the development of pay incentive plans: A field experiment. *Journal of Applied Psychology,* 1969, **53,** 467–471.

Zajonc, R. B. Social facilitation. *Science,* 1965, **149,** 269–274.

Zajonc, R. B., & Sales, S. M. Social facilitation of dominant and subordinate responses. *Journal of Experimental Social Psychology,* 1966, **2,** 160–168.

A Social Influence Interpretation of Worker Motivation

Mario Sussmann
Robert P. Vecchio

When considering the topic of worker motivation, one is initially overwhelmed by the abundance of different theories and approaches that are present in the organizational literature (Adams, 1965; Campbell & Pritchard, 1976; Campbell, Dunnette, Lawler, & Weick, 1970; Lawler, 1973; Porter & Lawler, 1968; Vroom, 1964). However, the major theories of worker motivation (both mechanistic and cognitive) have largely ignored a fundamental issue concerning the origins of worker behavior. Specifically, this omission stems from an assumption that factors which appear to precede changes in behavior operate in a unilateral fashion: and workers (it is assumed) do not exercise an appreciable degree of personal volition, that is, they *do not decide to accept influence attempts*. This theoretical omission sidesteps the question of the process whereby influence attempts are accepted/rejected as well as the varieties of influence that exist. Rather than define "influence processes," one can instead attempt to define the "basis of acceptance." However, the latter view does not present the worker as an active participant in the determination of his or her behavior. Presented in this paper is a process view of social influence that specifies the manner and nature of socially induced changes in worker behavior.

An influence attempt is defined here as a social occasion wherein one individual exhibits behaviors, emits verbal utterances, and so on, with the intent of altering the behavior of another or others to a desired end. The scope of this discourse is restricted to work related behaviors (especially, but not exclusively, behaviors related to worker productivity). Of concern here are occasions of socially dependent influence. That is to say, influence that originates from outside the target person can be distinguished from influence that originates primarily from within the target person (e.g., the socially independent process of a competency motive or exploratory motive). Furthermore, it is recognized that influence is unlikely to be unilateral. Rather, it is most commonly a reciprocal process in that the target person's response to an influence attempt likely will alter the variety, frequency, intensity, and/or direction of future influence attempts.

For the moment, the focus is on the behavior (i.e., response to an influence attempt) of the person who occupies a "subordinate" position (i.e., in the formal, organizational sense of subordinate) because subordinate behavior traditionally has been the primary interest of theories of worker motivation. However, as will be illustrated, influence can be more broadly conceptualized so as to include the impact of subordinate behavior on supervisor behavior (specifically, supervisor's influence attempts).

From *Academy of Management Review*, 1982, **7**, 177–186. Reprinted by permission.

SOCIAL INFLUENCE PROCESSES

Kelman's (1961) work on identifying qualitatively distinct processes of opinion change has particular relevance to the goals of this paper. These processes are termed compliance, identification, and internalization. If Kelman's terms are extended to work settings, it may be said that *compliance* is concerned with whether a worker accepts an influence attempt because of a desire to obtain a favorable outcome or to avoid an unfavorable outcome. *Identification* refers to whether a worker exhibits behaviors derived from another or others because these behaviors contribute to a person's self-image. The third type of influence process, *internalization,* refers to whether a worker accepts an influence attempt because the encouraged actions are congruent with a personal value system and/or are intrinsically rewarding to the individual.

French and Raven's (1959) view of social power suggests five major sources of influence: reward, coercive, legitimate, referent, and expert. Each of these five may be viewed as being relatively more closely aligned with one of the three processes proposed by Kelman. Specifically, French and Raven's reward and coercive power possesses a strong conceptual similarity with Kelman's notion of compliance. Also, the social power bases of referent power are most in allegiance with Kelman's process of identification. And, finally, legitimate power may be viewed as being potentially the power source for an internalization influence process. Therefore, French and Raven's analysis of social power may be viewed as overlapping with Kelman's typology such that French and Raven's power bases provide a more elaborate conceptual foundation for influence attempts. These influence attempts, in turn, are directed at (or, perhaps more properly, are translated into) specific psychological processes (Kelman, 1961) and succeed or fail in altering behavior as a function of individual and situational contingencies.

Etzioni (1975) has offered an approach that examines social power and worker response within the framework of a structurally oriented organizational analysis. Etzioni considered the influence-motivation problem as one of *compliance,* a term that indicates the relation between the influence agent's power and the influencee's involvement (by involvement is meant a cathectic-evaluative orientation of an actor to an object).

In Etzioni's typology of power, coercive power refers to the administration of pain or the threat to do so. Remunerative or utilitarian power refers to allocation of rewards such as pay, benefits, services, and commodities. Among two types of normative power, pure normative power refers to the allocation of symbolic rewards based on prestige, esteem, and ritualistic symbols, and social power refers to the apportionment of interpersonal rewards and acceptance. There also are four types of involvement: alienative (a negative and hostile orientation); calculative (based on the material gain in an economic relationship); and two types of moral involvement (devotion to ideas, groups, movements, organizations, leaders), with a distinction between "pure moral" commitment and "social" commitment, paralleling the distinction between pure normative and social power. In a proposal that anticipated contingency theories, congruent types of compliance are defined as occasions in which a type of power is paired with a corresponding type of involvement (coercive with alienative, remunerative-utilitarian with calculative, normative with moral); all other combinations are incongruent.

A comparison of Kelman's and Etzioni's typologies shows that Etzioni offers two types of relationship (coercive power and remunerative-utilitarian power) but Kelman writes only of compliance. On the other hand, Kelman's distinction between identification (social power, social commitment) and internalization (pure normative power—pure moral commitment) appears to be particularly useful because Kelman also postulates a cost difference between identification and internalization: the internalization process clearly is the one that does not require surveillance (in contrast with compliance) or the presence/salience (in contrast with identification) of the power agent and might be seen as the most effective and parsimonious means of control. Yet, an important difference remains: Kelman's three processes are located at the individual level of analysis, whereas Etzioni's compliance is defined as a relation between an individual process (involvement) and an organizational process (power).

INDIVIDUAL AND SITUATIONAL MODERATORS

Individual differences variables, one may reasonably assume, moderate the impact of influence attempts such that a given type of influence attempt will be more successful with a given group of individuals. Imagine, for example, the outcome of the use of coercive/reward power in order to bring about simple compliance. In such an instance, one would find that the influence attempt was or was not successful as a partial function of such predispositions as willingness to comply with incentives, intimidation, bribery, or threats. It would be suspected that animals, children, and those adults who possess little desire for autonomy would be most responsive to influence attempts that are designed to bring about simple compliance and that are based on coercive/reward power.

Some individual differences moderators that have been the focus of considerable organizational research include growth need strength (Hackman & Oldham, 1976), Protestant work ethic (Blood, 1969; Mirels & Garrett, 1971), and internal versus external locus-of-control (Rotter, 1966). It is suspected that these value system indices are likely to be most relevant for social influence attempts directed at an internalization process. That is to say, influence attempts that essentially are appeals to the target's value system will be differentially effective as a function of the target's value system.

A value system having implications across all three influence models has been advanced by Kohlberg (1963, 1969). Kohlberg proposes that an individual passes through three identifiable stages of value maturity. At the first level, the preconventional, an individual is most concerned with the consequences of his or her behavior. At the second (conventional) level, an individual is most concerned with meeting the expectations of family, immediate group, or nation because it is valuable as an end in itself. The final, or postconventional, level is characterized by an individual's effort to define and apply these values or principles apart from external norms and potential sanctions.

It can be argued that Kohlberg's typology maps, aptly, into the social influence processes. Specifically, the more an influence attempt is based on simple reward/coercive power and seeks to evoke compliance, the more successful the influence attempt will be if it is directed towards individuals whose value system is best characterized as hedonistic/utilitarian. Influence attempts based on referent power should be most effective with individuals who have a strong desire for social conformity. And, finally, influence heavily directed toward appealing to an individual's values will be most effective with persons who are strongly concerned with value issues. It is worthy of note that a recent motivational study that employed the Kohlberg typology (Vecchio, 1981) reported support for the hypothesis that individual values moderate worker response to incentive schemes.

In addition to individual differences moderators, one might expect situational factors to play an important role in moderating the differential effectiveness of the various influence approaches. Situational attributes of possible importance job autonomy and job challenge. Organizational level (a potentially significant situational factor) may be of particular importance to the influence process view of motivation. For example, one might find that different influence processes are used more frequently at different organizational levels, such that internalization influence attempts are used more frequently in higher organizational levels and compliance-based influence attempts are employed more commonly at lower organizational levels. Although such a finding would be of a purely descriptive nature, it should be possible to document the differential effectiveness of these influence processes at different levels.

At a still broader level of conceptualization, the organizational power types proposed by Etzioni offer a further framework for matching the type of influence attempt with situational attributes. That is to say, specific types of influence attempts may appear most appropriate (congruent) and be most effective within specific organizational power structures.

Up to this point, the importance has been shown of several situational and individual attributes as moderators of the relationship between influence attempts and individual motivation. However, the translation of individual motivation (often conceptualized as effort and/or strength of a behavioral intention) into performance requires the specification of individual and situational attributes that serve as moderators of the relationship between individual motivation and performance (Lawler, 1971; Porter & Lawler, 1968; Vroom, 1964). These specific attributes can be best summarized by the terms "ability," and "availability of the behavior."

The intersection of situational attributes, individual differences attributes, and influence attempts yields a complex and theoretically rich framework for hypothesizing specific interactions. However, before discussing such effects it is necessary to link the influence processes with clusters of relevant dependent variables. That is to say, not only is the presently proposed model deliberately explicit with respect to the impact of situational and individual differences moderators (and their interactions), but it also explicitly specifies theoretically relevant intermediate variables and it ties relevant dependent variables to associated processes.

Therefore, it is suggested that each influence process is most directly relevant for only certain outcome/process variables.

RELEVANT VARIABLES

Before linking intermediary variables to their associated processes, one must consider the constructs and variables commonly investigated in the area of worker motivation. These constructs and variables have various conceptual commonalities that permit a simple clustering in the interest of parsimony.

The intermediary process variables may be defined as those dimensions that describe individuals' behaviors, intentions, and cognitive and emotional states within an organizationally-relevant setting. These process variables appear to describe the specific details of Etzioni's "involvement." Two trends have emerged within the literature for identifying these variables. For the first approach, clusters of these variables are identified and relationships with their antecedents, concomitants, and consequents are explored (Porter & Steers, 1973). Alternatively, many authors have dropped the strict dichotomy between overt behaviors and attitudinal, conative, and cognitive antecedents/concomitants. These authors tend (implicitly) to conceive of acts as including both overt and covert aspects, and they describe work behavior as a process involving a sequence of stages (Mobley, 1977; Mobley, Horner, & Hollingsworth, 1978; Mobley, Griffith, Hand, & Meglino, 1979; Porter & Lawler, 1968; Steers & Rhodes, 1978). The second approach has the potential advantage of emphasizing the importance of individual processes that mediate overt actions and observable outcomes. Thus, the second route of viewing behavior as a unit of overt and covert processes (by covert is meant those latent processes that can reasonably be deduced from overt behaviors) has been adopted for this paper.

Based on a review of the recent literature, three sets of intermediary process variables and a suspected sequence were derived. The first set of variables centers on the issue of the extent to which work events and attributes are related to the individual's value system. Therefore, these variables are termed *value-related*. This set is similar to Katz's (1964) motivational patterns of intrinsic satisfaction, goal internalization, and acceptance of organizational rules. Four variables were identified for this set: (a) importance of success versus failure at work for a person's self-esteem—a variable identified by Rabinowitz and Hall (1977) as one conceptualization of job involvement; (b) the extent to which one's job and/or work is a "central life interest" (Dubin, 1956)—a variable also interpreted by Rabinowitz and Hall (1977) as a manifestation of the "importance of self-esteem" conceptualization of job involvement; (c) the worker's expectation of pleasant/unpleasant feelings as a result of success versus failure (Lawler, 1969)—a variable best summarized as intrinsic motivation; and (d) the extent of belief in and acceptance of values pertinent to the work role—these values can consist of organizational goals, but they may be specific to a particular profession or occupation (Gouldner, 1957). As "acceptance of organizational goals and values," this variable is identical to the first component of "organizational commitment" (Porter, Steers, Mowday, & Boulian, 1974).

The second set, which includes two variables, represents the extent to which work role, occupation, and organizational membership mark the individual's self-image and the degree to which the individual derives satisfaction from interpersonal relations and primary-group relationships (Katz, 1964) in organizations. This set therefore may be labeled *identity-related*. More specifically, the variables in this set may be termed: (a) importance of the job or the work role for a person's self-concept; and (b) social attachment to the organization. Importance of the job for self-concept is the second conceptualization of job involvement as elaborated by Rabinowitz and Hall (1977). According to these authors, this variable also can be understood as the degree of psychological identification with work. Social attachment refers to the desire to remain within one's organization and to remain a member of the organization. It corresponds therefore to the third component of "organizational commitment" (Porter et al., 1974).

The third set of variables is comprised of utility-related aspects of the job—for example Katz's (1964) instrumental system and instrumental rewards. These aspects will be referred to with the inclusive variable level of "job outcome utility." This variable consists of extrinsic factors and is reflected in terms such as role attraction (Mobley, Hand, Baker, & Meglino, 1979) and valance of the work role (Vroom, 1964). Also, it is parallel to satisfaction with specific extrinsic facets of the job (Lawler, 1973). Subjective evaluations of job outcomes are thought to be a function not only of the absolute attractiveness of outcomes, but also of social comparisons (Adams, 1965; Katzell, 1964; Locke, 1969).

These three sets of variables—value-related, identity-related, and utilitarian—may be understood as antecedents of those *behavioral intentions* that are, in turn, related to overt behavior. Thus, the variable now considered corresponds to Fishbein's (1967) "behavioral intentions" (BI). This variable is used in Mobley's turnover model (Miller, Katerberg, & Hulin, 1979; Mobley, 1977; Mobley et al., 1978). In the Porter et al. (1974) "organizational commitment" scheme, this variable appears as "willingness to exert effort on behalf of the organization." It must be noted that Porter et al.'s "willingness to exert effort" is far less specific than such variables as intentions to quit, attend, and produce efficiently, which usually are criteria for prediction. Thus, willingness to exert effort might appear as an antecedent to specific intentions.

Lastly, the proposed process generates overt activity. Examples of this variable are production behavior, quitting, attending, and job performance (the latter is defined as production behavior projected on an evaluative dimension of effectiveness).

A SOCIAL INFLUENCE FRAMEWORK

The entire sequence, consisting of the influence attempts, the three sets of antecedent variables, BI, and overt behavior, is portrayed in Figure 1. Cardinal emphasis is placed on the concept that BI is determined by the three categories of antecedents identified herein. A major corollary of this contention is that in order to change motivation, one has to alter one, two, or all three of these categories. That is to say, motivation change is mediated by changes in the three sets of antecedent variables.

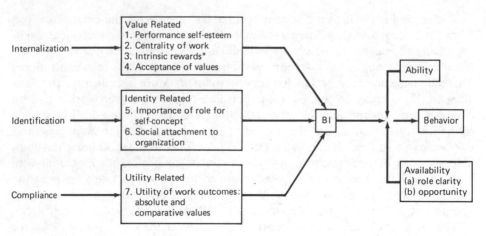

*Includes desire for competence, mastery.

FIGURE 1
Influence processes and sequence.

Logically, the question then must be asked as to how these antecedent variables can be modified. Kelman's (1961) aforementioned processes of influence appear to correspond closely to the character of the three BI-antecedent categories.

1 Compliance is defined by Kelman as acceptance of influence in order to gain specific rewards and to avoid punishments. It is a process wherein behavior is controlled by its contingencies; or, in the terminology of expectancy theory, by expectancies of differently valued outcomes. These notions are similar to the variable "utility of work outcomes." It is proposed here, therefore, that motivation is influenced through the mediary of *utility* by the process of *compliance*.

2 Identification refers to the process of accepting influence in order to engage in a satisfying role-relationship with another person or a group. It is behavior controlled by role acceptance, the involvement in the work role in terms of its importance for the self-concept, the commitment to a group, or the attractiveness of membership in an organization. Therefore, this variety of motivation is influenced through the mediary of *identity-related* variables (i.e., importance of the work role for the self-concept, and social attachment to the organization) by the process of *identification*.

3 Internalization refers to the acceptance of influence because it is congruent with a worker's value system and/or because it is intrinsically rewarding. With regard to the work behavior variables listed above, internalization can be understood to exert control through the importance of success and failure for self-esteem, the place of work as a central life interest, the importance of intrinsic rewards, and acceptance of organizational goals and values. Thus, in such cases, motivation is influenced through the mediary of *value-related* variables by the process of *internalization*.

The relationship between the Kelman influence processes and the dependent and process variables is shown at the left-hand side of Figure 1. The incorporation of the dependent and process variables within the Kelman scheme represents an important elaboration of Kelman's work. The proposed framework and inherent process may be summarized as follows: Among the three variables that influence overt behavior directly, BI is the motivational construct. Motivation, in turn, is a function of value-related, identity-related, and/or utility-related categories of person variables. These three categories are controlled by the interpersonal influence process of internalization, identification, and compliance, respectively.

A relationship exists between Kelman's interpersonal influence processes and Etzioni's types of organizational power. Pure normative organizational power (Etzioni) parallels an internalization interpersonal influence process (Kelman), social power corresponds to identification, and utilitarian and coercive power correspond to Kelman's compliance. In the present framework, this paper proposes to distinguish between *positive* (reward based) and *negative* (punitive oriented) compliance, in order to provide the connections with utilitarian and coercive power. Figure 2 portrays this integration of structural (macro-level) with interpersonal and individual (micro-level) processes. On the left-hand side of Figure 2 are Etzioni's types of power, which at the level of interpersonal influence attempts appear as Kelman-type influence processes (second column). The de-

FIGURE 2
An expanded motivation framework.

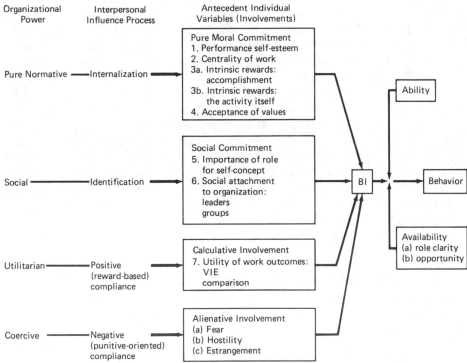

Solid arrows indicate congruent (appropriate) links.

pendent and process variables are clustered, as in Figure 1, with the difference that now the corresponding involvement labels are: pure moral commitment for the value-related variables, social commitment for the identity-related variables, and calculative involvement for the utility-related variables. A cluster is added to describe alienative involvement (consisting of responses such as fear, hostility, and estrangement). These clusters are then seen as antecedents of BI. The right-hand side of Figure 2 is identical to the right-hand side of Figure 1.

The *validity* of the proposed view of social influence is suggested by a consideration of popular methods of motivating workers. For example, O. B. Mod and incentive-type schemes appear to be representative of influence attempts that are based on a simple compliance process. Such approaches seek to use extrinsic factors to bring about behavior change (with little or no attention given to appealing to higher order processes).

Identification-based motivational techniques are best represented by modeling techniques. For example, Goldstein and Sorcher (1974) proposed the use of behavioral modeling, which recently was tested by Latham and Saari (1979) and found to be an effective training technique. Also, studies reported by Burnaska (1976) and Kraut (1976) exemplify the social-learning theory approach to modifying work behavior (Davis & Luthans, 1980a).

Job enrichment, by contrast, appears to be directed toward altering the behavior of workers who are more seriously concerned with value-related issues (by offering opportunities for psychological rewards via job redesign). Job enrichment investigators have reported difficulty with respect to motivating individuals who are low on higher-order growth need strength (e.g., the case of the hard-core unemployed). This gives testimony to the validity of the proposition that an internalization influence attempt is most effective with only certain individuals (Hulin, 1971).

In summary, the major approaches to motivating workers (i.e., organizational intervention approaches) can be viewed as being aligned with each of the proposed influence processes. Although the effectiveness of the various intervention approaches is potentially *moderated* by individual and situational contingencies, the possibility exists that the simultaneous use of multiple approaches may result in relatively greater effectiveness (relative to employing a single motivational approach). This second, *additive* strategy is based on evidence—reviewed by Porras (1979) and Porras and Berg (1978)—that suggests that the number of OD techniques employed in intervention projects (or intervention mix) is positively related with effectiveness.

A SOCIALLY INDEPENDENT MOTIVATIONAL PROCESS

There is a motivational process that has received little consideration in the organizational literature. This process has been ignored, perhaps, because it may be accurately described as a process that is somewhat socially independent. "Socially independent" here means that the relevant behavior originates within the worker with little (at least apparent) external inducement. Nonetheless, the behavior can be characterized as purposeful and seemingly goal-oriented, although the goal is totally internal to the worker. This socially independent motivational process has been termed a competence or mastery motive (White, 1959). This motivational process also encompasses exploratory behavior. Despite its generally socially independent nature, it nonetheless is possible to imagine an influence attempt directed at an individual's competence motive. Such an influence attempt would be one that offered novel and challenging job assignments.

In the vein of socially independent motivational processes, the recently proposed concept of behavioral self-management should be mentioned (Davis & Luthans, 1980b; Luthans & Davis, 1979; Manz & Sims, 1980). Based on concepts derived from cognitive behavior modification (Meichenbaum, 1977), behavioral self-management has been offered as a device for self-directing one's own behavior in desired directions.

IMPLICATIONS

By extending and elaborating the proposed framework, it is possible to deduce several implications for supervisory behaviors that would be directed toward motivating workers. For this extension, it is necessary to introduce a feedback loop from worker behavior to a supervisor or, more generally, an evaluator. In this process (see Figure 3), the supervisor compares the observed behavior of the worker with a standard or prior expectations. The supervisor then determines whether a further influence attempt is warranted. If so, the supervisor decides the nature of the influence attempt (compliance, internalization, and/or identification). From a purely descriptive standpoint, the framework represents a cyclical view of social influence, with the supervisor changing influence strategies as a function of worker behavior. It might be argued that this view places a substantial emphasis on worker behavior as a determinant of supervisor behavior. At first glance, this seems like supervision turned upside-down in that the supervisor's influence attempts are "shaped" by the behavior of the worker. However, once the cycle begins, a reciprocal causation process is set in motion so that the question of primary control of one person over the other becomes pointless.

Taking the descriptive stance a bit further, it might be demonstrated empirically that different types of supervisors prefer different influence modes. For ex-

FIGURE 3
A social influence view of supervisor behavior.

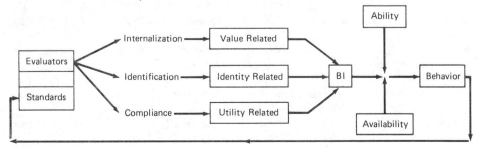

ample, highly authoritarian supervisors might prefer to use compliance influence modes; human-relations oriented supervisors might prefer to use identification influence modes. Also, supervisors might be observed to use different modes of influence when operating in different levels of an organization.

From a prescriptive standpoint, the proposed influence framework suggests that supervisors should be attentive to individual worker differences for preferred inducements. For example, to increase worker motivation, a supervisor should be sensitive to differences in subordinates' preferences for compliance-identification-internalization inducement schemes. It might be possible to demonstrate that more effective supervisors are aware of and make use of subordinate's inducement preferences when attempting to influence the latter's behavior. Such a finding would have important implications for a prescriptive application of the proposed framework.

The above-mentioned extension to supervisor behavior is consistent with the currently popular contingency view of leadership. Clearly, the framework's implications for supervision point to an optimal "matching" of (a) supervisor's preferred style of influence, (b) individual predisposition to respond to specific influence modes, and (c) situational variables that dictate what is socially-appropriate (i.e., normative) for the employment of specific influence models. The view of the supervisor within the proposed framework, in essence, is best summarized as a view of the supervisor "as motivator."

SUMMARY

This paper has outlined a viewpoint that argues that worker motivation cannot be adequately understood without relating the concept of motivation to attempts on the part of organizational agents to "motivate" people. Such attempts usually take place by means of manipulating outcomes that are made contingent on the actions of individuals. The variables were identified that operate at the individual level (motivation), the interpersonal level (influence), and the organizational level (power). A framework was presented for tying these variables together, and concepts from both micro-level and macro-level approaches were integrated in a relatively meso-level approach. Also, specific testable predictions were generated from a proposed theoretical integration.

REFERENCES

Adams, J. S. Inequity in social exchange. In L. Berkowitz (Ed.), *Advances in experimental social psychology* (Vol. 2). New York: Academic Press, 1965, 267–299.

Blood, M. R. Work values and job satisfaction. *Journal of Applied Psychology*, 1969, 53, 456–459.

Burnaska, R. F. The effects of behavior upon managers' behaviors and employees' perceptions. *Personnel Psychology*, 1976, 29, 329–335.

Campbell, J. P., & Pritchard, R. D. Motivation theory in industrial and organizational psychology. In M. Dunnette (Ed.), *Handbook of industrial and organizational psychology*. Chicago: Rand-McNally, 1976, 63–130.

Campbell, J. P., Dunnette, M. D., Lawler, E. E., & Weick, K. E. *Managerial behavior, performance and effectiveness*. New York: McGraw-Hill, 1970.

Davis, T. R. V., & Luthans, F. A social learning approach to organizational behavior. *Academy of Management Review*, 1980a, 5, 281–290.

Davis, T. R. V., & Luthans, F. A social learning approach to training and development: Guidelines for application. *Proceedings of the 12th Annual Meeting of the American Institute for Decision Sciences*, 1980b, 1, 399–401.

Dubin, R. Industrial workers' worlds: A study of the "central life interests" of industrial workers. *Social problems*. 1956, 3, 131–142.

Etzioni, A. *A comparative analysis of complex organizations* (Rev. ed.). New York: Free Press, 1975.

Fishbein, M. (Ed.). *Readings in attitude theory and measurement*. New York: Wiley, 1967.

French, J. R. P., & Raven, B. The bases of social power. In D. Cartwright (Ed.), *Studies in social power*. Ann Arbor, Mich.: Institute for Social Research, 1959, 150–167.

Goldstein, A. P., & Sorcher, M. *Changing supervisory behavior*. New York: Pergamon Press, 1974.

Gouldner, A. W. Cosmopolitans and locals: Toward an analysis of latent social roles. *Administrative Science Quarterly*, 1957, 2, 281–292.

Hackman, J. R., & Oldham, G. R. Motivation through the design of work: Test of a theory. *Organizational Behavior and Human Performance*, 1976, 16, 250–279.

Hulin, C. L. Individual differences and job enrichment: The case against general treatments. In J. R. Maher (Ed.), *New perspectives in job enrichment*. New York: Van Nostrand, 1971, 159–191.

Katz, D. The motivational basis of organizational behavior. *Behavioral Science*, 1964, 9, 131–146.

Katzell, R. A. Personal values, job satisfaction, and job behavior. In H. Borow (Ed.), *Man in a world of work*. Boston: Houghton Mifflin, 1964, 314–363.

Kelman, H. C. Processes of opinion change. *Public Opinion Quarterly*, 1961, 25, 57–78.

Kohlberg, L. Moral development and identification. In H. Stevenson (Ed.), *Child psychology*, 62nd Yearbook of the National Society for the study of Education. Chicago: University of Chicago Press, 1963, 383–431.

Kohlberg, L. The cognitive-developmental approach to socialization. In D. A. Goslin (Ed.), *Handbook of socialization theory and research*. Chicago: Rand-McNally, 1969, 347–480.

Kraut, A. I. Developing managerial skills via modeling techniques: Some positive research findings—a symposium. *Personnel Psychology*, 1976, 29, 325–369.

Latham, G. P., & Saari, L. M. Application of social-learning theory to training supervisors through behavioral modeling. *Journal of Applied Psychology*, 1979, 64, 239–246.

Lawler, E. E., III. Job design and employee motivation. *Personnel Psychology*, 1969, 22, 426–435.

Lawler, E. E., III. *Pay and organizational effectiveness*. New York: McGraw-Hill, 1971.

Lawler, E. E., III. *Motivation in work organizations*. Monterey, Cal.: Brooks/Cole, 1973.

Locke, E. A. What is job satisfaction? *Organizational Behavior and Human Performance*, 1969, 4, 309–336.

Luthans, F., & Davis, T. R. V. Behavioral self-management—the missing link in managerial effectiveness. *Organizational dynamics*, 1979, 8, 42–60.

Manz, C. C., & Sims, H. P. Self-management as a substitute for leadership: A social learning theory perspective. *Academy of Management Review*, 1980, 5, 361–367.

Meichenbaum, D. *Cognitive behavior modification: An integrative approach*. New York: Plenum, 1977.

Miller, E. E., Katerberg, R., & Hulin, C. L. Evaluation of the Mobley, Horner, and Hollingsworth model of employee turnover. *Journal of Applied Psychology*, 1979, 64, 509–517.

Mirels, H. L., & Garrett, J. B. The Protestant ethic as a personality variable. *Journal of Consulting and Clinical Psychology,* 1971, 36, 40–44.

Mobley, W. H. Intermediate linkages in the relationship between job satisfaction and employee turnover. *Journal of Applied Psychology,* 1977, 62, 237–240.

Mobley, W. H., Horner, S. O., & Hollingsworth, A. T. An evaluation of precursors of hospital employee turnover. *Journal of Applied Psychology,* 1978, 63, 408–414.

Mobley, W. H., Griffeth, R. W., Hand, H. H., & Meglino, B. M. Review and conceptual analysis of the employee turnover process. *Psychological Bulletin,* 1979, 86, 493–522.

Mobley, W. H., Hand, H. H., Baker, R. L., & Meglino, B. M. Conceptual and empirical analysis of military recruit training attrition. *Journal of Applied Psychology,* 1979, 64, 10–18.

Porras, J. I. The comparative impact of different OD techniques and intervention intensities. *Journal of Applied Behavioral Sciences,* 1979, 15, 156–178.

Porras, J. I., & Berg, P. O. The impact of organization development. *Academy of Management Review,* 1978, 3, 249–266.

Porter, L. W., & Lawler, E. E., III. *Managerial attitudes and performance.* Homewood, Ill.: Irwin, 1968.

Porter, L. W., & Steers, R. M. Organizational, work and personal factors in employee turnover and absenteeism. *Psychological Bulletin,* 1973, 80, 151–176.

Porter, L. W., Steers, R. M., Mowday, R. T., & Boulian, P. V. Organizational commitment, job satisfactions and turnover among psychiatric technicians. *Journal of Applied Psychology,* 1974, 59, 603–609.

Rabinowitz, S., & Hall, D. T. Organizational research and job involvement. *Psychological Bulletin,* 1977, 84, 265–288.

Rotter, J. B. Generalized expectancies for internal versus external control of reinforcement. *Psychological Monographs,* 1966, 80, (1, Whole No. 609).

Steers, R. M., & Rhodes, R. S. Major influences on employee attendance: A process model. *Journal of Applied Psychology,* 1978, 63, 391–407.

Vecchio, R. P. An individual differences interpretation of conflicting predictions generated by equity theory and expectancy theory. *Journal of Applied Psychology,* 1981, 66, 470–481.

Vroom, V. H. *Work and motivation.* New York: Wiley, 1964.

White, R. Motivation reconsidered: The concept of competence. *Psychological Review,* 1959, 66, 297–334.

The Development and Enforcement of Group Norms

Daniel C. Feldman

Group norms are the informal rules that groups adopt to regulate and regularize group members' behavior. Although these norms are infrequently written down or openly discussed, they often have a powerful, and consistent, influence on group members' behavior (Hackman, 1976).

Most of the theoretical work on group norms has focused on identifying the types of group norms (March, 1954) or on describing their structural characteris-

From *Academy of Management Review,* 1984, **9,** 47–53. Reprinted by permission.

tics (Jackson, 1966). Empirically, most of the focus has been on examining the impact that norms have on other social phenomena. For example, Seashore (1954) and Schachter, Ellertson, McBride, and Gregory (1951) use the concept of group norms to discuss group cohesiveness; Trist and Bamforth (1951) and Whyte (1955a) use norms to examine production restriction; Janis (1972) and Longley and Pruitt (1980) use norms to illuminate group decision making; and Asch (1951) and Sherif (1936) use norms to examine conformity.

This paper focuses on two frequently overlooked aspects of the group norms literature. First, it examines *why* group norms are enforced. Why do groups desire conformity to these informal rules? Second, it examines *how* group norms develop. Why do some norms develop in one group but not in another? Much of what is known about group norms comes from post hoc examination of their impact on outcome variables; much less has been written about how these norms actually develop and why they regulate behavior so strongly.

Understanding how group norms develop and why they are enforced is important for two reasons. First, group norms can play a large role in determining whether the group will be productive or not. If the work group feels that management is supportive, group norms will develop that facilitate—in fact, enhance—group productivity. In contrast, if the work group feels that management is antagonistic, group norms that inhibit and impair group performance are much more likely to develop. Second, managers can play a major role in setting and changing group norms. They can use their influence to set task-facilitative norms; they can monitor whether the group's norms are functional; they can explicitly address counterproductive norms with subordinates. By understanding how norms develop and why norms are enforced, managers can better diagnose the underlying tensions and problems their groups are facing, and they can help the group develop more effective behavior patterns.

WHY NORMS ARE ENFORCED

As Shaw (1981) suggests, a group does not establish or enforce norms about every conceivable situation. Norms are formed and enforced only with respect to behaviors that have some significance for the group. The frequent distinction between task maintenance duties and social maintenance duties helps explain why groups bring selected behaviors under normative control.

Groups, like individuals, try to operate in such a way that they maximize their chances for task success and minimize their chances of task failure. First of all, a group will enforce norms that facilitate its very survival. It will try to protect itself from interference from groups external to the organization or harassment from groups internal to the organization. Second, the group will want to increase the predictability of group members' behaviors. Norms provide a basis for predicting the behavior of others, thus enabling group members to anticipate each other's actions and to prepare quick and appropriate responses (Shaw, 1981; Kiesler & Kiesler, 1970).

In addition, groups want to ensure the satisfaction of their members and prevent as much interpersonal discomfort as possible. Thus, groups also will enforce norms that help the group avoid embarrassing interpersonal problems. Certain topics of conversation might be sanctioned, and certain types of social interaction might be openly discouraged. Moreover, norms serve an expressive function for groups (Katz & Kahn, 1978). Enforcing group norms gives group members a chance to express what their central values are, and to clarify what is distinctive about the group and central to its identity (Hackman, 1976).

Each of these four conditions under which group norms are most likely to be enforced is discussed in more detail below.

1 *Norms are likely to be enforced if they facilitate group survival.* A group will enforce norms that protect it from interference or harassment by members of other groups. For instance, a group might develop a norm not to discuss its salaries with members of other groups in the organization, so that attention will not be brought to pay inequities in its favor. Groups might also have norms about not discussing internal problems with members of other units. Such discussions might boomerang at a later date if other groups use the information to develop a better competitive strategy against the group.

Enforcing group norms also makes clear what the "boundaries" of the group are. As a result of observation of deviant behavior and the consequences that ensue, other group members are reminded of the *range* of behavior that is acceptable to the group (Dentler & Erikson, 1959). The norms about productivity that frequently develop among piecerate workers are illustrative here. By observing a series of incidents (a person produces 50 widgets and is praised; a person produces 60 widgets and receives sharp teasing; a person produces 70 widgets and is ostracized), group members learn the limits of the group's patience: "This far, and no further." The group is less likely to be "successful" (i.e., continue to sustain the low productivity expectations of management) if it allows its jobs to be reevaluated.

The literature on conformity and deviance is consistent with this observation. The group is more likely to reject the person who violates group norms when the deviant has not been a "good" group member previously (Hollander, 1958, 1964). Individuals can generate "idiosyncrasy credits" with other group members by contributing effectively to the attainment of group goals. Individuals expend these credits when they perform poorly or dysfunctionally at work. When a group member no longer has a positive "balance" of credits to draw on when he or she deviates, the group is much more likely to reject the deviant (Hollander, 1961).

Moreover, the group is more likely to reject the deviant when the group is failing in meeting its goals successfully. When the group is successful, it can afford to be charitable or tolerant towards deviant behavior. The group may disapprove, but it has some margin for error. When the group is faced with failure, the deviance is much more sharply punished. Any behavior that negatively influences the success of the group becomes much more salient and threatening to group members (Alvarez, 1968; Wiggins, Dill & Schwartz, 1965).

2 *Norms are likely to be enforced if they simplify, or make predictable, what behavior is expected of group members.* If each member of the group had to decide individually how to behave in each interaction, much time would be lost performing routine activities. Moreover, individuals would have more trouble predicting the behaviors of others and responding correctly. Norms enable group members to anticipate each other's actions and to prepare the most appropriate response in the most timely manner (Hackman, 1976; Shaw, 1981).

For instance, when attending group meetings in which proposals are presented and suggestions are requested, do the presenters really want feedback or are they simply going through the motions? Groups may develop norms that reduce this uncertainty and provide a clearer course of action, for example, make suggestions in small, informal meetings but not in large, formal meetings.

Another example comes from norms that regulate social behavior. For instance, when colleagues go out for lunch together, there can be some awkwardness about how to split the bill at the end of the meal. A group may develop a norm that gives some highly predictable or simple way of behaving, for example, split evenly, take turns picking up the tab, or pay for what each ordered.

Norms also may reinforce specific individual members' roles. A number of different roles might emerge in groups. These roles are simply expectations that are shared by group members regarding who is to carry out what types of activities under what circumstances (Bales & Slater, 1955). Although groups obviously create pressure toward uniformity among members, there also is a tendency for groups to create and maintain *diversity* among members (Hackman, 1976). For instance, a group might have one person whom others expect to break the tension when tempers become too hot. Another group member might be expected to keep track of what is going on in other parts of the organization. A third member might be expected to take care of the "creature" needs of the group—making the coffee, making dinner reservations, and so on. A fourth member might be expected by others to take notes, keep minutes, or maintain files.

None of these roles are *formal* duties, but they are activities that the group needs accomplished and has somehow parcelled out among members. If the role expectations are not met, some important jobs might not get done, or other group members might have to take on additional responsibilities. Moreover, such role assignments reduce individual members' ambiguities about what is expected specifically of them. It is important to note, though, that who takes what role in a group also is highly influenced by individuals' personal needs. The person with a high need for structure often wants to be in the note-taking role to control the structuring activity in the group; the person who breaks the tension might dislike conflict and uses the role to circumvent it.

3 *Norms are likely to be enforced if they help the group avoid embarrassing interpersonal problems.* Goffman's work on "facework" gives some insight on this point. Goffman (1955) argues that each person in a group has a "face" he or she presents to other members of a group. This "face" is analogous to what one would call "self-image," the person's perceptions to himself or herself and how he or she would like to be seen by others. Groups want to insure that no one's self-image is damaged, called into question, or embarrassed. Consequently, the group will establish norms that discourage topics of conversation or situations in which face is too likely to be inadvertently broken. For instance, groups might develop norms about not discussing romantic involvements (so that differences in moral values do not become salient) or about not getting together socially in people's homes (so that differences in taste or income do not become salient).

A good illustration of Goffman's facework occurs in the classroom. There is always palpable tension in a room when either a class is totally unprepared to discuss a case or a professor is totally unprepared to lecture or lead the discussion. One part of the awkwardness stems from the inability of the other partner in the interaction to behave as he or she is prepared to or would like to behave. The professor cannot teach if the students are not prepared, and the students cannot learn if the professors are not teaching. Another part of the awkwardness, though, stems from self-images being called into question. Although faculty are aware that not all students are serious scholars, the situation is difficult to handle if the class as a group does not even show a pretense of wanting to learn. Although students are aware that many faculty are mainly interested in research and consulting, there is a problem if the professor does not even show a pretense of caring to teach. Norms almost always develop between professor and students about what level of preparation and interest is expected by the other because both parties want to avoid awkward confrontations.

4 *Norms are likely to be enforced if they express the central values of the group and clarify what is distinctive about the group's identity.* Norms can provide the social justification for group activities to its members (Katz & Kahn, 1978). When the production group labels rate-busting deviant, it says: "We care more about maximizing group security than about individual profits." Group norms also convey what is distinctive about the group to outsiders. When an advertising agency labels unstylish clothes deviant, it says: "We think of ourselves, personally and professionally, as trend-setters, and being fashionably dressed conveys that to our clients and our public."

One of the key expressive functions of group norms is to define and legitimate the power of the group itself over individual members (Katz & Kahn, 1978). When groups punish norm infraction, they reinforce in the minds of group members the authority of the group. Here, too, the literature on group deviance sheds some light on the issue at hand.

It has been noted frequently that the amount of deviance in a group is rather small (Erikson, 1966; Schur, 1965). The group uses norm enforcement to show the *strength* of the group. However, if a behavior becomes so widespread that it becomes impossible to control, then the labeling of the widespread behavior as deviance becomes problematic. It simply reminds members of the *weakness* of the group. At this point, the group will redefine what is deviant more narrowly, or it will define its job as that of keeping deviants *within bounds* rather than that of obliterating it altogether. For example, though drug use is and always has been illegal, the widespread use of drugs has led to changes in law enforcement over time. A greater distinction now is made between "hard" drugs and other controlled substances; less penalty is given to those apprehended with small amounts than large amounts; greater attention is focused on capturing large scale smugglers and traffickers than the occasional user. A group, unconsciously if not consciously, learns how much behavior it is capable of labeling deviant *and* punishing effectively.

Finally, this expressive function of group norms can be seen nicely in circumstances in which there is an inconsistency between what group members *say* is the group norm and how people actually *behave*. For instance, sometimes groups will engage in a lot of rhetoric about how much independence its managers are allowed and how much it values entrepreneurial effort; yet the harder data suggest that the more conservative, deferring, or dependent managers get rewarded. Such an inconsistency can reflect conflicts among the group's expressed values. First, the group can be ambivalent about independence; the group knows it needs to encourage more entrepreneurial efforts to flourish, but such efforts create competition and threaten the status quo. Second, the inconsistency can reveal major subgroup differences. Some people may value and encourage entrepreneurial behavior, but others do not—and the latter may control the group's rewards. Third, the inconsistency can reveal a source of the group's self-consciousness, a dichotomy between what the group is really like and how it would like to be perceived. The group may realize that it is too conservative, yet be unable or too frightened to address its problem. The expressed group norm allows the group members a chance to present a "face" to each other and to outsiders that is more socially desirable than reality.

HOW GROUP NORMS DEVELOP

Norms usually develop gradually and informally as group members learn what behaviors are necessary for the group to function more effectively. However, it also is possible for the norm development process to be short-cut by a critical event in the group or by conscious group decision (Hackman, 1976).

Most norms develop in one or more of the following four ways: explicit statements by supervisors or co-workers; critical events in the group's history; primacy; and carry-over behaviors from past situations.

1 *Explicit statements by supervisors or co-workers.* Norms that facilitate group survival or task success often are set by the leader of the group or powerful members (Whyte, 1955b). For instance, a group leader might explicitly set norms about not drinking at lunch because subordinates who have been drinking are more likely to have problems dealing competently with clients and top management or they are more likely to have accidents at work. The group leader might also set norms about lateness, personal phone calls, and long coffee breaks if too much productivity is lost as a result of time away from the work place.

Explicit statements by supervisors also can increase the predictability of group members' behavior. For instance, supervisors might have particular preferences for a way of analyzing problems or presenting reports. Strong norms will be set to ensure compliance with these preferences. Consequently, supervisors will have increased certainty about receiving work in the format requested, so they can plan accordingly; workers will have increased certainty about what is expected, so they will not have to outguess their boss or redo their projects.

Managers or important group members also can define the specific role expectations of individual group members. For instance, a supervisor or a co-worker might go up to a new recruit after a meeting to give the proverbial advice: "New recruits should be seen and not heard." The senior group member might be trying to prevent the new recruit from appearing brash or incompetent or from embarrassing other group members. Such interventions set specific role expectations for the new group member.

Norms that cater to supervisor preferences also are frequently established even if they are not objectively necessary to task accomplishment. For example, although organizational norms may be very democratic in terms of everybody calling each other by their first names, some managers have strong preferences about being called Mr., Ms., or Mrs. Although the form of address used in the work group does not influence group effectiveness, complying with the norm bears little cost to the group member, whereas noncompliance could cause daily friction with the supervisor. Such norms help group members avoid embarrassing interpersonal interactions with their managers.

Fourth, norms set explicitly by the supervisor frequently express the central values of the group. For instance, a dean can set very strong norms about faculty keeping office hours and being on campus daily. Such norms reaffirm to members of the academic community their teaching and service obligations, and they send signals to individuals outside the college about what is valued in faculty behavior or distinctive about the school. A dean also could set norms that allow faculty to consult or do executive development two or three days a week. Such norms, too, legitimate other types of faculty behavior and send signals to both insiders and outsiders about some central values of the college.

2 *Critical events in the group's history.* At times there is a critical event in the group's history that established an important precedent. For instance, a group member might have discussed hiring plans with members of other units in the organization, and as a result new positions were lost or there was increased competition for good applicants. Such indiscretion can substantially hinder the survival and task success of the group; very likely the offender will be either formally censured or informally rebuked. As a result of such an incident, norms about secrecy might develop that will protect the group in similar situations in the future.

An example from Janis's *Victims of Groupthink* (1972) also illustrates this point nicely. One of President Kennedy's closest advisors, Arthur Schlesinger, Jr., had serious reservations about the Bay of Pigs invasion and presented his strong objections to the Bay of Pigs plan in a memorandum to Kennedy and Secretary of State Dean Rusk. However, Schlesinger was pressured by the President's brother, Attorney General Robert Kennedy, to keep his objections to himself. Remarked Robert Kennedy to Schlesinger: "You may be right or you may be wrong, but the President has made his mind up. Don't push it any further. Now is the time for everyone to help him all they can." Such critical events led group members to silence their views and set up group norms about the bounds of disagreeing with the president.

Sometimes group norms can be set by a conscious decision of a group after a particularly good or bad experience the group has had. To illustrate, a group might have had a particularly constructive meeting and be very pleased with how much it accomplished. Several people might say, "I think the reason we got so much accomplished today is that we met really early in the morning before the rest of the staff showed up and the phone started ringing. Let's try to continue to meet at 7:30 a.m." Others might agree, and the norm is set. On the other hand, if a group notices it accomplished way too little in a meeting, it might openly discuss setting norms to cut down on ineffective behavior (e.g., having an agenda, not interrupting others while they are talking). Such norms develop to facilitate task success and to reduce uncertainty about what is expected from each individual in the group.

Critical events also can identify awkward interpersonal situations that need to be avoided in the future. For instance, a divorce between two people working in the same group might have caused a lot of acrimony and hard feeling in a unit, not only between the husband and wife but also among various other group members who got involved in the marital problems. After the unpleasant divorce, a group might develop a norm about not hiring spouses to avoid having to deal with such interpersonal problems in the future.

Finally, critical events also can give rise to norms that express the central, or distinctive, values of the group. When a peer review panel finds a physician or lawyer guilty of malpractice or malfeasance, first it establishes (or reaffirms) the rights of professionals to evaluate and criticize the professional behavior of their colleagues. Moreover, it clarifies what behaviors are inconsistent with the group's self-image or its values. When a faculty committee votes on a candidate's tenure, it, too, asserts the legitimacy of influence of senior faculty over junior faculty. In addition, it sends (hopefully) clear messages to junior faculty about its values in terms of quality of research, teaching, and service. There are important "announcement effects" of peer reviews; internal group members carefully re-examine the group's values, and outsiders draw inferences about the character of the group from such critical decisions.

3 *Primacy.* The first behavior pattern that emerges in a group often sets group expectations. If the first group meeting is marked by very formal interaction between supervisors and subordinates, then the group often expects future meetings to be conducted in the same way. Where people sit in meetings or rooms frequently is developed through primacy. People generally continue to sit in the same seats they sat in at their first meeting, even though those original seats are not assigned and people could change where they sit at every meeting. Most friendship groups of students develop their own "turf" in a lecture hall and are surprised/dismayed when an interloper takes "their" seats.

Norms that develop through primacy often do so to simplify, or make predictable, what behavior is expected of group members. There may be very little task impact from where people sit in meetings or how formal interactions are. However, norms develop about such behaviors to make life much more routine and predictable. Every time a group member enters a room, he or she does not have to "decide" where to sit or how formally to behave. Moreover, he or she also is much more certain about how other group members will behave.

4 *Carry-over behaviors from past situations.* Many group norms in organizations emerge because individual group members bring set expectations with them from other work groups in other organizations. Lawyers expect to behave towards clients in Organization I (e.g., confidentiality, setting fees) as they behaved towards those in Organization II. Doctors expect to behave toward patients in Hospital I (e.g., "bedside manner," professional distance) as they behaved in Hospital II. Accountants expect to behave towards colleagues at Firm I (e.g., dress code, adherence to statutes) as they behaved towards those at Firm II. In fact, much of what goes on in professional schools is giving new members of the profession the same standards and norms of behavior that practitioners in the field hold.

Such carry-over of individual behaviors from past situations can increase the predictability of group members' behaviors in new settings and facilitate task accomplishment. For instance, students and professors bring with them fairly constant sets of expectations from class to class. As a result, students do not have to relearn continually their roles from class to class; they know, for instance, if they come in late to take a seat quietly at the back of the room without being told. Professors also do not have to relearn continually their roles; they know, for instance, not to mumble, scribble in small print on the blackboard, or be vague when making course assignments. In addition, presumably the most task-successful norms will be the ones carried over from organization to organization.

Moreover, such carry-over norms help avoid embarrassing interpersonal situations. Individuals are more likely to know which conversations and actions provoke annoyance, irritation, or embarrassment to their colleagues. Finally, when groups carry over norms from one organization to another, they also clarify what is distinctive about the occupational or professional role. When lawyers maintain strict rules of confidentiality, when doctors maintain a consistent professional distance with patients, when accountants present a very formal physical appearance, they all assert: "These are the standards we sustain *independent* of what we could 'get away with' in this organization. This is *our* self-concept."

SUMMARY

Norms generally are enforced only for behaviors that are viewed as important by most group members. Groups do not have the time or energy to regulate each and every action of individual members. Only those behaviors that ensure group survival, facilitate task accomplishment, contribute to group morale, or express the group's central values are likely to be brought under normative control. Norms that reflect these group needs will develop through explicit statements of supervisors, critical events in the group's history, primacy, or carry-over behaviors from past situations.

Empirical research on norm development and enforcement has substantially lagged descriptive and theoretical work. In large part, this may be due to the methodological problems of measuring norms and getting enough data points either across time or across groups. Until such time as empirical work progresses, however, the usefulness of group norms as a predictive concept, rather than as a post hoc explanatory device, will be severely limited. Moreover, until it is known more concretely why norms develop and why they are strongly enforced, attempts to *change* group norms will remain haphazard and difficult to accomplish.

REFERENCES

Alvarez, R. Informal reactions to deviance in simulated work organizations: A laboratory experiment. *American Sociological Review,* 1968, 33, 895–912.

Asch, S. Effects of group pressure upon the modification and distortion of judgment. In M. H. Guetzkow (Ed.), *Groups, leadership, and men.* Pittsburgh: Carnegie, 1951, 117–190.

Bales, R. F., & Slater, P. E. Role differentiation in small groups. In T. Parsons, R. F. Bales, J. Olds, M. Zelditch, & P. E. Slater (Eds.), *Family, socialization, and interaction process.* Glencoe, Ill.: Free Press, 1955, 35–131.

Dentler, R. A., & Erikson, K. T. The functions of deviance in groups. *Social Problems,* 1959, 7, 98–107.

Erickson, K. T. *Wayward Puritans.* New York: Wiley, 1966.

Goffman, E. On face-work: An analysis of ritual elements in social interaction. *Psychiatry,* 1955, 18, 213–231.

Hackman, J. R. Group influences on individuals. In M. Dunnette (Ed.), *Handbook of industrial and organizational psychology.* Chicago: Rand McNally, 1976, 1455–1525.

Hollander, E. P. Conformity, status, and idiosyncrasy credit. *Psychological Review,* 1958, 65, 117–127.

Hollander, E. P. Some effects of perceived status on responses to innovative behavior. *Journal of Abnormal and Social Psychology,* 1961, 63, 247–250.

Hollander, E. P. *Leaders, groups, and influence.* New York: Oxford University Press, 1964.

Jackson, J. A conceptual and measurement model for norms and roles. *Pacific Sociological Review,* 1966, 9, 35–47.

Janis, I. *Victims of groupthink: A psychological study of foreign-policy decisions and fiascos.* New York: Houghton-Mifflin, 1972.

Katz, D., & Kahn, R. L. *The social psychology of organizations.* 2nd ed. New York: Wiley, 1978.

Kiesler, C. A., & Kiesler, S. B. *Conformity.* Reading, Mass.: Addison-Wesley, 1970.

Longley, J., & Pruitt, D. C. Groupthink: A critique of Janis' theory. In Ladd Wheeler (Ed.), *Review of personality and social psychology.* Beverly Hills: Sage, 1980, 74–93.

March, J. Group norms and the active minority. *American Sociological Review,* 1954, 19, 733–741.

Schachter, S., Ellertson, N., McBride, D., & Gregory, D. An experimental study of cohesiveness and productivity. *Human Relations,* 1951, 4, 229–238.

Schur, E. M. *Crimes without victims.* Englewood Cliffs, N.J.: Prentice-Hall, 1965.

Seashore, S. *Group cohesiveness in the industrial work group.* Ann Arbor: Institute for Social Research, University of Michigan, 1954.

Shaw, M. *Group dynamics.* 3rd ed. New York: Harper, 1936.

Trist, E. L., & Bamforth, K. W. Some social and psychological consequences of the longwall method of coal-getting. *Human Relations,* 1951, 4, 1–38.

Whyte, W. F. *Money and motivation.* New York: Harper, 1955a.

Whyte, W. F. *Street corner society*. Chicago: University of Chicago Press, 1955b.
Wiggins, J. A., Dill, F., & Schwartz, R. D. On status-liability. *Sociometry*, 1965, 28, 197–209.

When Friends Leave: A Structural Analysis of the Relationship between Turnover and Stayers' Attitudes

David Krackhardt
Lyman W. Porter

One of the fundamental dilemmas facing those studying organizational phenomena is that all such phenomena are simultaneously micro and macro. That is, individual actors behave in organizations in ways that are influenced by the larger context in which they find themselves. The dilemma stems from the difficulty of keeping the importance of both of these perspectives in focus. We have a tendency to focus on one arena or the other, perhaps because of our training (as psychologists or sociologists, for example).

This propensity to focus narrowly survives despite admonitions from many scholars in the field. Probably the most famous of these is Lewin's familiar dictum about behavior being a function of the person and the environment (Lewin, 1966: 166). He translated this axiom into a force-field theory of cognitions and behavior that became a cornerstone of social psychology. The study of the micro side of organizations has certainly benefited from the stream of research that has resulted (e.g., Salancik and Pfeffer, 1978; Staw, 1980b). But the original emphasis that Lewin placed on the larger social context has been missing in such work.

At the macro level, a few organizational sociologists have introduced some psychology into their models. Notable among these is Burt (1982), who incorporated the work of the psychologist Stevens (1962) into his theory of action. The contribution that psychology makes to his understanding of behavior, however, is minor: Burt restricts himself to rational and purposive action within the structure surrounding the actor.

Thus, on the one hand, organizational psychology and social psychology have explored individuals' values, beliefs, perceptions, and motives, which can lead to their observed behavior. On the other hand, organizational sociology has focused on the structural constraints to such behavior. The purpose of this paper is to demonstrate that the combination of both orientations can lead to new insights into organizational phenomena. This demonstration employs a distinctly macro, structural lens to look at a current micro organizational research question—the effect that turnover has on the attitudes of those who remain. The result confirms

Condensed from the *Administrative Science Quarterly*, 1985, **30**(2), 242–261. Copyright © 1985 by Cornell University. 0001-8392/85/3002-0242. Reprinted by permission.

the power of structural constraints, but at the same time retains the richness of the psychological explanations.

TURNOVER AND THE PSYCHOLOGY OF STAYERS: A MICRO PERSPECTIVE

The field of organizational behavior is witnessing a miniparadigmatic shift in the study of turnover (Dalton and Todor, 1979). Instead of looking for causes of turnover, as is traditionally done, a handful of researchers (e.g., Staw, 1980a; Steers and Mowday, 1981; Mobley, 1982) maintain the question should be asked: "What effect does turnover have on people who stay in the organization?"

It has been suggested that this is not a simple question. Mowday, Porter, and Steers (1982) argued that there are both positive and negative consequences for stayers when a coworker leaves. On the positive side, turnover creates internal promotion opportunities for those who remain (Dalton and Todor, 1979; Staw, 1980a). Another positive outcome stems from the potentially dissonant situation employees face when their coworkers leave. Mowday (1981) predicted that one way employees can resolve this dissonance is to increase their satisfaction with the job and organization to justify their own decision to stay. An additional benefit may arise if those who left were not carrying their weight in the workload (Dalton and Todor, 1979). One study found that many of the turnovers among bank tellers were those of poor performers (Dalton, Krackhardt, and Porter, 1981). Mowday, Porter, and Steers (1982) suggested that stayers in such situations will benefit and presumably be more satisfied with their jobs.

Conversely, the turnover could leave behind more discouraged, less satisfied coworkers. Each of the reasons for positive consequences mentioned above could be turned around to predict negative consequences. For example, Mowday, Porter, and Steers (1982) noted that the termination of a coworker could require more work of those who remain to make up for the work not being accomplished by the person who left. This would be particularly true if the person who left was a valued employee.

Clearly, one cannot easily predict universally the effects of turnover on the attitudes of stayers. At this stage of development, more empirical work is needed to stabilize any such predictions. One study, that of Mowday's (1981) work on government agencies, provides a starting point for building such a stable set of predictions. He questioned 540 employees in seven agencies of state and county governments in a midwestern state and found that those who were most committed and satisfied with their jobs were more likely to attribute the dominant cause of the coworkers' departures to reasons other than job dissatisfaction.

As Mowday (1981) noted, it was difficult to isolate the cognitive process behind these attributions. For example, an explanation of these results could lie in the nature of the work setting each of the respondents faced. Those who were in work groups where the work was satisfying could be realistic in their perceptions that coworkers were leaving for reasons other than dissatisfaction; those who were in jobs that were less desirable may have equally realistically perceived coworkers leaving for reasons of dissatisfaction. Thus, the observed relationship between attitudes and perceived reasons for turnover could be spurious. To control for spuriousness it is necessary to observe several people's reactions to the identical turnover event.

Mowday's work also pulls together two of the most frequently studied psychological variables in turnover research: job satisfaction and organizational commitment. While based on distinct concepts, they are frequently correlated with each other and with turnover (Mowday, Porter, and Steers, 1982). Perhaps the most important distinction between them can be inferred from their definitions. Job satisfaction focuses on the daily experience and nature of the workplace and work activities. The focus of commitment, on the other hand, is on the organization as a whole, on its goals and values (Angle and Perry, 1981). It is often reflected in the employee's desire to remain a member of the organization, in spite of any specific job to which he or she might be assigned (Porter et al., 1974; Mowday, Steers, and Porter, 1979).

Many of the processes described earlier can lead to changes in either job satisfaction or commitment, depending on the focus of the meaning that the observer gives to the turnover event. For example, if coworkers leave because they dislike the kind of work they are doing, this may remind the stayer of how dissatisfying his or her work is. On the other hand, if the stayer believes that organizational policies are responsible for the miserable lot that the leaver has just escaped, then the stayer's commitment to the organization may also suffer.

TURNOVER IN FRIENDSHIP DYADS: A SOCIAL PSYCHOLOGICAL PERSPECTIVE

Since it is so difficult to predict negative vs. positive consequences, Mowday, Porter, and Steers (1982) provided a set of moderating variables. One of these, the social relationship the stayer has to the leaver, they stated may be critical: When the person leaving is a close friend, the effect on the stayer "may be particularly traumatic" (p. 148).

But Mowday, Porter, and Steers (1982) did not offer specific predictions as to how the close friendship might affect the attitudes of stayers. However, the literature on friendships does provide some guidelines. Perhaps the most useful model to organize the possible outcomes is Heider's (1958) balance theory. In this model, a triangle of relationships is described between an observer (self), another person, and an object of common interest. In this case, the observer (stayer) is faced with a coworker (who is a friend) and the job (Figure 1). For the purpose of exposition, it is assumed that the link between each pair of vertices is positive prior to the departure of the coworker. That is, the triangle is balanced: The observer has positive affect for the job, the observer has positive affect for the coworker, and the coworker has positive affect toward the job.

How this triangle might change (or not change) as a result of the termination of the coworker is depicted in Figure 1 (Effects A, B, and C). In each of these predictions, it is assumed that positive attitudes held toward the friends remain, or at least do not become negative. This assumption is supported in friendship studies,

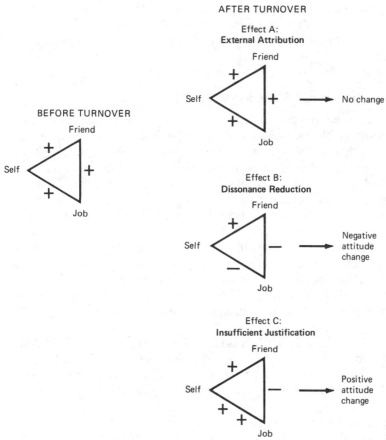

FIGURE 1
Possible effects of turnover of friend on stayer.

where such links are generally stable over long periods of time (e.g., Newcomb et al., 1967).

The first prediction is that no change in attitude toward the job would occur. This could happen if the employee attributed exogenous reasons to the friend's departure (Effect A). In this way, an attribution of job satisfaction to the friend can be maintained in the face of the friend's leaving (e.g., "My friend liked the job, but she had to leave because of school"). Mowday (1981) proposed a similar argument to explain his results, referring to such external attributions as the "pull" forces of turnover.

Effect B in Figure 1 depicts the possibility of a negative change in attitude resulting from a friend's leaving. In this scenario, the employee attributes dissatisfaction to the friend who left. This creates dissonance, which is resolved in the triangle by the stayer becoming more dissatisfied with his or her job.

Effect C represents a possibility not predicted directly from balance theory but that has some support in dissonance studies. If the person observes a coworker leaving and attributes dissatisfaction to the leaver, then the person's decision to stay may require more justification (Staw, 1976; 1980b). One way this justification could occur is for the stayer to develop more and stronger positive attitudes toward the workplace.

TURNOVER EMBEDDED IN NETWORK STRUCTURES

These scenarios represent the possibilities at the micro level between two people and their job. However, the workplace is seldom restricted to two people in their organization. Instead, each of N employees must balance N-1 such triangles in his or her head. Few probably actually do so, but it is likely that such forces on a person's psychology are to some extent additive at least figuratively. That is, if many of a person's friends leave, then the effects described in Figure 1 are likely to be stronger than if only one friend leaves. Moreover, the closer the friends are to the person, the stronger the effect is likely to be. Viewed from a more macro perspective, this phenomenon dictates that effects of turnover on stayers will not be uniformly nor randomly distributed among the stayers in the organization. Rather, these effects will be localized and focused on those stayers who are closest to those who left. The social network, then, describes the topology of forces that reverberate throughout an organization when someone leaves (Lewin, 1966; Burt, 1977).

The friendship network in Figure 2 illustrates this proposed effect. Each letter represents an employee; a line connecting two employees indicates that the two employees are friends. Thus, A is a friend of B and C but not of the remaining employees (D through H). If A were to leave, it is proposed that B and C would be most strongly affected.

A person who is not a friend but is seen as a friend of a friend is more apt to have more influence than someone who is not seen as a friend of a friend. By extension, one is more affected by a friend of a friend of a friend than by someone further out in the friendship chain. Thus, it is proposed that A's termination would affect D more than E and that H and G would be least affected.

Another contextual effect must be considered when moving from simple dyads to the entire network. An individual is influenced by those who stay as well as by those who leave. That is, in Figure 1, if the person's friend does not leave, then

FIGURE 2
Hypothetical friendship network.

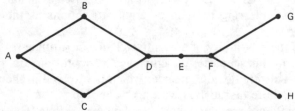

the triangle in "Before Turnover" is reinforced. If many of the coworkers who remain are friends and only one friend leaves, then the impact that this termination will have on the individual will be attenuated.

This balancing effect of leavers vs. stayers is depicted in Figure 3. Four extreme scenarios are represented. In each case, person A has eight coworkers, four of whom leave. Scenario 1 (in the upper left corner of Figure 3) predicts the maximum impact on person A of the four turnovers. That is, since A is close to all four leavers and not close to any of the four stayers, then whatever impact the turnover will have would be relatively large. At the other extreme (scenario 4), when A is close to the stayers and not close to the leavers, then the impact of the turnovers would be least. Scenarios 2 and 3 represent two more moderate effects; however, they represent moderate positions for different reasons. In scenario 2, the impact is neutral because each of the actors is not concerned (either directly or indirectly) to A; thus, there is little impact from either stayers or leavers. In scenario 3, the relatively strong impact of those who left is balanced by the impact of an equal number of coworkers who stayed.

To be consistent with the psychological foundation of the thesis of this paper, however, we must make one final modification to the above structural arguments. This modification is based on W. I. Thomas' maxim, "If men define sit-

FIGURE 3
Four extreme scenarios depicting various degrees of impact from leavers.

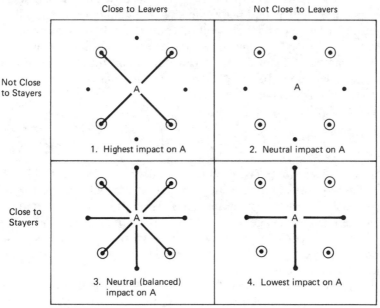

Circled dots represent Leavers.
Uncircled dots represent Stayers.
A line connecting a dot (coworker) to A indicates that A perceives the coworker to be a close friend.

uations as real they are real in their consequences'' (in Volkart, 1951: 81). Person A's leaving will affect person B, assuming that person B *perceives* that person A is a friend. The effect is attenuated if person B perceives that person A is only a friend of a friend, and so on. For example, in Figure 2, if person D does not perceive person A to be a friend of B or C, and thus person C sees no connection at all between self and A, then the effect of A leaving will not be felt by D, even though in ''reality'' A is connected indirectly to D.

Burt (1982) recognized the importance of actors' perceptions of networks as the true constraints to their behaviors. The problem arises when one tries to measure such perceptions. Burt's solution was an interesting one. He borrowed from Steven's (1971) law of psychophysics that an individual's perception of stimuli is a direct power function of the actual ''objective'' stimuli. In Burt's (1982: 174–175) model, the exponent of the power function becomes a parameter to be estimated from the data. To our knowledge, his is the only attempt to deal with this problem in a social network context. The psychologist's first criticism of this approach would be that the assumptions underlying the power function are tenuous at best. Such perceptions, the psychologist would continue, should be measured directly, if at all possible. However the measurement issue is resolved, we argue that the predictions outlined for Figure 1 will be heavily moderated by the perceived social structure of the actors. Specifically, the effect of turnover on coworkers will depend, it is hypothesized, on how close in the friendship network the leaver was to the stayer *as perceived by the stayer*.

The purpose of this study was to explore the issues proposed by these models. A structural perspective dictates that before making individual predictions about the effects of turnover, we consider the entire context as defined by the perceived social network. To explore this contextual effect, we examined the relationship between turnover and subsequent organizational attitudes of those who remain and, in particular, how this relationship is moderated by the perceived position of leavers in the friendship network.

METHODS

Sample

The sites for this study were three fast-food restaurants located in three different suburban areas. Fast-food restaurants were selected because of their history of high turnover (typically 200–400 percent annually). Three-fourths of the employees in the sample were under the age of 18, with tenure averaging less than seven months in each site. No significant differences existed among employees at the three sites in tenure, age, or sex. Sites did vary somewhat in size: 16 employees in Site A, 27 in Site B, and 20 in Site C.

Most of the employees were high school students working part time (at least 20 hours per week). Social relationships were important to these people. Frequently, during the course of this study, we saw employees return to the restaurant during their off-hours to socialize with both on-duty and off-duty coworkers. Few of them depended on this income for a living, and thus they were not trapped financially into keeping the job.

Overall Design

A pre-post natural quasi-experimental design was used to study this phenomenon. At Time 1, a questionnaire was administered that included network questions and attitude items. One month later, at Time 2, a second questionnaire with the attitude items was administered. The major treatment variable, turnover, was recorded during the interval between Time 1 and Time 2 at each of the sites. Using this design, we could determine the relationship each respondent had to each of the coworkers who left, and we could assess the degree of change in stayers' attitudes subsequent to the turnover of their coworkers.

The questionnaires were administered individually by the researchers to each employee. He or she was asked to complete it at home, seal it in the envelope provided, and bring it to work the next day, when the researchers would collect them. Since network questionnaires of this type cannot be anonymous, care was taken to assure the respondent that his or her participation was voluntary and that all responses would be kept in strict confidence. . . .

Operationalization of the Independent Variable

As mentioned previously, a strong argument can be made that it is the *perception* of the network that influences an individual's behavior and attitudes, not the actual set of network links (Burt, 1982). To date, no study of organizational networks has directly measured such perceived structures. The reason for this is simple: it is a formidable task, since the length of the questionnaire would increase linearly with the square of the size of the organization. The task is manageable, however, with organizations the size of the restaurants used in this study. Given the important role that perceptions play in the proposed model, we devised the following method for assessing directly each employee's perceived network in the restaurant.

In the first questionnaire, each person in the workgroup was asked to record who they perceived to be a friend of whom. While simple on the surface, this substantial task required that employees consider all possible pairs of friends in the restaurant. To accomplish this, the respondent was told to check the names of all those listed whom he or she thought would be considered a friend by employee #1 (for example, "Henry"). Then, the same list was repeated on the next page, and the respondent was asked to check all names of those whom he or she thought would be considered a friend of employee #2 ("Rita"). This process was repeated a total of N times (for N employees). In this way, we could assess each person's perception of everyone's friends, their own as well as their coworkers'. These data allowed us to construct, for example, Henry's perception of the entire network in the group, Rita's perception of this network, and so on.

These friendship links were combined with subsequent turnover data to create the independent variable in this study, hereafter referred to as the IMPACT index. The assumption behind this index is that those who leave differentially affect those who stay. This variable is a summary indication of how much potential influence there is on an individual stayer from friends who terminated, relative to those friends who stayed (see Figures 2 and 3). . . .

DISCUSSION

The insufficient justification model in Figure 1 received the strongest support from the data. In general, dissatisfaction was attributed to those who left. This suggests that external attributions, if there were any, were not strong enough to justify the coworker's departure. Thus the model of Effect A depicted in Figure 1 is not supported. Effect B in Figure 1, while predicting correctly the attributed negative link between coworker and job, was incorrect in its prediction of the subsequent dissatisfaction of the stayer. Effect C correctly identified both the negative link between coworker and job and the positive subsequent change in stayers' attitudes.

It is worth noting that the two dependent variables, organizational commitment and job satisfaction, did not respond in identical patterns. While commitment was correlated with IMPACT at Time 1 and Time 2, the change in commitment was not. It is reasonable to expect this, given the strength of the correlation at Time 1. If the employee knows that a close coworker is about to leave, and at the same time knows that he himself or she herself is going to stay, then the insufficient justification process proposed earlier is likely to be operating at Time 1. Given this, one would expect that little change would be observed.

This anticipatory effect does not explain the satisfaction pattern. Correlations with the change in satisfaction subsequent to the turnover of coworkers indicate that the employees were affected by the turnover itself. If the insufficient justification was enough to force stayers to be positively disposed toward the organization at Time 1, why did not the same forces work to improve their satisfaction at Time 1, also? There are two possible explanations of this inconsistency, one based on methods, the second based on theory.

The inconsistency may be a result of the satisfaction measures, which are partially ipsative (Smith, 1967). That is, they measure satisfaction only in a relative sense. Consequently, an increase in a satisfaction score could result from a person becoming more satisfied or from a person perceiving that others are less satisfied. This makes the interpretation of these change scores somewhat tentative as compared, for example, to Likert scales. In contrast, the Organizational Commitment Questionnaire is a standardized instrument whose psychometric properties are well established (Mowday, Steers, and Porter, 1979). The OCQ score provides an absolute indication of commitment. As such, increases or decreases in commitment are readily interpretable.

The problem lies not in the advantages or disadvantages of either ipsative or nonipsative scales (cf. Smith, 1967; Kerlinger, 1973). Rather, of concern here is that the difference in results between the satisfaction and commitment measures could be partly a function of how they were measured. While this is a possibility, it should be remembered that these results are based on correlation, not on absolute differences. The fact that IMPACT is positively related to satisfaction at Time 2 can be interpreted as meaning that those with high IMPACT scores reported themselves to be relatively more satisfied than their coworkers. This interpretation is not substantially different than that given to the similar positive correlation to commitment: those with high IMPACT scores report themselves to be relatively more committed than their coworkers. The similarity in interpretation can be extended to the change scores in both satisfaction and commitment. Thus, while the two measures do exhibit different psychometric properties, there is no reason to assume these differences would lead to the observed discrepancies between the satisfaction and commitment results.

A more interesting and theoretically based explanation lies in another model of work attitude formation, social information processing theory (Salancik and Pfeffer, 1978). Suppose employee A is about to leave, and B is A's good friend. A's behavior during these last weeks may include providing B with an earful of why it is that A is leaving (complaining about the work, the supervisor, etc.). B's evaluation of the work during this time is influenced by A on two counts. First, since A is a friend, the frequency of interaction will be higher, allowing A more opportunity to provide negative social cues. Second, and equally important, since B perceives A to be a friend, B may take cues coming from A more seriously than cues coming from a stranger. Thus, not only are the social cues from A more frequent, but also, B's receptivity to such cues is enhanced by the friendship link. Once A has terminated, this source of negative information about the workplace also diminishes, resulting in a higher percentage of positive social cues about the work. Hence, B's job attitude toward the job itself improves. Moreover, since the job is more immediate to the employees' experience of work than is an evaluation of the organization, it would seem reasonable that shared communications would focus more frequently on the job than on the organization. Organizational commitment, then, was probably not as susceptible to social information cues; thus, changes in this attitude were less likely to be affected by the turnover itself and more likely to be governed by the anticipation of turnover as described previously.

External Validity

More work on the attributions made by coworkers is necessary before definitive conclusions can be drawn about this process. While interesting results were observed in this study, many unanswered questions remain. One primary question is whether these results are generalizable to other jobs and other kinds of work environments. There are at least three reasons this group of subjects might be considered atypical. As was noted earlier, most of these employees were adolescents. Their first concerns were high school and social relationships, not a career (Greenberger, Steinberg, and Ruggiero, 1982).

What impact this might have on the effect of friends leaving, however, is not clear. On the one hand, a career-oriented individual might take the departure of a friend more seriously, especially if the move provides information about better job opportunities. On the other hand, a career-oriented individual might consider the current work opportunities to be more important information than whether friends stay or leave. In addition, the importance attached to social relationships by the adolescents may enhance the effects of turnover of close friends. On balance, then, it is difficult to predict whether this sample would react differently because of their age to turnover of friends than would more career-oriented samples of employees.

The second reason this sample could be considered atypical is the motivation the employees have for working at all. Fast-food employees work for extra spending money, not for survival. They are not trapped in the job, at least not for economic reasons. They are freer to quit than would be the case if they were career-oriented. Consequently, when someone does leave, the event does not carry with it the gravity it might in a normal job environment. The effect of friends leaving in such "normal" environments, then, might be amplified by the seriousness of the turnover.

Third, in a similar vein, turnover runs at about 200 percent annually in these restaurants. It is part of the culture in the fast-food industry. When someone leaves, it is not particularly interesting news. In environments in which turnover is far less frequent, a single event is likely to be taken more seriously by observers, especially close friends. Thus, we would expect the effects in more typical career-oriented locations to be even stronger than the ones observed in this study.

Although there is thus reason to believe that this sample is substantially different from other kinds of organizations, it would be expected that the effects noted in this study would show up more clearly in a career-oriented workplace than they did in fast-food restaurants. It would be interesting to study more traditional organizations to determine whether such a conjecture withstands empirical testing.

CONCLUSION

The question addressed in this paper was spawned from an interest in micro-organizational phenomena: turnover and employee attitudes. Indeed, the question has been proposed and studied largely by scholars in the micro tradition (Staw, 1980a; Mobley, 1982; Mowday, Porter, and Steers, 1982). The approach taken here to answer this question, however, draws specifically on the sociological literature on informal structures (Burt, 1982). While it is difficult to generalize beyond these data, the results demonstrate a substantial and significant influence of the friendship structure on the relationship between turnover and stayers' attitudes. A strictly micro approach to answering this question would have searched for individual differences or traits to explain the changes in attitudes, thereby missing the structural contribution discovered here.

Conversely, the structure per se provides little insight into why the employees may have responded the way that they did. In particular, a structural theory would not have predicted the positive (or negative, for that matter) attitude changes resulting from turnover of specific others. The richness of the social psychological literature allows us to understand and explore more fully the effects the structure had.

As has been noted, these results are limited in scope to adolescent-dominated fast-food restaurants. But the central point of this paper can be generalized far beyond these sites: social networks are powerful forces in organizations, forces that influence micro-level motives as well as more aggregated phenomena. By setting the study of individual behavior in organizations in such contextual frameworks, we will better approach the ideal that Lewin proposed fifty years ago.

REFERENCES

Angle, Harold L., & James L. Perry. (1981). "An empirical assessment of organizational commitment and organizational effectiveness." *Administrative Science Quarterly,* 26:1–14.

Burt, Ronald S. (1977). "Positions in multiple network systems, Part one: A general conception of stratification and prestige in a system of actors cast as a social typology." *Social Forces,* 56: 106–131.

Burt, Ronald S. (1982). *Toward a structural theory of action: Network models of social structure, perception, and action.* New York: Academic Press.

Dalton, Dan R., David Krackhardt, & Lyman Porter. (1981). "Functional turnover: An empirical investigation." *Journal of Applied Psychology,* 66: 716–721.

Dalton, Dan R., & William D. Todor. (1979). "Turnover turned over: An expanded and positive perspective." *Academy of Management Review,* 4: 225–235.

Greenberger, Ellen, Laurence D. Steinberg, & Mary Ruggiero. (1982). "A job is a job is a job . . . Or is it?" *Work and Occupations,* 9: 79–96.

Heider, Fritz. (1958). *The psychology of interpersonal relations.* New York: Wiley.

Kerlinger, Fred N. (1973). *Foundations of behavioral research.* New York: Holt, Rinehart & Winston.

Krackhardt, David. (1985). "Variations in perceived structures: Cognitive networks, local aggregated networks, and voted networks." Paper presented at the Annual Social Network Conference, Palm Beach, CA.

Lewin, Kurt. (1966). *Principles of topological psychology.* (Originally published in 1936.) New York: McGraw-Hill.

Mobley, William H. (1982). *Employee turnover: Causes, consequences and control.* Reading, MA: Addison-Wesley.

Mowday, Richard T. (1981). "Viewing turnover from the perspective of those who remain: The relationship of job attitudes to attributions of the cause of turnover." *Journal of Applied Psychology,* 66: 120–123.

Mowday, Richard T., Lyman W. Porter, & Richard M. Steers. (1982). *Employee-organization linkages: The psychology of commitment, absenteeism, and turnover.* New York: Academic Press.

Mowday, Richard T., Richard M. Steers, & Lyman W. Porter. (1979). "The measurement of organizational commitment." *Journal of Vocational Behavior,* 14: 224–227.

Newcomb, Theodore M., Kathryn E. Koenig, Richard Flacks, & Donald P. Warwick. (1967). *Persistence and change: Bennington College and its students after twenty-five years.* New York: Wiley.

Porter, Lyman W., Richard M. Steers, Richard T. Mowday, & Paul V. Boulian. (1974). "Organizational commitment, job satisfaction, and turnover among psychiatric technicians." *Journal of Applied Psychology,* 59: 603–609.

Salancik, Gerald R., & Jeffrey Pfeffer. (1978). "A social information processing approach to job attitudes and task design." *Administrative Science Quarterly,* 23: 224–253.

Smith, L. H. (1967). *Some properties of ipsative, normative, and forced choice normative measures.* Philadelphia: Franklin Institute Research Laboratories.

Staw, Barry M. (1976). "Knee-deep in the Big Muddy: A study of escalating commitment to a chosen course of action." *Organizational Behavior and Human Performance,* 16: 27–44.

Staw, Barry M. (1980a). "The consequences of turnover." *Journal of Occupational Behavior*, 1: 253–273.

Staw, Barry M. (1980b). "Rationality and justification in organizational life." In Barry M. Staw and Larry L. Cummings (eds.), *Research in Organizational Behavior*, 2: 45–80. Greenwich, CT: JAI Press.

Steers, Richard M., & Richard T. Mowday. (1981). "Employee turnover and post-decision accommodation processes." In Barry M. Staw and Larry L. Cummings (eds.), *Research in Organizational Behavior*, 3: 235–281.

Stevens, S. S. (1962). "The surprising simplicity of sensory metrics." *American Psychologist*, 17: 29–39.

Stevens, S. S. (1971). "Issues in psychophysical measurement." *Psychological Review*, 78: 426–450.

Volkart, E. H. (1951). *Social behavior and personality*. New York: Social Science Research Council.

Corporations, Culture and Commitment: Motivation and Social Control in Organizations

Charles O'Reilly

Corporate culture is receiving much attention in the business press. A recent article in *Fortune* describes how the CEO at Black & Decker "transformed an entire corporate *culture*, replacing a complacent manufacturing mentality with an almost manic, market-driven way of doing things."[1] Similarly, the success of Food Lion (a $3 billion food-market chain that has grown at an annual rate of 37% over the past 20 years with annual returns on equity of 24%) is attributed to a culture which emphasizes "hard work, simplicity, and frugality."[2] Other well-known firms such as 3M, Johnson & Johnson, Apple, and Kimberly-Clark have been routinely praised for their innovative cultures.[3] Even the success of Japanese firms in the U.S. has been partly attributed to their ability to change the traditional culture developed under American managers. Peters and Waterman report how a U.S. television manufacturing plant, under Japanese management, reduced its defect rate from 140 to 6, its complaint rate from 70% to 7%, and the turnover rate among employees from 30% to 1%, all due to a changed management philosophy and culture.[4]

Even more dramatic is the turnaround at the New United Motors Manufacturing Incorporated (NUMMI) plant in Fremont, California. When General Motors closed this facility in 1982, it was one of the worst plants in the GM assembly division with an 18 percent daily absenteeism rate and a long history of conflict in its labor relations. The plant reopened as a joint venture between Toyota and GM in 1983. Over 85 percent of the original labor force was rehired, and workers are

Condensed from the *California Management Review*, 31(4), 9–25. Copyright © 1989 by the Regents of the University of California. Reprinted by permission.

still represented by the UAW. Although the technology used is vintage 1970s and the plant is not as automated as many others within GM and Toyota, productivity is almost double what GM gets in other facilities. In 1987, it took an estimated 20.8 hours to produce a car at NUMMI versus 40.7 in other GM plants and 18.0 at Toyota. Quality of the NUMMI automobiles is the highest in the GM system, based on both internal audits and owner surveys, and absenteeism is at 2 percent compared to 8 percent at other GM facilities. What accounts for this remarkable success? According to one account, "At the system's core is a *culture* in which the assembly line workers maintain their machines, ensure the quality of their work, and improve the production process."[5]

But a culture is not always a positive force. It has also been implicated when firms run into difficulties. The CEO of financially troubled Computerland, William Tauscher, has attempted to restructure the firm, noting that "a low-cost culture is a must."[6] Henry Wendt, CEO of SmithKline Beckman, has attributed his firm's current difficulties to complacency. "We've been victims of our own success. . . . I want to create a new culture."[7] Corporate culture has also been implicated in problems faced by Sears, Caterpillar, Bank of America, Polaroid, General Motors, and others. Even difficulties in mergers and acquisitions are sometimes attributed to cultural conflicts which make integration of separate units difficult. Failure to merge two cultures can lead to debilitating conflict, a loss of talent, and an inability to reap the benefits of synergy.

But what is really meant when one refers to a firm's "culture"? Do all organizations have them? Are they always important? Even if we can identify cultures, do we know enough about how they work to manage them? Four major questions need to be answered:

- What is culture?
- From a manager's perspective, when is culture important?
- What is the process through which cultures are developed and maintained?
- How can cultures be managed?

WHAT IS CULTURE?

If culture is to be analyzed and managed, it is important that we be clear about what is meant by the term. Failure to clearly specify what "culture" is can result in confusion, misunderstanding, and conflict about its basic function and importance.

Culture as Control

Clearly, little would get done by or in organizations if some control systems were not in place to direct and coordinate activities. In fact, organizations are often seen to be efficient and effective solely because control systems operate.[8]

But what is a "control system"? A generic definition might be that a control system is "the knowledge that someone who knows and cares is paying close attention to what we do and can tell us when deviations are occurring?" Although broad, this definition encompasses traditional formal control systems ranging from planning and budgeting systems to performance appraisals. According to this definition, control systems work when those who are monitored are aware that someone who matters, such as a boss or staff department, is paying attention and is likely to care when things aren't going according to plan.

Several years ago a large toy manufacturer installed, at considerable expense, a management-by-objectives (MBO) performance and appraisal system. After a year or so, top management became aware that the system was working well in one part of the organization but not another. They conducted an investigation and discovered the reason for the failure. In the part of the organization where MBO was working well, senior management was enthusiastic and committed. They saw real benefits and conveyed their belief up and down the chain of command. In the part of the organization where the system had failed, senior management saw MBO as another bureaucratic exercise to be endured. Subordinate managers quickly learned to complete the paperwork but ignore the purpose. The lesson here was that a control system, no matter how carefully designed, works only when those being monitored believe that people who matter care about the results and are paying close attention. When Jan Carlzon became head of SAS Airline, he was concerned about the poor on-time record. To correct this, he personally requested a daily accounting of the on-time status of all flights. In the space of two years, SAS on-time record went from 83% to 97%.[9]

In designing formal control systems, we typically attempt to measure either outcomes or behaviors. For example, in hospitals it makes no sense to evaluate the nursing staff on whether patients get well. Instead, control systems rely on assessing behaviors. Are specified medical procedures followed? Are checks made at appropriate times? In other settings, behavior may not be observable. Whenever possible, we then attempt to measure outcomes. Sales people, for instance, are usually measured on their productivity, since the nature of their job often precludes any effective monitoring of their behavior. In other situations, control systems can be designed that monitor both behaviors and outcomes. For example, for some retail sales jobs both behaviors (how the customer is addressed, how quickly the order is taken, whether the sales floor is kept stocked) and outcomes (sales volume) can be measured.

However, it is often the case that neither behavior nor outcomes can be adequately monitored.[10] These are the activities that are nonroutine and unpredictable, situations that require initiative, flexibility, and innovation. These can be dealt with only by developing social control systems in which common agreements exist among people about what constitutes appropriate attitudes and behavior.

Culture may be thought of as a potential social control system. Unlike formal control systems that typically assess outcomes or behaviors only intermittently, social control systems can be much more finely tuned. When we care about those with whom we work and have a common set of expectations, we are "under control" whenever we are in their presence. If we want to be accepted, we try to live up to their expectations. In this sense, social control systems can operate more extensively than most formal systems. Interestingly, our response to being monitored by formal and social control systems may also differ. With formal systems people often have a sense of external constraint which is binding and unsatisfying. With social controls, we often feel as though we have great autonomy, even though paradoxically we are conforming much more.

Thus, from a management perspective, culture in the form of shared expectations may be thought of as a social control system. Howard Schwartz and Stan Davis offer a practical definition of culture as "a pattern of beliefs and expectations shared by the organization's members. These beliefs and expectations produce norms that powerfully shape the behavior of individuals and groups."[11]

Culture as Normative Order

What Schwartz and Davis are referring to as culture are the central norms that may characterize an organization. Norms are expectations about what are appropriate or inappropriate attitudes and behaviors. They are socially created standards that help us interpret and evaluate events. Although their content may vary, they exist in all societies and, while often unnoticed, they are pervasive. For instance, in our society we have rather explicit norms about eye-contact. We may get uncomfortable when these are violated. Consider what happens when someone doesn't look at you while speaking or who continues to look without pause. In organizations we often find peripheral or unimportant norms around issues such as dress or forms of address. In the old railroads, for example, hats were a must for all managers, while everyone addressed each other with a formal "mister."

More important norms often exist around issues such as quality, performance, flexibility, or how to deal with conflict. In many organizations, it is impolite to disagree publicly with others. Instead, much behind-the-scenes interaction takes place to anticipate or resolve disputes. In other organizations, there may be norms that legitimate and encourage the public airing of disputes. Intel Corporation has an explicit policy of "constructive confrontation" that encourages employees to deal with disagreements in an immediate and direct manner.

In this view, the central values and styles that characterize a firm, perhaps not even written down, can form the basis for the development of norms that attach approval or disapproval to holding certain attitudes or beliefs and to acting in certain ways. For instance, the fundamental value of aggressiveness or competition may, if widely held and supported, be expressed as a norm that encourages organizational participants to stress winning competition. Pepsico encourages competition and punishes failure to compete.[12] Service is a pivotal norm at IBM; innovation is recognized as central at 3M. It is through norms—the expectations shared by group members and the approval or disapproval attached to these expectations—that culture is developed and maintained.

However, there is an important difference between the guiding beliefs or vision held by top management and the daily beliefs or norms held by those at lower levels in the unit or organization. The former reflect top managements' beliefs about how things ought to be. The latter define how things actually are. Simply because top management is in agreement about how they would like the organization to function is no guarantee that these beliefs will be held by others. One CEO spoke at some length about the glowing corporate philosophy that he believed in and felt characterized his firm's culture. After spending some time talking to mid-level managers in the organization, a very different picture emerged. A central norm shared by many of these managers was "Good people don't stay here." It is a common occurrence to find a noble sounding statement of corporate values framed on the wall and a very different and cynical interpretation of this creed held by people who have been around long enough to realize what is really important.

Moreover, norms can vary on two dimensions: the intensity or amount of approval/disapproval attached to an expectation; and the crystallization or degree of consensus or consistency with which a norm is shared. For instance, when analyzing an organization's culture it may be that for certain values there can be wide consensus but no intensity. Everyone understands what top management values, but there is no strong approval or disapproval attached to these beliefs or behaviors. Or, a given norm, such as innovation, can be positively valued in one group (e.g., marketing or R&D) and negatively valued in another (manufacturing or personnel). There is intensity but no crystallization.

It is only when there exist both intensity and consensus that strong cultures exist. This is why it is difficult to develop or change culture. Organizational members must come to know and share a common set of expectations. These must, in turn, be consistently valued and reinforced across divisions and management levels.[13] Only when this is done will there be both intensity and consensus. Similarly, a failure to share the central norms or to consistently reinforce them may lead to vacuous norms, conflicting interpretations, or to micro-cultures that exist only within subunits.

To have a strong culture, an organization does not have to have very many strongly held values. Only a few core values characterize strong culture firms such as Mars, Marriott, Hewlett-Packard, and Walmart. What is critical is that these beliefs be widely shared and strongly held; that is, people throughout the organization must be willing to tell one another when a core belief is not being lived up to. . . .

Culture and Commitment

Culture is critical in developing and maintaining levels of intensity and dedication among employees that often characterize successful firms. This strong attachment is particularly valuable when the employees have knowledge that is instrumental to the success of the organization or when very high levels of motivation are required. When IBM bought ROLM, the critical resource was not the existing product line but the design and engineering expertise of ROLM's staff. A failure to gain the commitment of employees during mergers and acquisitions can diminish or destroy the value of the venture. In contrast, a highly dedicated workforce represents a significant competitive advantage. Under turbulent or changing conditions, relying on employees who wait to be told exactly what to do can be a liability.

How, then, do strong culture organizations develop intensity and commitment? A 20-year veteran of IBM was quoted in a *Wall Street Journal* article as saying, "I don't know what a cult is and what it is those bleary-eyed kids selling poppies really do, but I'm probably that deeply committed to the IBM company."[14] To understand this process, we need to consider what commitment is and how it is developed. By understanding the underlying psychology of commitment, we can then think about how to design systems to develop such an attachment among employees.

Organizational Commitment   What is meant by the term "organizational commitment"? It is typically conceived of as an individual's psychological bond to the organization, including a sense of job involvement, loyalty, and a belief in the values of the organization. There are three processes or stages of commitment: *compliance, identification,* and *internalization.*[15] In the first stage, *compliance,* a person accepts the influence of others mainly to obtain something from others, such as pay. The second stage is *identification* in which the individual accepts influence in order to maintain a satisfying, self-defining relationship. People feel pride in belonging to the firm. The final stage of commitment is *internalization* in which the individual finds the values of the organization to be intrinsically rewarding and congruent with personal values.

Conceiving of commitment as developing in this manner allows us to understand how a variety of organizations—ranging from cults to strong culture corporations—generate commitment among their members. In fact, these organizations can be categorized based on the type of commitment displayed by their members. Cults and religious organizations, for example, typically have members who have internalized the values of the organization and who become "deployable agents," or individuals who can be relied upon to go forth and proselytize.[16] Japanese organizations, Theory Z, and strong culture firms are characterized by members who have a strong identification with the organization. These employees identify with the firm because it stands for something they value. In typical corporations, members comply with directions but may have little involvement with the firm beyond self-interest; that is, there is no commitment with the firm beyond that of a fair exchange of effort for money and, perhaps, status.

HOW CULTURE IS DEVELOPED

How do people become committed to organizations? Why, for example, would someone choose to join a cult? How do firms such as NUMMI get the incredible levels of productivity from their employees (as one team member said, "I like the new system so much it scares me. I'm scared because it took me 18 years to realize that I blew it at GM. Now we have a chance to do things a different way.")? The answer to this puzzle is simultaneously simple and nonobvious. As Jerry Salancik has noted, "commitment is too easy," yet it relies on an understanding of human motivation that is counter-intuitive.[17]

Constructing Social Realities

Most discussions of motivation assume a stable set of individual needs and values.[18] These are seen as shaping expectations, goals, and attitudes. In turn, these are presumed to guide behavior and people's responses to situations. In Maslow's theory, for instance, people are assumed to have a hierarchy of needs.[19] The managerial consequence of this view can be seen in our theories of job design in which jobs are supposed to be designed to take advantage of the desire of people to grow and self-actualize.[20] But are such theories correct? The empirical evidence is weak at best.[21] In spite of numerous efforts to demonstrate the effect of needs and personality, there is little support for the power of individual differences to predict behavior.

Consider the results of two experiments. In the first, Christian seminary students were approached and given one of two requests. Both asked them to extemporaneously address a visiting class in a discussion of the parable of the Good Samaritan. They were told to walk over to a classroom building to do this. In one condition they were informed that the class was already there and that they should hurry. In the other condition they were told that the class would arrive in several minutes. As they walked to the classroom, all subjects passed an old man (the "victim") dressed in shabby clothes and in obvious need of help. The experimenters were interested in what proportion of Christian seminarians thinking of the Good Samaritan would stop and help this person. Surprisingly, in the condition in which the subjects were told to hurry, only 30 percent paid any attention. Think about this. Seventy percent of a group of individuals with religious values who were training to be ministers failed to stop. Ninety-five percent of those who were not in a hurry, stopped to help.

In another experiment, researchers observed when students using a campus restroom washed their hands. They discovered that when another person was visible in the restroom, 90 percent washed their hands. When no other person was visible, less than 20 percent did so.

What explains these and other findings? What often seems to account for behavior are the expectations of others. As individuals, we are very susceptible to the informational and normative influence of others. We pay attention to the actions of others and learn from them. "In actuality, virtually all learning phenomena resulting from direct experience occur on a vicarious basis by observing other people's behavior and its consequences for them." We watch others and form expectations about how and when we should act.[22]

Yet, we are not sensitive to how much of our world is really a social construction—one that rests on shared agreements. We often tend to underestimate the degree to which situations and the expectations of others can constrain and shape behavior. Strong situations—ones in which there are very clear incentives and expectations about what constitutes appropriate attitudes and behavior—can be very powerful. When we care what others think, the power of these norms or social expectations can be heightened.

Mechanisms for Developing Culture

How can cultures be developed and managed in organizations? All organizations—from cults to strong culture corporations—draw on the same underlying psychology and create situations characterized by strong norms that focus people's attention, provide clear guidance about what is important, and provide for group reinforcement of appropriate attitudes and behavior. Four common mechanisms are used to accomplish this. What varies across these organizations is not what is done but only the degree to which these mechanisms are used.

Participation   The first mechanism that is critical in developing or changing a culture are systems that provide for participation. These systems encourage people to be involved and send signals to the individual that he or she is valued. These may range from formal efforts such as quality circles and advisory boards to less formal efforts such as suggestion systems and opportunities to meet with top managers and informal social gatherings. What is important about these processes is that people are encouraged to make incremental choices and develop a sense of responsibility for their actions. In some cases, such as work design, the specific choices made may be less important for future success than the fact that people had the chance to make them.

From a psychological perspective, choice is often associated with commitment. When we choose of our own volition to do something, we often feel responsible.[23] When the choice is volitional, explicit, public, and irrevocable, the commitment is even more binding.[24] For instance, direct sales companies have learned that by getting the customer to fill out the order sheet, they can cut cancellations dramatically. A large number of psychological experiments have convincingly shown that participation can lead to both commitment and enjoyment, even when people are induced to engage in physically and emotionally stressful activities such as eating earthworms and becoming bone marrow donors.[25]

How do organizations use participation? Marc Galanter has documented how members of the Unification Church use processes of incremental commitment to recruit cult members.[26] Individuals are invited to dinner, convinced to spend the weekend for a seminar, and in some cases, induced to remain permanently with their new found "friends." Interestingly, there is no evidence that people who join cults under these circumstances are suffering from any psychopathology. Religious organizations often use elaborate systems of incremental choice and participation leading to greater and greater involvement. Japanese-managed automobile companies in the U.S. also have elaborate systems of selection and orientation that rely heavily on these approaches, as do American "strong culture" firms.

Management as Symbolic Action   The second mechanism commonly seen in strong culture organizations is that of clear, visible actions on the part of management in support of the cultural values.[27] In organizations, participants typically want to know what is important. One way we gain this information is to carefully watch and listen to those above us. We look for consistent patterns. When top management not only says that something is important but also consistently behaves in ways that support the message, we begin to believe what is said. When the CEO of Xerox, David Kearns, began his quest for improved quality, there was some initial uncertainty about whether he meant it. Over time, as the message was repeated again and again, and as resources continued to be devoted to the quality effort, norms developed setting expectations about the role and importance of quality throughout the corporation.[28]

An important function of management is to provide interpretations of events for the organization's members. Without a shared meaning, confusion and conflict can result. Managers need to be sensitive to how their actions are viewed. Interpreting (or reinterpreting) history, telling stories, the use of vivid language, spending time, and being seen as visible in support of certain positions are all potential ways of shaping the organization's culture. This does not mean that managers need to be charismatic. However, managers need to engage in acts of "mundane symbolism." By this they can insure that important issues get suitable amounts of time, that questions are continually asked about important topics, and that the subject gets on the agenda and it is followed up.

The appropriate use of symbols and ceremonies is also important. When Jerry Sanders, CEO of Advanced Micro Devices, decided to shift the firm's strategy toward innovation, he not only made substantive changes in budget, positions, and organizational structure, he also used a symbol. As a part of the many talks he had with employees describing the need to change, Sanders would also describe how important it was to invest in areas that others could not easily duplicate—such as investing in proprietary products. He would describe how a poor farmer would always need a cash crop at the end of the year if he was to survive. But if he began to prosper, a smart farmer would begin to plant crops that others might not be able to afford—crops, for example, that took more than a year to come to fruition; crops like asparagus. The notion of asparagus became a visible and important symbol for change within AMD, even to the point where managers begin referring to revenues from new proprietary products as "being measured on asparagus."

Symbols are not a substitute for substance, and ceremonies cannot replace content. Rather, many of the substantive changes that occur in organizations, such as promotions or reorganizations, have multiple meanings and interpretations. Over time, people may lose a clear sense for what the superordinate goals are and why their jobs are important. In strong culture organizations, managers frequently and consistently send signals helping to renew these understandings. They do this by continually calling attention to what is important, in word and in action.

Information from Others   While clear messages from management are an important determinant of a culture, so too are consistent messages from coworkers. If control comes from the knowledge that someone who matters is paying attention, then the degree to which we care about our coworkers also gives them a certain control over us. Years ago, several researchers conducted an experiment in which subjects were placed in a room to complete a questionnaire. While they were doing this, smoke began to flow from an air vent. While 75% of the subjects who were alone responded by notifying the experimenter of a possible fire, only 38% did so when in the company of two other subjects. When these other two were confederates of the experimenter and deliberately said nothing, only 10% of the subjects responded. One conclusion from this and other similar experiments is that we often take our cue from others when we are uncertain what to do.

In organizations, during periods of crisis or when people are new to the situation, they often look to others for explanations of what to do and how to interpret events. Strong cultures are typically characterized by consensus about these questions. In these settings there are often attempts made to insure a consistency of understanding and to minimize any us-them attitudes between parts of the organization. For instance, strong culture firms often pride themselves on the equality of treatment of all employees. At Mars, all employees punch a time clock and no one has a private secretary. At Gore-Tex, Walmart, Disney, and others there are no employees or managers, only associates, team members, and hosts. At NUMMI, Honda, and Nissan there are no private dining rooms for managers and both managers and workers often wear uniforms. In the Rajneesh Commune, everyone wore clothes with the color magenta.

The goal here is to create a strong social construction of reality by minimizing contradictory interpretations. In cults, this is often done by isolating the members from family and friends. Some religious organizations do this by encouraging extensive involvement in a variety of church activities and meetings. Japanese firms expect after work socializing. At NUMMI, for instance, each work team is given a semiannual budget to be spent only on team-sponsored activities where the entire team participates. In corporations, 60 hour work weeks can also isolate people from competing interpretations. Some electronics firms in Silicon Valley have provided employee T-shirts with slogans such as "Working 80 hours a week and loving it." With this commitment of time, workers may be as isolated as if they had joined a cult.

Comprehensive Reward Systems A final mechanism for promoting and shaping culture is the reward system, but not simply monetary rewards. Rather, these systems focus on rewards such as recognition and approval which can be given more frequently than money. These rewards also focus on the intrinsic aspects of the job and a sense of belonging to the organization. Recognition by your boss or coworkers for doing the right thing can be more potent in shaping behavior than an annual bonus. In the words of a popular management book, the trick is to catch someone doing something right and to reward it on the spot. While tokens such as scrolls or badges can be meaningless, under the right circumstances they can also be highly valued.

It is easy to desire one type of behavior while rewarding another. Often management professes a concern for quality while systematically rewarding only those who meet their goals, regardless of the quality. Innovation may be espoused but even the slightest failure is punished. At its simplest, people usually do what they are rewarded for and don't do what they're punished for. If this is true and to be taken seriously, then a simple analysis of what gets management's attention should give us a sense for what the culture supports. Who gets promoted? At 3M, one important aspect of success is to be associated with a new product introduction. If innovation is espoused, but doing things by-the-book is what is rewarded, it doesn't take a psychologist to figure out what the firm actually values. In fact, if there are inconsistencies between what top management says and what is actually rewarded, the likely outcome will be confusion and cynicism.

MANAGING CULTURE

Each of these can affect the development of a shared set of expectations. As shown in Figure 1, the process begins with words and actions on the part of the group's leaders. Even if no explicit statements are made, subordinates will attempt to infer a pattern. If management is credible and communicates consistently, members of the group may begin to develop consistent expectations about what is important. When this consensus is also rewarded, clear norms can then emerge.

Whether or not these norms constitute a desirable culture depends on the critical tasks to be accomplished and whether the formal control system provides sufficient leverage to attain these. If culture *is* important, four steps can help a manager understand how to manage it.

• Identify the strategic objectives of the unit. Once identified, specify the short-term objectives and critical actions that need to be accomplished if the strategic objectives are to be accomplished.
• Analyze the existing values and norms that characterize the organization. This can be done by focusing on what people in the unit feel is expected of them by their peers and bosses and what is actually rewarded. What does it take to get

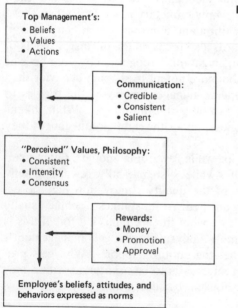

FIGURE 1

ahead? What stories are routinely told? Who are the people who exemplify the group? Look for norms that are widely shared and strongly felt.

• Once these are identified, look for norms that may hinder the accomplishment of critical tasks; norms that would help but are not currently present; and conflicts between what is needed and what is currently rewarded.

• Once these are identified, programs can be designed to begin to shape or develop the desired norms. These can draw upon the psychological mechanisms discussed previously.

The logic here is straightforward and links culture to those activities critical for the implementation of strategy and for generating widespread understanding and commitment among the organization's members. Obviously, these actions take time and management resources to accomplish. However, to ignore them is to ignore a social control system that may already be operating in the organization. The issue is whether this system is helping or hindering. Managers need to be sensitive to what the central organizational norms are and how they can affect them. To not be sensitive to these issues is to ignore the advice of a CEO who said, "We will either be a victim or a successful result of our culture."

REFERENCES

1 *Fortune,* January 2, 1989.
2 *Fortune,* August 15, 1988.
3 *Fortune,* June 6, 1988.
4 T. Peters and R. H. Waterman, *In Search of Excellence: Lessons From America's Best-Run Companies* (New York, NY: Harper & Row, 1982), p. 32.
5 *Fortune,* January 30, 1989.
6 *Business Week,* October 10, 1988.
7 *Business Week,* October 10, 1988.
8 A. Wilkins and W. Ouchi, "Efficient Cultures: Exploring the Relationship between Culture and Organizational Performance," *Administrative Science Quarterly,* 28 (1983): 468–481; O. Williamson, *Markets and Hierarchies* (New York, NY: The Free Press, 1975).
9 J. Carlzon, *Moments of Truth* (Cambridge, MA: Ballinger, 1987).
10 S. Dornbusch and W. R. Scott, *Evaluation and the Exercise of Authority* (San Francisco, CA: Jossey-Bass, 1975).
11 H. Schwartz and S. Davis, "Matching Corporate Culture and Business Strategy," *Organizational Dynamics* (1981), pp. 30–48.
12 *Fortune,* April 10, 1989.
13 D. Feldman, "The Development and Enforcement of Group Norms," *Academy of Management Review,* 9 (1984): 45–53.
14 *Wall Street Journal,* April 7, 1986.
15 C. O'Reilly and J. Chatman, "Organizational Commitment and Psychological Attachment: The Effects of Compliance, Identification and Internalization on Prosocial Behavior," *Journal of Applied Psychology,* 71 (1986): 492–499.
16 W. Appel, *Cults in America* (New York, NY: Holt, Rinehart and Winston, 1983); D. Gerstel, *Paradise Incorporated: Synanon* (San Francisco, CA: Presidio Press, 1982).
17 G. Salancik, "Commitment Is Too Easy!" *Organizational Dynamics* (Summer 1977), pp. 62–80.

18 For example, see F. Herzberg, B. Mausner, and B. Snyderman, *The Motivation to Work* (New York, NY: John Wiley, 1959); A. Maslow, *Motivation and Personality* (New York, NY: Harper & Row, 1970).

19 Maslow, op. cit.

20 For example, see J. R. Hackman and G. Oldham, *Work Redesign* (Reading, MA: Addison-Wesley, 1980).

21 For example, see G. Salancik and J. Pfeffer, "A Social Information Processing Approach to Job Attitudes and Task Design," *Administrative Science Quarterly,* 23 (1978): 224–253.

22 For example, see S. Milgram, *Obedience to Authority* (New York, NY: Harper & Row, 1969); A. Bandura, *Social Learning Theory* (Englewood Cliffs, NJ: Prentice-Hall, 1977).

23 For example, see R. Caldini, *Influence: The New Psychology of Modern Persuasion* (New York, NY: Quill, 1984).

24 Salancik, op. cit.

25 For example, see I. Janis and L. Mann, *Decision Making: A Psychological Analysis of Conflict, Choice, and Commitment* (New York, NY: Free Press, 1977).

26 M. Galanter, "Psychological Induction into the Large Group: Findings from a Modern Religious Sect," *American Journal of Psychiatry,* 137 (1980): 1574–1579.

27 J. Pfeffer, "Management as Symbolic Action: The Creation and Maintenance of Organizational Paradigms," in L. Cummings and B. Staw, eds., *Research in Organizational Behavior,* Volume 3 (Greenwich, CT: JAI Press, 1981).

28 G. Jacobsen and J. Hillkirk, *Xerox: American Samuri* (New York, NY: Collier Books, 1986).

QUESTIONS FOR DISCUSSION

1 What relationship exists between group aspiration level and individual performance on the job?

2 What motivationally relevant functions do groups serve in organizations? How could you use this information to increase employee motivation?

3 Under what circumstances would you expect competition among group members for rewards to result in higher performance than cooperation? When might cooperation lead to higher performance? Explain why such differences occur.

4 If you were a manager trying to increase performance among your subordinates, would you use group or individual incentives? Why?

5 Porter, Lawler, and Hackman use expectancy theory to explain how group processes influence individual motivation to perform. What other theories of motivation might be useful in explaining group influences? Explain.

6 Several articles (in previous chapter) have suggested that members should be carefully selected and trained so as to diminish differences between individual and organizational goals. What predictions might you make about decisions made in organizations which adopt this suggestion? What steps might an organization take to increase the effectiveness of decision making and yet maintain goal congruence?

7 Compare the relative costs and benefits to a supervisor of attempting to use each of Kelman's three interpersonal influence processes (compliance, identification, and internalization) to motivate subordinates.

8 To what extent could each of the social influence processes identified in the article by Sussmann and Vecchio be used by managers to motivate their *bosses* (as opposed to their subordinates)?

9 Explain how the concept of "group norm" relates to different theories of employee motivation (goal-setting, expectancy, social learning, etc.).

10 Suppose that a manager who has been newly appointed to head a particular organizational unit finds that he or she is confronted with a norm in that unit that can be summarized as follows: "Don't make waves, but also don't exert yourself beyond a minimally adequate level of effort." How could the manager, utilizing a knowledge of motivational theory, proceed to attempt to change this norm?

11 How might information about social networks be useful to a manager in understanding the behavior of individual employees?

12 O'Reilly discusses the powerful influence of organizational culture on motivation. How would you explain this relationship from an "expectancy" theory perspective?

13 As a new manager entering an organization, how would you go about assessing the organizational culture and its influence on the motivation and commitment of your employees?

6

JOB ATTITUDES AND PERFORMANCE

One of the most controversial issues in the field of motivation concerns the relationship between job attitudes and employee performance. The origins of the controversy stem from disagreements not only about the potential causal relationships between these two variables but also about the meanings and measurements of the two. For example, what do we mean by an attitude and how should we most accurately measure attitudes? What constitutes good job performance? Should we measure job performance at the individual level or at the group level? Should we focus on short-term results or long-term? And finally, do positive attitudes lead to good performance or does good performance lead to positive attitudes? Alternatively, is there a third intervening variable that moderates or in some way affects the relationship between the two? How we resolve this controversy has a major impact both on theory development and on managerial practice.

To begin with, let us consider what we mean by job attitudes. Briefly defined, an "attitude" represents a predisposition to respond in a favorable or unfavorable way to persons or objects in one's environment. When we say we "like" something or "dislike" something, we are in effect expressing an attitude toward the person or object. When we look at the specific attitude of job satisfaction, for example, we are considering the extent to which one's job or job experiences are pleasurable or unpleasurable.

Three important assumptions underlie the concept of attitudes. First, an attitude is a hypothetical construct. We cannot actually see attitudes, although we can often see the behavioral consequences. Instead, we have to infer the existence of attitudes from people's statements and behaviors. Second, an attitude is a unidimensional construct; it usually ranges from very positive to very negative. As such, an attitude can be measured along a continuum. Third, attitudes are be-

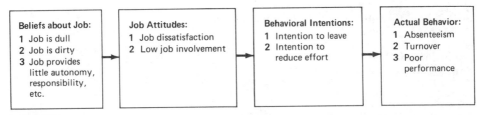

EXHIBIT 1
A conceptual model of job attitudes. (After Fishbein, 1967.)

lieved to be somewhat related to subsequent behavior, although this relationship is unclear, as we shall see.

Traditionally, job attitudes have been described as consisting of three related parts: (1) beliefs about the job, (2) the attitude itself, and (3) the behavioral intentions that result from the attitude. As shown in Exhibit 1, negative beliefs about the job (e.g., this is a dull, dirty job) lead to negative job attitudes (e.g., job dissatisfaction), which in turn lead to behavior intentions (e.g., intent to leave). These behavioral intentions are then often translated into actual behavior, such as leaving the organization, assuming the person is able to carry out the intention. Or, an individual who is dissatisfied may decide to put forth less effort on the job as a way of expressing his or her frustrations with the job. In both cases, the traditional model suggests that behaviors (including performance) are largely influenced by attitudes.

Recently, this traditional model has been questioned as being too simple a representation of what actually happens inside people. As we shall see, there are alternative ways to conceptualize such attitudes and their consequences. In the first article that follows, Iaffaldano and Muchinsky review the results of studies focusing on the satisfaction-performance relationship. In the next article, Staw reconsiders the old adage "a happy worker is a productive worker." Here we see a discussion of a dispositional approach to the concept of job attitudes. Finally, Organ looks at the same topic but focuses on the outcome variable performance instead of on attitudes. That is, he argues that we may need to redefine what we mean by performance in the study of the satisfaction-performance controversy. Together, these three articles attempt to elaborate on the general issue of how—or whether—attitudes relate to job performance. Throughout, implications for management will emerge.

Job Satisfaction and Job Performance:
A Meta-Analysis

Michelle T. Iaffaldano
Paul M. Muchinsky

The elusive relation between job satisfaction and job performance has intrigued organizational researchers for nearly 50 years. In their classic review of the early literature in this area, Brayfield and Crockett (1955) credited Kornhauser and Sharp (1932) with the initial investigation of attitudes and productivity in an industrial setting. Although the flurry of research on this topic has abated somewhat in the past few years, the current literature continues to be highlighted with reports of new theoretical and empirical developments. Indeed, the *Journal of Vocational Behavior*'s yearly research review still references studies that relate job satisfaction to job performance (e.g., Bartol, 1981).

To keep pace with this ever-expanding volume of research, several summaries of the job satisfaction-job performance literature have appeared, both from an empirical perspective (Brayfield & Crockett, 1955; Herzberg, Mausner, Peterson, & Capwell, 1957; Srivastva et al., 1975; Vroom, 1964) and a theoretical orientation (Schwab & Cummings, 1970). These reviewers attempted to reconcile the inconsistencies among individual study results by concluding that there is no strong pervasive relation between workers' job satisfaction and productivity. Specifically, Vroom (1964) reported a median correlation of +.14 from the 20 studies he reviewed, and Brayfield and Crockett reported that there was insufficient evidence that employee attitudes "bear any simple . . . or for that matter, appreciable . . . relationship to performance on the job" (1955, p. 408). However, Herzberg et al. (1957) were somewhat more optimistic, and although the correlations they compiled were generally low, they concluded that further attention to satisfaction in relation to worker output was warranted.

Despite these generally negative conclusions by reviewers, investigations into the connection between these two variables proliferated along several lines. One area that received much attention was the question of causality between satisfaction and performance (cf. Lawler & Porter, 1967; Organ, 1977; Schwab & Cummings, 1970; Siegel & Bowen, 1971). Another area of concern has been the search for moderators of the satisfaction-performance relation, such as the contingency of rewards (Jacobs & Solomon, 1977; Lawler, 1973), situational constraints (Bhagat, 1982; Herman, 1973), self-esteem (Jacobs & Solomon, 1977; Lopez, 1982), pressures for production (Triandis, 1959), and reciprocity norms (Organ, 1977). A third line of research has focused on methodological/measurement techniques for increasing the magnitude of the satisfaction-performance relation obtained (Fisher, 1980; Jacobs & Solomon, 1977; Triandis, 1959).

One impetus behind researchers' proclivity for studying the satisfaction-performance relation appears to be the assumption that the two variables should

Condensed from *Psychological Bulletin*, 1985, **97**, 251–273. Copyright © 1985 by the American Psychological Association. Adapted by permission.

be related, and that further research will reveal this as-yet-undiscovered truth. However, the new studies often served only to increase the existing data base in this area to the point where it is now highly fractionated. What appears to be needed is an integration of the already documented results into some descriptive yet quantitative form. The recent emergence of a new approach to research integration, meta-analysis, offers this possibility.

Glass (1976) proposed the term *meta-analysis* to refer to the "statistical analysis of a large collection of analysis results from individual studies, for the purpose of integrating the findings" (p. 3). He and his colleagues typically used and advocated a specific methodology that included quantifying an effect size for each study and then relating (via regression analysis) the magnitude of effect to various descriptive contextual characteristics of the studies to determine the causes of variation in study findings (e.g., Smith & Glass, 1977). In general, this form of meta-analysis has been used by several researchers to derive generalizations from the literature on a wide variety of topics. Glass, McGaw, and Smith (1981) and Hunter, Schmidt, and Jackson (1982) provided extensive bibliographies of meta-analytic investigations of this sort.

Concurrently with Glass's work on meta-analysis, Schmidt and Hunter and their colleagues developed an extensive set of procedures for demonstrating the generalizability of employment test validities (cf. Pearlman, Schmidt, & Hunter, 1980; Schmidt, Gast-Rosenberg, & Hunter, 1980; Schmidt & Hunter, 1977; Schmidt, Hunter, & Pearlman, 1981). They regarded their validity generalization method as an extension of Glassian meta-analysis, because both sets of procedures emphasized statistical integration by determining a mean effect size across studies. They cited the major conceptual difference between the two approaches as being the direct focus that validity generalization procedures place on the role of statistical artifacts in influencing the variance in observed effects across studies (Schmidt et al., 1980).

Although Schmidt and Hunter's validity generalization procedures were originally proposed in the context of personnel selection, the formulas have recently been developed into a general technique of meta-analysis, applicable to the integration of research in virtually any domain (Hunter et al., 1982). The rationale behind the procedure remains the same, however, in that a large proportion (if not all) of the variation in findings across studies is assumed to be the result of seven statistical artifacts: (a) sampling error due to small sample sizes, (b) criterion unreliability, (c) predictor unreliability, (d) range restriction, (e) criterion contamination and deficiency, (f) slight differences in factor structure between different tests measuring similar constructs, and (g) computational and typographical errors (Schmidt & Hunter, 1977). Recent studies within several content domains demonstrated that Schmidt and Hunter's procedure, which corrects for just the first four of these artifacts, can explain a substantial amount of the variation found in effect sizes (Fisher & Gitelson, 1983; Linn, Harnisch, & Dunbar, 1981; Mabe & West, 1982; Terborg, Lee, Smith, Davis, & Turbin, 1982).

Aside from their specific results, Mabe and West's (1982) review demonstrated the complementary nature of the Glassian and Hunter et al. (1982) approaches to meta-analysis. Whereas Hunter et al.'s (1982) technique used a confirmatory perspective and attempted to assess the theoretical true relation between the variables in question, Glass et al.'s (1981) approach was more exploratory in nature, attempting to discern qualitative aspects of the studies themselves that can account for the obtained results. Although Hunter et al. criticized Glass's use of large numbers of coded characteristics as capitalizing on chance, they did acknowledge the use of the Glassian approach as a supplementary step to their own procedure when the estimated variance of effect sizes (i.e., after corrections for artifacts have been made) across studies is substantially greater than zero.

PRESENT STUDY

The present study attempts to synthesize and integrate our existing knowledge of the job satisfaction-job performance literature by using the meta-analytic techniques of Hunter et al. (1982) and Glass et al. (1981). Although previous narrative reviews (Brayfield & Crockett, 1955; Herzberg et al., 1957; Vroom, 1964) drew some tentative conclusions regarding the nature of this relation, the statistical integration now available with these two forms of meta-analysis offers the prospect of more exact conclusions regarding the true theoretical correlation between these two variables and a delineation of what types of study conditions moderate this relation in practice. Results of a meta-analytic review of the satisfaction-performance literature may demonstrate that the true magnitude of this relation is, substantially different from the low positive correlation that reviewers have found (e.g., Brayfield & Crockett, 1955; Herzberg et al., 1957; Vroom, 1964). . . .

DISCUSSION

Perhaps the most immediately striking result of this analysis is the correspondence between the (uncorrected) frequency-weighted mean correlation ($\bar{r}_{xy}$) obtained here and that reported by Vroom (1964). On the basis of the 20 estimates available at the time, Vroom reported the mean correlation between job satisfaction and job performance to be $+.14$. Those who questioned Vroom's (1964) conclusion may find it disconcerting that 20 years and at least 200 satisfaction-performance correlations later, the average correlation was found here to be nearly the same ($+ .146$). Despite such psychometric and methodological advances as the development of refined measures of job satisfaction (e.g., the JDI), the recognition of the need to use larger sample sizes, and the increased use of longitudinal designs, the results of researchers' efforts to obtain high satisfaction-performance correlations have on the average not been more fruitful than those attempts reviewed by Vroom. Results of the chi-square analysis echo this conclusion in that there were no significant differences in the magnitude of observed satisfaction-performance correlations over the four time periods examined (prior to 1960, 1960–1969, 1970–1979, and 1980–1983). The standard deviation of this distribution of correlations ($\sigma_{r_{xy}}^2 = .029$; $SD = .17$), however, indicates that there is some sizable variability between studies in the correlations obtained. Hence, conclusions drawn from these results would necessarily be less precise than if the observed variance ($\sigma_{r_{xy}}^2$) had been virtually zero. . . .

SUBSTANTIVE IMPLICATIONS

The conclusion that job satisfaction and job performance are only slightly related has many practical implications. The ideals of high job satisfaction and high productivity are valued in our society, and attempts to design work so as to jointly achieve these goals are continuous. Indeed, both management and union representatives generally endorse the notion that greater productivity would result if workers were more satisfied (Katzell & Yankelovich, 1975). Thus, the finding that these two variables are not highly correlated questions the assumptions implicit in our organizational programs and policies, our research endeavors, and even in the expectations of those who review the satisfaction-performance literature.

Katzell and Yankelovich (1975) exemplified this implicit assumption in their review of policy-related satisfaction-performance research. Their intention was to determine how productivity and job satisfaction could be increased jointly. Although they concluded that this goal could not usually be achieved, they lamented their failure to find strong satisfaction-performance linkages.

> We *wish* (italics added) we could announce that our search had been completely *successful* (italics added), that it had clearly disclosed the secret of motivating people so that they are both satisfied with their work and productive in it. *Unfortunately* (italics added) . . . the facts are still too incomplete and equivocal to permit that. (Katzell & Yankelovich, 1975, p. ix)

The implicit assumption that satisfaction and performance are ecologically related may have contributed to the publication of many empirical studies that disconfirmed this assumption. The name often given to such research is the *debunking paradigm*. Rosenthal (1979) observed that there is a bias against publishing nonsignificant findings in the belief that they are generally not noteworthy. It seems that articles addressing the satisfaction-performance relation have not been affected by this bias in that most published studies find a nonsignificant relation between these two variables.

Thirty years ago organizational theorists endorsed the prescription that a happy worker is a productive worker. Subsequent research has dispelled this assumption; however, there still exists residual support for its veracity, although often amended by a host of contingency factors. Support for the belief is evidenced in such popularized managerial techniques as job enrichment, participative decision making, and autonomous work groups. All these are undergirded by the tenet that worker satisfaction can be increased, which in turn will lead to improved performance. Indeed, some researchers hypothesized that the stronger the relation between satisfaction and performance (other things being equal; Lawler & Porter, 1967), the more effective the organization. Some theorists proposed it is the quality of work, not the quantity, which is enhanced by having a satisfied work force. Yet other researchers sought conditions under which satisfaction and performance are more closely aligned, such as the contingency of rewards (Cherrington, Reitz, & Scott, 1971), the degree of stimulation in the work (Baird, 1976), and organizational pressure (Bhagat, 1982). The product of this research has been the formulation of models proposing under what conditions, or for what people (i.e., those with high self-esteem), satisfaction and performance will be more strongly related.

The empirical support for these contingency models, however, has not been overly positive. As was previously noted, only eight of the 217 satisfaction-performance correlations exceeded .44, and this degree of association leaves 80% of the variance in one variable unexplained by the other. Perhaps it is the manifest importance of these dual criteria for the world of work, or their hoary lineage in organizational research, but few other empirical relations have embraced the null hypothesis so often yet continued to foster additional research. Dunnette (1966) noted that fads influence the selection of research topics, and the degree of empirical support a topic receives often affects its longevity. It appears that the satisfaction-performance relation qualifies as a long-standing fad among organizational researchers, and researchers feel compelled to reinvestigate the topic despite a profusion of empirical nonsupport.

Given the significance of both variables in our work lives, it seems unlikely that investigations of their co-relation will ever completely dissipate. What we have learned to date is that under most employment conditions the two variables are only slightly related to each other. Under selected experimentally created employment conditions, the extent of their interrelation can be enhanced to some degree; however, these conditions are the exception, not the rule. To the extent that high worker satisfaction and high worker performance are desirable objectives, efforts to enhance both simultaneously by organizational interventions would be facilitated by their showing a nonindependent relation. The findings indicate, however, that in most cases each objective will have to be met by a different intervention, as efforts to embellish both concurrently are not likely to be successful. In fact, evidence exists that some interventions produce an enhancement in one variable and a diminution in the other.

CONCLUSIONS

In summary, this study represents a meta-analysis of one of the most often investigated topics in all of organizational research—the relation between satisfaction and performance. This topic is replete with major implications for both theoreticians and practitioners alike. Our results indicate, similar to the findings reported in the earlier reviews published over 20 years ago, that satisfaction and performance are only slightly related to each other. The amount of empirical support for the satisfaction-performance relation does not approximate the degree to which this relation has been espoused in theories of organizational design. It is almost as if the satisfaction-performance relation is itself what Chapman and Chapman (1969) called an illusory correlation, a perceived relation between two variables that we logically or intuitively think should interrelate, but in fact do not. Although we do not preclude the possibility that future architects of organizational structure may develop methods of designing work that result simultaneously in high productivity and worker satisfaction, we conclude such a covariant relation does not exist to any substantial degree in the literature published to date.

REFERENCES

Baird, L. S. (1976). Relationship of performance to satisfaction in stimulating and nonstimulating jobs. *Journal of Applied Psychology, 61,* 721–727.

Bartol, K. M. (1981). Vocational behavior and career development, 1980: A review. *Journal of Vocational Behavior, 19,* 123–162.

Bhagat, R. S. (1982). Conditions under which stronger job performance–job satisfaction relationships may be observed: A closer look at two situational contingencies. *Academy of Management Journal, 25,* 772–789.

Brayfield, A. H., & Marsh, M. M. (1957). Aptitudes, interests, and personality characteristics of farmers. *Journal of Applied Psychology, 41,* 98–103.

Chapman, L. J., & Chapman, J. P. (1969). Illusory correlation as an obstacle to the use of valid psycho-diagnostic signs. *Journal of Abnormal Psychology, 74,* 271–280.

Cherrington, D. J., Reitz, H. J., & Scott, W. E. (1971). Effects of contingent and noncontingent reward on the relationship between satisfaction and task performance. *Journal of Applied Psychology, 55,* 531–536.

Dunnette, M. D. (1966). Fads, fashions, and folderol in psychology. *American Psychologist, 21,* 343–352.

Fisher, C. D. (1980). On the dubious wisdom of expecting job satisfaction to correlate with performance. *Academy of Management Review, 5,* 607–612.

Fisher, C. D. & Gitelson, R. (1983). A meta-analysis of the correlates of role conflict and ambiguity. *Journal of Applied Psychology, 68,* 320–333.

Glass, G. V. (1976). Primary, secondary, and meta-analysis of research. *Educational Researcher, 5*(10), 3–8.

Glass, G. V., McGaw, B., & Smith, M. L. (1981). *Meta-analysis in social research.* Beverly Hills, CA: Sage.

Herman, J. B. (1973). Are situational contingencies limiting job attitude–job performance relationships? *Organizational Behavior and Human Performance, 10,* 208–224.

Herzberg, F., Mausner, B., Peterson, R. O. & Capwell, D. F. (1957). *Job attitudes: Review of research and opinion.* Pittsburgh, PA: Psychological Service of Pittsburgh.

Hunter, J. E., Schmidt, F. L., & Jackson, G. B. (1982). *Meta-analysis: Cumulating research findings across studies.* Beverly Hills, CA: Sage.

Jacobs, R., & Solomon, T. (1977). Strategies for enhancing the prediction of job performance from job satisfaction. *Journal of Applied Psychology, 62,* 417–421.

Katzell, R. A., & Yankelovich, D. (1975). *Work, productivity, and job satisfaction: An evaluation of policy-related research.* New York: Psychological Corp.

Kornhauser, A., & Sharp, A. (1932). Employee attitudes: Suggestions from a study in a factory. *Personnel Journal, 10,* 393–401.

Lawler, E. E. (1973). *Motivation in work organizations.* Monterey, CA: Brooks/Cole.

Lawler, E. E., & Porter, L. W. (1967). The effect of performance on job satisfaction. *Industrial Relations, 7,* 20–28.

Linn, R. L., Harnisch, D. L., & Dunbar, S. B. (1981). Validity generalization and situational specificity: An analysis of the prediction of first-year grades in law school. *Applied Psychological Measurement, 5,* 281–289.

Lopez, E. M. (1982). A test of the self-consistency theory of the job performance–job satisfaction relationship. *Academy of Management Journal, 25,* 335–348.

Mabe, P. A., & West, S. G. (1982). Validity of self-evaluation of ability: A review and meta-analysis. *Journal of Applied Psychology, 67,* 280–296.

Organ, D. W. (1977). A reappraisal and reinterpretation of the satisfaction-cause-performance hypothesis. *Academy of Management Review, 2,* 46–53.

Pearlman, K., Schmidt, F. L., & Hunter, J. E. (1980). Validity generalization results for tests used to predict job proficiency and training success in clerical occupations. *Journal of Applied Psychology, 65*, 373–406.

Rosenthal, R. (1979). The "file drawer problem" and tolerance for null results. *Psychological Bulletin, 86*, 638–641.

Schmidt, F. L., Gast-Rosenberg, I., & Hunter, J. E. (1980). Validity generalization results for computer programmers. *Journal of Applied Psychology, 65*, 643–661.

Schmidt, F. L., Hunter, J. E., & Pearlman, K. (1981). Task differences as moderators of aptitude test validity in selection: A red herring. *Journal of Applied Psychology, 66*, 166–185.

Schwab, D. P., & Cummings, L. L. (1970). Theories of performance and satisfaction: A review. *Industrial Relations, 9*, 408–430.

Siegel, J. P., & Bowen, D. (1971). Satisfaction and performance: Causal relationships and moderating effects. *Journal of Vocational Behavior, 1*, 263–269.

Smith, M. L., & Glass, G. V. (1977). Meta-analysis of psychotherapy outcome studies. *American Psychologist, 32*, 752–760.

Srivastva, S., Salipante, P. F., Cummings, T. G., Notz, W. W., Bigelow, J. D., & Waters, J. A. (1975). *Job satisfaction and productivity: An evaluation of policy related research on productivity, industrial organization and job satisfaction: Policy development and implementation*. Cleveland, OH: Department of Organizational Behavior, Case Western Reserve University.

Terborg, J. R., Lee, T. W., Smith, F. J., Davis, G. A., & Turbin, M. S. (1982). Extension of the Schmidt and Hunter validity generalization procedure to the prediction of absenteeism behavior from knowledge of job satisfaction and organizational commitment. *Journal of Applied Psychology, 67*, 440–449.

Triandis, H. C. (1959). A critique and experimental design for the study of the relationship between productivity and job satisfaction. *Psychological Bulletin, 56*, 309–312.

Vroom, V. H. (1964). *Work and motivation*. New York: Wiley.

Organizational Psychology and the Pursuit of the Happy/Productive Worker

Barry M. Staw

What I am going to talk about in this article is an old and overworked topic, but one that remains very much a source of confusion and controversy. It is also a topic that continues to attract the attention of managers and academic researchers alike, frequently being the focus of both popular books and scholarly articles. The issue is how to manage an organization so that employees can be both happy and productive—a situation where workers and managers are both satisfied with the outcomes.

The pursuit of the happy/productive worker could be viewed as an impossible dream from the Marxist perspective of inevitable worker–management conflict.

From the *California Management Review, 28*(4), 40–53. Copyright © [1986] by the Regents of the University of California. Reprinted by permission of The Regents.

Such a goal could also be seen as too simple or naive from the traditional industrial relations view of outcomes being a product of necessary bargaining and compromise. Yet, from the psychological perspective, the pursuit of the happy/productive worker has seemed a worthwhile though difficult endeavor, one that might be achieved if we greatly increase our knowledge of work attitudes and behavior. In this article, I will examine this psychological perspective and try to provide a realistic appraisal of where we now stand in the search for satisfaction and productivity in work settings.

APPROACHES TO THE HAPPY/PRODUCTIVE WORKER

One of the earliest pursuits of the happy/productive worker involved the search for a relationship between satisfaction and productivity. The idea was that the world might be neatly divided into situations where workers are either happy and productive or unhappy and unproductive. If this were true, then it would be a simple matter to specify the differences between management styles present in the two sets of organizations and to come up with a list of prescriptions for improvement. Unfortunately, research has never supported such a clear relationship between individual satisfaction and productivity. For over thirty years, starting with Brayfield and Crockett's classic review of the job satisfaction-job performance literature,[1] and again with Vroom's discussion of satisfaction-performance research,[2] organizational psychologists have had to contend with the fact that happiness and productivity may not necessarily go together. As a result, most organizational psychologists have come to accept the argument that satisfaction and performance may relate to two entirely different individual decisions—decisions to participate and to produce.[3]

Though psychologists have acknowledged the fact that satisfaction and performance are not tightly linked, this has not stopped them from pursuing the happy/productive worker. In fact, over the last thirty years, an enormous variety of theories have attempted to show how managers can reach the promised land of high satisfaction and productivity. The theories shown in Table 1 constitute only an abbreviated list of recent attempts to reach this positive state.

None of the theories in Table 1 have inherited the happy/productive worker hypothesis in the simple sense of believing that job satisfaction and performance generally co-vary in the world *as it now exists*. But, these models all make either indirect or direct assumptions that *it is possible* to achieve a world where both

TABLE 1
PATHS TO THE HAPPY/PRODUCTIVE WORKER

Worker Participation	The Pursuit of Excellence
Supportive Leadership	Socio-Technical Systems
9–9 Systems	Organizational Commitment
Job Enrichment	High Performing Systems
Behavior Modification	Theory Z
Goal Setting	Strong Culture

satisfaction and performance will be present. Some of the theories focus on ways to increase job satisfaction, with the implicit assumption that performance will necessarily follow; some strive to directly increase performance, with the assumption that satisfaction will result; and some note that satisfaction and performance will be a joint product of implementing certain changes in the organization.

Without going into the specifics of each of these routes to the happy/productive worker, I think it is fair to say that most of the theories in Table 1 have been oversold. Historically, they each burst on the scene with glowing and almost messianic predictions, with proponents tending to simplify the process of change, making it seem like a few easy tricks will guarantee benefits to workers and management alike. The problem, of course, is that as results have come in from both academic research and from wider practical application, the benefits no longer have appeared so strong nor widespread. Typically, the broader the application and the more well-documented the study (with experimental controls and measures of expected costs and benefits), the weaker have been the empirical results. Thus, in the end, both managers and researchers have often been left disillusioned, skeptical that any part of these theories are worth a damn and that behavioral science will ever make a contribution to management.

My goal with this article is to *lower our expectations*—to show why it is so difficult to make changes in both satisfaction and performance. My intention is not to paint such a pessimistic picture as to justify not making any changes at all, but to inoculate us against the frustrations of slow progress. My hope is to move us toward a reasoned but sustainable pursuit of the happy/productive worker—away from the alternating practice of fanfare and despair.

CHANGING JOB ATTITUDES

Although organizational psychologists have accepted the notion that job satisfaction and performance do not necessarily co-vary, they have still considered job attitudes as something quite permeable or subject to change. This "blank state" approach to job attitudes comes from prevailing psychological views of the individual, where the person is seen as a creature who constantly appraises the work situation, evaluates the merits of the context, and formulates an attitude based on these conditions. As the work situation changes, individuals are thought to be sensitive to the shifts, adjusting their attitudes in a positive or negative direction. With such an approach to attitudes, it is easy to see why job satisfaction has been a common target of organizational change, and why attempts to redesign work have evolved as a principal mechanism for improving job satisfaction.

Currently, the major debate in the job design area concerns whether individuals are more sensitive to objective job conditions or social cues. In one camp are proponents of job redesign who propose that individuals are highly receptive to concrete efforts to improve working conditions. Hackman and Oldham, for example, argue that satisfaction can be increased by improving a job in terms of its variety (doing a wider number of things), identity (seeing how one's various tasks make a meaningful whole), responsibility (being in charge of one's own work and its quality), feedback (knowing when one has done a good job), and significance (the meaning or relative importance of one's contribution to the organization or society in general).[4] In the opposing camp are advocates of social information processing. These researchers argue that jobs are often ambiguous entities subject to multiple interpretations and perceptions.[5] Advocates of social information processing have noted that the positive or negative labeling of a task can greatly determine one's attitude toward the job, and that important determinants of this labeling are the opinions of co-workers who voice positive or negative views of the work. These researchers have shown that it may be as easy to persuade workers that their jobs are interesting by influencing the *perception* of a job as it is to make objective changes in the work role.

The debate between job design and social information processing has produced two recent shifts in the way we think about job attitudes. First, organizational psychology now places greater emphasis on the role of cognition and subjective evaluation in the way people respond to jobs. This is probably helpful, because even though we have generally measured job conditions with perceptual scales, we have tended to confuse these perceptions with objective job conditions. We need to be reminded that perceptions of job characteristics do not necessarily reflect reality, yet they can determine how we respond to that reality.

The second shift in thinking about job attitudes is a movement toward situationalism, stressing how even slight alterations in job context can influence one's perception of a job. It is now believed that people's job attitudes may be influenced not only by the objective properties of the work, but also by subtle cues given off by co-workers or supervisors that the job is dull or interesting. I think this new view is a mistake since it overstates the role of external influence in the determination of job attitudes. The reality may be that individuals are quite resistant to change efforts, with their attitudes coming more as a function of personal disposition than situational influence.

THE CONSISTENCY OF JOB ATTITUDES

Robert Kahn recently observed that, although our standard of living and working conditions have improved dramatically since World War II, reports of satisfaction on national surveys have not changed dramatically.[6] This implies that job satisfaction might be something of a "sticky variable," one that is not so easily changed by outside influence. Some research on the consistency of job attitudes leads to the same conclusion. Schneider and Dachler, for example, found very strong consistency in satisfaction scores over a 16-month longitudinal study (averaging .56 for managers and .58 for non-managers).[7] Pulakos and Schmitt also found that high school students' pre-employment expectations of satisfaction correlated significantly with ratings of their jobs several years later.[8] These findings, along with the fact that job satisfaction is generally intertwined with both life satisfaction and mental health, imply that there is some ongoing consistency in job attitudes, and that job satisfaction may be determined as much by dispositional properties of the individual as any changes in the situation.

A Berkeley colleague, Joseph Garbarino, has long captured this notion of a dispositional source of job attitudes with a humorous remark, "I always told my children at a young age that their most important decision in life would be whether they wanted to be happy or not; everything else is malleable enough to fit the answer to this question.'' What Garbarino implies is that job attitudes are fairly constant, and when reality changes for either the better or worse, we can easily distort that reality to fit our underlying disposition. Thus, individuals may think a great deal about the nature of their jobs, but satisfaction can result as much from the unique way a person views the world around him as from any social influence or objective job characteristics. That is, individuals predisposed to be happy may interpret their jobs in a much different way than those with more negative predispositions.

The Attitudinal Consistency Study

Recently, I have been involved with two studies attempting to test for dispositional sources of job attitudes. In the first study, Jerry Ross and I reanalyzed data from the National Longitudinal Survey, a study conducted by labor economists at Ohio State.[9] We used this survey to look at the stability of job attitudes over time and job situations. The survey's measure of attitudes were not very extensive but did provide one of the few available sources of data on objective job changes.

The National Longitudinal Survey data revealed an interesting pattern of results. We found that job satisfaction was fairly consistent over time, with significant relationships among job attitudes over three- and five-year time intervals. We also found that job satisfaction showed consistency *even when people changed jobs*. This later finding is especially important, since it directly contradicts the prevailing assumptions of job attitude research.

Most job design experiments and organizational interventions that strive to improve job attitudes change a small aspect of work, but look for major changes in job satisfaction. However, the National Longitudinal Survey data showed that when people changed their place of work (which would naturally include one's supervisor, working conditions, and procedures), there was still significant consistency in attitudes. One could, of course, argue that people leave one terrible job for another, and this is why such consistency in job attitudes arises. Therefore, we checked for consistency across occupational changes. The National Longitudinal Survey showed consistency not only across occupational changes, but also when people changed *both* their employers and their occupations. This evidence of consistency tells us that people may not be as malleable as we would like to think they are, and that there may be some underlying tendency toward equilibrium in job attitudes. If you are dissatisfied in one job context, you are also likely to be dissatisfied in another (perhaps better) environment.

The Dispositional Study

The consistency data from the National Longitudinal Survey, while interesting, do not tell us what it is that may underlie a tendency to be satisfied or dissatisfied on the job. Therefore, Nancy Bell (a doctoral student at the Berkeley Business

School), John Clausen (a developmental sociologist at Berkeley), and I undertook a study to find some of the dispositional sources of job satisfaction.[10] We sought to relate early personality characteristics to job attitudes later in life, using a very unusual longitudinal data source.

There are three longitudinal personality projects that have been running for over fifty years at Berkeley (the Berkeley Growth Study, the Oakland Growth Study, and the Guidance Study), and they have since been combined into what is now called the Intergenerational Study. Usually when psychologists speak of longitudinal studies, they mean data collected from one or two year intervals. These data span over 50 years. Usually, when psychologists refer to personality ratings, they mean self-reports derived from the administration of various questionnaires. Much of the Intergenerational Study data are clinical ratings derived from questionnaires, observation, and interview materials evaluated by a different set of raters for each period of the individual's life. Thus, these data are of unusual quality for psychological research.

Basically what we did with data from the Intergenerational Study was to construct an affective disposition scale that measured a very general positive-negative orientation of people. We then related this scale to measures of job attitudes at different periods in people's lives. The ratings used for our affective disposition scale included items such as "cheerful," "satisfied with self," and "irritable" (reverse coded), and we correlated this scale with measures of job and career satisfaction. The results were very provocative. We found that affective dispositions, from as early as the junior-high-school years, significantly predicted job attitudes during middle and late adulthood (ages 40–60). The magnitude of correlations was not enormous (in the .3 to .4 range). But, these results are about as strong as we usually see between two attitudes measured on the same questionnaire by the same person at the same time—yet, these data cut across different raters and over fifty years in time.

What are we to conclude from this personality research as well as our reanalyses of the National Longitudinal Survey? I think we can safely conclude that there is a fair amount of consistency in job attitudes and that there may be dispositional as well as situational sources of job satisfaction. Thus, it is possible that social information processing theorists have been on the right track in viewing jobs as ambiguous entities that necessitate interpretation by individuals. But, it is also likely that the interpretation of jobs (whether they are perceived as positive or negative) can come as much from internal, dispositional causes (e.g., happiness or depression) as external sources. Consequently, efforts to improve job satisfaction via changes in job conditions will need to contend with stable personal dispositions toward work—forces that may favor consistency of equilibrium in the way people view the world around them.

THE INTRANSIGENCE OF JOB PERFORMANCE

Although we have not conducted research on the consistency of performance or its resistance to change, I think there are some parallels between the problems of changing attitudes and performance. Just as job attitudes may be constrained by individual dispositions, there are many elements of both the individual and work situation that can make improvements in job performance difficult.[11]

Most of the prevailing theories of work performance are concerned with individual motivation. They prescribe various techniques intended to stimulate, reinforce, or lure people into working harder. Most of these theories have little to say about the individual's limits of task ability, predisposition for working hard, or the general energy or activity level of the person. Somewhat naively, our theories have maintained that performance is under the complete control of the individual. Even though there are major individual differences affecting the quantity or quality of work produced, we have assumed that *if the employee really wants to perform better, his or her performance will naturally go up.*

There already exist some rather strong data that refute these implicit assumptions about performance. A number of studies[12] have shown that mental and physical abilities can be reliable predictors of job performance, and it is likely that other dispositions (e.g., personality characteristics) will eventually be found to be associated with effective performance of certain work roles. Thus, influencing work effort may not be enough to cause wide swings in performance, unless job performance is somewhat independent of ability (e.g., in a low skill job). Many work roles may be so dependent on ability (such as those of a professional athlete, musician, inventor) that increases in effort may simply not cause large changes in the end product.

In addition to ability, there may also be other individual factors that contribute to the consistency of performance. People who work hard in one situation are likely to be the ones who exert high effort in a second situation. If, for example, the person's energy level (including need for sleep) is relatively constant over time, we should not expect wide changes in available effort. And, if personality dimensions such as dependability and self-confidence can predict one's achievement level over the lifecourse,[13] then a similar set of personal attributes may well constitute limitations to possible improvements in performance. Already, assessment centers have capitalized on this notion by using personality measures to predict performance in many corporate settings.

Performance may not be restricted just because of the individual's level of ability and effort, however. Jobs may *themselves* be designed so that performance is not under the control of the individual, regardless of ability or effort. Certainly we are aware of the fact that an assembly line worker's output is more a product of the speed of the line than any personal preference. In administrative jobs too, what one does may be constrained by the work cycle or technical procedures. There may be many people with interlocking tasks so that an increase in the performance of one employee doesn't mean much if several tasks must be completed sequentially or simultaneously in order to improve productivity. Problems also arise in situations where doing one's job better may not be predicated upon a burst of energy or desire, but upon increases in materials, financial support, power, and resources. As noted by Kanter, the administrator must often negotiate, hoard, and form coalitions to get anything done on the job, since there are lots of actors vying for the attention and resources of the organization.[14] Thus, the nature of the organization, combined with the abilities and efforts of individuals to maneuver in the organization, may serve to constrain changes in individual performance.

ASSESSING THE DAMAGE

So far I have taken a somewhat dark or pessimistic view of the search for the happy/productive worker. I have noted that in terms of satisfaction and performance, it may not be easy to create perfect systems because both happiness and performance are constrained variables, affected by forces not easily altered by our most popular interventions and prescriptions for change. Should organizational psychologists therefore close up shop and go home? Should we move to a more descriptive study of behavior as opposed to searching for improvements in work attitudes and performance?

I think such conclusions are overly pessimistic. We need to interpret the stickiness of job attitudes and performance not as an invitation to complacency or defeat, but as a realistic assessment that it will take very strong treatments to move these entrenched variables. Guzzo, Jackson, and Katzell have recently made a similar point after a statistical examination (called meta-analysis) of organizational interventions designed to improve productivity.[15] They noted that the most effective changes are often *multiple treatments,* where several things are changed at once in a given organization. Thus, instead of idealistic and optimistic promises, we may literally need to throw the kitchen sink at the problem.

The problem of course is that we have more than one kitchen sink! As noted earlier, nearly every theory of organizational behavior has been devoted to predicting and potentially improving job attitudes and performance. And, simply aggregating these treatments is not likely to have the desired result, since many of these recommendations consist of conflicting prescriptions for change. Therefore, it would be wiser to look for compatible *systems* of variables that can possibly be manipulated in concert. Let us briefly consider three systems commonly used in organizational change efforts and then draw some conclusions about their alternative uses.

THREE SYSTEMS OF ORGANIZATIONAL CHANGE

The Individually-Oriented System

The first alternative is to build a strong individually-oriented system, based on the kind of traditional good management that organizational psychologists have been advocating for years. This system would emphasize a number of venerable features of Western business organizations such as:

- Tying extrinsic rewards (such as pay) to performance.
- Setting realistic and challenging goals.
- Evaluating employee performance accurately and providing feedback on performance.
- Promoting on the basis of skill and performance rather than personal characteristics, power, or connections.

- Building the skill level of the workforce through training and development.
- Enlarging and enriching jobs through increases in responsibility, variety, and significance.

All of the above techniques associated with the individually-oriented system are designed to promote both satisfaction and productivity. The major principle underlying each of these features is to structure the work and/or reward system so that high performance is either intrinsically or extrinsically rewarding to the individual, thus creating a situation where high performance contributes to job satisfaction.

In practice, there can be numerous bugs in using an individually-oriented system to achieve satisfaction and performance. For example, just saying that rewards should be based on performance is easier than knowing what the proper relationship should be or whether there should be discontinuities at the high or low end of that relationship. Should we, for instance, lavish rewards on the few highest performers, deprive the lowest performers, or establish a constant linkage between pay and performance? In terms of goal-setting, should goals be set by management, workers, or joint decision making, and what should the proper baseline be for measuring improvements? In terms of job design, what is the proper combination of positive social cues and actual job enrichment that will improve motivation and satisfaction?

These questions are important and need to be answered in order to "fine-tune" or fully understand an individually-oriented system. Yet, even without answers to these questions, we already know that a well-run organization using an individually-oriented system *can* be effective. The problem is we usually don't implement such a system, either completely or very well, in most organizations. Instead, we often compare poorly managed corporations using individually-oriented systems (e.g., those with rigid bureaucratic structures) with more effectively run firms using another motivational system (e.g., Japanese organizations), concluding that the individual model is wrong. The truth may be that the individual model may be just as correct as other approaches, but we simply don't implement it as well.

The Group-Oriented System

Individually-oriented systems are obviously not the only way to go. We can also have a group-oriented system, where satisfaction and performance are derived from group participation. In fact, much of organizational life could be designed around groups, if we wanted to capitalize fully on the power of groups to influence work attitudes and behavior.[16] The basic idea would be to make group participation so important that groups would be capable of controlling both satisfaction and performance. Some of the most common techniques would be:

- Organizing work around intact groups.
- Having groups charged with selection, training, and rewarding of members.
- Using groups to enforce strong norms for behavior, with group involvement in off-the-job as well as on-the-job behavior.

- Distributing resources on a group rather than individual basis.
- Allowing and perhaps even promoting intergroup rivalry so as to build within-group solidarity.

Group-oriented systems may be difficult for people at the top to control, but they can be very powerful and involving. We know from military research that soldiers can fight long and hard, not out of special patriotism, but from devotion and loyalty to their units. We know that participation in various high-tech project groups can be immensely involving, both in terms of one's attitudes and performance. We also know that people will serve long and hard hours to help build or preserve organizational divisions or departments, perhaps more out of loyalty and altruism than self-interest. Thus, because individuals will work to achieve group praise and adoration, a group-oriented system, effectively managed, can potentially contribute to high job performance and satisfaction.

The Organizationally-Oriented System

A third way of organizing work might be an organizationally-oriented system, using the principles of Ouchi's Theory Z and Lawler's recommendations for developing high-performing systems.[17] The basic goal would be to arrange working conditions so that individuals gain satisfaction from contributing to the entire organization's welfare. If individuals were to identify closely with the organization as a whole, then organizational performance would be intrinsically rewarding to the individual. On a less altruistic basis, individuals might also gain extrinsic rewards from association with a high-performing organization, since successful organizations may provide greater personal opportunities in terms of salary and promotion. Common features of an organizationally-oriented system would be:

- Socialization into the organization as a whole to foster identification with the entire business and not just a particular subunit.
- Job rotation around the company so that loyalty is not limited to one subunit.
- Long training period with the development of skills that are specific to the company and not transferable to other firms in the industry or profession, thus committing people to the employing organization.
- Long-term or protected employment to gain organizational loyalty, with concern for survival and welfare of the firm.
- Decentralized operations, with few departments or subunits to compete for the allegiance of members.
- Few status distinctions between employees so that dissension and separatism are not fostered.
- Economic education and sharing of organizational information about products, financial condition, and strategies of the firm.
- Tying individual rewards (at all levels in the firm) to organizational performance through various forms of profit sharing, stock options, and bonuses.

The Japanese have obviously been the major proponents of organizationally-oriented systems, although some of the features listed here (such as profit sharing) are very American in origin. The odd thing is that Americans have consistently followed an organizationally-oriented system for middle and upper management and for members of professional organizations such as law and accounting firms. For these high-level employees, loyalty may be as valued as immediate performance, with the firm expecting the individual to defend the organization, even if there does not seem to be any obvious self-interest involved. Such loyalty is rarely demanded or expected from the lower levels of traditional Western organizations.

EVALUATING THE THREE SYSTEMS

I started this article by noting that it may be very difficult to change job performance and satisfaction. Then I noted that recognition of this difficulty should not resign us to the present situation, but spur us to stronger and more systemic actions—in a sense, throwing more variables at the problem. As a result, I have tried to characterize three syndromes of actions that might be effective routes toward the happy/productive worker.

One could build a logical case for the use of any of the three motivational systems. Each has the potential for arousing individuals, steering their behavior in desired ways, and building satisfaction as a consequence of high performance. Individually-oriented systems work by tapping the desires and goals of individuals and by taking advantage of our cultural affinity for independence. Group-oriented systems work by taking advantage of our more social selves, using group pressures and loyalty as the means of enforcing desired behavior and dispensing praise for accomplishments. Finally, organizationally-oriented systems function by building intense attraction to the goals of an institution, where individual pleasure is derived from serving the collective welfare.

If we have three logical and defensible routes toward achieving the happy/productive worker, which is the best path? The answer to this question will obviously depend on how the question is phrased. If "best" means appropriate from a cultural point of view, we will get one answer. As Americans, although we respect organizational loyalty, we often become suspicious of near total institutions where behavior is closely monitored and strongly policed—places like the company town and religious cult. If we define "best" as meaning the highest level of current performance, we might get a different answer, since many of the Japanese-run plants are now outperforming the American variety. Still, if we phrase the question in terms of *potential* effectiveness, we may get a third answer. Cross-cultural comparisons, as I mentioned, often pit poorly managed individually-oriented systems (especially those with non-contingent rewards and a bureaucratic promotion system) against more smoothly running group or organizationally-oriented systems. Thus, we really do not know which system, managed to its potential, will lead to the greatest performance.

Mixing the Systems

If we accept the fact that individual, group, and organizationally-oriented systems may each do *something* right, would it be possible to take advantage of all three? That is, can we either combine all three systems into some suprasystem or attempt to build a hybrid system by using the best features of each?

I have trepidations about combining the three approaches. Instead of a stronger treatment, we may end up with either a conflicted or confused environment. Because the individually-oriented system tends to foster competition among individual employees, it would not, for example, be easily merged with group-oriented systems that promote intragroup solidarity. Likewise, organizationally-oriented systems that emphasize how people can serve a common goal may not blend well with group-oriented systems that foster intergroup rivalry. Finally, the use of either a group- or organizationally-oriented reward system may diminish individual motivation, since it becomes more difficult for the person to associate his behavior with collective accomplishments and outcomes. Thus, by mixing the motivational approaches, we may end up with a watered-down treatment that does not fulfill the potential of *any* of the three systems.

In deciding which system to use, we need to face squarely the costs as well as benefits of the three approaches. For example, firms considering an individually-oriented system should assess not only the gains associated with increases in individual motivation, but also potential losses in collaboration that might result from interpersonal competition. Similarly, companies thinking of using a group-oriented system need to study the tradeoffs of intergroup competition that can be a byproduct of increased intragroup solidarity. And, before thinking that an organizationally-oriented system will solve all the firm's problems, one needs to know whether motivation to achieve collective goals can be heightened to the point where it outweighs potential losses in motivation toward personal and group interests. These trade-offs are not trivial. They trigger considerations of human resource policy as well as more general philosophical issues of what the organization wants to be. They also involve technical problems for which current organizational research has few solutions, since scholars have tended to study treatments in isolation rather than the effect of larger systems of variables.

So far, all we can be sure of is that task structure plays a key role in formulating the proper motivational strategy. As an example, consider the following cases: a sales organization can be divided into discrete territories (where total performance is largely the sum of individual efforts), a research organization where several product groups are charged with making new developments (where aggregate performance is close to the sum of group efforts), and a high-technology company where success and failure is due to total collaboration and collective effort. In each of these three cases, the choice of the proper motivational system will be determined by whether one views individual, group, or collective efforts as the most important element. Such a choice is also determined by the degree to which one is willing to sacrifice (or trade-off) a degree of performance from other elements of the system, be they the behavior of individuals, groups, or the collective whole. Thus, the major point is that each motivational system has its relative strengths and weaknesses—that despite the claims of many of our theories of management, there is no simple or conflict-free road to the happy/productive worker.

CONCLUSION

Although this article started by noting that the search for the happy/productive worker has been a rather quixotic venture, I have tried to end the discussion with some guarded optimism. By using individual, group, and organizational systems, I have shown how it is *at least possible* to create changes that can overwhelm the forces for stability in both job attitudes and performance. None of these three approaches are a panacea that will solve all of an organization's problems, and no doubt some very hard choices must be made between them. Yet, caution need not preclude action. Therefore, rather than the usual academic's plea for further research or the consultant's claim for bountiful results, we need actions that are flexible enough to allow for mistakes and adjustments along the way.

REFERENCES

1 A. H. Brayfield and W. H. Crockett, "Employee Attitudes and Employee Performance," *Psychological Bulletin,* 51 (1955):396–424.

2 Victor H. Vroom, *Work and Motivation* (New York, NY: Wiley, 1969).

3 James G. March and Herbert A. Simon, *Organizations* (New York, NY: Wiley, 1958).

4 Richard J. Hackman and Greg R. Oldham, *Work Redesign* (Reading, MA: Addison-Wesley, 1980).

5 E.g., Gerald R. Salancik and Jeffrey Pfeffer, "A Social Information Processing Approach to Job Attitudes and Task Design," *Administrative Science Quarterly,* 23 (1978):224–253.

6 Robert Kahn, (1985).

7 Benjamin Schneider and Peter Dachler, "A Note on the Stability of the Job Description Index," *Journal of Applied Psychology,* 63 (1978):650–653.

8 Elaine D. Pulakos and Neal Schmitt, "A Longitudinal Study of a Valence Model Approach for the Prediction of Job Satisfaction of New Employees," *Journal of Applied Psychology,* 68 (1983):307–312.

9 Barry M. Staw and Jerry Ross, "Stability in the Midst of Change: A Dispositional Approach to Job Attitudes," *Journal of Applied Psychology,* 70 (1985):469–480.

10 Barry M. Staw, Nancy E. Bell, and John A. Clausen, "The Dispositional Approach to Job Attitudes: A Lifetime Longitudinal Test," *Administrative Science Quarterly* (March 1986).

11 See, Lawrence H. Peters, Edward J. O'Connor, and Joe R. Eulberg, "Situational Constraints: Sources, Consequences, and Future Considerations," in Kendreth M. Rowland and Gerald R. Ferris, eds., *Research in Personnel and Human Resources Management,* Vol. 3 (Greenwich, CT: JAI Press, 1985).

12 For a review, see Marvin D. Dunnette, "Aptitudes, Abilities, and Skills," in Marvin D. Dunnette, ed., *Handbook of Industrial and Organizational Psychology* (Chicago, IL: Rand McNally, 1976).

13 As found by John Clausen, personal communications, 1986.

14 Rosabeth M. Kanter, *The Change Masters* (New York, NY: Simon & Schuster, 1983).

15 Richard A. Guzzo, Susan E. Jackson, and Raymond A. Katzell, "Meta-analysis Analysis," in Barry M. Staw and Larry L. Cummings, eds., *Research in Organizational Behavior,* Volume 9 (Greenwich, CT: JAI Press, 1987).

16 See, Harold J. Leavitt, "Suppose We Took Groups Seriously," in E. L. Cass and F. G. Zimmer, eds., *Man and Work in Society* (New York: NY: Van Nostrand, 1975).

17 William Ouchi, *Theory Z: How American Business Can Meet the Japanese Challenge* (Reading, MA: Addison-Wesley, 1981); Edward E. Lawler, III, "Increasing Worker Involvement to Enhance Organizational Effectiveness," in Paul Goodman, ed., *Change in Organizations* (San Francisco, CA: Jossey-Bass, 1982).

A Restatement of the Satisfaction-Performance Hypothesis

Dennis W. Organ

It appears that management scholars will not, perhaps cannot, let the job satisfaction-performance hypothesis fade away. Over 30 years have elapsed since Brayfield and Crockett (1955) reviewed a large body of evidence generally unsupportive of the proposition that there is any "appreciable" relationship between these variables, let alone the idea that "job satisfaction causes performance." Nearly a decade later, Vroom (1964) saw no reason to alter this conclusion. Yet recently we have seen two independent meta-analytic reviews updating the assessment of the empirical record (Iaffaldano and Muchinsky, 1985; Petty, McGee, & Cavender, 1984). Interestingly, the former review came to much the same conclusions as the earlier assessments, suggesting that high productivity and worker satisfaction form only "an illusory correlation . . . between two variables that we logically think should interrelate, but in fact do not" (Iaffaldano & Muchinsky, 1985, p. 270). On the other hand, Petty et al. (1984) concluded that the support for this relationship is perhaps greater than indicated by previous reviews. But even more interesting is the continued fascination of the management research community with an issue presumably settled by previous investigation.

Perhaps the fascination derives from the discomforting discrepancy between the empirical record and the apparently strong intuitive belief among practitioners (Gannon & Noon, 1971; Katzell & Yankelovich, 1975) that job satisfaction is indeed an important determinant of productivity. On the one hand, management scholars certainly do not feel obligated to have their research confirm conventional wisdom and may even take pride in the ability to disconfirm apparent common sense with scientific data. On the other hand, perhaps management theorists also feel an abiding need to explain such contradictions in such as way as to offer points of reconciliation between research findings and the opinions of presumably intelligent, experienced observers of work behavior.

Over a decade ago, Organ (1977) suggested that one means of reconciling the discrepancy lay in the various meanings we might attach to the concept "performance." Conceivably, the practitioner attaches multiple meanings to this term, including such non-productivity or extra-role dimensions as cooperation, informal modes of helping coworkers and superiors, and generalized tendencies toward compliance. Research measures of performance may not adequately cap-

From *Journal of Management*, 1988, **14**(4), 547–557. Reprinted by permission.

ture the variance in some of these more qualitative aspects of the practitioner's conception of performance. Organ drew upon social psychological exchange theory (e.g., Blau, 1964) to offer a defensible rationale why job satisfaction might account for more variance in informal helping and compliance than in more narrow measures of productivity or in-role performance.

However, Organ (1977) had scant data to support his argument. Furthermore, though concerned with the interpretation of the concept "performance," he took no note of the strong possibility that the "satisfaction" part of the proposition also demands scrutiny. Just what is it in what we call "satisfaction" that particularly influences "performance" of the sort that practitioners have in mind?

The purpose of this paper is to contribute toward a more precise and defensible version of the satisfaction-performance hypothesis by (a) reviewing recent empirical work that addresses extra-role contributions as "performance" correlates of satisfaction; (b) specifying the "satisfaction" referent that is tied to extra-role contributions and doing so in a way that links the issue to a potentially rich body of theory; and (c) considering the problems and prospects for both research and practice of the resulting reformulation of the satisfaction-performance proposition.

"PERFORMANCE" AS ORGANIZATIONAL CITIZENSHIP BEHAVIOR

Bateman and Organ (1983) used the term "citizenship behavior" to denote helpful, constructive gestures exhibited by organization members and valued or appreciated by officials, but not related directly to individual productivity nor inhering in the enforceable requirements of the individual's role. Bateman and Organ cited two rationales, either or both of which could support conceptually a link between job satisfaction and individual citizenship behavior. The first, drawn from social exchange concepts (e.g., Blau, 1964) suggests that individuals will feel bound by the norm of reciprocity when given the resources, treatment, and opportunities that induce satisfaction. Furthermore, given the constraints exerted by technology, work flow, and individual skills on productivity, they frequently will choose to reciprocate in the form of such citizenship behaviors as cooperation, supportiveness of the supervisor, helping behaviors, and gestures that enhance the reputation of the work unit internal and external to the organization. The second rationale, drawn from extensive naturalistic experiments on prosocial and altruistic behavior (e.g., as summarized in Brown, 1985, pp. 56–60) notes the accumulating evidence for a "mood state" or "positive affect" explanation of many forms of helping behavior. Thus, if job satisfaction represents the chronic or modal mood state of an organizational member, then presumably those most satisfied should have a characteristic predisposition toward prosocial gestures within the organization environment, and among those prosocial acts would number various forms of citizenship behavior.

Bateman and Organ (1983) tested the satisfaction-citizenship behavior hypothesis in a two-wave, two-variable cross-correlation panel research design, using a homemade measure of citizenship behavior that included 30 items on which immediate supervisors rated nonacademic university employees. The Job Descriptive Index (JDI: Smith, Kendall, & Hulin, 1969) provided measures of overall and facet satisfaction. The researchers found at each time of testing a static correlation of .41 between overall satisfaction and citizenship behavior. They could not, however, reject the null hypothesis of some common cause of both variables, because the cross-lagged correlations were approximately equal to each other and to both static correlations.

Smith, Organ, and Near (1983), working with a shorter but more refined measure of Organizational Citizenship Behavior (OCB), tested its relationship to satisfaction—in this instance, defined by the "Me at Work" semantic differential scale from Scott's (1967) measure—among 220 employees of two large banks. The researchers identified a two-factor structure in the OCB measure. Altruism, representing OCB gestures aimed at specific individuals, correlated .31 with job satisfaction. Compliance (or perhaps more aptly termed "conscientiousness"), which seemed to capture more impersonal forms of citizenship striving, correlated .21 with satisfaction. Separate causal models constructed from the interrelationships among these and other variables confirmed the link between satisfaction and Altruism, but not the link with Compliance.

Puffer (1987) guided by the concept "prosocial behavior," devised a measure of extra-role contributions by appliance salespeople whose earnings depended solely on sales commissions. Prosocial behavior (as rated by superiors) correlated .27 with a measure of "satisfaction with material rewards." Puffer also contributed a note of discriminant validity in this context, because the prosocial measure correlated only .16 with actual sales performance, which in turn correlated only .18 with satisfaction.

Motowidlo (1984) extended these findings to leader performance. Among 134 managers, he noted a correlation of .27 between managerial satisfaction and independent ratings by superiors of the manager's display of consideration toward subordinates. To the extent that certain forms of consideration and supportiveness of group members qualify as OCB, Motowidlo's finding adds a note of generality and robustness to the satisfaction-OCB hypothesis.

More recently, Motowidlo, Packard, and Manning (1986) have tested the flip side of the satisfaction-OCB hypothesis—i.e., that job-related distress inhibits the flow of OCB gestures. Motowidlo et al. surveyed the extent of prosocial behaviors by nurses toward patients, colleagues, and physicians. They found consistently negative correlations between self-reports of job stress and five different measures of prosocial behaviors; the absolute value of the correlations averaged about .20. In a path-analytic reconstruction of the linkages among the measured variables, they found that feelings of depression mediated the relation between job stressors and prosocial behaviors.

Thus, five published studies, using varied subject groups and procedurally independent assessments of the important variables, have reported significant relationships between measures of OCB and job satisfaction. The correlations range from the teens to over .40, with a weighted mean in the high twenties to low thirties—somewhat greater than Vroom's (1964) estimate of .14 from studies of satisfaction and traditional performance measures, or the .15 of Iaffaldano and Muchinsky's (1985) meta-analysis.

Interestingly, Iaffaldano and Muchinsky found that the correlations were significantly higher when the performance measures used in past studies were either subjective or global in nature. It seems likely that those types of performance measures would be the ones most likely to capture variance in some forms of OCB. Katzell and Yankelovich (1975), reporting the results of a survey of 563 managers and 69 union leaders, noted that respondents in both groups attached to the definition of "productivity" such attributes as "loyalty" and "less tangible features such as the absence of disruption . . . " (pp. 19–20) and other factors "even when their impact on output cannot be measured easily" (p. 103). It therefore seems likely that subjective, global ratings of subordinates' performance or productivity will reflect varying but substantial estimates of their tendencies to render OCB.

It would seem, then, that when we take into account what practitioners include in their concept of performance, that the empirical record provides some support for the "common sense" notion that satisfaction is related to performance.

But is this the same thing as saying "a happy worker is a productive worker," even when "productive" is couched in the terms described above? This inference follows only if we equate satisfaction with happiness and/or assume that job satisfaction scores bear a monotonic relationship to the psychological state of "happiness." The interpretation of the OCB-satisfaction correlation requires first some analysis of the underlying referent of satisfaction measures.

"SATISFACTION" AS FAIRNESS

There are well-developed theories of job satisfaction (e.g., Locke, 1976) and some measures of job satisfaction (such as the JDI) that are well-grounded and systematically developed from such theories. However, in recent years it seems that job satisfaction researchers have had little inclination to qualify or interpret their findings in light of some of the characteristic "behaviors" of job satisfaction scores or to consider possible distinguishable referents of such scores. Yet there do exist some data and relevant theoretical frameworks that permit some elaboration upon such referents.

Almost by convention, we use the term "job satisfaction" and "job attitudes" interchangeably. Measures of job satisfaction are based on the techniques of attitude scale construction. And psychologists (e.g., Berkowitz, 1980) have long defined attitude in terms of constituent cognitions (beliefs) and affect (feeling). Not unreasonably, therefore, job satisfaction measures are assumed to reflect cognitions and affect in roughly equal proportion. Thus, Locke (1976, p. 1300) defines job satisfaction as "a pleasurable or positive emotional state [affect] resulting from the appraisal [cognition] of one's job or job experiences." Similarly, Smith, Kendall, and Hulin (1969) regard "job satisfactions" as "feelings or affective responses to facets of the situation," but in the next sentence "hypothesize that these feelings are associated with a perceived difference between what is expected as a fair return . . . and what is experienced . . . " (Smith, et al., 1976, p. 6). Both Locke and Smith et al. seem to imply that responses of job satisfaction directly reflect affect but, because cognitions are such a direct and immediate determinant of these feelings, both components of attitude are strongly represented in responses.

However, Campbell (1976) has reviewed a series of studies of "quality of life" that show satisfaction measures behaving quite differently from happiness measures. Andrews and Withey (1976) factor analyzed 12 global subjective measures of well-being, finding that satisfaction-type measures load on a factor suggestive of "cognition" (i.e., a controlled assessment of external circumstances). Happiness-type measures load on what appears to be an "affect" factor, or the individual's internal emotional state. The two sets of measures correlate around .50, but correlate differently with other things; for example, the cognition measures correlate positively with age, whereas the affect indicators correlate negatively. Organ and Near (1985), reviewing these findings, suggested that job satisfaction measures capture more cognition than affect.

In support of this argument, Brief and Robertson (1987) found that a separate job cognitions measure was far superior to measures of positive and negative affect in accounting for unique variance in job satisfaction scores of 144 subjects.

Thus, consistent with recent work by Zajonc (1980), it appears that cognition and affect are not as tightly conjoined as once thought. They can operate in semi-independent fashion. And to the extent that they are separable, it appears that job satisfaction measures reflect more cognition than affect, not necessarily affect as a direct result of cognitions.

But what kind of cognition? To confront this question requires drawing upon some observations about the behavior of job satisfaction responses—how they are distributed and broken down—and the developing theory of social cognition (Folger, 1986).

The distribution of job satisfaction scores is almost invariably negatively skewed. Smith et al. (1969) reported this finding in the large samples with which they developed the JDI, even after weighting the neutral (i.e., "?") response closer to the dissatisfied response; presumably the skewness was even more pronounced with the neutral response given a value midway between the positive and negative responses. This is precisely the type of distribution found by Helson (1964) when subjects were asked to render psychophysical judgments of various stimuli when accompanied by an anchor or reference stimulus. The distribution of responses is negatively skewed, and subjects' judgments are less variable as well as more accurate in the vicinity of the value of the anchor stimulus. Helson (1964) has suggested that the same phenomenon that underlies subjective perception of audible tones, color, and other physical stimuli might also characterize judgments of social stimuli and attitudinal objects.

Indeed, Smith et al. (1969) drew upon Helson's adaptation level theory in developing the theoretical basis of the JDI as a measure of job satisfaction. They regard responses to the JDI items as resulting from comparisons of job circumstance to some anchor point. They also comment frequently on the respondent's "frame of reference." It seems that they implicitly regard this frame of reference as functioning like a standard of fairness, as they conclude that "satisfaction can be regarded as an evaluation of equitableness of treatments or conditions" (Smith et al., 1969, p. 166).

Herzberg, Mausner, and Snyderman's (1959) analysis of secondary or internal states, correlated with critical incidents of satisfaction and dissatisfaction, revealed that "feelings of fairness or unfairness" were the psychological state related to dissatisfaction. Fairness was seldom referred to in connection with satisfaction episodes.

We have some basis, then, for thinking that job satisfaction measures reflect more cognition than affect and that the cognition in question is an appraisal or comparison of the situation with a standard of fairness. The empirical distribution of scores, when coupled with Herzberg et al. (1959), suggest that most of the available scale or range of responses is used by subjects to appraise outcomes up to the approximate point regarded as fair or equitable. Thus, Smith et al. (1969) find the distribution " . . . sloping off steeply toward the satisfied end and gently toward the dissatisfied end" (pp. 79–80). This echoes Blau (1964), who marshals considerable support for the premise that outcomes that bring a person's situation up to the normatively expected level are more important than those that surpass it.

To interpret job satisfaction responses as largely representing judgments of fairness is not to imply any specific rule of fairness, such as the proportionate contributions rule in Adams' Equity Theory (1965). Blau (1964) has argued convincingly that any expectation—whether based on social comparison, past experience, the going rate, or prior implied promise—can and often does function much like a standard of justice with a quasi-moral character. More recently Leventhal (1980) has broadened our awareness of alternatives to the contributions rule, noting that needs, equality, conventional agreement, or status—but more typically some mix of the foregoing—can operate as rules of justice.

Thinking about job satisfaction in this fashion finds a useful point of contact with Folger's (1986) theory and experimental research concerning "referent cognitions." Folger argues that dissatisfaction is "inherently referential," in the sense that outcomes are compared with a referent cognition (p. 147). The psychological closeness or availability of a referent cognition is a function of the ease with which it can be imagined. The referent cognition, or "what the outcomes might have been," may derive from social comparison, but could also take the form of a previously held expectation or a promise made to the subject alone (in fact, in the experiments reviewed by Folger, 1986, the manipulation of referent cognition always takes the form of a stated or implied promise of what the probable outcomes would be). Folger has found that dissatisfaction is an interactive function of (a) the discrepancy between actual outcomes and the referent cognition; (b) the perceived likelihood of amelioration of outcomes; and (c) the perceived justification for the events or actions that caused the outcomes to fall short of referent cognition. He concludes that the combination of these factors determines whether outcomes determine "mere discontent" (affect?) or a sense of injustice (Folger, 1986, p. 151).

Folger raises as a problem for future research how responses to unfairness go beyond verbal expressions of satisfaction/dissatisfaction. Perhaps in organizations an important overt response is the extent of OCB.

WHY IS OCB A FUNCTION OF FAIRNESS?

One rationale for restraining OCB in response to cognitions of unfairness would make use of the terms drawn from Adams' (1965) Equity theory (i.e., a form of reducing inputs in order to effect equity). However, one need not endorse the proportionate contributions rule as the definitive criterion of justice in order to suggest that people perceiving unfairness will withhold something. But are they likely to diminish performance in terms of explicit job requirements? To do so invites potential sanctions and/or sacrifice of the incremental rewards provided by the system, and such a tactic probably would be painful for professionals and skilled artisans whose egos and self-esteem are so closely bound to pride in performance. A less painful, more flexible means of responding to perceived unfairness lies in calculated, discriminating withholding of discretionary gestures of the sort suggested by OCB.

Yet to characterize this response as merely an attempt to reestablish equity somehow seems to miss the point. It does not seem likely that an individual, perceiving himself or herself as a victim of injustice, really believes that the situation is made right by any degree of reduction of OCB, even though the response is elicited by conceptions of justice. What is suggested is that perceived unfairness evokes a fundamental redefinition of the relationship between the individual and the organization. The change is interpretable as one from social exchange, described by Blau (1964) as consisting of diffuse obligations and precise terms of exchange. Contributions are now limited to those of a contractually binding character.

In contrast, someone who senses general fairness in a social exchange relationship with the organization need not quibble over whether this or that mundane contribution tips the balance of equity. In any given instance, there is ambiguity about the value of the gesture and what should represent its appropriate recompense. Similarly, there is ambiguity concerning what degree of reciprocation is binding for any specific valued outcome. What is important is that the person be able to think of the organization as a microcosm of a just world (Lerner, 1980). If the long-run dynamic is toward fairness, the ambiguity attendant to the here-and-now discretionary contribution is tolerable. Indeed, there comes to mind a possible advantage to organizational reward systems that strive for long-term, global appraisals of fairness rather than one-to-one correspondence of micro-reward for micro-contribution. The inherent ambiguity of such a system frees the individual to contribute in discretionary fashion without thinking that this will be acquiescence to exploitation; on the other hand, there is enough cognitive slippage in attribution of the cause of the behavior to permit the person to infer some degree of intrinsic causation (Deci, 1975).

Interpreting the correlation between OCB and satisfaction as essentially a functional relationship between OCB and fairness cognitions finds support in a study by Scholl, Cooper, and McKenna (1987). They constructed a 10-item, self-report measure of "extra-role behavior," based on examples of such discretionary behavior as offered by Katz and Kahn (1978). Items included suggestions for improvement, helping others with problems, taking on extra responsibility, and continuing education. Scores on this measure correlated .41 with a measure of the person's report of perceived pay equity vis-à-vis others with a similar job. A smaller, but still statistically significant ($p < .01$) correlation was found between the extra-role behavior and report of pay equity in the context of the larger organization as a system. These correlations are quite in line with the trend of relationships elsewhere reported between OCB (or Prosocial Behavior) and the more general measures of job satisfaction.

THE FAIRNESS-OCB HYPOTHESIS: PROBLEMS AND IMPLICATIONS

Although recasting the satisfaction-performance hypothesis in terms of a fairness-OCB proposition has a reasonable logical basis and some degree of empirical support, and possibly resolves some issues, we still must reckon with some loose ends and with the plausibility of what it implies for theory, research, and practice.

Theory and Research

The discussion has assumed a direction of causality not inferrable from the research on OCB. The one longitudinal study attempting to ascertain cause-effect (Bateman & Organ, 1983) could not unequivocally do so. Causal models have been tested only against correlational data. Arguably, the correlation could reflect OCB as cause of satisfaction, either because OCB often elicits at the very least informal reinforcements from coworkers or superiors or because it brings satisfaction in its own right. One must also consider the justification phenomenon: having rendered OCB, a person might well experience a cognitive strain toward positive evaluation of the various dimensions of job circumstance. More convincing evidence that fairness cognitions temporally precede OCB is required before we can confidently develop theoretical frameworks within this area.

Another problem that arises is how to fit the person within the issue. Schneider and Dachler (1978) and Staw, Bell, and Clausen (1986) have marshalled impressive data arguing that satisfaction could be largely a dispositional variable. Does it seem plausible to think that this represents stable tendencies to perceive fairness or unfairness? Or is it more reasonable to anchor dispositional causes of satisfaction in something like Watson and Clark's (1984) concept of negative affectivity as a trait? A recent study (Atich, Brief, Burke, Robinson, & Webster, 1987) found a correlation of only $-.24$ between negative affectivity and job satisfaction, but the correlation was $-.46$ with life satisfaction, suggesting that this trait may be less influential in satisfaction measures as the domain of satisfaction becomes more circumscribed.

Whether the disposition accounting for stability in measured job satisfaction is primarily affective or cognitive, it presents a serious challenge to researchers trying to sort out causal paths among the person, environment, and OCB. Almost certainly there are feedback loops among those variables: for example, OCB has consequences that might well augment any disposition to exercise OCB, and, conversely, to withhold OCB.

If cognitions are taken as the major influence on OCB, what then do we make of the extensive social psychological research implicating affect as the cause of helping behavior (Brown, 1985)—research that apparently inspired much of the work examining the correlation between job satisfaction and OCB? Perhaps a distinction should be drawn between one-shot episodes of helping in nonorganizational contexts versus sustained patterns over time of OCB in the work environment. Conceivably more refined measures of OCB in the future would show that affect is more influential in certain types of OCB (e.g., helping a coworker in a direct, personal way), whereas fairness cognitions (net of affect) have more to do with less personal forms of OCB.

Addressing these questions would seem to require, at a minimum, the use of separate measures of affect as experienced at work and indices of fairness cognitions in respect to outcomes.

Management Practice

If OCB contributes appreciably to organizational effectiveness, if it is at least somewhat independent of in-role performance level, and if it is in considerable degree determined by fairness cognitions, what then follow as implications for management?

First, considering the apparent variety of fairness criteria and their weightings by different individuals (Leventhal, 1980), it would seem prudent for organizational officials to eschew any pure formula for fair outcomes based on any one criterion (e.g., a pay formula mechanically determined by measured in-role performance). A studied compromise among various criteria (e.g., technical excellence, market valuations, tenure, status), runs less risk of triggering cognitions of unacceptable unfairness (the tradeoff being, of course, that no group is likely to see perfect fairness). Perhaps organization theorists have overemphasized the virtues of a reward system dictating a one-to-one correspondence between increments of reward and specific individual actions; a system that permits some degree of ambiguity in this regard, yet on an overall basis continues to approximate most participants' notions of fairness, has much to recommend it.

Second, to the extent that stable dispositions enter into characteristic appraisals of fairness, some consideration of this tendency is important at selection time. Evidence that a given individual has some sort of persecution complex, reporting consistent victimization by unfair systems, employers, teachers, should be weighed against promise of ability to contribute in-role.

Finally, just as job satisfaction surveys have aided not only researchers but practitioners as well, perhaps organization officials would benefit by systematic inclusion of specific measures of fairness cognitions in periodic surveys.

REFERENCES

Adams, J. S. (1965). Inequity in social exchange. In L. Berkowitz (Ed.), *Advances in experimental psychology* (Vol. 2, pp. 267–299). New York: Academic Press.

Andrews, F. M., & S. B. Withey. (1976). *Social indicators of well-being.* New York: Plenum Press.

Atich, J. M., Brief, A. P., Burke, M. J., Robinson, B. S., & Webster, J. (1987, August). *Should negative affectivity remain an unmeasured variable in the study of job stress?* Paper presented at the meeting of the Academy of Management, New Orleans.

Bateman, T. S., & Organ, D. W. (1983). Job satisfaction and the good soldier: The relationship between affect and employee "citizenship." *Academy of Management Journal, 26,* 587–595.

Berkowitz, L. (1980). *A survey of social psychology.* New York: Holt, Rinehart, & Winston.

Blau, P. (1964). *Exchange and power in social life.* New York: Wiley.

Brayfield, A. H., & Crockett, W. H. (1955). Employee attitudes and employee performance. *Psychological Bulletin, 52,* 396–424.

Brief, A. P., & Robertson, L. (1987, August). *Job attitude organization: An exploratory study.* Paper presented at the meeting of the Academy of Management, New Orleans.

Brown, R. (1985). *Social psychology.* New York: Free Press.

Campbell, A. (1976). Subjective measures of well-being. *American Psychologist, 31,* 117–124.

Deci, E. L. (1975). *Intrinsic motivation.* New York: Plenum.

Folger, R. (1986). Rethinking equity theory. In Bierhof, H. W., Cohen, R. L., & Greenberg, J. (Eds.), *Justice in social relations* (pp. 145–162). New York: Plenum.

Gannon, M. J., & Noon, J. P. (1971). Management's critical deficiency. *Business Horizons, 14,* 49–56.

Helson, H. (1964). Current trends and issues in adaptation-level theory. *American Psychologist, 19,* 26–38.

Herzberg, F. H., Mausner, B., & Snyderman, B. S. (1959). *The motivation to work.* New York: Wiley.

Iaffaldano, M. T., & Muchinsky, P. M. (1985). Job satisfaction and job performance: A Meta-Analysis. *Psychological Bulletin, 97,* 251–273.

Katz, D., & Kahn, R. L. (1978). *The social psychology of organizations.* New York: Wiley.

Katzell, R. A., & Yankelovich, D. (1975). *Work, productivity, and job satisfaction.* New York: The Psychological Corporation.

Lerner, M. J. (1980). *The belief in a just world: A fundamental delusion.* New York: Plenum.

Leventhal, G. S. (1980). What should be done with Equity Theory? New approaches to the study of fairness in social relationships. In K. G. Gergen, M. S. Greenberg, & R. H. Willis (Eds.), *Social exchange: Advances in theory and research* (pp. 27–55). New York: Plenum.

Locke, E. A. (1976). The nature and causes of job satisfaction. In M. D. Dunnette (Ed.), *Handbook of industrial and organizational psychology* (pp. 1297–1349). Chicago: Rand McNally.

Motowidlo, S. J. (1984). Does job satisfaction lead to consideration and personal sensitivity? *Academy of Management Journal, 27,* 910–915.

Motowidlo, S. J., Packard, J. S., & Manning, M. R. (1986). Occupational stress: Its causes and consequences for job performance. *Journal of Applied Psychology, 71,* 618–629.

Organ, D. W. (1977). A reappraisal and reinterpretation of the satisfaction-cause-performance hypothesis. *Academy of Management Review, 2,* 46–53.

Organ, D. W., & Near, J. P. (1985). Cognition vs. affect in measures of job satisfaction. *International Journal of Psychology, 20,* 241–253.

Petty, M. M., McGee, G. W., & Cavender, J. W. (1984). A meta-analysis of the relationships between job satisfaction and individual performance. *Academy of Management Review, 9,* 712–721.

Puffer, S. M. (1987). Prosocial behavior, noncompliant behavior, and work performance among commission salespeople. *Journal of Applied Psychology, 72,* 615–621.

Schneider, B., & Dachler, P. (1978). A note on the stability of the job descriptive index. *Journal of Applied Psychology, 63,* 650–653.

Scholl, R. W., Cooper, E. A., & McKenna, J. F. (1987). Referent selection in determining equity perceptions: Differential effects on behavioral and attitudinal outcomes. *Personnel Psychology, 40,* 113–124.

Scott, W. E., Jr. (1967). The development of semantic differential scales as measures of "morale." *Personnel Psychology, 20,* 179–198.

Smith, C. A., Organ, D. W., & Near, J. P. (1983). Organizational citizenship behavior: Its nature and antecedents. *Journal of Applied Psychology, 68,* 653–663.

Smith, P. C., Kendall, L. M., & Hulin, C. L. (1969). *The measurement of satisfaction in work and retirement.* Chicago: Rand McNally.

Staw, B. M., Bell, N. E., & Clausen, J. A. (1986). The dispositional approach to job attitudes: A lifetime longitudinal test. *Administrative Science Quarterly, 31,* 56–77.

Vroom, V. H. (1964). *Work and motivation.* New York: Wiley.

Watson, D., & Clark, L. A. (1984). Negative affectivity: The disposition to experience aversive emotional states. *Psychological Bulletin, 96,* 465–490.

Zajonc, R. B. (1980). Feeling and thinking: Preferences need no inferences. *American Psychologist, 35,* 151–175.

CHAPTER 7

EMPLOYEE ATTACHMENT
TO ORGANIZATIONS

Much of the book up to this point has focused on what has been called the "decision to produce," that is, what causes someone to work harder on a job. With this chapter, we shift our focus somewhat and consider the "decision to participate." In other words, this chapter examines factors that influence people's willingness to remain with the organization and become involved in organizational activities. We do this by looking at two related issues. First, we consider the topic of organizational commitment, the process by which people become psychologically attached to an organization. Employee commitment has received increased attention in recent years as companies have sought ways to enhance employee involvement and contributions to overall organizational effectiveness.

Following this, we consider several causes of employee withdrawal in the forms of absenteeism and turnover. The question of why employee absenteeism and turnover deserve attention can be answered in several ways. Perhaps the most direct answer lies in considering the costs and consequences associated with such behavior. Each year, turnover and absenteeism cost industry billions of dollars in lost productivity, while employees lose considerable income. In view of the current economic problems facing industrialized countries and the increased competition in the marketplace, such losses can have a severe impact on the national economy. Moreover, absenteeism and turnover cost the organization in many ways, including increased selection and recruitment costs, increased training and development costs, increased organizational disruption, and possible demoralization of those who remain. For people who actually leave the organization, there is a loss of seniority and nonvested benefits, possible loss of friendships, and possible disruption for their families if relocation is necessary for new jobs. Again, both the individual and the organization can lose in such situations.

On the other hand, it would be inaccurate to assume that such withdrawal is associated with negative consequences only. Several positive outcomes are also possible. With respect to absenteeism, temporary withdrawal can allow employees some relief from a highly stressful or boring job. The employee may be better able to cope when he or she returns after a short hiatus. In addition, for those organizations that have a policy of job rotation, temporary absences often allow other employees to gain needed experience with different aspects of the work situation.

Employee turnover can also lead to positive outcomes on occasion. In some cases, turnover can lead to improved performance when those leaving either have burned out on the job or have such negative attitudes that they adversely affect output. In such cases, we would expect new employees to bring a fresh approach to the job situation. Moreover, turnover can in some cases prove beneficial where it reduces entrenched conflict that has built up over the years. The departure of someone whom others consider abrasive, for example, can relax tensions for those remaining. In addition, turnover can sometimes increase both mobility and morale by allowing room for internal growth and promotion. Finally, turnover can at times allow for increased innovation, as new people and new ideas enter the workplace.

Hence, absenteeism and turnover can be both functional and dysfunctional for individuals and organizations. As we shall see in several of the selections that follow, the question is not so much *why* turnover or absenteeism as *which* turnover or absenteeism. That is, which employees are leaving (or being absent) and which are remaining? Under which circumstances are people most likely to leave or be absent? And, finally, which actions can management initiate that will cause the more valued employees to want to remain?

This chapter consists of three readings. The first, by Neale and Northcraft, reviews the research and conceptual work on organizational commitment. Particular attention is given to understanding which factors are most likely to influence the development of commitment in organizations. Included here are the four factors of visibility, explicitness, irreversibility, and volition. Based on this discussion, a model of the development of commitment among new employees is reviewed.

Next, we turn to the subject of absenteeism and turnover. The reading by Rhodes and Steers briefly reviews the various approaches to the subject, including the use of both economic and psychological frames of reference in analysis of the subject. Based on a review of the available literature, a diagnostic model of attendance is presented that accounts for both voluntary and involuntary absenteeism.

Following this, Mobley introduces us to a model of employee turnover. This model focuses on the intermediate linkages that exist between job attitudes and the employee's ultimate decision to stay with or leave an organization. Taken together, these three articles provide a good overview to the literature on organizational attachment and on what managers can do to facilitate a more stable, committed, dedicated workforce.

Factors Influencing
Organizational Commitment

Margaret A. Neale
Gregory B. Northcraft

Once the organization has extended an offer to an applicant and that individual has decided to enter into a psychological contract by accepting the offer, then the applicant becomes an organizational member. However, the preparation needed to become a functioning part of the organization has just begun. The applicant must now become schooled in and committed to the organization's goals, objectives, and ways of conducting business.

Simply defined, organizational commitment is the relative strength of an individual's identification with and involvement in a particular organization.[1] It usually includes three factors: (1) a strong belief in the organization's goals and values; (2) a willingness to exert considerable effort on behalf of the organization; and (3) a strong desire to continue as an organizational member. Organizational commitment, then, is not simply loyalty to an organization. Rather, it is an ongoing process through which organizational actors express their concern for the organization and its continued success and well-being.

There are many reasons why an organization should want to increase the level of organizational commitment among its members. For example, research has found that the more committed the employee is to the organization, the greater the effort expended by the employee in performing tasks.[2] In addition, highly committed workers are likely to remain with the organization for longer periods of time—that is, there is a positive relationship between the level of organizational commitment and job tenure.[3] Finally, given the contribution a highly productive, trained employee can make to organizational productivity, keeping such an employee should be a high priority for the organization. Because highly committed employees wish to remain associated with the organization and advance organizational goals, they are less likely to leave. Thus, high levels of organizational commitment are associated with low levels of employee turnover.[4]

FACTORS INFLUENCING COMMITMENT

Once individuals select membership in an organization, what is it about their early experiences that leads them to be more or less committed to the organization? To answer this question, we must first consider exactly what leads to the phenomenon of commitment. Gerald Salancik suggests that four major factors lead to commitment.[5] The visibility, explicitness, and irreversibility of our behaviors and personal volition for our behaviors are the factors that commit us to our acts.

Condensed from G. B. Northcraft & M. A. Neale, *Organizational Behavior: A Management Challenge*. Hinsdale, Ill.: The Dryden Press, 1990, Chapter 11. All rights reserved.

Visibility

One major determinant of how committing a particular behavior may be is how observable that behavior is to others. Behaviors that are secret or unobserved do not have a committing force behind them because they cannot be linked to a specific individual. One of the most simple and straightforward ways to commit individuals to an organization is to make their association with the organization public information. If they are part of the organization, they (by association) support that organization and its goals. Many organizations are already taking advantage of this visibility notion to increase employee commitment. When a new employee joins an organization, the employee's photograph and a formal announcement are sent to the local newspapers, in-house publications, and other such outlets to inform others of the new arrival. As suggested in the opening vignette, the new employee may also be outfitted in the company's uniform—an obvious and visible sign of organizational membership.

Maintaining *visibility* is not a difficult task. For instance, it takes about the same time for inspectors to write a number after their task is completed as it does to write their names, or for the company to provide a nameplate on a door as to leave it blank. Very little additional effort is required to associate individuals with their work, their accomplishments, and their organization. The more visible individuals and their contributions, the more committed they are likely to be to the organization.

On some occasions, however, an organization does not want its members clearly associated with their acts. For example, there is a conscious attempt through the use of uniforms to reduce the visibility of individual soldiers, prison guards, and police officers so a particular individual is not associated with some of the more unpleasant tasks. Thus, the uniform in this case clearly identifies the individual as a soldier or police officer, but the individual within the uniform is not unique. In addition, organizations may decrease the visibility of individuals performing onerous tasks or tasks with a high likelihood of failure. This reduced visibility is likely to enhance the willingness of an individual to take on a task with negative overtones.

Explicitness and Irreversibility

Visibility alone is not sufficient to commit individuals to their actions. It must be combined with explicitness; the more explicit the behavior, the less deniable it is. Thus, *explicitness* is the extent to which the individual cannot deny that the behavior occurred. How explicit the behavior is depends on two factors: its observability and its unequivocality. When a behavior cannot be observed but only inferred, it is less explicit. For example, if I left a sensitive document on my desk and later heard one of my subordinates talking about the content of that document, I could not know that the subordinate had been in my office and read the document. At best, I might suspect that he or she had, but all I know for sure is that this sensitive information is now public. If I had seen that subordinate reading the document in my office, then I would know which subordinate released the information. Equivocality is the difficulty of pinning down the act or behavior. It can be seen in the way people qualify the statements they make (such as "It sometimes seems to me that . . . " versus "I think . . . ").

Irreversibility, on the other hand, means that the behavior is permanent—it cannot easily be revoked or undone. The importance of irreversibility can be observed in the circumstances that committed Great Britain and France to building the Concorde.[6] The Minister of Aviation, James Avery, included a clause in the 1961 agreement with France that made both France's and Britain's decision to produce the Concorde virtually irreversible. The clause required that if either of the two partners withdrew from the collaboration, the entire development cost up to that point would be borne by the withdrawing party. Interestingly, the more rational it became to withdraw (because of escalating costs), the more committed the parties were to continuing. This type of commitment is typically referred to as behavioral commitment or escalation.

Organizations also are aware of the committing aspect of irreversible acts. Many organizations have developed benefit packages that are not transferable from one firm to another. The irreversible loss of these benefits, should an individual choose to leave the organization, commits the individual to continued employment. Training an employee in a skill that is specific to the organization or developing an employee's abilities to match the unique constellation of an organization's expectations also reduces the likelihood that the person will disengage from the organization.

Consider, for example, the cost a bookkeeper might incur in learning a particular accounting software package. Consider the much greater cost to this individual of relearning if this accounting package is unique to the organization. This is an example of knowledge that is very useful within a particular organization but may be completely irrelevant elsewhere. The time contributed to learning this system has a payoff in the current organization, but may be irreversibly lost if the bookkeeper were to transfer to any other organization.

Other factors influence a person's perceived attachment to the organization. Personal or family-related factors may foster an individual's commitment to an organization. Children in school, the cost of housing in other parts of the country, the circle of friends and acquaintances, and the spouse's job are all personal factors that may bind a person to an organization.

Of course, the commitment may be more to the status quo than to the organization. Imagine that an organization were to offer its employees a promotion that required relocation of the employee's family. The personal factors that may have initially enhanced the employee's commitment to the organization may now be enhancing a similar commitment to a locality. The unique problems of dual-career couples are a salient example of the factors that tie individuals to an area.

An organization may attempt to compete with the personal factors that tie an individual to a locality by creating a network of relationships at work that become important. Developing work or project teams or fostering collaborations among specific coworkers are primary ways to connect workers to the organization.

Further dependencies upon coworkers are fostered when employees are unable to develop relationships outside the organization because of frequent moves.

All of these are attempts to entangle the individual in organizational relationships. The greater the employee's entanglement with these relationships, the more costly termination would be to the employee. Employees' perceptions of the irreversibility of their positions in an organization develop naturally over time. The longer they are employed by an organization, the more their skills are tailored to the unique demands of that firm. What they know and how they think about a business become, in reality, what they know and how they think about the particular way their organization does business.

In fact, given the committing nature of organization-specific skills, it is probably against the best interests of the organization to encourage employees to develop general skills that would make them more attractive to other organizations. Developing generalized skills reduces the uniqueness of an individual's fit with a particular organization while simultaneously increasing that individual's attractiveness to others. The organization should clearly consider the potential costs and benefits of encouraging such skill development.

The irreversibility of behavior is important because it influences the psychological contract. Consider, for example, the plight of college-student cadets who had joined the Reserve Officers Training Corps (ROTC) in the late 1960s and early 1970s. Some were required to sign two-year contracts and others were not. During the Vietnam War, joining ROTC was viewed as a way to avoid the draft or to control the site and type of war experience one could expect. Because the war and thus the need for military personnel was limited, a lottery based on birth dates was designed to rank the order in which young men were subject to being drafted into the services. If you were assigned a low number through the lottery process, the odds were that you would soon receive a draft notice. If you were assigned a high number in the draft lottery, you were almost assured of not being drafted.

Barry Staw, a researcher with an interest in organizational commitment, examined the impact on ROTC cadets' behaviors of having a birth date with a very low probability of being drafted into the service.[7] Among those who had joined ROTC to avoid the draft, one would expect little reason to continue with the program. This was true, but only for those who had not signed a contract committing them to a specific period of service. While those without a contract began to be openly hostile toward ROTC, those with a contract became increasingly attached to the program. Thus, the irrevocable nature of the contract they had signed now influenced their commitment to the organization, regardless of the fact that the reason for their joining ROTC no longer existed.

These findings suggest that when the instrumental nature of our associations ceases to exist, we justify our continued association with emotional, rational, or socially desirable trappings. Once we have accepted a position, then the perceived attractiveness of that position and our commitment to that position and the organization increase. Of course, this commitment increase also occurs when we accept a marriage proposal, buy a home, or make any choice we perceive to be irrevocable (or revocable only at great cost).

Volition

We have been considering the importance of irreversibility in the commitment process, but there is still a piece of this puzzle missing. For example, if someone makes an irrevocable choice under duress or pressure, does that choice commit the person? Suppose your supervisor assigns you the task of firing several subordinates. How might you feel about the appropriateness of firing the employees if your supervisor applies a great deal of pressure on you to perform this task ("Either fire them or I will fire you!") or applies very little pressure ("Please terminate the following employees.")? It is likely that if you carry out your supervisor's instructions, you will feel more justified in terminating the employees when there is little pressure than you will when there is considerable pressure to comply. If there is very little pressure applied to get you to comply, then you are more likely to believe that the employees deserved to be fired. (After all, you did terminate the individuals; they must have deserved it.) However, if your supervisor applied considerable pressure to you and then you fired the employees, you are more likely to perceive that you had little choice in the matter. That is, you made the choice to act, but it was not of your own volition; you were forced to make that decision.

Volition, then, and its observable equivalent—personal responsibility—is the fourth mechanism that binds us to our actions. Without volition, behaviors are not committing. "Since I have no choice," one might reason, "I really cannot be held responsible for the consequences of my behavior." When trying to separate ourselves from our actions, we might protest that we do not like what we are doing, but the money was too good to refuse. Another way in which we try to distance ourselves from certain behaviors (usually those associated with unpleasant circumstances) is to insist that we have little personal responsibility for the behavior or the outcome. For example, in trying to explain why he did not turn in a paper by the deadline, a graduate student might report that his car had been stolen and the only copy of the paper was in the car at the time. Because he could not control the stealing of his car, he believes that his not meeting the deadline was not volitional.

If we reconsider the ROTC example, volition was certainly a factor. Because many ROTC cadets had avoided signing a contract, those who signed such a contract must have done it of their own volition. Those who signed contracts but had no other reasons for being in ROTC (the lottery indicated they had a low probability of being drafted) must be in ROTC because they enjoyed it. Thus, they became more committed because they were choosing to be cadets.

Enhancing employees' personal responsibility for their actions is critical to establishing and maintaining their commitment to the task and the organization. A number of organizational interventions acknowledge the importance of personal volition. For example, organizations are designing tasks in ways that increase an individual's personal responsibility for performing or scheduling them.

A second form of organizational intervention that emphasizes volition or personal responsibility is *participative decision making.* If a work group is involved in making a decision or solving a problem, its members will be more committed to the implementation of that decision or solution than if they were simply informed

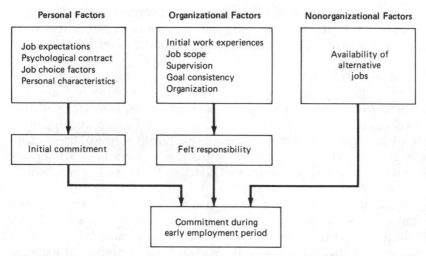

FIGURE 1
Major determinants of organizational commitment during early membership.
(From R. T. Mowday, L. W. Porter, & R. M. Steers, *Employee-Organization Linkages:
The Psychology of Commitment, Absenteeism, and Turnover.* New York: Academic
Press, 1982, p. 56.)

of it. Their reasoning might be that if they chose to participate in the development of a solution, then they must be committed to it. This feeling of personal responsibility in turn increases employees' stake in the solution's successful implementation.

We have established that visibility, explicitness and irreversibility, and volition are important to the creation of commitment. Further, commitment to the organization and its goals is important because individuals adjust their attitudes and expectations in situations to which they are committed. While enhancing organizational commitment is an ongoing process, it is probably most critical early in an employee's association with an organization to assure continued attachment.

Mowday, Porter, and Steers suggest a number of factors that may lead to greater organizational commitment early in an employee's tenure with an employer.[8] Their complete model is pictured in Figure 1. According to this model, commitment depends on (1) personal factors such as the employee's initial level of commitment (deriving from initial job expectations, the psychological contract, and so on), (2) organizational factors such as an employee's initial work experiences and subsequent sense of responsibility, and (3) nonorganizational factors, such as the availability of alternative jobs. Each of these three factors will be discussed in turn.

Personal Factors The primary personal factor is the amount of potential attachment an employee brings to work on the first day—the employee's propensity to develop a stable attachment to the organization. Individuals who are highly committed to an organization on their first day are likely to stay with the organization.[9] Individuals who are highly committed at entry are likely to be willing to take on additional responsibilities and contribute more to the organization.

This early commitment process may become a self-reinforcing cycle. That is, if individuals, early in their tenure with an organization, put forth extra effort, then they may justify that extra effort by being more committed to the organization.

Organization Factors Such organizational factors as job scope—the job's feedback, autonomy, challenge, and significance—increase behavioral involvement. The ability to participate actively in task-related decision making will also influence level of commitment. Consistency between work-group and organizational goals will increase commitment to those goals. Finally, organizational characteristics such as concern for employees' best interests or employee ownership are also positively associated with increased commitment to the organization.[10]

Nonorganizational Factors The primary nonorganizational factor that enhances commitment is the availability of alternatives after the initial choice has been made. Research has found that Master's in Business Administration (MBA) students who did not take the job with the highest salary (insufficient external justification for the choice) reported significantly higher levels of job commitment six months later when no other job offers had been received than when alternative positions were available. Individuals who had accepted the position offering the highest salary (sufficient external justification for the choice) reported approximately equal levels of job commitment, regardless of whether subsequent alternative offers existed or not. Thus, it seems that the highest level of initial commitment occurs among those who (1) have insufficient external justification for their initial choice and (2) view the choice as relatively irrevocable; that is, believe they have had no subsequent opportunities to change their initial decision.[11]

Commitment to the organization and its goals is a major factor in predicting performance. Thus it is critical that organizations have mechanisms to enhance the development of organizational commitment among new employees. In fact, one way in which organizations with high levels of employee commitment differ from organizations with low levels of employee commitment is that the former are "strong culture" firms. For employees to be part of a strong culture, they must be educated as to the expectations and practices of the organization. The extent of their commitment to their jobs and the organization may well hinge on their ability to understand, accept, and become a part of the **organizational culture**—"the way we do things around here."[12]

NOTES

1 R. T. Mowday, L. W. Porter, and R. M. Steers, *Employee-Organization Linkages: The Psychology of Commitment, Absenteeism, and Turnover* (New York: Academic Press, 1982).

2 R. M. Steers, "Antecedents and Outcomes of Organizational Commitments," *Administrative Science Quarterly* 22 (1977): 46–56.

3 See, for example, R. T. Mowday, R. M. Steers, and L. W. Porter, "The Measurement of Organizational Commitment," *Journal of Vocational Behavior* 14 (1979): 224–247; Steers, "Antecedents and Outcomes of Organizational Commitments"; and J. L. Koch

and R. M. Steers, "Job Attachment, Satisfaction, and Turnover among Public Employees," *Journal of Vocational Behavior* 12 (1978): 119–128.

4 H. Angle and J. Perry, "An Empirical Assessment of Organizational Commitment and Organizational Effectiveness," *Administrative Science Quarterly* 26 (1981): 1–14; Mowday, Steers, and Porter, "The Measurement of Organizational Commitment"; and Steers, "Antecedents and Outcomes of Organizational Commitments."

5 The following section draws heavily from G. R. Salancik, "Commitment Is Too Easy!," *Organizational Dynamics* (Summer 1977): 207–222.

6 Ibid.

7 B. M. Staw, cited in G. R. Salancik, "Commitment Is Too Easy!," *Organizational Dynamics* (Summer 1977): 207–222.

8 Mowday, Porter, and Steers, *Employee-Organization Linkages: The Psychology of Commitment, Absenteeism and Turnover.*

9 W. Crampon, R. Mowday, F. Smith, and L. W. Porter, "Early Attitudes Predicting Future Behavior," paper presented at the 38th annual meeting of the Academy of Management, San Francisco, August 1978.

10 See, for example, R. M. Steers and S. R. Rhodes "Major Influences on Employee Attendance: A Process Model," *Psychological Bulletin* 63 (1978): 391–407. Steers, "Antecedents and Outcomes," 46–56.

11 C. A. O'Reilly and D. Caldwell, "Job Choice: The Impact of Intrinsic and Extrinsic Factors on Subsequent Satisfaction and Commitment," *Journal of Applied Psychology* 65 (1980): 559–565.

12 J. S. Ott, *The Organizational Culture Perspective* (Chicago, Ill.: Dorsey Press, 1989).

Major Causes of Absenteeism

Susan R. Rhodes
Richard M. Steers

BACKGROUND FOR MODEL DEVELOPMENT

As one reviews the available research on employee absenteeism, one is struck by the general absence, until recently, of any systematic or comprehensive theory development. As Nicholson (1977, p. 232) pointed out, much of the early research focused on "tentative speculations and propositions *ex post facto* to case studies, and a number of more general theories of organizational behavior in which absence is only a minor element." Following Nicholson, these findings and theories can be categorized into three types of explanatory models: (1) *pain-avoidance models,* in which absence behavior is viewed as a flight from negative work experiences; (2) *adjustment-to-work models,* in which absence is seen as resulting largely from employee responses to changes in job conditions leading to a renegotiation of the psychological contract; (3) *decision models,* in which absence behavior is viewed primarily as a rational (or at least quasi-rational) deci-

Condensed from Susan R. Rhodes & Richard M. Steers, *Managing Employee Absenteeism.* Reading, Mass.: Addison-Wesley, 1990, pp. 33–42, 55–63.

sion to attain valued outcomes. In addition, a final category called "integrated models" can be identified that attempt to go beyond narrow sets of parameters and offer a more complex view of the causes of attendance.

Pain-Avoidance Models

Pain-avoidance models have guided much of absence research over the years (see Hackett and Guion, 1985) and have their origins in the early job satisfaction research. The underlying assumption is that job dissatisfaction (or negative job attitudes in general) represents the primary cause of absenteeism. Although concluding that there was little empirical evidence for a job satisfaction–performance relationship, Brayfield and Crockett (1955) ventured the opinion that dissatisfied workers would be absent more if their work dissatisfaction was symptomatic of being in a punishing situation. Moreover, Argyle (1972) noted that when work is satisfying people will show up to enjoy it.

Several meta-analyses of the absence–job satisfaction relationship, although presenting somewhat conflicting results, tend to support the conclusion that the pain-avoidance model is overly simplistic (Farrell and Stamm, 1988; Hackett and Guion, 1985; McShane, 1984). McShane's review of twenty-four published studies supported the notion that employees who are dissatisfied with various aspects of their jobs are more likely to be absent. The relationship was strongest for overall and work satisfaction, but coworker, pay, and supervision dissatisfaction also led to higher absenteeism. His results indicated that satisfaction with promotions was the only dimension unrelated to absenteeism. Finally, he found job satisfaction to be more highly related to frequency of absences than to number of days lost.

Farrell and Stamm's (1988) study found significant negative weighted correlations between overall job satisfaction and both total time absent and absence frequency. Finally, Hackett and Guion's meta-analysis results showed that less than 4 percent of the variance in absence measures was explained by overall job satisfaction and its dimensions. Although they did find all corrected mean correlations to be negative, they concluded that the strength of the relationship was very weak. They further argued against third factor variables moderating the job satisfaction–absence relationship in that too much of the variance in correlations reported across studies could be accounted for by statistical artifacts. Although these studies offer slightly different viewpoints on the absence–job satisfaction relationship, none of them reported particularly strong mean correlations.

In addition to the meta-analysis technique, which is based on bi-variate correlations, an examination of multivariate studies of absence in which satisfaction is included as one of the variables is revealing. When considered along with other variables (for example, demographic, prior absenteeism, organizational), work attitudes (including overall job satisfaction, organizational commitment, job involvement) generally were not found to be significant predictors of absenteeism. Nonsignificant absence-attitude findings were reported for overall job satisfaction, satisfaction with supervision, and satisfaction with pay, working conditions, coworkers, and equipment. In Popp and Belohlav's study, overall satisfaction was a significant predictor of absence frequency but accounted for the smallest amount of variance among the significant variables.

When taken together, the meta-analysis and the multivariate studies provide little support for the "absence as pain-avoidance" theory. Therefore, like Hackett and Guion (1985), we conclude that it is not fruitful to test further any models that are based on the assumption that dissatisfaction is the primary cause of absence. However, sufficient findings are present to warrant the inclusion of attitudinal variables in more comprehensive models of employee absenteeism. Attitudes can at times serve to "pull" the individual toward the organization assuming the attitudes are positive, and the reverse can be expected when attitudes are more negative.

Adjustment-to-Work Models

In adjustment-to-work models, absence from work is viewed as a consequence of organizational socialization and other adaptive processes in response to job demands. Included among adjustment models are the earlier theorizing of Hill and Trist (1953) and Gibson (1966), as well as the more recent models of Rosse and Miller (1984) and Chadwick-Jones et al. (1982).

Hill and Trist's Model Following Hill and Trist (1953), absence is viewed as one of the means of withdrawal from stressful work situations. Other means of withdrawal include turnover and accidents. In the early phase of "induction crisis," turnover is often the preferred mode of withdrawal. During this phase, newcomers typically lack knowledge about absence norms. Unsanctioned absence is the characteristic mode during the middle period of "differential transit." After this, in the "settled connection" phase, the individual substitutes sanctioned absences for unsanctioned absences, and levels of absence are reduced. This model is described as basically one of organizational socialization. That is, in becoming aware of the absence culture of the firm, individuals internalize these norms such that a change in withdrawal behavior consistent with the norms occurs. Accidents become a means of withdrawal if the sanctioned outlets for withdrawal are insufficient.

In providing evidence based on collective trends of accidents and absence to explain individual reactions, Hill and Trist's theory can only be considered to be highly speculative. Not only is there no direct evidence supporting their model, but also it is not clear that testable hypotheses could be developed from it (Chadwick-Jones et al., 1982). Their theory, however, makes a contribution by introducing the concept of social norms of absence.

Gibson's Model Gibson (1966) set forth a comprehensive conceptual model of organizational behavior to explain absence behavior based on the contractual relationship between the individual and the organization. According to Gibson's model, individuals and organizations enter into an exchange relationship in which the individual agrees to contribute his or her competencies in exchange for certain rewards, and the organization agrees to provide rewards for a certain level of effort on the part of the individual. Fundamental to the satisfactory implementation of the contract is the attitude of commitment to both the contract's intent and its terms, or what is termed "authenticity." The more the tasks and rewards of the organization are viewed as satisfying the individual's needs, the stronger will be the individual's identification with and commitment to the organization.

Gibson then applied the model to explain conflicting research in the absence literature. Work identification was viewed as a strong influence on absence behavior, and any factor that served to increase identification operated to reduce absence. Other important influences on absence behavior were the ease of legitimating absences, and the perceived authenticity of management. Using his framework, he explained research findings on the relationship between absence and gender, length of service, age, job status, size of organization, and cosmopolitans and locals. Although the research findings he presented appear to be consistent with his theory, they in no way represent a test of his theory. Moreover, as Chadwick-Jones et al. (1982) point out, there is a considerable gap in the level of abstraction of the conceptual model and the methods and data used to support it. Finally, although Gibson provided propositions that were suitable for testing, there have been no following comprehensive tests of his model by absenteeism researchers.

Rosse and Miller's Model More recently Rosse and Miller (1984) focused on the adaptive responses or coping mechanisms available to a worker in coping with his or her work environment. Absence behavior is one of the adaptive responses available to the worker. Because their model was developed in response to the question "What do workers do when they are dissatisfied?" it is concerned with behavioral shifts and is not meant to be a general theory of behavior. According to this view, then, absence behavior would represent a break from normal routine. Although their approach is primarily an adjustment model, it also contains elements of a decision model.

According to Rosse and Miller, a stimulus event (for example, the first warm, sunny day of spring) leads to a state of relative dissatisfaction. This relative state equates with an awareness of a new standard, a negative response (or affect) resulting from not being at the new standard, and an action tendency to achieve the new standard. Next, the individual is viewed as considering behavioral alternatives to achieve the better state. Factors influencing the person's consideration include personal experience, exposure to role models, the presence of clear social norms, and the perception of constraints (that is, ability-induced or environmentally-induced limitations to behavior). The result of this consideration is a set of alternatives, ordered according to the perceived likelihood that they will lead to the person's being better off. The alternative chosen will be the one resulting in the highest positive utility, defined as "the anticipation that the behavior will improve the person's situation" (p. 211).

The environmental responses to the behavior will be experienced by the person as either positive, neutral, or negative. If the consequences are positive, the source of relative dissatisfaction has been eliminated, and successful adaptation has occurred. On the other hand, if the consequences are positive or neutral, the source of relative dissatisfaction is still present, and the individual continues to repeat the adaptation cycle until successful adaptation occurs.

Rosse and Miller's model was examined empirically by a correlational field study designed and carried out prior to the development of the full model (Rosse and Hulin, 1985). As such, the study was not intended to be a formal test, but Rosse and Hulin concluded that the results provided an empirical basis for the model. Their findings indicated that job satisfaction indices were good predictors of intentions to quit, turnover, change attempts, and health symptoms. On the other hand, only satisfaction with work content and coworkers were related to absence behavior. According to Rosse and Miller, however, an adequate test of the model requires a longitudinal within-subject design permitting analysis of work perceptions, decision processes, enacted behavior, and the consequences of that behavior on subsequent cycles. This requires rigorous, labor-intensive studies.

In summary, Rosse and Miller's model makes three useful contributions. First, it focuses on absence as one of several behavioral responses available to individuals in dealing with relative dissatisfaction. This means that it is necessary to consider the relationship between absence and other behaviors. Second, it draws attention to the dynamic nature of absence behavior. Third, in acknowledging that the stimuli leading to relative dissatisfaction can come from within the work environment or outside it, absence behavior as an adaptive response can be viewed within the context of the individual's total life space.

Chadwick-Jones, Nicholson, and Johns's Model   The final adjustment model can be distinguished from the other models discussed thus far in that it focuses on the notion of social exchange rather than individual motivations. Moreover, the amount of absences taken is influenced by the prevailing absence culture. This framework was first developed by Chadwick-Jones et al. (1982) and later expanded by Nicholson and Johns (1985).

In viewing absence as part of a social exchange, Chadwick-Jones et al. stress that this is not simply an exchange that occurs between the individual and the organization, as in Gibson's model, but also one that occurs among individuals in the organization. First, the exchange between the individuals and the organization is a "negative exchange" in that the employees are withholding their presence from work, perhaps to make up for workload pressures, stress, or the constraints imposed by fixed work schedules. In some cases, management might tacitly collude with employees in the exchange, for example, in encouraging employees to use up sick days rather than lose them. Second, among employees, absences might be allocated to ensure that workload pressures can be met. Employees might take turns in being absent: "If you were absent last week, then it's all right for me to be absent tomorrow."

Because the absence of one person affects others in the organization, the absence culture sets limits on the appropriate levels of absence. Although interindividual variations in absence do occur, these differences operate within the limits prescribed by the particular culture. Chadwick-Jones et al. (1982, p. 7) define absence culture as "the beliefs and practices influencing the totality of ab-

CULTURAL SALIENCE
(Horizontal integration)

		Low salience	High salience
PSYCHOLOGICAL CONTRACT (Vertical integration)	High trust	Type I **Dependent** Deviant absence	Type II **Moral** Constructive absence
	Low trust	Type III **Fragmented** Calculative absence	Type IV **Conflictual** Defiant absence

FIGURE 1
A typology of organizational absence cultures. (From N.
Nicholson & G. Johns, 1985, The absence of culture and the
psychological contract: Who's in control of absence? *Academy of
Management Review*, **10**, 402. Reprinted with permission.)

sences—their frequency and duration—as they currently occur within an employee group or organization.'' Employees are aware, albeit imperfectly, of the
nature of this culture. The absence culture then influences the absence norm,
which is what employees "collectively recognize (usually with management col-
lusion) as suitable and appropriate for people in the job, their unit, their organization, given the particular conditions, both physical and social, of tasks, pay,
status, and discipline'' (p. 7).

Following Nicholson and Johns (1985), variations in absence cultures across
organizations or groups are predicted to arise from the degree of salience of the
culture and the level of trust inherent in the psychological contract (see Fig. 1).
First, the *salience* of the culture refers to the degree of distinctiveness of beliefs
about absence, assumptions underlying employment, and views toward self-
control. The more salient the culture, the more homogeneous it is and the more it
impacts the individual directly, frequently resulting in clear norms regarding attendance behavior. On the other hand, cultures that are less salient exert more
subtle influences on behavior and lead to greater individual variations in absences. Cultural salience is influenced by the organization's absence control system, its technology, and social ecology. Second, the level of *trust* refers to
whether the tasks surrounding one's job are high or low in discretion. The four
types of absence cultures are: (1) the *dependent* culture (low salience, high trust),
characterized by deviant absence; (2) the *moral* culture (high salience, high
trust), typified by constructive absence; (3) the *fragmented* culture (low salience,
low trust), characterized by calculative absence; and (4) the *conflictual* culture
(high salience, low trust) with its resultant defiant absence.

This absence culture framework makes a significant contribution to our understanding of absence behavior in recognizing how constraints can be placed on individual behavior by the collective reality of the organization. Group norms defining what constitutes acceptable behavior must be recognized as an important

factor here. However, such an approach can be somewhat limited because it does not give sufficient attention to individual variations in behavior within an absence culture. That is, there is an equally important need to recognize individual differences as a factor in absenteeism.

Decision Models

Two primary streams of influence have contributed to the development of decision models of absence. These are the rational decision models provided by economists and sociologists and the expectancy-valence framework posited by organizational psychologists. What these groups have in common is that they view absence behavior as largely rational in nature and determined by the individual's subjective evaluation of the costs and benefits associated with absence and its alternative.

Economic Models Economists have drawn on microeconomic theory and labor-economics analysis. First, Gowler (1969) presented a model of the labor supply of the firm. According to this model, absence is used by employees as a way to restore the balance of effort-rewarded ratios disturbed by fluctuations in levels of overtime. Second, following Gowler's lead, Allen, drawing on the concepts of work-leisure tradeoff and income substitution effects, developed a model of work attendance. According to his model, absence permits the worker to control wage levels and other rewards for work when considering desired levels of work, leisure, and risk. Absence results when the benefits of not working on any particular day are greater than the costs. Third, economists have examined the effect of the wage and fringe benefit structure on absence. For example, we know that when fringe benefits are not tied to hours worked, an incentive for absence is created. This is due to the fact that as work hours decrease, the paid benefits per hour increase, thus creating an income effect that fosters absence. Supporting the models based on economic theory are studies showing an increase in absence associated with an increase in the difference between a worker's marginal rate of substitution of income for leisure and his or her marginal wage rate (Dunn and Youngblood, 1986), increased fringe benefits (Allen, 1981; Chelius, 1981), and higher levels of paid sick and absence days (Dalton and Perry, 1981; Winkler, 1980).

Psychological Models Perhaps the most prominent psychological model of decision-making that has been applied to absence behavior is the expectancy-valence theory of employee motivation as developed by Vroom (1964) and extended by Lawler and Porter (1967). This approach integrates decision theory with an analysis of motivational processes. Individuals are regarded as making choices about their behavior based on the probability that they will receive valued outcomes. Although the theory was not originally developed to explain absence, Lawler and Porter argue that it could apply to absence behavior. And although there has not been an empirical test of expectancy-valence theory in relation to absence behavior, the theory has had a pervasive influence on the study of absenteeism (for example, Ilgen and Hollenback, 1977; Morgan and Herman, 1976). Moreover, it had an influence on the development of the original Steers and Rhodes (1978, 1984) model, particularly in explaining the linkage between satisfaction with the job situation and attendance motivation.

Absence behavior is also treated in equity theory (Adams, 1965) as one of the means of restoring equity with regard to the ratio of outcomes received from work and one's inputs in comparison with a relevant other. Absence is a form of leaving the field in order to restore equity. Although notions of equity have been explored in absence research, the ambiguous role of absence in equity theory and the minor role it plays does not make the theory suitable for examining absence behavior.

Finally, integrating psychological and economic approaches to time valuation, Youngblood (1984) viewed absence as a function of motivation processes associated with both work and nonwork domains. First, similar to pain-avoidance models, absence was considered to be a reactive response to an unfavorable work environment. Second, drawing from economic theory, absence was viewed as reflecting proactive behavior for the purpose of restructuring the workweek. Correlational research results provided support for his framework. Youngblood's theory with supporting research suggests the importance of considering the centrality of the nonwork domain in understanding absence rather than simply viewing absence as "organizational" behavior.

TOWARD A DIAGNOSTIC MODEL OF ATTENDANCE

Based on the above discussion and the progress that has been made in recent years on the topic, we are now in a position to use this current knowledge to build a diagnostic model of employee attendance. The proposed model is designed to be integrative in that it incorporates new empirical and theoretical developments and because it includes both avoidable and unavoidable absence. Although this model is similar to the original formulation by Steers and Rhodes in focusing on the individual employee's decision to attend, it differs in its increased attention to absence culture, organizational practices, societal context, and perceived ability to attend. These developments follow from recent literature and are included here in an effort to delineate more clearly the major factors influencing such behavior. The model is also meant to be diagnostic in that it is designed to be used not just by researchers but also by managers interested in better understanding the particular forces for absenteeism in their own organizations. . . . It is hoped that this model will also continue the research tradition in the field of absenteeism by making use of what we currently know and by challenging others to continue the developmental process.

The *diagnostic model* of employee attendance will be described in three parts: (1) major influences on attendance motivation; (2) major influences on perceived ability to attend and actual attendance; and (3) the role of societal context and reciprocal relationships (see Fig. 2). Throughout, it is important to recognize that this is not an organizational or group model of absence; rather, the primary unit of analysis is individual behavior. Thus, the more macro variables are relevant to

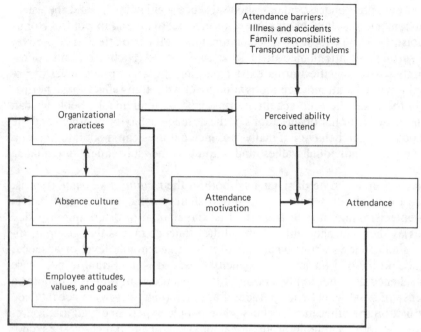

FIGURE 2
A diagnostic model of employee attendance.

the extent that they influence individual attendance. In suggesting this paradigm, we recognize that any effort to model complex social behavior can lead to a situation in which some important variables might receive less attention than they deserve. Moreover, causal patterns are often complex or reciprocal, and this point too is sometimes lost or simplified in modeling attempts. Even so, while recognizing the limitations of parsimony, we have attempted in this model to highlight what appear to be the more salient factors that have a fairly significant and consistent influence on absence behavior.

Influences on Attendance Motivation

At least three sets of highly interactive factors can be identified that have an influence on an employee's attendance motivation. These are (1) the prevailing absence culture; (2) organizational policies and practices with respect to the workplace; and (3) employee attitudes, values and goals. Hence, such influences can be found at the individual, group, and organizational levels throughout the organization. Let us see how each of these work.

Absence Culture As discussed earlier in the paper, the concept of absence culture as originally introduced by Chadwick-Jones et al. (1982) and Johns and Nicholson (1982; see also Nicholson and Johns, 1985) represents one of the signal contributions to the study of employee absence. Absence culture can be defined as "the set of shared understandings about absence legitimacy . . . and the established 'custom and practice' of employee absence behavior and its control (Johns and Nicholson, 1982, p. 136). Absence cultures can influence attendance motivation and subsequent attendance in at least three ways (Nicholson and Johns, 1985). First, where specific norms exist regarding the appropriate level of absence, an individual's attendance motivation level will often reflect these norms. Second, in the case where no specific norms exist, an individual's behavior can be influenced by his or her observations of the absence behavior of others and the consequences of such behavior. Finally, absence cultures can moderate the relationship between individual values and attitudes and subsequent attendance motivation.

Absence cultures can be distinguished both in their *cultural salience* (that is, the degree to which all members of a group share similar or divergent beliefs about absenteeism) and in their *trust* (that is, the amount of discretion provided employees by their management). High cultural salience means that group members have similar views about what constitutes an acceptable level of absence; low salience means that far less homogeneity exists. It is important to note here that high salience does not imply a norm of low absenteeism; rather, it denotes a shared sense of what level or magnitude of absence (high or low) is acceptable.

High trust, on the other hand, occurs when people experience high job discretion (as we see, for example, in professional jobs), leading to a high-trust psychological contract that reinforces the work ethic and internalized commitment to the organization. Low trust results when people experience lower job discretion (for example, assembly line workers) and typically leads to a more detached view of organizational participation and commitment. As noted earlier in the paper, (see Fig. 1), these two aspects of absence culture combine to determine which of four "cultures" emerge in an organization (Nicholson and Johns, 1985).

In the final analysis, the nature and quality of these two variables determine the extent to which absence culture influences attendance motivation. For example, when an absence culture is highly salient, it can represent the primary influence on an individual's motivation to attend. On the other hand, when an absence culture is low in salience, other factors (for example, organizational practices or employee attitudes) typically emerge to have a stronger influence on attendance motivation).

Organizational Practices   In addition to variations in absence cultures, we must also recognize differences in organizational practices as a major influence on attendance motivation. Such practices can provide either the "push" or the "pull" necessary to encourage attendance. Four such practices can be identified: (1) the nature of an organization's absence control policies; (2) the work design or task interdependencies that characterize a particular job; (3) organizational recruitment and selection practices; and (4) expressed job expectations by management. Although other factors could be added to this list, let us look at these four examples.

First, a company's *absence control policies* represent a particularly salient force for attendance. These policies embody what management thinks constitute acceptable—and unacceptable—levels of absence and reasons for absence. Some companies are noted for their "rigorous" policies and policy enforcement; others are often seen as "lax." Moreover, it is not uncommon to find companies that apply significantly different control policies to managers and nonmanagers; indeed, minimal absence controls are often seen as a fringe benefit for managers. Sometimes these control policies are determined solely by corporate representatives; at other times they follow from contractual negotiations with unions. In any case, they are meant to reflect the basic ground rules governing "acceptable behavior" for whatever group they apply to.

Second, the nature of the job itself can influence motivation. Such *work design factors* as work cycle time, role discretion, and task identity, as well as resulting job stressors can often influence how employees see their role in the organization. As noted by Nicholson and Johns (1985, p. 401), "technological and bureaucratic experience may encourage them to see themselves as isolated, dispensable functionaries whose temporary absence is of no fundamental purpose, or they may see themselves as people whose coordinated commitment and reliable attendance is vital to organizational success." Because nonmanagerial positions are more likely to be characterized by low degrees of job discretion, task interdependencies, and perceived importance to the organization, it is not surprising that attendance values at this level tend to be weaker.

A third influence on attendance behavior is the *recruitment and selection practices* of the organization. Recruitment and selection practices determine what kinds of people are hired and what kinds are not. To the extent that companies examine job applicants' previous attendance and tardiness records from earlier employment or other pertinent information, it is less likely that absence-prone individuals will actually be hired.

And, finally, to the extent that management communicates *clear job expectations* regarding acceptable levels of absence to both current and prospective employees, we would expect a higher attendance norm. One way to convey such expectations for prospective employees is through the use of realistic job previews (Wanous, 1980), where prospective employees are fully informed concerning job duties and expectations. For current employees, such expectations can be transmitted by management through the communication of attendance policies, measuring employee attendance, and performance appraisal and reward practices.

Employee Attitudes, Values, and Goals Interacting with absence culture and organizational practices in determining attendance motivation is a third critical variable, namely the differences found across employees with respect to their attitudes, values, and goals. These differences can vary considerably from person to person, depending upon what is salient for the individual at a particular point in time. As noted earlier, *work-related attitudes* (for example, job involvement) can play a significant role in determining how employees view the psychological contract between employees and management, as well as how committed they are to coming to work (Farrell and Stamm, 1988; Hackett, 1988). Moreover, attendance motivation can be affected by variations in *personal work ethics,* as well as the *centrality of work* to the employees (that is, how important work is in his

or her life goals). In employees who have other interests outside that take prece-
dence (for example, family responsibilities, hobbies) or to the extent that the
work ethic itself is low, we would expect to see a resulting attitude that is conducive to high absenteeism. And, finally, changes in *employee job expectations*
(for example, when an employee becomes more "marketable" and begins to re-
examine what he or she expects from the job) can influence an employee's view
of the importance of coming to work.

Other examples of employee characteristics that can influence attendance can
be identified. Whatever the specific set of characteristics, it is important to remember the *interactive* nature between these characteristics and absence culture
and organizational practices. For example, variations in work design (for example, a speed-up on the assembly line) or changes in an absence control policy can
influence job attitudes. Moreover, a consistently poor work ethic among a group
of employees can cause a company to "tighten up" on its absence control policies because the employees might be seen as less trustworthy or committed. And
the specificity, consistency of enforcement, and severity of absence control policies can clearly influence cultural salience and the trust dimension of an absence
culture. Hence, as shown in Fig. 2, these three sets of factors—absence culture;
organizational practices; and employee attitudes, values, and goals—interact
with each other in a variety of ways ultimately to determine an employee's motivation or desire to come to work.

Influences on Perceived Ability to Attend and Attendance

The second part of the proposed model deals with the link between attendance
motivation and actual attendance. As indicated (see Fig. 2), attendance motivation leads to actual attendance as constrained by an employee's perceived ability
to attend. This perceived ability on the part of the employee, in turn, is influenced by both attendance barriers and organizational practices. At least three attendance barriers can be noted. First, there is the issue of actual *illness or accidents* that physically prevent someone from attending. No responsible company
wants sick employees to come to work. Second, *family responsibilities* (for example, a sick child at home) can prevent an otherwise healthy individual from
attending. This problem is especially serious for single parents or parents with
several children, and the severity of the problem is likely to increase as more
young mothers enter the labor force. And, finally, a variety of *transportation
problems* (for example, a car breakdown, missing one's bus) can inhibit attendance in spite of one's motivational level.

These problems can sometimes be alleviated with the help of the company
through such means as company-sponsored day care, car or van pooling, and
physical fitness programs. Such organizational practices have become popular
solutions in recent years to the problem of how we make it easier for motivated
employees to get to work.

As noted in the model, these absence barriers combine with organizational relief efforts and are then assessed by the employee to determine his or her perceived ease of attending. Clearly, the way employees interpret a situation—as op-

posed to how it "really" is—will influence their actual behavior, and such employees will often see the same situation quite differently. For example, a snowstorm or a car breakdown might cause one employee to yield; whereas another employee might see these events as a challenge to be met. However they see it, the resulting perceptions concerning what is possible or not possible can represent a major influence on subsequent attendance.

Societal Context and Reciprocal Relationships

Finally, it is important to recognize that this sequence of interactive events, although not represented explicitly in Fig. 2, is enacted within a particular societal context. Two aspects of this context are particularly relevant to our analysis here. First, general *societal norms* concerning work or the value of work can influence both employee characteristics and organizational practices. Consider the example of work ethics. In Japan, for instance, societal norms stress hard work and the value of being a dedicated employee. It is not surprising, therefore, to find a low average absence rate of one-half percent, compared to almost 5 percent in the United States. Employees in Japan are more committed to coming to work, and companies respond with commensurate and supportive organizational practices. Few control policies are needed because for all practical purposes there is no problem.

Norms can also vary across segments of a larger society, based on such factors as geographic region, occupational grouping, and so forth. For example, occupational groups that are characterized by unionization often feel less commitment to the organization and more to the union, a fact that is capable of influencing absence behavior. Moreover, many companies prefer to open new divisions or plants in rural areas, where it is believed that employee work values and attendance norms are stronger. Finally, norms concerning child-care responsibilities are often different for women and men.

In fact, one could argue that societal norms influence almost all aspects of employee and corporate behavior. Some countries (most notably those in Western Europe) place a high societal value on efficient public transportation systems, thereby alleviating transportation problems for most employees. Moreover, in some societies like Japan, China, and Korea, it is customary for grandparents to assume child-care responsibility for working parents, thus making ability to attend somewhat easier. Thus, the pervasive nature of societal norms and practices should not be overlooked in our efforts better to understand behavior in the workplace.

In addition to societal norms, *economic and labor market conditions* can influence employee characteristics and organizational practices. For example, in periods of tight employment, companies can be reticent to enforce control policies rigorously for valued employees for fear of losing them. Moreover, recruitment and selection practices might not lead to the hiring of "ideal" employees when few job candidates are available. On an individual level, when economic conditions are poor, employees might be more likely to do their best to attend so as not to risk being discharged.

Thus attendance behavior must be viewed within an appropriate societal context. In addition, however, we must recognize several reciprocal relationships that exist within any social dynamic. For example, actual absence behavior is not only influenced by the many variables we have discussed here but also it, in turn, feeds back to influence some of its precursors. High absenteeism within a company, for example, might influence management to tighten its control policies; conversely, high attendance might lead to the opposite effect. High attendance or absenteeism can also influence absence culture, by either reinforcing or challenging the existing culture. Finally, high or low attendance can affect employee attitudes in either positive or negative ways. Hence, the diagnostic model presented here is a dynamic one, where major forces on behavior must be viewed as being in a constant state of flux and where a significant change in one variable can set off a chain reaction that ultimately affects many of the other variables, including attendance behavior itself.

REFERENCES

Adams, J. C. (1965). "Injustice in Social Exchange." In L. Berkowitz (ed.), *Advances in Experimental Social Psychology* (Vol. 2). New York: Academic Press.

Allen, S. G. (1981). "An Empirical Model of Work Attendance." *The Review of Economics and Statistics, 63,* pp.77–87.

Argyle, M. (1972). *The Social Psychology of Work.* Harmondsworth: Penguin.

Brayfield, A., and Crockett, W. (1955). "Employee Attitudes and Employee Performance." *Psychological Bulletin, 52,* pp. 396–424.

Chadwick-Jones, J. K., Nicholson, N., and Brown, C. (1982). *Social Psychology of Absenteeism.* New York: Praeger.

Chelius, J. R. (1981). "Understanding Absenteeism: The Potential Contribution of Economic Theory." *Journal of Business Research, 9,* pp. 409–418.

Dalton, D. R., and Perry, J. L. (1981). "Absenteeism and the Collective Bargaining Agreement: An Empirical Test." *Academy of Management Journal, 24,* pp. 425–431.

Dunn, L. F., and Youngblood, S. A. (1986). "Absenteeism as a Mechanism for Approaching an Optimal Labor Market Equilibrium: An Empirical Study." *The Review of Economics and Statistics, 68,* pp. 668–674.

Farrell, D., and Stamm, C. L. (1988). "Meta-Analysis of the Correlates of Employee Absence." *Human Relations, 41,* pp. 211–227.

Gibson, R. O. (1966). "Toward a Conceptualization of Absence Behavior." *Administrative Sciences Quarterly, 11,* pp. 107–133.

Gowler, D. (1969). "Determinants of the Supply of Labour to the Firm." *Journal of Management Studies, 6,* pp. 73–95.

Hackett, R. D. (1988). "Yet Another Look at the Relationship of Employee Absenteeism to Job Satisfaction." Hamilton, Canada: Series #290.

Hackett, R. D., and Guion, R. M. (1985). "A Reevaluation of the Absenteeism-Job Satisfaction Relationship." *Organizational Behavior and Human Decision Processes, 35,* pp. 340–381.

Hill, J. M. M., and Trist, E. L. (1953). "A Consideration of Industrial Accidents as a Means of Withdrawal from the Work Situation." *Human Relations, 6,* pp. 357–380.

Ilgen, D., and Hollenback, J. H. (1977). "The Role of Job Satisfaction in Absence Behavior." *Organizational Behavior and Human Performance, 19,* pp. 148–161.

Johns, G., and Nicholson, N. (1982). "The Meaning of Absence: New Strategies for Theory and Research." In B. M. Staw and L. L. Cummings (eds.), *Research in Organizational Behavior* (Vol. 4). Greenwich, CT:JAI.

McShane, S. L. (1984). "Job. Satisfaction and Absenteeism: A Meta-Analytic Re-Examination." *Canadian Journal of Administrative Sciences, 1*, pp. 61–77.

Morgan, L. G., and Herman, J. B. (1976). "Perceived Consequences of Absenteeism." *Journal of Applied Psychology, 61*, pp. 738–742.

Nicholson, N. (1977). "Absence Behavior and Attendance Motivation: A Conceptual Synthesis." *Journal of Management Studies, 14*, pp. 231–252.

Nicholson, N., and Johns, G. (1985). "The Absence Culture and the Psychological Contract—Who's in Control of Absence?" *Academy of Management Review, 10*, pp. 397–407.

Porter, L. W., and Lawler, E. E. (1968). *Managerial Attitudes and Performance.* Homewood, Ill.: Dorsey Press.

Rosse, J. G., and Hulin, C. L. (1985). "Adaptation to Work: An Analysis of Employee Health, Withdrawal, and Change." *Organizational Behavior and Human Decision Processes, 36*, pp. 324–347.

Rosse, J. G., and Miller, H. E. (1984). "Relationship between Absenteeism and Other Employee Behaviors." In P. S. Goodman and R. S. Atkin (eds.), *Absenteeism: New Approaches to Understanding, Measuring, and Managing Absence*, pp. 194–228. San Francisco: Jossey-Bass.

Steers, R. M., and Rhodes, S. R. (1978). "Major Influences on Employee Attendance: A Process Model." *Journal of Applied Psychology, 63*, pp. 391–407.

———. (1984). "Knowledge and Speculation about Absenteeism." In P. S. Goodman and R. S. Atkin (eds.), *Absenteeism: New Approaches to Understanding, Measuring, and Managing Absence*, pp. 229–275. San Francisco: Jossey-Bass.

Vroom, V. (1964). *Work and Motivation.* New York: Wiley.

Wanous, J. P. (1975). "Tell It Like It Is at Realistic Job Previews." *Personnel, 52*,(4), pp. 50–60.

———. (1980). *Organizational Entry: Recruitment, Selection, and Socialization of Newcomers.* Reading, Mass.: Addison-Wesley.

Winkler, D. R. (1980). "The Effects of Sick-Leave Policy on Teacher Absenteeism." *Industrial and Labor Relations Review, 33*, pp. 232–239.

Youngblood, S. A. (1984). "Work, Nonwork, and Withdrawal." *Journal of Applied Psychology, 69*, pp.106–117.

Intermediate Linkages in the Relationship between Job Satisfaction and Employee Turnover

William H. Mobley

Reviews of the literature on the relationship between employee turnover and job satisfaction have reported a consistent negative relationship (Brayfield and Crockett, 1955; Locke, 1975; Porter and Steers, 1973; Vroom, 1964). Locke (1976) noted that while the reported correlations have been consistent and significant they have not been especially high (usually less than 40).

Reprinted from *Journal of Applied Psychology*, 1977, **62**, 237–240. Copyright © 1977 American Psychological Association. Reprinted by permission.

It is probable that other variables mediate the relationship between job satisfaction and the act of quitting. Based on their extensive review, Porter and Steers (1973) concluded the following.

Much more emphasis should be placed in the future on the psychology of the withdrawal *process*. . . . Our understanding of the manner in which the actual decision is made is far from complete (p. 173).

The present paper suggests several of the possible intermediate steps in the withdrawal decision process (specifically, the decision to quit a job). Porter and Steers (1973) suggest that expressed "intention to leave" may represent the next logical step after experienced dissatisfaction in the withdrawal process. The withdrawal decision process presented here suggests that thinking of quitting is the next logical step after experienced dissatisfaction and that "intention to leave," following several other steps, may be the last step prior to actual quitting.

A schematic representation of the withdrawal decision process is presented in Figure 1. Block A represents the process of evaluating one's existing job, while Block B represents the resultant emotional state of some degree of satisfaction-dissatisfaction. A number of models have been proposed for the process inherent in Blocks A and B—for example, the value-percept discrepancy model (Locke, 1969, 1976), an instrumentality-valence model (Vroom, 1964), a met-expectations model (Porter & Steers, 1973), and a contribution/inducement ratio (March & Simon, 1958). Comparative studies that test the relative efficacy of these and other alternative models of satisfaction continue to be needed.

Most studies of turnover examine the direct relationship between job satisfaction and turnover. The model presented in Figure 1 suggests a number of possible mediating steps between dissatisfaction and actual quitting. Block C suggests that one of the consequences of dissatisfaction is to stimulate thoughts of quitting. Although not of primary interest here, it is recognized that other forms of withdrawal less extreme than quitting (e.g., absenteeism, passive job behavior) are possible consequences of dissatisfaction (see e.g., Brayfield & Crockett, 1955; Kraut, 1975).

Block D suggests that the next step in the withdrawal decision process is an evaluation of the expected utility of search and of the cost of quitting. The evaluation of the expected utility of search would include an estimate of the chances of finding an alternative to working in the present job, some evaluation of the desirability of possible alternatives, and the costs of search (e.g., travel, lost work time, etc.). The evaluation of the cost of quitting would include such considerations as loss of seniority, loss of vested benefits, and the like. This block incorporates March and Simon's (1958) perceived ease of movement concept.

If the costs of quitting are high and/or the expected utility of search is low, the individual may reevaluate the existing job (resulting in a change in job satisfaction), reduce thinking of quitting, and/or engage in other forms of withdrawal behavior. Research is still needed on the determinants of alternative forms of withdrawal behavior and on how the expression of withdrawal behavior changes as a function of time and of changes in or reevaluation of the environment.

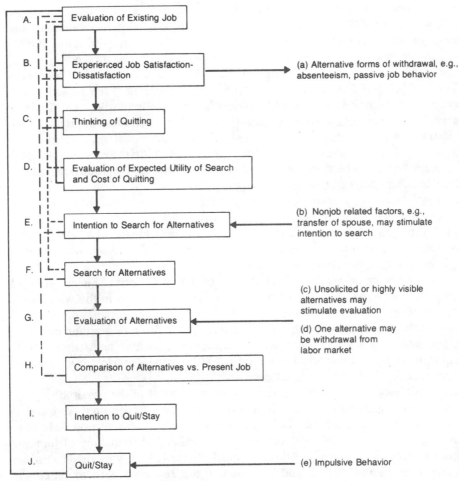

FIGURE 1
The employee turnover decision process.

If there is some perceived chance of finding an alternative and if the costs are not prohibitive, the next step, Block E, would be behavioral intention to search for an alternative(s). As noted by Arrow (b) in Figure 1, non-job-related factors may also elicit an intention to search (e.g., transfer of spouse, health problem, etc.). The intention to search is followed by an actual search (Block F). If no alternatives are found, the individual may continue to search, reevaluate the expected utility of search, reevaluate the existing job, simply accept the current state of affairs, decrease thoughts of quitting, and/or engage in other forms of withdrawal behavior (e.g., absenteeism, passive job behavior).

If alternatives are available, including (in some cases) withdrawal from the labor market, an evaluation of alternatives is initiated (Block G). This evaluation process would be hypothesized to be similar to the evaluation process in Block A. However, specific job factors the individual considers in evaluating the present job and alternatives may differ (see Hellriegel & White, 1973; and Kraut, 1975, for a discussion of this point). Independent of the preceding steps, unsolicited or highly visible alternatives may stimulate this evaluation process.

The evaluation of alternatives is followed by a comparison of the present job to alternatives(s) (Block H). If the comparison favors the alternative, it will stimulate a behavioral intention to quit (Block 1), followed by actual withdrawal (Block J). If the comparison favors the present job, the individual may continue to search, reevaluate the expected utility of search, reevaluate the existing job, simply accept the current state of affairs, decrease thoughts of quitting, and/or engage in other forms of withdrawal behavior.

Finally, Arrow (e) gives recognition to the fact that for some individuals, the decision to quit may be an impulsive act involving few, if any, of the preceding steps in this model. The relative incidence and the individual and situational determinants of an impulsive versus a subjectively rational decision process presents yet another area of needed research.

The model being described is heuristic rather than descriptive. There may well be individual differences in the number and sequence of steps in the withdrawal decision process, in the degree to which the process is conscious, and as noted earlier, in the degree to which the act of quitting is impulsive rather than based on a subjectively rational decision process. One value of such an heuristic model is to guide thinking and empirical research toward a valid descriptive model that can account for such individual differences.

There is a lack of research evaluating all or even most of the possible steps in the withdrawal decision process. There have been a few studies that have tested one or two of the intermediate linkages proposed in the present note. Mobley[*] found high negative correlations between satisfaction and frequency of thinking of quitting (Blocks A and C). Atkinson and Lefferts (1972), who dealt with the association between Blocks C and J, found that the frequency with which people thought about quitting their job was significantly related to actual termination. Kraut (1975), looking at the associations among Blocks B, I, and J, found significant correlations between expressed intention to stay and subsequent employee participation. These correlations were much stronger than relationships between expressed satisfaction and continued participation. Finally, Armknecht and Early's (1972) review is relevant to the relationships between Blocks D and/or F and Block J. They concluded that voluntary terminations are closely related to economic conditions.

Each of these studies fails to look at a complete withdrawal decision process. Such research would appear to be sorely needed. Several researchable questions that follow from the withdrawal decision process described in the present note were mentioned earlier. Additional questions include the following. Do individuals evaluate the expected utility of search? If so, what are the determinants and consequences of this evaluation? What are the consequences and determinants of behavior in the face of an unsuccessful search? In such cases, do individuals persist in search, reevaluate their existing jobs, reevaluate the cost of search, or engage in other forms of withdrawal? Is the process and/or content for evaluating alternative jobs the same as for evaluating the present job? Does satisfaction with the present job change as a function of the availability or evaluation of alternatives?

Attention to these sorts of questions rather than a continued replication of the direct relationship between job satisfaction and turnover would appear to be warranted. Particularly useful would be the longitudinal analysis of the variables and linkages suggested by the model. Such research would be responsive to Porter and Steers' (1973) conclusion that more emphasis should be placed on the psychology of the withdrawal decision process.

REFERENCES

Armknecht, P. A., & Early, J. F. Quits in manufacturing: A study of their causes. *Monthly Labor Review*, 1972, **11**, 31–37.

Atkinson, T. J., & Lefferts, E. A. The prediction of turnover using Herzberg's job satisfaction technique. *Personnel Psychology*, 1972, **25**, 53–64.

Brayfield, A. H., & Crockett, W. H. Employee attitudes and employee performance. *Psychological Bulletin*, 1955, **52**, 396–424.

Hellriegel, D., & White, G. E. Turnover of professionals in public accounting: A comparative analysis. *Personnel Psychology*, 1973, **26**, 239–249.

Kraut, A. I. Predicting turnover of employees from measured job attitudes. *Organizational Behavior and Human Performance*. 1975, **13**, 233–243.

Locke, E. A. What is job satisfaction? *Organizational Behavior and Human Performance*, 1969, **4**, 309–336.

Locke, E. A. Personnel attitudes and motivation. *Annual Review of Psychology*, 1975, **26**, 457–480.

Locke, E. A. The nature and consequences of job satisfaction. In M. D. Dunnette (Ed.), *Handbook of industrial and organizational psychology*. Chicago: Rand-McNally, 1976.

March, J. G., & Simon, H. A. *Organizations*. New York: Wiley, 1958.

Porter, L. W., & Steers, R. M. Organizational, work, and personal factors in employee turnover and absenteeism. *Psychological Bulletin*, 1973, **80**, 151–176.

Vroom, V. H. *Work and motivation*. New York: Wiley, 1964.

QUESTIONS FOR DISCUSSION

1 What managerial implications follow from the Steers and Rhodes model of employee absenteeism?

2 How would you design a work environment aimed at minimizing voluntary absenteeism?

3 Absenteeism in several Asian countries (such as Japan) is substantially lower than that in most western countries (including those in North America and Europe). What factors explain these differences?

4 Using Mobley's model of the individual's decision to leave an organization, how would you as a manager determine a subordinate's intent to leave? How would you increase the likelihood that individuals who have considered leaving will end up staying?

5 If you as a manager had a high rate of turnover among your employees, how would you determine the cause of this high turnover?

6 Considering the biases and moderators affecting the attribution process, what cautions would you give a manager who is attempting to decide why a particular subordinate left the organization?

7 What are the underlying assumptions of the theory of cognitive dissonance? Is a cognitive dissonance theory a need theory of motivation? Explain.

8 Cherrington discusses several organization factors which influence commitment. Can you think of additional organization factors?

9 Would you expect organizational commitment to be more highly related to job performance or organizational citizenship behaviors? Why?

10 Do you think that organizational commitment can be developed through operant conditioning?

CHAPTER 8

CROSS-CULTURAL INFLUENCES ON MOTIVATION

Questions relating to motivation and work behavior are not restricted to national or cultural boundaries. In this day of almost instantaneous communication across continents, high-speed international jet travel, and a proliferation of multinational companies, it is more important than ever to examine whether motivational factors affect individuals' job satisfaction and performance similarly from one country or culture to another, or whether there are wide variations across countries and cultures (Steers and Miller, 1988). This turns out not to be an easy question to answer, in terms of providing definitive and convincing evidence, since it is possible to point to elements of similarities and differences. What does seem to be clear, however, is that it is possible to gain a better understanding of work motivation in one's own culture by comparing its values, attitudes, and practices to those in other cultures. This is analogous to the traveler who goes abroad and upon returning sees his or her own country quite differently than before. Without such an experience (either directly or vicariously) it is difficult to gain a perspective on what is unique to one's own set of circumstances.

For this chapter we have chosen the title "Cross-cultural Influences. . . . " However, we could as effectively have used the term "Cross-national influences. . . . " It is important to remember, however, that although cultures and nations frequently overlap, they do not always correspond directly to each other. Belgium and Canada, for example, tend to have two distinct cultures contained within one country, and, likewise, one culture can overlap more than a single country (as in the case of Norway, Sweden, and Denmark). The basic point is that when the term "cross-cultural" is used it generally signifies that "cross-national" is also implied, though there can be definite exceptions, as noted.

In considering different influences on motivation across nations and their associated cultures, it is helpful to define briefly what is meant by the term culture.

Unfortunately, as Ajiferuke and Boddewyn (1970) have pointed out, "Culture is one of those terms that defy a single all-purpose definition, and there are almost as many meanings of culture as people using the term." Nevertheless, a typical social science definition is that put forth by Kroeber and Parsons (1958, p. 583): "the transmitted and created content and patterns of values, ideas, and other symbolic-meaningful systems as factors in the shaping of human behavior and the artifacts produced through that behavior." A more succinct definition provided by a management scholar who has carried out extensive cross-cultural studies is: "the collective programming of the mind which distinguishes the members of one human group from another", or, as he has also put it: "culture is to a human collectivity what personality is to an individual" (Hofstede, 1980, p. 25).

The critical or central issue in cross-national analyses of motivational influences is whether individuals' responses to organizations' practices are more or less universal and therefore whether those practices can be transferred from one culture to another with essentially similar results (Nath, 1988). Perhaps a better way to put the question is: To what extent can what is learned about motivation in the work situation in one culture (e.g., the United States) be applied in another culture (e.g., Egypt) with predictable outcomes? As implied earlier, the research evidence to date does not provide clear-cut answers to this type of question. Part of the reason is that research methodologies and conceptual foundations have not been sufficiently developed to permit unambiguous interpretation of findings. For example, when significant differences are found between motivational patterns (e.g., the values attached to different possible work incentives) across countries, it is extremely difficult to pin down the causes for these differences (or similarities, for that matter). While improved research designs can help in this regard, it is still a major problem to disentangle the effects of culture from those of other key variables such as type of technology, size of organization, nature of specific legal statutes, and the like. Even if these factors can be controlled some way in an effective research design, the question still remains as to what it is about the culture or country that is in fact causing the differences (or lack of them).

Despite all of the nettlesome complexities involved in interpreting data and information obtained in cross-cultural or cross-national comparisons, it remains important to attempt to do so. For one thing, it helps provide a good antidote to ethnocentrism (a belief in the inherent superiority of one's own culture or group). No nation or culture has a monopoly on the best ways of doing something. This is especially so when it comes to understanding motivation at work and attempting to implement practices based on this knowledge. Second, it is always easier to understand something by comparison rather in an absolute sense. Thus, our comprehension of a particular situation (e.g., motivation in U.S. organizations) is enhanced. Third, the world is increasingly moving toward greater intercultural and international exchanges of knowledge and individuals, and, therefore, many more people than in the past will find that their work careers will involve experiences in more than a single culture.

The readings in this chapter focus on how cross-cultural or cross-national differences can affect employee motivation. First, on a general level, Adler examines several contemporary western theories of motivation to see how they apply internationally. That is, can a theory of motivation developed in the United States, for example, incorporate factors from other countries that are important for understanding motivation and behavior. Consider the issue of "pay for performance," for instance. In the United States, considerable emphasis is given to tying pay raises to individual performance. What happens to this approach in several European countries, where personal income tax escalates rapidly in the higher income brackets to the point where most, if not all, the pay raise goes for taxes? What happens to the motivational value of the reward? Or, consider what happens to individual pay for performance systems in several Asian countries where group achievement is prized and individual (that is, independent) effort is not? Again, what happens to the original theory? Issues such as these are considered in this first reading.

Following this general discussion, we turn our attention to motivational problems in specific countries. It is clearly not possible in the space allowed to cover the subject in a global fashion. Instead, we will focus on the issue of employee motivation in two very different Asian countries, Japan and China. This comparison (along with comparisons with North America) allow us to gain a sense of the complexities of motivating employees around the world. First, Lincoln examines employee work attitudes and motivation in Japan and compares this situation with the American situation. This article clearly demonstrates how culture can have a profound impact on employee behavior. Next, Tung examines motivational practices in China. Here we can see the influence of a socialist economy and political system on employee behavior and management practice. Throughout, implications for management are considered.

REFERENCES

Ajiferuke, M., & Boddewyn, J. Culture and other explanatory variables in management studies. *Academy of Management Journal,* 1970, **13**, 153–163.

Hofstede, G. *Culture's consequence: International differences in work-related values.* Beverly Hills, Calif.: Sage, 1980.

Kroeber, A., & Parsons, T. The concepts of culture and of the social system. *American Sociological Review,* 1958, **23**, 582–583.

Nath, R. *Comparative management: A regional view.* Cambridge, Mass.: Ballinger, 1988.

Steers, R. M., & Miller, E. A. Management in the 1990s: The management challenge. *Academy of Management Executive,* 1988, **2**, 21–23.

Cross-Cultural Motivation

Nancy J. Adler

What causes high employee productivity and job satisfaction? What energizes employees to behave in certain ways? What directs and channels their behavior to accomplish organizational goals? How do organizations maintain desired behavior? What forces in employees and their environment reinforce or discourage them in their course of action?

Numerous motivation theories address these questions and, like the leadership theories, most have been developed and tested in the United States. Each attempts to explain why human beings behave in the ways they do and what managers can do to encourage certain types of behavior while discouraging others. Let's look at a few of the more well-recognized motivation theories and determine if they are universal or culture bound.

MASLOW'S NEED HIERARCHY

Maslow (15), an American psychologist, suggested that human beings' five basic needs form a hierarchy: from physiological, to safety, to social, to esteem, to self-actualization needs. According to Maslow, the higher order needs (e.g., esteem and self-actualization) only become activated, and thus motivate behavior, after lower order needs have been satisfied.

Does Maslow's theory, which he based on Americans, hold for workers outside of the United States?* Hofstede (8) suggests that it does not. For instance, in countries high on uncertainty avoidance (such as Greece and Japan) as compared with lower uncertainty avoidance countries (such as the United States), security motivates most workers more strongly than does self-actualization. More workers in high uncertainty avoidance countries consider job security and life-time employment as more important than a very interesting or challenging job. Social needs tend to dominate the motivation of workers in countries (such as Sweden, Norway, and Denmark) that stress the quality of life (Hofstede's femininity dimension) over productivity (Hofstede's masculinity dimension). Workers in more collectivist countries, such as Pakistan, also tend to stress social needs over the more individualistic ego and self-actualization needs.

Numerous research studies testing Maslow's hierarchy demonstrate similar but not identical rank ordering of needs across cultures. Studies include research on such diverse cultures as Peru (24, 27), India (11), the Middle East (1), Mexico (22), and Anglophone and Francophone Canada (12). For example, one study

From N. J. Adler, *International Dimensions of Organizational Behavior,* Boston: PWS-KENT Publishing Company, 1986, pp. 127–133. Copyright © by Wadsworth, Inc. Reprinted by permission of PWS-KENT Publishing Company, a division of Wadsworth, Inc.

*While Maslow's hierarchy has been questioned within the United States, it has become one of the accepted bases for explaining and understanding behavior within organizations; generalizing from this United States–based acceptance to worldwide applicability is questioned in this chapter.

shows that Liberian managers express similar needs to those of managers in South Africa, Argentina, Chile, India, and other developing countries, while demonstrating higher security and self-esteem needs than managers in more developed countries (9). In another study, the need hierarchy of Libyan executives failed to replicate the rank ordering of needs in the United States; the conclusion was that Maslow's hierarchy varies from culture to culture (2). Another study found results more consistent with Maslow's findings: in a study involving the United States, Mexico, Puerto Rico, Venezuela, Japan, Thailand, Turkey, and Yugoslavia, workers in the twenty-six surveyed industrial plants ranked self-actualization most highly and security among the two least important needs. In all eight countries the more highly educated managers ranked self-actualization as more important and security as less important than did their less educated colleagues (21). In a fourteen-country study, Haire *et al.* (4) found that although managers in each culture want similar things from their jobs, they differ in what they think their jobs are currently giving them.

While the conflicting pattern of research fails to be definitive, it strongly indicates that we should not assume Maslow's hierarchy to hold universally. As aptly summarized by researchers O'Reilly and Roberts (20):

> Studies have found that an individual's frame of reference will determine the order of importance of his needs. It has also been found that his frame of reference is in part determined by his culture. Therefore, it can be said that an individual's needs are partially bound by culture.

Human needs may well include fundamental or universal aspects, but their importance and the ways in which they express themselves is different in different cultures.

McCLELLAND'S THREE MOTIVES

McClelland, another American theorist, suggested that three important motives drive workers: the needs for achievement, power, and affiliation (17). Although McClelland has focused more recently on executives' needs for power (18), he initially emphasized the need for achievement as fundamental in explaining why some societies produce more than others (19). For example, in his famous studies in India he found that entrepreneurs trained in the need for achievement did better than did untrained entrepreneurs (also see 10).

Comparative research on McClelland's achievement motivation has shown it to be relatively robust across cultures. For example, managers in New Zealand appear to follow the pattern developed in the United States (7). However, similar to his analysis of Maslow's need hierarchy, Hofstede questions the universality of McClelland's three needs (8). Hofstede begins by pointing out that the word *achievement* itself is hardly translatable into any language other than English (8:55). In his research, Hofstede found that countries with a high need for achievement also have a high need to produce (Hofstede's masculinity dimension) and a strong willingness to accept risk (Hofstede's weak uncertainty avoidance). Anglo-American countries such as the United States, Canada, and Great

Britain (weak uncertainty avoidance combined with masculinity) follow the high achievement motivation pattern, while countries such as Chile and Portugal (strong uncertainty avoidance combined with femininity) follow the low achievement motivation pattern. While helpful in explaining human behavior, McClelland's three motives have not been shown to be universal.

HERZBERG'S TWO FACTOR THEORY

Herzberg (5, 6) suggested that certain extrinsic factors (those associated with the environment surrounding a job) only have the power to de-motivate while other intrinsic factors (those associated with the job itself) have the power to energize, or motivate, behavior. The extrinsic or hygiene factors largely correspond to Maslow's lower order physiological and safety needs. They include factors associated with job dissatisfaction such as working conditions, supervision, relations with co-workers, salary, company policy, and administration. Intrinsic factors or motivators largely corresponding to Maslow's higher order needs, include the work itself, responsibility, recognition for work well done, advancement, and achievement.

Hofstede (8) again points out that culture influences factors that motivate and demotivate behavior. According to his dimensions, it is not surprising that the highly individualistic, productivity-oriented (masculine) American culture has focused on job enrichment (the restructuring of individual jobs to increase productivity), whereas the more feminine and slightly more collective societies of Sweden and Norway developed socio-technical systems and approaches to the quality of working life (the restructuring of employees into work groups to achieve the same ends).

Herzberg's two-factor theory has also been tested outside of the United States. Results in New Zealand failed to replicate those in the United States: in New Zealand, supervision and interpersonal relationships appear to contribute significantly to satisfaction and not merely to reducing dissatisfaction (7). Similarly, in a Panama Canal Zone study researchers found non-United States citizens (including those of the Republic of Panama, the West Indies, Latin America, Europe, Asia, and Canada) to cite certain hygiene factors as satisfiers with greater frequency than did their American counterparts (3).

Similar to other motivation theories, the universality of Herzberg's two-factor theory cannot be assumed. In every culture certain factors act as motivators while others act as hygiene factors. The specific factors and their relative importance appears particular to each culture, and, all too frequently, to each situation. Managers should enter a new culture asking which factors are important, and not assume that their prior experience is transferable.

VROOM'S EXPECTANCY THEORY

Expectancy theories (25, 26; also see 13) claim that people are driven by the expectation that their acts will produce results. Workers assess both their ability to perform a task and the probable type of reward for successful performance (for example, continued employment or a paycheck). According to expectancy theories, the likelihood that an action will lead to certain outcomes or goals (E), multiplied by attractiveness of the outcome (V, its valence) equals motivation ($M = E \times V$) (14:95). Expectancy theories depend on the extent to which employees believe they have control over the outcomes of their efforts as well as the manager's ability to identify desired rewards, both of which vary across cultures. While expectancy theories have clearly advanced our understanding of motivation, they are equally clearly culturally dependent.

People in different cultures vary in the amount of control they believe they have over their environment. Most Americans strongly believe that they control their environment. American managers believe that they directly influence the world in which they work (that is, they have a high level of internal attribution). By contrast, many managers in other parts of the world believe that they only partially control their work environment and the outcomes of their own behavior (that is, they attribute the causes of some events to external circumstances). For example, Moslem managers believe that things will happen only if God wills them to happen (external attribution), whereas most American managers believe hard work will get the job done (internal attribution). Expectancy theories work best in explaining cultures that emphasize internal attribution.

The rewards people want from work also vary greatly across cultures. As discussed in reference to Maslow, security is very important to some people, congenial relationships are paramount to others, and individual status and respect (career advancement) are dominant for others. In a classic study, Sirota and Greenwood (23) investigated the work goals of 19,000 employees in a large multinational electrical equipment manufacturer operating in forty-six countries and reported the results for the twenty-five countries with at least 40 employees, including Argentina, Australia, Austria, Belgium, Brazil, Canada, Chile, Colombia, Denmark, Finland, France, Germany, India, Israel, Japan, Mexico, New Zealand, Norway, Peru, South Africa, Sweden, Switzerland, the United Kingdom, the United States, and Venezuela. In all countries, the five most important goals concerned achievement, especially individual achievement. Next in importance were the immediate environment, general features of the organization, and employment conditions such as pay and work hours. Some of the major differences among the cultural groups included: (a) English speaking countries were higher on individual achievement and lower on the desire for security; (b) French countries, while similar to the English speaking countries, gave greater importance to security and somewhat less to challenging work; (c) Northern European countries expressed less interest in "getting ahead" and work recognition goals and put more emphasis on job accomplishment; in addition, they showed more concern for people and less for the organization as a whole (it was important for them that the job not interfere with their personal lives); (d) Latin countries found individual achievement somewhat less important, especially southern Europeans who placed the highest emphasis on job security. Both groups of Latin countries emphasized fringe benefits; (e) Germany was high on security and fringe benefits, and among the highest on "getting ahead"; and (f) Japan was low on advancement, but was also second highest on challenge and lowest on autonomy, with strong emphasis on good working conditions and a friendly working environment (23).

Expectancy theories are universal to the extent that they do not specify the types of rewards that motivate a given group of workers. Managers themselves must determine the level and type of rewards most sought after by a particular people. While Sirota and Greenwoods' conclusions support the idea that basic human needs are similar, they highlight that culture and environment determine how these needs can best be met.

International management literature is replete with examples of overgeneralization, due to the dominance of American reward structures. For example, raising the salaries of a particular group of Mexican workers motivated them to work *fewer,* not more, hours. As the Mexicans explained, "We can now make enough money to live and enjoy life [one of their primary values] in less time than previously. Now, we do not have to work so many hours." In another example, an expatriate manager in Japan decided to promote one of his Japanese sales representatives to manager (a status reward). To the surprise of the expatriate boss, the promotion diminished the new Japanese manager's performance. Why? Japanese have a high need for harmony—to fit in with their work colleagues. The promotion, an individualistic reward, separated the new manager from his colleagues, embarrassed him, and therefore diminished his motivation to work.

When modified for the extent to which managers believe they control their work environment and for the specific types of rewards desired, expectancy theories appear to hold outside of the United States, even in countries as culturally dissimilar to the United States as Japan (16).

MOTIVATION IS CULTURE BOUND

Most motivation theories in use today were developed in the United States by Americans and about Americans. Of those which were not, many have been strongly influenced by American theoretical work. Americans' strong emphasis on individualism has led to the expectancy and equity theories of motivation: theories that emphasize rational, individual thought as the primary basis of human behavior. The emphasis placed on achievement is not surprising given Americans' willingness to accept risk and their high concern for performance. The theories therefore do not offer universal explanations of motivation; rather, they reflect the values system of Americans (see 8).

Unfortunately, American as well as non-American managers have tended to treat American theories as the best or only way to understand motivation. They are neither. American motivation theories, while assumed to be universal, have failed to provide consistently useful explanations outside the United States. Managers must therefore guard against imposing their domestic American management theories onto their multinational business practices.

REFERENCES

1 Badawy, M. K. "Managerial Attitudes and Need Orientations of Mideastern Executives: An Empirical Cross-Cultural Analysis," *Academy of Management Proceedings,* vol. 39 (1979), pp. 293–297.
2 Buera, A.; and Glueck, W. "Need Satisfaction of Libyan Managers," *Management International Review,* vol. 19, no. 1 (1979), pp. 113–123.
3 Crabbs, R. A. "Work Motivation in the Culturally Complex Panama Canal Company," *Academy of Management Proceedings* (1973), pp. 119–126.
4 Haire, Mason; Ghiselli, Edwin E.; and Porter, Lyman W. "Cultural Patterns in the Role of the Manager," *Industrial Relations,* vol. 2, no. 2 (February 1963), pp. 95–117.
5 Herzberg, F.; Mausner, B.; and Snyderman, B. *The Motivation to Work,* 2nd ed. (New York: John Wiley & Sons, 1959).
6 Herzberg, F. "One More Time: How Do You Motivate Employees?" *Harvard Business Review* (January–February 1968), pp. 54–62.
7 Hines, G. H. "Achievement, Motivation, Occupations and Labor Turnover in New Zealand," *Journal of Applied Psychology,* vol. 58, no. 3 (1973), pp. 313–317.
8 Hofstede, Geert. "Motivation, Leadership and Organization: Do American Theories Apply Abroad?" *Organizational Dynamics* (Summer 1980), pp. 42–63.
9 Howell, P.; Strauss, J.; and Sorensen, P. F. "Research Note: Cultural and Situational Determinants of Job Satisfaction among Management in Liberia," *Journal of Management Studies* (May 1975), pp. 225–227.
10 Hundal, P. S. "A Study of Entrepreneurial Motivation: Comparison of Fast- and Slow-Progressing Small Scale Industrial Entrepreneurs in Punjab, India," *Journal of Applied Psychology,* vol. 55, no. 4 (1971), pp. 317–323.
11 Jaggi, B. "Need Importance of Indian Managers," *Management International Review,* vol. 19, no. 1 (1979), pp. 107–113.
12 Jain, C H.; and Kanungo, R. *Behavioral Issues in Management: The Canadian Context* (Toronto: McGraw-Hill Ryerson Ltd., 1977), pp. 85–99.
13 Lawler, E. E., III. "Job Design and Employee Motivation," *Personnel Psychology,* vol. 22 (1969), pp. 426–435.
14 Lawler, E. E., III. *Pay and Organizational Effectiveness: A Psychological View* (New York: McGraw–Hill, 1971).
15 Maslow, Abraham H. "A Theory of Human Motivation," *Psychology Review* (July 1943), pp. 370–396.
16 Matsui, T.; and Terai, I. "A Cross-Cultural Study of the Validity of the Expectancy Theory of Work Motivation," *Journal of Applied Psychology,* vol. 60, no. 2 (1979), pp. 263–265.
17 McClelland, D. C.; Atkinson, J. W.; Clark, R. A.; and Lowell, E. L. *The Achievement Motive* (New York: Appleton-Century-Crofts, 1953).
18 McClelland, D. C.; and Burnham, D. H. "Power is the Great Motivator," *Harvard Business Review,* vol 54, no. 2, pp. 100–110.
19 McClelland, D. C. *The Achieving Society* (Princeton, N.J.: Van Nostrand, 1961).
20 O'Reilly, Charles A.; and Roberts, Karlene H. "Job Satisfaction Among Whites and Nonwhites," *Journal of Applied Psychology,* vol. 57, no. 3 (1973), pp. 295–299.
21 Reitz, H. J. "The Relative Importance of Five Categories of Needs Among Industrial Workers in Eight Countries," *Academy of Management Proceedings* (1975), pp. 270–273.
22 Reitz, Joseph; and Grof, Gene. *Similarities and Differences Among Mexican Workers, in Attitudes to Worker Motivation* (Bloomington, Ind.: Indiana University, 1973).

23 Sirota, David; and Greenwood, Michael J. "Understanding Your Overseas Work-force," *Harvard Business Review,* vol. 14 (January–February 1971), pp. 53–60.

24 Stephens, D.; Kedia, B.; and Ezell, D. "Managerial Need Structures in U.S. and Peruvian Industries," *Management International Review,* vol. 19 (1979), pp. 27–39.

25 Vroom, V. H. *Work and Motivation* (New York: John Wiley & Sons, 1964).

26 Vroom, V. H.; and Yetton, P. W. *Leadership and Decision Making* (Pittsburgh, Penn.: University of Pittsburgh Press, 1973).

27 Williams, L. K.; Whyte, W. F.; and Green, C. S. "Do Cultural Differences Affect Workers' Attitudes?" *Industrial Relations,* vol. 5 (1966), pp. 105–117.

Employee Work Attitudes and Management Practice in the U.S. and Japan: Evidence from a Large Comparative Survey

James R. Lincoln

What do we really know about the work motivation of the Japanese and the role of Japanese management practice in shaping it? How deeply rooted in the culture of Japan and the psyches of the Japanese people is the legendary commitment and the discipline of the Japanese labor force? How important are Japanese work patterns and the internal management of the Japanese firm for explaining the Japanese economic miracle, as compared with the macro forces of state guidance, *keiretsu* enterprise groupings, corporate strategy, and low-cost capital? If Japanese management practice does provide part of the explanation for the cooperation and productivity of the Japanese, does it only work with Japanese employees? That is to say, how transportable is Japanese management style: do overseas Japanese firms produce similar results with foreign workers? Do American and European firms that organize in "Japanese" fashion achieve the labor discipline, cooperation, and commitment that seem to characterize Japan?

Attempts to answer these and similar questions have filled the pages of the business press as well as scholarly journals in the nearly 8 years since the publication of *Theory Z* and *The Art of Japanese Management* marked the onset of Japanese management boom.[1] The quality of these accounts has ranged widely. Too many are ill-informed and opportunistic efforts to capitalize on the explosive demand for information on Japan and Japanese business. Others are thoughtful, incisive discussions by expert journalists, scholars, and consultants able to bring to bear on the issue rich experience from studying, living, and working in Japan. Notably absent until quite recently is much prominent commentary by the Japanese themselves, who, to a surprising extent, have followed the lead and absorbed the claims of Western observers of the Japanese management scene.[2]

Even the recent expert testimony of writers like Abegglen, Dore, and Vogel on Japanese organization and its lessons for the West is based much more on long

From the *California Management Review,* 32(1), 89–106. Copyright © 1989 by the Regents of the University of California. Reprinted by permission of The Regents.

personal experience, intuitive understanding, and generally "soft" journalistic research.[3] What does quantitative social science have to say about the contrasts in work motivation and worker productivity between Japan and the U.S.? Though the United States arguably has the world's largest, best-funded, and technically most sophisticated behavioral science community, surprisingly little of this research expertise has been aimed at a problem of critical contemporary importance to Americans: the nature, scope, and origins of the Japanese labor productivity advantage in manufacturing.

This article reviews a large survey research investigation of 106 factories in the U.S. (central Indiana) and Japan (Kanagawa Prefecture) and 8,302 of their employees. Between 1981 and 1983, my colleagues and I interviewed factory executives about the management style and organization of the plant and distributed questionnaires to representative samples of employees. To the best of our knowledge, the resulting data is the largest and most detailed body of survey information on American and Japanese factory workers and their employing organizations.

ARE WORK ATTITUDES DIFFERENT IN JAPAN AND THE U.S.?

The Japanese Are Less Satisfied . . .

A twofold question motivated our research: how do the work attitudes of Japanese manufacturing employees differ between Japan and the U.S.; and do those differences depend on the management and organization of the factory? Let's take the question of work attitudes first. We sought to measure through questionnaire items two attitude dimensions: job satisfaction and commitment to the company. Many would expect Japanese workers to score higher than Americans on both. The long hours, low absenteeism and turnover, the productivity and esprit de corps, the careers spent within a single company, the reluctance even to take time off for vacation—these are all well-documented patterns of Japanese worker behavior. Surely they suggest that job satisfaction and commitment to a particular company are extraordinarily high in Japan.

As Table 1 shows, however, what we initially found was quite different. If our survey data are to be believed, it appears that commitment to the company is essentially the same in our American and Japanese employee samples. The specific questionnaire items in the six-item factor-weighted scale likewise either show no difference or the Americans appear to give the "more committed" response. Is the much-touted loyalty of the Japanese employee, then, a myth? Does the stability and discipline of Japanese labor have no basis in the attitudes and values of Japanese workers? These results seemed so at odds with expectations and the impressions of previous scholars that we were quite taken aback.

On the other hand, Table 1 *does* show large country differences in the job satisfaction items, but the direction is *contrary* to expectations. American employees seem much more satisfied with their jobs than do the Japanese. We were not, in fact, surprised by this finding. Every prior survey contrasting Japanese and Western work attitudes has likewise found work satisfaction to be lowest among the Japanese.[4]

TABLE 1
DESCRIPTIVE STATISTICS FOR MEASURES OF
ORGANIZATIONAL COMMITMENT AND JOB SATISFACTION

	U.S. mean (SD)	Japan mean (SD)
Organizational Commitment Scale[a] (alpha = .75, U.S.; .79, Japan).	2.13(.469)	2.04 (.503)[b]
"I am willing to work harder than I have to in order to help this company succeed." (1 = strongly disagree, 5 = strongly agree)	3.91(.895)	3.44 (.983)[b]
"I would take any job in order to continue working for this company." (same codes)	3.12(1.14)	3.07 (1.13)
"My values and the values of this company are quite similar." (same codes)	3.15(1.06)	2.68 (.949)[b]
"I am proud to work for this company." (same codes)	3.70(.943)	3.51 (1.02)[b]
"I would turn down another job for more pay in order to stay with this company." (same codes)	2.71(1.17)	2.68 (1.08)
"I feel very little loyalty to this company." (1 = strongly agree, 5 = strongly disagree)	3.45(1.13)	3.40 (1.03)
Job Satisfaction Scale (alpha = .78, U.S.; .65, Japan).	1.54(.449)	.962 (.350)[b]
"All in all, how satisfied would you say you are with your job?" (0 = not at all, 4 = very)	2.95(1.12)	2.12 (1.06)[b]
"If a good friend of yours told you that he or she was interested in working at a job like yours at this company, what would you say?" (0 = would advise against it, 1 = would have second thoughts, 2 = would recommend it)	1.52(.690)	.909 (.673)[b]
"Knowing what you know now, if you had to decide all over again whether to take the job you now have, what would you decide?" (0 = would not take job again, 1 = would have some second thoughts, 2 = would take job again)	1.61(6.30)	.837 (.776)[b]
"How much does your job measure up to the kind of job you wanted when you first took it?" (0 = not what I wanted, 1 = somewhat, 2 = what I wanted)	1.20(.662)	.427 (.591)[b]

[a]Factor weighted composite of commitment (satisfaction) items. "Alpha" is Cronbach's measure of internal consistency reliability.
[b]Difference in means between countries significant at p < .001.

How are we to interpret these results? Any first-year MBA student knows that high job satisfaction does not spell high work motivation.[5] As Ronald Dore suggests, low job satisfaction in Japan may imply a restless striving for perfection, an ongoing quest for fulfillment of lofty work values and company goals.[6] By the same token, American observers have cautioned that the high percentages of the

U.S. workforce routinely reporting satisfaction with their jobs may be more cause for concern than complacency.[7] It may signal low expectations and aspirations, a willingness to settle for meager job rewards, and a preoccupation with leisure-time pursuits.[8]

Another possibility, of course, is that the Japan-U.S. differences in work attitudes we found are due, not to real cultural contrasts in work motives and values, but to measurement biases.[9] Many would argue that a distinctly American impulse is to put the best face on things, to be upbeat and cheerful, to appear in control and successful even when uncertainty is high and the future looks bleak. The Japanese, it appears, bias their assessments in the opposite direction. From the Japanese mother who turns aside praise of her child's piano playing with: *"ie, mada heta desu!"* (no, it is still bad) to the Japanese politicians who, despite Japan's booming economy, persist in protesting the country's weak and dependent posture in world affairs—the Japanese seem to color their evaluations of nearly everything with a large dose of pessimism, humility, and understatement.

. . . But More Committed.

In order to better understand the country differences in our sample's work attitudes, we estimated a statistical simultaneous equations model which assumed that satisfaction and commitment are each caused by the other (and by other variables as well). The results showed that commitment to the company is strongly determined by job satisfaction but the reverse relation is weak to nonexistent.[10] Moreover, with the causal reciprocity thus statistically controlled, we found satisfaction still lower in Japan but commitment to the company proved substantially higher. Our initial impression of no commitment difference, it appeared, was due to our earlier failure to adjust for the very large gap in reported job satisfaction. The resulting picture of Japanese work attitudes as combining low job satisfaction and high organizational commitment is not inconsistent with what some theories hold to be a state of strong work motivation. We thus took this evidence as support for our hypothesis that the discipline of the Japanese work force does have some basis in the work attitudes of Japanese employees.

WORK ATTITUDES AND JAPANESE-STYLE ORGANIZATION

What then about the other questions we raised—particularly the extent to which management and organization have something to do with Japan-U.S. differences in work attitudes? Much has been written on the distinctiveness of Japanese management and its power to motivate work effort and loyalty among employees. While our survey could not address all the ways the Japanese firm is thought to be successful at mobilizing its human assets, we were nonetheless able to examine several such hypotheses.

Seniority Systems Breed Workforce Commitment

First, consider the age and seniority of the worker. The pervasive age and seniority-grading (*nenko*) of Japanese organizations is a much discussed and documented phenomenon.[11] Once maligned as arational and feudalistic, more and more economic and organizational theory has come to recognize the inner logic to seniority systems, particularly in work settings where skills are hard to measure and are peculiar to the firm.[12] Moreover, part of the motivational logic to an employment system that couples permanent employment with seniority compensation is that it builds loyalty and identification with the company's goals. With time spent in the organization individuals accumulate investments and incur opportunity costs. To realize a fair return on these investments they must stick with the company and work to maximize its success. Moreover, the psychological phenomenon of cognitive dissonance—the need to seek congruence or equilibrium between one's acts and one's cognitions—leads people to justify to themselves their past organizational investments by embracing the company's values and goals as their own.

Younger Japanese are much more likely to share American-style values of leisure, consumption, and affluence—which evokes endless fretting by Japanese elders over its dire implications for Japan's future productivity and economic growth.

Our survey found, as previous studies had, that age and seniority are strong predictors of company commitment and job satisfaction. Moreover, we found pervasive evidence that these and other work attitudes were more age-dependent in Japan. Part of the reason, it appears, is that rewards and opportunities are more likely to be explicitly tied to age and seniority than in the American workplace. Another reason has less to do with age or seniority per se than with differences among generations. Given Japan's rapid postwar social change, older Japanese are apt to have the scarcity- and production-mentality typical of populations in the early stages of economic development. Younger Japanese are much more likely to share American-style values of leisure, consumption, and affluence. The latter fact evokes endless fretting by Japanese elders over the erosion of traditional values and its dire implications for Japan's future productivity and economic growth.

Strong Social Bonds Foster Positive Work Attitudes

One of the very distinctive features of Japanese work organization is the cohesiveness of work groups and the strong social bonds that develop between superiors and subordinates.[13] Our survey findings underscore these patterns. The Japanese employees in our sample reported an average of more than two close friends on the job, while the Americans averaged fewer than one. Moreover, the much-noted Japanese practice of *tsukiai* (work group socializing over food and drink) appears in our finding that Japanese employees were far more likely than Americans to get together after hours with workmates and supervisors. Our study found that employees enmeshed in such networks of coworker relationships, whether Japanese or American, had more positive attitudes toward the company and the job. The clear implication in that a rise in the cohesion of the U.S. workplace to the level typical of Japanese firms would help to narrow the U.S. "commitment gap" with Japan.

There is still the question of whether work group cohesion in the Japanese company is an outcome of rational management efforts at job and organizational design. The alternative interpretation is that Japanese people are simply culturally inclined to cluster into tight-knit cliques.[14] The cultural explanation has many advocates, and certainly a strong case can be made that Japanese values motivate people to bind themselves to groups. On the other side is all the evidence that the Japanese workplace is organized in ways that seem consciously aimed at fostering enterprise community.

AUTHORITY AND STATUS HIERARCHIES

Are Japanese Hierarchies "Flat?"

A number of observers have pointed to the shape of the management pyramid in Japanese companies as an example of organizational architecture whose logic is that of fostering commitment to the firm. While American executives and consultants commonly allude (often as a rationale for middle-management reductions at home) to the lean and flat hierarchies of Japanese firms,[15] most scholars generally agree that finely graded hierarchies and narrow spans of control are typical of Japanese organization.[16]

Japanese companies are on the average smaller, more specialized to particular industries, and less likely to use the decentralized, multidivisional structures typical of large, diversified U.S. firms.[17] These traits imply smaller corporate staffs and economies in the deployment of middle-level functional managers. But within a particular plant or business unit, one tends to find levels proliferating, as well as status rankings (based largely on seniority) which bear little direct relation to decision making and responsibility.

Does the shape of Japanese managerial hierarchies play a role in promoting workforce discipline, integration, and commitment? A number of thoughtful observers believe that they do. A finely layered management pyramid implies opportunities for steady progression up long career paths, a critical factor in motivation when employees expect to spend their working lives within a single firm. Status differentiation also works to avert the polarization and alienation, common in U.S. and British manufacturing, when a rigid class division is drawn between homogeneous "management" and "labor" groups. Japanese hierarchies incorporate many small steps which break up this homogeneity and serve as career ladders. Yet the inequality in status and reward between peak management and production rank-and-file is typically much smaller than in comparably-sized U.S. firms.[18] To many observers, this kind of structure figures importantly in the company-wide community and commitment for which the Japanese company is renowned.

Our survey of 51 Japanese factories and 55 American plants showed the Japanese organizations, despite their smaller mean size (461 vs. 571 employees), averaging 5.5 management levels compared with 4.9 for the American plants.

The samples did not differ in average first-line supervisor's span of control, but we did find some evidence in the Japanese plants of more organizational subunits for the same number of employees; a pattern indicative of smaller spans of control.

Do Flat Hierarchies Produce Positive Work Attitudes?

Japanese plants may have taller hierarchies, but *in both countries* plants with more levels proved to have less committed and satisfied employees.[19] This was the only instance where an organizational design feature typical of U.S. manufacturing appeared to have the motivational advantage. And even here there were some indications that the Japanese approach had merit. We found clear and consistent evidence across a large number of indicators that work attitudes, behaviors, and relations were far less determined by the employee's status position than in the U.S. As we argued above, this is part of the motivational logic of a finely graded hierarchy—to blur the boundaries and reduce the distance between echelons and hence the potential for conflict.

Do Narrow Spans of Control Mean Domineering Supervisors?

Another highly distinctive feature of Japanese authority hierarchies is the nature of supervision and the quality of the superior-subordinate relationship. Rather than bosses exercising direct authority and issuing commands to subordinate employees, Japanese supervisors seem to function as counselor and confidante to their work groups, building communication and cohesion with a minimum of direct, authoritarian control.[20] In sharp contrast to American workers who generally favor an arm's-length, strictly business, low-intensity relationship with their supervisors, workforce surveys in Japan regularly turn up evidence that Japanese employees prefer a paternalistic, diffuse, and personal supervisory style.[21]

Our study revealed a number of differences in Japanese and U.S. patterns of supervision.[22] The Japanese were much more likely to get together socially with supervisors outside of work. This, of course, is part of *tsukiai,* the Japanese practice of after hours socializing with workgroups. The Japanese were also much less likely than the American respondents to report that their supervisors: "*let them alone unless they asked for help.*"[23] Moreover, such contact with supervisors raised the morale of the Japanese employees but lowered that of the Americans. Finally, we found clear evidence in the American sample that narrow supervisory spans of control reduced commitment and satisfaction. This was not the case in Japan. It appears that narrow spans in the American workplace have a connotation, absent in Japan, of "close and domineering supervision."

These findings paint a consistent picture: frequent supervisor-subordinate interactions have a positive quality in Japanese work settings which is missing in the U.S. While American manufacturing employees keep their distance from supervisors, Japanese employees seek such contact and through it develop stronger bonds to the work group and the organization as a whole.

DECISION-MAKING STRUCTURES

Japanese Organizations Are Centralized but Participatory . . .

Japanese decision-making styles are commonly characterized as participatory, consensus-seeking, and "bottom-up."[24] At the management level, they involve less formal delegation of authority to individual managers and more informal networking (*nemawashi*) to draw people into the decision process. The ironic result is that the formal structure of Japanese decision making appears quite centralized. High-level executives bear at least symbolic responsibility for many decisions which, in U.S. firms, are typically delegated.[25]

The *ringi* system exemplifies this pattern. A middle-level manager drafts a document proposing a course of action (*ringi-sho*). It then circulates up through the hierarchy, acquiring the "chops" (personal stamps) of other managers symbolizing their participation in the decision and willingness to commit to it.

At the shop- or office-floor level, participation operates through small group activities such as quality circles, production teams, and high-responsibility systems that hold workers accountable for quality, minor maintenance, and clean-up in the conduct of their tasks.[26]

We measured decision making in our Japanese and U.S. plants in three ways. First, we used a modification of the standard Aston scale of centralization.[27] For each of 37 standard decision-items, the chief executive of the plant was asked to report the hierarchical level where: the formal authority for the decision was located; and where, in practice, the decision was usually made. Averaged over the 37 decisions, we found strong evidence that, compared with U.S. plants, authority was more centralized in the Japanese plants but there was also more *de facto* participation by lower ranks.

Secondly, in the Japanese plants, we measured the prevalence of *ringi* by asking whether, for each of the 37 decisions, the *ringi* system was used. Averaged across the 51 Japanese plants, our informants reported that the *ringi* method was applied to approximately one-third of this set of decisions.

Finally, we measured quality circle participation from our questionnaire survey of employees. We found that 81% of the Japanese plants had quality circle programs in which 94% of the employees of those plants participated; 62% of the U.S. plants had circles and 44% of their employees were members.

Our survey results are thus consistent with the impressions of more casual observers: Japanese organizations centralize authority but decentralize participation in decisions. The *ringi* system is used to a substantial degree in decision making in Japanese factories. And quality circle participating is close to universal in Japanese plants, though it is reasonably widespread in American plants as well.[28]

. . . A Pattern Which Produces Positive Work Attitudes in Both Countries.

The question then becomes: do Japanese decision-making practices help shape the work attitudes of Japanese employees? As with work group cohesion, the motivational payoff to participation has been a central theme in management theory, at least since the Hawthorne studies. We found *in both countries* that organizations which in Japanese fashion coupled formal centralization with de facto participation had more committed and satisfied employees.

Why? This outcome fits the general proposition that Japanese-style management works in the U.S. as well as in Japan. But it is not obvious why this particular configuration should have greater motivational value than one in which formal and *de facto* authority are aligned and both decentralized. Our reasoning is that formal decentralization (as the Aston scale measures it) taps delegation of specialized decision-making roles to lower management positions. First- and second-line supervisors in American manufacturing commonly enjoy a good deal of power over narrow jurisdictional areas. Yet that kind of delegation opens up few opportunities for participation either by the rank-and-file *or* by supervisors in other areas.

When formal authority stays high in the organization but widespread participation occurs, the power of lower management is reduced and decision making becomes the diffuse, participatory kind typical of Japanese organization, not the individualistic, compartmentalized delegation found in American firms. Clark has argued that Japanese middle managers are delegated so little formal authority that they have no choice but to negotiate with their employees in order to get things done.[29] In his view, the networking and consensus-seeking found in Japanese organizations are a direct response to their centralized authority structures.

Ringi and Quality Circles Also Produce Positive Work Attitudes

What about the specific participatory practices of *ringi* and quality circles? Do they also foster job satisfaction and commitment to a company? Our data suggest that they do. In the sample of Japanese plants, we found a statistically significant positive association between a plant's use of the *ringi* system and the employee's commitment to the firm. This was a noteworthy finding, for the majority of our employee sample were rank-and-file people who would not ordinarily be involved in the *ringi* process. The use of *ringi* is probably symptomatic of a generally participatory decision-making climate which has motivational value for workers and managers alike.

There are good reasons to suppose that quality circle programs are quite different in the U.S. and Japan. Owing in large part to the centralized oversight of the Japan Union of Scientists and Engineers, quality circle programs in Japanese industry generally comprise a much more uniform set of practices than in the United States. They require a high level of technical training on the part of production workers and a substantial commitment of resources on the part of the firm. American quality circle programs, with much less centralized guidance from professional and managerial bodies, are generally a hodgepodge. Few such programs exhibit the rigor and structure of Japanese practice.

Yet quality circle participation proved to be positively associated with job satisfaction and organizational commitment in both the U.S. and Japan. Moreover, the effect was stronger in the U.S. sample. The reason may in part lie in the later inception of American quality circles which give them a novelty value that has worn off the more established Japanese programs. Recent observers of Japanese quality circle programs have commented on growing problems of maintaining worker interest and motivation.[30]

In summary, our evidence, with rather remarkable consistency, suggests that Japanese-style decision-making arrangements (quality circles, *ringi,* centralized authority combined with dispersed participation), have positive effects on the work attitudes of Japanese and American employees alike. The fact that such arrangements are much more prevalent in Japanese industry suggests a partial explanation for the Japanese edge in labor discipline and commitment.

COMPANY-SPONSORED EMPLOYEE SERVICES

Yet another distinctive feature of the Japanese employment system is the large bundle of services, programs, and social activities that Japanese firms sponsor and provide for their employees. Such services figure significantly in the traditional portrait of Japanese "paternalism" in industry.[31] The array of programs, activities, classes, ceremonies, peptalks, calisthenics, songs, and other practices that Japanese firms employ in the quest of building community and commitment among the workforce is downright dizzying.[32]

How effective are such programs as motivational devices? Would more ceremonies, company picnics, sports teams, newsletters, and the like create a stronger bond between the U.S. manufacturing worker and the firm? Or, as many Western observers seem to think, are individualistic British and American workers likely to be contemptuous of overt management gestures at creating a happy corporate family?[33] Once again, a case can be made that employee services in Japan are a reflection, not a cause, of Japanese work values and attitudes. Cultural and historical forces have bred within companies an inclusive enterprise community one sign of which is a profusion of company-planned activities and services.

Individualistic or not, the Americans in our sample appeared to react every bit as favorably as the Japanese to company-sponsored employee-oriented services.

Still, there are some indications in the historical record that Japanese employers set upon welfarism (along with permanent employment and other labor practices) as a rational instrument for curbing labor militancy and creating, in a time of labor shortage, a more docile and dependent workforce.[34] Its timing coincided with the era of "welfare capitalism" in the United States (the 1920s), which large firms ushered in for similar purposes of managing an unruly labor force and appeasing the growing ranks of muckrakers and progressivist reformers. Why welfarism seemed to "stick" in Japan but faded in the U.S., at least until the postwar period, may be due to several forces: the milder impact on Japan of the Great Depression (which in the U.S. led many firms to jettison expensive welfare programs); the heightened stress on industrial discipline produced by militarist and imperialistic policies; and, for cultural reasons, the greater receptivity of Japanese workers to corporate paternalism and the principle of an enterprise family.[35]

Employee Services Are More Abundant in Japan . . .

Our strategy for measuring the level of welfare, social, and ceremonial activity was a relatively simple one. We inquired of our informants in each plant whether a list of nine company-sponsored activities/services were present. The list included: outside training, inhouse training, an employee newsletter, company ceremonies, company-sponsored sports and recreation programs, new employee orientation programs, an employee handbook, regular plant-wide information-sharing/"pep-talk" sessions, and a morning calisthenics program.

Our hypothesis was that such programs are more prevalent in Japanese firms. That proved to be the case for most of them, specifically: in-house training (by a small margin), formal ceremonies (present in all Japanese plants), sports and recreational activities, formal orientation programs, peptalks, and morning exercise sessions (nonexistent in the U.S. plants we studied). On the other hand, the American plants were more likely to encourage and support enrollment in high school and college coursework (by a large margin) and (by a small one) to provide employees with a company handbook. We found no difference between Japanese and U.S. plants in the likelihood of publishing a company newspaper. The indices proposed by summing these items had acceptable internal consistency reliability levels of .60 in the Japanese sample and .62 in the U.S. sample, indicating that these services tended to cluster in the same firms.

. . . But Raise Commitment and Satisfaction in Both Countries.

When we estimated the effect of the services index on employee commitment to the company and satisfaction with the job, we found almost identical positive associations in the two countries. Individualistic or not, the Americans in our sample appeared to react every bit as favorably as the Japanese to company-sponsored employee-oriented services. Once again the lesson seems clear: were such services in American industry to rise to the level typical of Japanese manufacturers, we should witness a corresponding shrinkage in the Japan-U.S. commitment gap.

ENTERPRISE UNIONS

Finally we consider the structure of unions and their implications for employee work attitudes. A legacy of the postwar Occupation reforms, Japanese unions are organized on a per-enterprise basis, concentrated in the largest firms, and combined into weak federations at higher levels.[36] They organize all regular (blue- and white-collar) employees, up to second-line supervision. Much debate has centered on whether Japanese enterprise unions are truly independent labor organizations in the Western sense. Some writers see them as highly dependent upon and easily coopted by the company, avoiding confrontations to advance their members' interests and working to build commitment to the firm. Hanami expresses this view well:

> There exists a climate of collusion . . . between the employers and the union representing the majority of employees . . . Basically the relationship is one of patronage and dependence, though the unions frequently put on an outward show of radical militancy in their utterances and behavior. [Moreover] the president of an enterprise union is in effect the company's senior executive in charge of labor relations.[37]

Yet other observers argue that, despite the constraints posed by dependence on a single firm, Japanese unions bargain hard on wage and benefit issues and have effectively coordinated their militancy in the annual Spring offensives (*shunto*) which present groups of employers with a set of unified wage demands.[38] A study by Koshiro concludes that union militancy has been an important factor behind rising aggregate wage levels in the postwar Japanese economy.[39]

U.S. Unions Foster Negative Work Attitudes, Japanese Unions Do Not

What, however, about the impact of unionism on employee work attitudes? Much survey research shows that U.S. union members report *lower* job satisfaction than do nonunion employees.[40] This pattern seems consistent with the goals of American union strategy: to aggregate grievances, foster an adversarial industrial relations climate, and drive a wedge between the worker and the firm.

Yet unionized workers are less likely to quit their jobs than nonunion employees.[41] One interpretation is that "true" dissatisfaction is probably no higher among union members but that the union politicizes the employment relation and encourages workers to inflate and publicize their grievances. In the nonunion workplace, by contrast, workers have no such vehicle for airing dissatisfactions and therefore act on them by simply terminating their relationship with the firm. This view, grounded in Albert Hirschman's "exit-voice-loyalty" model,[42] is also supported by evidence that grievance rates are higher in union shops even when objective working conditions are no worse.[43]

We would not anticipate finding similar union effects on the work attitudes of Japanese unionists. Indeed, a reasonable argument can be made for the opposite prediction: that enterprise unions build support for and loyalty to the company—that they are, in effect, one more Japanese management device for building motivation and commitment.

Our data do not show that. We find no statistically significant effect of union membership on job satisfaction, although we do find a slight tendency for company commitment to be lower in union plants. Thus, it does not appear that Japanese unions are in some sense instruments of a proactive policy of building discipline and dedication in the workforce. On the other hand, what we find in the

U.S. still poses a decisive contrast with the Japan case. Consistent with other research, our survey produced strong and clear evidence that unions in U.S. factories give rise to sharply more negative employee work attitudes. Holding constant a large number of variables pertaining to the pay, status, job, skills, and gender of the worker, plus the size, age, and technology of the plant, company commitment and job satisfaction in our Indiana sample were markedly lower among the unionized plants.

The implications appear to be as follows. Japanese unions are not the agents of management that some critics hold them to be. But neither do they present the challenge to harmonious labor-management relations or high workforce morale that U.S. unions historically have posed. Since enterprise-specific unions are generally absent from the U.S. economy, we have no evidence on how they might perform in an American setting.

Some circumstantial evidence from the New United Motors Manufacturing, Inc. (NUMMI) plant in Fremont, California (the Toyota-GM joint venture), suggests, however, that U.S. workers may react very well to Japanese-style collective bargaining.[44] The union at NUMMI is a local of the United Auto Workers, but it made a number of concessions to the company in the area of work rules and job classifications. In turn, the company provides the union with space in the plant, shares information extensively, and enlists the cooperation of the union in enforcing policy with respect to absenteeism, quality, safety, and other issues. Though a small dissident movement has been formed, the level of labor-management cooperation and the productivity and discipline of the workforce at NUMMI has few parallels in the American auto industry. The special relationship between the company and the UAW local, reminiscent of the interdependence between enterprise unions and firms in Japan, is clearly part of the reason.

DISCUSSION

What conclusions can be drawn from our survey evidence on Japanese and U.S. work attitudes and the role of plant organization and management practice in shaping them? First, though a preliminary reading of the data sends mixed signals, the Japanese employee's combination of high commitment coupled with low satisfaction is in line with the hypothesis of a highly motivated Japanese workforce. Second, we found quite consistent evidence that "Japanese-style" management and employment methods, whether practiced by Japanese or U.S. plants, produce very similar gains in employee work attitudes (see the summary of findings in Table 2). These include cohesive work groups, quality circles, participatory (but not delegated) decision making, and company-sponsored services. The fact that such practices are more widely deployed in Japanese than in U.S. industry does suggest they may provide part (though we would hardly argue all) of the reason for the Japan-U.S. "commitment gap" in manufacturing.

Other management and employment practices we examined are not directly comparable across countries and our results cannot therefore be interpreted in this way. They nonetheless testify that tangible differences in Japanese and U.S.

TABLE 2
DO "JAPANESE"-STYLE MANAGEMENT PRACTICES PRODUCE COMPANY COMMITMENT
AND JOB SATISFACTION IN JAPAN *and* IN THE U.S.?

"Japanese" management/employment practice	Impact on work attitudes
Long-term employment and age/seniority grading	Positive in both countries[a]
Cohesive work groups	Positive in both countries
Dense supervision; close supervisor-subordinate contact	Positive in Japan; negative in U.S.
"Tall," finely-layered hierarchies	Negative in both countries; but contributes to management-labor consensus in Japan
Formal centralization/de facto decentralization of decision-making	Positive in both countries
Ringi system	Positive in Japan[b]
Quality circle participation	Positive in both countries
Welfare services	Positive in both countries
Unions (enterprise-specific in Japan; industry/occupation-specific in the U.S.)	Weak negative to null in Japan; strongly negative in U.S.

[a]In the sense that psychological attachment to the firm is found in both countries to rise with age and seniority.
[b]No comparable measure from the U.S. survey.

management translate into competitive advantages for Japanese firms in the area of employee motivation and cooperative industrial relations. In both countries, rising age and seniority engender increasingly positive work attitudes. As career employment and seniority promotion and compensation are more central to Japanese than U.S. employment practice, Japanese companies are better able to capitalize on these motivational returns. The Japanese system of enterprise unions offers collective bargaining in an atmosphere of mutual dependence and cooperation, and, in sharp contrast to U.S. unions, does little to foster tension between the worker and the firm.

Our findings seem to contradict the argument that Japanese management styles are only effective with employees who hold Japanese-type work values. The credibility of this view, which has much face validity, is also undercut by the apparent success of Japanese manufacturing firms in managing their U.S. operations and their American employees. Japanese management is no panacea, and mindless attempts to copy from the Japanese are doubtless doomed to failure. Still, our study strongly suggests that Japanese management practices are in part responsible for the work motivation of Japanese employees and that similar practices in the American workplace yield similar returns. Careful attempts on the part of U.S. managers to move in the direction of Japanese organizational design and human resource management may well yield some long-run competitive payoffs for American manufacturing.

REFERENCES

1 William G. Ouchi, *Theory Z: How American Business Can Meet the Japanese Challenge* (Reading, MA: Addison-Wesley, 1981); Richard Tanner Pascale and Anthony G. Athos, *The Art of Japanese Management: Applications for American Managers* (New York, NY: Simon and Schuster, 1981).

2 But see, Masahiko Aoki, "Risk Sharing in the Corporate Group," in Masahiko Aoki, ed., *The Economic Analysis of the Japanese Firm* (Amsterdam: North-Holland, 1984) pp. 259–264; Taishiro Shirai, ed., *Contemporary Industrial Relations in Japan* (Madison, WI: University of Wisconsin Press, 1983).

3 James C. Abegglen and George Stalk, Jr., *Kaisha: The Japanese Corporation* (New York, NY: Basic Books, 1985); Ronald Dore, *Flexible Rigidities* (Stanford, CA: Stanford University Press, 1986); Ronald Dore, *Taking Japan Seriously* (Stanford, CA: Stanford University Press, 1987); Ezra F. Vogel, *Comeback* (New York, NY: Simon and Schuster, 1985).

4 See the review in James R. Lincoln and Kerry McBride, "Japanese Industrial Organization in Comparative Perspective," *Annual Review of Sociology,* 13 (1987): 289–312.

5 See, for example, Charles Perrow, *Complex Organizations: A Critical Essay,* 3rd edition (Glenview, IL: Scott, Foresman, 1986).

6 Ronald Dore, *British Factory, Japanese Factory: The Origins of Diversity in Industrial Relations* (Berkeley, CA: University of California Press, 1973).

7 Robert Blauner, "Work Satisfaction and Industrial Trends in Modern Society," in Walter Galenson and Seymour Martin Lipset, eds., *Labor and Trade Unionism* (New York, NY: John Wiley, 1960), pp. 339–360; HEW Report, *Work in America* (Cambridge, MA: MIT Press, 1973).

8 John H. Goldthorpe, David Lockwood, F. Bechhofer, and J. Platt, *The Affluent Worker: Industrial Attitudes and Behavior* (London: Cambridge University Press, 1968).

9 Dore, 1973, op. cit.

10 James R. Lincoln and Arne L. Kalleberg, "Work Organization and Workforce Commitment: A Study of Plants and Employees in the U.S. and Japan," *American Sociological Review,* 50 (1985): 738–760; James R. Lincoln and Arne L. Kalleberg, *Culture, Control, and Commitment: A Study of Work Organization and Work Attitudes in the U.S. and Japan* (Cambridge: Cambridge University Press, 1989).

11 Kazuo Koike, "Internal Labor Markets: Workers in Large Firms," in Taishiro Shirai, ed., op. cit., pp. 29–62.

12 Edward Lazear, "Why Is There Mandatory Retirement?" *Journal of Political Economy,* 87 (1979): 1261–1284.

13 Robert E. Cole, "Permanent Employment in Japan: Facts and Fantasies," *Industrial and Labor Relations Review,* 26 (1972): 612–630; Thomas P. Rohlen, *For Harmony and Strength* (Berkeley, CA: University of California Press, 1974).

14 See, for example, Chie Nakane, *Japanese Society* (Berkeley, CA: University of California Press, 1970).

15 Thomas J. Peters and Robert H. Waterman, Jr., *In Search of Excellence: Lessons from America's Best-Run Companies* (New York, NY: Harper and Row, 1982).

16 Michael Y. Yoshino, *Japan's Managerial System: Tradition and Innovation* (Cambridge, MA: MIT Press, 1968); Dore, 1973, op. cit.; Richard Tanner Pascale, "Zen and the Art of Management," *Harvard Business Review,* 56 (1978): 153–162.

17 Rodney C. Clark, *The Japanese Company* (New Haven, CT: Yale, 1979).

18 Abegglen and Stalk, op. cit.

19 Lincoln and Kalleberg, 1985, op. cit.

20 Dore, 1973, op. cit.; Cole, 1972, op. cit.

21 Robert M. Marsh and Hiroshi Mannari, *Modernization and the Japanese Factory* (Princeton, NJ: Princeton University Press, 1977); Arthur M. Whitehill and Shinichi Takezawa, *The Other Worker: A Comparative Study of Industrial Relations in the U.S. and Japan* (Honolulu, HI: East-West Center Press, 1968).

22 Lincoln and Kalleberg, 1989, op. cit., Chapter 4.

23 Pascale and Athos, op. cit., p. 183.

24 Ouchi, op. cit.

25 Ezra F. Vogel, *Modern Japanese Organization and Decision-Making* (Berkeley, CA: University of California Press, 1975); Yoshino, op. cit.

26 Robert E. Cole, *Work, Mobility, and Participation* (Berkeley, CA: University of California Press, 1979).

27 D.S. Pugh, D.J. Hickson, C.R. Hinings, and C. Turner, "Dimensions of Organization Structure," *Administrative Science Quarterly,* 13 (1968): 65–91; James R. Lincoln, Mitsuyo Hanada, and Kerry McBride, "Organizational Structures in Japanese and U.S. Manufacturing," *Administrative Science Quarterly,* 31 (1986): 338–364.

28 Robert E. Cole, *Strategies for Learning: Small Group Activities in American, Japanese, and Swedish Industry* (Berkeley, CA: University of California Press, 1989).

29 Clark, op. cit.

30 Kunio Odaka, "The Japanese Style of Workers' Self-Management: From the Voluntary to the Autonomous Group," in Velnko Rus, Akihiro Ishikawa, and Thomas Woodhouse, eds., *Employment and Participation* (Tokyo: Chuo University Press, 1982), p. 323.

31 John W. Bennett and Iwao Ishino, *Paternalism in the Japanese Economy* (Minneapolis, MN: University of Minnesota Press, 1963).

32 See, for example, Dore, 1973, op. cit.; Rohlen, op. cit.; Marsh and Mannari, op. cit.

33 See, for example, Goldthorpe et al., op. cit.

34 Cole, 1979, op. cit.

35 Yoshino, op. cit.

36 H. Kawada, "Workers and Their Organizations," In Bernard Karsh and Solomon B. Levine, eds., *Workers and Employers in Japan* (Tokyo: University of Tokyo Press), pp. 217–268; Shirai, op. cit.

37 Tadashi Hanami, *Labor Relations in Japan Today* (Tokyo: Kodansha International, Ltd., 1979), p. 56.

38 Jean Bounine-Cabale, Ronald Dore, and Kari Tapiola, "Flexibility in Japanese Labor Markets," Report of the OECD Team, 1988.

39 Kazutoshi Koshiro, "The Quality of Life in Japanese Factories," in Taishiro Shirai, ed., *Contemporary Industrial Relations in Japan* (1983), pp. 63–88.

40 Richard B. Freeman and James L. Medoff, *What Do Unions Do?* (New York, NY: Basic Books, 1984), Chapter 9.

41 Ibid., p. 139.

42 Albert O. Hirschman, *Exit, Voice, and Loyalty* (Cambridge, MA: Harvard University Press, 1970).

43 Freeman and Medoff, op. cit., p. 139.

44 Clair Brown and Michael Reich, "When Does Union-Management Cooperation Work: A Look at NUMMI and GM-Van Nuys," in Daniel J.B. Mitchell and Jane Wildhorn, eds., *Can California Be Competitive and Caring?* (Los Angeles, CA: Institute of Industrial Relations, University of California, 1989), pp. 115–147.

Motivation in Chinese Industrial Enterprises

Rosalie L. Tung

In Tung (1981), the ways that Chinese industrial enterprises motivate their workers were analyzed according to the paradigm advanced by Katz and Kahn (1978): rule enforcement, external rewards, and internalized motivation. Since then, China has embarked on a multitude of reforms designed to spur economic productivity and performance to advance the goals of the Four Modernizations, including developments in industry, agriculture, military defense, and science and technology. These included the restructuring of the administrative system in factories, more specifically the division of responsibility between the party secretary and the factory director; the introduction of stock ownership plans to engender greater employee commitment; the reform of the wage and bonus systems along the principle of "to each according to his work" to increase productivity; the introduction of a labor contract system to allow enterprises the right to hire and fire to promote economic efficiency; and the implementation of laws and regulations to facilitate joint venture operations with foreign entities to enable the importation of advanced technology and management know-how. In short, China has become one vast social laboratory where different organizational and motivational policies and practices are experimented with to determine their impact on organizational efficiency and effectiveness.

In this paper, the focus will be on the reforms that have taken place in the motivational devices employed by Chinese industrial enterprises to increase worker productivity. Essentially, the country still relies on the three motivational patterns identified by Katz and Kahn. The primary difference is one of emphasis. The emphasis of one dimension over another has oscillated with the political vicissitudes over the past decade. In periods of greater political openness, external rewards were paramount. During times of political retrenchment, ideology and internalized motivation have assumed a greater role.

To understand and analyze the motivational patterns and reforms in Chinese industrial enterprises, it is important to discuss the types and nature of industrial enterprises in the country.

TYPES AND NATURE OF CHINESE INDUSTRIAL ENTERPRISES

Beginning in 1978–1979, Chinese industrial enterprises can be classified into four major categories:

1 *State-owned enterprises.* These constitute the industrial backbone of China's economy. In the past, state-owned enterprises were considered superior and hence were emphasized. With the reforms, alternative means of ownership were

This paper was written especially for this volume.

encouraged. State-owned enterprises accounted for 83 percent of the country's industrial output in 1975, decreased to 74 percent in 1983, and 70 percent in 1988.

2 *Collectively owned enterprises in cities, townships, and rural areas.* Under this type of ownership, "the means of production and products belong to the laborers of the collectives concerned." In 1975, collectively owned enterprises accounted for 17 percent of the country's total industrial output. This share increased to 25 percent in 1984.

3 *Individually owned enterprises.* The 1978 Chinese Constitution authorized the establishment of the individual economy. In 1985, there were approximately 11.6 million individually owned enterprises employing 18 million workers and accounting for 0.2 percent of China's total industrial output.

4 *Other economic forms, such as joint ventures with foreign entities.* In 1980, other economic forms comprised approximately 0.6 percent of the country's industrial output; this share increased to 1.2 percent in 1984 (*Statistical Yearbook of China,* various years).

Labor management practices vary across these four categories of industrial enterprises. For example, enterprises with foreign investment had the right to recruit employees through examination and other selection procedures. They also had the right to fire workers. Collectively owned enterprises also enjoyed these rights and could recruit workers according to production needs. Furthermore, enterprises with foreign investment and collectively owned enterprises had more flexibility with regard to the distribution of wages and bonuses.

In this paper, the focus will be on the motivational devices adopted by state-owned enterprises for two reasons. One, state-owned enterprises still comprise the bulk of China's industrial economy. Two, state-owned enterprises, compared with other categories of ownership, appear to operate at lower levels of efficiency. In an investigative report of various types of ownerships in several major cities and townships, the Chinese Industrial Economy Association found that collectively owned enterprises and foreign investment enterprises, which were responsible for their own profits and losses, generally showed greater "rigor and vitality," whereas state-owned enterprises were often deficient in "competition and risk." Furthermore, the association found that underemployment was prevalent in state-owned enterprises. They estimated that approximately 20 to 30 percent of the workers and staff in these factories were redundant. The association attributed this sad state of affairs to the fact that state-owned enterprises still operated as "appendages of administrative departments." For this reason, employees in state-owned enterprises were reluctant to undertake risks to forge ahead (*Renmin Ribao,* 1988). According to Chamberlain, state-owned enterprises were essentially "governed by administrative rather than economic imperative" (1987, p. 634). Consequently, efficiency and profitability were not the critical concerns of the factory administration. Rather "hoarding and hiding resources were rational forms of behavior, serving to consolidate and expand a given unit's bureaucratic power." In 1986, it was estimated that roughly one-third of the state-owned enterprises failed to meet their production targets ("Third wave," 1988).

PATTERNS OF MOTIVATION

As noted earlier, the three motivational patterns identified by Katz and Kahn (1978) are still in vogue in Chinese industrial enterprises. These are (1) rule enforcement, whereby organizational members accept role prescriptions and organizational directives because of their legitimacy; (2) external rewards, whereby incentives tied to desired behavioral outcomes are instrumental in achieving specific rewards; and (3) internalized motivation, whereby organizational goals are internalized and become part of the individual's own value system.

Rule Enforcement

Compared to their western counterparts, Chinese industrial personnel—managers, technicians, and workers (the former two are referred to as "cadres" in China)—are given exact and detailed prescriptions of what is expected of them as members of the factory, workshop, or work unit. Since 1978, the government has granted factories greater powers of decision-making autonomy. In 1984, state-owned enterprises were granted 10 rights. The most salient ones as they relate to workers' motivation were (1) the right to enter into labor contracts with employees, (2) the right of the factory director to manage production functions with minimal interference from the party committee attached to each enterprise, and (3) the right of the enterprise to retain profits after paying taxes (Laaksonen, 1988). Each of these rights is examined briefly.

Labor Contract System In the past, employees in state-owned enterprises were protected by the system of lifetime employment. This was referred to as the policy of the "iron rice bowl." In 1984, under the 10 rights granted to industrial enterprises, a factory can enter into a labor contract with an employee for a specific time period and the person can be fired for cause. This represented a major departure in Chinese labor practices and has important implications for improving worker efficiency: Employees who are hired under the new contract system have to meet minimal performance standards; otherwise, they face the threat of dismissal. To date, only a fairly small percentage of employees in state-owned enterprises are hired under a contract system. In June 1988, it was estimated that only 7.9 percent of the employees in state-owned enterprises were recruited under such labor contracts. Furthermore, it is still very difficult to dismiss workers for unsatisfactory performance. According to a Chinese manager, firing a worker is "harder than going to heaven" (Horsley, 1988, p. 52). A Hong Kong newspaper even related accounts of factory managers who were "beaten or killed" for taking disciplinary actions against their employees, such as reducing salaries and bonuses and dismissing employees ("Hong Kong," 1988).

Separating the Party Committee from the Factory Administration Prior to 1978, factory directors had operated under the leadership of the party committee attached to each enterprise. The principle of division of responsibility between the party committee and the factory administration was introduced in 1978. The powers of the factory director were subsequently increased in 1984 when the factory director responsibility system was implemented. Under this system, the factory director assumed full responsibility for directing and managing the production functions in the enterprise (Laaksonen, 1988). Another planned change is to replace the system of appointing managers and factory directors with one of "competitive bidding" ("Breakthrough in reforms," 1988, p. 37). After the political unrest in June 1989, the government has tried to strengthen the role of the party. While the factory director is still responsible for the day-to-day administration of the enterprise, all strategic economic decisions now have to be made jointly with the party secretary. Another change is in the area of personnel promotion decisions. Until June 1989, factory directors could make such promotion decisions without consulting the party secretary. Now these recommendations must be endorsed by the party secretary, who may introduce political criteria in assessing the person's overall qualifications ("Foreign investors," 1990).

The debate over the criterion of being "Red" (i.e., political soundness) versus being "expert" (i.e., technical competence) has plagued the operations of Chinese industrial enterprises over the decades. During times of political upheaval, such as the Cultural Revolution (1966–1976), being Red was emphasized at the expense of economic efficiency. With economic modernization as a primary objective, the criterion of expertness became paramount. Thus, technical expertise and competence became major considerations in promotion decisions. This can help raise organizational efficiency.

Making Enterprises Responsible for Their Own Profits and Losses   In the past, state-owned enterprises were not treated as independent accounting units responsible for their own profits and losses. All their revenues were turned over to the state, and all their expenditures (including losses) were absorbed by the state. Thus, there was little or no incentive to overfulfill assigned production quotas. In the past decade, enterprises were gradually converted into independent economic units responsible for their own profits and losses. After paying taxes, the enterprise could retain their profits for use in factory expansion, salary increase, and distribution as bonuses. Furthermore, the amount of bonus to be received by the workers was tied directly to the factory's overall profitability.

Another step in this direction was the enactment of the bankruptcy laws. This provision could serve as a deterrent to inefficient management practices and lax worker attitude because enterprises which lost money had to reduce worker wages. If the enterprise consistently operated at a loss, it could be forced to merge with others. In Beijing, for example, 14 enterprises which failed to meet their 1988 production quotas had to reduce their workers' wages. In addition, 5 other firms had to go out of business. As part of their reorganization plans, they had to "invite bids for new management contracts" or merge with other factories ("Workers fail," 1989, p. 48).

Despite these changes, the state still remained as the "macroscopic manager of all enterprises" (Wu & Jin, 1988–89, p. 26). Consequently, the government still sets minimum production targets, allocates essential raw materials, and purchases and markets a fixed percentage of the output of state-owned enterprises. In addition, the government prescribes the overall policies and guidelines that industry should follow in their overall operations. In the "Report to the Third Plenary Session of the Thirteenth Chinese Communist Party Central Committee," then-Premier Zhao Ziyang stressed the need to rely upon macroeconomic controls. Zhao said:

> To exercise macro-control, it is necessary to make comprehensive use of economic, administrative, legal and disciplinary means as well as conduct extensive political and ideological work. [It is] . . . unwise to abandon administrative means prematurely or offhandedly. Otherwise economic chaos will ensue. The purpose of strengthening administrative means is to better promote the reforms.

Zhao stressed continued adherence to the four cardinal principles of following the socialist road, accepting the dictatorship of the proletariat, following the leadership of the Communist Party, and abiding by the principles of Marxism-Leninism-Mao Zedong thought (Zhao, p. iii). After the events of June fourth, there has been a revision back to greater central governmental control. As such, rule enforcement will continue to serve as an important motivational device in Chinese industrial enterprises.

External Rewards

The principal forms of material incentives used are wages (based on time or piecework), subsidies, bonuses, other welfare benefits provided to workers, and establishment of a direct link between the enterprise's or work unit's performance and the amount of profits to be retained for its own use (Tung, 1982).

Wages, Subsidies, and Bonuses In the past, China's wage policy was governed by two principles. On the one hand, there was opposition to a wide wage spread. On the other hand, China was opposed to absolute egalitarianism. While the government has not discarded the first principle, the slogan during the 1980s has been, "To be rich is glorious!" In a 1988 survey of 1000 students in Beijing's middle schools and universities about their attitude toward money and their goals and aspirations in life, 83.5 percent indicated that they "thought money was indispensable in this world" and 91.8 percent "hoped to have higher incomes" ("Survey conducted," 1988).

In 1986, the average annual income of staff and workers in state-owned enterprises was 1414 yuan. For the same year, the difference between the highest- and the lowest-paid employee in state-owned enterprises was roughly eightfold. The highest-paid government employee earned 500 yuan per month and the lowest-paid worker received 60 yuan per month (*Statistical Yearbook of China,* 1987). Accounting for inflation, the real value of wages in China has increased at an average annual rate of 8.7 percent between 1979 to 1987 ("Reform of labor," 1988). The wages are fairly uniform across enterprises in different industries but are generally higher along the coastal cities and provinces, where the cost of living is higher.

Wages are paid on a time or piecework basis. Time-based wages are determined directly by the duration of labor and are therefore paid according to the work done over a certain period of time. Under the piecework system, the worker is paid in direct proportion to the quantity of work or items produced. Piecework wages are suited to many different kinds of work, especially work involving physical strength, such as loading, unloading, and transportation. In 1986, 58.7 percent of the wages in state-owned enterprises were time-based and 9.1 percent were on a piecework basis.

In addition to time and piecework wages, overtime pay and bonuses are given as rewards for extra work done by laborers. During the Cultural Revolution, bonuses were discontinued. In 1977, bonuses were reintroduced. While bonuses were intended to motivate workers to increase their performance and/or productivity, they often failed to produce the desired results because many factories distributed bonuses indiscriminately. For example, prior to 1979, the factory bonus fund was fixed at 5 percent of the total wage bill. Since the bonus fund was fixed, to be released upon the factory's fulfillment of the production target, there was little incentive for the factory director and the workers to overfulfill the assigned quota; hence there was no desire to increase productivity. To make bonuses a motivational device for increasing performance, beginning in 1979, the size of the bonus fund was tied to the overall profitability of the factory (Walder, 1987). As a result, bonus payments escalated. In 1980, for example, in a survey of 90 work units in Chongqing, it was found that bonuses accounted for 40 percent of the workers' wages. To bring this situation under control, the government introduced a harsh "bonus tax" in 1984 on all bonus funds exceeding one-third of the annual wage bill. More specifically, enterprises which distributed bonuses amounting to 4 to 5 months' of the factory's wage bill had to pay a 30 percent bonus tax; those paying 5 to 6 months' of bonuses were subject to a 100 percent tax rate; and those meting out more than 6 months' bonuses had to pay a 300 percent tax. As a result of this bonus tax, by 1984, bonuses leveled off and accounted for only 16.8 percent of the wage bill of state-owned enterprises.

In addition to wages and bonuses, Chinese workers enjoy generous sickness, injury, disability, maternity, retirement, death, and other benefits (Tung, 1982). In 1986, subsidies accounted for 13.4 percent of the total amount paid out in wages for state-run enterprises. This was borne in full by the government.

For salary increases and bonuses to be used effectively as motivational devices, they have to be tied directly to the workers' skill level and work performance. In other words, the principle of "to each according to need" has to be changed to "to each according to work." However, egalitarian distribution still prevails. Thus the attempt to link rewards with performance as a "key to raising efficiency . . . remains the least reformed aspect of industrial management" (Tidrick & Chen, 1987, p. 1). Attempts at overcoming egalitarianism in the allocation of pay increases and bonuses have met with opposition for several reasons. First, there was disagreement among the workers on how to assess an employee's skill level. Young workers favored written examinations, whereas older workers preferred practical tests. Second, workers argued over the weights assigned to the mix of criteria (performance, financial need, and seniority) to determine salary increases and the size of a bonus. In fact, by mid-1980, the group evaluation process for pay increases was likened to a life-and-death struggle. The situation deteriorated to the point where workers would refuse to undertake a job or improve performance unless there were monetary incentives associated with such activities. The workers developed "an increasingly calculative ... mentality" with respect to the amount of effort to be expended on a project (Walder, 1987, pp. 27–29). In short, the use of external rewards not only failed to reinforce "the efficacy of a 'payment by result' approach, [but] ... tended to create a system of 'effort according to the amount of reward'" (Hong & Lansbury, 1987, p. 160).

Those workers who favored the elimination of egalitarianism were ostracized and became the subjects of verbal attacks. Two phenomena soon emerged: the "red eye" disease, whereby average workers became jealous of the rate busters; and "white eye" disease, whereby average workers ostracized the high performers. To restore harmony, many factory administrators simply meted out salary increments and bonuses fairly equally, "rotating the high bonuses to different workers each month" (Walder, 1987, p.29).

Internalized Motivation

In China, internalized motivation is almost synonymous with moral encouragement. Moral encouragement involves the principle of "fighting the self"—one who is prepared to sacrifice self-interest for the general welfare and progress of all others and the state. As Hu Qili, a member of China's Politburo stated, ideological work "should be used as a moral booster to unite and encourage the people in their struggle" toward the goals of the Four Modernizations ("Ideological work," 1988, p. 10). Internalized motivation also involves the application of the principle of "from each according to ability," whereby all workers should do their best regardless of wage. The principal means of moral encouragement used are socialist labor emulation drives and political indoctrination or education.

Socialist Emulation Drives While the government has always emphasized the need for moral encouragement, *Guangming Ribao,* a leading Chinese daily, acknowledged the difficulty of conducting ideological indoctrination in the 1980s because revolutionary slogans, which played a key role in the early decades of the establishment of the People's Republic, can no longer excite people's consciousness. In the past, the models for socialist labor emulation were drawn from revolutionary heroes who, through hard work and labor, helped establish the People's Republic. Now, the people held up as models for socialist emulation are of two principal types: those with high moral principles who dedicate themselves wholeheartedly to the people and the motherland, and the Horatio Algers of China, that is, those who amassed wealth as a result of their labor. Senior party officials and the media have encouraged the rural community, which accounts for over 80 percent of China's population, to aspire to the goal of a "household with an annual income of 10,000 yuan" ("Thoughts on building," 1988, p. 22). With the current emphasis on material incentives, models in the latter category appear to exert a far greater influence on the mass populace as borne out by the survey findings of 1000 Beijing middle school and university students, the overwhelming majority of whom believed that wealth was a desired goal ("Survey conducted," 1988). In other words, the everything-depends-on-money ideology appears to hold sway in the era of economic modernization (Sklair, 1987).

Political Indoctrination After the events of June 4, the government has strengthened the role of the party and reemphasized the need for greater efforts in the area of political and ideological indoctrination. Beijing has attributed the unrest in large part, to "slack ideological control." In all industrial enterprises, including those with foreign investment, workers are once again compelled to sing revolutionary songs during work hours to ignite their ideological fervor. In addition, the party committees attached to the factories have revived revolutionary song contests, a practice common during the Cultural Revolution. While such contests have not been abandoned under the policy of economic modernization, these sessions took place after work. Now these contests have moved center stage and are conducted during work hours ("Foreign investors," 1990, p. 2).

In line with this renewed emphasis on ideological control, bookstores throughout China have reported that books on Marxism-Leninism-Mao Zedong thought have once again resurfaced as best-sellers. A reason for this is cadres are now required to write examinations on ideology. To mark the ninety-sixth birthday of Mao Zedong, the government announced that young people who were "disillusioned with western philosophies" are once again "rediscovering the truth in the works of the late Great Helmsmen" ("China claims," 1990, p. 2). Beijing, however, quickly reiterated that Mao Zedong was a man and not a god and that Mao Zedong thought was not the product of one man but represented the "collective wisdom of his comrades-in-arms, the Party and the revolutionary people." Hence there should be no personality cult around one individual (Tung, 1982).

DISCUSSION

In the past, China has relied on a combination of rule enforcement, external rewards, and internalized motivation to spur workers to improve on-the-job performance and increase productivity. Despite problems associated with the implementation of each of these devices, there is every indication that this combined approach will continue in the future. In the case of rule enforcement, unless China moves completely away from central planning, administrative directives and procedures will be used. The government recognizes that in order to manage a country as large as China, administrative procedures cannot be abandoned overnight; otherwise, it can result in chaos. Throughout the 1980s, however, there has been a shift toward greater reliance upon economic means over administrative guidelines. It appears that this trend will continue in the 1990s and beyond.

In the area of material incentives, it appears that China cannot reverse the course. It is highly unlikely that the mass populace will be willing to forsake the increased standard of living they have experienced under economic modernization. However, much remains to be done to overcome absolute egalitarianism; otherwise, the use of salary and bonuses as motivational devices may prove futile.

In the case of moral encouragement, it appears that the government will be reluctant to relinquish such a potent weapon. This motivational device was largely responsible for the significant economic strides made by the country in the first two decades of the establishment of the People's Republic. A key to its continued success as an effective motivational device is for the government to demonstrate its relevance in an environment where people aspire toward material gains. It appears that as China imports western products and technology to fuel its modernization efforts, "spiritual pollution" is inevitable. The Chinese on the mainland will increasingly resemble their counterparts in capitalist economies. As Sklair (1987, p. 191) noted, "In the absence of other models legitimized by the party and the state, the newly rich will simply copy the capitalist lifestyles of Hong Kong." This will constitute one of the major challenges confronting the country's leaders.

REFERENCES

Breakthrough in reforms. (1988, November 30). *Federal Broadcast Information Service.*

Chamberlain, H. B. (1987). Party-management relations in Chinese industries: Some political dimensions of economic reforms. *China Quarterly,* December, 631–661.

China claims the young are rediscovering Mao. (1990, January 1). *Asian Wall Street Journal,* p. 2.

Foreign investors in China grow jittery as the party steps up role in factories. (1990, January 1) *Asian Wall Street Journal,* p. 2.

Hong, N. S., & Lansbury, R. D. (1987). The workers' congress in Chinese enterprises. In M. Warner (Ed.), *Management reforms in China.* New York: St. Martin's Press.

Hong Kong paper views bankruptcy law. (1988, November 6). *Hong Kong Standard: China Today Supplement.*

Horsley, J. P. The Chinese workforce. (1988). *China Business Review,* May–June, pp. 50–55.

Ideological work: Field for reform. (1988, July 25–31). *Beijing Review.*

Katz, F., & Kahn, R. (1978). *The social psychology of organizations.* New York: Wiley.

Laaksonen, O. (1988). *Management in China during and after Mao in enterprises, government and party.* Berlin, Germany: Walter de Gruyter.

Reform of labor and wage system. (1988, October 24–30). *Beijing Review.*

Renmin Ribao views state enterprises. (1988, August 25). *Federal Broadcast Information Service.*

Sklair, L. (1987). Capitalist efficiency without exploitation—Some indications from Shenzhen. In M. Warner (Ed.), *Management reforms in China.* New York: St. Martin's Press.

Statistical Yearbook of China. Hong Kong: Longman Group (Far East) Ltd. Various years.

Survey conducted on students' concepts of value. (1988, August 22). *Federal Broadcast Information Service,* p. 32.

Third wave: Enterprise mergers. (1988, October 17–23). *Beijing Review.*

Tidrick, G., & Chen, J. (1987). The essence of the industrial reforms. In G. Tidrick & J. Chen (Eds.), *China's Industrial Reforms.* New York: Oxford University Press.

Thoughts on building spiritual civilization. (1988, July 20). *Federal Broadcast Information Service.*

Tung, R. L. (1981). Patterns of motivation in Chinese industrial enterprises. *Academy of Management Review,* **6**(3), 481–489.

Tung, R. L. (1982). *Chinese industrial society after Mao.* Lexington, Mass.: Lexington Books.

Walder, A. G. (1987). Wage reforms and the web of factory interests. *China Quarterly,* March, 22–41.

Workers fail to meet goals, wages reduced. (1989, January 31). *Federal Broadcast Information Service.*

Wu, J. & Jin, L. (1988–89). Sharing enterprises: An approach to further reform. *Chinese Economic Studies,* **22**(2), 24–37.

Zhao, Z. (1988, November 14–20). Report to the Third Plenary Session of the Thirteenth CPC Central Committee. *Beijing Review,* pp. i–viii.

QUESTIONS FOR DISCUSSION

1 If you were transferred into a multinational corporation in Japan and you wanted to apply the need theories and equity theories in managing your Japanese employees, what considerations would you have to take into account in this new environment?

2 Do you think that the differences in organizational commitment and job satisfaction between Japanese and American employees are due more to cultural factors or national factors—or some other set of factors.

3 Discuss the implications of a socialist economy and political system for equity theory and for goal-setting theory.

4 International operations require an understanding of the culture, economy, and political system of the host country. List several specific cultural and national factors which you think play an important role in the motivation and work behavior of employees in different countries.

5 Compare Lincoln's discussion of culture and commitment with O'Reilly's discussion of organizational culture and commitment.

6 How would you manage a group of culturally diverse employees (e.g., 50 percent Americans and 50 percent Japanese)? What problems might you encounter? What positive outcomes might occur in such a culturally diverse group?

7 What do you think the differences would be between managing non-American employees in the United States and managing them in their native country?

PART FOUR

TECHNIQUES OF
MOTIVATION

CHAPTER 9

GOAL-SETTING AND SELF-MANAGEMENT

As we pointed out in Chapters 1 and 4, theories of motivation that emphasize a *cognitive* perspective—that is, how individuals think about themselves and their environmental context—have become increasingly prominent in organizational psychology. In this chapter we take a look at a particular cognitive approach—goal-setting—that has been intensively and extensively investigated in recent years. The goal-setting approach emphasizes the role of intentions, or deliberate determinations to act, as major causes of motivated behavior. In other words, this approach assumes that if a person makes a commitment to an objective or desired endpoint, such a goal will in fact strongly influence the subsequent behavior of that person. It follows from this line of reasoning, of course, that to motivate someone it is crucial to obtain the person's commitment to a particular goal.

The first article, by Latham and Locke, describes goal-setting as a motivational technique and provides an overview of early research that demonstrates its effects. These two authors, who have been primary developers of this approach as it applies to organizational settings, emphasize that the goals that seem to have the greatest positive effects on performance are those that are both specific (not vague) *and* challenging (not easy). The second article, by Locke et al., examines in more detail the factors that determine *whether* individuals will make a commitment to particular goals. Their analysis focuses on three major categories of determinants, roughly analogous to our categorization of theoretical approaches to motivation in Part Two of this book: factors in the person, such as expectancies or self-administered intrinsic rewards; factors in the environment, such as supervision and peer influence; and person-environment interactions, such as participation and competition. The last article in the chapter by Manz deals with the notion of "self-influence" or self-management as it impacts people's behavior. The ideas discussed in this article draw on various theories of motivation that were reviewed in Part Two, particularly social learning theory and the concept of intrinsic motivation. They also strongly relate to goal-setting with its emphasis on the role of deliberate intentions in determining behavior.

Goal Setting—A Motivational Technique That Works

Gary P. Latham
Edwin A. Locke

The problem of how to motivate employees has puzzled and frustrated managers for generations. One reason the problem has seemed difficult, if not mysterious, is that motivation ultimately comes from within the individual and therefore cannot be observed directly. Moreover, most managers are not in a position to change an employee's basic personality structure. The best they can do is try to use incentives to direct the energies of their employees toward organizational objectives.

Money is obviously the primary incentive, since without it few if any employees would come to work. But money alone is not always enough to motivate high performance. Other incentives, such as participation in decision making, job enrichment, behavior modification, and organizational development, have been tried with varying degrees of success. A large number of research studies have shown, however, that one very straightforward technique—goal setting—is probably not only more effective than alternative methods, but may be the major mechanism by which these other incentives affect motivation. For example, a recent experiment on job enrichment demonstrated that unless employees in enriched jobs set higher, more specific goals than do those with unenriched jobs, job enrichment has absolutely no effect on productivity. Even money has been found most effective as a motivator when the bonuses offered are made contingent on attaining specific objectives.

THE GOAL-SETTING CONCEPT

The idea of assigning employees a specific amount of work to be accomplished—a specific task, a quota, a performance standard, an objective, or a deadline—is not new. The task concept, along with time and motion study and incentive pay, was the cornerstone of scientific management, founded by Frederick W. Taylor more than 70 years ago. He used his system to increase the productivity of blue collar workers. About 20 years ago the idea of goal setting reappeared under a new name, management by objectives, but this technique was designed for managers.

In a 14-year program of research, we have found that goal setting does not necessarily have to be part of a wider management system to motivate performance effectively. It can be used as a technique in its own right.

Laboratory and Field Research

Our research program began in the laboratory. In a series of experiments, individuals were assigned different types of goals on a variety of simple tasks—ad-

From *Organizational Dynamics*, Autumn, 1979. Copyright © 1979 by American Management Association. Reprinted by permission. All rights reserved.

dition, brainstorming, assembling toys. Repeatedly it was found that those as-signed hard goals performed better than did people assigned moderately difficult or easy goals. Furthermore, individuals who had specific, challenging goals out-performed those who were given such vague goals as to "do your best." Finally, we observed that pay and performance feedback led to improved performance only when these incentives led the individual to set higher goals.

While results were quite consistent in the laboratory, there was no proof that they could be applied to actual work settings. Fortunately, just as Locke pub-lished a summary of the laboratory studies in 1968, Latham began a separate se-ries of experiments in the wood products industry that demonstrated the practical significance of these findings. The field studies did not start out as a validity test of laboratory theory, but rather as a response to a practical problem.

In 1968, six sponsors of the American Pulpwood Association became con-cerned about increasing the productivity of independent loggers in the South. These loggers were entrepreneurs on whom the multimillion-dollar companies are largely dependent for their raw material. The problem was twofold. First, these entrepreneurs did not work for a single company; they worked for themselves. Thus they were free to (and often did) work two days one week, four days a sec-ond week, five half-days a third week, or whatever schedule they preferred. In short, these workers could be classified as marginal from the standpoint of their productivity and attendance, which were considered highly unsatisfactory by conventional company standards. Second, the major approach taken to alleviate this problem had been to develop equipment that would make the industry less dependent on this type of worker. A limitation of this approach was that many of the logging supervisors were unable to obtain the financing to purchase a small tractor, let alone a rubber-tired skidder.

Consequently, we designed a survey that would help managers determine "what makes these people tick." The survey was conducted orally in the field with 292 logging supervisors. Complex statistical analyses of the data identified three basic types of supervisor. One type stayed on the job with their men, gave them instructions and explanations, provided them with training, read the trade magazines, and had little difficulty financing the equipment they needed. Still, the productivity of their units was at best mediocre.

The operation of the second group of supervisors was slightly less mecha-nized. These supervisors provided little training for their workforce. They simply drove their employees to the woods, gave them a specific production goal to at-tain for the day or week, left them alone in the woods unsupervised, and returned at night to take them home. Labor turnover was high and productivity was again average.

The operation of the third group of supervisors was relatively unmechanized. These leaders stayed on the job with their men, provided training, gave instruc-tions and explanations, and in addition, set a specific production goal for the day or week. Not only was the crew's productivity high, but their injury rate was well below average.

Two conclusions were discussed with the managers of the companies sponsor-ing this study. First, mechanization alone will not increase the productivity of logging crews. Just as the average tax payer would probably commit more mathematical errors if he were to try to use a computer to complete his income tax return, the average logger misuses, and frequently abuses, the equipment he purchases (for example, drives a skidder with two flat tires, doesn't change the oil filter). This increases not only the logger's downtime, but also his costs which, in turn, can force him out of business. The second conclusion of the survey was that setting a specific production goal combined with supervisory presence to ensure goal commitment will bring about a significant increase in productivity.

These conclusions were greeted with the standard, but valid, cliché, "Statistics don't prove causation." And our comments regarding the value of machinery were especially irritating to these managers, many of whom had received degrees in engineering. So one of the companies decided to replicate the survey in order to check our findings.

The company's study placed each of 892 independent logging supervisors who sold wood to the company into one of three categories of supervisory styles our survey had identified—namely, (1) stays on the job but does not set specific production goals; (2) sets specific production goals but does not stay on the job; and (3) stays on the job and sets specific production goals. Once again, goal setting, in combination with the on-site presence of a supervisor, was shown to be the key to improved productivity.

TESTING FOR THE HAWTHORNE EFFECT

Management may have been unfamiliar with different theories of motivation, but it was fully aware of one label—the Hawthorne effect. Managers in these wood products companies remained unconvinced that anything so simple as staying on the job with the men and setting a specific production goal could have an appreciable effect on productivity. They pointed out that the results simply reflected the positive effects any supervisor would have on the work unit after giving his crew attention. And they were unimpressed by the laboratory experiments we cited—experiments showing that individuals who have a specific goal solve more arithmetic problems or assemble more tinker toys than do people who are told to "do your best." Skepticism prevailed.

But the country's economic picture made it critical to continue the study of inexpensive techniques to improve employee motivation and productivity. We were granted permission to run one more project to test the effectiveness of goal setting.

Twenty independent logging crews who were all but identical in size, mechanization level, terrain on which they worked, productivity, and attendance were located. The logging supervisors of these crews were in the habit of staying on the job with their men, but they did not set production goals. Half of the crews were randomly selected to receive training in goal setting; the remaining crews served as a control group.

The logging supervisors who were to set goals were told that we had found a way to increase productivity at no financial expense to anyone. We gave the ten supervisors in the training group production tables developed through time-and-motion studies by the company's engineers. These tables made it possible to determine how much wood should be harvested in a given number of manhours. They were asked to use these tables as a guide in determining a specific production goal to assign their employees. In addition, each sawhand was given a tallymeter (counter) that he could wear on his belt. The sawhand was asked to punch the counter each time he felled a tree. Finally, permission was requested to measure the crew's performance on a weekly basis.

The ten supervisors in the control group—those who were not asked to set production goals—were told that the researchers were interested in learning the extent to which productivity is affected by absenteeism and injuries. They were urged to "do your best" to maximize the crew's productivity and attendance and to minimize injuries. It was explained that the data might be useful in finding ways to increase productivity at little or no cost to the wood harvester.

To control for the Hawthorne effect, we made an equal number of visits to the control group and the training group. Performance was measured for 12 weeks. During this time, the productivity of the goal-setting group was significantly higher than that of the control group. Moreover, absenteeism was significantly lower in the groups that set goals than in the groups who were simply urged to do their best. Injury and turnover rates were low in both groups.

Why should anything so simple and inexpensive as goal setting influence the work of these employees so significantly? Anecdotal evidence from conversations with both the loggers and the company foresters who visited them suggested several reasons.

Harvesting timber can be a monotonous, tiring job with little or no meaning for most workers. Introducing a goal that is difficult, but attainable, increases the challenge of the job. In addition, a specific goal makes it clear to the worker what it is he is expected to do. Goal feedback via the tallymeter and weekly record-keeping provide the worker with a sense of achievement, recognition, and accomplishment. He can see how well he is doing now as against his past performance and, in some cases, how well he is doing in comparison with others. Thus the worker not only may expend greater effort, but may also devise better or more creative tactics for attaining the goal than those he previously used.

NEW APPLICATIONS

Management was finally convinced that goal setting was an effective motivational technique for increasing the productivity of the independent woods worker in the South. The issue now raised by the management of another wood products company was whether the procedure could be used in the West with the company logging operations in which the employees were unionized and paid by the hour. The previous study had involved employees on a piece-rate system, which was the practice in the South.

The immediate problem confronting this company involved the loading of logging trucks. If the trucks were underloaded, the company lost money. If the trucks were overloaded, however, the driver could be fined by the Highway Department and could ultimately lose his job. The drivers opted for underloading the trucks.

For three months management tried to solve this problem by urging the drivers to try harder to fill the truck to its legal net weight, and by developing weighing scales that could be attached to the truck. But this approach did not prove cost effective, because the scales continually broke down when subjected to the rough terrain on which the trucks traveled. Consequently, the drivers reverted to their former practice of underloading. For the three months in which the problem was under study the trucks were seldom loaded in excess of 58 to 63 percent of capacity.

At the end of the three-month period, the results of the previous goal setting experiments were explained to the union. They were told three things—that the company would like to set a specific net weight goal for the drivers, that no monetary reward or fringe benefits other than verbal praise could be expected for improved performance, and that no one would be criticized for failing to attain the goal. Once again, the idea that simply setting a specific goal would solve a production problem seemed too incredible to be taken seriously by the union. However, they reached an agreement that a difficult, but attainable, goal of 94 percent of the truck's legal net weight would be assigned to the drivers, provided that no one could be reprimanded for failing to attain the goal. This latter point was emphasized to the company foremen in particular.

Within the first month, performance increased to 80 percent of the truck's net weight. After the second month, however, performance decreased to 70 percent. Interviews with the drivers indicated that they were testing management's statement that no punitive steps would be taken against them if their performance suddenly dropped. Fortunately for all concerned, no such steps were taken by the foremen, and performance exceeded 90 percent of the truck's capacity after the third month. Their performance has remained at this level to this day, seven years later.

The results over the nine-month period during which this study was conducted saved the company $250,000. This figure, determined by the company's accountants, is based on the cost of additional trucks that would have been required to deliver the same quantity of logs to the mill if goal setting had not been implemented. The dollars-saved figure is even higher when you factor in the cost of the additional diesel fuel that would have been consumed and the expenses incurred in recruiting and hiring the additional truck drivers.

Why could this procedure work without the union's demanding an increase in hourly wages? First, the drivers did not feel that they were really doing anything differently. This, of course, was not true. As a result of goal setting, the men began to record their truck weight in a pocket notebook, and they found themselves bragging about their accomplishments to their peers. Second, they viewed goal setting as a challenging game: "It was great to beat the other guy."

Competition was a crucial factor in bringing about goal acceptance and commitment in this study. However, we can reject the hypothesis that improved performance resulted solely from competition, because no special prizes or formal recognition programs were provided for those who came closest to, or exceeded, the goal. No effort was made by the company to single out one "winner." More important, the opportunity for competition among drivers had existed before goal setting was instituted; after all, each driver knew his own truck's weight, and the truck weight of each of the 36 other drivers every time he hauled wood into the yard. In short, competition affected productivity only in the sense that it led to the acceptance of, and commitment to, the goal. It was the setting of the goal itself and the working toward it that brought about increased performance and decreased costs.

PARTICIPATIVE GOAL SETTING

The inevitable question always raised by management was raised here: "We know goal setting works. How can we make it work better?" Was there one best method for setting goals? Evidence for a "one best way" approach was cited by several managers, but it was finally concluded that different approaches would work best under different circumstances.

It was hypothesized that the woods workers in the South, who had little or no education, would work better with assigned goals, while the educated workers in the West would achieve higher productivity if they were allowed to help set the goals themselves. Why the focus on education? Many of the uneducated workers in the South could be classified as culturally disadvantaged. Such persons often lack self-confidence, have a poor sense of time, and are not very competitive. The cycle of skill mastery, which in turn guarantees skill levels high enough to prevent discouragement, doesn't apply to these employees. If, for example, these people were allowed to participate in goal setting, the goals might be too difficult or they might be too easy. On the other hand, participation for the educated worker was considered critical in effecting maximum goal acceptance. Since these conclusions appeared logical, management initially decided that no research was necessary. This decision led to hours of further discussion.

The same questions were raised again and again by the researchers. What if the logic were wrong? Can we afford to implement these decisions without evaluating them systematically? Would we implement decisions regarding a new approach to tree planting without first testing it? Do we care more about trees than we do about people? Finally, permission was granted to conduct an experiment.

Logging crews were randomly appointed to either participative goal setting, assigned (nonparticipative) goal setting, or a do-your-best condition. The results were startling. The uneducated crews, consisting primarily of black employees who participated in goal setting, set significantly higher goals and attained them more often than did those whose goals were assigned by the supervisor. Not surprisingly, their performance was higher. Crews with assigned goals performed no better than did those who were urged to do their best to improve their productivity. The performance of white, educationally advantaged workers was higher with assigned rather than participatively set goals, although the difference was not statistically significant. These results were precisely the opposite of what had been predicted.

Another study comparing participative and assigned goals was conducted with typists. The results supported findings obtained by researchers at General Electric years before. It did not matter so much *how* the goal was set. What mattered was *that* a goal was set. The study demonstrated that both assigned and participatively set goals led to substantial improvements in typing speed. The process by which these gains occurred, however, differed in the two groups. In the participative group, employees insisted on setting very high goals regardless of whether they had attained their goal the previous week. Nevertheless, their productivity improved—an outcome consistent with the theory that high goals lead to high performance.

In the assigned-goal group, supervisors were highly supportive of employees. No criticism was given for failure to attain the goals. Instead, the supervisor lowered the goal after failure so that the employee would be certain to attain it. The goal was then raised gradually each week until the supervisor felt the employee was achieving his or her potential. The result? Feelings of accomplishment and achievement on the part of the worker and improved productivity for the company.

These basic findings were replicated in a subsequent study of engineers and scientists. Participative goal setting was superior to assigned goal setting only to the degree that it led to the setting of higher goals. Both participative and assigned-goal groups outperformed groups that were simply told to "do your best."

An additional experiment was conducted to validate the conclusion that participation in goal setting may be important only to the extent that it leads to the setting of difficult goals. It was performed in a laboratory setting in which the task was to brainstorm uses for wood. One group was asked to "do your best" to think of as many ideas as possible. A second group took part in deciding with the experimenter, the specific number of ideas each person would generate. These goals were, in turn, assigned to individuals in a third group. In this way, goal difficulty was held constant between the assigned-goal and participative groups. Again, it was found that specific, difficult goals—whether assigned or set through participation—led to higher performance than did an abstract or generalized goal such as "do your best." And, when goal difficulty was held constant, there was no significant difference in the performance of those with assigned as compared with participatively set goals.

These results demonstrate that goal setting in industry works just as it does in the laboratory. Specific, challenging goals lead to better performance than do easy or vague goals, and feedback motivates higher performance only when it leads to the setting of higher goals.

It is important to note that participation is not only a motivational tool. When a manager has competent subordinates, participation is also a useful device for increasing the manager's knowledge and thereby improving decision quality. It can lead to better decisions through input from subordinates.

A representative sample of the results of field studies of goal setting conducted by Latham and others is shown in Figure 1. Each of these ten studies compared the performance of employees given specific challenging goals with those given "do best" or no goals. Note that goal setting has been successful across a wide variety of jobs and industries. The effects of goal setting have been recorded for as long as seven years after the onset of the program, although the results of most

FIGURE 1

REPRESENTATIVE FIELD STUDIES OF GOAL SETTING

Researcher(s)	Task	Duration of study or of significant effects	Percent of change in performance[a]
Blumenfeld & Leidy	Servicing soft drink coolers	Unspecified	+27
Dockstader	Keypunching	3 mos.	+27
Ivancevich	Skilled technical jobs	9 mos.	+15
Ivancevich	Sales	9 mos.	+24
Kim and Hamner	5 telephone service jobs	3 mos.	+13
Latham and Baldes	Loading trucks	9 mos.[b]	+26
Latham and Yukl	Logging	2 mos.	+18
Latham and Yukl	Typing	5 weeks	+11
Migliore	Mass production	2 years	+16
Umstot, Bell, and Mitchell	Coding land parcels	1–2 days[c]	+16

[a]Percentage changes were obtained by subtracting pre-goal-setting performance from post-goal-setting performance and dividing by pre-goal-setting performance. Different experimental groups were combined where appropriate. If a control group was available, the percentage figure represents the difference of the percentage changes between the experimental and control groups. If multiple performance measures were used, the median improvement on all measures was used. The authors would like to thank Dena Feren and Vicki McCaleb for performing these calculations.

[b]Performance remained higher for seven years.

[c]Simulated organization.

studies have been followed up for only a few weeks or months. The median improvement in performance in the ten studies shown in Figure 1 was 17 percent.

A CRITICAL INCIDENTS SURVEY

To explore further the importance of goal setting in the work setting, Dr. Frank White conducted another study in two plants of a high-technology, multinational corporation on the East Coast. Seventy-one engineers, 50 managers, and 31 clerks were asked to describe a specific instance when they were especially productive and a specific instance when they were especially unproductive on their present jobs. Responses were classified according to a reliable coding scheme. Of primary interest here are the external events perceived by employees as being responsible for the high-productivity and low-productivity incidents. The results are shown in Figure 2.

The first set of events—pursuing a specific goal, having a large amount of work, working under a deadline, or having an uninterrupted routine—accounted for more than half the high-productivity events. Similarly, the converse of these—goal-blockage, having a small amount of work, lacking a deadline, and suffering work interruptions—accounted for nearly 60 percent of the low-productivity events. Note that the first set of four categories are all relevant to goal setting and the second set to a lack of goals or goal blockage. The goal category itself—that of pursuing an attainable goal or goal blockage—was the one most frequently used to describe high- and low-productivity incidents.

FIGURE 2
EVENTS PERCEIVED AS CAUSING HIGH AND LOW PRODUCTIVITY*

Events	Percent of times event caused	
	High productivity	Low productivity
Goal pursuit/Goal Blockage	17.1	23.0
Large amount of work/Small amount of work	12.5	19.0
Deadline or schedule/No deadline	15.1	3.3
Smooth work routine/Interrupted routine	5.9	14.5
Intrinsic/Extrinsic factors	50.6	59.8
Interesting task/Uninteresting task	17.1	11.2
Increased responsibility/Decreased responsibility	13.8	4.6
Anticipated promotion/Promotion denied	1.3	0.7
Verbal recognition/Criticism	4.6	2.6
People/Company conditions	36.8	19.1
Pleasant personal relationships/Unpleasant personal relationships	10.5	9.9
Anticipated pay increase/Pay increase denied	1.3	1.3
Pleasant working conditions/Unpleasant working conditions	0.7	0.7
Other (miscellaneous)	—	9.3

*N = 152 in this study by Frank White.

The next four categories, which are more pertinent to Frederick Herzberg's motivator-hygiene theory—task interest, responsibility, promotion, and recognition—are less important, accounting for 36.8 percent of the high-productivity incidents (the opposite of these four categories accounted for 19.1 percent of the lows.) The remaining categories were even less important.

Employees were also asked to identify the responsible agent behind the events that had led to high and low productivity. In both cases, the employees themselves, their immediate supervisors, and the organization were the agents most frequently mentioned.

The concept of goal setting is a very simple one. Interestingly, however, we have gotten two contradictory types of reaction when the idea was introduced to managers. Some claimed it was so simple and self-evident that everyone, including themselves, already used it. This, we have found, is not true. Time after time we have gotten the following response from subordinates after goal setting was introduced: "This is the first time I knew what my supervisor expected of me on this job." Conversely, other managers have argued that the idea would not work, precisely *because* it is so simple (implying that something more radical and complex was needed). Again, results proved them wrong.

But these successes should not mislead managers into thinking that goal setting can be used without careful planning and forethought. Research and experience suggest that the best results are obtained when the following steps are followed:

Setting the Goal

The goal set should have two main characteristics. First, it should be specific rather than vague: "Increase sales by 10 percent" rather than "Try to improve sales." Whenever possible, there should be a time limit for goal accomplishment: "Cut cost by 3 percent in the next six months."

Second, the goal should be challenging yet reachable. If accepted, difficult goals lead to better performance than do easy goals. In contrast, if the goals are perceived as unreachable, employees will not accept them. Nor will employees get a sense of achievement from pursuing goals that are never attained. Employees with low self-confidence or ability should be given more easily attainable goals than those with high self-confidence and ability.

There are at least five possible sources of input, aside from the individual's self-confidence and ability, that can be used to determine the particular goal to set for a given individual.

The scientific management approach pioneered by Frederick W. Taylor uses time and motion study to determine a fair day's work. This is probably the most objective technique available, but it can be used only where the task is reasonably repetitive and standardized. Another drawback is that this method often leads to employee resistance, especially in cases where the new standard is substantially higher than previous performance and where rate changes are made frequently.

More readily accepted, although less scientific than time and motion study, are standards based on the average past performance of employees. This method was used successfully in some of our field studies. Most employees consider this approach fair but, naturally in cases where past performance is far below capacity, beating that standard will be extremely easy.

Since goal setting is sometimes simply a matter of judgment, another technique we have used is to allow the goal to be set jointly by supervisor and subordinate. The participative approach may be less scientific than time and motion study, but it does lead to ready acceptance by both employee and immediate superior in addition to promoting role clarity.

External constraints often affect goal setting, especially among managers. For example, the goal to produce an item at a certain price may be dictated by the actions of competitors, and deadlines may be imposed externally in line with contract agreements. Legal regulations, such as attaining a certain reduction in pollution levels by a certain date, may affect goal setting as well. In these cases, setting the goal is not so much the problem as figuring out a method of reaching it.

Finally, organizational goals set by the board of directors or upper management will influence the goals set by employees at lower levels. This is the essence of the MBO process.

Another issue that needs to be considered when setting goals is whether they should be designed for individuals or for groups. Rensis Likert and a number of other human relations experts argue for group goal setting on grounds that it promotes cooperation and team spirit. But one could argue that individual goals better promote individual responsibility and make it easier to appraise individual performance. The degree of task interdependence involved would also be a factor to consider.

Obtaining Goal Commitment

If goal setting is to work, then the manager must ensure that subordinates will accept and remain committed to the goals. Simple instruction backed by positive support and an absence of threats or intimidation were enough to ensure goal acceptance in most of our studies. Subordinates must perceive the goals as fair and reasonable and they must trust management, for if they perceive the goals as no more than a means of exploitation, they will be likely to reject the goals.

It may seem surprising that goal acceptance was achieved so readily in the field studies. Remember, however, that in all cases the employees were receiving wages or a salary (although these were not necessarily directly contingent on goal attainment). Pay in combination with the supervisor's benevolent authority and supportiveness were sufficient to bring about goal acceptance. Recent research indicates that whether goals are assigned or set participatively, supportiveness on the part of the immediate superior is critical. A supportive manager or supervisor does not use goals to threaten subordinates, but rather to clarify what is expected of them. His or her role is that of a helper and goal facilitator.

As noted earlier, the employee gets a feeling of pride and satisfaction from the experience of reaching a challenging but fair performance goal. Success in reaching a goal also tends to reinforce acceptance of future goals. Once goal setting is introduced, informal competition frequently arises among the employees. This further reinforces commitment and may lead employees to raise the goals spontaneously. A word of caution here, however: We do not recommend setting up formal competition, as this may lead employees to place individual goals ahead of company goals. The emphasis should be on accomplishing the task, getting the job done, not "beating" the other person.

When employees resist assigned goals, they generally do so for one of two reasons. First, they may think they are incapable of reaching the goal because they lack confidence, ability, knowledge, and the like. Second, they may not see any personal benefit—either in terms of personal pride or in terms of external rewards like money, promotion, recognition—in reaching assigned goals.

There are various methods of overcoming employee resistance to goals. One possibility is more training designed to raise the employee's level of skill and self-confidence. Allowing the subordinate to participate in setting the goal—deciding on the goal level—is another method. This was found most effective among uneducated and minority group employees, perhaps because it gave them a feeling of control over their fate. Offering monetary bonuses or other rewards (recognition, time off) for reaching goals may also help.

The last two methods may be especially useful where there is a history of labor-management conflict and where employees have become accustomed to a lower level of effort than currently considered acceptable. Group incentives may also encourage goal acceptance, especially where there is a group goal, or when considerable cooperation is required.

Providing Support Elements

A third step to take when introducing goal setting is to ensure the availability of necessary support elements. That is, the employee must be given adequate resources—money, equipment, time, help—as well as the freedom to utilize them in attaining goals, and company policies must not work to block goal attainment.

Before turning an employee loose with these resources, however, it's wise to do a quick check on whether conditions are optimum for reaching the goal set. First, the supervisor must make sure that the employee has sufficient ability and knowledge to be able to reach the goal. Motivation without knowledge is useless. This, of course, puts a premium on proper selection and training and requires that the supervisor know the capabilities of subordinates when goals are assigned. Asking an employee to formulate an action plan for reaching the goal, as in MBO, is very useful, as it will indicate any knowledge deficiencies.

Second, the supervisor must ensure that the employee is provided with precise feedback so that he will know to what degree he's reaching or falling short of his goal and can thereupon adjust his level of effort or strategy accordingly. Recent research indicates that, while feedback is not a sufficient condition for improved performance, it is a necessary condition. A useful way to present periodic feedback is through the use of charts or graphs that plot performance over time.

Elements involved in taking the three steps described are shown in Figure 3, which illustrates in outline form our model of goal setting.

CONCLUSION

We believe that goal setting is a simple straightforward and highly effective technique for motivating employee performance. It is a basic technique, a method on which most other methods depend for their motivational effectiveness. The currently popular technique of behavior modification, for example, is mainly goal setting plus feedback, dressed up in academic terminology.

However, goal setting is no panacea. It will not compensate for underpayment of employees or for poor management. Used incorrectly, goal setting may cause rather than solve problems. If, for example, the goals set are unfair, arbitrary, or unreachable, dissatisfaction and poor performance may result. If difficult goals are set without proper quality controls, quantity may be achieved at the expense of quality. If pressure for immediate results is exerted without regard to how they are attained, short-term improvement may occur at the expense of long-run profits. That is, such pressure often triggers the use of expedient and ultimately costly methods—such as dishonesty, high-pressure tactics, postponing of maintenance expenses, and so on—to attain immediate results. Furthermore, performance goals are more easily set in some areas than in others. It's all too easy, for example, to concentrate on setting readily measured production goals and ignore employee development goals. Like any other management tool, goal setting works only when combined with good managerial judgment.

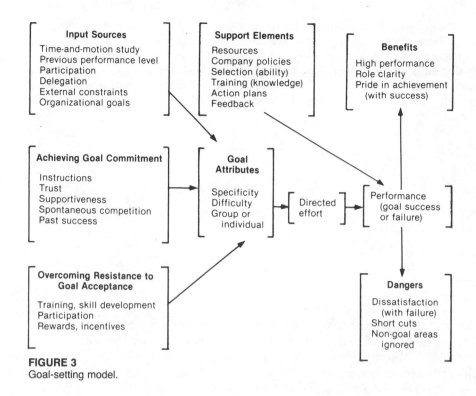

FIGURE 3
Goal-setting model.

SELECTED BIBLIOGRAPHY

A summary of the early (mainly laboratory) research on goal setting may be found in E. A. Locke's "Toward a Theory of Task Motivation and Incentives" (*Organization Behavior and Human Performance*, May 1968). More recent reviews that include some of the early field studies are reported by G. P. Latham and G. A. Yukl's "Review of Research on the Application of Goal Setting in Organizations" (*Academy of Management Journal*, December 1975) and in R. M. Steers and L. W. Porter's "The Role of Task-Goal Attributes in Employee Performance" (*Psychological Bulletin*, July 1974).

An excellent historical discussion of management by objectives, including its relationship to goal-setting research, can be found in G. S. Odiorne's "MBO: A Backward Glance" (*Business Horizons*, October 1978).

A thorough review of the literature on participation, including the relationship of participation and goal setting, can be found in a chapter by E. A. Locke and D. M. Schweiger, "Participation in Decision-Making: One More Look," in B. M. Staw's edited work, *Research in Organizational Behavior* (Vol.1, Greenwich, JAI Press, 1979). General Electric's famous research on the effect of participation in the appraisal interview is summarized in H. H. Meyer, E. Kay, and J. R. P. French, Jr.'s "Split Roles in Performance Appraisal" (*Harvard Business Review*, January–February 1965).

The relationship of goal setting to knowledge of results is discussed in E. A. Locke, N. Cartledge, and J. Koeppel's "Motivational Effects of Knowledge of Results: A Goal

Setting Phenomenon?'' (*Psychological Bulletin,* December 1968) and L. J. Becker's "Joint Effect of Feedback and Goal Setting on Performance: A Field Study of Residential Energy Conservation" (*Journal of Applied Psychology,* August 1978). Finally, the role of goal setting in virtually all theories of work motivation is documented in E. A. Locke's "The Ubiquity of the Technique of Goal Setting in Theories of and Approaches to Employee Motivation" (*Academy of Management Review,* July 1978).

The Determinants of Goal Commitment

Edwin A. Locke
Gary P. Latham
Miriam Erez

Reviews of the literature have shown that goal setting theory is among the most scientifically valid and useful theories in organizational science (Mento, Steel, & Karren, 1987; Miner, 1980; Pinder, 1984; Tubbs, 1986). The effectiveness of goal setting, however, presupposes the existence of goal commitment (Erez & Kanfer, 1983; Latham & Yukl, 1975a; Locke, 1968; Locke & Latham, 1984); it is virtually axiomatic that if there is no commitment to goals, then goal setting does not work. Naylor, Pritchard, and Ilgen (1980) have made goal commitment a key element in their general motivation theory.

A practical demonstration of the importance of goal commitment was given by Erez and Zidon (1984) in a laboratory study. They found a significant dropoff in performance as goal commitment declined in response to increasingly difficult goals. In field settings, noncommitment to organizational goals can result in restriction of output or "soldiering" (Mathewson, 1931; Roethlisberger & Dickson, 1939/1956; Taylor, 1911/1967). For example, in the famous bank-wiring observation room study at Hawthorne, the workers' personal goals (despite some inconsistencies in their reports) clearly were lower than the officially assigned goals or bogies (pp. 412–413) indicating less than full acceptance of management's goals.

Coch and French's (1948) classic study of participation was designed specifically to compare procedures for overcoming resistance by factory workers to changes in work standards or goals accompanying product changes (see also Cadwell, 1970; Goodman, 1979; Perkins, Nivea, & Lawler, 1983; Tushman, 1974). Organizational change, driven by rapid changes in technology and the world economy, is even more a fact of life today than in the past. Thus, understanding the factors that both inhibit and promote goal commitment is of great practical as well as theoretical importance.

From *Academy of Management Review,* 1988, **13**(1), 23–39. Reprinted by permission.

Some confusion exists in the use of the terms goal acceptance and goal commitment. In 1969, Locke implied that goal acceptance referred to initial agreement with a goal, whereas commitment referred to resistance to changing the goal later. The terms are used differently now, however. Commitment is the more inclusive concept because it refers to one's attachment to or determination to reach a goal, regardless of the goal's origin. Thus it can apply to any goal, whether self-set, participatively set, or assigned. Acceptance is one type of commitment; it refers specifically to commitment to a goal which is assigned (Locke, Shaw, Saari, & Latham, 1981).

It is possible that subsequent research will demonstrate the utility of a more marked separation of the concepts of acceptance and commitment, but thus far, such a distinction has not been shown to be useful. For example, Earley and Kanfer (1985, p. 382) in their study found that commitment and acceptance measures formed one, highly homogeneous index (alpha = .95). Leifer and McGannon (1986) found that a variety of alleged commitment and acceptance measures formed four separate factors; however, only one factor, that related to commitment, was associated with performance. Thus, the generic term *commitment* is used throughout this paper. The purpose of this review is to summarize and integrate research findings on the determinants of goal commitment.

MEASUREMENT OF COMMITMENT

A precondition for discovering the factors that affect goal commitment is the ability to measure it, or more specifically, to measure it in a way that will show systematic relationships between it and (a) prior causal factors, and (b) subsequent action (performance).

Commitment has been measured directly, indirectly, and by inference. Examples of direct questions are: "How committed are you to attaining the goal set?" and "To what degree do you accept the goal set?" (Earley, 1985b; Earley & Kanfer, 1985; Latham & Steele, 1983). The use of direct questions assumes that subjects can introspect well enough to detect varying degrees of commitment, and that the scales used allow people to indicate those degrees.

Leifer and McGannon (1986) used a direct approach in the study noted earlier. They found that the commitment factor that was related to performance included items which asked subjects how enthusiastic they were about trying for their goal. This emotion-focused factor not only was a more valid predictor of performance but showed higher variance than the more cognitively focused factor containing items which simply asked subjects if they were committed (personal communication, 1987).

An indirect measure of commitment is the discrepancy between an assigned goal level and the personal goal the subject claims actually to be trying to attain (Hannan, 1975). Earley (1985a, 1985b) found that the direct and indirect types of measures were highly correlated (.76 and .90, in two studies). The indirect method, of course, can be used only to measure commitment to assigned or participatively set goals. Asking subjects to set their own goals and then to indicate their personal goals makes no sense.

A third way to measure commitment is by inference from performance. While performance cannot be a catch-all measure of commitment, since performance can be caused by other factors such as ability, judicious use of inference from performance seems both theoretically and empirically justified. Theoretically, Salancik (1977) argued that behavior or action is the ultimate *proof* of commitment and thus, by implication, the most accurate measure of it. Commitment, he argued, quoting from others, is "the binding of the individual to behavioral acts." He claimed that "action is a necessary ingredient of commitment" (p. 4). Thus, "a person who is committed to a goal will try harder to achieve it than if he is not" (p. 27). Empirically, commitment inferences from performance levels can be justified if performance goal level, ability, and so forth, were or can be assumed to have been controlled or randomized. Further, commitment could be inferable from goal choice, whereas lack of commitment could be inferable from goal rejection; that is, at the time of choice it seems virtually axiomatic that people will choose the goal to which they are most committed (all forces and influences considered). Similarly, individuals who resist change, that is, resist changing from a current to a new goal, logically would seem to be uncommitted or less committed to the new goal. (The causes of such commitment or lack thereof, of course, still need to be explained.) It should also be noted that inference is not confined to the use of behavioral measures. Inference is also involved when direct, self-report measures of commitment are made. One is inferring that the verbal report corresponds to an actual psychological state. The inference in the case of behavior is simply more risky due to possible confounding variables.

A problem in the measurement of commitment exists if commitment affects performance, but the person is unable to report it accurately. This could result from poor introspection (see Schweiger, Anderson, & Locke, 1985, for a discussion of the validity of introspection). Latham, Mitchell, and Dossett (1978) reported the results of a study in which actual commitment differences may have existed but could not be reported accurately by the subjects. They found that offering a monetary incentive affected the performance of engineers and scientists, even though this difference was not mediated by differences in reported goal commitment or goal difficulty.

It may be possible to solve the introspection problem by using within-subject designs (e.g., Erez & Zidon, 1984). These should be more sensitive to different degrees of commitment than between-subject designs because scale interpretations should be uniform across conditions.

Goal commitment researchers also must decide whether to administer commitment questions to subjects, before, during, or after performance. Measuring before prevents post hoc rationalization; measuring after reveals if subjects changed their goals during performance. However, the results of research on the effects of both goal content and "learning without awareness" suggest that it does not matter when such variables are measured; the same results are obtained in both cases (Locke & Bryan, 1968; Spielberger, 1965). Similarly, Earley and Kanfer (1985) found no difference in results when goal commitment was measured both before and after performance.

COMMITMENT-PERFORMANCE RELATIONSHIP

Researchers have had difficulty demonstrating the effect of goal commitment on performance because, in the majority of studies, goal commitment has been easily achieved (Locke, Shaw, Saari, & Latham, 1981). Often, the small amount of variability that has been found was unrelated to performance (e.g., Dumont & Grimes, 1982; Frost & Mahoney, 1976; Huber & Neale, 1986; Ivancevich & McMahon, 1977b, 1977c, 1982; Locke, 1982; Locke, Frederick, Lee, & Bobko, 1984; London & Oldham, 1976; Mento, Cartledge, & Locke, 1980; Oldham, 1975; Pritchard & Curtis, 1973; Yukl & Latham, 1978). However, when steps are taken to deliberately increase variability, the importance of goal commitment can be demonstrated. For example, Erez and Zidon's (1984; phase 2) results (shown in Figure 1) indicate that when commitment dropped markedly in response to increasingly difficult goals, performance dropped accordingly.

Several other studies also have generated sufficient variability in goal commitment to yield significant relationships between commitment and performance (Earley, 1985a, 1985b, 1986; Earley & Kanfer, 1985; Erez, 1986; Erez & Arad, 1986; Erez, Earley, & Hulin, 1985; Hannan, 1975; Kolb, Winter, & Berlew, 1968; Locke & Shaw, 1984; Locke, Frederick, Buckner, & Bobko, 1984.) Ivancevich and McMahon (1977a) and Organ (1977) obtained mixed results.

The level at which the data are analyzed also can affect the commitment-performance relationship. Earley (1985b) reported that goal commitment was re-

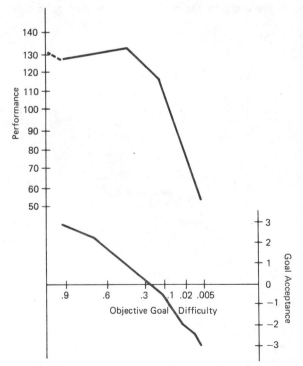

FIGURE 1
Mean performance and goal acceptance scores for different levels of objective goal difficulty in phase 2. (Adapted from Erez & Zidon, 1984.)

lated to performance within each of a number of goal difficulty levels. When he combined subjects across goal levels, however, goal commitment was no longer significant as either a main or an interaction effect. In contrast, the goal difficulty effect was highly significant.

It is important to observe that the overall correlation of commitment and performance across goal levels can be negative (Locke, Frederick, Buckner, & Bobko, 1984) because very hard goals, which lead to high performance, generally are accepted to a lesser degree than easy goals which lead to low performance.

It should be noted that even easy goals are not always fully accepted. However, goal rejection by subjects in an easy goal condition may not mean the same thing as goal rejection by subjects in a hard goal condition. Rejection in the former case may entail setting a harder personal goal (Locke, Mento, & Katcher, 1978), whereas rejection in the latter case may entail setting an easier personal goal.

In summary, theory as well as empirical research suggest that there is indeed a relationship between goal commitment and performance. Thus, there is a need to understand the factors that affect goal commitment. The remainder of this paper analyzes the literature dealing with the determinants of goal commitment.

Figure 2 shows an inductive model of commitment. Determinants of commitment are put into three categories: external influences (authority, peer influence, and external rewards); interactive influences (participation and competition); and internal factors (expectancy and internal rewards). It is assumed that the external and interactive factors undergo cognitive processing but this has not been ad-

FIGURE 2
Commitment model.

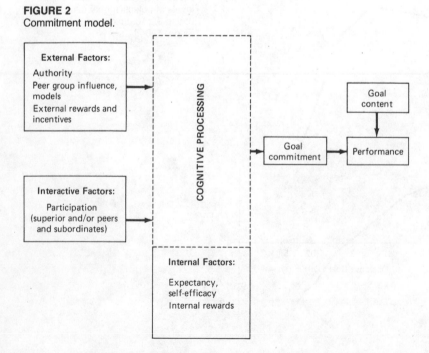

dressed in the research to date; thus, it is not discussed here. Campbell (1982) discussed some of these factors in his review of the goal choice literature, but there is only a small degree of overlap between the literature covered in his review and the one presented here.

DETERMINANTS OF COMMITMENT

External Influences

Legitimate Authority Most goal-setting studies have focused on the effects of assigned goals. The subjects or employees were asked to try for a specific level of performance on a task. Overwhelmingly, people tried to do what was asked of them (Latham & Lee, 1986). Studies that measured personal goals after the goals were assigned show that the two are highly correlated (Garland, 1983). This is not to say that instructions from an authority figure will always be obeyed; they will not (Bandura, 1986; Locke, Bryan, & Kendall, 1968). However, people usually choose to obey an authority figure because they judge the requests/assignments to be legitimate.

When an experimenter instructs a subject to try for a certain goal, he or she also affects the goals the subjects subsequently choose for themselves. For example, when subjects are asked on one or more trials to try for an assigned goal and subsequently are allowed to set their own goals on another trial, the self-set goal is similar in difficulty to the previously assigned goal (Locke, Frederick, Buckner, & Bobko, 1984; Locke, Frederick, Lee, & Bobko, 1984; Huber & Neale, 1986). This occurs despite the fact that people report that they are free to set any goal they want (Locke, Frederick, Buckner, & Bobko, 1984). Thus, commitment to an assigned goal may endure beyond the period of the actual assignment.

It appears that goal commitment reflects compliance with legitimate authority or power (French & Raven, 1959). This type of authority certainly exists in both laboratory and field settings. It may account for the high degree of similarity of results found in the two settings (Latham & Lee, 1986). In the laboratory, the experimenter is an authority figure. An experiment, by its nature, is a "demand situation" (Orne, 1962). Similarly, in industry, most employees consider it the supervisor's or manager's right to tell them what to do, because doing what one is told is inherent in the employment contract. Oldham (1975) found supervisory legitimacy to be significantly related to the intent to work hard to attain an assigned goal.

Salancik (1977) argued that assigned goals lead to commitment because (a) assigning the goal implies that the recipient is capable of reaching the goal, and (b) listening to the assignment without objection is itself a form of consent. These may, in fact, be two of the mechanisms by which legitimate authority affects a subordinate's behavior.

A number of studies suggest specific aspects of authority figures that may enhance their effectiveness. Although not all of these studies directly measured goal commitment, the results indicate that further exploration of these factors is worthwhile. For example, Ronan, Latham, and Kinne (1973) found that supervisors of logging crews who stayed on the job after assigning goals obtained higher productivity from their crews than those who assigned goals to their crews but did not remain on the job with them. One explanation for this finding is that the supervisor's *physical presence* enhanced goal commitment, although other explanations cannot be ruled out.

Latham and Saari (1979b) and Dossett, Cella, Greenberg, and Adrian (1983) explored the effects of supervisory supportiveness (Likert, 1961) on goal commitment and performance. Generally, correlations between supportiveness and commitment have not been significant because commitment has been uniformly high. But supportiveness has led to higher goals being set and/or higher performance (e.g., Likert, 1967, p. 53ff). Latham and Yukl (1975b) found that goal setting had no effect if management was perceived as indifferent to the goals that were set either by or for logging crews. Based on these findings, additional studies of supportiveness seem warranted.

Trust in authority is another dimension that has long been stressed as important to employee motivation by organizational development practitioners. Existing research provides supportive evidence for the effects of trust. In a study by Earley (1986) tire tread layers in England and in the United States were assigned goals by either union stewards or supervisors. In the U.S. sample, these two sources had no differential effect on goal commitment, but in the English sample, there was more commitment when the rationale for the goals was explained by the union steward than when it was explained by the supervisors. Earley argued that in England, workers trust their union stewards more than they do their supervisors. These results support those of Oldham (1975) who found perceptions of trust to be significantly related to the intent to work hard for an assigned goal.

The exertion of *pressure* on subordinates by those in authority may also affect goal commitment. Both Andrews and Farris (1972) and Hall and Lawler (1971) found that pressure from superiors (and others) was related positively to performance of scientists and engineers. Excessive pressure was found to be dysfunctional (Andrews & Farris, 1972; Forward & Zander, 1971; Likert, 1967). Goal commitment, however, was not actually measured in these studies.

Peer (Group) Influence As noted earlier, the effect of peer pressure on performance is a well-known phenomenon in industry. Historically the focus has been on documenting how peer pressure combines with past instances of ratecutting to enhance commitment to worker-originated group goals that are lower than management's assigned or preferred goals. As noted earlier, Taylor (1911/ 1967) called this phenomenon "systematic soldiering." Later it became known as "restriction of output" and was documented in the now classic studies of Mathewson (1931) and Roethlisberger and Dickson (1939). Commitment to uniform production standards is determined to a great extent by the level of group cohesion. Seashore (1954) found that high cohesion led to more uniform productivity within groups than did low cohesion, clearly implying an effect of commitment. Group commitment to high performance is facilitated by management support (Seashore, 1954), by the congruence between standards urged on the group by others and the members' own desires (Zander & Ulberg, 1971), and by the attachment of high importance to group goals and group success (Forward & Zander, 1971; Schacter, Ellertson, McBride, & Gregory, 1951; Zander & Ulberg, 1971).

Matsui, Kakuyama, and Onglatco (1986) found that in two-person groups, commitment was higher for subjects who were assigned both group and individual goals than it was for subjects who were assigned only individual goals for their segment of the group task. Commitments that carry responsibility to others can generate social pressures to follow through (Bandura, 1986).

Peers (and others) also may affect performance by acting as role models (Bandura, 1986). Rakestraw and Weiss (1981) found that modeling affected goal level. A specific, positive effect of peer modeling on goal commitment was found by Earley and Kanfer (1985).

Values, Incentives, and Rewards   Expectancy, operant, and social learning theorists would all agree, at least by implication, that commitment to actions is affected by incentives and rewards. For example, expectancy theorists predict that the value (valence) of the perceived outcomes and the estimated probability that effort and performance would lead to such outcomes would affect commitment/choice and, thereby, performance. The evidence seems consistent with this belief.

1 General Valence and Instrumentality   Yukl and Latham (1978) found an overall measure of goal instrumentality to be significantly related to goal commitment for female typists. Mento, et al. (1980) found significant relationships between general valence ratings and goal acceptance in two laboratory studies involving a perceptual speed task. Using the same task, Locke and Shaw (1984) found a significant relationship between the overall valence of winning and commitment to winning a monetary prize in a competitive setting. These findings show that monetary rewards can increase the level of goal commitment and, presumably, performance for some individuals.

In a study using within-subject design and a number comparison task, Matsui, Okada, and Mizuguchi (1981) found that the overall instrumentality of attaining hard goals was higher than that of attaining easy goals. Goal commitment was not measured, but performance change across goal conditions was highly correlated with the difference in valence ratings across goal conditions. This suggests more commitment to high performance in the high goal (and thus, high instrumentality) condition than in the low goal condition.

Dachler and Mobley (1973) found complex measures of general expected utility (based on combined expectancy, valence, and instrumentality ratings) to be significantly related to both current and future production goals of blue-collar employees in two plants. These self-chosen goals can be inferred as the ones to which the employees were most committed.

2 Monetary Incentives   Locke et al. (1968) hypothesized that monetary incentives affect performance by affecting goal level or goal commitment. Although several studies show that these incentives can affect performance independently of goal level (Campbell, 1984; Huber, 1985a; London & Oldham, 1976; Pritchard & Curtis, 1973; Terborg, 1976; Terborg & Miller, 1978), only one of these studies (Pritchard & Curtis, 1973) actually measured goal commitment. They found no effect of incentives on reported commitment. The performance results suggest, however, that commitment could have played a role in some of these studies since other factors (goal level, etc.) were controlled. Oldham (1975) found that a pay-focused instrumentality rating was significantly related to the intention to attain an assigned goal.

Mowen, Middlemist, and Luther (1981) reported the existence of an interesting interaction effect between money and goals. Under a piece-rate system, high goals resulted in higher performance than medium or easy goals. But, when subjects were paid a bonus *only* if they attained their goal, performance was lower when the goal was hard than when it was moderately difficult or easy. It may be that under the hard goal and task-and-bonus system, subjects were not committed to their goals because they believed there was no chance of earning the bonus. Under a task-and-bonus system, partial success, in the sense of coming close to the goal, is not rewarded. In contrast, the piece-rate payment system rewards partial success, because payment is based on performance, not goal attainment. When hard goals are assigned without tangible rewards, people can feel some accomplishment even if they do not fully attain the goals. Under such conditions one would expect commitment to hard goals to be higher than under a task-and-bonus system.

3 Punishment Latham and Saari (1982) found that unionized truck drivers committed themselves to a goal-setting program under four conditions: (a) that it would not lead to layoffs, (b) that monetary incentives (viewed as potentially punitive) would not be used, (c) that the goals would be voluntary, and (d) that supervisors would be supportive of attempts to reach the goals, and the truckers would not be punished for failure. The program was successful as long as the employees believed that these terms were being met. When the employees concluded that these conditions were not being met, they interpreted the program as punitive, and rejected it by using an extreme form of goal rejection, a wildcat strike.

Interactive Factors

Participation Findings about the effect participation has on goal commitment are contradictory. The first series of studies questioning importance of participation were conducted at General Electric by Meyer and his associates (French, Kay, & Meyer, 1966; Meyer, Kay, & French, 1965). Their widely disseminated conclusion was that it is not so important how a goal is set as it is that a goal, in fact, be set.

Latham and Yukl (1975b) found that participatively set goals led to higher performance than assigned goals only among uneducated woods workers. This difference may have been due to the higher goals that were set in the participative condition; goal commitment was not measured. Subsequently, a series of nine (five field and four laboratory) experiments comparing participative and assigned goal setting was conducted by Latham and his colleagues. Eight of the studies found no differences in goal commitment regardless of whether the goal was assigned or set participatively, when goal difficulty was held constant [Dossett, Latham, & Mitchell, 1979 (2 studies); Latham & Marshall, 1982; Latham & Saari,

1979a; Latham & Steele, 1983; Latham et al. 1978; Latham, Steele, & Saari, 1982; Latham & Yukl, 1976]. The exception was Latham and Saari's study (1979b), in which the participation effect probably was cognitive not motivational, because the participative subjects asked more questions regarding task requirements than the assigned goal subjects.

Ivancevich (1976, 1977) also failed to find consistent differences in the effects of participative and assigned goals on various performance measures in two field studies. Dossett et al. (1983) found no effect on commitment or performance attributable to participation in a field study.

These null findings are consistent with conclusions drawn from reviews of the participation literature in general (Locke & Schweiger, 1979; Locke, Feren, McCaleb, Shaw, & Denny, 1980) and with those drawn from reviews of the participation in goal-setting literature in particular (Schweiger & Leana, 1986; Latham & Lee, 1986; Latham & Yukl, 1975a). A meta-analysis of the goal-setting literature by Mento et al. (1987) which focused on effect size rather than direction as in the case of the other reviews, found only a borderline effect (approximately 4 percent) in favor of participation. Such a finding is considered trivial (Fowler, 1985). Citing Lykken (1968), Flowler argued that molar psychological variables share on the average about 4 to 5 percent common variance. Tubbs (1986) also found that participation had a negligible effect in another meta-analysis of goal-setting studies even when goal difficulty was not held constant.

However, a series of experiments conducted by Erez and her colleagues has found results consistently favoring participative over assigned goal setting (Earley, 1985b; Earley & Kanfer, 1985; Erez, 1986; Erez, Earley, & Hulin, 1985; Erez & Arad, 1986). In addition, these studies found significant relationships between goal commitment and performance. A key reason for the latter finding is that Erez's procedures, as a package, produced a much wider range of goal commitment among various experimental groups than did Latham et al.'s. In Erez, Earley, and Hulin (1985), for example, the range in goal commitment among subgroups was from 1.70 to 6.75 on a 7-point scale in the first study and 4.20 to 6.50 in the second. In Erez and Arad (1986) the range was 3.58 to 5.79. In Erez (1986) it was 4.24 to 5.91. In contrast the largest range reported by Latham within one study (on a 5-point scale) was 3.63 to 4.08 (Latham & Steele, 1983).

It is important to note that Latham and Erez actually agree about the effectiveness of participative goal setting; both found it to be effective. They disagree only about the effectiveness of assigned goal setting. Latham found it to be as effective as participative goal setting, whereas Erez did not. In order to resolve this contradiction, Erez, Latham, and Locke (1987) jointly designed and conducted four experiments. A key finding of these experiments was that the "Tell and Sell" style (cf. Maier, 1958; Tannenbaum & Schmidt, 1958) of assigning goals used by Latham and his colleagues was as effective as setting goals participatively, whereas the "Tell" style of assigning goals used by Erez and her colleagues was significantly less effective in terms of commitment and performance than setting goals participatively.

The effectiveness of different goal-setting styles may differ depending on cultural values. Erez and Earley (in press) found that assigned and participative goal setting produced similar effects on commitment, but different effects on performance among U.S. and Israeli subjects. (Commitment was correlated with performance for the Israeli but not for the U.S. subjects.) Americans performed equally well in both cases. The Israelis performed more poorly under assigned goals than participative goals, a result consonant with their more collectivistic value orientation (Hofstede, 1980). Latham used only American and Canadian subjects in his studies; they are certainly more individualistic than Kibbutz members. There are other differences between the Latham and Erez studies which may have contributed in minor ways to the differences in results (e.g., differential self-efficacy inductions; see Latham, Erez, & Locke, 1987 for details).

Another possible interactive factor is competition. Mueller (1983) tested Locke's (1968) hypothesis that competition can increase performance if it leads to the setting of and/or commitment to high goals. The hypothesis was supported with regard to goal difficulty. Subjects in the competitive condition set significantly higher goals and performed significantly better than those who were not in the competitive condition. However, competition did not affect the commitment of subjects in either the assigned or self-set goal conditions. It remains to be seen whether subsequent studies will show commitment as well as goal level effects of competition.

Internal Factors

Expectancy of Success and Self-Efficacy Expectancy theorists (Dachler & Mobley, 1973; Vroom, 1964) argue that one's choices are affected by one's perceived chances of performing well on a task. Results of a number of studies indicate that commitment declines as the goal becomes more difficult and/or as the person's perceived chances of reaching it decline. A dramatic effect of commitment was obtained in the experiment noted earlier by Erez and Zidon (1984). In the second phase of a two-part experiment, technicians were shown bogus goal acceptance norms allegedly based on the responses of high level professionals. These norms suggested the appropriateness of low commitment to more difficult goals. The result was a high level of goal rejection and low performance in response to the more difficult goals.

Many studies find that goal commitment is lower for more objectively difficult goals (presumably associated with lower expectancies) than less objectively difficult goals (e.g., Dumont & Grimes, 1982; Earley, 1985a, 1985b; Erez, Earley, & Hulin, 1985; Hanges, 1987; Hannan, 1975; Locke, 1982; Locke, Frederick, Buckner, & Bobko, 1984). However, Huber (1985b), Oldham (1975), and Shalley and Oldham (1985) found no such effect, and Locke (1982) and Garland (1983) found that even impossible goals could motivate high performance in the short term. Huber and Neale (1986) and Mento et al. (1980) found that rated subjective expectancy of success significantly affected commitment.

Self-efficacy is related to expectancy of success. Bandura defines self-efficacy as a judgment of "how well one can execute courses of action required to deal with prospective situations" (1982, p. 122; see also 1986). This concept, broader in scope than expectancy, includes a judgment of one's total capability of performing a task (see Gist, 1987). Because self-efficacy ratings are performance-based, they do not apply to goals as such. However, one could predict that the chances of accepting a hard goal would be higher when self-efficacy for a task is high as opposed to low. Bandura and Cervone (1983, 1986) found that when subjects were given feedback indicating performance below the level of the assigned goal, subsequent effort was higher for those with high self-efficacy than for those with low self-efficacy. Locke, Frederick, Lee, and Bobko (1984) found that self-efficacy was significantly related to commitment to self-set goals, but not to assigned goals, a finding consistent with previous comments regarding restriction of range, since it was found that the variance in commitment was significantly higher for self-set than for assigned goals.

Earley (1985a) found that information about how to perform the task increased goal commitment, and Earley (1986) found that such information affected self-efficacy, and, thereby, goal commitment and performance. Earley (1985b) also found an effect of self-efficacy on goal commitment.

Self-Administered Rewards Masters, Furman, and Barden (1977) found that self-administered rewards in the form of statements such as "I did very good [sic]" led to such dramatic improvements among 5- and 6-year-old children that subjects in all goal conditions reached asymptote. This did not occur when the children were given tangible prizes for goal attainment. Possibly the effect of the self-reward was to increase the children's self-efficacy (Bandura, 1982) and thus commitment.

Ivancevich and McMahon (1982) found no relationship between goal commitment and performance. However, goal setting plus self-generated feedback led to higher organizational commitment and performance than did goal setting plus feedback given by the supervisor. The reason for this is not clear, but, perhaps, the self-generated feedback was either more accepted or seen as more meaningful than feedback provided by others. There may be a parallel here with the Masters et al. study (1977) described above in which self-reward had a greater effect on motivation than rewards given by others.

DISCUSSION

This review has theoretical, methodological, and practical implications. Theoretically, it has been shown that there is a logical relationship between goal commitment and performance. Methodologically, such a relationship can be shown using various types of measures but requires the existence of a reasonable degree of variance in goal commitment. Leifer and McGannon's finding (personal communication, 1987) that emotion-focused measures of commitment are more valid and produce more variance than cognitively focused measures is worth further exploration. Practically, the evidence regarding the factors that affect the degree (and, thus, by implication the range) of goal commitment has been summarized.

Legitimate authority is a key determinant of goal commitment. The relationship between goal commitment and authority was discussed many years ago by Barnard (1938) who proposed that the source of authority does not reside in the superior, but in the acceptance of that authority by subordinates. According to Barnard, individuals must assent to authority and will do so if (a) they understand the communicated order, (b) they believe that the order is consistent with organizational objectives and their personal interests, and (c) they are mentally and physically able to comply with the order. Barnard coined the concept *zone of indifference* within which orders will be accepted by a person without question. However, if obeying the order results in a negative balance, the person will no longer comply with authority. In most goal-setting studies, the instructions appear to have remained within the zone of indifference. More research on the effects of authority would be useful, especially regarding characteristics or actions of authority figures (e.g., physical presence, use of pressure, supportiveness, and trust) that affect commitment.

Gaining goal commitment also can be discussed and researched in the context of a wider organizational issue pertaining to the exercise of authority, that of leadership. It seems clear that productive goal setting for self and others (including identifying the organizational mission or purpose) is a key activity of successful managers and leaders (Bennis & Nanus, 1985; Boyatzis, 1982; Kotter, 1982). Bennis and Nanus (1985) argued that communicating the goals or mission of the organization to subordinates in a way that will be clear and compelling, that is, that will get subordinates committed, is a requirement of effective leadership (e.g., Locke & Somers, 1987). The same viewpoint has been expressed by Peters and Waterman (1982). They stressed the importance of managers reinforcing the core organizational values by taking value-relevant actions themselves (e.g., answering customer calls in order to emphasize the importance of good customer relations).

To better understand the effect of peer influence, more group goal-setting studies are needed. Studies of the effects of modeling would especially be useful (Bandura, 1986).

More studies need to use commitment measures and within-subject designs to see whether findings such as that by Mowen et al. (1981) regarding the effects of rewards can be explained by commitment differences.

Further research on the effects of participation on commitment may be of limited usefulness at this time since the reasons for the differences between Latham et al.'s and Erez et al.'s results now seem clear. A recent meta-analysis of participation studies by Wagner and Gooding (1986) found that, excluding percept-percept correlations, the mean correlation between participation and commitment was a mere $.10(R^2 = .01)$. Competition as a possible commitment-inducing activity is clearly in need of further study.

Since self-efficacy affects goal commitment, different ways of increasing self-efficacy should be examined. Bandura (1986) stessed inactive mastery (practice), modeling, and persuasion as the three key methods. However, Earley's (1986) results suggest that giving the employee task strategy information also can be a powerful way to raise confidence. Self-reward also merits further study.

The factors known to affect goal commitment not only have implications for future practice, but they also can help to explain (even reinterpret) the results of previous studies. Consider the famous Coch and French (1948) study of workers in a pajama factory. Despite the authority exercised by supervisors and an incentive bonus for goal attainment, workers routinely showed lowered productivity after product changeovers which involved the establishment of new standards and piece rates.

Coch and French observed that workers felt that they could not attain the new standards and banded together to restrict production at a low level. Thus, even though legitimate authority and incentives were present, there seemed to be a lack of trust and support, low self-efficacy, and group norms in opposition to the assigned standards. The low self-efficacy apparently negated the effect of the incentive, because the workers did not think they could produce enough to earn it.

Coch and French instituted a "participation" intervention that overcame worker resistance. However, Bartlem and Locke (1981) noted that the participative groups were given a much more detailed and compelling explanation of the need for the product change than was the control (nonparticipative) group. This difference may have been equivalent to the difference between the "Tell" and "Tell and Sell" styles—a distinction that explained in large part the contradictory findings of Erez and Latham regarding assigned goals.

In addition, participative groups in the Coch and French study were given additional training and new piece rates were set by studying the workers themselves rather than using standard times. Undoubtedly, the effect of these interventions would be to raise self-efficacy and trust. In turn, increased self-efficacy would make the incentives effective because the workers would believe that they could attain them. Thus these delineated factors seem to explain both the rejection of goals by the control group and the acceptance of goals by the experimental groups.

Unfortunately, not enough is known abut the relative importance of the various determinants of goal commitment to permit meaningful predictions of their effects on commitment when there are conflicting elements. This should be the subject of future studies. Bandura (1986) indicated that low self-efficacy can negate the effects of incentives because people will not be motivated by incentives if they think they cannot earn them. Thus, it may be that rewards are less fundamental than self-efficacy. Further it can be hypothesized that in the face of a reward system that is seen as inappropriate or unfair, group norms may develop which restrict performance (cf., Coch & French, 1948; Seashore, 1954).

Individual and cultural values as determinants of the effects of various goal-setting procedures on commitment also need exploration. It was noted earlier that Erez and Earley (in press) found that cultural values were a strong moderator of the effects of assigned goals when "Tell" instructions were employed.

Motive and value measurement at the individual level within a given culture also may prove worthwhile. For example, people may accept goals partly because they enjoy being challenged; thus, commitment may be related to individual differences in achievement motivation.

The effect of (role, goal) conflict on goal commitment has not been studied, but the clinical literature suggests that conflict can be debilitating and may adversely influence performance as well as affect (stress, etc.). For example, an individual may be rewarded for one type of activity (e.g., quantity of production) while being asked to make another activity a top priority (e.g., making quality products).

Less commitment to both quantity and quality goals or lowered commitment to one at the expense of the other could result.

Finally, McCaul, Hinsz, and McCaul (in press) found that when subjects publicly announced their goals in a group setting and posted their names and goals publicly, this led to higher reported commitment and greater task persistence (but not performance level) than when these were stated privately on a questionnaire. Public announcement of the goal is an issue that harks back to Lewin's (1947, 1952) classic studies of methods of changing food habits. Lewin, however, did not manipulate public vs. private announcement as a separate variable. The McCaul et al. study suggests that this variable is worth further exploration.

REFERENCES

Andrews, F. M., & Farris, G. F. (1972) Time pressure and performance of scientists and engineers: A five-year panel study. *Organizational Behavior and Human Performance,* 8, 185–200.

Bandura, A. (1982) Self-efficacy mechanism in human agency. *American Psychologist,* 37, 122–147.

Bandura, A. (1986) *Social foundations of thought and action: A social cognitive theory.* Englewood Cliffs, NJ: Prentice-Hall.

Bandura, A., & Cervone, D. (1983) Self-evaluative and self-efficacy mechanisms governing the motivational effects of goal systems. *Journal of Personality and Social Psychology,* 45, 1017–1028.

Bandura, A., & Cervone, D. (1986) Differential engagement of self-reactive influence in cognitive motivation. *Organizational Behavior and Human Decision Processes,* 38, 92–113.

Barnard, C. I. (1938) *The functions of the executive.* Cambridge, MA: Harvard University Press.

Bartlem, C. S., & Locke, E. A. (1981) The Coch and French study: A critique and reinterpretation. *Human Relations,* 34, 555–566.

Bennis, W., & Nanus, B. (1985) *Leaders.* New York: Harper & Row.

Boyatzis, R. E. (1982) *The competent manager.* New York: Wiley.

Cadwell, R. B. (1970) *Barriers to planned change: A study of two business organizations.* Dublin, Ireland: Irish National Productivity Committee, Development Division.

Campbell, D. J. (1982) Determinants of choice of goal difficulty level: A review of situational and personality influences. *Journal of Occupational Psychology,* 55, 79–95.

Campbell, D. J. (1984) The effects of goal-contingent payment on the performance of a complex task. *Personnel Psychology,* 37, 23–40.

Coch, L., & French, J. R. P. (1948) Overcoming resistance to change. *Human Relations,* 1, 512–532.

Dachler, H. P., & Mobley, W. H. (1973) Construct validation of an instrumentality-expectancy-task-goal model of work motivation: Some theoretical boundary conditions. [Monograph]. *Journal of Applied Psychology,* 58, 397–418.

Dossett, D. L., Cella, A., Greenberg, C. L., & Adrian, N. (1983) *Goal setting, participation and leader supportiveness effects on performance.* Paper presented at the meeting of the American Psychological Association, Anaheim, CA.

Dossett, D. L., Latham, G. P., & Mitchell, T. R. (1979) The effects of assigned versus participatively set goals, KR, and individual differences when goal difficulty is held constant. *Journal of Applied Psychology,* 64, 291–298.

Dumont, P. F., & Grimes, A. J. (1982) *The hard-impossible threshold: A pragmatic limitation of the task goal model and a link to individual difference theories.* Paper presented at the meeting of the American Institute for Decision Sciences, San Francisco.

Earley, P. C. (1985a) Influence of information, choice and task complexity upon goal acceptance, performance, and personal goals. *Journal of Applied Psychology,* 70, 481–491.

Earley, P. C. (1985b) *The influence of goal setting methods on performance, goal acceptance, self-efficacy expectations, and expectancies across levels of goal difficulty.* Paper presented at the meeting of the American Psychological Association, Los Angeles.

Earley, P. C. (1986) Supervisors and shop stewards as sources of contextual information in goal setting: A comparison of the U.S. with England. *Journal of Applied Psychology,* 71, 111–117.

Earley, P. C., & Kanfer, R. (1985) The influence of component participation and role models on goal acceptance, goal satisfaction and performance. *Organizational Behavior and Human Decision Processes,* 36, 378–390.

Erez, M. (1986) The congruence of goal setting strategies with socio-cultural values, and its effect on performance. *Journal of Management,* 12, 83–90.

Erez, M., & Arad, R. (1986) Participative goal setting: Social, motivational and cognitive factors. *Journal of Applied Psychology,* 71, 591–597.

Erez, M., & Earley, P. C. (in press) Comparative analysis of goal setting across cultures. *Journal of Applied Psychology.*

Erez, M., Earley, P. C., & Hulin, C. L. (1985) The impact of participation on goal acceptance and performance: A two-step model. *Academy of Management Journal,* 28, 50–66.

Erez, M., & Kanfer, F. H. (1983) The role of goal acceptance in goal setting and task performance. *Academy of Management Review,* 8, 454–463.

Erez, M., & Zidon, I. (1984) Effect of goal acceptance on the relationship of goal difficulty to performance. *Journal of Applied Psychology,* 69, 69–78.

Forward, J., & Zander, A. (1971) Choice of unattainable group goals and effects on performance. *Organizational Behavior and Human Performance,* 6, 184–199.

Fowler, R. L. (1985) Testing for substantive significance in applied research by specifying non-zero effect null hypotheses. *Journal of Applied Psychology,* 70, 215–218.

French, J. R. P., Kay, E., & Meyer, H. H. (1966) Participation and the appraisal system. *Human Relations,* 19, 3–20.

French, J., & Raven, B. H. (1959) The bases of social power. In D. Cartwright (Ed.), *Studies in social power* (pp. 150–167). Ann Arbor, MI: Institute for Social Research.

Frost, P. J., & Mahoney, T. A. (1976) Goal setting and the task process: I. An interactive influence on individual performance. *Organizational Behavior and Human Performance,* 17, 328–350.

Garland, H. (1983) The influence of ability, assigned goals, and normative information on personal goals and performance: A challenge to the goal attainability assumption. *Journal of Applied Psychology,* 68, 20–30.

Gist, M. E. (1987) Self-efficacy: Implications for organizational behavior and human resource management. *Academy of Management Review,* 12, 472–485.

Goodman, P. S. (1979) *Assessing organizational change: Rushton quality of work experiment.* New York: Wiley.

Hall, D. T., & Lawler, E. E. (1971) Job pressures and research performance. *American Scientist,* 59(1), 64–73.

Hanges, P. (1987) *Using regression analysis to empirically verify catastrophe models.* Paper presented at the meeting of the Society of Industrial and Organizational Psychology, Atlanta.

Hannan, R. L. (1975) *The effects of participation in goal setting on goal acceptance and performance: A laboratory experiment.* Unpublished doctoral dissertation, University of Maryland.

Hofstede, G. (1980) *Culture's consequences.* Beverly Hills, CA: Sage.

Huber, V. L. (1985a) Comparison of monetary reinforcers and goal setting as learning incentives. *Psychological Reports,* 56, 223–235.

Huber, V. L. (1985b) Effects of task difficulty, goal setting, and strategy on performance of a heuristic task. *Journal of Applied Psychology,* 70, 492–504.

Huber, V. L., & Neale, M. A. (1986) Effects of cognitive heuristics and goals on negotiator performance and subsequent goal setting. *Organizational Behavior and Human Decision Processes,* 38, 342–365.

Ivancevich, J. M. (1976) Effects of goal setting on performance and job satisfaction. *Journal of Applied Psychology,* 61, 605–612.

Ivancevich, J. M. (1977) Different goal setting treatments and their effects on performance and job satisfaction. *Academy of Management Journal,* 20, 406–419.

Ivancevich, J. M., & McMahon, J. T. (1977a) A study of task-goal attributes, higher order need strength and performance. *Academy of Management Journal,* 20, 552–563.

Ivancevich, J. M., & McMahon, J. T. (1977b) Black-white differences in a goal-setting program. *Organizational Behavior and Human Performance,* 20, 287–300.

Ivancevich, J. M., & McMahon, J. T. (1977c) Education as a moderator of goal setting effectiveness. *Journal of Vocational Behavior,* 11, 83–94.

Ivancevich, J. M., & McMahon, J. T. (1982) The effects of goal setting, external feedback, and self-generated feedback on outcome variables: A field experiment. *Academy of Management Journal,* 25, 359–372.

Kolb, D., Winter, S. K., & Berlew, D. E. (1968) Self-directed change: Two studies. *Journal of Applied Behavioral Science,* 4, 453–471.

Kotter, J. P. (1982) *The general managers.* New York: Free Press.

Latham, G. P., Erez, M., & Locke, E. A. (1987) Resolving scientific disputes by the joint design of crucial experiments by the antagonists: Application to the Erez-Latham dispute regarding participation in goal setting. Unpublished manuscript, University of Washington, Graduate School of Business Administration.

Latham, G. P., & Lee, T. W. (1986) Goal setting. In E. A. Locke (Ed.), *Generalizing from laboratory to field settings* (pp. 101–117). Lexington, MA: Lexington Books.

Latham, G. P., & Marshall, H. A. (1982) The effects of self-set, participatively set and assigned goals on the performance of government employees. *Personnel Psychology,* 35, 399–404.

Latham, G. P., Mitchell, T. R., & Dossett, D. L. (1978) Importance of participative goal setting and anticipated rewards on goal difficulty and job performance. *Journal of Applied Psychology,* 63, 163–171.

Latham, G. P., & Saari, L. M. (1979a) The effects of holding goal difficulty constant on assigned and participatively set goals. *Academy of Management Journal,* 22, 163–168.

Latham, G. P., & Saari, L. M. (1979b) Importance of supportive relationships in goal setting. *Journal of Applied Psychology,* 64, 151–156.

Latham, G. P., & Saari, L. M. (1982) The importance of union acceptance for productivity improvement through goal setting. *Personnel Psychology,* 35, 781–787.

Latham, G. P., & Steele, T. P. (1983) The motivational effects of participation versus goal setting on performance. *Academy of Management Journal,* 26, 406–417.

Latham, G. P., Steele, T. P., & Saari, L. M. (1982) The effects of participation and goal difficulty on performance. *Personnel Psychology,* 35, 677–686.

Latham, G. P., & Yukl, G. A. (1975a) A review of research on the application of goal setting in organizations. *Academy of Management Journal,* 18, 824–845.

Latham, G. P., & Yukl, G. A. (1975b) Assigned versus participative goal setting with educated and uneducated woods workers. *Journal of Applied Psychology,* 60, 299–302.

Latham, G. P., & Yukl, G. A. (1976) Effects of assigned and participative goal setting on performance and job satisfaction. *Journal of Applied Psychology,* 61, 166–171.

Leifer, R., & McGannon, K. (1986) *Goal acceptance and goal commitment: Their differential impact on goal setting theory.* Paper presented at the meeting of the Academy of Management, Chicago.

Lewin, K. (1947) Frontiers in group dynamics. *Human Relations,* 1, 5–42.

Lewin, K. (1952) Group decision and social change. In T. Newcomb & E. Hartley (Eds.), *Readings in social psychology* (pp. 330–344). New York: Holt, Rinehart & Winston.

Likert, R. (1961) *New patterns of management.* New York: McGraw-Hill.

Likert, R. (1967) *The human organization.* New York: McGraw-Hill.

Locke, E. A. (1968) Toward a theory of task motivation and incentives. *Organizational Behavior and Human Performance,* 3, 157–189.

Locke, E. A. (1982) Relation of goal level to performance with a short work period and multiple goal levels. *Journal of Applied Psychology,* 67, 512–514.

Locke, E. A., & Bryan, J. F. (1968) Goal setting as a determinant of the effects of knowledge of score on performance. *American Journal of Psychology,* 81, 398–406.

Locke, E. A., Bryan, J. F., & Kendall, L. M. (1968) Goals and intentions as mediators of the effects of monetary incentives on behavior. *Journal of Applied Psychology,* 52, 104–121.

Locke, E. A., Feren, D. B., McCaleb, V. M., Shaw, K. N., & Denny, A. T. (1980) The relative effectiveness of four methods of motivating employee performance. In K. Duncan, M. Gruneberg, & D. Wallis (Eds.), *Changes in working life* (pp. 363–388). New York: Wiley.

Locke, E. A., Frederick, E., Buckner, E., & Bobko, P. (1984) Effects of previously assigned goals on self-set goals and performance. *Journal of Applied Psychology,* 69, 694–699.

Locke, E. A., Frederick, E., Lee, C., & Bobko, P. (1984) Effect of self-efficacy, goals and task strategies on task performance. *Journal of Applied Psychology,* 69, 241–251.

Locke, E. A., & Latham, G. P. (1984) *Goal-setting: A motivational technique that works.* Englewood Cliffs, NJ: Prentice-Hall.

Locke, E. A., Mento, A. J., & Katcher, B. L. (1978) The interaction of ability and motivation in performance: An exploration of the meaning of moderators. *Personnel Psychology,* 31, 269–280.

Locke, E. A., & Schweiger, D. M. (1979) Participation in decision-making: One more look. In B. M. Staw (Ed.), *Research in organizational behavior* (Vol. 1, pp. 265–339). Greenwich, CT: JAI Press.

Locke, E. A., & Shaw, K. N. (1984) Atkinson's inverse-U curve and the missing cognitive variables. *Psychological Reports,* 55, 403–412.

Locke, E. A., Shaw K. N., Saari, L. M., & Latham, G. P. (1981) Goal setting and task performance: 1969–1980. *Psychological Bulletin,* 90, 125–152.

Locke, E. A., & Somers, R. L. (1987) The effects of goal emphasis on performance on a complex task. *Journal of Management Studies,* 24, 405–411.

London, M., & Oldham, G. R. (1976) Effects of varying goal types and incentive systems on performance and satisfaction. *Academy of Management Journal,* 19, 537–546.

Lykken, D. T. (1968) Statistical significance in psychological research. *Psychological Bulletin*, 70, 151–159.

Maier, N. R. F. (1958) *The appraisal interview*. New York: Wiley.

Masters, J. C., Furman, W., & Barden, R. C. (1977) Effects of achievement standards, tangible rewards, and self-dispensed achievement evaluations on children's task mastery. *Child Development*, 48, 217–224.

Mathewson, S. B. (1931) *Restriction of output among unorganized workers*. New York: Viking Press.

Matsui, T., Kakuyama, T., & Onglatco, M. L. (1986) *Goals, feedback, and task performance: Group versus individual*. Unpublished manuscript.

Matsui, T., Okada, A., & Mizuguchi, R. (1981) Expectancy theory prediction of the goal theory postulate, the harder the goals, the higher the performance. *Journal of Applied Psychology*, 66, 54–58.

McCaul, K. D., Hinsz, V. B., & McCaul, H. S. (in press) The effects of commitment to performance goals on effort. *Journal of Applied Social Psychology*.

Mento, A. J., Cartledge, N. D., & Locke, E. A. (1980) Maryland vs. Michigan vs. Minnesota: Another look at the relationship of expectancy and goal difficulty to task performance. *Organizational Behavior and Human Performance*, 25, 419–440.

Mento, A. J., Steele, R. P., & Karren, R. J. (1987) A meta-analytic study of the effects of goal setting on task performance: 1966–1984. *Organizational Behavior and Human Decision Processes*, 39, 52–83.

Meyer, H. H., Kay, E., & French, J. R. P. (1965) Split roles in performance appraisal. *Harvard Business Review*, 43(1), 123–129.

Miner, J. B. (1980) *Theories of organizational behavior*. Hinsdale, IL: Dryden.

Mowen, J. C., Middlemist, R. D., & Luther, D. (1981) Joint effects of assigned goal level and incentive structure on task performance: A laboratory study. *Journal of Applied Psychology*, 66, 598–603.

Mueller, M. E. (1983) *The effects of goal setting and competition on performance: A laboratory study*. Unpublished master's thesis, University of Minnesota.

Naylor, J. C., Pritchard, R. D., & Ilgen, D. R. (1980) *A theory of behavior in organizations*. New York: Academic Press.

Oldham, G. R. (1975) The impact of supervisory characteristics on goal acceptance. *Academy of Management Journal*, 18, 461–475.

Organ, D. W. (1977) Intentional vs. arousal effects of goal-setting. *Organizational Behavior and Human Performance*, 18, 378–389.

Orne, M. T. (1962) On the social psychology of the psychological experiment with particular reference to demand characteristics. *American Psychologist*, 17, 776–783.

Perkins, D. N. T., Nieva, V. G., & Lawler, E. E. (1983) *Managing creation: The challenge of building a new organization*. New York: Wiley.

Peters, T. J., & Waterman, R. H. (1982) *In search of excellence*. New York: Harper & Row.

Pinder, C. C. (1984) *Work motivation*. Glenview, IL: Scott, Foresman.

Pritchard, R. D., & Curtis, M. I. (1973) The influence of goal setting and financial incentives on task performance. *Organizational Behavior and Human Performance*, 10, 175–183.

Rakestraw, T. L., & Weiss, H. (1981) The interaction of social influence and task experience on goals, performance and performance satisfaction. *Organizational Behavior and Human Performance*, 27, 326–344.

Roethlisberger, F. J., & Dickson, W. J. (1939/1956) *Management and the worker*. Cambridge, MA: Harvard University Press.

Ronan, W. W., Latham, G. P., & Kinne, S. B. (1973) Effects of goal setting and supervision on worker behavior in an industrial situation. *Journal of Applied Psychology,* 58, 302–307.

Salancik, G. R. (1977) Commitment and the control of organizational behavior and belief. In B. M. Staw & G. Salancik (Eds.), *New directions in organizational behavior* (pp. 1–54). Chicago: St. Clair.

Schacter, S., Ellertson, N., McBride, D., & Gregory, D. (1951) An experimental study of cohesiveness and productivity. *Human Relations,* 4, 229–238.

Schweiger, D. M., Anderson, C. R., & Locke, E. A. (1985) Complex decision-making: A longitudinal study of process and performance. *Organizational Behavior and Human Decision Processes,* 36, 245–272.

Schweiger, D. M., & Leana, C. R. (1986) Participation in decision making. In E. A. Locke (Ed.), *Generalizing from laboratory to field settings* (pp. 147–166). Lexington, MA: Lexington Books.

Seashore, S. E. (1954) *Group cohesiveness in the industrial work group.* Ann Arbor: Survey Research Center, Institute for Social Research, University of Michigan.

Shalley, C. E., & Oldham, G. R. (1985) Effects of goal difficulty and expected external evaluation on intrinsic motivation: A laboratory study. *Academy of Management Journal,* 28, 628–640.

Spielberger, C. D. (1965) Theoretical and epistemological issues in verbal conditioning. In S. Rosenberg (Ed.), *Directions in psycholinguistics* (pp. 149–200). New York: Macmillan.

Tannenbaum, R., & Schmidt, E. (1958) How to choose a leadership pattern. *Harvard Business Review,* 36(2), 95–101.

Taylor, F. W. (1911/1967) *Principles of scientific management.* New York: Norton.

Terborg, J. R. (1976) The motivational components of goal setting. *Journal of Applied Psychology,* 61, 613–621.

Terborg, J. R., & Miller, H. E. (1978) Motivation, behavior and performance: A closer examination of goal setting and monetary incentives. *Journal of Applied Psychology,* 63, 29–39.

Tubbs, M. E. (1986) Goal setting: A meta-analytic examination of the empirical evidence. *Journal of Applied Psychology,* 71, 474–483.

Tushman, M. (1974) *Organizational change: An exploratory study and a case history.* Ithaca, NY: New York State School of Industrial and Labor Relations, Cornell University.

Vroom, V. (1964) *Work and motivation.* New York: Wiley.

Wagner, J. A., & Gooding, R. Z. (1987) Shared influence and organizational behavior: A meta-analysis of situational variables expected to moderate participation-outcome relationships. *Academy of Management Journal,* 30, 524–541.

Yukl, G. A., & Latham, G. P. (1978) Interrelationships among employee participation, individual differences, goal difficulty, goal acceptance, goal instrumentality, and performance. *Personnel Psychology,* 31, 305–323.

Zander, A., & Ulberg, C. (1971) The group level of aspiration and external social pressures. *Organizational Behavior and Human Performance,* 6, 362–378.

Self-Leadership: Toward an Expanded Theory of Self-Influence Processes in Organizations

Charles C. Manz

Recently, significant attention has been devoted to a previously neglected aspect of organizational behavior—the influence organization members exert over themselves. This "new" managerial focus has emerged primarily from the social learning theory literature (Bandura, 1977a) and related work in self-control (Bandura, 1969; Cautela, 1969; Goldfried & Merbaum, 1973; Kanfer, 1970; Mahoney & Arnkoff, 1978, 1979; Mahoney & Thoresen, 1974; Thoresen & Mahoney, 1974). In the organization literature, this process generally has been referred to as self-management (Andrasik & Heimberg, 1982; Luthans & Davis, 1979; Manz & Sims, 1980; Marx, 1982; Mills, 1983).

This paper, stimulated by the earlier work, proposes an expanded and more comprehensive theory of the self-influence of organization members. First, the fundamental importance, and the need for greater integration, of the self-influence processes into organizational theories are discussed. Second, an overview of conceptualization of self-management thus far in the organization literature is presented. It is argued that while these treatments are useful, they provide an incomplete view of self-influence; therefore, an expanded "self-leadership" perspective is proposed that emphasizes purposeful leadership of self toward personal standards and "natural" rewards that hold greater intrinsic motivational value. Implications for theory, research, and practice are discussed.

RECOGNIZING SELF-CONTROL SYSTEMS

Organizations impose multiple controls of varying character on employees. Tannenbaum (1962), for example, argued that "organization implies control" (p. 237). Lawler and Rhode (1976) pointed out that control systems try to exert influence by identifying appropriate behavior, providing means to monitor behavior that is taking place, and coordinating, rewarding, and punishing this behavior. One view suggests that the control process involves applying rational, manageable, control mechanisms (work standards, appraisal and reward systems, etc.) to influence employees through external means to assure that the organization achieves its goals.

An alternative view, however, shifts the perspective of the control system-controllee interface significantly. Simply stated, this perspective views each person as possessing an internal self-control system (Manz, 1979; Manz, Mossholder, & Luthans, in press). Organizational control systems in their most basic form provide performance standards, evaluation mechanisms, and systems of reward and punishment (Lawler, 1976; Lawler & Rhode, 1976). Similarly, individ-

From *Academy of Management Review*, 1986, **11**(3), 585–600. Reprinted by permission. The author thanks the participants in "The Not For Prime Time Workshop" for their helpful comments on an earlier draft of this paper.

uals possess self-generated personal standards, engage in self-evaluation processes, and self-administer rewards and punishments in managing their daily activities (Bandura, 1977a; Mahoney & Thoresen, 1974; Manz & Sims, 1980). Even though these mechanisms take place frequently, in an almost automatic manner, this makes them no less powerful.

Furthermore, while organizations provide employees with certain values and beliefs packaged into cultures, corporate visions and so forth, people too possess their own systems of values, beliefs, and visions (however vague) for their future. In addition, the counterparts of organizational rules, policies, and operating procedures are represented internally in the form of behavioral and psychological scripts (Abelson, 1981; Gioia & Poole, 1984; Schank & Abelson, 1977) or "programs" (Carver & Scheier, 1982) held at various levels of abstraction.

The point is—organizations provide organizational control systems that influence people but these systems do not access individual action directly. Rather, the impact of organizational control mechanisms is determined by the way they influence, in intended as well as unintended ways, the self-control systems within organization members. This logic is portrayed graphically in Figure 1.

While this perspective is not new, an analysis of theory and research in the field reveals that it has not been well integrated into organizational management. The literature does include cognitive mediation of external stimuli (e.g., social learning theory views—Davis & Luthans, 1980; Manz & Sims, 1980; attributed causes to observed physical actions—Feldman, 1981; Green & Mitchell, 1979; Mitchell, Green, & Wood, 1981; Mitchell, Larson, & Green, 1977; Staw, 1975) but does not adequately recognize the self-influence system as a focal point (rather than a mediator) for enhanced understanding and practice of organizational management. The perspective shown in Figure 1, on the other hand, suggests that the self-influence system is the ultimate system of control. In addition, it suggests that this internal control system must receive significant attention in its own right before maximum benefits for the organization and employee are realized.

Recent work on cybernetic (control) theory provides a useful perspective for making concrete the nature of employee self-regulating systems (Carver & Scheier, 1981, 1982). Based on the negative feedback loop, Carver and Scheier (1981) present an insightful view of self-regulating processes involving: (a) input perceptions of existing conditions, (b) comparison of the perception with an existing reference value (standard), (c) output behaviors to reduce discrepancies from the standard, and (d) a consequent impact on the environment. From this view, an employee attempting to achieve a given production standard would operate within a closed loop of control aimed at minimizing deviations from standards in existing performance. Unless an environmental disturbance of some kind occurred, this self-regulating process theoretically could occur indefinitely.

Carver and Scheier (1981, 1982) further speculated, based on the work of Powers (1973a, 1973b), that standards emerge from a hierarchical organization of control systems. That is, standards for a particular control system loop (X units of production) derive from superordinate systems of control. Thus, an employee working to achieve a minimum deviation from a production standard at one level

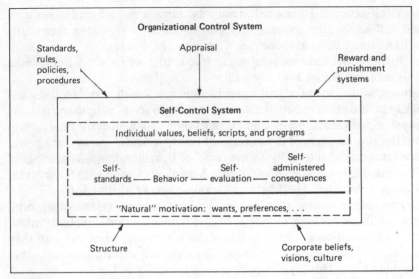

FIGURE 1
The organizational and self-control systems.

may serve higher level systems aimed at higher level standards (meeting job responsibilities, being a conscientious employee, being a good person).

From an organizational perspective, recognizing and facilitating employee self-regulating systems pose a viable and more realistic view of control than views centered entirely on external influence. In addition, overreliance on external controls can lead to a number of dysfunctional employee behaviors: "rigid bureaucratic behavior," (performance of only those behaviors that are rewarded by the control system), inputting of invalid information into management information systems, and so forth (Camman & Nadler, 1976; Lawler, 1976; Lawler & Rhode, 1976).

It is instructive at this point to address current views of employee self-management and then to present an expanded self-leadership view of self-regulatory processes.

EMPLOYEE SELF-MANAGEMENT

Most relevant treatments of self-management to date focused on strategies designed to facilitate behaviors targeted for change (e.g., Andrasik & Heimberg, 1982; Luthans & Davis, 1979; Manz & Sims, 1980). This work generally reflects the view that behaviors are not performed for their intrinsic value but because of their necessity or because of what the performer will receive for his/her performance. A widely recognized definition of self-control, one that illustrates this view, is: "A person displays self-control when in the relative absence of immediate external constraints (performs without external assistance) he or she engages in behavior whose previous probability has been less than that of alternatively available behaviors (a less attractive behavior but one that is implied to be more desirable)'' (text added) (Thoresen & Mahoney, 1974, p. 12).

Several specific self-management strategies can be identified. Mahoney and Arnkoff (1978, 1979) provided a useful array of strategies that were applied in clinical contexts. These include: self-observation, self-goal setting, cueing strategies, self-reinforcement, self-punishment, and rehearsal. Much of the employee self-management literature has centered on adaptations of these self-control strategies for addressing management problems (Andrasik & Heimberg, 1982; Luthans & Davis, 1979; Manz & Sims, 1980, 1981). Luthans and Davis (1979) provided descriptions of cueing strategy interventions across a variety of work contexts. Physical cues such as a wall graph to chart progress on target behaviors and a magnetic message board were used to self-induce desired behavioral change in specific cases. Manz and Sims (1980) explicated the relevance of the broader range of self-control strategies, especially as substitutes for formal organizational leadership. Self-observation, cueing strategies, self-goal setting, self-reward, self-punishment, and rehearsal were each discussed in terms of their applicability to organizational contexts. Andrasik and Heimberg (1982) developed a behavioral self-management program for individualized self-modification of targeted work behaviors. Their approach involved pinpointing a specific behavior for change, observing the behavior over time, developing a behavioral change plan involving self-reward or some other self-influence strategy, and adjusting the plan based on self-awareness of a need for change.

In terms of cybernetic self-regulating systems (Carver & Scheier, 1981, 1982), these employee self-management perspectives can be viewed as providing a set of strategies that facilitate behaviors that serve to reduce deviations from higher level reference values that the employee may or may not have helped establish. That is, the governing standards at higher levels of abstraction (cf., Powers, 1973a, 1973b)—for example, what it means to be a good employee based on organizational or professional values—can remain largely externally defined even though lower level standards to reach the goals may be personally created. Mills (1983) argued that factors such as the normative system and professional norms can exercise just as much control over the individual as a mechanistic situation in which the performance process is manipulated directly. The implication is that, unlike the perspective suggested in Figure 1, the aims of the "self-managed employee" can be, in actuality, externally controlled by existing higher level external standards.

This view is consistent with arguments that employee self-control is perhaps more an illusion than a reality (Dunbar, 1981) and that self-managed individuals are far from loosely supervised or controlled (Mills, 1983). In addition, it has been argued that self-management strategies themselves are behaviors that require reinforcement in order to be maintained (Kerr & Slocum, 1981; Manz & Sims, 1980; Thoresen & Mahoney, 1974). Because of this dependence on external reinforcement, it could be argued that the self-management approach violates Thoresen and Mahoney's (1974) definition cited earlier, " . . . in the relative absence of immediate external constraints . . . '' in the long run. That is, while *immediate* external constraints or supports may not be required, *longer-term* reinforcement is. Again, self-management is subject to external control.

TOWARD A BROADER VIEW OF SELF-INFLUENCE PROCESSES

In developing a broader perspective, self-influence should be viewed as more than a set of strategies designed to facilitate employee behaviors that help meet standards. For some individuals being ''less controlled'' (not meeting socially based standards) may represent active self-controlled choice.

In addressing the question ''What is truly self-controlled behavior?'' one can become immersed in metaphysical arguments on the nature of free-will (cf., Dennett, 1984). Rychlak (1979) suggested that the crucial concern is a telic one— that is, the underlying reason one is performing the behavior. For example, is the individual performing because he/she wants to or because of a belief that he/she ''should?'' Interestingly, Marx (1982) suggested management of one's ''should/ want ratio'' (p. 439) as a self-control strategy for avoiding becoming over-burdened with activities that must be done (''shoulds'') relative to those that one likes to do (''wants'').

Following this line of reasoning, the differences between self-management and external control can become clouded depending on the perspective adopted. Consider a person who truly wants to deal with a problem behavior to achieve a freely chosen personal standard, but despite systematic persistent use of self-management strategies does not succeed. In such a case, calling on another person or organization to establish constraints for his/her behavior (i.e., giving up ''self-management'') may be the most effective means to achieve a personal goal. Again, Thoresen and Mahoney's (1974) definition of self-control is violated. Yet, acting on the environment to produce constraints may be the most viable avenue for exercising self-influence in such cases.

Schelling (1980) addressed a host of internal struggles (e.g., inducing over withholding on income taxes to assure a surplus of personal funds later), all of which exemplify relying on external constraints to exercise ''self-command.'' Bandura's (1977a, 1978) notion of reciprocal determinism, which recognized an interdependent relationship between one's behavior and the environment, is useful here. That is, acting on the environment to cause it to influence or control one's behavior in a personally desired way can be a legitimate form of self-influence (albeit one step removed). Indeed, self-constraints (e.g., lack of confidence, inadequate ability) can sometimes produce greater limitations on one's freedom to behave than rigid external controls.

The question ''Who is more or less self-controlled, the person who uses self-management to achieve standards imposed by someone else or the person who chooses externally controlled situations to achieve personally chosen standards?'' illustrates the heart of this discussion. The position taken in this paper is that true self-leadership is based on the personal meaningfulness and ''ownership'' of the individual's governing standards. Invoking external influence to achieve personally chosen standards is a legitimate form of self-leadership. Self-imposing self-management strategies to reach externally defined and personally undesired standards, however, is a form of "self-management" that masks external control.

TOWARD A THEORY OF SELF-LEADERSHIP

In this section, a self-leadership view is proposed. Here, self-leadership is conceptualized as a comprehensive self-influence perspective that concerns leading oneself toward performance of naturally motivating tasks as well as managing oneself to do work that must be done but is not naturally motivating. It includes the self-management of immediate behaviors and in addition, similar to the notion of "double loop learning" (Argyris, 1982a, 1982b), it challenges the appropriateness of operating standards that govern the employee self-influence system as the reasons for the behavior. Three critical elements of self-leadership that distinguish it and contribute to our understanding of self-influence beyond the previous work include: (a) that it allows for addressing a wider range (higher level) of *standards* for self-influence, (b) that it more fully incorporates the role of *intrinsic work motivation,* and (c) that it suggests some additional *strategies* for employee self-control. Each of these elements is discussed below.

STANDARDS FOR SELF-INFLUENCE

A standard establishes a target or goal for performance and can serve a primary controlling function. Locke, Shaw, Saari, and Latham (1981) pointed out that goals direct attention, mobilize effort, increase persistence, and motivate strategy development. Thus, when goals or standards are established by an external source they can serve as a significant external influence or control mechanism.

The ability of standards to influence employees is based in part on knowledge of one's progress in meeting the standards that is received from external sources. Thus, external feedback can have an impact on employee self-control. Ilgen, Fisher, and Taylor (1979) indicated that excessive external feedback can place external limits on self-influence. They suggested that in order to shift to an internal locus of control in persons, the frequency of feedback (from external sources) likely will need to be changed (reduced) to allow increased self-monitoring. Despite its importance a systematic review of the role of feedback in employee influence is beyond the scope of the current discussion (cf., Taylor, Fisher, & Ilgen, 1984).

Consequently, the focus here is on the standards themselves. The position taken is that a self-leadership view facilitates a broader higher-level perspective on individuals' guiding standards than does the existing work on employee self-management. Figure 2 illustrates a philosophical difference between the concepts of self-management and self-leadership relating to this issue. The figure relies on a cybernetic control system perspective of self-influence (Carver & Scheier, 1981, 1982). The aim of this system is to reduce deviations from operating standards which are defined hierarchically by increasingly abstract perceptions about the relation between work and self. Conceptually, self-management can be viewed as a set of strategies that aids employees in structuring their work environment, in establishing self-motivation, and so forth, that facilitates appropriate behaviors for achieving minimal deviations from primarily lower-level behavioral standards. Self-leadership, on the other hand, encompasses self-management behavior but it is also concerned with leading the self-influence system at superordinate levels.

Self-management, for example, might be exercised by establishing a performance self-goal/standard of calling on six customers daily, in order to meet sales quotas, and then providing a self-reward each day for meeting this goal. Self-leadership, on the other hand, allows for self-leading of the higher level standards that provide the reasons for the self-managed behaviors—e.g., "Why does one want to meet a sales quota . . . be a good salesperson or be in sales at all . . . be a conscientious provider for one's family . . . be a good person?"

A central distinction between self-management and the proposed self-leadership perspective is a difference in focus. Self-management is largely concerned with a set of behavioral and cognitive strategies that reflect a rational view of what people ought to be doing—for example, stop smoking (Thoresen & Mahoney, 1974), finish a report (Luthans & Davis, 1979), reduce non-productive informal conversations (Manz & Sims, 1980). Self-leadership goes beyond this to place significant emphasis on the intrinsic value of tasks. While employee self-management theorists likely would recognize the relevance of intrinsic motivation factors for self-management, the existing focus in the literature on strategies that facilitate "appropriate" behaviors tends to distract potential developments in this vein. The self-leadership view proposed here is intended to stimulate a

FIGURE 2
A cybernetic control system view of the role of self-management and self-leadership.

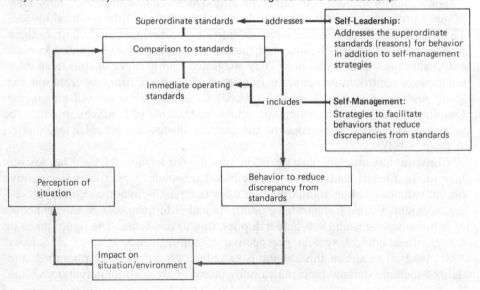

broader view of self-influence that includes the important role of the intrinsically appealing aspects of work ("natural" rewards) and how important these aspects are in defining why behavior is performed.

Intrinsic Motivation in Self-Regulation

Self-management emphasizes rewards that are separate from the task and that are received for its completion (e.g., self-praise, external recognition, and rewards). A broader self-leadership view explicitly recognizes rewards that result from performing activities themselves. These can be described as "natural" rewards (Manz, 1983a, 1983b) because they are a natural part of the task performance process and derive from natural intrinsic responses. Self-leadership goes beyond self-management to address redefining one's tasks and one's relationship with and/or perception of tasks so that desired performance results from a natural motivational process. Particular emphasis is taken from the intrinsic motivation literature (cf., Deci, 1971, 1975a; Deci & Ryan, 1980) and especially, cognitive evaluation theory (Deci, 1975a, 1975b).

Cognitive evaluation theory, based on the work of White (1959) and de Charms (1986), was founded on the assumption that behavior is caused by internal states (Deci, 1975b). Although the validity of cognitive evaluation theory has not received universal support (e.g., Farr, 1976; Farr, Vance, & McIntyre, 1977; Phillips & Lord, 1980; Scott, 1975), an impressive body of evidence has been gathered in its support both from Deci and his colleagues (Benware & Deci, 1975; Deci, 1971, 1975a; Deci, Nezlek, & Sheinman, 1981; Deci & Ryan, 1980) and from others (Calder & Staw, 1975; Daniel & Esser, 1980; Greene & Lepper, 1974; Kruglanski, Alon, & Lewis, 1972; Lepper & Greene, 1975; Lepper, Greene, & Nisbett, 1973). Thus, while this view is subject to potential arguments, for example from more functional viewpoints (Scott, 1975), this assumption as part of a broader view of behavioral causes is accepted here. Notably, social learning theory relies on a reciprocal determinism view in which behavior is caused by internal states as well as external influences, and each of these three components (behavior, internal processes, and external forces) influences each other in a reciprocal fashion (Bandura, 1978). This comprehensive reciprocal determinism view is the assumptive framework upon which conceptual development is based in this paper.

In cognitive evaluation theory (Deci, 1975a), an individual's *feelings of self-determination and competence* are central to the experience of intrinsic motivation. Specifically, rewards that increase these intrinsic outcomes will increase intrinsic motivation. Deci (1975a) suggested that the natural inclination to pursue feelings of competence and self-determination leads to a behavioral pattern. This pattern includes a search for reasonable challenges and an expenditure of effort to overcome these challenges. The logic is that by overcoming such challenges, feelings of competence and self-control will be enhanced.

In a similar vein, Bandura (1977a, 1977b, 1982) viewed individual self-efficacy perceptions as central to social learning theory. He pointed out that perceived self-efficacy will influence the amount of effort and persistence expended in the face of adversity. Bandura (1977b, 1982) also indicated that the strongest contributor to positive self-efficacy perceptions is one's personal performance history.

In performance appraisal, Bernardin and Beatty (1984) suggested that the tendency of raters to be lenient in their evaluations may stem from a perception of a low personal capability (low self-efficacy) to cope with the likely negative reaction of the ratee. They suggested training to assess rater efficacy perceptions followed by training to allow raters to experience mastery of progressively difficult rating tasks. This approach was designed to facilitate increases in rater self-efficacy perceptions which were assumed to result in more accurate evaluations by raters. Again, a greater sense of competence is linked to one's willingness and motivation to perform a task.

By combining the work of Deci and the literature of self-efficacy, it could be concluded that an important aspect of self-influence is the process of establishing intrinsic motivation by enhancing one's feelings of competence and self-control (more generally one's perceptions of self-efficacy). Furthermore, a primary objective of self-leadership practice should be to enhance self-efficacy perceptions which are reciprocally related to performance. That is, enhanced self-efficacy should lead to higher performance through its impact on effort and persistence. A history of higher performance in turn will have a positive impact on future self-efficacy perceptions (Bandura, 1977b).

In addition to feelings of competence and self-control, a third intrinsic motivation factor, the task performer's *feelings of purpose,* is addressed. This additional component is consistent with literature emphasizing the importance of purpose and belief in one's work for fostering task performance. Examples of this are provided in the Japanese management literature (Hatvany & Pucik, 1981a, 1981b; Ouchi, 1981a, 1981b; Ouchi & Jaeger, 1978; Pascale & Athos, 1981; Sullivan, 1983), work that emphasizes the importance of shared vision (e.g., a corporate philosophy) (Hatvany & Pucik, 1981a; Ouchi & Price, 1978), and the job characteristic "task significance" addressed in the job design literature (Hackman & Oldham, 1975). The essential idea is that a reason (purpose) for doing one's work that extends beyond the rewards, reprimands, and so forth, is important. The shared values component of the recently proposed McKinsey "7 S's" approach for characterizing organizations is consistent with this latter phenomenon (Pascale & Athos, 1981; Peters & Waterman, 1982).

One view suggests that feelings of purpose most probably result from worthwhile contributions to something or someone other than oneself (i.e., altruism) (Manz, 1983a). In this sense, "external" corporate philosophies or visions can foster internal purpose if they are defined in an altruistic fashion. It may be that this altruistic component is coupled with an egoistic motive (e.g., altruistic egoism, Selye, 1974). On the other hand, evidence has been gathered suggesting that altruism is part of human nature apart from "selfish" ends (Hoffman, 1981). One American production plant that has displayed highly motivated and committed workers, for example, has as its motto "people helping people" (Manz, 1983b). Examination of Japanese organizations often reveals a similar concern for purposeful (altruistic) ends.

Strategies for Self-Leadership Practice

Self-leadership, with its emphasis on the intrinsic motivational aspects of work, suggests several strategies that can complement existing self-management strategies (cf., Andrasik & Heimberg, 1982; Manz & Sims, 1980). These additional strategies are based on employees wanting to, rather than feeling they should, perform task behaviors.

Work Context Strategies Briefly, one self-leadership approach involves choosing, to the extent possible, work environments that enhance the natural impact of the physical work setting on performance. A long distance runner who chooses to run in pleasant surroundings as opposed to a conventional quarter-mile track uses this approach. In addition, a sense of *competence* can result from successfully navigating new, challenging terrain. Feelings of *self-determination* are enhanced by the runner's control over running routes, and the positive health benefits (*purpose*) are provided to the runner as well. Together these elements stemming from a chosen desirable work context should have a positive impact on motivation and performance.

A subtle, yet no less powerful, aspect of the work context involves social psychological elements such as group norms, corporate values, and existing interpersonal employee interaction patterns. Two more global concepts that have received significant attention in the literature are: organizational climate (e.g., Field & Abelson, 1982; Hellriegel & Slocum, 1974; Schneider, 1975) and corporate culture (e.g., Deal & Kennedy, 1982; Marshall, 1982; Pettigrew, 1979). Again, an individual is using a work context self-leadership strategy by choosing and working to create a social psychological work context that contributes to natural enjoyment of task performance.

Task Performance Process Strategies Another approach for exercising self-leadership is to build natural rewards into the *process* of performing, that is, to focus on *how* the task is performed. The challenge for the self-leading individual is to discover what activities provide him/her with "natural" rewards and then to build these activities into the task process, where possible.

A manager, for example, may have a choice regarding whether to explain a new work procedure to a subordinate through a memo or face-to-face communication. If documentation is not essential, a manager might choose oral communication because he/she finds the task process to be more enjoyable (more naturally rewarding). These kinds of work process choices that continually arise become the base from which self-leadership can be exercised. If an individual can establish a reasonable level of self-awareness regarding what kinds of activities he/she enjoys and perform work consistent with these preferences (where this is possible without jeopardizing performance), self-leadership is enhanced.

An open-ended search for activities that provide natural rewards would be difficult and highly inefficient. Fortunately, the three natural reward elements: feelings of competence, self-control, and purpose, can guide in identifying and building activities into one's work. In essence, the process becomes a self-performed job analysis and job redesign, within the limits of one's job specifications (although these too might be negotiated and modified). While an expanded view of cognitive evaluation theory is suggested here as a flexible and general basis for self-initiated job redesign, other theoretical views could be used to provide some specific alternative strategies. A self-initiated job characteristics approach (e.g., Hackman & Oldham, 1975; Sims, Szilagyi, & Keller, 1975) to job redesign might be one way of exercising self-leadership within these broad guidelines. In this approach, individuals use their discretion to define certain aspects of the performance process to establish enhanced natural motivation potential for work performance.

Other types of self-leadership strategies could be identified beyond those centered on the work context or process discussed above. For example, choice of a vocational field or a particular job position in itself can represent a powerful self-leadership strategy with considerable potential for affecting the intrinsic enjoyment and motivation derived from work. Another important type of self-leadership strategy focuses on management of thought processes, the subject of the following discussion.

Self-Leadership of Thought Patterns Perhaps the ultimate goal of self-leadership practice should be to enhance the effectiveness of employees in managing their own thought patterns. For example, in addition to systematically managing one's own behavior or altering the physical context or the process by which work is performed, one can manage his/her mental representation of the work. In a sense, the job is redesigned mentally rather than physically.

Any job holds both desirable and undesirable elements for a performer. To the extent that one's mental energy is focused on unpleasant aspects of the work (fatigue, pressure, uncertainty, etc.) the work process likely will be experienced unfavorably. On the other hand, if desirable elements (challenge, learning, variety, etc.) become the focus of one's mental energy, the potential for motivation can be established. This view holds obvious similarities to popularized notions such as the power of "positive thinking" (Peale, 1956). There exists more than a little merit, however, to the notion that an existing reality is more in the mind of the beholder than in any physical sense (e.g., Beck, 1970; Ellis, 1970; Meichenbaum, 1974).

Leadership approaches that center on managing meaning and vision (Berlew, 1979; House, 1977) incorporate parallel logic. Berlew (1979) discussed an essentially charismatic approach to leadership that provides employees with, among other things, "common vision" (e.g., purpose) and the opportunity for organization members to "feel stronger and more in control of their own destinies" (a sense of competence and self-control) (p. 347). The logic of self-leadership of thought is similar except that the worker takes an active part in mentally establishing worthwhile states for himself/herself.

Recent applications of the schema concept to organizational behavior (e.g., Gioia & Poole, 1984; Hastie, 1981; Langer, 1978; Taylor & Crocker, 1981), derived from a schema-based, information-processing view (e.g., Graesser, Woll, Kowalski, & Smith, 1980), make it apparent that such mental functioning, that has been characterized as being "automatic," almost "thoughtless," goes beyond descriptive power. That is, if consistent (similar to habitual) ways of processing information develop (e.g., relying on stereotypes—Hamilton, 1979), individuals need not be passive subjects but can and frequently do experience these thought processes in a "thoughtful" way (Gioia & Manz, 1985; Gioia & Poole, 1984). By actively self-managing mental activity (schemas or otherwise) desired thought patterns can be pursued.

It is beyond the scope of this paper to address a detailed analysis of how this can be achieved. It has been suggested elsewhere (Manz, 1983a), however, that desired thought patterns might be developed by managing internal verbalizations or self-talk (Meichenbaum & Cameron, 1974), imagery (Bandura, 1969; Cautela, 1966, 1967, 1971; Mahoney, 1974), and one's belief systems (Ellis, 1975; Ellis & Whiteley, 1979). A general illustrative example could be a conscious effort to increase mental energy devoted to work elements that provide natural reward value over those that do not. The objective is to foster the development of new thought patterns that aid rather than hinder motivation and performance.

Overall, it has been argued that a broader self-influence view (self-leadership) recognizes not only strategies for self-managing behaviors to meet existing standards, but also addresses the higher-level standards (reasons for behavior) themselves. Thus, self-leadership concerns itself with self-leading ongoing self-influence (cybernetic) systems. An important aspect of this self-leadership process centers on "natural" rewards that foster intrinsic motivation to more fully integrate "wants" with "shoulds" in establishing a more comprehensive view of employee self-influence. In particular, the theoretical view developed here suggests that intrinsic motivation derived from feelings of competence, self-control, and purpose is an important component of self-leadership.

SELF-LEADERSHIP:
SOME IMPLICATIONS FOR THEORY AND PRACTICE

Some distinctions have been drawn between existing employee self-management perspectives and a more comprehensive self-leadership view. Self-leadership is conceptualized as a process that encompasses behaviorally focused self-management strategies and further addresses self-regulation of higher-level control standards to more fully recognize the role of intrinsic motivation. Such an expanded view poses significant implications for both theory and practice.

It suggests the existence of at least three self-influence perspectives. The first, labeled here as employee *self-regulation,* consists of an ongoing cybernetic control process aimed at reducing deviation from existing standards that are arranged hierarchically. Usually, self-regulation in the short run occurs automatically and adjustments are made to help reduce discrepancies from established reference points. Control can be anchored to the existing external (e.g., organization) control system where self-regulation serves as a process to satisfy this system.

Employee self-management consists of a set of self-management strategies that are designed to facilitate behaviors that help meet standards. In the immediate time period (i.e., negative feedback loop) these standards may be established by the self-managed individual (e.g., a self-set goal of X units of output on a given day). The self-management strategies (including self-set goals), however, tend to serve as mechanisms for reducing deviation from standards in higher-level control loops (meet job specifications, be a "good" employee, etc.). The focus is on behaviors to facilitate performance of what "should" be done.

The *self-leadership* perspective proposed in this paper represents a broader view of self-influence. This view includes self-management strategies to foster functional behaviors for meeting standards; it also addresses how appropriate or how desirable the standards are themselves. In addition, the self-leadership view goes beyond a behavioral focus to more fully recognize the importance of intrinsic motivation. Recognition of individual "wants," in addition to "shoulds," is viewed as a legitimate aspect of self-influence. The self-leadership view more accurately reflects the concept of free will as an issue of why behavior is performed, not just whether it is personally chosen, by addressing the legitimacy of governing standards and the intrinsic based "wants" of the individual.

These different concepts indicate a need to distinguish the specific view of self-influence that is adopted by management theories. Theories that provide for employee autonomy (e.g., self-management) actually may represent efforts to control employees through achieving greater deviation reduction at higher levels of control. One study (Manz & Angle, 1985), for example, described an insurance firm that introduced self-managed work groups (almost universally viewed as a mechanism for increasing worker autonomy) apparently to increase control over insurance sales people in complying with company procedures and goals.

Indeed, the whole notion of employee freedom and autonomy in existing management theories deserves closer scrutiny in the light of differing perspectives on employee self-influence. Future research should address the implications of different kinds of autonomy and self-control at different levels of control (e.g., over immediate behavior, over work system standards, over the organizational mission, etc.). Questions such as "What are the implications (in terms of commitment, performance, ethics, etc.) of worker involvement strategies that seek employee participation to meet goals established by executive management vs. programs that involve employees in establishing higher-level organizational and personal goals?" are especially relevant.

The self-leadership view posited in this paper also suggests several self-leadership strategies that are based on the intrinsic motivational aspects of work. They offer the potential to make employee self-control more universal. After all, if the ideal of having employees experience their work as a naturally enjoyed activity can be achieved, theoretically, autonomous work performance should be as natural as play. The logic here is similar to early participative management theorists (e.g., Argyris, 1964; McGregor, 1960), who suggested that when a person is performing because of the reward value of the task process itself, the potential for greater commitment to the task is established.

Realistically, however, such an ideal is likely to remain an objective that can be continuously pursued by never completely achieved. As a consequence, self-leadership for every employee may not be feasible. Some persons will be better candidates for self-leadership than others. For example, if the values and beliefs of the organization are not sufficiently congruent with those of the employees the potential for breakdowns in the control process and for suboptimized outcomes is increased. Conversely, the feasibility of self-leadership for a specific employee whose work values are highly discrepant from the organization's may seem quite low. Such a situation may pose a difficult dilemma; should the organization opt for employee compliance based on external control or should it accept lower organizationally valued employee output in the short run in order to encourage employee commitment and self-leadership capability in order to let the two value systems hopefully converge over time? Not every employee may appear to warrant the investment entailed in the latter alternative, but achieving the ideal of an organization consisting of highly committed self-led employees may require that such hard choices be made.

CONCLUSIONS

The recent attention to self-influence processes has challenged researchers and practitioners to rethink many of their fundamental assumptions regarding organizational research and practice. Indeed, employee self-control should be viewed as a central element of important organizational processes such as leadership, control, and management in general. The employee self-management literature, however, typically has centered on a set of behaviorally focused strategies that tend to divert attention away from, or overlook, the reasons the behavior is being self-managed.

A more comprehensive self-leadership perspective has been proposed to more fully address the higher-level standards/reasons that employee self-influence is performed and to suggest self-influence strategies that allow the intrinsic value of work to help enhance individual performance. Further research and theoretical development is needed to address several central elements of self-influence—for example, the derivation of personal standards at multiple hierarchical levels, human thought patterns, self-influence strategies that build motivation into target behaviors—that have been neglected in the employee self-management literature. This paper is intended to be a first step in advancing the existing literature toward such a broader self-leadership perspective.

REFERENCES

Abelson, R. P. (1981) Psychological status of the Script Concept. *American Psychologist,* 36, 715–729.
Andrasik, F., & Heimberg, J. S. (1982) Self-management procedures. In L. W. Frederikson (Ed.), *Handbook of organizational behavior management* (pp. 219–247). New York: Wiley.
Argyris, C. (1964) *Integrating the individual and the organization.* New York: Wiley.
Argyris, C. (1982a) *Reasoning, learning and action: Individual and organizational.* San Francisco: Jossey-Bass.
Argyris, C. (1982b) The executive mind and double-loop learning. *Organizational Dynamics,* 11, 5–22.

Bandura, A. (1969) *Principles of behavior modification.* New York: Holt, Rinehart, and Winston.

Bandura, A. (1977a) *Social learning theory.* Englewood Cliffs, NJ: Prentice-Hall.

Bandura, A. (1977b) Self-efficacy: Towards a unifying theory of behavioral change. *Psychological Review,* 84, 191–215.

Bandura, A. (1978) The self system in a reciprocal determinism. *American Psychologist,* 33, 344–358.

Bandura, A. (1982) Self-efficacy mechanism in human agency. *American Psychologist,* 37, 122–147.

Beck, A. T. (1970) Cognitive therapy: Nature and the relation to behavior therapy. *Behavior Therapy,* 1, 184–200.

Benware, C., & Deci, E. L. (1975) Attitude change as a function on the inducement for espousing a pro-attitudinal communication. *Journal of Experimental Social Psychology,* 11, 271–278.

Berlew, D. E. (1979) Leadership and organizational excitement. In D. A. Kolb, I. M. Rubin, & J. M. McIntyre (Eds.), *Organizational psychology: A book of readings* (pp. 343–356). Englewood Cliffs, NJ: Prentice-Hall.

Bernardin, H. J., & Beatty, R. W. (1984) *Performance appraisal: Assessing human behavior at work.* Boston: Kent Publishing Co.

Calder, B. J., & Staw, B. M. (1975) The self-perception of intrinsic and extrinsic motivation. *Journal of Personality and Social Psychology,* 35, 599–605.

Camman, C., & Nadler, D. (1976) Fit control systems to your managerial style. *Harvard Business Review,* 54(1), 65–72.

Carver, C. S., & Scheier, M. F. (1981) *Attention and self-regulation: A control theory approach to human behavior.* New York: Springer-Verlag.

Carver, C. S., & Scheier, M. F. (1982) Control theory: A useful conceptual framework for personality—social, clinical, and health psychology. *Psychological Bulletin,* 92, 111–135.

Cautela, J. R. (1966) Treatment of compulsive behavior by covert sensitization. *Psychological Record,* 16, 33–41.

Cautela, J. R. (1967) Covert sensitization. *Psychological Reports,* 20, 459–468.

Cautela, J. R. (1969) Behavior therapy and self-control: Techniques and implications. In C. M. Franks (Ed.), *Behavior therapy: Appraisal and status* (pp. 323–340). New York: McGraw-Hill.

Cautela, J. R. (1971) *Covert modeling.* Paper presented at the Association for the Advancement of Behavior Therapy, Washington, DC.

Daniel, T. L., & Esser, J. K. (1980) Intrinsic motivation as influenced by rewards, task interest, and task structure. *Journal of Applied Psychology,* 65, 566–573.

Davis, T. R. V., & Luthans, F. (1980) A social learning approach to organizational behavior. *Academy of Management Review,* 5, 281–290.

Deal, T. E., & Kennedy, A. A. (1982) *Corporate cultures.* Reading, MA: Addison-Wesley.

deCharms, R. (1968) *Personal causation: The internal affective determinants of behavior.* New York: Academic Press.

Deci, E. L. (1971) Effects of externally mediated rewards on intrinsic motivation. *Journal of Personality and Social Psychology,* 18, 105–115.

Deci, E. L. (1975a) *Intrinsic motivation.* New York: Plenum.

Deci, E. L. (1975b) Notes on the theory and metatheory of intrinsic motivation. *Organizational Behavior and Human Performance,* 15, 130–145.

Deci, E. L., Nezlek, J., & Sheinman, S. (1981) Characteristics of the rewarder and intrinsic motivation of the rewardee. *Journal of Personality and Social Psychology,* 40, 1–10.

Deci, E. L., & Ryan, R. (1980) The empirical exploration of intrinsic motivational processes. In L. Berkowitz (Ed.), *Advances in experimental social psychology* (Vol. 13, pp. 39–80). New York: Academic Press.

Dennett, D. C. (1984) *Elbow room: The varieties of free will worth wanting.* Cambridge, MA: The MIT Press.

Dunbar, R. L. M. (1981) Designs for organizational control. In W. Starbuck & P. Nystrom (Eds.), *Handbook of organizations* (pp. 85–115). New York: Oxford University Press.

Ellis, A. (1970) *The essence of rational psychotherapy: A comprehensive approach to treatment.* New York: Institute for Rational Living.

Ellis, A. (1975) *A new guide to rational living.* Englewood Cliffs, NJ: Prentice-Hall.

Ellis, A., & Whiteley, J. M. (Eds.) (1979) *Theoretical and empirical foundations of rational emotive therapy.* Monterey, CA: Brooks/Cole.

Farr, J. L. (1976) Task characteristics, reward contingency, and intrinsic motivation. *Organizational Behavior and Human Performance, 16,* 294–307.

Farr, J. L., Vance, R. J., & McIntyre, R. M. (1977) Further examination of the relationship between reward contingency and intrinsic motivation. *Organizational Behavior and Human Performance, 20,* 31–53.

Feldman, J. M. (1981) Beyond attribution theory: Cognitive processes in performance evaluation. *Journal of Applied Psychology, 66,* 127–148.

Field, R. H. G., & Abelson, M. A. (1982) Climate: A reconceptualization and proposed model. *Human Relations, 35,* 131–201.

Gioia, D. A., & Manz, C. C. (1985) Linking cognition and behavior: A script processing interpretation of vicarious learning. *Academy of Management Review, 10,* 527–539.

Gioia, D. A., & Poole, P. P. (1984) Scripts in organizational behavior. *Academy of Management Review, 9,* 449–459.

Goldfried, M. R., & Merbaum, M. (Eds.) (1973) *Behavior change through self-control.* New York: Holt, Rinehart, and Winston.

Graesser, A. C., Woll, S. B., Kowalski, D. J., & Smith, D. A. (1980) Memory for typical and atypical actions in scripted activities. *Journal of Experimental Psychology, 6,* 503–515.

Green, S. G., & Mitchell, T. R. (1979) Attributional processes of leaders in leader-member interactions. *Organizational Behavior and Human Performance, 23,* 429–458.

Greene, D., & Lepper, M. R. (1974) Effects of extrinsic reward on children's subsequent intrinsic interest. *Child Development, 45,* 1141–1145.

Hackman, J. R., & Oldham, G. R. (1975) Development of the job diagnostic survey. *Journal of Applied Psychology, 60,* 159–170.

Hamilton, D. L. (1979) A cognitive-attributional analysis of stereotyping. In L. Berkowitz (Ed.), *Advances in experimental social psychology* (Vol. 12, pp. 53–84). New York: Academic Press.

Hastie, R. (1981) Schematic principles in human memory. In E. T. Higgins, C. P. Herman, and M. P. Sanna (Eds.), *Social cognition* (Vol. 1, pp. 39–88). Hillsdale, NJ: Erlbaum.

Hatvany, N., & Pucik, V. (1981a) An integrated management system: Lessons from the Japanese experience. *Academy of Management Review, 6,* 469–480.

Hatvany, N., & Pucik, V. (1981b) Japanese management practices and productivity. *Organizational Dynamics, 9,* 5–21.

Hellriegel, D., & Slocum, J. W., Jr. (1974) Organizational climate: Measures, research and contingencies. *Academy of Management Journal, 17,* 255–280.

Hoffman, M. L. (1981) Is altruism part of human nature? *Journal of Personality and Social Psychology, 40,* 121–137.

House, R. J. (1977) A 1976 theory of charismatic leadership. In J. G. Hunt & L. L. Larson (Eds.), *Leadership: The cutting edge* (pp. 189–207). Carbondale, IL: Southern Illinois University Press.

Ilgen, D., Fisher, C., & Taylor, M. S. (1979) Consequences of individual feedback on behavior in organizations. *Journal of Applied Psychology*, 64, 349–371.

Kanfer, F. H. (1970) Self-regulation: Research, issues and speculations. In C. Neuringer & J. L. Michael (Eds.), *Behavior modification in clinical psychology* (pp. 178–220). New York: Appleton-Century-Crofts.

Kerr, S., & Slocum, J. W., Jr. (1981) Controlling the performance of people in organization. In W. Starbuck & P. Nystrom (Eds.), *Handbook of organizations* (pp. 116–134). New York: Oxford University Press.

Kruglanski, A. W., Alon, S., & Lewis, T. (1972) Retrospective misattribution and task enjoyment. *Journal of Experimental Social Psychology*, 8, 493–501.

Langer, E. J. (1978) Rethinking the role of thought in social interaction. In J. H. Harvey, W. J. Ickes, & R. F. Kidd (Eds.), *New directions in attribution research* (Vol. 2, pp. 35–58). Hillsdale, NJ: Erlbaum.

Lawler, E. E. (1976) Control systems in organizations. In M. D. Dunnette (Ed.), *Handbook of industrial and organizational psychology* (pp. 1247–1291). Chicago: Rand-McNally.

Lawler, E. E., & Rhode, J. G. (1976) *Information and control in organizations*. Pacific Palisades, CA: Goodyear.

Lazarus, R. S. (1956) Subception: Fact or artifact? a reply to Eriksen. *Psychology Review*, 63, 343–347.

Lepper, M. R., & Greene, D. (1975) Turning play into work: Effects of adult surveillance and extrinsic rewards on children's intrinsic motivation. *Journal of Personality and Social Psychology*, 31, 479–486.

Lepper, M. R., Greene, D., & Nisbett, R. E. (1973) Undermining children's intrinsic interest with extrinsic rewards: A test of the overjustification hypothesis. *Journal of Personality and Social Psychology*, 28, 129–137.

Locke, E., Shaw, K., Saari, L., & Latham, G. (1981) Goal setting and task performance: 1969–1980. *Psychological Bulletin*, 90, 125–152.

Luthans, F., & Davis, T. (1979) Behavioral self-management (BSM): The missing link in managerial effectiveness. *Organizational Dynamics*, 8, 42–60.

Mahoney, M. J. (1974) *Cognition and behavior modification*. Cambridge: Ballinger.

Mahoney, M. J., & Arnkoff, D. B. (1978) Cognitive and self-control therapies. In S. L. Garfield & A. E. Borgin (Eds.), *Handbook of psychotherapy and therapy change* (pp. 689–722). New York: Wiley.

Mahoney, M. J., & Arnkoff, D. B. (1979) Self-management: Theory, research and application. In J. P. Brady & D. Pomerleau (Eds.), *Behavioral medicine: Theory and practice* (pp. 75–96). Baltimore: Williams and Williams.

Mahoney, M. J., & Thoresen, C. E. (Eds.) (1974) *Self-control: Power to the person*. Monterey, CA: Brooks/Cole.

Manz, C. C. (1979) Sources of control: A behavior modification perspective. *Proceedings: Eastern Academy of Management*, 82–88.

Manz, C. C. (1983a) *The art of self-leadership: Strategies for personal effectiveness in your life and work*. Englewood Cliffs, NJ: Prentice-Hall.

Manz, C. C. (1983b) Improving performance through self-leadership. *National Productivity Review*, 2, 288–297.

Manz, C. C., & Angle, H. L. (1985) *Does group self-management mean a loss of personal control?: Triangulating on a paradox*. Paper presented at the annual meeting of the National Academy of Management, San Diego.

Manz, C. C., Mossholder, K. W., & Luthans, F. (in press) An integrated perspective of self-control in organizations. *Administration and Society.*

Manz, C. C., & Sims, H. P., Jr. (1980) Self-management as a substitute for leadership: A social learning theory perspective. *Academy of Management Review,* 5, 361–367.

Manz, C. C., & Sims, H. P., Jr. (1981) Vicarious learning: The influence of modeling on organizational behavior. *Academy of Management Review,* 6, 105–113.

Marshall, J. (1982) Organizational culture: Elements in its portraiture and some implications for organization functioning. *Group and Organization Studies,* 7, 367–384.

Marx, R. D. (1982) Relapse prevention of managerial training: A model for maintenance of behavior change. *Academy of Management Review,* 7, 433–441.

McGregor, D. (1960) *The human side of the enterprise.* New York: McGraw-Hill.

Meichenbaum, D. (1975) Self-instructional methods. In F. H. Kanfer & A. P. Goldstein (Eds.), *Helping people change.* (pp. 357–391). New York: Pergamon.

Meichenbaum, D., & Cameron, R. (1974) The clinical potential of modifying what clients say to themselves. In M. J. Mahoney & C. E. Thoresen (Eds.), *Self-control: Power to the person* (pp. 263–290). Monterey, CA: Brooks/Cole.

Mills, P. K. (1983) Self-management: Its control and relationship to other organizational properties. *Academy of Management Review,* 8, 445–453.

Mitchell, T. R., Green, S. G., & Wood, R. E. (1981) An attributional model of leadership and the poor performing subordinate: Development and validation. In B. Staw & L. Cummings (Eds.), *Research in organizational behavior* (Vol. 3, pp. 197–234). Greenwich, CT: JAI Press.

Mitchell, T. R., Larson, J. R., & Green, S. G. (1977) Leader behavior, situational moderators and group performance: An attributional analysis. *Organizational Behavior and Human Performance,* 18, 254–268.

Ouchi, W. G. (1981a) *Theory Z: How American business can meet the Japanese challenge.* Reading, MA: Addison-Wesley.

Ouchi, W. G. (1981b) Organizational paradigms: A commentary of Japanese management and theory Z organizations. *Organizational Dynamics,* 10, 36–43.

Ouchi, W. G., & Jaeger, A. M. (1978) Type Z organization: Stability in the midst of mobility. *Academy of Management Review,* 3, 305–313.

Ouchi, W. G., & Price, R. L. (1978) Hierarchies, clans and theory Z: a new perspective on organizational development. *Organizational Dynamics,* 7, 25–44.

Pascale, R. T., & Athos, A. G. (1981) *The art of Japanese management.* New York: Simon and Schuster.

Peale, N. V. (1956) *The power of positive thinking.* New York: Spire Books.

Peters, T. J., & Waterman, R. H., Jr. (1981) *In search of excellence: Lessons from America's best run companies.* New York: Harper & Row.

Pettigrew, A. M. (1979) On studying organizational cultures. *Administrative Science Quarterly,* 24, 570–581.

Phillips, J. S., & Lord, R. G. (1980) Determinants of intrinsic motivation: Locus of control and competence information as components of Deci's cognitive evaluation theory. *Journal of Applied Psychology,* 65, 211–218.

Powers, W. T. (1973a) *Behavior: The control of perception.* Chicago: Aldine.

Powers, W. T. (1973b) Feedback: Beyond behaviorism. *Science,* 179, 351–356.

Rychlak, J. F. (1979) *Discovering free will and personal responsibility.* New York: Oxford University Press.

Schank, R. C., & Abelson, R. P. (1977) *Scripts, plans, goals and understanding.* Hillsdale, NJ: Erlbaum.

Schelling, T. C. (1980) The intimate contest for self-command. *The Public Interest,* No. 60, 94–118.

Schneider, B. (1975) Organizational climates: An essay. *Personal Psychology,* 28, 447–479.

Scott, W. E., Jr. (1975) The effects of extrinsic rewards on intrinsic motivation: A critique. *Organizational Behavior and Human Performance,* 15, 117–129.

Şelye, H. (1974) *Stress without distress.* New York: Signet.

Sims, H. P., Jr., Szilagyi, A. D., & Keller, R. (1975) The measurement of job characteristics. *Academy of Management Journal,* 19, 195–212.

Staw, B. M. (1975) Attribution of the "causes" of performance: A general alternative interpretation of cross-sectional research on organizations. *Organizational Behavior and Human Performance,* 13, 414–432.

Sullivan, J. G. (1983) A critique of theory Z. *Academy of Management Review,* 8, 132–142.

Taylor, M. S., Fisher, C. D., & Ilgen, D. R. (1984) Individuals' reactions to performance feedback in organizations: A control theory perspective. In K. Rowland & G. Ferris (Eds.), *Research in personnel and human resources management,* (Vol. 2, pp. 81–124). JAI Press.

Taylor, S. E., & Crocker, J. (1981) Schematic bases of social information processing. In E. T. Higgins, C. P. Herman, & M. P. Zanna (Eds.), *Social cognition* (Vol. 1, pp. 89–134). Hillsdale, NJ: Erlbaum.

Tannenbaum, A. (1962) Control in organizations: Individual adjustment and organizational performance. *Administrative Science Quarterly,* 1, 236–257.

Thoresen, C. E., & Mahoney, M. J. (1974) *Behavioral self-control.* New York: Holt, Rinehart, and Winston.

White, R. W. (1959) Motivation reconsidered: The concept of competence. *Psychology Review,* 66, 297–333.

QUESTIONS FOR DISCUSSION

1 Locke asserts that "rational human action is goal directed." Do you agree with this statement? What actions in organizations do you expect would *not* conform to Locke's aphorism?

2 Goal-setting theory takes a cognitive perspective, while reinforcement theory (Chapter 3) focuses more on the environment and does not rely on cognitive concepts per se. Despite these differences in focus, how are these two theories similar? What management practices would be consistent with both theories?

3 Goal-setting theory suggests that performance outcomes are highest when goals are specific and challenging. How would you, as a manager, determine whether your employees' goals meet these criteria?

4 What do expectancy theory and goal-setting theory each predict about difficult goals? If there are differences, how would you reconcile them?

5 On which theories of motivation (discussed in this book) is the "self-leadership" technique based?

6 List and describe the types of employees and job positions which would be most suited to self-leadership. Justify your responses.

7 In *The Determinants of Goal Commitment,* Locke et al. present some of the recent developments in the area of goal-setting research. How does this recent research increase

your understanding of the motivation process beyond that which was presented in the Latham and Locke article?

8 Which theories of motivation are used by Locke et al. to explain goal commitment? Which other theories might also be useful? Why?

9 Do you think that the mechanisms prescribed to achieve goal commitment (in Locke et al.) would be applicable in Japan? In China? Why would they or would they not work?

CHAPTER 10

WORK DESIGN

Early managerial approaches to job design (discussed in Chapter 1) focused primarily on attempts to simplify an employee's required tasks insofar as possible in order to increase production efficiency. It was felt that, since workers were largely economically motivated, the best way to maximize output was to reduce tasks to their simplest forms and then reward workers with money on the basis of units of output—a piece-rate incentive plan. In theory, such a system would simultaneously satisfy the primary goals of both the employees and the company. Evidence of such a philosophy can be seen in the writings of Taylor and other scientific management advocates.

This approach to simplified job design reached its zenith from a technological standpoint in assembly-line production techniques such as those used by automobile manufacturers. (Piece-rate incentive systems have been largely omitted here, however.) On auto assembly lines, in many cases, the average length of "work cycle" (i.e., the time allowed for an entire "piece" of work) ranges from 30 seconds to 1½ minutes. This means that workers repeat the same task an average of at least 500 times per day. Such a technique, efficient as it may be, is not without its problems, however. As workers have become better educated and more organized, they have begun demanding more from their jobs. Not only is this demand shown in recurrent requests for shorter hours and higher wages, but it is also shown in several undesirable behavior patterns, such as increased turnover, absenteeism, dissatisfaction, and sabotage.

While organizational psychologists and practicing managers have long sought ways of reducing such undesirable behavior, only recently have they begun to study it rigorously in connection with the task performed. Now there exists a considerable body of knowledge concerning ways to attack the problem of job redesign as it affects motivation, performance, and satisfaction. Somewhat surprisingly, many of the new "solutions" bear a striking resemblance to the old craft type of technology of pre-assembly-line days.

Considerable evidence has come to light recently in support of positive behavioral and attitudinal consequences of such job enrichment efforts. In general, such efforts have tended to result in (1) significantly reduced turnover and absenteeism; (2) improved job satisfaction; (3) improved quality of products; and (4) some, though not universal, improvements in productivity and output rates. On the negative side, the costs often associated with such programs are generally identified as (1) increased training time and expense and (2) occasionally, additional retooling costs where dramatic shifts toward group assembly teams have been instituted.

A major thrust of many of the contemporary efforts at job redesign research represents a blend of two central factors. On the one hand, researchers are concerned with studying the motivational processes associated with redesigning jobs. On the other hand, they are equally concerned with the practical applications of such knowledge as it affects attempts to improve the work environment. In this sense, investigations in this area have generally represented applied research in the truest sense.

HERZBERG'S TWO-FACTOR THEORY

One of the earliest researchers in the area of job redesign as it affects motivation was Frederick Herzberg. Herzberg and his associates began their initial work on factors affecting work motivation in the mid-1950s. Their first effort entailed a thorough review of existing research to that date on the subject (Herzberg, Mausner, Peterson, & Capwell, 1957). On the basis of this review, Herzberg carried out his now famous survey of 200 accountants and engineers, from which he derived the initial framework for his theory of motivation. The theory, as well as the supporting data, was first published in 1959 (Herzberg, Mausner, & Snyderman, 1959) and was subsequently amplified and developed in a later book (Herzberg, 1966).

On the basis of his survey, Herzberg discovered that employees tended to describe satisfying experiences in terms of factors that were intrinsic to the content of the job itself. These factors were called "motivators" and included such variables as achievement, recognition, the work itself, responsibility, advancement, and growth. Conversely, dissatisfying experiences, called "hygiene" factors, resulted largely from extrinsic, non-job-related factors, such as company policies, salary, coworker relations, and supervisory style (See Exhibit 1). Herzberg argued, on the basis of these results, that eliminating the causes of dissatisfaction (through hygiene factors) would not result in a state of satisfaction. Instead, it would result in a neutral state. Satisfaction (and motivation) would occur only as a result of the use of motivators.

The implications of this model of employee motivation are clear: motivation can be increased through basic changes in the nature of an employee's job (that is, job enrichment). Thus, jobs should be redesigned to allow for increased chal-

Models	Basic Components of the Model
Two-Factor Theory (Herzberg)	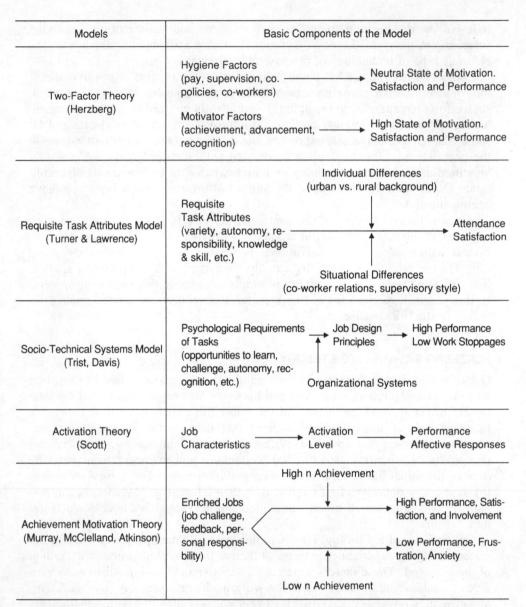
Requisite Task Attributes Model (Turner & Lawrence)	
Socio-Technical Systems Model (Trist, Davis)	
Activation Theory (Scott)	
Achievement Motivation Theory (Murray, McClelland, Atkinson)	

EXHIBIT 1
Conceptual models of the motivational properties of tasks. (From R. M. Steers & R. T. Mowday. The motivational properties of tasks. *Academy of Management Review*, 1977, **2**, 645–658. Reprinted by permission.)

lenge and responsibility, opportunities for advancement and personal growth, and recognition.

Herzberg differentiated between what he described as the older and less effective job redesign efforts, known as job *enlargement,* and the newer concept of job *enrichment* (Paul, Robertson, & Herzberg, 1969). The term "job enlargement," as used by Herzberg, means a *horizontal* expansion of an employee's job, giving him or her more of the same kinds of activities but not altering the necessary skills. "Job enrichment," on the other hand, means a *vertical* expansion of an employee's job, requiring an increase in the skills repertoire which ostensibly leads to increased opportunities. As Paul et al. (1969, p. 61) described it, job enrichment "seeks to improve both efficiency and human satisfaction by means of building into people's jobs, quite specifically, a greater scope for personal achievement and recognition, more challenging and responsible work, and more opportunity for individual advancement and growth."

Since its inception, Herzberg's theory has been subject to several important criticisms. For example, it has been noted (King, 1970), that the model itself has five different theoretical interpretations and that the available research evidence is not entirely consistent with any of these interpretations. Second, a number of scholars believe the model does not give sufficient attention to individual differences (although Herzberg himself would dispute this) and assumes that job enrichment benefits all employees. Research evidence suggests that individual differences are, in fact, an important moderator of the effects of job enrichment. Finally, research also has generally failed to support the existence of two independent factors (motivators and hygiene factors). Even so, the model has enhanced our understanding of motivation at work.

One of the most significant contributions of Herzberg's work was the tremendous impact it had on stimulating thought, research, and experimentation in the area of motivation at work. This contribution should not be overlooked. Before 1959, little research had been carried out on *work* motivation (with the notable exception of Viteles, 1953, and Maier, 1955), and the research that did exist was largely fragmentary. Maslow's work on need hierarchy theory and Murray's, McClelland's, and Atkinson's work on achievement motivation theory were concerned largely with laboratory-based findings or clinical observations, and neither had seriously addressed the problems of the workplace at that time. Herzberg filled this void by specifically calling attention to the need for increased understanding of the role of motivation in work organizations.

Moreover, he did so in a systematic manner and in language that was easily understood by a large body of managers. He advanced a theory that was simple to grasp, was based on some empirical data, and—equally important—offered specific action recommendations for managers to improve employee motivational levels. In doing so, he forced organizations to examine closely a number of possible misconceptions concerning motivation. For example, Herzberg argued that money should not necessarily be viewed as the most potent force on the job. Moreover, he stated that other "context" factors in addition to money which surround an employee's job (such as fringe benefits and supervisory style) should not be expected to affect motivation markedly either. He advanced a strong case that managers must instead give considerable attention to a series of "content" factors (such as opportunities for achievement, recognition, and advancement) that have an important bearing on behavior. According to Herzberg, it is these content factors, and not money or other context factors, that are primarily related to work motivation. These contributions are often overlooked in the heated debates over the validity of the empirical data behind the theoretical formulations.

Herzberg, in addition, probably deserves a good deal of credit for acting as a stimulus to other researchers who have advocated alternative theories of *work* motivation. A multitude of research articles have been generated as a result of the so-called "Herzberg controversy." Some of these articles (e.g., Bockman, 1971; Whitset & Winslow, 1967) strongly support Herzberg's position, while others (e.g., House & Wigdor, 1967; Vroom, 1964) seriously question the research methodology underlying the theory. Such debate is healthy for any science. The serious student of motivation should consider Herzberg's theory—and any other theory—to be one attempt at modeling work behavior. As such, the theory should be dissected and/or modified in a continuing effort to develop comprehensive and accurate predictors of human behavior on the job. In other words, it appears that a fruitful approach to this "controversial" theory would be to learn from it that which can help us develop better models, rather than to accept or reject the model totally.

ADDITIONAL EARLY MODELS OF JOB DESIGN

In addition to Herzberg's model, several other early models of job design can be identified (see Exhibit 1). These are (1) the requisite task attributes model, (2) the sociotechnical systems model, (3) activation theory, and (4) achievement motivation theory. While a detailed examination of these models is beyond the scope of this chapter, we can briefly review how these various models differ in their approach to the motivational properties of tasks.

The *requisite task attributes model,* proposed by Turner and Lawrence (1965), argued that an enriched job (that is, a job characterized by variety, autonomy, responsibility, etc.) would lead to increased attendance and job satisfaction. The model was similar to Herzberg's in that it viewed job enrichment as a motivating variable. It differed from Herzberg's in that Turner and Lawrence included absenteeism as a dependent variable. Moreover, Turner and Lawrence acknowledged the existence of two sets of important moderators in the job scope-outcome relationship. First, it was found in their study that workers from urban settings were more satisfied with low-scope jobs than workers from rural settings. Second, it was found that situational factors (such as supervisory style and coworker relations) also moderated the impact of job scope on satisfaction and absenteeism. This acknowledgement of the role of individual and situational variables represents a significant contribution to our understanding of the ways in which job redesign affects employee attitudes and behavior. In fact, much of the subsequent work on the topic has taken the lead from the work of Turner and Lawrence.

A second and popular model, advanced by Trist and Davis, is known as the *sociotechnical systems model*. This model suggests that an appropriate starting point for understanding job design is to consider the psychological requirements of tasks in order for them to be motivating. These principles include the need for a job to provide (1) reasonably demanding content, (2) an opportunity to learn, (3) some degree of autonomy or discretion in decisions affecting the job, (4) social support and recognition, and (5) a feeling that the job leads to a desirable future.

On the basis of these principles, job design principles are derived which suggest, in brief, that enriched jobs meet these psychological requirements. As a consequence, enriched jobs would be expected to lead to such outcomes as high job performance and low labor stoppages. An important aspect of the sociotechnical model is that it clearly acknowledges the role of the social context (or organizational system) in which job redesign attempts are made. That is, the model argues that such changes cannot be successfully implemented without acknowledging and taking into account various social and organizational factors that also influence people's desire to perform on the job (reward system, work group norms, supervisory relations, etc.). Hence, the sociotechnical systems approach attempts to be a truly systematic (that is, comprehensive) approach to work design.

Activation theory focuses on the physiological processes involved in job redesign (Scott, 1966). Activation, defined as the degree of excitation of the brain stem reticular formation, has been found in laboratory experiments to have a curvilinear relationship to performance. Research has demonstrated that performance suffers at very low or very high levels of activation. Hence, jobs that are dull or repetitive may lead to low levels of performance because they fail to activate. On the other hand, more enriched jobs should lead to a state of activation with a resulting increase in performance. While many questions remain concerning the empirical support for activation theory, it does suggest how job design can affect employees physiologically, a relationship ignored in previous research.

Finally, *achievement motivation theory*, proposed by Murray (1938) and refined by McClelland and Atkinson, also examines the process by which changes in the job situation influence behavior. The focus of this approach, however, is on employee personality, specifically, an employee's need for achievement. In essence, achievement motivation theory posits that employees with a high need for achievement will be more likely to respond favorably to enriched jobs than employees with a low need for achievement. Enriched jobs cue, or stimulate, the achievement motive, typically leading to higher levels of performance, involvement, and satisfaction. For employees with a low need for achievement, however, an enriched job may be threatening; that is, they may feel overchallenged. As a result, they may experience increased frustration and anxiety and exhibit lower performance.

In conclusion, we have seen that several models of job design exist. Each model tends to focus on one aspect of the job situation (e.g, personality, social context, or physiological response) and, therefore makes a useful contribution by expanding our understanding of the relevant variables that must be included in a comprehensive model of work design. As the readings in this chapter will demonstrate, when one or more features of these models are implemented and job designs are actually changed, opinions about their efficacy for improving "quality of work life" are mixed. Results overall tend to be positive, but not uniformly so, and it is clear that the kinds of approaches discussed later in the chapter are not simple and do not constitute any type of panacea. In other words, there are a number of complexities involved in job design changes that are intended to improve the quality of work life. Nevertheless, these kinds of efforts have the *potential* for bringing about beneficial effects on the way the employee relates to the work situation, to supervision, and to the organization.

OVERVIEW

The readings that follow present a comprehensive portrait of work design quality-of-work-life (QWL) issues. In the initial article, by Hackman, the concept of job design is examined in some detail, with particular attention to job design as a change strategy. The job characteristics model is presented, along with supporting evidence. Moreover, several principles for enriching jobs are reviewed. Finally, guidelines for instituting job redesign are suggested.

In the second article, Walton updates much of the QWL literature by focusing on how organizations can develop personnel policies that center on commitment instead of control. Implications for management are discussed.

The third article, by Lawler and Mohrman, examines the more specific topic of quality circles. The point is made here that while quality circles serve a definite role in employee motivation and performance, their success can be enhanced and sustained only if such techniques are embedded in a larger, more systematic approach to participative management.

Finally, another article by Lawler and Mohrman attempts to tie together several issues relating to work design into a general approach to high-involvement management. This last article emphasizes the managerial implications of the work design and participative management research, including the importance of sharing knowledge, power, and rewards with all organizational stakeholders involved in performance enhancement efforts.

REFERENCES

Bockman, V. M. The Herzberg controversy. *Personnel Psychology*, 1971, **24**, 155–189.
Herzberg, F. *Work and the nature of man*. Cleveland: World Publishing, 1966.
Herzberg, F., Mausner, B., Peterson, R. O., & Capwell, D. F. *Job attitudes: Review of research and opinion*. Pittsburgh: Psychological Services of Pittsburgh, 1957.
Herzberg, F., Mausner, B., & Snyderman, B. *The motivation to work*. New York: Wiley, 1959.
House, R. J., & Wigdor, L. A. Herzberg's dual-factor theory of job satisfaction and motivation. *Personnel Psychology*, 1957, **20**, 369–390.
King, N. Clarification and evaluation of the two-factor theory of job satisfaction. *Psychological Bulletin*, 1970, **74**, 18–31.
Maier, N. R. F. *Psychology in industry*, 2d ed. Boston: Houghton Mifflin, 1955.
Murray, H. A. *Explorations in personality*. New York: Oxford University Press, 1938.

Myers, M. S. *Every employee a manager*. New York: McGraw-Hill, 1970.

Paul W. J., Robertson, K. B., & Herzberg, F. Job enrichment pays off. *Harvard Business Review*, 1969, **47**(2), 61–78.

Scott, W. E. Activation theory and task design. *Organizational Behavior and Human Performance*, 1966, **1**, 3–30.

Turner, A. N., & Lawrence P. R. *Industrial jobs and the worker*. Boston: Harvard University, Graduate School of Business Administration, 1965.

Viteles, M. S. *Motivation and morale in industry*. New York: Norton, 1953.

Vroom, V. H. *Work and motivation*. New York: Wiley, 1964.

Whitset, D. A., & Winslow, E. K. An analysis of studies critical of the motivation-hygiene theory. *Personnel Psychology*, 1967, **20**, 391–416.

Work Design

J. Richard Hackman

Every five years or so, a new behavioral science "solution" to organizational problems emerges. Typically such a solution is first tried out—with great success—in a few forward-looking organizations. Then it is picked up by the management journals and the popular press and spreads across the country. And finally, after a few years, it fades away as disillusioned managers, union leaders, and employees come to agree that the solution really does not solve much of anything.

It looks as if the redesign of work is to be the solution of the mid-1970s. The seeds of this strategy for change were planted more than two decades ago, with the pioneering research of Charles Walker and Robert Guest (1952), Frederick Herzberg and his associates (Herzberg, Mausner, and Snyderman, 1959; Herzberg, 1966), Louis Davis (1957, 1966), and a few others. Successful tests of work redesign were conducted in a few organizations and were widely reported. Now, change programs involving work redesign are flooding the nation, stories on "how we profited from job enrichment" are appearing in management journals, and the labor community is struggling to determine how it should respond to the tidal wave that seems to be forming (Gooding, 1972).

The question of the moment is whether the redesign of work will evolve into a robust and powerful strategy for organizational change—or whether, like so many of its behavioral science predecessors, it will fade into disuse as practitioners experience failure and disillusionment in its applications. The answer is by no means clear.

Present evidence regarding the merits of work redesign can be viewed as optimistic or pessimistic, depending on the biases of the reader. On the one hand, numerous published case studies of successful work redesign projects show that work redesign can be an effective tool for improving both the quality of the work experience of employees and their on-the-job productivity. Yet it also is true that numerous failures in implementing work redesign have been experienced by organizations around the country—and the rate of failure shows no sign of diminishing. Reif and Luthans (1972), for example, summarize a survey, conducted in the mid-1960s, in which only four of forty-one firms implementing job enrichment described their experiences with the technique as "very successful." Increasingly, other commentators are expressing serious doubts about whether job enrichment is really as effective as it has been cracked up to be (Fein, 1974; Gomberg, 1973; Hulin and Blood, 1968).

Unfortunately, existing research findings and case reports are not very helpful in assessing the validity of the claims made by either the advocates or the skeptics of work redesign. In particular, an examination of the literature cited in Hackman (1975a) leads to the following conclusions:

From J. R. Hackman & J. L. Suttle (Eds.), *Improving Life at Work*. Glenview, Ill.: Scott, Foresman, 1977. Copyright © 1977 by Scott, Foresman and Company. Reprinted by permission.

1 Reports of work redesign successes tend to be more evangelical than thoughtful; for example, little conceptualizing is done that would be useful either as a guide to implementation of work redesign in other settings or as a theoretical basis for research on its effects.

2 The methodologies used in evaluating the effects of changes in work design often are weak or incomplete. Therefore, findings reported may be ambiguous and open to alternative explanations.

3 Although informal sources and surveys suggest that the failure rate for work redesign projects is moderate to high, few documented analyses are available of projects that failed. This is particularly unfortunate because careful analyses of failures often are among the most effective tools for exploring the applicability and the consequences of this or any other organizational change strategy.

4 Most published reports focus almost exclusively on assessing the positive and negative effects of specific changes in work content. Conclusions are then drawn about the general worth of work redesign as a change strategy. Yet there is an *interaction* between the content of the changes and the organizational context in which they are installed; identical job changes may have quite different effects in different organizational settings (or when installed using different processes). Existing literature has little to say about the nature or dynamics of such interactions.

5 Rarely are economic data (that is, direct and indirect dollar costs and benefits) analyzed and discussed when conclusions are drawn about the effects of work redesign projects, even though many such projects are undertaken in direct anticipation of economic gains.

In sum, it appears that despite the abundance of writing on the topic, there is little definite information about why work redesign is effective when it is, what goes wrong when it is not, and how the strategy can be altered to improve its general usefulness as an approach to personal and organizational change.

This paper attempts to advance current understanding about such questions. It reviews what is known about how the redesign of work can help improve life in organizations and attempts to identify the circumstances under which the approach is most likely to succeed. It reviews current practice for planning and installing work redesign and emphasizes both the pitfalls that may be encountered and the change strategies that have been shown to be especially effective. And, at the most general level, it asks whether this approach to organizational change is indeed worth saving, or whether it should be allowed to die.

WHAT IS WORK REDESIGN?

Whenever a job is changed—whether because of a new technology, an internal reorganization, or a whim of a manager—it can be said that work redesign has taken place. The present use of the term is somewhat more specialized. Throughout this paper, work redesign is used to refer to any activities that involve the alteration of specific jobs (or interdependent systems of jobs) with the intent of increasing both the quality of the employees' work experience and their on-the-job productivity. This definition of the term is deliberately broad, to include the great diversity of changes that can be tried to achieve these goals. It subsumes such terms as *job rotation, job enrichment,* and *sociotechnical systems design,* each of which refers to a specific approach to or technique for redesigning work.

There are no simple or generally accepted criteria for a well-designed job, nor is there any single strategy that is acknowledged as the proper way to go about improving a job. Instead, what will be an effective design for one specific job in a particular organization may be quite different from the way the job should be designed or changed in another setting. There are, nonetheless, some common-alities in most work redesign experiments that have been carried out to date. Typically changes are made that provide employees with additional responsibili-ties for planning, setting up, and checking their own work; for making decisions about methods and procedures; for establishing their own work pace within broad limits; and sometimes for relating directly with the client who receives the results of the work. Often the net effect is that jobs which previously had been simplified and segmented into many small parts (in the interest of efficiency from an engineering perspective) are put back together again and made the responsi-bility of individual workers (Herzberg, 1974).

An early case of work redesign (reported by Kilbridge, 1960) is illustrative. The basic job involved the assembly of small centrifugal pumps used in washing machines. Prior to redesign, the pumps were assembled by six operators on a conveyor line, with each operator performing a particular part of the assembly. The job was changed so that each worker assembled an entire pump, inspected it, and placed his own identifying mark on it. In addition, the assembly operations were converted to a batch system in which workers had more freedom to control their work pace than they had had under the conveyor system. Kilbridge reports that after the job had been enlarged, total assembly time decreased, quality im-proved, and important cost savings were realized.

In another case, the responsibilities of clerks who assembled information for telephone directories at Indiana Bell Telephone Company were significantly ex-panded (Ford, 1973). Prior to the change, a production line model was used to assemble directory information. Information was passed from clerk to clerk as it was processed, and each clerk performed only a very small part of the entire job. There were a total of twenty-one different steps in the workflow. Jobs were changed so that each qualified clerk was given responsibility for all the clerical operations required to assemble an entire directory—including receiving, pro-cessing, and verifying all information. (For large directories, clerks were given responsibility for a specific alphabetical section of the book.) Not only did the new work arrangement improve the quality of the work experience of the em-ployees, but the efficiency of the operation increased as well—in part because clerks made fewer errors, and so it was no longer necessary to have employees who merely checked and verified the work of others.

In recent years, work redesign increasingly has been used as part of a larger change package aimed at improving the overall quality of life and productivity of people at work. A good example is the new General Foods pet food manufactur-ing plant in Topeka, Kansas (Walton, 1972, 1975b). When plans were developed for the facility in the late 1960s, corporate management decided to design and manage the plant in full accord with state-of-the-art behavioral science knowledge. Nontraditional features were built into the plant from the beginning—including the physical design of the facilities, the management style, information and feedback systems, compensation arrangements, and career paths for individual employees. A key part of the plan was the organization of the work force into teams. Each team (consisting of from seven to fourteen members) was given nearly autonomous responsibility for a significant organizational task. In addition to actually carrying out the work required to complete that task, team members performed many activities that traditionally had been reserved for management. These included coping with manufacturing problems, distributing individual tasks among team members, screening and selecting new team members, and participating in organizational decision-making (Walton, 1972). The basic jobs performed by team members were designed to be as challenging as possible, and employees were encouraged to further broaden their skills in order to be able to handle even more challenging work. Although not without problems, the Topeka plant appears to be prospering, and many employees experience life in the organization as a pleasant and near revolutionary change from their traditional ideas about what happens at work.

The Uniqueness of Work Redesign as a Strategy for Change

The redesign of work differs from most other behavioral science approaches to changing life in organizations in at least four ways (Hackman, 1975b). Together, these four points of uniqueness make a rather compelling case for work redesign as a strategy for initiating organizational change.

1 *Work redesign alters the basic relationship between a person and what he or she does on the job.* When all the outer layers are stripped away, many organizational problems come to rest at the interface between *people* and the *tasks* they do. Frederick Taylor realized this when he set out to design and manage organizations "scientifically" at the beginning of this century (Taylor, 1911). The design of work was central to the scientific management approach, and special pains were taken to ensure that the tasks done by workers did not exceed their performance capabilities. As the approach gained credence in the management community, new and more sophisticated procedures for analyzing work methods emerged, and industrial engineers forged numerous principles of work design. In general, these principles were intended to maximize overall production efficiency by minimizing human error on the job (often accomplished by partitioning the work into small, simple segments), and by minimizing time and motion wasted in doing work tasks.

It turned out, however, that many workers did not like jobs designed according to the dictates of scientific management. In effect, the person-job relationship had been arranged so that achieving the goals of the organization (high productivity) often meant sacrificing important personal goals (the opportunity for interesting, personally rewarding work). Taylor and his associates attempted to deal with this difficulty by installing financial incentive programs intended to make workers want to work hard toward organizational goals, and by placing such an elaborate set of supervisory controls on workers that they scarcely could behave otherwise. But the basic incongruence between the person and the work remained, and people-problems (such as high absenteeism and turnover, poor quality work, and high worker dissatisfaction) became increasingly evident in work organizations.

In the past several decades, industrial psychologists have carried out a large number of studies intended to overcome some of the problems that accompanied the spread of scientific management. Sophisticated strategies for identifying those individuals most qualified to perform specific jobs have been developed and validated. New training and attitude change programs have been tried. And numerous motivational techniques have been proposed to increase the energy and commitment with which workers do their tasks. These include development of human relations programs, alteration of supervisory styles, and installation of complex piece-rate and profit-sharing incentive plans. None of these strategies have proven successful. Indeed, some observers report that the quality of the work experience of employees today is more problematic than it was in the heyday of scientific management (cf. *Work in America,* 1973).

Why have behavioral scientists not been more successful in their attempts to remedy motivational problems in organizations and improve the quality of work life of employees? One reason is that psychologists (like managers and labor leaders) have traditionally assumed that the *work itself was inviolate*—that the role of psychologists is simply to help select, train, and motivate people within the confines of jobs as they have been designed by others. Clearly, it is time to reject this assumption and to seek ways to change both people and jobs in order to improve the fit between them.

The redesign of work as a change strategy offers the opportunity to break out of the "givens" that have limited previous attempts to improve life at work. It is based on the assumption that the work itself may be a very powerful influence on employee motivation, satisfaction, and productivity. It acknowledges (and attempts to build on) the inability of people to set aside their social and emotional needs while at work. And it provides a strategy for moving away from extrinsic props to worker motivation and to move instead toward *internal* work motivation that causes the individual to do the work because it interests him, challenges him, and rewards him for a job well done.

2 *Work redesign directly changes behavior—and it tends to stay changed.* People do the tasks they are given. How well they do them depends on many factors, including how the tasks are designed. But no matter how the tasks are designed, people do them.

On the other hand, people do *not* always behave in ways that are consistent with their attitudes, their levels of satisfaction, or what they cognitively know they should do. Indeed, it is now well established that one's attitudes often are *determined* by the behaviors one engages in—rather than vice versa, as traditionally has been thought (Bem, 1970; Kiesler, Collins, and Miller, 1969). This is especially true when individuals perceive that they have substantial personal freedom or autonomy in choosing how they will behave (Steiner, 1970).

Enriching jobs, then, may have twin virtues. First, behavior is changed; and second, because enriched jobs usually bring about increased feelings of autonomy and personal discretion, the individual is likely to develop attitudes that are supportive of his new on-the-job behaviors (cf. Taylor, 1971). Work redesign does not, therefore, rely on changing attitudes first (for example, inducing the worker to care more about the work outcomes, as in zero defects programs) and hoping that the attitude change will generalize to work behavior. Instead, the strategy is to change the *behavior,* and to change it in a way that gradually leads to a more positive set of attitudes about the work, the organization, and the self.

Moreover, after jobs are changed, it usually is difficult for workers to slip back into old ways. The old ways simply are inappropriate for the new tasks, and the structure of those tasks reinforces the changes that have taken place. Thus, one need not worry much about the kind of backsliding that occurs so often after training or attitude modification activities, especially those that occur off-site. The task-based stimuli that influence the worker's behavior are very much on-site, every hour of the day. And once those stimuli are changed, behavior is likely to stay changed—at least until the job is again redesigned.

3 *Work redesign offers—and sometimes forces into one's hands—numerous opportunities for initiating other organizational changes.* When work is redesigned in an organization so that many people are doing things differently than they used to, new problems inevitably surface and demand attention. These can be construed solely as *problems,* or they can be treated as *opportunities* for further organizational change activities. For example, technical problems are likely to develop when jobs are changed—offering opportunities to smooth and refine the work system as a system. Interpersonal issues also are likely to arise, almost inevitably between supervisors and subordinates and sometimes between peers who have to relate to one another in new ways. These issues offer opportunities for developmental work aimed at improving the social and supervisory aspects of the work system.

Because such problems are literally forced to the surface by the job changes, all parties may feel a need to do something about them. Responses can range from using the existence of a problem to justify that "job enrichment doesn't work," to simply trying to solve the problem quickly so the work redesign project can proceed, to using the problem as a point of entry for attacking other organizational issues. If the last stance is taken, behavioral science professionals may find themselves pleasantly removed from the old difficulty of selling their wares to skeptical managers and employees who are not really sure there is anything wrong. Eventually a program of organizational change and development may evolve that addresses organizational systems and practices that, superficially at least, seem unrelated to how the work itself is designed (Beer and Huse, 1972).

4 *Work redesign, in the long term, can result in organizations that rehumanize rather than dehumanize the people who work in them.* Despite the popular infla-

tion of the work ethic issue in recent years, there is convincing evidence that organizations can and do sometimes stamp out part of the humanness of their members—especially people's motivations toward growth and personal development (cf. Kornhauser, 1965).

Work redesign can help individuals regain the chance to experience the kick that comes from doing a job well, and it can encourage them to once again *care* about their work and about developing the competence to do it even better. These payoffs from work redesign go well beyond simple job satisfaction. Cows grazing in the field may be satisfied, and employees in organizations can be made just as satisfied by paying them well, by keeping bosses off their backs, by putting them in pleasant work rooms with pleasant people, and by arranging things so that the days pass without undue stress or strain.

The kind of satisfaction at issue here is different. It is a satisfaction that develops only when individuals are stretching and growing as human beings, increasing their sense of competence and self-worth. Whether the creation of opportunities for personal growth is a legitimate goal for work redesign activities is a value question deserving long discussion; the case for the value of work redesign strictly in terms of *organizational* health easily can rest on the first three points discussed above. But personal growth is without question a central component of the overall quality of work life in organizations, and the impact of work redesign on the people who do the work, as human beings, should be neither overlooked nor underemphasized. . . .

DESIGNING WORK FOR INDIVIDUALS

A model specifying how job characteristics and individual differences interact to affect the satisfaction, motivation, and productivity of individuals at work has been proposed by Hackman and Oldham (1976). The model is specifically intended for use in planning and carrying out changes in the design of jobs. It is described below and then is used as a guide for discussion of diagnostic procedures and change principles that can be used in redesigning the jobs of individuals.

The Job Characteristics Model

The basic job characteristics model is shown in Figure 1. As illustrated in the figure, five core job dimensions are seen as creating three critical psychological states that, in turn, lead to a number of beneficial personal and work outcomes. The links among the job dimensions, the psychological states, and the outcomes are shown to be moderated by individual growth need strength. The major classes of variables in the model are reviewed briefly below.

Psychological States   The three following psychological states are postulated as critical in affecting a person's motivation and satisfaction on the job:

1 Experienced meaningfulness: The person must experience the work as generally important, valuable, and worthwhile.

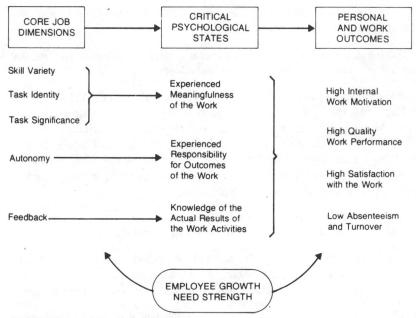

| CORE JOB DIMENSIONS | CRITICAL PSYCHOLOGICAL STATES | PERSONAL AND WORK OUTCOMES |

Skill Variety
Task Identity
Task Significance

Experienced Meaningfulness of the Work

Autonomy

Experienced Responsibility for Outcomes of the Work

Feedback

Knowledge of the Actual Results of the Work Activities

High Internal Work Motivation

High Quality Work Performance

High Satisfaction with the Work

Low Absenteeism and Turnover

EMPLOYEE GROWTH NEED STRENGTH

FIGURE 1
The job characteristics model of work motivation.

2 Experienced responsibility: The individual must feel personally responsible and accountable for the results of the work he performs.

3 Knowledge of results: The individual must have an understanding, on a fairly regular basis, of how effectively he is performing the job.

The more these three conditions are present, the more people will feel good about themselves when they perform well. Or, following Hackman and Lawler (1971), the model postulates that internal rewards are obtained by an individual when he *learns* (knowledge of results) that he *personally* (experienced responsibility) has performed well on a task that he *cares about* (experienced meaningfulness). These internal rewards are reinforcing to the individual and serve as incentives for continued efforts to perform well in the future. When the person does not perform well, he does not experience reinforcement, and he may elect to try harder in the future so as to regain the rewards that good performance brings. The net result is a self-perpetuating cycle of positive work motivation powered by self-generated rewards. This cycle is predicted to continue until one or more of the three psychological states is no longer present, or until the individual no longer values the internal rewards that derive from good performance.

Job Dimensions Of the five job characteristics shown in Figure 1 as fostering the emergence of the psychological states, three contribute to the experienced meaningfulness of the work, and one each contributes to experienced responsibility and to knowledge of results.

The three job dimensions that contribute to a job's *meaningfulness* are skill variety, task identity, and task significance.

Skill variety—the degree to which a job requires a variety of different activities that involve the use of a number of different skills and talents.

When a task requires a person to engage in activities that challenge or stretch his skills and abilities, that task almost invariably is experienced as meaningful by the individual. Many parlor games, puzzles, and recreational activities, for example, achieve much of their fascination because they tap and test intellectual or motor skills. When a job draws on several skills of an employee, that individual may find the job to be of very high personal meaning even if, in any absolute sense, it is not of great significance or importance.

Task identity—the degree to which the job requires completion of a whole and identifiable piece of work—that is, doing a job from beginning to end with a visible outcome.

If an employee assembles a complete product or provides a complete unit of service, he should find the work more meaningful than if he were responsible for only a small part of the whole job, other things (such as skill variety) being equal.

Task significance—the degree to which the job has a substantial impact on the lives or work of other people, whether in the immediate organization or in the external environment.

When an individual understands that the results of his work may have a significant effect on the well-being of other people, the experienced meaningfulness of the work usually is enhanced. Employees who tighten nuts on aircraft brake assemblies, for example, are much more likely to perceive their work as meaningful than are workers who fill small boxes with paper clips, even though the skill levels involved may be comparable.

The job characteristic predicted to prompt employee feelings of personal *responsibility* for the work outcomes is autonomy, which is defined as follows:

Autonomy—the degree to which the job provides substantial freedom, independence, and discretion to the individual in scheduling the work and in determining the procedures to be used in carrying it out.

To the extent that autonomy is high, work outcomes will be viewed by workers as depending substantially on their *own* efforts, initiatives, and decisions, rather than on the adequacy of instructions from the boss or on a manual of job procedures. In such circumstances, individuals should feel strong personal responsibility for the successes and failures that occur on the job.

The job characteristic that fosters *knowledge of results* is feedback, which is defined as follows:

Feedback—the degree to which carrying out the work activities required by the job results in the individual obtaining direct and clear information about the effectiveness of his performance.

It is often useful to combine the scores of a job on the five dimensions described above into a single index reflecting the overall potential of the job to prompt self-generated work motivation in job incumbents. Following the model diagrammed in Figure 1, a job high in motivating potential must be high on at least one (and hopefully more) of the three dimensions that lead to experienced meaningfulness, *and* high on autonomy and feedback as well. The presence of these dimensions creates conditions for all three of the critical psychological states to be present. Arithmetically, scores of jobs on the five dimensions are combined as follows to meet this criterion:

$$
\begin{array}{l}
\text{Motivating} \\
\text{Potential} \\
\text{Score (MPS)}
\end{array} = \left[\frac{\text{Skill} + \text{Task} + \text{Task}}{\text{Variety}\ \text{Identity}\ \text{Significance}}{3} \right] \times \text{Autonomy} \times \text{Job Feedback}
$$

As can be seen from the formula, a near-zero score of a job on either autonomy or feedback will reduce the overall MPS to near-zero; a near-zero score on one of the three job dimensions that contribute to experienced meaningfulness cannot, by itself, do so.

Individual Growth Need Strength   Growth need strength is postulated to moderate how people react to complex, challenging work at two points in the model shown in Figure 1: first at the link between the objective job dimensions and the psychological states, and again between the psychological states and the outcome variables. The first link means that high growth need individuals are more likely (or better able) to *experience* the psychological states when their objective job is enriched than are their low growth need counterparts. The second link means that individuals with high growth need strength will respond more positively to the psychological states, when they are present, than will low growth need individuals.

Outcome Variables   Also shown in Figure 1 are several outcomes that are affected by the level of self-generated motivation experienced by people at work. Of special interest as an outcome variable is internal work motivation (Lawler and Hall, 1970; Hackman and Lawler, 1971). This variable taps directly the contingency between effective performance and self-administered affective rewards. Typical questionnaire items measuring internal work motivation include: (1) "I feel a great sense of personal satisfaction when I do this job well"; (2) "I feel bad and unhappy when I discover that I have performed poorly on this job."; and (3) "My own feelings are *not* affected much one way or the other by how well I do on this job" (reversed scoring).

Other outcomes listed in Figure 1 are the quality of work performance, job satisfaction (especially satisfaction with opportunities for personal growth and development on the job), absenteeism, and turnover. All of these outcomes are predicted to be affected positively by a job high in motivating potential.

Validity of the Job Characteristics Model

Empirical test of the job characteristic model of work motivation is reported in detail elsewhere (Hackman and Oldham, 1976). In general, results are supportive, as suggested by the following overview:

1 People who work on jobs high on the core job characteristics are more motivated, satisfied, and productive than are people who work on jobs that score low on these characteristics. The same is true for absenteeism, although less strongly so.

2 Responses to jobs high in objective motivating potential are more positive for people who have strong needs for growth than for people with weak growth needs. The moderating effect of individual growth need strength occurs both at the link between the job dimensions and the psychological states and at the link between the psychological states and the outcome measures, as shown in Figure 1. (This moderating effect is not, however, obtained for absenteeism.)

3 The job characteristics operate *through* the psychological states in influencing the outcome variables, as predicted by the model, rather than influencing the outcomes directly. Two anomalies have been identified, however: (a) results involving the feedback dimension are in some situations less strong than results obtained for the other dimensions (perhaps in part because individuals receive feedback at work from many sources—not just the job), and (b) the linkage between autonomy and experienced responsibility does not operate exactly as specified by the model in affecting the outcome variables (Hackman and Oldham, 1976). . . .

Principles for Enriching Jobs

The core job dimensions specified in the job characteristic model are tied directly to a set of action principles for redesigning jobs (Hackman, Oldham, Janson, and Purdy, 1975; Walters and Associates, 1975). As shown in Figure 2, these principles specify what types of changes in jobs are most likely to lead to improvements in each of the five core job dimensions, and thus to an increase in the motivating potential of the job as a whole.

FIGURE 2
Principles for changing jobs.

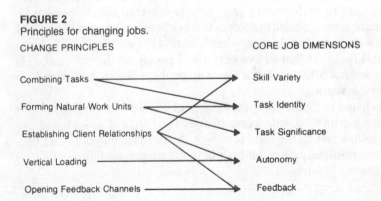

Principle #1: Forming Natural Work Units A critical step in the design of any job is the decision about how the work is to be distributed among the people who do it. Numerous considerations affect that decision, such as technological constraints, level of worker training and experience, efficiency from an industrial or systems engineering perspective, and equity of individual work loads. Work designed on the basis of these factors usually is distributed among employees rationally and logically. The problem is that the logic used often does not include the needs of employees for personally meaningful work.

Consider, for example, a typing pool consisting of one supervisor and ten typists who do all the typing for one division of an organization. Jobs are delivered in rough draft or dictated form to the supervisor, who distributes them as evenly as possible among the typists. In such circumstances the individual letters, reports, and other tasks performed by a given typist in one day or week are randomly assigned. There is no basis for identifying with the work or with the person or department for whom it is performed, or for placing any personal value on it.

By contrast, creating natural units of work increases employee "ownership" of the work and improves the chances that employees will view their work as meaningful and important rather than as irrelevant and boring. In creating natural units of work, one must first identify the basic work items. In the typing pool example, that might be "pages to be typed." Then these items are grouped into natural and meaningful categories. For example, each typist might be assigned continuing responsibility for all work requested by a single department or by several smaller departments. Instead of typing one section of a large report, the individual will type the entire piece of work, with knowledge of exactly what the total outcome of the work is. Furthermore, over time the typist will develop a growing sense of how the work affects co-workers or customers who receive the completed product. Thus, as shown in Figure 2, forming natural units of work increases two of the core dimensions that contribute to experienced meaningfulness—task identity and task significance.

Because it is still important that work be distributed so that the system as a whole operates efficiently, work loads must be arranged so that they are divided equitably. The principle of natural work units simply requires that these traditional criteria be supplemented so that, as far as possible, the tasks that arrive at an employee's work station form an identifiable and meaningful whole.

Principle #2: Combining Tasks The very existence of a pool made up entirely of persons whose sole function is typing reflects a fractionalization of jobs that sometimes can lead to such hidden costs as high absenteeism and turnover and extra supervisory time. The principle of combining tasks is based on the assumption that such costs often can be reduced by taking existing and fractionalized tasks and putting them back together again to form a new and larger module of work. At the Medfield, Massachusetts plant of Corning Glass Works, for example, the job of assembling laboratory hot plates was redesigned by combining a number of tasks that had been separate. After the change, each hot plate was assembled from start to finish by one operator, instead of going through several separate operations performed by different people.

Combining tasks (like forming natural work units) contributes in two ways to the experienced meaningfulness of the work. First, task identity is increased. The hot plate assembler, for example, can see and identify with a finished product ready for shipment, rather than with a nearly invisible junction of solder. Moreover, as more tasks are combined into a single worker's job, the individual must use a greater variety of skills in performing the job, further increasing the meaningfulness of the work.

Principle #3: Establishing Client Relationships Jobs designed according to traditional criteria often provide workers with little or no contact with the ultimate user of their product or service. As a consequence, workers may have difficulty generating high commitment and motivation to do the job well.

By establishing direct relationships between workers and their clients, jobs often can be improved in three ways. First, feedback increases because additional opportunities are created for the employees to receive direct praise or criticism of their work outputs. Second, skill variety may increase, because of the need to develop and exercise one's interpersonal skills in managing and maintaining the relationship with the client. Finally, autonomy will increase to the degree that individuals are given real personal responsibility for deciding how to manage their relationships with the people who receive the outputs of their work.

Creating client relationships can be viewed as a three-step process: (1) identifying who the client actually is; (2) establishing the most direct contact possible between the worker and the client; and (3) establishing criteria and procedures so that the client can judge the quality of the product or service received and relay his judgments directly to the worker. Especially important (and, in many cases, difficult to achieve) is identification of the specific criteria by which the work output is assessed by the client, and ensuring that both the worker and the client understand these criteria and agree with them.

Principle #4: Vertical Loading In vertical loading, the intent is to partially close the gap between the "doing" and the "controlling" aspects of the job. Thus, when a job is vertically loaded, responsibilities and controls that formerly were reserved for management are given to the employee as part of the job. Among ways this might be achieved are the following:

• Giving job incumbents responsibility for deciding on work methods and for advising or helping to train less experienced workers;

• Providing increased freedom in time management, including decisions about when to start and stop work, when to take breaks, and how to assign work priorities;

• Encouraging workers to do their own troubleshooting and to manage work crises, rather than calling immediately for a supervisor;

• Providing workers with increased knowledge of the financial aspects of the job and the organization, and increased control over budgetary matters that affect their work.

Vertically loading a job inevitably increases *autonomy*. And, as shown in Figure 1, this should lead to increased feelings of personal responsibility and accountability for the work outcomes.

Principle #5: Opening Feedback Channels   In virtually all jobs there are ways to open channels of feedback to individuals, to help them learn not only how well they are performing their jobs but also whether their performance is improving, deteriorating, or remaining at a constant level. Although there are various sources from which information about performance can come, it usually is advantageous for a worker to learn about his performance directly as he does the job—rather than from management on an occasional basis.

Job-provided feedback is more immediate and private than supervisor-supplied feedback, and it increases workers' feelings of personal control over their work. Moreover, it avoids many of the potentially disruptive interpersonal problems that can develop when a worker can find out how he is doing only from direct messages or subtle cues from the boss.

Exactly what should be done to open channels for job-provided feedback varies from job to job and from organization to organization. Often the changes involve simply removing existing blocks that isolate the individual from naturally occurring data about performance, rather than generating entirely new feedback mechanisms. For example:

• Establishing direct client relationships (discussed above) often removes blocks between the worker and natural external sources of data about the work.

• Quality control efforts often eliminate a natural source of feedback, because all quality checks are done by people other than the individuals responsible for the work. In such situations, any feedback that workers do receive may be belated and diluted. Placing most quality control functions in the hands of workers will dramatically increase the quantity and quality of data available to them about their performances.

• Tradition and established procedure in many organizations dictate that records about performance be kept by a supervisor and transmitted up (not down) the organizational hierarchy. Sometimes supervisors even check the work and correct any errors themselves. The worker who made the error never knows it occurred and is therefore denied the very information that could enhance both internal work motivation and the technical adequacy of his performance. In many cases, it is possible to provide standard summaries of performance records directly to the workers. This would give the employees personally and regularly the data they need to improve their effectiveness.

• Computers and other automated machines sometimes can be used to provide individuals with data now blocked from them. Many clerical operations, for example, are now performed on computer consoles. These consoles often can be programmed to provide the clerk with immediate feedback in the form of a CRT display or a printout indicating that an error has been made. Some systems even have been programmed to provide the operator with a positive feedback message when a period of error-free performance has been sustained.

The principles for redesigning jobs reviewed above, although illustrative of the kinds of changes that can be made to improve the jobs of individuals in organizations, obviously are not exhaustive. They were selected for attention here because of the links (Figure 2) between the principles and the core job dimension in the motivational model presented earlier. Other principles for enriching jobs (which, although often similar to those presented here, derive from alternative conceptual frameworks) are presented by Ford (1969), Glaser (1975), Herzberg (1974), and Katzell and Yankelovich (1975). . . .

GUIDELINES FOR INSTALLING PLANNED CHANGES IN JOBS

We move now to exploration of issues that arise in the actual installation of changes in the design of work. The material presented below is based on observations and interviews conducted by the author and his associates over the past three years in numerous organizations where work redesign activities were being planned, implemented, or evaluated.

In general, we have found job enrichment to be failing as least as often as it is succeeding. And the reasons for the failures, in many cases, appear to have more to do with the way planned changes are *implemented* in organizations than with the intrinsic merit of the changes. Again and again we have seen good ideas about the redesign of work die because the advocates of change were unable to gain acceptance for their ideas or because unexpected roadblocks led to early termination of the change project.

Our findings are summarized below as six prescriptive guides for implementing changes in jobs. Each guide includes a discussion of pitfalls that frequently are encountered in work redesign projects, as well as ingredients that were common to many of the more successful projects we observed.

Guide 1: Diagnose the Work System Prior to Change

It is now clear that work redesign is not effective in all organizational circumstances. Yet rarely is a systematic diagnosis carried out beforehand to determine whether meaningful change is feasible, given the jobs being considered, the people who will be involved, and the social, organizational, or cultural environment in which the work is performed. As a result, faulty initial assumptions often go uncorrected, and the change project may be doomed before it is begun.

The choice of the job to be changed, for example, often seems to be almost random. Perhaps a manager will decide that a given job seems right for enrichment. Or he will settle on a job because it is peripheral to the major work done in the organization—thereby minimizing the risk of severe disruption if something should go wrong. Or a job will be selected because everything seems wrong with it—the work is not getting done on time or correctly, employees are angry about everything from their pay to the cleanliness of the restrooms, grievances are excessive, and so on. The hope, apparently, is that somehow redesigning the job will fix everything all at once.

Yet it must be recognized that some jobs, given existing technological constraints, are about as good as they ever can be. Work redesign in such situations is at best a waste of time. Other jobs have so much wrong with them that is irrelevant to how enriched they are that job enrichment could not conceivably bring about a noticeable improvement—and instead might add even more complexity to an already chaotic situation. When such matters are overlooked in planning for work redesign, the result often is a change effort that fails simply because it is aimed at an inappropriate target.

Similarly, differences in employee readiness to handle contemplated changes in jobs only infrequently are assessed before a project is installed. Line managers often express doubts that employees can handle proposed new responsibilities or skepticism that employees will enjoy working on an enriched job. Sometimes, as planning for work redesign proceeds, managers become convinced of the contrary. But only rarely are change projects designed with full cognizance that employees are likely to differ in their psychological readiness for enriched work.

Even less frequently is explicit assessment made of the readiness of managers to deal with the kinds of problems that inevitably arise when a major organizational change is made. In one case, the management team responsible for a job enrichment project nearly collapsed when the first serious change-related problem emerged. Time and energy that were needed for the project were spent instead working on intrateam issues that has been flushed out by the problem. And another "job enrichment failure" occurred while the managers talked and talked. An adequate diagnosis of the readiness of the management team for change-management would have increased the likelihood that the problematic intrateam issues would have been dealt with *before* the work redesign activities were initiated.

The commitment of middle and top management to job enrichment also rarely received diagnostic attention in the observations we observed. Whether organizational change activities must begin at the top—or whether work redesign is a strategy for change that can spread from the bottom up—remains an important and unresolved question (Beer and Huse, 1972). It is almost always true, however, that middle and top management can terminate a project they find unsatisfactory, whether for good reasons or on a whim. In one case, a high-level executive agreed to serve as sponsor for a project without really understanding what the changes would involve. When difficulties in implementation developed, the executive concluded that he had been misled—and the project found itself out from under its protective umbrella and in serious organizational jeopardy. In another case, a single vice-president was counted on to protect a fledgling project from meddling by others who favored alternative approaches to organizational change. When the vice-president departed the organization to attend a several-month executive development training program, his temporary replacement terminated job enrichment activities and substituted a training program more to his own liking. In both cases, an early assessment of the attitudes of key top managers would have revealed the need to develop a broader and better informed base of high-level support for the projects.

A number of organizations we studied did conduct diagnoses of the work system before changes were installed. Almost invariably these studies identified problems or issues that required attention prior to the beginning of the job changes. Such diagnoses are not easy to make. They involve the raising of anxieties at a time when most participants in a project are instead seeking comfort and assurance that everything will turn out all right. Moreover, the tools and methodologies required for undertaking such diagnoses only now are beginning to become available (cf. Hackman and Oldham, 1975; Jenkins, Nadler, Lawler, and Cammann, 1975; Sirota and Wolfson, 1972). Our observations suggest, however, that the diagnostic task may be one of the most crucial in a work redesign project.

Guide 2: Keep the Focus on the Work Itself

Redesigning a job often appears seductively simple. In practice, it is a rather challenging undertaking. It requires a good deal more energy than most other organizational development activities, such as attitude improvement programs, training courses, and objective-setting practices (Ford, 1971).

There are many reasons why it is so hard to alter jobs. At the purely bureaucratic level, the entire personnel-and-job description apparatus often must be engaged to get the changes approved, documented, and implemented. If the organization is unionized, the planned changes often must be negotiated beforehand—sometimes a formidable task. Simple inertia often tempts managers to add lots of window dressing to make things appear different, rather than actually to change what people do on their jobs. Finally, when even one job in an organization is changed, many of the interfaces between that job and related ones must be dealt with as well. In even moderately complex work systems, this is no small matter.

Because of these and other forces against change, work redesign projects frequently are carried out that have very little impact on the work itself. A project carried out in the stock transfer department of a large bank is illustrative (Frank and Hackman, in press). At the end of the project the informal word among managers was, "We tried job enrichment and it failed." But our research data (which measured the objective characteristics of jobs before and after the change) showed that, although all manner of things did change as part of the job enrichment project, the work itself was not among them. Our correlational analyses of data collected in that organization showed that there were very positive relationships between the amount of skill variety, autonomy, and feedback in various jobs and the satisfaction, motivation, performance, and attendance of the job incumbents. These across-job relationships were present prior to the change project and they were there afterwards. But it was also true that those people who held the "good" jobs before the change also held them afterward, and those people whose jobs originally were routine, repetitive, and virtually without feedback had essentially identical jobs after the work was "redesigned." Workers had been formed into small groups, supervision had been changed, names of jobs and work units had been altered, and a general stirring about had taken place. But the *jobs* were not changed much, and the effect (after about six months) was a slight deterioration in worker satisfaction and motivation. This deterioration, apparently, was due more to the failure of the project to live up to expectations than to the changes that had actually taken place.

It is easy, apparently, for those responsible for work redesign activities to delude themselves about what is actually being altered in such projects, and thereby to avoid the rather difficult task of actually changing the structure of the work people do. One way of ensuring that a project stays focused on the work is to base change activities firmly on a theory of work design.

No doubt some theories are better than others. Our observations suggest, however, that the specific details of various theories may not be as important as the fact that *some* theory is used to guide the implementation of change. In addition to keeping the changes focused on the original objective of restructuring the work, a good theory can help identify the kinds of data needed to plan and evaluate the changes and can alert implementors to special problems and opportunities that may develop as the project unfolds.

The theory must, however, be appropriate for the changes that are contemplated. Therein lies one of the major difficulties of the stock transfer project described above. The project originally was designed on the basis of motivation-hygiene theory, which deals exclusively with the enrichment of jobs performed by individuals. The changes that actually were made, however, involved the creation of enriched *group* tasks. Because the theory did not address the special problems of designing work for groups (how to create conditions that encourage members to share with one another their special task-relevant skills), those responsible for implementation found the theory of limited use as a guide for planning and installing the changes. Gradually the theory dropped from their attention. Without the benefit of theory specified guidelines for change, the project became increasingly diffuse and eventually addressed many issues that had little or nothing to do with the work. All this is not to imply that these other issues were unrelated to the change or were improper. However, they cannot be made as substitutes for changes in the work itself.

Guide 3: Prepare Ahead of Time for Unexpected Problems

When substantial changes are made in jobs, shock waves may be created that reverberate throughout adjacent parts of the organization. If insufficient attention is given to such spin-off effects of job changes, they may backfire and create problems that negate (or even reverse) expected positive outcomes.

The site of the backfire varies from case to case. In one company, employees who prepared customer accounts for computer processing were given increased autonomy in scheduling their work and in determining their own work pace. This resulted in a less predictable schedule of data input to the computer system. Because the data processing department had not been involved in the project until the changes were already made, serious computer delays were encountered while data processing managers struggled to figure out how to respond to the new and irregular flow of work. The net result was an increase in antagonism between computer operations and the employees whose jobs had been enriched—and a decrease in the promptness of customer service.

In another company work was redesigned to give rank-and-file employees a number of responsibilities that previously had been handled by their supervisors.

The employees (who dealt with customers of the company by telephone) were given greater opportunities for personal initiative and discretion in dealing with customers, and initially seemed to be prospering in their new responsibilities. But later observations revealed a deterioration in morale, especially in the area of supervisor-subordinate relationships. Apparently the supervisors had found themselves with little work to do after the change (because the employees were handling much of what the supervisors had done before). When supervisors turned to higher management for instructions, they were told to "develop your people—that's what a manager's job is." The supervisors had little idea what "developing your people" involved, and many of them implemented that instruction by looking over the employees' shoulders and correcting each error they could find. Resentment between the supervisor and the employee groups soon developed, and more than overcame any positive benefits that had accrued from the changes in the job (Lawler, Hackman, and Kaufman, 1973).

Problems such as those described above often can be avoided by developing contingency plans ahead of time to deal with the inevitable spin-off problems that crop up whenever jobs are changed. Such plans can be advantageous in at least two ways. First, employees, managers, and consultants all will share an awareness that problems are likely to emerge elsewhere in the work system as the change project develops. This simple understanding may help keep surprise and dismay at manageable levels when the problems do appear and so may decrease the opportunity for people to conclude prematurely that "the project failed."

Second, preplanning for possible problems can lead to an objective increase in the readiness of all parties to deal with those problems that do emerge. Having a few contingency plans filed away can increase the chances that change-related problems will be dealt with before they get out of hand—and before they create a significant drain on the energy and morale needed to keep the change project afloat.

Not all contingency plans can be worked out in detail beforehand. Indeed, they probably should not be. Until a project is underway one cannot know for sure what the specific nature of the most pressing needs and problems will be. But one can be ready to deal with common problems that may appear. For example, the training department can be alerted that some training may be required if managers find themselves in difficulty supervising the employees after the work is redesigned. And those responsible for the reward system can be asked to engage in some contingency planning on the chance that the new work system may require nontraditional compensation arrangements. One does not *begin* with these matters. But one is well advised to anticipate that some of them will arise, and to be prepared to deal with them when and if they do.

Guide 4: Evaluate Continuously

When managers or consultants are asked whether a work redesign project has been evaluated, the answer nearly always is affirmative. But when one asks to see the evaluation, the response frequently is something like, "Well, let me tell you . . . only one week after we did the actual job changes this guy who had been on the lathe for fifteen years came up to me, and he said . . . " Such anecdotes are interesting, but they provide little help to managers and union officials as they consider whether work redesign is something that should be experimented with further and possibly diffused throughout the organization. Nor is it the stuff of which generalizable behavioral science knowledge is made.

Sometimes hard data are pointed to, such as financial savings resulting from reductions in personnel in the unit where the work redesign took place. Such data can validly document an improvement in worker productivity, but they are of little value in understanding the full richness of what has happened, or why. And, of great importance in unionized organizations, they are hardly the kind of data that will engage the enthusiasm of the bargaining unit for broader application of work redesign.

There are many good reasons why adequate evaluations of work redesign projects are not done—not having the capability to translate human gains into dollars and cents, not being able to separate out the influence of the job changes on measured productivity and unit profitability from the many other factors that influence these outcomes, having an organization-wide accounting system that cannot provide data on the costs of absenteeism, turnover, training, and extra supervisory time, not really trusting measures of job satisfaction, and so on.

These reasons can be convincing, at least until one asks what was done to try to overcome the problems and gets as a response, "Well, we really didn't think we could get the accountants to help out, so. . . . " And one is left with several unhappy hypotheses: (1) nobody knows how to do a decent evaluation—nor how to get help in doing one; or (2) management does not consider systematic evaluation an essential part of the change activity; or (3) the desire of the people responsible for the program to have it appear successful is so strong that they cannot afford the risk of an explicit evaluation.

In a retailing organization, for example, job enrichment was sold to top management by a single individual. And soon the program came to be known throughout the organization as "Joe's program." Joe, understandably, developed a considerable personal interest in managing the image of the program within the organization. When offered the chance for a systematic evaluation of the project to be conducted at no cost to the organization, Joe showed considerable initial hesitation, and finally declined the offer. Later discussions revealed that although he recognized the potential usefulness of the information he would gain from an outside evaluation, that benefit was more than countered by the risk of losing his personal control over the image of the project that eventually would emerge.

Because of the pressure on lower-level managers and consultants to make job enrichment programs at least *appear* successful, it often is necessary for top management or union leaders to insist that serious and systematic evaluations of such programs take place. For such evaluations to be valid and useful, management must attempt to create an organizational climate in which the evaluation is viewed as an occasion for *learning*—rather than as an event useful mainly for assessing the performance and competence of those who actually installed the changes.

Such a stance permits interim disappointments and problems to be used as times for reconsideration and revision of the change project, rather than as a cause for disillusionment and abandonment. And it encourages those responsible for managing the change to learn as they go how most effectively to design, install, and manage enriched jobs. This is a matter of considerable importance, because there is no neat package for redesigning work in organizations and there probably never will be.

Taking a learning orientation to work redesign is, however, a costly proposition. It is expensive to collect trustworthy data for use in monitoring a project throughout its life, and to experiment actively with different ways of changing jobs. It is painful to learn from failure, and to try again. Yet such costs may actually be among the better investments an organization contemplating work redesign can make. Paying such costs may be the only realistic way for the organization to develop the considerable knowledge and expertise it will need to reap the full benefits of work redesign as a strategy for change.

Guide 5: Confront the Difficult Problems Early

Individuals responsible for work redesign projects often find it tempting to get the project sold to management and union leadership, and only then to begin negotiations on the difficult problems that must be solved before the project can actually be carried out. This seems entirely reasonable. If such problems are raised *before* the project is agreed to, the chances are increased that it will never get off the ground. It appears, nevertheless, that in the long run it may be wiser to risk not doing a project for which the tough issues cannot be resolved beforehand than to do one under circumstances that require compromise after compromise to keep the project alive after it has begun.

. Vigilance by those responsible for the change is required to ensure that the tough issues are not swept under the rug when the project is being considered. Among such issues (that too often are reserved for later discussion) are:

• The nature and extent of the commitment of management and union leaders, including the circumstances under which a decision may be made to terminate the project. It is especially important to make sure that both management and union leadership realize that problems will emerge in the early stages of a project, and that a good deal of energy may be required to protect and nurture the project during such down phases.

• The criteria against which the project ultimately will be evaluated and the means by which the evaluation will be done, including measures that will be used. Given that there are serious measurement difficulties in assessing any work redesign project, it is important to make sure that all parties, including management and union sponsors, are aware of these difficulties and are committed at the outset to the evaluation methodology.

• The way that learnings gained in the project (whether they are "successful tactics we discovered" or "roadblocks we unexpectedly encountered") will be made available to people who can use them as guides for future action, in the same or in other organizations.

Guide 6: Design Change Processes That Fit with Change Objectives

Most work redesign projects provide employees with increased opportunities for autonomy and self-direction in carrying out the work of the organization. Employees are allowed to do their work with a minimum of interference, and they are assumed to have the competence and sense of responsibility to seek appropriate assistance when they need it. The problem is that far too often the process of *implementing* job enrichment is strikingly incongruent with that intended end state.

It appears unrealistic to expect that a more flexible, bottom-loaded work system can be created using implementation procedures that are relatively rigid and bureaucratic, and that operate strictly from the top down. Yet again and again we observed standard, traditional, organizational practices being used to install work redesign. More often than not employees were the last to know what was happening, and only rarely were they given any real opportunity to actively participate in and influence the changes. In many situations they were never told the reasons why the changes were being made.

What happens during the planning stages of a work redesign project is illustrative of such incongruence between means and ends. Typically, initial planning for work redesign (including decision-making about what jobs will be changed) is done privately by managers and consultants. Diagnostic work, if performed at all, is done using a plausible cover story—such as telling employees that they are being interviewed "as part of our regular program of surveying employee attitudes." (The rationale is that employee expectations about change should not be raised prematurely; the effect often is that suspicions are raised instead.) Eventually managers appear with a fully determined set of changes that are installed in traditional top-down fashion. If employees resist and mistrust the changes, managers are surprised and disappointed. As one said: "I don't understand why they did not respond more enthusiastically. Don't they realize how we are going to make their work a lot more involving and interesting?" Apparently he did not see the lack of congruence between the goals being aspired to and the means being used, between "what we want to achieve" and "how we're going to achieve it."

As an alternative approach, managers might choose to be public and participative in translating from theory through diagnosis to the actual steps taken to modify jobs. Such an approach could be advantageous for a number of reasons.

First, when diagnostic data are collected and discussed openly, everyone who will be affected by the changes has the chance to become involved in the redesign activities and knowledgeable about them, and so everyone is less threatened. In one organization, managers initially were very skeptical about employee participation in planning for job changes. After employees had become involved in the project, however, a number of managers commented favorably on the amount of energy employees contributed to the planning activities and on the constructive attitudes they exhibited.

Second, the quality of the diagnostic data may be improved. If employees know that changes in their own work will be made partly on the basis of their responses to the diagnostic instruments, they may try especially hard to provide valid and complete data.

Third, chances are increased that learnings will emerge from the project that can be used to develop better action principles of work redesign for future applications. The involvement of people from a diversity of organizational roles in diagnostic and change-planning activities should facilitate attempts to piece together a complete picture of the change project—including the reasons that various changes were tried, what went wrong (and what went right), and what might be done differently next time.

Fourth, expectations about change will be increased when employees are involved in diagnostic and change-planning processes. Rather than being something to be avoided, therefore, heightened employee expectations can serve as a positive force for change. For example, such expectations might counter the conservatism that inevitably creeps into changes planned and implemented downwards through several hierarchical levels in an organization.

Despite these potential advantages, it is not easy to carry off a fully participative work redesign project. Nor do openness and employee participation guarantee success. Indeed, some experienced commentators have argued explicitly against employee participation in planning job changes, because (1) participation may contaminate the change process with "human relations hygiene" (Herzberg, 1966), (2) employees are not viewed as competent to redesign their own jobs, or (3) job design is viewed solely as a management function (Ford, 1969).

Our observations of work redesign projects turned up a few projects in which employee participating was actively used in the change process. And the ideas for change that employees proposed in these cases did focus mainly on the removal of roadblocks from the work and on the improvement of hygiene items. This is consistent with the predictions of Ford (1969) that employee suggestions usually deal more with the context of work than with its motivational core.

The circumstances under which employees participated in work redesign activities in these organizations, however, were far from optimal. Often employees simply were asked, "What would you suggest?" and given little time to consider their responses. In no case were employees provided with education in the theory and strategy of job redesign before being asked for suggestions. And in all cases we studied, employees had no real part in the final decision-making about what changes actually would be made. They were contributors to the change process, but not partners in it.

To develop and utilize the *full* potential of employees as resources for change would be an exciting undertaking, and a major one. It could require teaching employees the basics of motivation theory, discussing with them state-of-the-art knowledge about the strategy and tactics of work redesign, and providing them with training and experience in planning and installing organizational innovations. Such an approach would be costly, perhaps too much so to be practical. But it would have the advantage of encouraging employees to become full collaborators in the redesign of their own work, thereby creating a process for improving jobs that is consistent with the ultimate objectives of the change. Moreover, and of special importance to the quality of work life in organizations, the approach would provide employees with greatly increased opportunities for furthering their own personal growth and development—and at the same time would significantly increase their value as human resources to the organization.

REFERENCES

Bakan, P., Belton, J. A., & Toth, J. C. Extraversion-introversion and decrement in an auditory vigilance task. In *Vigilance: A symposium,* edited by D. N. Buckner and J. J. McGrath. New York: McGraw-Hill, 1963.

Beer, M., & Huse, E. F. A systems approach to organization development. *Journal of Applied Behavioral Science,* **8** (1972): 79–101.

Bem, D. J. *Beliefs, attitudes and human affairs.* Monterey, Calif.: Brooks/Cole, 1970.

Berlyne, D. E. Arousal and reinforcement. *Nebraska Symposium on Motivation,* **15** (1967).

Best, F. Flexible work scheduling: Beyond the forty-hour impasse. In *The future of work,* edited by F. Best. Englewood Cliffs, N.J.: Prentice-Hall, 1973.

Blood, M. R., & Hulin, C. L. Alienation, environmental characteristics, and worker responses. *Journal of Applied Psychology,* **51** (1967): 284–290.

Calame, B. E. Wary labor eyes job enrichment. *Wall Street Journal,* February 26, 1973, p. 12.

Davis, L. E. Toward a theory of job design. *Journal of Industrial Engineering,* **8** (1957): 19–23.

Davis, L. E. The design of jobs. *Industrial Relations,* **6** (1966): 21–45.

Davis, L. E. Developments in job design. In *Personal goals and work design,* edited by P. B. Warr. London: Wiley, 1975.

Davis, L. E., & Trist, E. L. Improving the quality of work life: Sociotechnical case studies. In *Work and the quality of life,* edited by J. O'Toole. Cambridge, Mass.: MIT Press, 1974.

Dunnette, M. D., Campbell, J. P., & Hakel, M.D. Factors contributing to job satisfaction and dissatisfaction in six occupational groups. *Organizational Behavior and Human Performance,* **2** (1967): 143–174.

Emery, F. E., & Trist, E. L. Socio-technical systems. In *Systems thinking,* edited by F. E. Emery. Middlesex, England: Penguin, 1969.

Engelstad, P. H. Socio-technical approach to problems of process control. In *Design of jobs,* edited by L. E. Davis and J. C. Taylor. Middlesex, England: Penguin, 1972.

Fein, M. Job enrichment: A reevaluation. *Sloan Management Review,* **15** (1974): 69–88.

Fiss, B. *Flexitime in federal government.* Washington, D.C.: Government Printing Office, 1974.

Ford, R. N. *Motivation through the work itself.* New York: American Management Association, 1969.

Ford, R. N. A prescription for job enrichment success. In *New perspectives in job enrichment,* edited by J. R. Maher. New York: Van Nostrand-Reinhold, 1971.

Ford, R. N. Job enrichment lessons from AT&T. *Harvard Business Review,* January–February, 1973, pp. 96–106.

Frank, L., & Hackman, J. R. A failure of job enrichment: The case of the change that wasn't. *Journal of Applied Behavioral Science,* in press.

Friedlander, F., & Brown, L. D. Organization development. *Annual Review of Psychology,* **25** (1974): 313–341.

Glaser, E. M. *Productivity gains through worklife improvement.* New York: The Psychological Corp., 1975.

Gomberg, W. Job satisfaction: Sorting out the nonsense. *AFL-CIO American Federationist,* June, 1973.

Gooding, J. *The job revolution.* New York: Walker, 1972.

Graen, G. B. Testing traditional and two-factor hypotheses concerning job satisfaction. *Journal of Applied Psychology,* **52** (1968): 343–353.

Gulowsen, J. A measure of work group autonomy. In *Design of jobs,* edited by L. E. Davis and J. C. Taylor. Middlesex, England: Penguin, 1972.

Hackman, J. R. *Improving the quality of work life: Work design.* Washington, D.C.: Office of Research, ASPER, U.S. Dept. of Labor, 1975(a).

Hackman, J. R. On the coming demise of job enrichment. In *Man and work in society,* edited by E. L. Cass and F. G. Zimmer. New York: Van Nostrand-Reinhold, 1975(b).

Hackman, J. R., & Lawler, E. E. Employee reactions to job characteristics. *Journal of Applied Psychology Monograph,* **55** (1971): 259–286.

Hackman, J. R., & Oldham, G. R. Development of the job diagnostic survey. *Journal of Applied Psychology,* **60** (1975): 159–170.

Hackman, J. R., & Oldham, G. R. Motivation through the design of work: Test of a theory. *Organizational Behavior and Human Performance,* **16** (1976): 250–279.

Hackman, J. R., Oldham, G. R., Janson, R., & Purdy, K. A new strategy for job enrichment. *California Management Review,* Summer 1975, pp. 57–71.

Herbst, P. G. *Autonomous group functioning.* London: Travistock, 1962.

Herzberg, F. *Work and the nature of man.* Cleveland: World, 1966.

Herzberg, F. The wise old turk. *Harvard Business Review,* September–October 1974, pp. 70–80.

Herzberg, F., Mausner, B., & Snyderman, B. *The motivation to work.* New York: Wiley, 1959.

Hinton, B. L. An empirical investigation of the Herzberg methodology and two-factor theory. *Organizational Behavior and Human Performance,* **3** (1968): 286–309.

House, R. J., & Wigdor, L. Herzberg's dual-factor theory of job satisfaction and motivation: A review of the evidence and a criticism. *Personnel Psychology,* **20** (1967): 369–398.

Hulin, C. L. Individual differences and job enrichment. In J. R. Maher (Ed.), *New perspectives in job enrichment.* New York: Van Nostrand-Reinhold, 1971.

Hulin, C. L., & Blood, M. R. Job enlargement, individual differences and worker responses. *Psychological Bulletin,* **69** (1968): 41–55.

Jenkins, G. D., Jr., Nadler, D. A., Lawler, E. E. III, & Cammann, C. Standardized observations: An approach to measuring the nature of jobs. *Journal of Applied Psychology,* **60** (1975): 171–181.

Katzell, R. A., & Yankelovich, D. *Work, productivity and job satisfaction.* New York: The Psychological Corporation, 1975.

Kiesler, C. A., Collins, B. E., & Miller, N. *Attitude change.* New York: Wiley, 1969.

Kilbridge, M. D. Reduced costs through job enrichment: A case. *The Journal of Business,* **33** (1960): 357–362.

King, N. A clarification and evaluation of the two-factor theory of job satisfaction. *Psychological Bulletin,* **74** (1970): 18–31.

Kornhauser, A. *Mental health of the industrial worker.* New York: Wiley, 1965.

Lawler, E. E. III, Hackman, J. R., & Kaufman, S. Effects of job redesign: A field experiment. *Journal of Applied Social Psychology,* **3** (1973): 49–62.

Lawler, E. E. III, & Hall, D. T. The relationship of job characteristics to job involvement, satisfaction, and intrinsic motivation. *Journal of Applied Psychology,* **54** (1970): 305–312.

Oldham, G. R. The motivational strategies used by supervisors: Relationships to effectiveness indicators. *Organizational Behavior and Human Performance,* **15** (1976): 66–86.

Paul, W. J., Jr., Robertson, K. B., & Herzberg, F. Job enrichment pays off. *Harvard Business Review,* March–April 1969, pp. 61–78.

Reif, W. E., & Luthans, F. Does job enrichment really pay off? *California Management Review,* Fall 1972, pp. 30–37.

Rice, A. K. *Productivity and social organization: The Ahmedabad experiment.* London: Tavistock, 1958.

Scott, W. E. Activation theory and task design. *Organizational Behavior and Human Performance,* **1** (1966): 3–30.

Scott, W. E. The behavioral consequences of repetitive task design: Research and theory. In *Readings in organizational behavior and human performance,* edited by L. L. Cummings and W. E. Scott. Homewood, Ill.: Irwin-Dorsey, 1969.

Scott, W. E., & Rowland, K. M. The generality and significance of semantic differential scales as measures of 'morale'. *Organizational Behavior and Human Performance,* **5** (1970): 576–591.

Sirota, D., & Wolfson, A. D. Job enrichment: Surmounting the obstacles. *Personnel,* July–August 1972, 8–19.

Special Task Force to the Secretary of the U.S. Dept. of Health, Education, and Welfare. *Work in America.* Boston, Mass.: MIT Press, 1973.

Steiner, I. D. Perceived freedom. In *Advances in experimental social psychology,* edited by L. Berkowitz. Vol. 5. New York: Academic Press, 1970.

Taylor, F. W. *The principles of scientific management.* New York: Harper, 1911.

Taylor, J. C. Some effects of technology in organizational change. *Human Relations,* **24** (1971): 105–123.

Thayer, R. E. Measurement of activation through self-report. *Psychological Reports,* **20** (1967): 663–678.

Thayer, R. E. Activation states as assessed by verbal report and four psychophysiological variables. *Psychophysiology* **7** (1970): 86–94.

Trist, E. L., Higgin, G. W., Murray, H., & Pollock, A. B. *Organizational choice.* London: Tavistock, 1963.

Turner, A. N., & Lawrence, P. R. *Industrial jobs and the worker.* Boston: Harvard Graduate School of Business Administration, 1965.

Vernon, H. M. *On the extent and effects of variety in repetitive work.* Industrial Fatigue Research Board Report No. 26. London: H. M. Stationery Office, 1924.

Vroom, V. *Work and motivation.* New York: Wiley, 1964.

Walker, C. R., & Guest, R. H. *The man on the assembly line.* Cambridge, Mass.: Harvard University Press, 1952.

Walters, R. W. A long-term look at the shorter work week. *Personnel Administrator,* July–August 1971.

Walters, R. W. & Associates. *Job enrichments for results.* Reading, Mass.: Addison-Wesley, 1975.

Walton, R. E. How to counter alienation in the plant. *Harvard Business Review,* November–December 1972, pp. 70–81.

Walton, R. E. The diffusion of new work structures: Explaining why success didn't take. *Organizational Dynamics,* Winter 1975, pp. 3–22(a).

Walton, R. E. From Hawthorne to Topeka and Kalmar. In *Man and work in society,* edited by E. L. Cass and F. G. Zimmer. New York: Van Nostrand-Reinhold, 1975(b).

Whitsett, D. A., & Winslow, E. K. An analysis of studies critical of the motivator-hygiene theory. *Personnel Psychology,* **20** (1967): 391–415.

Worthy, J. C. Organizational structure and employee morale. *American Sociological Review,* **15** (1950): 169–179.

From Control to Commitment in the Workplace

Richard E. Walton

The larger shape of institutional change is always difficult to recognize when one stands right in the middle of it. Today, throughout American industry, a significant change is under way in long-established approaches to the organization and management of work. Although this shift in attitude and practice takes a wide variety of company-specific forms, its larger shape—its overall pattern—is already visible if one knows where and how to look.

Consider, for example, the marked differences between two plants in the chemical products division of a major U.S. corporation. Both make similar products and employ similar technologies, but that is virtually all they have in common.

The first, organized by businesses with an identifiable product or product line, divides its employees into self-supervising 10- to 15-person work teams that are collectively responsible for a set of related tasks. Each team member has the training to perform many or all of the tasks for which the team is accountable, and pay reflects the level of mastery of required skills. These teams have received assurances that management will go to extra lengths to provide continued employment in any economic downturn. The teams have also been thoroughly briefed on such issues as market share, product costs, and their implications for the business.

Not surprisingly, this plant is a top performer economically and rates well on all measures of employee satisfaction, absenteeism, turnover, and safety. With its employees actively engaged in identifying and solving problems, it operates with fewer levels of management and fewer specialized departments than do its sister plants. It is also one of the principal suppliers of management talent for these other plants and for the division manufacturing staff.

In the second plant, each employee is responsible for a fixed job and is required to perform up to the minimum standard defined for that job. Peer pressure keeps new employees from exceeding the minimum standards and from taking other initiatives that go beyond basic job requirements. Supervisors, who manage daily assignments and monitor performance, have long since given up hope for anything more than compliance with standards, finding sufficient difficulty in getting their people to perform adequately most of the time. In fact, they and their workers try to prevent the industrial engineering department, which is under pressure from top management to improve operations, from using changes in methods to "jack up" standards.

From *Harvard Business Review,* March–April 1985, 77–84. Copyright © 1985 by the President and Fellows of Harvard College. All rights reserved.

A recent management campaign to document an "airtight case" against employees who have excessive absenteeism or sub-par performance mirrors employees' low morale and high distrust of management. A constant stream of formal grievances, violations of plant rules, harassment of supervisors, wildcat walkouts, and even sabotage has prevented the plant from reaching its productivity and quality goals and has absorbed a disproportionate amount of division staff time. Dealings with the union are characterized by contract negotiations on economic matters and skirmishes over issues of management control.

No responsible manager, of course, would ever wish to encourage the kind of situation at this second plant, yet the determination to understand its deeper causes and to attack them at their root does not come easily. Established modes of doing things have an inertia all their own. Such an effort is, however, in process all across the industrial landscape. And with that effort comes the possibility of a revolution in industrial relations every bit as great as that occasioned by the rise of mass production the better part of a century ago. The challenge is clear to those managers willing to see it—and the potential benefits, enormous.

APPROACHES TO WORK-FORCE MANAGEMENT

What explains the extraordinary differences between the plants just described? Is it that the first is new (built in 1976) and the other old? Yes and no. Not all new plants enjoy so fruitful an approach to work organization; not all older plants have such intractable problems. Is it that one plant is unionized and the other not? Again, yes and no. The presence of a union may institutionalize conflict and lackluster performance, but it seldom causes them.

At issue here is not so much age or unionization but two radically different strategies for managing a company's or a factory's work force, two incompatible views of what managers can reasonably expect of workers and of the kind of partnership they can share with them. For simplicity, I will speak of these profound differences as reflecting the choice between a strategy based on imposing *control* and a strategy based on eliciting *commitment*.

The "Control" Strategy

The traditional—or control-oriented—approach to work-force management took shape during the early part of this century in response to the division of work into small, fixed jobs for which individuals could be held accountable. The actual definition of jobs, as of acceptable standards of performance, rested on "lowest common denominator" assumptions about workers' skill and motivation. To monitor and control effort of this assumed caliber, management organized its own responsibilities into a hierarchy of specialized roles buttressed by a top-down allocation of authority and by status symbols attached to positions in the hierarchy.

For workers, compensation followed the rubric of "a fair day's pay for a fair day's work" because precise evaluations were possible when individual job requirements were so carefully prescribed. Most managers had little doubt that labor was best thought of as a variable cost, although some exceptional companies guaranteed job security to head off unionization attempts.

In the traditional approach, there was generally little policy definition with regard to employee voice unless the work force was unionized, in which case damage control strategies predominated. With no union, management relied on an open-door policy, attitude surveys, and similar devices to learn about employees' concerns. If the work force was unionized, then management bargained terms of employment and established an appeal mechanism. These activities fell to labor relations specialists, who operated independently from line management and whose very existence assumed the inevitability and even the appropriateness of an adversarial relationship between workers and managers. Indeed, to those who saw management's exclusive obligation to be to a company's shareowners and the ownership of property to be the ultimate source of both obligation and prerogative, the claims of employees were constraints, nothing more.

At the heart of this traditional model is the wish to establish order, exercise control, and achieve efficiency in the application of the work force. Although it has distant antecedents in the bureaucracies of both church and military, the model's real father is Frederick W. Taylor, the turn-of-century "father of scientific management," whose views about the proper organization of work have long influenced management practice as well as the reactive policies of the U.S. labor movement.

Recently, however, changing expectations among workers have prompted a growing disillusionment with the apparatus of control. At the same time, of course, an intensified challenge from abroad has made the competitive obsolescence of this strategy clear. A model that assumes low employee commitment and that is designed to produce reliable if not outstanding performance simply cannot match the standards of excellence set by world-class competitors. Especially in a high-wage country like the United States, market success depends on a superior level of performance, a level that, in turn, requires the deep commitment, not merely the obedience—if you could obtain it—of workers. And as painful experience shows, this commitment cannot flourish in a workplace dominated by the familiar model of control.

The "Commitment" Strategy

Since the early 1970s, companies have experimented at the plant level with a radically different work-force strategy. The more visible pioneers—among them, General Foods at Topeka, Kansas; General Motors at Brookhaven, Mississippi; Cummins Engine at Jamestown, New York; and Proctor & Gamble at Lima, Ohio—have begun to show how great and productive the contribution of a truly committed work force can be. For a time, all new plants of this sort were nonunion, but by 1980 the success of efforts undertaken jointly with unions—GM's cooperation with the UAW at the Cadillac plant in Livonia, Michigan, for example—was impressive enough to encourage managers of both new and existing facilities to rethink their approach to the work force.

Stimulated in part by the dramatic turnaround at GM's Tarrytown assembly plant in the mid-1970s, local managers and union officials are increasingly talking about common interests, working to develop mutual trust, and agreeing to sponsor quality-of-work-life (QWL) or employee involvement (EI) activities. Although most of these ventures have been initiated at the local level, major exceptions include the joint effort between the Communication Workers of America and AT&T to promote QWL throughout the Bell System and the UAW-Ford EI program centrally directed by Donald Ephlin of the UAW and Peter Pestillo of Ford. In the nonunion sphere, the spirit of these new initiatives is evident in the decision by workers of Delta Airlines to show their commitment to the company by collecting money to buy a new plane.

More recently, a growing number of manufacturing companies has begun to remove levels of plant hierarchy, increase managers' spans of control, integrate quality and production activities at lower organizational levels, combine production and maintenance operations, and open up new career possibilities for workers. Some corporations have even begun to chart organizational renewal for the entire company. Cummins Engine, for example, has ambitiously committed itself to inform employees about the business, to encourage participation by everyone, and to create jobs that involve greater responsibility and more flexibility.

In this new commitment-based approach to the work force, jobs are designed to be broader than before, to combine planning and implementation, and to include efforts to upgrade operations, not just maintain them. Individual responsibilities are expected to change as conditions change, and teams, not individuals, often are the organizational units accountable for performance. With management hierarchies relatively flat and differences in status minimized, control and lateral coordination depend on shared goals, and expertise rather than formal position determines influence.

People Express, to cite one example, started up with its management hierarchy limited to three levels, organized its work force into three- or four-person groups, and created positions with exceptionally broad scope. Every full-time employee is a "manager": flight managers are pilots who also perform dispatching and safety checks; maintenance managers are technicians with other staff responsibilities; customer service managers take care of ticketing, security clearance, passenger boarding, and in-flight service. Everyone, including the officers, is expected to rotate among functions to boost all workers' understanding of the business and to promote personal development.

Under the commitment strategy, performance expectations are high and serve not to define minimum standards but to provide "stretch objectives," emphasize continuous improvement, and reflect the requirements of the marketplace. Accordingly, compensation policies reflect less the old formulas of job evaluation than the heightened importance of group achievement, the expanded scope of individual contribution, and the growing concern for such questions of "equity" as gain sharing, stock ownership, and profit sharing. This principle of economic sharing is not new. It has long played a role in Dana Corporation, which has many unionized plants, and is a fundamental part of the strategy of People Express, which has no union. Today, Ford sees it as an important part of the company's transition to a commitment strategy.

Equally important to the commitment strategy is the challenge of giving employees some assurance of security, perhaps by offering them priority in training and retraining as old jobs are eliminated and new ones created. Guaranteeing employees access to due process and providing them the means to be heard on such issues as production methods, problem solving and human resource policies and practices is also a challenge. In unionized settings, the additional tasks include making relations less adversarial, broadening the agenda for joint problem solving and planning, and facilitating employee consultation.

Underlying all these policies is a management philosophy, often embodied in a published statement, that acknowledges the legitimate claims of a company's multiple stakeholders—owners, employees, customers, and the public. At the center of this philosophy is a belief that eliciting employee commitment will lead to enhanced performance. The evidence shows this belief to be well-grounded. In the absence of genuine commitment, however, new management policies designed for a committed work force may well leave a company distinctly more vulnerable than would older policies based on the control approach. The advantages—and risks—are considerable.

THE COSTS OF COMMITMENT

Because the potential leverage of a commitment-oriented strategy on performance is so great, the natural temptation is to assume the universal applicability of that strategy. Some environments, however, especially those requiring intricate teamwork, problem solving, organizational learning, and self-monitoring, are better suited than others to the commitment model. Indeed, the pioneers of the deep commitment strategy—a fertilizer plant in Norway, a refinery in the United Kingdom, a paper mill in Pennsylvania, a pet-food processing plant in Kansas— were all based on continuous process technologies and were all capital and raw material intensive. All provided high economic leverage to improvements in workers' skills and attitudes, and all could offer considerable job challenge.

Is the converse true? Is the control strategy appropriate whenever—as with convicts breaking rocks with sledgehammers in a prison yard—work can be completely prescribed, remains static, and calls for individual, not group, effort? In practice, managers have long answered yes. Mass production, epitomized by the assembly line, has for years been thought suitable for old-fashioned control.

But not any longer. Many mass producers, not least the automakers, have recently been trying to reconceive the structure of work and to give employees a significant role in solving problems and improving methods. Why? For many reasons, including to boost in-plant quality, lower warranty costs, cut waste, raise machine utilization and total capacity with the same plant and equipment, reduce operating and support personnel, reduce turnover and absenteeism, and speed up implementation of change. In addition, some managers place direct value on the fact that the commitment policies promote the development of human skills and individual self-esteem.

The benefits, economic and human, of worker commitment extend not only to continuous-process industries but to traditional manufacturing industries as well. What, though, are the costs? To achieve these gains, managers have had to invest extra effort, develop skills and relationships, cope with higher levels of ambiguity and uncertainty, and experience the pain and discomfort associated with changing habits and attitudes. Some of their skills have become obsolete, and some of their careers have been casualties of change. Union officials, too, have had to face the dislocation and discomfort that inevitably follow any upheaval in attitudes and skills. For their part, workers have inherited more responsibility and, along with it, greater uncertainty and a more open-ended possibility of failure.

Part of the difficulty in assessing these costs is the fact that so many of the following problems inherent to the commitment strategy remain to be solved.

Employment Assurances

As managers in heavy industry confront economic realities that make such assurances less feasible and as their counterparts in fiercely competitive high-technology areas are forced to rethink early guarantees of employment security, pointed questions await.

Will managers give lifetime assurances to the few, those who reach, say, 15 years' seniority, or will they adopt a general no-layoff policy? Will they demonstrate by policies and practices that employment security, though by no means absolute, is a higher priority item that it was under the control approach? Will they accept greater responsibility for outplacement?

Compensation

In one sense, the more productive employees under the commitment approach deserve to receive better pay for their better efforts, but how can managers balance this claim on resources with the harsh reality that domestic pay rates have risen to levels that render many of our industries uncompetitive internationally? Already, in such industries as trucking and airlines, new domestic competitors have placed companies that maintain prevailing wage rates at a significant disadvantage. Experience shows, however, that wage freezes and concession bargaining create obstacles to commitment, and new approaches to compensation are difficult to develop at a time when management cannot raise the overall level of pay.

Which approach is really suitable to the commitment model is unclear. Traditional job classifications place limits on the discretion of supervisors and encourage workers' sense of job ownership. Can pay systems based on employees' skill levels, which have long been used in engineering and skilled crafts, prove widely effective? Can these systems make up in greater mastery, positive motivation, and work-force flexibility what they give away in higher average wages?

In capital-intensive businesses, where total payroll accounts for a small percentage of costs, economics favor the move toward pay progression based on deeper and broader mastery. Still, conceptual problems remain with measuring skills, achieving consistency in pay decisions, allocating opportunities for learning new skills, trading off breadth and flexibility against depth, and handling the effects of "topping out" in a system that rewards and encourages personal growth.

There are also practical difficulties. Existing plants cannot, for example, convert to a skill-based structure overnight because of the vested interests of employees in the higher classifications. Similarly, formal profit- or gain-sharing plans like the Scanlon Plan (which shares gains in productivity as measured by improvements in the ratio of payroll to the sales value of production) cannot always operate. At the plant level, formulas that are responsive to what employees can influence, that are not unduly influenced by factors beyond their control, and that are readily understood, are not easy to devise. Small stand-alone businesses with a mature technology and stable markets tend to find the task least troublesome, but they are not the only ones trying to implement the commitment approach.

Yet another problem, very much at issue in the Hyatt-Clark bearing plant, which employees purchased from General Motors in 1981, is the relationship between compensation decisions affecting salaried managers and professionals, on the one hand, and hourly workers, on the other. When they formed the company, workers took a 25% pay cut to make their bearings competitive but the managers maintained and, in certain instances increased, their own salaries in order to help the company attract and retain critical talent. A manager's ability to elicit and preserve commitment, however, is sensitive to issues of equity, as became evident once again when GM and Ford announced huge executive bonuses in the spring of 1984 while keeping hourly wages capped.

Technology

Computer-based technology can reinforce the control model or facilitate movement to the commitment model. Applications can narrow the scope of jobs or broaden them, emphasize the individual nature of tasks or promote the work of groups, centralize or decentralize the making of decisions, and create performance measures that emphasize learning or hierarchical control.

To date, the effects of this technology on control and commitment have been largely unintentional and unexpected. Even in organizations otherwise pursuing a commitment strategy, managers have rarely appreciated that the side effects of technology are not somehow "given" in the nature of things or that they can be actively managed. In fact, computer-based technology may be the least deterministic, most flexible technology to enter the workplace since the industrial revolution. As it becomes less hardware-dependent and more software-intensive and as the cost of computer power declines, the variety of ways to meet business requirements expands, each with a different set of human implications. Management has yet to identify the potential role of technology policy in the commitment strategy, and it has yet to invent concepts and methods to realize that potential.

Supervisors

The commitment model requires first-line supervisors to facilitate rather than direct the work force, to impart rather than merely practice their technical and administrative expertise, and to help workers develop the ability to manage themselves. In practice, supervisors are to delegate away most of their traditional functions—often without having received adequate training and support for their new team-building tasks or having their own needs for voice, dignity, and fulfillment recognized.

These dilemmas are even visible in the new titles many supervisors carry—"team advisers" or "team consultants," for example—most of which imply that supervisors are not in the chain of command, although they are expected to be directive if necessary and assume functions delegated to the work force if they are not being performed. Part of the confusion here is the failure to distinguish the behavioral style required of supervisors from the basic responsibilities assigned them. Their ideal style may be advisory, but their responsibilities are to achieve certain human and economic outcomes. With experience, however, as first-line managers become more comfortable with the notion of delegating what subordinates are ready and able to perform, the problem will diminish.

Other difficulties are less tractable. The new breed of supervisors must have a level of interpersonal skill and conceptual ability often lacking in the present supervisory work force. Some companies have tried to address this lack by using the position as an entry point to management for college graduates. This approach may succeed where the work force has already acquired the necessary technical expertise, but it blocks a route of advancement for workers and sharpens the dividing line between management and other employees. Moreover, unless the company intends to open up higher level positions for these college-educated supervisors, they may well grow impatient with the shift work of first-line supervision.

Even when new supervisory roles are filled—and filled successfully—from the ranks, dilemmas remain. With teams developed and functions delegated, to what new challenges do they turn to utilize fully their own capabilities? Do those capabilities match the demands of the other managerial work they might take on? If fewer and fewer supervisors are required as their individual span of control extends to a second and a third work team, what promotional opportunities exist for the rest? Where do they go?

Union-Management Relations

Some companies, as they move from control to commitment, seek to decertify their unions, and, at the same time, strengthen their employees' bond to the company. Others—like GM, Ford, Jones & Laughlin, and AT&T—pursue cooperation with their unions, believing that they need their active support. Management's interest in cooperation intensified in the late 1970s, as improved work-force effectiveness could not by itself close the competitive gap in many industries and wage concessions became necessary. Based on their own analysis

EXHIBIT 1
WORK FORCE STRATEGIES

	Control	Transitional	Commitment
Job design principles	Individual attention limited to performing individual job. Job design deskills and fragments work and separates doing and thinking. Accountability focused on individual. Fixed job definition.	Scope of individual responsibility extended to upgrading system performance, via participative problem-solving groups in QWL, EI, and quality circle programs. No change in traditional job design or accountability.	Individual responsibility extended to upgrading system performance. Job design enhances content of work emphasizes whole task, and combines doing and thinking. Frequent use of teams as basic accountable unit. Flexible definition of duties, contingent on changing conditions.
Performance expectations	Measured standards define minimum performance. Stability seen as desirable.		Emphasis placed on higher, "stretch objectives," which tend to be dynamic and oriented to the marketplace.
Management organization: structure, systems, and style	Structure tends to be layered, with top-down controls. Coordination and control rely on rules and procedures. More emphasis on prerogatives and positional authority. Status symbols distributed to reinforce hierarchy.	No basic changes in approaches to structure, control, or authority. A few visible symbols change.	Flat organization structure with mutual influence systems. Coordination and control based more on shared goals, values, and traditions. Management emphasis on problem solving and relevant information and expertise. Minimum status differentials to de-emphasize inherent hierarchy.

Compensation policies	Variable pay where feasible to provide individual incentive. Individual pay geared to job evaluation. In downturn, cuts concentrated on hourly payroll.	Typically no basic changes in compensation concepts. Equality of sacrifice among employee groups.	Variable rewards to create equity and to reinforce group achievements: gain sharing, profit sharing. Individual pay linked to skills and mastery. Equality of sacrifice.
Employment assurances	Employees regarded as variable costs.	Assurances that participation will not result in loss of job. Extra effort to avoid layoffs.	Assurances that participation will not result in loss of job. High commitment to avoid or assist in reemployment. Priority for training and retaining existing work force.
Employee voice policies	Employee input allowed on relatively narrow agenda. Attendant risks emphasized. Methods include open-door policy, attitude surveys, grievance procedures, and collective bargaining in some organizations. Business information distributed on strictly defined "need to know" basis.	Addition of limited, ad hoc consultation mechanisms. No change in corporate governance. Additional sharing of information.	Employee participation encouraged on wide range of issues. Attendant benefits emphasized. New concepts of corporate governance. Business data shared widely.
Labor-management relations	Adversarial labor relations; emphasis on interest conflict.	Thawing of adversarial attitudes; joint sponsorship of QWL or EI; emphasis on common fate.	Mutuality in labor relations; joint planning and problem solving on expanded agenda. Unions, management, and workers redefine their respective roles.

of competitive conditions, unions sometimes agreed to these concessions but expanded their influence over matters previously subject to management control.

These developments open up new questions. Where companies are trying to preserve the non-union status of some plants and yet promote collaborative union relations in others, will unions increasingly force the company to choose? After General Motors saw the potential of its joint QWL program with the UAW, it signed a neutrality clause (in 1976) and then an understanding about automatic recognition in new plants (in 1979). If forced to choose, what will other managements do? Further, where union and management have collaborated in promoting QWL, how can the union prevent management from using the program to appeal directly to the workers about issues, such as wage concessions, that are subject to collective bargaining?

And if, in the spirit of mutuality, both sides agree to expand their joint agenda, what new risks will they face? Do union officials have the expertise to deal effectively with new agenda items like investment, pricing, and technology? To support QWL activities, they already have had to expand their skills and commit substantial resources at a time when shrinking employment has reduced their membership and thus their finances.

THE TRANSITIONAL STAGE

Although some organizations have adopted a comprehensive version of the commitment approach, most initially take on a more limited set of changes, which I refer to as a "transitional" stage or approach. The challenge here is to modify expectations, to make credible the leaders' stated intentions for further movement, and to support the initial changes in behavior. These transitional efforts can achieve a temporary equilibrium, provided they are viewed as part of a movement toward a comprehensive commitment strategy.

The cornerstone of the transitional stage is the voluntary participation of employees in problem-solving groups like quality circles. In unionized organizations, union-management dialogue leading to a jointly sponsored program is a condition for this type of employee involvement, which must then be supported by additional training and communication and by a shift in management style. Managers must also seek ways to consult employees about changes that affect them and to assure them that management will make every effort to avoid, defer, or minimize layoffs from higher productivity. When volume-related layoffs or concessions on pay are unavoidable, the principle of "equality of sacrifice" must apply to all employee groups, not just the hourly work force.

As a rule, during the early stages of transformation, few immediate changes can occur in the basic design of jobs, the compensation system, or the management system itself. It is easy, of course, to attempt to change too much too soon. A more common error, especially in established organizations, is to make only "token" changes that never reach a critical mass. All too often managers try a succession of technique-oriented changes one by one: job enrichment, sensitivity training, management by objectives, group brainstorming, quality circles, and so on. Whatever the benefits of these techniques, their value to the organization will rapidly decay if the management philosophy—and practice—does not shift accordingly.

A different type of error—"overreaching"—may occur in newly established organizations based on commitment principles. In one new plant, managers allowed too much peer influence in pay decisions; in another, they underplayed the role of first-line supervisors as a link in the chain of command; in a third, they overemphasized learning of new skills and flexibility at the expense of mastery in critical operations. These design errors by themselves are not fatal, but the organization must be able to make mid-course corrections.

RATE OF TRANSFORMATION

How rapidly is the transformation in work-force strategy, summarized in Exhibit 1, occurring? Hard data are difficult to come by, but certain trends are clear. In 1970, only a few plants in the United States were systematically revising their approach to the work force. By 1975, hundreds of plants were involved. Today, I estimate that at least a thousand plants are in the process of making a comprehensive change and that many times that number are somewhere in the transitional stage.

In the early 1970s, plant managers tended to sponsor what efforts there were. Today, company presidents are formulating the plans. Not long ago, the initiatives were experimental; now they are policy. Early change focused on the blue-collar work force and on those clerical operations that most closely resemble the factory. Although clerical change has lagged somewhat—because the control model has not produced such overt employee disaffection, and because management has been slow to recognize the importance of quality and productivity improvement—there are signs of a quickened pace of change in clerical operations.

Only a small fraction of U.S. workplaces today can boast of a comprehensive commitment strategy, but the rate of transformation continues to accelerate, and the move toward commitment via some explicit transitional stage extends to a still larger number of plants and offices. This transformation may be fueled by economic necessity, but other factors are shaping and pacing it—individual leadership in management and labor, philosophical choices, organizational competence in managing change, and cumulative learning from change itself.

SUGGESTED READINGS

Irving Bluestone, "Labor's Stake in Improving the Quality of Working Life," *The Quality of Working Life and the 1980s,* ed. Harvey Kolodny and Hans van Beinum (New York: Praeger, 1983).

Robert H. Guest, "Quality of Work Life—Learning from Tarrytown," HBR July–August 1979, p. 76.

Janice A. Klein, "Why Supervisors Resist Employee Involvement," HBR September–October 1984, p. 87.

John F. Runcie, "'By Days I Make the Cars'," HBR May–June 1980, p. 106.

W. Earl Sasser and Frank S. Leonard, "Let First-Level Supervisors Do Their Job," HBR March–April 1980, p. 113.

Leonard A. Schlesinger and Janice A. Klein, "The First-Line Supervisor: Past, Present and Future," *Handbook of Organizational Behavior*, ed. Jay W. Lorsch (Englewood Cliffs, N.J.: Prentice-Hall, 1983).

Richard E. Walton, "Work Innovations in the United States," HBR July–August 1979, p. 88; "Improving the Quality of Work Life," HBR May–June 1974, p. 12; "How to Counter Alienation in the Plant," HBR November–December 1972, p. 70.

Richard E. Walton and Wendy Vittori, "New Information Technology: Organizational Problem or Opportunity?" *Office: Technology and People*, No. 1, 1983, p. 249.

Richard E. Walton and Leonard A. Schlesinger, "Do Supervisors Thrive in Participative Work Systems?" *Organizational Dynamics*, Winter 1979, p. 25.

Quality Circles: After the Honeymoon

Edward E. Lawler III
Susan A. Mohrman

The strengths and weaknesses of quality circles, a widely practiced approach to improving organizational performance, have appeared in numerous articles. Both critics and proponents agree that quality circles are typically characterized by a successful start-up or honeymoon period; the initial circles are characterized by high levels of enthusiasm and tend to produce a number of good suggestions. Problems with quality circles typically develop after they become an organizationwide activity, when an effort is made to sustain them over several years. We're going to review several reasons why quality circles typically are difficult to sustain and then look at approaches that deal with the institutionalization and maintenance problems associated with quality circles.

THE STRUCTURE OF CIRCLES

Quality circles are a parallel-structure approach to getting employees involved in problem solving. A parallel structure is a structure separate and distinct from an organization's regular ongoing activities; so it operates in a special way. In quality circle programs, groups are composed of volunteers from a work area that meet for a few hours every week or two with a special type of leader or facilitator to look at productivity and quality problems. In order to produce change, these groups must sell their ideas to the regular work organization. Because they are a form of parallel organization, they have certain inherent strengths and weaknesses characteristic of all such organizations.

One strength of quality circles is that they allow organizations to deal with issues that are not dealt with in the regular organization, either because of insufficient time, inappropriate definition of responsibilities and goals, or lack of inter-

From *Organizational Dynamics*, Spring, 1987, 42–54. Copyright © 1987 by American Management Association, New York. Reprinted by permission. All rights reserved.

est on the part of management or staff personnel. In addition, parallel structures can often start quickly and cause only minimal disruption to the organization's performance. The creation of quality circles requires no obvious changes in the regular organization's structure, activities, or responsibilities; nevertheless, circles permit problem solving by individuals who might not otherwise have the opportunity to become involved in this activity. In many organizations quality circles are the only participative management device that managers are willing to accept. They feel this sense of acceptance because quality circles disrupt the status quo only minimally and therefore help keep managerial authority firmly in place.

The problems associated with parallel structures are also significant. Since they are generally viewed as an auxiliary program, they are subject to cancellation. In addition, their kinds of power and problem-solving activities are limited. For example, quality circles typically have the power only to recommend innovations; the decision-making domain remains with the regular organization. Quality circles are authorized to deal only with changes in work methods and procedures or with organizational systems likely to improve quality and productivity. Because they involve only a portion of the employees, parallel organizations can lead to an "in" and "out" group situation and a negative backlash by nonparticipants. Finally, the norms and behaviors in parallel-structure activities may differ dramatically from those that govern the regular organization. Thus participants who are treated as responsible, thinking contributors in the quality circle meeting may receive very different treatment in their daily experiences in the organization. This can lead to internal tension.

Research on quality circles has shown that they go through a series of predictable phases. The first phase, or honeymoon period, is typically very positive. During this phase a small number of groups is formed; these groups are strongly motivated to produce good ideas and improvements, and as a result the organization often realizes significant gains. This period of success is usually followed by the widespread dissemination of quality circles. The organization then counts the number of quality circles and assumes that the more circles there are, the more things are improving.

After the expansion program has triggered the spread of circles throughout the organization, the first significant disillusionment with circles usually sets in. The reasons for this backlash are numerous: the resistance of middle managers, failure to implement some of the ideas generated, nonproductive groups, the extra cost of operating the extensive support systems that groups require, and the failure of some early ideas to produce the level of savings projected. While the initial groups received much high-level attention from sponsors or champions of the process, later groups were usually started more mechanically. Later circles have to compete for management attention; in addition, they are started in an environment in which political or personal dissension has polarized reactions to the quality circle process. At this point, some organizations decide that quality circles were a mistake and abandon them. Other organizations recognize that quality circles have had a positive impact and ask what can be done either to sustain them or to move beyond them to a different form of employee involvement.

These questions show a desire to build upon the good features of quality circles and to carry them forward to other kinds of organizational performance improvement approaches.

In our view, quality circles can be an important first step toward organizational effectiveness through employee involvement. Indeed, there are a number of other participative approaches that can build upon the work done in quality circles; there are also some things that can be done to sustain quality circles as an effective parallel structure. The remainder of this article considers various options for companies that have or are considering a quality circle program, such as ways to extend and strengthen the quality circle process and the parallel-structure approach in general. We will also discuss an alternative approach in which teams that are part of the regular organizational structure are responsible for decision making and problem solving. We begin by examining the contributions of quality circles in establishing employee involvement in an organization.

EMPLOYEE INVOLVEMENT:
WHERE DO QUALITY CIRCLES FIT IN?

In thinking about what kind of participative structures are appropriate, an organization must address two important issues: (1) what concerns must be dealt with in a participative manner and (2) how much decision-making authority will be delegated.

Exhibit 1 illustrates the range of choices in these two areas. It differentiates decision styles according to the relative influence of the actual performers of the

EXHIBIT 1
Impact of various participative structures on organizational decision making.

Decision Domains

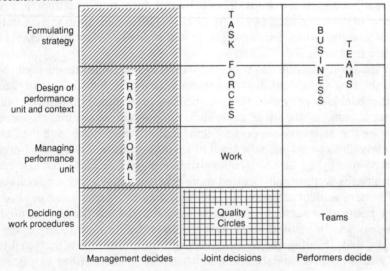

Location of Decision

work and the management structure. It also considers different kinds of decisions ranging from those involving corporate strategy to those related to particular work methods and procedures. As it notes, managers traditionally make all the important strategy, structure, and work-design decisions, as well as most of the ongoing decisions about work procedures.

Quality circles change organizational decision making by providing a vehicle through which the performers can influence their work. Employees can suggest better work methods, procedures, and occasionally organization design alternatives. On the other hand, quality circles are generally discouraged from considering broader policies, strategies, personnel matters, and structures. Quality circle ideas usually must be approved by the regular management and staff structure, making them the result of joint rather than delegated decision making; the upshot of this is that circles are frequently seen as an organizational burden. Instead of transferring responsibility to those who perform the work, they increase the demands on management and staff.

Nevertheless, the use of quality circles does make the organization more participative, and this use can prepare it for other types of participative activities. First, the training programs that are part of most quality circle efforts provide a number of employees with important problem-solving and group-process skills; they also provide some managers and supervisors with experience as participative leaders. These skills are necessary in virtually every form of participative management.

In addition, quality circles typically establish employee involvement as a credible strategy. Their usually positive results demonstrate conclusively that people at all levels have useful ideas and can contribute meaningful suggestions when given the opportunity. Furthermore, the high volunteer rate usually associated with quality circles convinces managers that people wish to participate.

Finally, quality circles often produce important ideas and ways to improve productivity and quality. The successful implementation of such ideas gives circle members a real sense of accomplishment; it also may lead to greater awareness of how employees can take more responsibility for organizational performance.

Organizations can move beyond quality circles in one of three ways. They can expand the kinds of decisions made by participative groups into the realms of strategy, design, and operations; this is generally accomplished by another parallel structure—the task force or task team. In an alternative approach, organizations can move from a joint decision-making model to one in which work teams are set up, thereby delegating authority downward into the group performing the work. Finally, they can treat the quality circle as the basic building block of participation, altering various aspects of the organizational context to support successfully quality-circle functioning. These three approaches will be discussed below.

TASK FORCES

In many respects, creating task forces or task teams is a small, natural step beyond quality circles because they expand the parallel structure approach. Task teams, which involve a cross section of the workforce, usually are assigned specific critical problems. Quality-circles training is very appropriate to the problem solving that task forces must do, and task forces often allow the organization to get broad input on problems that quality circles do not normally deal with. For example, they can deal with issues of policy, organization design, and occasionally even corporate strategy. Depending on the kind of participation that the organization wants to give these task teams, they can either decide on policy, strategy, and other organizational issues, or they can simply make recommendations on what should be done.

Like quality circles, task teams are easy to establish and, in many cases, quite productive. Furthermore, like quality circles, they are not expected to last forever. The task teams themselves have specific life expectancies based on the type of problem they address. New task teams have to be constantly formed if an organization wants to maintain this form of participation. Forming new task teams makes sense if there are always issues to be addressed by the organization, particularly in a dynamic environment requiring constant change and adaptation.

The advantage of task teams is that they can include both the production employees who are a part of quality circles and management people as well. Although some managers who don't like the idea of sharing decision making with lower-level employees may resist task teams, the teams themselves partially eliminate management resistance because managers are included on the task force.

However, task forces share an important problem with quality circles: Only a limited number of people can participate at any one time. As a result, task forces are not a broad participation vehicle. However, because of the limited life expectancy of any particular task team, a number of employees may eventually have the opportunity to serve on one. Because of the increased scope of decisions and the opportunity to involve more people at more organizational levels, task teams can be an important, useful structure for any organization that wishes to broaden the influence that performers have. Companies such as Honeywell and Xerox have successfully expanded their original quality-circle program in some of their facilities to include wide usage of task teams.

WORK TEAMS

Work teams are groups of employees who have the responsibility for producing a product or service. They make most decisions associated with their production activities: They schedule and assign work, decide on methods, and in some cases select their members, decide on their pay, and pick their managers or leaders. Unlike quality circles, work teams are not parallel structures; they are a means of performing the regular production work of an organization. They are sometimes called autonomous work groups, self-managing teams, or semiautonomous groups. As is shown in Exhibit 1, they typically allow employees to make decisions about work methods and procedures and to influence decisions about the day-to-day management of the work area.

Historically, the work team concept grew up quite independently of quality circles. Teams have been strongly recommended as a participative organization design feature for decades, particularly for organizations designed by socio-technical systems approaches. Many new plants in the United States that have been designed to maximize employee involvement have utilized the work-team model: TRW, Digital Equipment, Procter and Gamble, and Johnson and Johnson have all built plants with teams. Teams are used because they lead to ongoing employee involvement in managing their own work activities. This can be con-trasted with the common principle that underlies the implementation of quality circles: The workforce should be involved in productivity and quality enhance-ment efforts. The former is a commitment to a philosophy on which all aspects of an organization are based; the latter is a limited commitment that may or may not fit the underlying management philosophy.

Going to teams is obviously a dramatic step beyond quality circles; in some respects, however, the former are a logical follow-up to the latter. In effect, cir-cles introduce the organization to participative processes by providing both train-ing for organizational members and real-life examples of how such processes work. In addition, circles may well raise issues that make individuals more aware of barriers to effective performance in the organization, thus making many people eager for new approaches. They may also clarify the ways in which a partici-pative approach conflicts with the traditional management model. Teams may reduce functional divisions by combining responsibility into a team, motivate employees to achieve improvements in performance, and reduce the need for supervision and staff. In light of what we have seen, such teams may seem to be a natural next step.

Despite the potential advantages of teams, we rarely see them occur as a follow-up to quality circles. There are a number of reasons for this. First, they represent a much more dramatic step toward participative management than most organizations are willing to take. As was pointed out, they do in fact require a shift in management philosophy. In addition, they do not naturally evolve from the quality-circle programs of most organizations. As will be considered next, they could evolve more directly if certain features of quality circles were de-signed to facilitate that evolution.

First, we must consider the design of the circles themselves. Quality circles typically take only volunteers from a particular work area and put them into a circle; this means that many people in a work area may not have experience with circles. The team concept does not allow for volunteers; for a team to be effec-tive, everyone in the work area must be a member. In addition, supervisors are critical to the success of a team. In many cases quality circles do not affect the supervisor, and indeed the supervisor's behavior may not be altered as a result of a quality-circle program.

If the intention is to move toward teams, these points lead to specific recom-mendations on quality-circle design. First, everyone in the work area should par-ticipate in the quality-circle program. Secondly, supervisors should be trained as facilitators and should learn the types of leadership skills associated with group decision making. Such training is necessary to prepare them for becoming team leaders.

If everyone (including the supervisor) is trained, teams may naturally evolve from a quality-circle program. This can occur because experience in the parallel organization can be directly transferred to the day-to-day work issues facing a group. We know of one FMC plant where this transition was indeed accomplished. What began as intact work groups that had special "quality circle" meetings to solve problems grew into work teams. Team members were gradually trained in and given responsibility for more aspects of their own management and operations. The FMC plant was fortunately structured so that their work groups fit easily into the work team model. This experience differed from that of a Honeywell plant, which made the transition to self-managing teams only after its plant was gutted and its technical system was redesigned to support them.

An effective team must have responsibility for producing a whole product or service. In many cases, organizations are structured on a functional basis and thus do not contain natural work teams. For example, in a traditionally structured organization machine operators who use the same kinds of equipment usually report to the same supervisor and report together. However, they typically are not a good team because they are responsible for running a machine rather than for producing a product or service. Because members of the work group are not interdependent, many of the gains that teams produce by doing their own coordination and by their problem solving of work quality issues are not available. Thus, even though everyone in a work group or everyone reporting to a particular supervisor is in the same quality circle, a team need not necessarily emerge. It is likely to emerge only if organization design issues are taken into account and circles are created that have appropriate areas of responsibility.

Some contextual issues must be resolved to enable the transition to work teams. For example, personnel practices are a major issue. One of the reasons why teams are productive is the cross training and consequent flexibility and knowledge of the team members. Pay systems based on inflexible job grades and job descriptions that do not provide increased pay for improved knowledge and skills discourage flexible contributions from team members. In addition, approaches that limit training to specific job-related skills do not develop a broad understanding of business issues in lower-level employees; they need some version of knowledge-based pay and emphasis on cross training and peer training. A work team environment's logic and philosophy differ in such fundamental ways that organizations making the transition to this environment will probably have to modify nearly all their existing personnel systems.

In summary, quality circles can lead to teams, but a number of design features must be built into quality circles if this is to happen. In addition to assuring that supervisors and other employees in the work area are trained, the organizational structure may need to be altered. The best way to form teams is not necessarily on the basis of existing work groups and relationships; new reporting relationships and structures typically are needed. In like manner, changes may be required in many of the major organizational systems, such as personnel practices, that must create a context conducive to work teams.

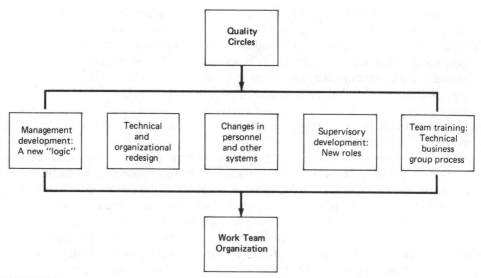

EXHIBIT 2
Possible organization design changes in the transition from quality circles to work teams.

One implication of this is that although circles may initially operate without major changes in organization design and important relationships, significant organization design changes may have to occur if there is to be movement from a parallel structure approach to one that incorporates work teams. Exhibit 2 summarized some of the changes that may be required in such a transition.

CREATING A SUPPORTIVE WORK ORGANIZATION FOR QUALITY CIRCLES

As has been stressed, one of the reasons quality circles often lose their momentum is that the existing organization is not designed to support the parallel structure created by the quality-circle program. People begin to perceive circles as a burden on the organization as they lose their initial enthusiasm and accomplishments are harder to come by. So far we have been emphasizing the development of task or work teams designed to replace or complement quality circles. These approaches in effect open up new participative avenues in the organization. Some characteristics of the existing organization can also be changed to make it more supportive of quality circles and to enhance those circles' effectiveness.

A major candidate for change is the reward system. There is a long history of very successful experience with gainsharing plans, like the Scanlon Plan, that involve the use of parallel organization structures. In these plans, a financial formula is developed for paying out to employees a portion of productivity and/or cost improvements. Experience with these plans shows that a combination of problem-solving groups and performance-improvement bonuses can be a viable long-term strategy for performance improvement.

There are Scanlon Plans in use today that have been in operation for over three decades, and they continue to be effective. A major reason for their long-term effectiveness is that, unlike quality circles, they affect everybody in the organization and reward performance improvement with an important incentive. The effect is to encourage everyone to think of ideas, participate in problem solving, and implement the ideas and suggestions that come out of the problem-solving process. In essence, because everyone in the organization shares in the success of the parallel structure, everyone tries to ensure that the structure works well.

As in the case of the movement to teams, we must point out that the transition to gainsharing may involve fundamental changes in philosophy. Gainsharing is based on the belief that all workers ought to share in financial performance improvements. Many quality-circle proponents are quite clear that the benefit to the employee should be intrinsic (outcomes such as satisfaction and pride) rather than financial. The premise of gainsharing is that financial results improve because of everyone's combined efforts; this may conflict with organizational assumptions that such results are the responsibility of management, and that incentives should properly reward managers alone for these results. Gainsharing calls for a broad sharing of information and training about the organization's financial performance, while traditional management thinking argues for keeping this information in the hands of senior management.

In most gainsharing installations, the parallel problem-solving approach is put in simultaneously with the bonus for organizational improvement. However, one need not necessarily follow this particular sequence; indeed, one could very readily follow the installation of quality circles with a gainsharing plan. One problem in the start-up of the typical gainsharing plan is that because there is so much to do, important activities get overlooked. The participative structures frequently do not receive adequate attention because of a tendency to focus solely on the financial part of the plan. In a typical gainsharing plan, for example, people must be trained in the workings of the bonus formula, as well as educated about cost and the organization's financial situation. In addition, problem solving and the suggestion process must be introduced. An alternative to an "all-at-one-time" implementation is to start with the problem-solving process and then move to gainsharing once there are structures and skills in place to generate gain.

Another factor may argue for the use of quality circles before putting a financial bonus in place. Gainsharing uses a fixed historical base to calculate improvements. If the organization has a lot of easily solved problems and is having financial difficulties, it may not make sense to share gains that are gathered from simply putting the house in order. If gainsharing is put in right away, these improvements will result in continual employee bonuses. In the case of an already effectively functioning organization, this usually is not a problem, although it may be in an organization that is performing poorly and needs gains simply to be competitive.

There are other features of the reward system that can be changed to reinforce quality-circle activity. For example, some companies in the United States that are committed to sustaining their quality circles have strongly emphasized nonfinancial recognition programs, including convention attendance, circles competitions for best improvement, and meetings with top management to acknowledge superior work. All these programs are potentially effective ways of reinforcing the importance of and sustaining interest in quality circles. Unfortunately, they do not deal with the issue of the nonparticipants; that is, they create neither a participation opportunity nor a reward for individuals who are not in groups.

One way to reduce the discrepancy between people's participative experiences in quality circles and their day-to-day work experiences is to use the human resources systems to develop and reward participative supervisory practices. Supervisors and managers at all levels can be trained in participative techniques, and appraisal, reward, and promotion can be linked to managerial style. Employees who experience a daily environment in which their supervisors solicit input, share information, and are open to suggestions are less likely to resent the time their coworkers spend in circle meetings. "Informal" problem solving is likely to become a regular part of the work setting, and the tension between the participative model of the quality circle and the daily management philosophy will be reduced.

Finally, changes in the information and education systems can help quality circles function more effectively. Most fundamentally, the information system can be designed to enable the regular sharing of key performance measures with all employees in a work unit. When employees in general and quality-circle members in particular are informed of important trends in work-area performance, they can set goals, initiate changes designed to improve performance, and experience satisfaction when performance improves. In addition, the widespread availability of such information, especially if measures are improving, can dispel both managers' and employees' misconceptions that circle meeting is nonproductive and actually impairs unit productivity. Such a clarification is important because the changes caused by quality circles more often have an indirect, cumulative impact on performance rates than a direct, immediately measurable one. Thus the trends can provide "hard" evidence that is often needed to persuade skeptics.

One problem in some quality circles is that the members often lack the economic and business education needed to make good suggestions and decisions. This problem can be partially solved by offering education in economics and organizational performance. Circles often stall after they have addressed the more obvious and easy-to-solve problems in a work area; the circle members do not have enough technical knowledge to go any further. This lack of knowledge may be overcome if technical staff groups provide technical assistance and training to the circles. In addition, the organization's information system can be opened up so that people throughout the organization have a better idea of costs, business performance, and even organizational strategy. Circles often come up with good ideas that are not practical because of strategy changes or business decisions they don't know about. Letting them in on more information can reduce their chances of going down blind alleys and coming up with suggestions for change that are impractical or that can't be implemented.

In summary, changes can be made to an existing organization to help sustain quality circles; Exhibit 3 illustrates these new approaches. The most important of

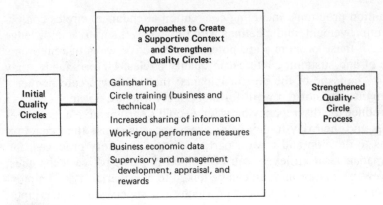

EXHIBIT 3
Strengthening the quality-circle approach.

the changes is probably the development of a gainsharing formula that will let everyone participate in the benefits of performance improvement. Other possible approaches include improved information and education for circle members and the use of training, appraisal, and rewards to develop participative supervision. The suggested reward, information, and education system changes involve changing the work organization in some important ways. In essence, they call for making it a more active organization for lower-level participants by giving them new kinds of knowledge, information, supervision, and rewards. This reinforces the fact that an organization that wants to sustain a participative parallel structure must become more participative in its day-to-day business.

A STRATEGY FOR INCREASING EMPLOYEE INVOLVEMENT

As the discussion has emphasized so far, things can be done in the organization to support the continued effectiveness of quality circles. On the other hand, quality circles can also be used as a starting point for an organization that wishes to move toward a more participative management approach. Which approach is best? The answer may be somewhat different for organizations that have never had quality circles than it is for organizations that have already engaged in quality-circle activity. Let us look first at the issues that confront the former type of organization.

Although quality circles can be a starting point in a move toward participative management, they are not necessarily the best place to start, nor are they guaranteed to lead to other forms of involvement. The argument so far clearly suggests that if they are to lead to more extensive forms of involvement, considerable planning, support, and transition help is needed. Indeed, one clear alternative is to skip quality circles entirely and go directly to teams and other participative structures; this approach has been used in the start-up of many new plants, and in such new organizations as People Express Airlines and American

Transtech. In most cases, this is the preferred strategy in a start-up situation; it causes the organization to move more quickly toward creating a participative culture and avoids implementing systems and processes that are out of keeping with a high involvement approach.

The situation may be different, however, in existing organizations. An existing organization may not be ready to move toward a team environment or an environment in which task forces make a number of important organizational decisions. In this case, quality circles can provide a possible first step toward other forms of employee involvement. One must decide at the beginning, however, whether quality circles are an end in themselves or a transition vehicle that will lead to other forms of involvement. As has been noted already, if an organization intends to move to teams and task forces, it must structure circles and train people differently. Finally, an organization with no experience in participation may want to start with a program like gainsharing that introduces a parallel organization structure and simultaneously changes the reward system. When this is successfully done, it can lead to relatively rapid improvement in organizational performance.

In conclusion, an organization without quality circles must plan on a sequence of change interventions that will lead to the type of participative organization desired. The right sequence depends on a number of things, including the technology and the current attitudes and values of the managers and employees. For example, the more traditional the existing organization, the more likely it is that quality circles are a good starting point. If the organization is ready for a more participative approach, then quality circles may be skipped as a first step.

The decisions confronting an organization that already has a quality-circle program are much different from those facing an organization with no program. In brief, organizations with quality circles typically face a choice between transitioning them or institutionalizing them. Institutionalizing them can be accomplished by performing the kind of support activities discussed earlier. Transforming them involves the formation of other kinds of parallel structures and/or the development of work teams as the primary focus of idea generation, problem solving, and employee involvement.

The choice between transformation and institutionalization is not an easy one. Our reading of the evidence is that transformation is likely to lead to the greatest long-term organizational effectiveness; however, it is clearly a difficult step to accomplish, as it involves the development of a new philosophy about managing. In addition, it requires significant changes in managerial behavior and the development of a long-term perspective on organizational performance. A major transition effort in an organization may not be practical or desirable for a number of reasons. For example, the resources may not be available to support it, or instability may be so great that no long-term commitments can be made. Finally, the power structure in the organization may not be receptive to more intensive forms of employee involvement. In this case, the best strategy may be either to allow quality circles to disappear entirely or to make the contextual and structural changes to assure that they continue to operate.

CONCLUSION

Quality circles are potentially useful in helping move an organization toward greater effectiveness. Their orientation and structures are consistent with a participative approach to management; as such, they pose the following challenge to traditional management approaches: How well can traditional approaches coexist with quality circles? Our view is that, in the long term, quality circles have trouble existing with traditional management approaches; under such conditions, they either face or require changes in major features of the organization. There is no road map for the use of quality circles. However, some of their strengths and weaknesses suggest that organizations should think carefully before choosing them as an approach to participative management. In most cases, it may be best to transition them to another form of cooperative program.

SELECTED BIBLIOGRAPHY

This article is a follow-up to an earlier article by Edward E. Lawler III and Susan Mohrman entitled "Quality Circles After the Fad" (*Harvard Business Review*, January–February 1985). Further information on some of the ideas suggested here can be found in Edward E. Lawler III, *High Involvement Management* (Jossey-Bass, 1986). For readers interested in finding out more about work-design and teams, a good basic reference is J. Richard Hackman and Greg R. Oldham, *Work Redesign* (Addison-Wesley, 1980). Further information on reward systems can be found in Edward E. Lawler III, *Pay and Organization Development* (Addison-Wesley, 1981).

Other related publications include Susan A. Mohrman, Gerald E. Ledford, Jr., Edward E. Lawler III, and Alan M. Mohrman, Jr., "Quality of Worklife and Employee Involvement" in C. L. Cooper and I. Robertson (Eds.), *International Review of Industrial and Organizational Psychology 1986* (John Wiley, 1986); Richard E. Walton, "From Control to Commitment in the Workplace" (*Harvard Business Review*, March–April 1985); and Richard E. Walton, "A Vision-Led Approach to Management Restructuring" (*Organizational Dynamics*, Spring 1986).

High-Involvement Management

Edward E. Lawler III
Susan A. Mohrman

In the literature on employee participation and involvement, managers often are cast as villains. Article after article points out that when organizations try to make the transition from a traditional control orientation to a high-involvement management style, many managers resist the new direction and fail to support the change process. One reason cited for their resistance is the managers' inability to

From *Organizational Dynamics*, April, 1989, 27–31. Copyright © 1989 by American Management Association, New York. Reprinted by permission. All rights reserved.

define their own role in the transition process; they have little ownership over the "new way of managing." Another reason is the managers' inability to make changes in management style on their own; they are trapped within traditional organizational systems that make it impossible for even the most committed manager to adopt high-involvement practices short of a corporatewide change effort.

Managers often are obstacles in the transition to a high-involvement management style. Such a transition requires a significant and, for many managers, undesirable change in their work role and behavior. However, managers need not become obstacles. They can do a number of things to facilitate the change process; indeed, they may even be able to lead it by creating in their particular work group or work area their own approach to high-involvement management.

Human resources professionals can help managers understand the value of a high-involvement management style and explain to them the ways in which they can involve employees in decision making that affects the business of their particular work area. First, however, the human resources professional must become thoroughly knowledgeable about all aspects of a high-involvement management culture.

High-involvement management can best be defined as an approach to management that encourages employee commitment to the success of the organization. Employees at all levels of the organization are given the right mix of information, knowledge, power, and rewards so that they can influence and be rewarded for organizational performance. Managers who want to adopt a high-involvement management style therefore need to learn what they can do to deliver new information, knowledge, power, and rewards to employees in their work area.

SHARING INFORMATION

Moving business information downward in the organization is perhaps the easiest thing a manager can do to encourage employee involvement—and HR professionals are in a position to encourage this flow throughout an organization. Provided that the manager himself or herself receives information about production, quality, service levels, and business plans, all he or she must do is be willing to share that information with others. The manager must regularly and honestly share valid data about the organization and the work unit's performance and future plans. The latter is especially important because without some sense of where the organization is going, employees will have difficulty identifying with and contributing to its success and business agenda.

In particular, employees need information about plans for new equipment, new work processes, and new schedules. This kind of information directly affects employees' lives and is their closest link to the future direction of the organization.

Information can be shared during regular state-of-the-business meetings that are held for all employees or during small, regular work-group meetings. Employees from other parts of the organization, such as members of staff groups and senior managers, can be invited to share information about the future direction of the organization. Of course, some managers may be reluctant to invite these employees because they do not want to expose to other parts of the organization what is occurring in their work area; nevertheless, this approach can be an effective way of communicating to employees what is going on in the organization. Particularly when the invited employee is a higher-level staff member or manager, this approach can communicate to employees the important status that their manager believes they have in the organization. In addition, the visiting employees can be familiarized with the concerns of the work group.

Perhaps the most effective communication links a manager can build are with customers and suppliers—both external and internal. Employees need to develop a sense that they are serving a customer, and they need to get feedback and reactions directly from that customer. The key word is "directly." All too often, employees who make a product or perform a service get information about customers through their supervisor or through employees outside the work group. As a result, the feedback tends to be diluted, and employees may view it as arbitrary and capricious. It simply does not have the same impact as when it is received directly from the customer who says "Service is poor," "The product failed for these reasons," or "It's an outstanding product; the best one I have ever owned."

Furthermore, if employees are being served by suppliers, they should be given the responsibility for giving feedback directly to those suppliers. By enabling employees to influence the behavior of their suppliers, they develop a greater sense of responsibility for the quality of their part of the work process.

In addition to promoting downward communication and customer-supplier communication, managers need to promote the upward flow of communication. They need to ensure that the views of employees in their work area are heard. A good place to start is with the manager's own work performance. The manager can regularly and systematically ask employees how he or she is doing. In this way, the manager can establish the principle that feedback and the upward flow of information are important.

To establish trust and overcome employee discomfort with informal, face-to-face feedback, the manager may want to collect such information through a simple attitude survey. Summarized results can then be shared and discussed during a work-group meeting. The human resources department should help managers design and conduct such surveys.

The upward flow of information must extend beyond the boundaries of a particular work unit. Managers need to carry suggestions and feedback on organizational directions and changes outside their particular work area and be sure that the feedback is processed and acted upon by upper management. Of course, the risks associated with this kind of upward communication are greater than they are when upward feedback is kept within the work unit. The probability increases that nothing will happen in reaction to the upward flow of information. If higher-level managers are not receptive to influence from below, a high-involvement manager may be criticized for being too demanding and for listening too much to employee concerns and ideas. Nevertheless, communication to upper management is highly desirable since it potentially allows employees to make significant changes in their work area and to have a strong impact on organizational performance.

SHARING KNOWLEDGE

Managers usually are in a position to add to the knowledge and expertise of the employees in their work area. To be effective, high-involvement management requires that employees know how the organization operates and how their particular work area operates. They also must understand and be capable of acting on the kind of financial and other information that is provided by the organization's information system. Without this knowledge, it is difficult for employees to be meaningful participants in decision making. It is also difficult for them to have an understanding of the business and feel responsible for the results that it produces.

Managers have the most control over knowledge about the operations of their particular work area or work unit. They can familiarize employees with all work done in the unit and encourage them to get broad training in the operation of that work unit. Training can take the form of peer cross-training or formal educational experiences. Employees should be encouraged to exchange information about the projects they are working on, the procedures they use, and the problems they encounter—either through routine meetings or through special quarterly updates. The important point is that employees know the overall operation of the work area so that they can understand and influence its performance.

Managers should also help employees develop an understanding of the larger context in which their work area operates. Formal training can be provided by staff personnel or by others who understand the operations of the organization. Such training may involve temporarily swapping employees with employees in other work areas so that they can see what happens to the product or service before it gets to them or after it leaves their particular work area.

In addition, HR and line managers can support formal training programs and classroom education for employees. These off-the-job learning experiences may cover topics such as business economics and the technical skills needed to operate the organization. The purpose is to develop employees who understand the operations of the organization and how their contribution fits in. They then will have the knowledge necessary to help make decisions that affect their work area.

SHARING POWER

To move power downward in an organization, managers must be willing to allow employees to influence a number of the decisions that affect their day-to-day worklife. Before power can be shared, however, knowledge and information must be shared, for power without knowledge and information is dangerous. Once employees know how the organization operates and have sufficient information about the organization, the issue of power can be addressed.

Advocates of job redesign argue that managers can and should allow employees to make a number of decisions concerning work methods and work procedures. Unfortunately, the sometimes trite refrain, "No one knows how to do a job better than the person performing it," is not always true. HR and other managers should make a regular practice of educating employees about alternative work methods. Consequently, redesigning jobs to include decision making about work methods and procedures must occur in tandem with educating employees about technical issues.

Quality circles, when successful, illustrate how groups of employees can make decisions that solve day-to-day operating problems. Managers play a key role in the process since they must not only commission the quality circle or task force but also provide time for the group to meet, be receptive to its recommendations, and provide resources for implementing those recommendations.

Goals can be powerful motivators of performance, and they can be effectively set by work groups or individual employees. Since participatively set goals are owned by everyone in the work unit, they typically are considered achievable by all employees in the work unit. Top-down goals, in contrast, often are seen as imposed and therefore do not receive the commitment of employees in the work unit. Once again, managers can play a key role by giving employees enough information and knowledge to permit them to set meaningful goals and by allowing employees to participate in the goal-setting process. In many cases, managers can also include employees in planning activities that focus on future directions for the organization. With sufficient information and knowledge, employees can help develop new work methods and new products and plan for new technologies and new work areas.

In one sense, HR and other managers who effectively move power downward—who are willing to share their supervisory or managerial power with their employees—can be a source of stress to other managers in the organization if those managers are not willing to share their power. Yet even when most managers in the organization are not behaving in a high-involvement manner, a manager can share certain kinds of decision making with the employees who work for him or her. In particular, decisions about work methods, work procedures, schedules, and goals can be shared.

In many high-involvement organizations, employees decide who will join their work unit and who will get a pay increase. They may even be involved in the evaluation of their manager or supervisor. Sharing that kind of power is an important part of the high-involvement approach because it engenders employee trust and motivation, but it may be difficult to achieve in organizations that are not oriented toward high-involvement management. In those organizations, a manager can, as a first step, solicit employee input on hiring decisions.

Having co-workers conduct performance appraisals and make reward decisions is a more difficult issue. Certainly, a manager can solicit input from an employee's co-workers when performance evaluations are made. In high-involvement organizations, this approach can be quite useful. In traditional organizations, however, it is more risky since it threatens the traditional hierarchy in ways that may cause other managers to oppose the idea of employee involvement. Moreover, this approach may harm the reputation of the HR or other manager who attempts to implement it.

SHARING REWARDS

Pay policies, employee benefits, career paths, and succession systems typically are planned and administered by an organization's human resources function and therefore are mostly beyond the control of individual managers. Nevertheless, managers have some ability to influence the distribution of rewards. Training, for example, can be an important reward and can be broadly and vigorously used by a manager to acknowledge excellent performance and promote employee involvement in decision making.

Some high-involvement organizations have implemented the principle of shared rewards by offering employees gainsharing or profit-sharing plans. Even without such formal programs, managers usually can influence the degree to which rewards and recognition are broadly shared within their work unit. When a project is successful, for example, they can make sure that everyone involved is acknowledged and that some kind of celebration is held in the work unit. The celebration can be as simple as buying pizzas for everyone or holding a meeting in which recognition is given by a senior manager, or it can be a special evening party, dinner, or weekend excursion. The important point is recognizing performance in the work unit as the product of every employee in that unit and sharing rewards and recognition for successful efforts with everyone involved.

Social rewards clearly are important to employees and are an effective means of distributing recognition for performance to lower levels of the organization. Such rewards, however, can be given only by individuals who are respected and whose opinion is valued. The manager's personal credibility and integrity play a key role in making social rewards effective.

A manager's feedback is more likely to be valued if he or she gives rewards only when employees believe they are deserved. Moreover, the feedback must be given with feeling. To ensure that the rewards given are valued by employees, managers should ask their employees whether rewards are given appropriately, at a meaningful time, and in a meaningful way. A manager's ability to give recognition, in short, is partly an earned ability and one that can be lost if the manager uses it unreasonably, too frequently, or inappropriately.

Improvements in the work itself can also be used as a reward. As employees gain more information and knowledge, they can be given more decision-making authority. Thus power and the ability to influence decisions is moved downward in a way that rewards learning and improved organizational performance.

Certainly, job evaluations are one feature of the reward system that managers can influence. When work is restructured, HR and line managers can urge that jobs be reevaluated. If they are and higher pay levels result, employees will have been rewarded for taking on additional power and responsibility.

Clear information from the HR department can make it easier for the line manager to help employees understand the organization's pay and promotion systems. (In many traditional work organizations, these systems are surrounded by great mystique and secrecy.) By explaining to employees how the pay system operates, managers can engender a more egalitarian feeling about the system and give employees a chance to influence their rewards through their own behavior. At least, this approach clarifies for employees what is possible and what is not within the context of the existing reward system. In addition, discussions about the organization's pay and promotion systems provide a great opportunity for managers to invite staff members to their work units to explain how the systems work and what employees can do to influence their own career situation.

With direction and support from HR professionals, most managers can make performance appraisal and career planning a participative process for their employees. They can jointly plan work activities with employees and agree upon performance goals and performance measures. They can invite employees' input before any evaluative discussion of performance begins. If the manager and employee strongly disagree about how well the employee has performed, the manager can ask a third party to listen to the different viewpoints and thereby resolve the situation in a fair and due-process-oriented way. In short, the manager can ensure that the performance-appraisal process itself is a two-way power-sharing experience in which employees have an understanding of how rewards are determined and how they can influence the rewards they receive.

Managers also can handle promotion decisions in a participative way. They can, for example, get peer data on who should be promoted. They can educate employees about career opportunities and support relevant training. They can hold career discussions with individual employees who have expressed an interest in being promoted and in moving into new positions. In short, managers can make the whole career-planning process much less mysterious and much more open to input and influence from employees in their work area. Combined with participative performance appraisals, this approach to career planning can empower employees to influence the reward system.

NOT WITHOUT RISKS

Some of the practices that managers can implement to develop a high-involvement management style are listed in Exhibit 1. No one of them constitutes a final or complete test for being an employee-involvement-oriented manager, but taken together they give a good picture of how a manager can practice high-involvement management. The manager who acts accordingly can move information, knowledge, power, and rewards downward in the organization and can go a long way toward establishing a high-involvement workplace. In most cases, all of these practices can be installed even in a relatively traditional work culture.

Nevertheless, high-involvement managers need to be warned that although they can survive in traditional organizations, they face risks. For example, many organizational systems are designed to operate in ways that cancel out or make difficult high-involvement management. Efforts to involve employees in career planning may be thwarted by the arbitrary top-down selection of "favorites" when opportunities arise. Information groups may refuse to provide business results.

Without the backing of HR and other higher-level managers, the manager who decides to operate in a high-involvement manner may be constantly running into

EXHIBIT 1
HIGH-INVOLVEMENT MANAGEMENT PRACTICES

- Having annual performance appraisals for all employees.
- Permitting substantial employee input into the performance-appraisal process.
- Holding career-counseling sessions with all employees at least every two years.
- Permitting substantial employee input into the career-counseling process.
- Being open to employees' suggestions about work methods and procedures.
- Testing new ideas and methods with employees to see if they agree.
- Implementing a method or suggestion that came from an employee.
- Holding frequent state-of-the-business meetings.
- Educating employees about how the business is measured and the economics of the business.
- Cross-training employees and exposing them to work that is done in other work areas.
- Holding regular meetings during which employees in the work area exchange information.
- Sharing success and recognition with all members of the work unit.
- Explaining the reward system to all employees.
- Having employees receive feedback directly from their customers.
- Permitting employees to give feedback to suppliers.
- Permitting employees to make operating decisions about how to do things.
- Educating employees about how their work unit fits into the larger organization.
- Giving employees a chance to participate in hiring decisions.

personnel, information, and other staff system conflicts and limitations that make it difficult to share information, knowledge, power, and rewards with employees. Because of these conflicts, employees may conclude that the whole effort to manage in a high-involvement way is destined to fail. It takes a skilled manager to overcome these conflicts and to convince employees that employee involvement is worth doing and can be done to a considerable degree.

Obviously, institutionalization of employee involvement is most difficult when the rest of the organization does not support it. In case after case, managers have successfully built high-involvement work units within traditional organizations only to see them crumble when they leave. Without overall systems support, high-involvement work units are fragile and may be eliminated by a new manager who is opposed to them. In that case, employees who support high-involvement management may become cynical and turned off; they may even feel worse than if they had never had the opportunity to work in a high-involvement environment. Thus, before encouraging the adoption of a high-involvement management style, the responsible HR manager must consider whether a high-involvement culture can stay in place long enough to make the effort worthwhile and safe for employees.

Finally, HR and other managers who wish to manage in a high-involvement manner must consider the career risks associated with this approach. In an organization that values traditional control-oriented practices, a high-involvement manager may be seen as weak and lacking the guts to manage in a top-down manner. Time spent informing and educating employees and solving task-oriented problems may be labeled "nonproductive." Ironically, a negative attitude about the high-involvement manager may develop even if the performance results of the work unit are outstanding. Other managers may wait expectantly to pounce on the first mistake made by the high-involvement work area to "prove" that high-involvement practices are a sign of managerial weakness.

Overall, then, high-involvement management clearly has risks associated with it for all concerned, including the HR professional who is trying to encourage this style. Those risks are substantially reduced when there is strong organizationwide support for high-involvement management and when the organization is changing its systems to encourage this approach. In that case, managers can move ahead with considerable confidence that they will be treated well and will not lose as a result of trying to install high-involvement management practices. Indeed, they may gain. Similarly, they will not have to worry about having a negative impact on their employees.

FOR THOSE WHO SUCCEED

Despite the risks that managers incur when they move to a high-involvement management style, the benefits of this approach may make the effort worthwhile. Managers who successfully move to a high-involvement management style can get superior performance from employees in their work unit. If the organization itself is moving toward high-involvement management, the pioneering manager who is successful at implementing this style may be seen as a valuable corporate resource and very promotable—an aspect the HR professional can emphasize. Finally, managing in a high-involvement manner is simply more personally satisfying and rewarding for many people, particularly those who view the use of authority based solely on position as undesirable and unreasonable.

A traditional organizational setting is not an ideal place to practice high-involvement management, but the manager who is willing to accept the risks can do it successfully. Every organizational study we have ever done has uncovered some low-profile high-involvement managers who were successfully managing in a way different from that of most managers in the organization. In some cases, because there were enough high-involvement managers, they were not obstacles to change but rather champions of it—in effect, changing the management style of the organization from the bottom up.

QUESTIONS FOR DISCUSSION

1 How might variations in job design affect employee motivation? Explain using (a) Maslow's need hierarchy and (b) expectancy theory.
2 Why might individual differences among employees play an important role in the impact of job characteristics on motivation?
3 What are the possible negative consequences of job redesign for the worker and the organization?
4 Do you think that it is possible to increase both organizational productivity and worker satisfaction? What are some common determinants of productivity and satisfaction?
5 What guidelines would you give to top management which is considering a change to a more participative organization?

6 What are some of the potential benefits to organizational effectiveness that can be derived from work designs which foster participation? Are there any potentially negative effects?

7 What criteria would you use to decide among the various participative structures described in "Quality Circles: After the Honeymoon"?

8 Discuss the potential impact of participative management on employee attitudes and employee attachment to the organization.

9 Why do you think that many organizations do not employ the "high-involvement management" approach? Why do you think an individual manager would avoid following such an approach even when top management advocates its use?

11

REWARD SYSTEMS
IN ORGANIZATIONS

One of the central issues—if not *the* central issue—in considering motivation in work situations concerns the reward systems utilized in and by organizations. Using the concept of reward in its broadest sense as something given in return for good received, we can see that reward systems in organizations involve exchange relationships. Organizations or those individuals functioning in their behalf (e.g., managers and supervisors) provide rewards to employees in exchange for "good received," that is, membership, attendance, and performance. The ways in which rewards are distributed within organizations and their relative amounts have considerable impact on the levels of employee motivation. Despite the obvious importance of reward systems to both employers and employees, experience has shown that they are neither simple nor easy to design and implement in ways that both parties will view as mutually beneficial and satisfactory.

TYPES OF REWARDS

There is a wide array of types of rewards that can be obtained in organizational settings, ranging from obvious ones such as pay, fringe benefits, and promotion, to praise, autonomy in decision making, and feelings of accomplishment and competency. These different types of rewards, however, can be classified along two major dimensions: intrinsic/extrinsic and systemwide/individual.

Intrinsic rewards are those that the individual provides himself or herself (e.g., feelings of accomplishment) as a result of performing some task. Extrinsic rewards, on the other hand, are those that are provided *to* the individual by someone else. Much of the conceptual work on intrinsic motivation is incorporated in the work of Deci (1975) and his *cognitive evaluation theory*. Briefly, this theory argues that an individual's level of effort on a task is determined largely by the nature of the rewards available for task accomplishment. Two processes by which rewards influence intrinsic motivation can be identified.

First, there is the notion of *locus of causality*. When behavior is intrinsically motivated, an individual's perceived locus of causality is thought to be internal; that is, individuals feel that task accomplishment is under their own control. Under such circumstances, they will engage in activities for *intrinsic* rewards. On the other hand, when individuals receive *extrinsic* rewards for task behavior, they will perceive their locus of causality to be external and will engage in those activities only when they believe that extrinsic rewards will be forthcoming. The important point here is that, according to Deci, providing extrinsic rewards on an intrinsically satisfying task leads to a shift from internal to external locus of causality. As Deci (1972) states:

> Interpreting these results in relation to theories of work motivation, it seems clear that the effects of intrinsic motivation and extrinsic motivation are not additive. When extrinsic rewards such as money can certainly motivate behavior, they appear to be doing so at the expense of intrinsic motivation; as a result, contingent pay systems do not appear to be compatible with participative management systems. (pp. 224–225)

The empirical evidence that has been obtained over the past several years with regard to the hypothesis that providing extrinsic rewards reduces the impact of intrinsic rewards is, however, decidedly mixed (Guzzo, 1979). This appears to be especially so the closer that situations approximate typical work settings.

Second, rewards can also influence intrinsic motivation through changes in feelings of *competence* and *self-determination*. Rewards or outcomes that reassure people they are competent or self-determining tend to increase their intrinsic motivation to perform. However, rewards or outcomes that convince people they are not competent or self-determining tend to decrease intrinsic motivation.

The balance of the chapter will focus primarily on extrinsic rewards, those provided by the organization or some designated official (e.g., supervisor) *to* the individual. In considering extrinsic versus intrinsic rewards, however, the reader should be aware that in the literature on motivation at work these terms sometimes take on other meanings. Guzzo (1979) has made the excellent point that any particular reward has multiple attributes (self-generated or not, immediate or delayed, of long or short duration, etc.). Thus, it is important to keep in mind that there are many variations of types of rewards within the two broad categories of extrinsic and intrinsic. As just one example among many that could be provided, consider that while a simple pat on the back from a supervisor and a promotion to a higher-status job with a significant increase in pay are both extrinsic rewards, their effects on the individual's performance may be quite different.

The other major dimension that can be used to classify types of rewards in organizational settings is the distinction emphasized by Katz (1964): systemwide rewards versus individual rewards. The distinction is this: systemwide rewards are those that are provided by the organization to everyone in a broad category of employees. Examples would be certain fringe benefits (e.g., medical insurance) that everyone in the organization receives simply by being an employee, or the

	Systemwide	Individual
Extrinsic	Example: Insurance benefits	Example: Large merit increase
Intrinsic	Example: Pride in being part of a "winning" organization	Example: Feeling of self-fulfillment

EXHIBIT 1
Types of rewards.

dining room facilities provided to all managers above a certain level. Individual rewards, on the other hand, are provided to particular individuals but not to all individuals in a category. Examples would be bonuses and merit increases.

If we combine the two dimensions, intrinsic/extrinsic and systemwide/individual, we have a convenient way of categorizing any particular type of reward, as shown in Exhibit 1. It is useful to keep this classification system in mind when considering the intended functions of reward systems that are discussed in the next section. A particular type of reward will often be very effective for one function, but very ineffective for another function.

FUNCTIONS OF REWARD SYSTEMS

Organizations provide rewards for many reasons. These were dicussed briefly at the beginning of Chapter 1 and are summarized in Exhibit 2 (utilizing categorization schemes suggested by March & Simon, 1958, and Katz, 1964). As can be seen, rewards in and from organizations can potentially motivate two broad categories of behavior: participation in the organization and performance in the organization. The first of these categories, participation, can in turn be divided into membership and attendance. "Membership" refers to the act of joining the organization as well as the decision to remain with it, and organizations clearly need to be concerned with both aspects. Thus, they devote considerable effort to

EXHIBIT 2
FUNCTIONS OF REWARDS SYSTEMS

A Participation
  1 Membership
    a Joining
    b Remaining
  2 Attendance (i.e., avoidance of absenteeism)
B Performance
  1 "Normal" role (job) performance
  2 "Extra-role behavior" (e.g., innovation, high commitment)

designing reward systems which will induce individuals to become members of the organization in the first place and which also will instill a strong desire to stay with it once having become a part of it. It should be clear, though, that although the *design* of a reward system affects decisions to join and subsequently remain (or leave), *implementation* of a reward system also affects how long a person will stay with a particular organization. From the organization's perspective, excessive turnover can be a major problem, and thus well-designed reward systems may not be effective because of faulty implementation in practice. The other participation category involves attendance or, in other words, the avoidance of absenteeism. Although absenteeism may not be as severe a problem for many organizations as the difficulties of attracting people to join the organization or the problem of excessive turnover, it is nevertheless a type of behavior that most organizations want to reduce. Therefore, one of the objectives in the design of reward systems is to motivate high levels of attendance.

The other major category of behavior that reward systems are designed to facilitate is that of job performance (or the "decision to produce" in March & Simon's terminology). Here, again, there are two distinct subcategories: "normal" or expected role (job) performance, and what is called "extra-role behavior." The former refers to performance that meets the minimal expected standards that the organization has designated for someone in a particular job. When this standard is met, the organization would consider that the employee's part of the psychological contract has been fulfilled. The employee has, in effect, exchanged adequate job performance for an agreed-upon level of compensation. Typically, to obtain an expected level of job performance the organization devotes considerable attention to the design and implementation of monetary compensation systems. The assumption is that if a pay system is set up in a way that appears fair and equitable in the amount and distribution of compensation, then most individuals in the organization can be depended upon to perform at least adequately if not outstandingly.

Extra-role behavior, on the other hand, goes "above and beyond" what is normally expected (by the organization) in the psychological contract. It is behavior that is spontaneous and innovative (Katz, 1964). Many examples could be offered, of course, such as the clerk who goes out of the way to placate a dissatisfied customer, or the manager who voluntarily stays overtime to solve some particular production problem. The essential point is that most organizations probably would not function very well if the only type of role behavior they received from all employees was routine minimally acceptable job performance. Hence, organizations need to find ways to motivate extra-role behavior from at least some of their employees (and particularly in certain types of circumstances—such as crises—that face organizations at particular times). The problem, from the organization's point of view, is that rewards which may be effective in generating normal job performance (such as certain systemwide rewards) may not be very useful in motivating extra-role behavior. Thus, to the extent that such extraordinary behavior is needed, the organization is presented with a considerable challenge in the design and application of reward systems, particularly as they involve individual extrinsic or intrinsic rewards.

IMPLEMENTATION AND ALLOCATION ISSUES

As noted several times already, the best-designed reward systems can often go awry in producing their intended results because of the manner in which they are implemented. Several of the articles in this chapter (see articles by Kerr and Pearce) deal directly with reward allocation and implementation problems. As one reviews the detailed discussions in these articles, it is useful to keep in mind several of the broad issues involved.

One important issue in implementing reward systems, and perhaps the most basic issue of all, concerns the evaluation or appraisal of performance. If rewards are to be distributed in such a way that they have a positive impact on an individual's motivation to participate and to perform, it is crucial that the organization have effective means for assessing the quality and quantity of performance. If the appraisal systems that organizations utilize are unreliable or lack reasonable validity, it can hardly be expected that rewards distributed on the basis of such systems can have much effect in the desired direction.

A second issue involves the questions of how and whether rewards are in fact related to performance. While it might seem obvious, at first glance, that rewards should be distributed directly in relation to differences in performance, there are many reasons organizations do not do so. One reason was discussed above, the problem of accurately appraising performance. Another reason would include the possibility that rewarding a particular type of performance will focus attention away from other desirable aspects of performance. In addition, there is the possibility that rewarding certain individuals or groups for high performance may have a negative effect on other individuals or groups. Also, many organizations believe they are relating rewards directly to performance when, in fact, the relationship is not seen or believed by those receiving the rewards. This, of course, reduces the motivational impact of the reward system. The message here is threefold: first, it is not an easy matter to set up reward systems that relate rewards closely to performance; second, it may not always be desirable to do so, from the organization's perspective; and, third, even when organizations are both willing and able to tie rewards closely to particular types of employee job behavior, the link may not be perceived as close by the recipients of the rewards.

Another issue in reward systems implementation is the question of how well the systems in a particular organization relate to the management style that characterizes that organization (Porter, Lawler, & Hackman, 1975). Organization theorists often distinguish between two broad categories of management style, an open/participative style versus a more traditional/authoritarian style. (Of course, many organizations, if not most, represent a blend of these two styles.) To the extent that a particular firm or agency is managed in accordance with one or the other of these styles, the more likely it is that a reward system will be ineffective if it is implemented in a way that is inconsistent with the particular management style. For example, a participative appraisal system coupled with a highly participative approach in the decisions regarding reward distribution is not likely to work well in an organization that is otherwise run in a very hierarchical, authoritarian manner. Likewise, attempting to have a rigid reward system based only on highly quantified and objective measures of performance is unlikely to have positive effects in an organization that prides itself on its open and participative way of operating.

A final implementation issue revolves around the question of whether there should be relative openness or secrecy regarding various aspects of monetary compensation. This issue is particularly acute in the management parts of organizations, where typically there are fairly wide variations in pay for individuals at roughly the same level of the organization. Organizations vary considerably in how "open" the information provided is. Some provide extensive information about how rates of pay are determined but not very much information, if any, about the amount. Other organizations provide relatively little information about either. A minority of organizations (and those usually are in the public sector) provide open information both about methods of determining pay and about amounts. The issue, then, for most organizations (particularly in the private sector) is not so much whether to be open or secret, but rather the degree of openness.

OVERVIEW

To begin, the fact that rewards that are intended to affect one type of behavior can actually end up encouraging other (nondesired) types of behavior is discussed in the article by Kerr. He illustrates his points with examples from both work organizations and society and concludes with suggestions about how organizations and managers may be able to increase the likelihood that rewards will actually produce their hoped-for effects.

Next, Pearce looks more specifically at the issue of merit pay and considers why such rewards often fail to achieve their intended objectives. In particular, the role of organizational uncertainty and complexity are mentioned as reasons for some failures of incentive compensation systems. This is followed by a discussion of how more effective reward systems can be designed. The third article, by Lawler, argues for the necessity of taking a strategic approach to compensation and rewards, tying rewards to the achievement of corporate strategic objectives. It is also argued that organization design and management policies must be compatible with and supportive of an effective reward system.

Finally, Hammer examines the research relating to gainsharing techniques in organizations. This approach to employee compensation and motivation has received widespread attention recently and this article assesses both the advantages and drawbacks to the technique.

REFERENCES

Deci, E. L. The effects of contingent and non-contingent rewards and controls on intrinsic motivation. *Organizational Behavior and Human Performance,* 1972, **8,** 217–229.

Deci, E. L. *Intrinsic motivation.* New York: Plenum, 1975.

Guzzo, R. A. Types of rewards, cognitions, and work motivation. *Academy of Management Review,* 1979, **4,** 75–86.

Katz, D. The motivational basis of organizational behavior. *Behavioral Science,* 1964, **9,** 131–146.

March, J. G., & Simon, H. A. *Organizations.* New York: Wiley, 1958.

Porter, L. W., Lawler, E. E., III, & Hackman, J. R. *Behavior in organizations.* New York: McGraw-Hill, 1975.

On the Folly of Rewarding A, While Hoping for B

Steven Kerr

Whether dealing with monkeys, rats, or human beings, it is hardly controversial to state that most organisms seek information concerning what activities are rewarded, and then seek to do (or at least pretend to do) those things, often to the virtual exclusion of activities not rewarded. The extent to which this occurs of course will depend on the perceived attractiveness of the rewards offered, but neither operant nor expectancy theorists would quarrel with the essence of this notion.

Nevertheless, numerous examples exist of reward systems that are fouled up in that behaviors which are rewarded are those which the rewarder is trying to *discourage,* while the behavior he desires is not being rewarded at all.

In an effort to understand and explain this phenomenon, this paper presents examples from society, from organizations in general, and from profit making firms in particular. Data from a manufacturing company and information from an insurance firm are examined to demonstrate the consequences of such reward systems for the organizations involved, and possible reasons why such reward systems continue to exist are considered.

SOCIETAL EXAMPLES

Politics

Official goals are "purposely vague and general and do not indicate . . . the host of decisions that must be made among alternative ways of achieving official goals and the priority of multiple goals . . . " (8, p. 66). They usually may be relied on to offend absolutely no one, and in this sense can be considered high acceptance, low quality goals. An example might be "build better schools." Operative goals are higher in quality but lower in acceptance, since they specify where the money will come from, what alternative goals will be ignored, etc.

The American citizenry supposedly wants its candidates for public office to set forth operative goals, making their proposed programs "perfectly clear," specifying sources and uses of funds, etc. However, since operative goals are lower in acceptance, and since aspirants to public office need acceptance (from at least 50.1 percent of the people), most politicians prefer to speak only of official goals, at least until after the election. They of course would agree to speak at the operative level if "punished" for not doing so. The electorate could do this by refusing to support candidates who do not speak at the operative level.

Instead, however, the American voter typically punishes (withholds support from) candidates who frankly discuss where the money will come from, rewards politicians who speak only of official goals, but hopes that candidates (despite the reward system) will discuss the issues operatively. It is academic whether it was

Reprinted from *Academy of Management Journal,* 1975, **18,** 769–783. Reprinted by permission.

moral of Nixon, for example, to refuse to discuss his 1968 "secret plan" to end the Vietnam war, his 1972 operative goals concerning the lifting of price controls, the reshuffling of his cabinet, etc. The point is that the reward system made such refusal rational.

It seems worth mentioning that no manuscript can adequately define what is "moral" and what is not. However, examination of costs and benefits, combined with knowledge of what motivates a particular individual, often will suffice to determine what for him is "rational."* If the reward system is so designed that it is irrational to be moral, this does not necessarily mean that immorality will result. But is this not asking for trouble?

War

If some oversimplification may be permitted, let it be assumed that the primary goal of the organization (Pentagon, Luftwaffe, or whatever) is to win. Let it be assumed further that the primary goal of most individuals on the front lines is to get home alive. Then there appears to be an important conflict in goals—personally rational behavior by those at the bottom will endanger goal attainment by those at the top.

But not necessarily! It depends on how the reward system is set up. The Vietnam war was indeed a study of disobedience and rebellion, with terms such as "fragging" (killing one's own commanding officer) and "search and evade" becoming part of the military vocabulary. The difference in subordinates' acceptance of authority between World War II and Vietnam is reported to be considerable, and veterans of the Second World War often have been quoted as being outraged at the mutinous actions of many American soldiers in Vietnam.

Consider, however, some critical differences in the reward system in use during the two conflicts. What did the GI in World War II want? To go home. And when did he get to go home? When the war was won! If he disobeyed the orders to clean out the trenches and take the hills, the war would not be won and he would not go home. Furthermore, what were his chances of attaining his goal (getting home alive) if he obeyed the orders compared to his chances if he did not? What is being suggested is that the rational soldier in World War II, *whether patriotic or not,* probably found it expedient to obey.

Consider the reward system in use in Vietnam. What did the man at the bottom want? To go home. And when did he get to go home? When his tour of duty was over! This was the case *whether or not* the war was won. Furthermore, concerning the relative chance of getting home alive by obeying orders compared to the chance if they were disobeyed, it is worth noting that a mutineer in Vietnam was far more likely to be assigned rest and rehabilitation (on the assumption that fatigue was the cause) than he was to suffer any negative consequence.

---

*In Simon's (10, pp. 76–77) terms, a decision is "subjectively rational" if it maximizes an individual's valued outcomes so far as his knowledge permits. A decision is "personally rational" if it is oriented toward the individual's goals.

In his description of the "zone of indifference," Barnard stated that "a person can and will accept a communication as authoritative only when . . . at the time of his decision, he believes it to be compatible with his personal interests as a whole" (1, p. 165). In light of the reward system used in Vietnam, would it not have been personally irrational for some orders to have been obeyed? Was not the military implementing a system which *rewarded* disobedience, while *hoping* that soldiers (despite the reward system) would obey orders?

Medicine

Theoretically, a physician can make either of two types of error, and intuitively one seems as bad as the other. A doctor can pronounce a patient sick when he is actually well, thus causing him needless anxiety and expense, curtailment of enjoyable foods and activities, and even physical danger by subjecting him to needless medication and surgery. Alternatively, a doctor can label a sick person well, and thus avoid treating what may be a serious, even fatal ailment. It might be natural to conclude that physicians seek to minimize both types of error.

Such a conclusion would be wrong.* It is estimated that numerous Americans are presently afflicted with iatrogenic (physician *caused*) illnesses (9). This occurs when the doctor is approached by someone complaining of a few stray symptoms. The doctor classifies and organizes these symptoms, gives them a name, and obligingly tells the patient what further symptoms may be expected. This information often acts as a self-fulfilling prophecy, with the result that from that day on the patient for all practical purposes is sick.

Why does this happen? Why are physicians so reluctant to sustain a type 2 error (pronouncing a sick person well) that they will tolerate many type 1 errors? Again, a look at the reward system is needed. The punishments for a type 2 error are real: guilt, embarrassment, and the threat of lawsuit and scandal. On the other hand, a type 1 error (labeling a well person sick) "is sometimes seen as sound clinical practice, indicating a healthy conservative approach to medicine" (9, p. 69). Type 1 errors also are likely to generate increased income and a stream of steady customers who, being well in a limited physiological sense, will not embarrass the doctor by dying abruptly.

Fellow physicians and the general public therefore are really *rewarding* type 1 errors and at the same time *hoping* fervently that doctors will try not to make them.

GENERAL ORGANIZATIONAL EXAMPLES

Rehabilitation Centers and Orphanages

In terms of the prime beneficiary classification (2, p. 42) organizations such as these are supposed to exist for the "public-in-contact," that is, clients. The or-

---

*In one study (4) of 14,867 films for signs of tuberculosis, 1,216 positive readings turned out to be clinically negative; only 24 negative readings proved clinically active, a ratio of 50 to 1.

phanage therefore theoretically is interested in placing as many children as possible in good homes. However, often orphanages surround themselves with so many rules concerning adoption that it is nearly impossible to pry a child out of the place. Orphanages may deny adoption unless the applicants are a married couple, both of the same religion as the child, without history of emotional or vocational instability, with a specified minimum income, and a private room for the child, etc.

If the primary goal is to place children in good homes, then the rules ought to constitute means toward that goal. Goal displacement results when these "means become ends-in-themselves that displace the original goals" (2, p. 229).

To some extent these rules are required by law. But the influence of the reward system on the orphanage's management should not be ignored. Consider, for example, that the:

1 Number of children enrolled often is the most important determinant of the size of the allocated budget.

2 Number of children under the director's care also will affect the size of his staff.

3 Total organizational size will determine largely the director's prestige at the annual conventions, in the community, etc.

Therefore, to the extent that staff size, total budget, and personal prestige are valued by the orphanage's executive personnel, it becomes rational for them to make it difficult for children to be adopted. After all, who wants to be the director of the smallest orphanage in the state?

If the reward system errs in the opposite direction, paying off only for placements, extensive goal displacement again is likely to result. A common example of vocational rehabilitation in many states, for example, consists of placing someone in a job for which he has little interest and few qualifications, for two months or so, and then "rehabilitating" him again in another position. Such behavior is quite consistent with the prevailing reward system, which pays off for the number of individuals placed in any position for 60 days or more. Rehabilitation counselors also confess to competing with one another to place relatively skilled clients, sometimes ignoring persons with few skills who would be harder to place. Extensively disabled clients find that counselors often prefer to work with those whose disabilities are less severe.*

Universities

Society *hopes* that teachers will not neglect their teaching responsibilities but *rewards* them almost entirely for research and publications. This is most true at the large and prestigious universities. Cliches such as "good research and good teaching go together" notwithstanding, professors often find that they must choose between teaching and research oriented activities when allocating their

*Personal interviews conducted during 1972–1973.

time. Rewards for good teaching usually are limited to outstanding teacher awards, which are given to only a small percentage of good teachers and which usually bestow little money and fleeting prestige. Punishments for poor teaching also are rare.

Rewards for research and publications, on the other hand, and punishments for failure to accomplish these, are commonly administered by universities at which teachers are employed. Furthermore, publication oriented resumés usually will be well received at other universities, whereas teaching credentials, harder to document and quantify, are much less transferable. Consequently it is rational for university teachers to concentrate on research, even if to the detriment of teaching and at the expense of their students.

By the same token, it is rational for students to act based upon the goal displacement which has occurred within universities concerning what they are rewarded for. If it is assumed that a primary goal of a university is to transfer knowledge from teacher to student, then grades become identifiable as a means toward the goal, serving as motivational, control, and feedback devices to expedite the knowledge transfer. Instead, however, the grades themselves have become much more important for entrance to graduate school, successful employment, tuition refunds, parental respect, etc., than the knowledge or lack of knowledge they are supposed to signify.

It therefore should come as no surprise that information has surfaced in recent years concerning fraternity files for examinations, term paper writing services, organized cheating at the service academies, and the like. Such activities constitute a personally rational response to a reward system which pays off for grades rather than knowledge.

BUSINESS RELATED EXAMPLES
Ecology

Assume that the president of XYZ Corporation is confronted with the following alternatives:

1 Spend $11 million for antipollution equipment to keep from poisoning fish in the river adjacent to the plant; or
2 Do nothing, in violation of the law, and assume a one in ten chance of being caught, with a resultant $1 million fine plus the necessity of buying the equipment.

Under this not unrealistic set of choices it requires no linear program to determine that XYZ Corporation can maximize its probabilities by flouting the law. Add the fact that XYZ's president is probably being rewarded (by creditors, stockholders, and other salient parts of his task environment) according to criteria totally unrelated to the number of fish poisoned, and his probable cause of action becomes clear.

Evaluation of Training

It is axiomatic that those who care about a firm's well-being should insist that the organization get fair value for its expenditures. Yet it is commonly known that firms seldom bother to evaluate a new GRID, MBO, job enrichment program, or whatever, to see if the company is getting its money's worth. Why? Certainly it is not because people have not pointed out that this situation exists; numerous practitioner oriented articles are written each year to just this point.

The individuals (whether in personnel, manpower planning, or whatever) who normally would be responsible for conducting such evaluations are the same ones often charged with introducing the change effort in the first place. Having convinced top management to spend the money, they usually are quite animated afterwards in collecting arigorous vignettes and anecdotes about how successful the program was. The last thing many desire is a formal, systematic, and revealing evaluation. Although members of top management may actually *hope* for such systematic evaluation, their reward systems continue to *reward* ignorance in this area. And if the personnel department abdicates its responsibility, who is to step into the breach? The change agent himself? Hardly! He is likely to be too busy collecting anecdotal "evidence" of his own, for use with his next client.

Miscellaneous

Many additional examples could be cited of systems which in fact are rewarding behaviors other than those supposedly desired by the rewarder. A few of these are described briefly below.

Most coaches disdain to discuss individual accomplishments, preferring to speak of teamwork, proper attitude, and a one-for-all spirit. Usually, however, rewards are distributed according to individual performance. The college basketball player who feeds his teammates instead of shooting will not compile impressive scoring statistics and is less likely to be drafted by the pros. The ballplayer who hits to right field to advance the runners will win neither the batting nor home run titles, and will be offered smaller raises. It therefore is rational for players to think of themselves first, and the team second.

In business organizations where rewards are dispensed for unit performance or for individual goals achieved, without regard for overall effectiveness, similar attitudes often are observed. Under most Management by Objectives (MBO) systems, goals in areas where quantification is difficult often go unspecified. The organization therefore often is in a position where it *hopes* for employee effort in the areas of team building, interpersonal relations, creativity, etc., but it formally *rewards* none of these. In cases where promotions and raises are formally tied to MBO, the system itself contains a paradox in that it "asks employees to set challenging, risky goals, only to face smaller paychecks and possibly damaged careers if these goals are not accomplished" (5, p. 40).

It is *hoped* that administrators will pay attention to long run costs and opportunities and will institute programs which will bear fruit later on. However, many organizational reward systems pay off for short run sales and earnings only. Under such circumstances it is personally rational for officials to sacrifice long term growth and profit (by selling off equipment and property, or by stifling research and development) for short term advantages. This probably is most pertinent in the public sector, with the result that many public officials are unwilling to implement programs which will not show benefits by election time.

As a final, clear-cut example of a fouled-up reward system, consider the cost-plus contract or its next of kin, the allocation of next year's budget as a direct function of this year's expenditures. It probably is conceivable that those who award such budgets and contracts really hope for economy and prudence in spending. It is obvious, however, that adopting the proverb "to him who spends shall more be given," rewards not economy, but spending itself.

TWO COMPANIES' EXPERIENCES

A Manufacturing Organization

A midwest manufacturer of industrial goods had been troubled for some time by aspects of its organizational climate it believed dysfunctional. For research purposes, interviews were conducted with many employees and a questionnaire was administered on a companywide basis, including plants and offices in several American and Canadian locations. The company strongly encouraged employee participation in the survey, and made available time and space during the workday for completion of the instrument. All employees in attendance during the day of the survey completed the questionnaire. All instruments were collected directly by the researcher, who personally administered each session. Since no one employed by the firm handled the questionnaires, and since respondent names were not asked for, it seems likely that the pledge of anonymity given was believed.

A modified version of the Expect Approval scale (7) was included as part of the questionnaire. The instrument asked respondents to indicate the degree of approval or disapproval they could expect if they performed each of the described actions. A seven point Likert scale was used, with one indicating that the action would probably bring strong disapproval and seven signifying likely strong approval.

Although normative data for this scale from studies of other organizations are unavailable, it is possible to examine fruitfully the data obtained from this survey in several ways. First, it may be worth noting that the questionnaire data corresponded closely to information gathered through interviews. Furthermore, as can be seen from the results summarized in Table 1, sizable differences between various work units, and between employees at different job levels within the same work unit, were obtained. This suggests that response bias effects (social desirability in particular loomed as a potential concern) are not likely to be severe.

Most importantly, comparisons between scores obtained on the Expect Approval scale and a statement of problems which were the reason for the survey revealed that the same behaviors which managers in each division thought dysfunctional were those which lower level employees claimed were rewarded. As compared to job levels 1 to 8 in Division B (see Table 1), those in Division A claimed a much higher acceptance by management of "conforming" activities. Between 31 and 37 percent of Division A employees at levels 1–8 stated that going along with the majority, agreeing with the boss, and staying on everyone's

TABLE 1
SUMMARY OF TWO DIVISIONS' DATA RELEVANT TO CONFORMING AND
RISK-AVOIDANCE BEHAVIORS
(Extent to Which Subjects Expect Approval)

Dimension	Item	Division and sample	Total responses	Percentage of workers responding		
				1, 2, or 3 Disapproval	4	5, 6, or 7 Approval
Risk avoidance	Making a risky decision based on the best information available at the time, but which turns out wrong.	A, levels 1–4 (lowest)	127	61	25	14
		A, levels 5–8	172	46	31	23
		A, levels 9 and above	17	41	30	30
		B, levels 1–4 (lowest)	31	58	26	16
		B, levels 5–8	19	42	42	16
		B, levels 9 and above	10	50	20	30
	Setting extremely high and challenging standards and goals, and then narrowly failing to make them.	A, levels 1–4	122	47	28	25
		A, levels 5–8	168	33	26	41
		A, levels 9+	17	24	6	70
		B, levels 1–4	31	48	23	29
		B, levels 5–8	18	17	33	50
		B, levels 9+	10	30	0	70
	Setting goals which are extremely easy to make and then making them.	A, levels 1–4	124	35	30	35
		A, levels 5–8	171	47	27	26
		A, levels 9+	17	70	24	6
		B, levels 1–4	31	58	26	16
		B, levels 5–8	19	63	16	21
		B, levels 9+	10	80	0	20
Conformity	Being a "yes man" and always agreeing with the boss.	A, levels 1–4	126	46	17	37
		A, levels 5–8	180	54	14	31
		A, levels 9+	17	88	12	0
		B, levels 1–4	32	53	28	19
		B, levels 5–8	19	58	21	11
		B, levels 9+	10	80	10	10

TABLE 1 (Continued)

				Percentage of workers responding		
Dimension	Item	Division and sample	Total responses	1, 2, or 3 Disapproval	4	5, 6, or 7 Approval
	Always going along with the majority.	A, levels 1–4	125	40	25	35
		A, levels 5–8	173	47	21	32
		A, levels 9+	17	70	12	18
		B, levels 1–4	31	61	23	16
		B, levels 5–8	19	68	11	21
		B, levels 9+	10	80	10	10
	Being careful to stay on the good side of everyone, so that everyone agrees that you are a great guy.	A, levels 1–4	124	45	18	37
		A, levels 5–8	173	45	22	33
		A, levels 9+	17	64	6	30
		B, levels 1–4	31	54	23	23
		B, levels 5–8	19	73	11	16
		B, levels 9+	10	80	10	10

good side brought approval; only once (level 5–8 responses to one of the three items) did a majority suggest that such actions would generate disapproval.

Furthermore, responses from Division A workers at levels 1–4 indicate that behaviors geared toward risk avoidance were as likely to be rewarded as to be punished. Only at job levels 9 and above was it apparent that the reward system was positively reinforcing behaviors desired by top management. Overall, the same "tendencies toward conservatism and apple-polishing at the lower levels" which divisional management had complained about during the interviews were those claimed by subordinates to be the most rational course of action in light of the existing reward system. Management apparently was not getting the behaviors it was *hoping* for, but it certainly was getting the behaviors it was perceived by subordinates to be *rewarding*.

An Insurance Firm

The Group Health Claims Division of a large eastern insurance company provides another rich illustration of a reward system which reinforces behaviors not desired by top management.

Attempting to measure and reward accuracy in paying surgical claims, the firm systematically keeps track of the number of returned checks and letters of complaint received from policyholders. However, underpayments are likely to provoke cries of outrage from the insured, while overpayments often are accepted in courteous silence. Since it often is impossible to tell from the physician's statement which of the two surgical procedures, with different allowable benefits, was performed, and since writing for clarifications will interfere with other standards used by the firm concerning "percentage of claims paid within two days of receipt," the new hiree in more than one claims section is soon acquainted with the informal norm: "When in doubt, pay it out!"

The situation would be even worse were it not for the fact that other features of the firm's reward system tend to neutralize those described. For example, annual "merit" increases are given to all employees, in one of the following three amounts:

1 If the worker is "outstanding" (a select category, into which no more than two employees per section may be placed): 5 percent

2 If the worker is "above average" (normally all workers not "outstanding" are so rated): 4 percent

3 If the worker commits gross acts of negligence and irresponsibility for which he might be discharged in many other companies: 3 percent.

Now, since (a) the difference between the 5 percent theoretically attainable through hard work and the 4 percent attainable merely by living until the review date is small and (b) since insurance firms seldom dispense much of a salary increase in cash (rather, the worker's insurance benefits increase, causing him to be further overinsured), many employees are rather indifferent to the possibility of obtaining the extra one percent reward and therefore tend to ignore the norm concerning indiscriminant payments.

However, most employees are not indifferent to the rule which states that, should absences or latenesses total three or more in any six-month period, the entire 4 or 5 percent due at the next "merit" review must be forfeited. In this sense the firm may be described as *hoping* for performance, while *rewarding* attendance. What it gets, of course, is attendance. (If the absence-lateness rule appears to the reader to be stringent, it really is not. The company counts "times" rather than "days" absent, and a ten-day absence therefore counts the same as one lasting two days. A worker in danger of accumulating a third absence within six months merely has to remain ill (away from work) during his second absence until his first absence is more than six months old. The limiting factor is that at some point his salary ceases, and his sickness benefits take over. This usually is sufficient to get the younger workers to return, but for those with 20 or more years' service, the company provides sickness benefits of 90 percent of normal salary tax-free! Therefore. . . .)

CAUSES

Extremely diverse instances of systems which reward behavior A although the rewarder apparently hopes for behavior B have been given. These are useful to illustrate the breadth and magnitude of the phenomenon, but the diversity increases the difficulty of determining commonalities and establishing causes. However, four general factors may be pertinent to an explanation of why fouled up reward systems seem to be so prevalent.

Fascination with an "Objective" Criterion

It has been mentioned elsewhere that:

> Most "objective" measures of productivity are objective only in that their subjective elements are a) determined in advance, rather than coming into play at the time of the formal evaluation, and b) well concealed on the rating instrument itself. Thus industrial firms seeking to devise objective rating systems first decide, in an arbitrary manner, what dimensions are to be rated, . . . usually including some items having little to do with organizational effectiveness while excluding others that do. Only then does Personnel Division churn out official-looking documents on which all dimensions chosen to be rated are assigned point values, categoi ies, or whatever. (6, p. 92)

Nonetheless, many individuals seek to establish simple, quantifiable standards against which to measure and reward performance. Such efforts may be successful in highly predictable areas within an organization, but are likely to cause goal displacement when applied anywhere else. Overconcern with attendance and lateness in the insurance firm and with number of people placed in the vocational rehabilitation division may have been largely responsible for the problems described in those organizations.

Overemphasis on Highly Visible Behaviors

Difficulties often stem from the fact that some parts of the task are highly visible while other parts are not. For example, publications are easier to demonstrate than teaching, and scoring baskets and hitting home runs are more readily observable than feeding teammates and advancing base runners. Similarly, the adverse consequences of pronouncing a sick person well are more visible than those sustained by labeling a well person sick. Team-building and creativity are other examples of behaviors which may not be rewarded simply because they are hard to observe.

Hypocrisy

In some of the instances described the rewarder may have been getting the desired behavior, notwithstanding claims that the behavior was not desired. This may be true, for example, of management's attitude toward apple-polishing in the manufacturing firm (a behavior which subordinates felt was rewarded, despite management's avowed dislike of the practice). This also may explain politicians' unwillingness to revise the penalties for disobedience of ecology laws, and the failure of top management to devise reward systems which would cause systematic evaluation of training and development programs.

Emphasis on Morality or Equity Rather than Efficiency

Sometimes consideration of other factors prevents the establishment of a system which rewards behaviors desired by the rewarder. The felt obligation of many Americans to vote for one candidate or another, for example, may impair their ability to withhold support from politicians who refuse to discuss the issues. Similarly, the concern for spreading the risks and costs of wartime military service may outweigh the advantage to be obtained by committing personnel to combat until the war is over.

It should be noted that only with respect to the first two causes are reward systems really paying off for other than desired behaviors. In the case of the third and fourth causes the system *is* rewarding behaviors desired by the rewarder, and the systems are fouled up only from the standpoints of those who believe the rewarder's public statements (cause 3), or those who seek to maximize efficiency rather than other outcomes (cause 4).

CONCLUSIONS

Modern organization theory requires a recognition that the members of organizations and society possess divergent goals and motives. It therefore is unlikely that managers and their subordinates will seek the same outcomes. Three possible remedies for this potential problem are suggested.

Selection

It is theoretically possible for organizations to employ only those individuals whose goals and motives are wholly consonant with those of management. In such cases the same behaviors judged by subordinates to be rational would be perceived by management as desirable. State-of-the-art reviews of selection techniques, however, provide scant grounds for hope that such an approach would be successful (for example, see 12).

Training

Another theoretical alternative is for the organization to admit those employees whose goals are not consonant with those of management and then, through training, socialization, or whatever, alter employee goals to make them consonant. However, research on the effectiveness of such training programs, though limited, provides further grounds for pessimism (for example, see 3).

Altering the Reward System

What would have been the result if:

1 Nixon had been assured by his advisors that he could not win reelection except by discussing the issues in detail?

2 Physicians' conduct was subject to regular examination by review boards for type 1 errors (calling healthy people ill) and to penalties (fines, censure, etc.) for errors of either type?

3 The President of XYZ Corporation had to choose between (a) spending $11 million dollars for antipollution equipment, and (b) incurring a fifty-fifty chance of going to jail for five years?

Managers who complain that their workers are not motivated might do well to consider the possibility that they have installed reward systems which are paying off for behaviors other than those they are seeking. This, in part, is what happened in Vietnam, and this is what regularly frustrates societal efforts to bring about honest politicians, civic-minded managers, etc. This certainly is what happened in both the manufacturing and the insurance companies.

A first step for such managers might be to find out what behaviors currently are being rewarded. Perhaps an instrument similar to that used in the manufacturing firm could be useful for this purpose. Chances are excellent that these managers will be surprised by what they find—that their firms are not rewarding what they assume they are. In fact, such undesirable behavior by organizational members as they have observed may be explained largely by the reward systems in use.

This is not to say that all organizational behavior is determined by formal rewards and punishments. Certainly it is true that in the absence of formal reinforcement some soldiers will be patriotic, some presidents will be ecology minded, and some orphanage directors will care about children. The point, however, is that in such cases the rewarder is not *causing* the behaviors desired but is only a fortunate bystander. For an organization to *act* upon its members, the formal reward system should positively reinforce desired behaviors, not constitute an obstacle to be overcome.

It might be wise to underscore the obvious fact that there is nothing really new in what has been said. In both theory and practice these matters have been mentioned before. Thus in many states Good Samaritan laws have been installed to protect doctors who stop to assist a stricken motorist. In states without such laws it is commonplace for doctors to refuse to stop, for fear of involvement in a subsequent lawsuit. In college basketball additional penalties have been instituted against players who foul their opponents deliberately. It has long been argued by Milton Friedman and others that penalties should be altered so as to make it irrational to disobey the ecology laws, and so on.

By altering the reward system the organization escapes the necessity of selecting only desirable people or of trying to alter undesirable ones. In Skinnerian terms (as described in 11, p. 704), "As for responsibility and goodness—as commonly defined—no one . . . would want or need them. They refer to a man's behaving well despite the absence of positive reinforcement that is obviously sufficient to explain it. Where such reinforcement exists, 'no one needs goodness.'"

REFERENCES

1 Barnard, Chester I. *The Functions of the Executive* (Cambridge, Mass.: Harvard University Press, 1964).
2 Blau, Peter M., and W. Richard Scott. *Formal Organizations* (San Francisco: Chandler, 1962).
3 Fiedler, Fred E. "Predicting the Effects of Leadership Training and Experience from the Contingency Model," *Journal of Applied Psychology*, Vol. 56 (1972), 114–119.
4 Garland, L. H. "Studies of the Accuracy of Diagnostic Procedures," *American Journal Roentgenological, Radium Therapy Nuclear Medicine*, Vol. 82 (1959), 25–38.
5 Kerr, Steven. "Some Modifications in MBO as an OD Strategy," *Academy of Management Proceedings*, 1973, pp. 39–42.
6 Kerr, Steven. "What Price Objectivity?" *American Sociologist*, Vol. 8 (1973), 92–93.
7 Litwin, G. H., and R. A. Stringer, Jr. *Motivation and Organizational Climate* (Boston: Harvard University Press, 1968).
8 Perrow, Charles. "The Analysis of Goals in Complex Organizations," in A. Etzioni (Ed.), *Readings on Modern Organizations* (Englewood Cliffs, N.J.: Prentice-Hall, 1969).
9 Scheff, Thomas J. "Decision Rules, Types of Error, and Their Consequences in Medical Diagnosis," in F. Massarik and P. Ratoosh (Eds.), *Mathematical Explorations in Behavioral Science* (Homewood, Ill.: Irwin, 1965).
10 Simon, Herbert A. *Administrative Behavior* (New York: Free Press, 1957).
11 Swanson, G. E. "Review Symposium: Beyond Freedom and Dignity," *American Journal of Sociology*, Vol. 78 (1972), 702–705.
12 Webster, E. *Decision Making in the Employment Interview* (Montreal: Industrial Relations Center, McGill University, 1964).

Why Merit Pay Doesn't Work:
Implications from Organization Theory

Jone L. Pearce

Compensation plans that base pay on an individual's recent performance, such as merit pay, enjoy prominence in both the professional compensation literature and in the popular imagination. Such plans have the attraction of clear communication of performance expectations and give employees the opportunity to increase their incomes through their own efforts. That these plans have become synonymous with "fairness" is reflected in the widespread support for President Reagan's call for merit pay for schoolteachers. Compensation textbooks and journals reflect the general belief in these plans through their devotion of substantial space to discussions of the design and implementation of such programs, despite the fact that individual performance-contingent pay makes up a very small portion of most employees' total compensation.

From D. B. Balkin & L. R. Gomez-Mejia (Eds.), *New Perspectives on Compensation* (pp. 169–178). Englewood Cliffs, N.J.: Prentice-Hall, 1987. Reprinted by permission.

In practice, however, we know that such pay programs are fraught with problems (see Winstanley 1982; Pearce and Perry 1983; Pearce, Stevenson, and Perry 1985). Edward Morse from Hay put it bluntly as 1986 drew to an end: "Our traditional reward systems have failed. The decline in U.S. productivity growth during the past 20 years signals loudly that our current [pay-for-performance] system is no longer meeting our needs" (p. 85). Although the limitations of these plans have been known for decades (see Sayles 1952; Whyte 1955; Meyer 1975), it is a rare author who does not end the list of "merit pay problems" with upbeat suggestions for the successful implementation of such programs (e.g., Hamner 1975).

Here it will be suggested that advice concerning the improvement of the implementation of such plans has not substantially improved their success. Real organizations are messy, indeterminate places, and a compensation idea that is not feasible except in pristine laboratory environments needs to be reexamined. Further, it will be proposed that the failure of individual merit pay plans should not reflexively be blamed on the practitioners struggling to put these programs in place. Rather, it will be suggested that these failures are the result of a flawed theoretical assumption behind individually contingent pay. Practicing managers are aware of the deficiencies of their own organizations' performance-contingent pay systems, but they have an incomplete rationale to explain these inadequacies. The result is frustration. Individually contingent pay, as an idea, needs to be analyzed in its organizational context. Therefore, in this paper, the implications of "organizational theory" for individually based pay are developed.

It is important to emphasize at the outset that the present argument is concerned only with the problems of merit pay based on *individual* performance, not on group or organizational performance-based merit pay or bonuses. Advocates of individual performance-based programs suggest that to be effective, performance expectations need to be clearly stated in advance. These true pay-for-performance systems (rather than the ones based mostly on retrospective subjective judgments) are the focus of the present discussion.

These pay programs are based on the assumption that overall organizational performance is the simple additive combination of individual employees' separate contributions. Alternatively, it will be proposed that the greater the uncertainty, interdependence, and complexity of organizational work, the greater the cooperation among employees required for successful organizational performance, and that individual performance-based pay can provide powerful disincentives for cooperation. This is not the traditional suggestion that money is not a powerful motivator (Deci 1975). Quite to the contrary, individually contingent pay programs can be pernicious because they so effectively direct and sustain individuals' motivation; but such plans can direct motivation away from the actions that are most functional for organizations.

The idea itself seems to hold such power that these programs are usually explained as failures of implementation or intention that, at best, suggest additions to the list of moderating or limiting conditions. Most often managers are blamed for not implementing such programs properly. For example, Hamner (1975) states that "it is not the merit pay theory that is defective. Rather, the history of the actual implementation of the theory is at fault" (p. 220).

This is not to suggest that individually based incentive pay programs are always correctly implemented but that too often evidence of "failure" receives reflexive condemnation rather than thoughtful analysis. This unexamined belief in the idea of pay for individual performance has led to a straining for explanations. The dazzle of high individual motivation has deflected theoretical attention away from a focus on what actions are being motivated. The following arguments and testable propositions derived from them are more fully developed in Pearce (1985).

ORGANIZATION THEORY AND MERIT PAY

Individual performance-contingent pay derives from an assumption that the organization's effectiveness is the simple additive combination of individual's separate performances. Such pay programs are based on the development of "compensation contracts" in which pay is linked to the employee's performance in an explicit agreement. The clarity, "fairness," and motivating potential of these compensation contracts distract us from the fact that the employee-employer relationship has not been based on such "fixed contracts" for the simple reason that this is a less productive relationship for the kinds of uncertain, interdependent, and complex work organizations undertake.

Uncertainty in Organizations

The authority relationship between supervisors and subordinates has been a long-standing interest of organization and management theorists. Simon's (1957) definition of authority bears repeating: Subordinates accept authority whenever they permit their behavior to be guided by the decision of a supervisor, *without independently examining the merits of that decision.* When exercising authority, the supervisor does not seek to convince subordinates, only to obtain acquiescence. Organization theorists have argued that the authority of supervisors is accepted by employees in exchange for wages. It is important to recognize that this "employment contract" is an open-ended one. In exchange for pay, employees offer not specific services but their undifferentiated time and effort, which can be directed by the supervisors as they see fit. This is because, as Simon notes, from the viewpoint of the organization, there is no point in offering inducements to employees unless their actions could be brought into the coordinated system of organizational actions through their acceptance of its authority. Simon argues that open-ended employment contracts allow organizations the flexibility to respond to future uncertainty.

If performance requirements are indeed uncertain, the writing of a fixed-compensation contract restricts the ability of managers to respond to these changes. Pay for individual performance attempts to modify these traditional employment contracts so that they are less open-ended and more like the closed-ended (behaviors specified in advance) contracts of the marketplace. Simon (1957) implies that under circumstances of uncertainty, closed-ended performance contracts would be difficult to write. If conditions are genuinely uncertain, how can these contracts be detailed in advance?

In practice, these pay programs are frequently adapted to uncertainty by combining "subjective judgment" with objective measures (Lawler, 1981). Such adaptions certainly help to retain open-ended authority relationships, but they have side effects of their own. For example, Carroll and Schneier (1982) note that the more subjective the rating criterion, the more rater judgment is required, not only regarding the degree to which the ratee meets the criterion but also regarding what the measure actually means. Therefore, as Lawler (1981) notes, subjectively based judgments require high levels of trust. Thus attempts to retain the authority relationship by using subjective supervisory judgments remove the clarity and fairness advantages of fixed contracts.

Recognition of the importance of uncertainty in organizational life helps us to understand otherwise inexplicable research findings. For example, researchers have found only a slight positive correlation between merit raises and performance ratings. Others usually interpret these data as missed opportunities to use a valued reward to increase motivation (e.g., Lawler 1971). Alternatively, supervisors may not tie such a salient reward to individually measured performance because they recognize not only that good performance is not completely represented in performance appraisals but also that these closed-ended contracts reduce their own ability to respond to unanticipated events. Supervisors face myriad uncertainties, requiring levels of flexibility that cannot be captured in individual performance contracts. Such supervisors use the discretion that merit raises afford to reward critical accomplishments, to cope with such concerns as inflation and salary compression, and to compensate for a particularly unattractive assignment or absence of an expected promotion. Pay does, in fact, serve a multitude of purposes in organizations, and mandating that it be dominated by an individual's measured performance in the most recent performance period impedes the ability of managers to manage.

Interdependence in Organizations

In describing the ways in which individually contingent pay interferes with the dependence of individuals on their organizations, it is useful to draw on Thompson's (1967) three-part categorization of dependence relations in organizations. First, individuals are most interdependent when they must work together, interacting during task performance, in order to complete their work. Individually contingent pay would rarely be advocated in the case of this "reciprocal interdependence," since credit and blame are virtually impossible to assign to individuals. However, Thompson's two other kinds of interdependence—sequential and pooled—are not readily seen as prohibiting individually contingent pay.

Sequentially dependent employees rely on others for either their inputs, for the disposal of their outputs, or for both. It is for this kind of interdependence that we have the most vivid descriptions of contingent pay dysfunctions (e.g., Whyte 1955; Babchuk and Goode 1951). Since the problems resulting from the use of individually contingent pay for sequentially dependent employees have been well documented, this discussion focuses on pooled interdependence.

Pooled interdependence is the collective dependence of employees on the continued success of the organization; Thompson argues that employees may not be directly interdependent with others for their task performance but are still jointly dependent with all other participants on their organization's ability to provide employment and other resources.

Individually contingent compensation contracts distract employees' attention from this more abstract dependence relationship and interfere with members' commitment to their colleagues and employer. By treating them as labor contractors, employees are encouraged to work only on activities represented in their contracts. Drawing on Kerr (1975), we might hope that they will cooperate with their colleagues and supervisors, but we are rewarding them for fulfilling the terms of a fixed contract.

Thus employees are seen by the organization and come to view themselves as "contractors," with a written "track record" provided by the compensation system that can be marketed to another employer. It can be speculated that it is this growing use of performance-based compensation contracts for professionals and managers, rather than massive changes in personal values, that has led to the popularly perceived shift among American managers and professionals from "organization men" (Whyte 1956) to "job-hopping professional managers" ("The Money Chase" 1981). Therefore, it should be no surprise to find that recent advocates of Japanese-style concern with fostering employee loyalty advocate abandoning individually contingent pay in favor of organizationwide bonuses (Ouchi 1981).

It is further suggested that pay for individual performance, since it provides incentives that run counter to the pooled interdependence among organization members, can actually undermine the quality of employer-employee relationships. Numerous scholars have attempted to articulate the positive attitude that frequently emerges among employees in their relationship with their employing organization (e.g., Pearce and Peters 1985). For example, Barnard (1938) describes the importance of "cooperation," and recently there has been a renewed interest in "organizational commitment" (Mowday, Porter, and Steers 1982; Wiener 1982).

These pay plans can damage organizational commitment, since they treat the employee as a labor contractor. Such contracts communicate that the employer is only concerned with the employee's performance as it is reflected in the "contract measures" and is, in effect, indifferent to past contributions and experience (since the employer pays only for the recent performance period), to the employee's potential for other kinds of work, and to any extenuating circumstances that may have influenced the recent performance measures. There is recent evidence that merit pay programs do have significant and long-lasting (fifteen months) negative effects on organizational commitment (Pearce and Porter 1985).

Complexity in Organizations

The work of Williamson (1975) illustrates the complexity of organizational work and helps to clarify why the fixed contracts of individually contingent pay can be dysfunctional for overall organizational effectiveness. This economist has sought to understand the conditions under which economic activity takes place either in markets—in which transactions involve exchange between autonomous economic entities—or in organizations. He suggests that organizations are more efficient than marketplace contracting under conditions of future uncertainty, complex transactions, and dependence on individuals willing to exploit their advantage.

Under these circumstances, employment contracts in organizational settings have certain advantages over labor market contracting that makes employment more efficient. Particularly relevant to the present discussion, Williamson argues that organizations are better able to encourage cooperation among opportunistic specialists (employees). Thus organizations are the more efficient forms under certain circumstances because they can more easily compensate individuals for cooperation.

Williamson's work has important implications for the design of pay systems. It suggests that despite its advantages of clarity and apparent fairness, market contracting is not suited to all types of economic exchange. Employment relationships dominate the labor market today because work has become more complex, more dependent on particular individuals, and must be conducted under conditions of future uncertainty. If such conditions are not present, Williamson suggests that it is more efficient to use marketplace contracting for services rather than employment.

Therefore, individually contingent pay, by tying an employee's pay to his or her performance during a specific time period, is an attempt to reformulate the employer-employee relationships into a pseudocontract between buyer and seller. Under conditions of uncertainty, interdependence, and complexity, such pseudocontracts cannot be completely specified. They can, at best, cover only a portion of the desired actions and become a forced and artificial representation of the kind of performance that would be most effective for the organization (a familiar problem for those who have had experience with merit pay programs). Further, since pay can be such a powerful motivator, all the problems in the use of pseudocontracting in organizations are made worse when pay is attached to fulfilling the terms of the contract.

Pay-for-individual-performance systems, despite their motivating power, would not, then, be expected to result in enhanced organizational effectiveness. Such systems build in disincentives for the management of uncertainty, interdependence, and complexity and so discourage the kinds of cooperative actions that lead the organizational form to be more efficient than labor contracting. If the organization does, in fact, have individual tasks that are predictable, simple, and independent, this analysis suggests that it would be more efficient to hire contractors than employees. Pay for individual performance is neither a labor contract (since the authority relationship remains) nor a conventional employment relationship (with rewards allocated based on *post hoc* judgments of overall employee historical and potential contributions). Thus organizations that use such forms of compensation would be expected to have less effective performance than those not using such systems, since their compensation system is working against the advantages of the organizational form. We certainly could not expect the greater overall organizational effectiveness implied by pay-for-performance advocates.

This suggests a reinterpretation of the research reporting that executives' pay is uncorrelated (Redling 1981; Perham 1971) or, at best, weakly associated (Patton 1961; Gomez-Mejia, Tosi, and Hinkin 1984) with their organizations' financial performance. Instead of deploring this evidence as representing a lack of "the will to pay for performance" (Redling 1981), it may more accurately reflect attempts to pay for performance that simply have no influence on corporate performance. Booz-Allen and Hamilton (1983) reported that while the "shareholder value" of Standard and Poor's 400 corporations declined 10.5 percent from 1970 to 1982, the use of performance-based bonuses for these firms' chief executive officers nearly doubled (from 23 percent of total compensation in 1971 to 41 percent in 1981). This appears to reflect an increasing effort to tie a larger proportion of executive pay to measures of performance. These compensation committees were apparently trying to pay for individual performance, despite the fact that organizational performance was declining during this period. This certainly doesn't prove that individually contingent pay caused the decline in firm performance, but it does suggest that the absence of a strong positive relationship between executive pay and firm performance does not necessarily reflect a lack of "the will to pay for performance." Rather, perhaps, corporate compensation committees have been using the wrong model of the ways in which individual's performances contribute to overall organizational performance.

IMPLICATIONS

The argument developed here has implications for both research and practice. Research hypotheses derived from these arguments need to be tested empirically; a discussion of possible tests appears in Pearce (1985).

Regarding compensation practice, this article was intended to help explain the gap between the popular belief in the power of merit pay and the actual track record of these programs by examining one of the relatively neglected assumptions behind individually contingent pay. At this point one could reasonably ask, Since virtually no compensation system is actually dominated by individual performance-contingent compensation, what practical difference does it make if an important assumption is flawed?

Such a large discrepancy between compensation practice and popular theory is demoralizing to practitioners and can lead to poor practice. Professional compensation specialists are led to feel uncomfortable that their own organization's actual system deviates so far from "accepted advice," and they have no way to explain coherently *why* true pay for performance plays such a limited role in their employees' overall compensation. This discussion is intended to confirm that there is no need to feel guilty about the small role of merit pay.

Virtually all compensation textbooks note that pay is intended to attract and retain employees as well as motivate greater individual performance (Nash and Carroll 1975; Ellig 1982; Wallace and Fay 1983). Wallace and Fay argue that compensation systems must meet employees' expectations for equity or fairness and that individual job performance is only one of many factors—including prevailing labor market wages, the responsibility of the position, and skill and knowledge requirements—that contribute to perceived compensation fairness. Pay systems are already burdened by spiraling labor market demand, pay compression, demands for comparable worth, inflation, and the like, and advocating that they also be harnessed as the primary short-term performance-contingent incentive is not realistic.

In conclusion, individually contingent pay plans are based on a false assumption. These plans attempt to mimic marketplace contracts under conditions of uncertainty, complexity, and dependence for which they are not appropriate. Pay can be a powerful incentive, but compensation specialists need to ensure that the dazzle of high performance motivation doesn't distract from a concern with *what* performance is being motivated. Paying people on the basis of their recent measured individual performance simply does not build on the relative advantages of the organizational form. Most kinds of organizations succeed because of cooperation among their members, not because of members' discrete, independent performances. Such cooperation is particularly critical among employees with either valuable expertise (which may be the basis for the organization's competitive advantage) or the discretion to commit the organization's resources (i.e., managers). It is simply not in the organization's interest to encourage short-term single-transaction expectations among such important employees. Pay is important, and the ways in which organizations dispense it tell us a lot about the actions they expect from their employees. Compensation theory could reflect organizational realities better if it had as great a concern for the organizational context in which employees must work as it does for their levels of individual effort.

REFERENCES

Babchuk, N., and W. J. Goode (1951), "Work Incentives in a Self-determined Group," *American Sociological Review* 16, 679–687.

Barnard, C. I. (1938), *The Functions of the Executive*. Cambridge, Mass.: Harvard University Press.

Booz-Allen, and Hamilton Inc. (1983), *Creating Shareholder Value: A New Mission for Executive Compensation*. New York: New York.

Carroll, S. J., and C. E. Schneier (1982), *Performance Appraisal and Review Systems: The Identification Measurement, and Development of Performance in Organizations*. Glenview, Ill.: Scott, Foresman.

Deci, E. L. (1975), *Intrinsic Motivation*. New York: Plenum.

Ellig, B. R. (1982), *Executive Compensation: A Total Pay Perspective*. New York: McGraw-Hill.

Gomez-Mejia, L. R., H. Tosi, and T. Hinkin (1984, August), *Organizational Determinants of Chief Executive Compensation*. Paper presented at the meeting of the Academy of Management, Boston.

Hamner, W. C. (1975), "How to Ruin Motivation with Pay," *Compensation Review* 7, no. 3, 17–27.

Kerr, S. (1975), "On the Folly of Rewarding A while Hoping for B," *Academy of Management Journal* 18, 769–783.

Lawler, E. E. (1971), *Pay and Organizational Effectiveness: A Psychological View*. New York: McGraw-Hill.

———(1981), *Pay and Organization Development*, Reading, Mass.: Addison-Wesley.

Morse, E. (Fall 1986), "Productivity Rewards for Non-Management Employees," in *Topics in Total Compensation*, ed. R. C. Ochsner. Greenvale, New York: A Panel Publication.

Meyer, H. H. (1975), "The Pay-for-Performance Dilemma," *Organizational Dynamics* 3, no. 3, 39–50.

"The Money Chase: Business School Solutions May Be Part of the U.S. Problem," *Time*, May 4, 1981, p. 20.

Mowday, R. T., L. W. Porter, and R. M. Steers (1982), *Employee-Organization Linkages: The Psychology of Commitment, Absenteeism, and Turnover*. New York: Academic Press.

Nash, A. N., and S. J. Carroll (1975), *The Management of Compensation*. Belmont, Calif.: Wadsworth.

Ouchi, W. G. (1981), *Theory Z*. Reading, Mass.: Addison-Wesley.

Patton, A. (1961), *Men, Money, and Motivation*. New York: McGraw-Hill.

Pearce, J. L. (1985), *An Organization Is Not the Sum of Its Employees: An Unexamined Assumption of Performance-contingent Compensation*. Working paper, Graduate School of Management, University of California, Irvine.

———, and J. L. Perry (1983), "Federal Merit Pay: A Longitudinal Analysis," *Public Administration Review* 43, 315–325.

———, and R. H. Peters (1985), "A Contradictory Norms View of Employer-Employee Exchange," *Journal of Management* 11, 19–30.

———, and L. W. Porter (1985), *Employee Responses to Formal Performance Appraisal Feedback*. Working paper, Graduate School of Management, University of California, Irvine.

———, W. B. Stevenson, and J. L. Perry (1985), "Managerial Compensation Based on Organizational Performance: A Time-Series Analysis of the Impact of Merit Pay," *Academy of Management Journal* 28, 261–279.

Perham, J. (1971), "What's Wrong with Bonuses?" *Dun's Review and Modern Industry* 98, 40–44.

Redling, E. T. (1981), "Myth vs. Reality: The Relationship Between Top Executive Pay and Corporate Performance," *Compensation Review* 13, no. 4, 16–24.

Sayles, L. R. (1952), "The Impact of Incentives on Inter-group Work Relations: A Management and Union Problem," *Personnel* 28, 483–490.

Simon, H. A. (1957), *Administrative Behavior*, 2nd ed. New York: Free Press.

Thompson, J. D. (1967), *Organizations in Action*. New York: McGraw-Hill.

Wallace, M. J., and C. H. Fay (1983), *Compensation Theory and Practice*. Boston: Kent.

Whyte, W. F. (1955), *Money and Motivation*. New York: Harper & Row.

———(1956), *The Organization Man*. New York: Simon & Schuster.

Wiener, Y. (1982), "Commitment and Organizations: A Normative View," *Academy of Management Review* 7, 418–428.

Williamson, O. E. (1975), *Markets and Hierarchies: Analysis and Antitrust Implications*. New York: Free Press.

Winstanley, N. B. (1982), "Are Merit Increases Really Effective?" *Personnel Administrator* 4, 37–41.

The Design of Effective Reward Systems

Edward E. Lawler III

Reward systems are one of the most prominent and frequently discussed features of organizations. Indeed, the organizational behavior and personnel-management literature is replete with examples of their functional and dysfunctional roles (see, for example, Whyte 1955). Too seldom, however, do writers examine thoroughly the potential impact of reward systems on organizational effectiveness and how they relate to the strategic objectives of the organization.

This chapter will focus on the strategic design choices that are involved in managing a reward system, and their relationship to organizational effectiveness, rather than on specific pay-system technologies. The details of pay-system design and management have been described in numerous books (e.g., Henderson 1979; Patten 1977; and Ellig 1982). The underlying assumption in this chapter is that a properly designed reward system can be a key contributor to organizational effectiveness. But careful analysis is required of the role reward systems should play in the strategic plan of the organization.

OBJECTIVES OF REWARD SYSTEMS

Reward systems in organizations have six kinds of impact that can influence organizational effectiveness: attraction and retention of employees, motivation of performance, motivation of skill development, cultural effects, reinforcement of structure, and cost.

Attraction and Retention

Research on job choice, career choice, and turnover clearly shows that the rewards an organization offers influences who is attracted to work for it and who will continue to work for it (see, for example, Lawler 1973; Mobley 1982). Overall, organizations that give the greatest rewards tend to attract and retain the most people. High reward levels apparently lead to high satisfaction, which in turn leads to lower turnover. Individuals who are currently satisfied with their jobs expect to remain so, and thus want to stay with the same organization.

The relationship between turnover and organizational effectiveness is not simple. It is often assumed that the lower the turnover rate, the more effective the organization is likely to be. Turnover is expensive. Replacing an employee can cost at least five times his or her monthly salary (Macy and Mirvis 1976). However, not all turnover is harmful to organizational effectiveness. Organizations may actually profit from losing poor performers. In addition, if replacement costs

From J. W. Lorsch (Ed.), *Handbook of Organizational Behavior* (pp. 255–271). Copyright ©1987, Englewood Cliffs, N.J.: Prentice Hall. Reprinted by permission.

are low, as they may be in unskilled jobs, it can be more cost effective to keep wages low and accept high turnover. Thus, the effect of turnover depends on its rate, the employees affected, and their replacement cost.

The objective should be to design a reward system that is very effective at retaining the most valuable employees. To do this, the system must distribute rewards in a way that will lead the more valuable employees to feel satisfied when they compare their rewards with those received by individuals performing similar jobs in other organizations. The emphasis here is on *external* comparisons, for it is the prospect of a better situation elsewhere that induces an employee to leave. One way to accomplish this is to reward everyone at a level above that prevailing in other organizations. This strategy can be very costly, however. Moreover, it can cause feelings of intraorganizational inequity. The better performers are likely to feel unfairly treated if they are rewarded at the same level as poor performers in the same organization, even though they fare better than their counterparts elsewhere. They may not quit, but they are likely to be dissatisfied, complain, look for internal transfers, and mistrust the organization.

The best solution is to have competitive reward levels and to base rewards on performance. This should satisfy the better performers and encourage them to stay with the organization. It should also attract achievement-oriented individuals, because they like environments in which their performance is rewarded. However, it is important that the better performers receive *significantly more* rewards than poor performers. Rewarding them only slightly more may simply make the better and poorer performers *equally* dissatisfied.

In summary, managing turnover means managing anticipated satisfaction. Ideally, rewards will be effectively related to performances. When this difficult task cannot be accomplished, an organization can try to reward individuals at an above-average level. If turnover is costly, this should be a cost-effective strategy, even if it involves giving out expensive rewards.

Research has shown that absenteeism and satisfaction are related, although not as strongly as satisfaction and turnover. When the workplace is pleasant and satisfying, individuals come to work regularly; when it isn't, they don't.

One way to reduce absenteeism is to administer pay in ways that maximize satisfaction. Several studies have also shown that absenteeism can be reduced by tying pay bonuses and other rewards to attendance (Lawler 1981). This approach is costly, but sometimes less costly than absenteeism. In many ways such a system is easier to administer than a performance-based one, because attendance is more readily measured. It is a particularly useful strategy in situations where both the work content and the working conditions are poor and do not lend themselves to meaningful improvements. If such improvements are possible, they are often the most effective and cost-efficient way to deal with absenteeism.

Motivation of Performance

Under certain conditions, reward systems have been shown to motivate performance (Lawler 1971; Vroom 1964). Employees must perceive that important rewards are tied in a timely fashion to effective performance. Individuals are inherently neither motivated nor unmotivated to perform effectively. Rather, they each use their own mental maps of what the world is like to choose behaviors that lead to outcomes that satisfy their needs. Thus, organizations get the kind of behavior that leads to the rewards their employees value. Performance motivation depends on the situation, how it is perceived, and the needs of people.

The most useful approach to understanding how people develop and act on their mental maps is called "expectancy theory" (Lawler 1973). Three concepts serve as the key building blocks of the theory.

Performance-Outcome Expectancy Each individual mentally associates every behavior with certain outcomes (rewards or punishments). In other words, people believe that if they behave in a certain way, they will get certain things. Individuals may expect, for example, that if they produce ten units, they will receive their normal hourly pay rate, while if they produce fifteen units, they will also receive a bonus. Similarly, they may believe that certain levels of performance will lead to approval or disapproval from members of their work group or their supervisor. Each performance level can be seen as leading to a number of different kinds of outcomes.

Attractiveness Each outcome has a certain attractiveness for each individual. Valuations reflect individual needs and perceptions, which differ from one person to another. For example, some workers may value an opportunity for promotion because of their needs for achievement or power, while others may not want to leave their current work group because of needs for affiliation with others. Similarly, a pension plan may have much greater value for older workers than for young employees on their first job.

Effort-Performance Expectancy Individuals also attach a certain probability of success to behavior. This expectancy represents the individual's perception of how hard it will be for him or her to achieve such behavior. For example, employees may have a strong expectancy (e.g., 90 percent) that if they put forth the effort, they can produce ten units an hour, but may feel that they have only a 50–50 chance of producing fifteen units an hour if they try.

Together, these concepts provide a basis for generalizing about motivation. An individual's motivation to behave in a certain way is greatest when he or she believes that the behavior will lead to certain outcomes (performance-outcome expectancy), feels that these outcomes are attractive, and believes that performance at a desired level is possible (effort-performance expectancy).

Given a number of alternative levels of behavior (ten, fifteen, or twenty units of production per hour, for example), a person will choose the level of performance with which the greatest motivational force is associated, as indicated by a combination of the relevant expectancies, outcomes, and values. In other words, he or she considers questions such as Can I perform at that level if I try? If I perform at that level, what will happen? and How do I feel about those things that will happen? The individual then decides to behave in a way that seems to have the best chance of producing positive, desired outcomes.

On the basis of these concepts, it is possible to construct a general model of behavior in organizational settings (see figure 1). Motivation is seen as a force

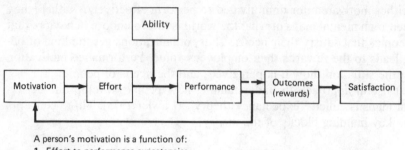

A person's motivation is a function of:
1 Effort-to-performance expectancies
2 Performance-to-outcome expectancies
3 Perceived attractiveness of outcomes

FIGURE 1
The expectancy-theory model.

impelling an individual to expend effort. Performance depends on both the level of the effort put forth *and* the individual's ability—which in turn reflects his or her skills, training, information, and talents. Effort thus combines with ability to produce a given level of performance. As a result of performance, the individual attains certain outcomes (rewards). The model indicates this relationship in a dotted line, reflecting the fact that people sometimes are not rewarded although they have performed. As this process of performance reward occurs repeatedly, the actual events provide information that influences an individual's perception (particularly expectancies) and thus influences motivation in the future. This is shown in the model by the line connecting the performance-outcome link with motivation.

Rewards can be both external and internal. When individuals perform at a given level, they can receive positive or negative outcomes from supervisors, coworkers, the organization's reward system, or other environmental sources. A second type of reward comes from the performance of the task itself (e.g., feelings of accomplishment, personal worth, achievement). In a sense individuals give these rewards to themselves when they feel they are deserved. The environment cannot give them or take them away directly; it can only make them possible.

The model also suggests that satisfaction is best thought of as a result of performance rather than as a cause of it. Strictly speaking, satisfaction does influence motivation in some ways. For instance, when it is perceived to come about as a result of performance, it can increase motivation because it strengthens people's beliefs about the consequences of performance. Also, satisfaction can lead to a decrease in the importance of certain outcomes (a satisfied need is no longer a motivation), and as a result, it can decrease motivation.

The expectancy model is a deceptively simple statement of the conditions that must exist if rewards are to motivate performance. It suggests that all an organization has to do is relate pay and other frequently valued rewards to obtainable levels of performance. But if the reward system is to be an effective motivator, the connection between performance and rewards must be visible, and a climate of trust and credibility must exist in the organization. The belief that performance will lead to rewards is essentially a prediction about the future. Individuals cannot make this kind of prediction unless they trust the system that is promising them the rewards. Unfortunately, it is not always clear how a climate of trust in the reward system can be established. However, as will be discussed later, research suggests that a high level of openness and the use of participation can contribute to trust in the pay system.

Skill Development

Just as reward systems can motivate performance they can motivate skill development. They can do this by tying rewards to skill development. To a limited degree most pay-for-performance systems do this indirectly by rewarding the performance that results from the skill. Pay systems that pay the holders of higher level, more complex jobs also reward skill development when and if it leads to obtaining a higher level job.

Technical ladders, which are often used in research and development settings, are intended to reward skill development more directly. As will be discussed later, some skill-based pay plans have recently been installed in some settings. They give individuals more pay as they develop specific skills. Like merit pay systems these systems are often difficult to manage because skill acquisition can be hard to measure. When they are well designed and administered, however, there is little question that they can motivate skill development (Lawler 1981).

The relationship between skill development and organizational effectiveness is not always a direct one. The nature of the technology an organization deals with or the availability of skilled labor may make this a low priority for an organization. Thus, although the reward system may be used to motivate skill development, in some instances this may not have a positive impact on organizational effectiveness.

Culture

Reward systems contribute to the overall culture or climate of an organization. Depending upon how they are developed, administered, and managed, reward systems can help create and maintain a human-resources-oriented, entrepreneurial, innovative, competence-based, bureaucratic, or participative culture.

Reward systems can shape culture precisely because of their important influence on motivation, satisfaction, and membership. The behaviors they evoke become the dominant patterns of behavior in the organization and lead to perceptions about what it stands for, believes in, and values.

Perhaps the most obvious connection between reward systems and culture concerns the practice of performance-based pay. A policy of linking—or not linking—pay and performance can have a dramatic impact on the culture because it so clearly communicates what the norms of performance are in the organization. Many other features of the reward system also influence culture. For example, relatively high pay levels can produce a culture in which people feel they are an elite group working for a top-flight company, while innovative pay practices such as flexible benefits can produce a culture of innovativeness. Finally, having employees participate in pay decisions can produce a participative culture in which employees are generally involved in business decisions and as a result are committed to the organization and its success.

Reinforcement and Definition of Structure

The reward system can reinforce and define the organization's structure (Lawler 1981). Because this effect is often not fully considered in the design of reward systems, their structural impact may be unintended. This does not mean it is insignificant. Indeed, the reward system can help define the status hierarchy, the degree to which people in technical positions can influence people in line-management positions, and the kind of decision structure used. As will be discussed later, the key issues here seem to be the degree to which the reward system is hierarchical and the degree to which it allocates rewards on the basis of movements up the hierarchy.

Cost

Reward systems are often a significant cost factor. Indeed, the pay system alone may represent over 50 percent of the organization's operating cost. Thus, it is important in strategically designing the reward system to focus on how high these costs should be and how they will vary as a function of the organization's ability to pay. For example, a well-designed pay system might lead to higher costs when the organization has the money to spend and lower costs when it does not. An additional objective might be to have lower overall reward-system costs than business competitors.

In summary, reward systems in organizations should be assessed from a cost-benefit perspective. The cost can be managed and controlled and the benefits planned for. The key is to identify the outcomes needed for the organization to be successful and then to design the reward system in such a way that these outcomes will be realized.

RELATIONSHIP TO STRATEGIC PLANNING

Figure 2 presents a way of viewing the relationship between strategic planning and reward systems. It suggests that once the strategic plan is developed, the organization needs to focus on the kinds of human resources, climate, and behavior that are needed to make it effective. The next step is to design reward systems that will motivate the right kind of performance, attract the right kind of people, and create a supportive climate and structure.

Figure 3 suggests another way in which the reward system needs to be taken into consideration in strategic planning. Before the strategic plan is developed, it is important to assess a variety of factors, including the current reward system, and to determine what kind of behavior, climate, and structure they foster. This

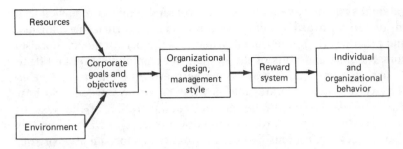

FIGURE 2
Goals and reward-system design.

step is needed to ensure that the strategic plan is based on a realistic assessment of the organization's current condition and the changes likely to be needed to implement the new strategic plan. This point is particularly pertinent to organizations that are considering going into new lines of business, developing new strategic plans, and acquiring new divisions.

Often, new lines of business require a different behavior and therefore a different reward system. Simply putting the old reward system in place can actually lead to failure in the new business. On the other hand, developing a new reward system for the new business can cause problems in the old business because of the comparisons that will be made between different parts of the same organization. The need for reward system changes must be carefully assessed before an organization enters into new business sectors.

DESIGN OPTIONS

Organizational reward systems can be designed and managed in virtually an infinite number of ways. A host of rewards can be distributed in a large number of ways. The rest of this chapter focuses on the visible extrinsic rewards that an organization can allocate to its members on a targeted basis: promotion, status symbols, and perquisites. Little attention will be given to such intrinsic rewards as feelings of responsibility, competence, and personal growth and development.

FIGURE 3
Determinants of strategic plan.

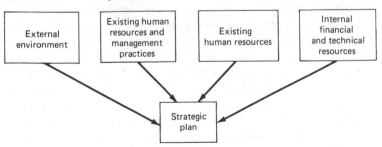

All organizational systems have a content or structural dimension as well as a process dimension. In a reward system, the content is the formal mechanisms, procedures, and practices (e.g., the salary structures, the performance-appraisal forms)—in short, the nuts and bolts of the system. Its communication and decision processes are also important. Key issues here are how much is revealed about how the reward system operates and how people are rewarded, and how much participation is allowed in the design and administration of the system. Many organizations administer rewards in a top-down, secretive way. Often this practice does not reflect a conscious choice. As discussed subsequently, organizations may wish to consider other ways that rewards can be administered.

Reward systems play important roles in organizational change efforts. They can aid or inhibit efforts to increase effectiveness. Ordinarily, major changes in other important organizational systems require a modification of the reward systems to ensure that all systems work well together. A key design decision then concerns the coordination of reward-system changes with other changes (for example, should they lead or lag?).

To begin the discussion of design choices, we will look at some key structural choices and then some key process choices. Finally the issue of pay and organizational change will be considered.

STRUCTURAL DECISIONS
Bases for Rewards

Job Based Traditionally in organizations such rewards as pay and perquisites have been based on the type of job a person does. Indeed, with the exception of bonuses and merit salary increases, the standard policy in most organizations is to evaluate the job, not the person, and then to set the reward level. This approach is based on the assumption that job worth can be determined and that the person doing the job is worth only as much to the organization as the job itself is worth. This assumption is in many respects valid, because such techniques as job-evaluation programs make it possible to determine what other organizations are paying people to do the same or similar jobs. A job-based reward system assures an organization that its compensation costs are not dramatically out of line with those of its competitors, and it gives a somewhat objective basis to compensation practices.

Skill Based An alternative to job-based pay that has recently been tried by a number of organizations is to pay individuals for their skills. In many cases this approach will not lead to pay rates very different from those of a job-based system. After all, people's skills are usually matched reasonably well with their jobs. A skill approach can, however, produce some different results in several respects. Often people have more skills than the job uses, in which case they would be paid more than under a job-based system. In other cases, newly appointed jobholders do not initially have all the skills associated with the position; they would have to earn the right to be paid whatever it is the job-related skills are worth.

Perhaps the most important changes introduced with skill-based or competence-based pay are in organizational climate and motivation. Instead of being rewarded for moving up the hierarchy, people are rewarded for increasing their skills and developing themselves. This policy can create a climate of concern for personal growth and development and produce a highly talented work force. It also can decrease the attractiveness of upward mobility and the traditional type of career progression. In factories where this system has been used, many people learn to perform multiple tasks, so that the work force becomes highly knowledgeable and flexible.

Skill-based pay tends to produce an interesting mix of positive and negative features as far as the organization is concerned (Lawler 1981). It typically produces somewhat higher pay levels for individuals, but this higher cost is usually offset by greater work-force flexibility. Lower staffing levels are also possible, there are fewer problems when absenteeism or turnover occur, and indeed absenteeism and turnover may be reduced, because people like the opportunity to utilize and be paid for a wide range of skills. On the other hand, skill-based pay can be rather challenging to administer. There is no easy way of determining how much a skill is worth, and skill assessment can often be difficult. Several systems have been developed for evaluating jobs and comparing them to the marketplace, but there are no analogous systems for workers' skills.

There are no well-established rules to determine which organizational situations best fit job-based pay and which best fit skill- or competence-based pay. In general, skill-based pay seems best suited to organizations that want to have a flexible, relatively permanent work force that is oriented toward learning, growth, and development. It also seems to fit particularly well with new plant start-ups and other situations in which the greatest need is for skill development. Despite its newness and the potential operational problems, skill-based pay seems to be a system that more and more organizations will be using.

Performance Based   Perhaps the key strategic decision made in the design of any reward system is whether or not it will be based on performance. Once this decision is made, other features of the system tend to fall into place. The major alternative to basing pay on performance is to tie it to seniority. Many government organizations, for example, base their rates on the job the person does and then on how long he or she has been in that job. In Japan, individual pay is often based on seniority, although individuals may receive bonuses based on corporate performance.

Most business organizations in the United States say that they reward individual performance and describe their pay system and their promotion system as merit-based. A true merit pay or promotion system is often more easily aspired to than done, however. It has been observed that many organizations would be better off if they did not try to relate pay and promotion to performance, but relied on other bases for motivating performance (Kerr 1975; Goldberg 1977; Hills 1979). It is difficult to specify what kind of performance is desired and often equally difficult to determine whether that performance has been demonstrated. There is ample evidence that a poorly designed and administered reward system can do more harm than good (see, for example, Whyte 1955; Lawler 1971). On the other hand, when pay is effectively related to the desired performance, it clearly helps to motivate, attract, and retain outstanding performers. Thus, when it is feasible, it is usually desirable to relate pay to performance.

How to relate pay to performance is often the most important strategic decision an organization makes. The options are numerous. The kind of pay reward that is given can vary widely, and many include such things as stock and cash. In addition, the interval between rewards can range from a few minutes to many years. Performance can be measured at various levels. Each individual may get a reward based on his or her own performance. In addition, rewards based on the performance of a particular group can be given to each of its members. Or everyone in the organization can be given an award based on the performance of the total organization. Finally, many different kinds of performance can be rewarded. For example, managers can be rewarded for sales increases, productivity volumes, their ability to develop their subordinates, their cost-reduction ideas, and so on.

Rewarding some behaviors and not others has clear implications for performance. Thus decisions about what is to be rewarded need to be made carefully and with attention to the overall strategic plan of the business (see, for example, Galbraith and Nathanson 1978; Salscheider 1981). Consideration needs to be given to such issues as short- versus long-term performance, risk taking versus risk aversion, division performance versus total corporate performance, ROI (return on investment) maximization versus sales growth, and so on. Once key performance objectives have been defined for the strategic plan, the reward system needs to be designed to motivate the appropriate performance. Decisions about such issues as the use of stock options (a long-term incentive), for example, should be made only after careful consideration of whether they will encourage the kind of behavior that is desired (see, for example, Crystal 1978; Ellig 1982). In large organizations, it is quite likely that the managers of different divisions should be rewarded for different kinds of performance. Growth businesses call for different reward systems from those of "cash cows," because the managers are expected to produce different results (see Stata and Maidique 1980, for an example).

A detailed discussion of the many approaches to relating pay and performance is beyond the scope of this chapter. Table 1 gives an idea of some of the design features that are possible in a reward system, and some of the advantages and disadvantages of each.

The first column in the table rates each plan in terms of its effectiveness in creating the perception that pay is tied to performance. In general, this indicates the degree to which the approach leads employees to believe that higher pay will follow good performance. Second, each plan is evaluated in terms of whether it produced the negative side effects often associated with performance-based pay plans (such as social ostracism of good performers, defensive behavior, and giving false data about performance). Third, each plan is rated as to its ability to encourage cooperation among employees. Finally, employee acceptance of the plan is indicated. The ratings were developed on the basis of a review of the lit-

TABLE 1
RATINGS OF VARIOUS PAY-INCENTIVE PLANS

		Tie pay to performance	Negative side effects	Encourage cooperation	Employee acceptance
Salary reward					
Individual plan	Productivity	4	1	1	4
	Cost effectiveness	3	1	1	4
	Superiors' rating	3	1	1	3
Group plan	Productivity	3	1	2	4
	Cost effectiveness	3	1	2	4
	Superiors' rating	2	1	2	3
Organizational plan	Productivity	2	1	3	4
	Cost effectiveness	2	1	2	4
Bonus					
Individual plan	Productivity	5	3	1	2
	Cost effectiveness	4	2	1	2
	Superiors' rating	4	2	1	2
Group plan	Productivity	4	1	3	3
	Cost effectiveness	3	1	3	3
	Superiors' rating	3	1	3	3
Organizational plan	Productivity	3	1	1	4
	Cost effectiveness	3	1	3	4
	Profit	2	1	2	4

Note: On a scale of 1 to 5, 1 = low and 5 = high.

erature and my experience with the different types of plans (see, for example, Lawler 1971).

Several patterns appear in the ratings. Pay to performance are seen as most closely linked in the individual plans; group plans are rated next; and organizational plans are rated lowest. In organizational plans, and to a lesser extent in group plans, an individual's pay is not directly a function of his or her behavior, but depends on the behavior of many others. In addition, when some types of performance measures (e.g., profits) are used, pay is influenced by external conditions that employees cannot control.

Bonus plans are generally seen as more closely tied to performance than pay-raise and salary-increase plans. The use of bonuses permit substantial variation in an individual's pay from one time period to another. With salary-increase plans, in contrast, such flexibility is very difficult because past raises tend not to be rescinded.

Approaches that use objective measures of performance are rated higher than those that rely on subjective measures. In general, objective measures enjoy higher credibility; that is, employees will often accept the validity of an objective measure, such as sales volume or units produced, when they will not accept a superior's evaluation of their performance. When pay is tied to objective measures, therefore, it is usually clearer to employees that it is determined by performance. Objective measures are also often publicly measurable. Thus the relationship between performance and pay is much more visible than when it is tied to a subjective, nonverifiable measure, such as a supervisor's rating. Overall, the data suggest that individually based bonus plans that rely on objective measures produce the strongest perceived connection between pay and performance.

The ratings indicate that most plans have little tendency to produce negative side effects. The notable exceptions here are individual bonus and incentive plans below the management level. These plans often lead to situations in which good performance leads to social rejection and ostracism, so that employees present false performance data and restrict their production. These side effects are particularly likely to appear where trust is low and subjective productivity standards are used.

In terms of the third criterion—encouraging cooperation—the ratings are generally higher for group and organizational plans than for individual plans. Under group and organizational plans, it is generally to everyone's advantage that an individual work effectively, because all share in the financial fruits of higher performance. This is not true under an individual plan. As a result, good performance is much more likely to be supported and encouraged by others when group and organizational plans are used.

Most performance-based pay plans achieve only moderate employee acceptance. The ratings show individual bonus plans to be least acceptable, particularly among nonmanagement employees, presumably because of their tendency to encourage competitive relationships between employees and the difficulty of administering such plans fairly.

No one performance-based pay plan represents a panacea, and it is unlikely that any organization will ever be completely satisfied with the approach it chooses. Furthermore, some of the plans that make the greatest contributions to organizational effectiveness do not make the greatest contributions to quality of work life, and vice versa. Still, the situation is not completely hopeless. When all factors are taken into account, group and organizational bonus plans that are based on objective data receive high ratings, as do individual-ievel salary-increase plans.

Many organizations employ multiple or combination reward systems. For example, they may use a salary-increase system that rewards workers for their individual performance while at the same time giving everybody in the division or plant a bonus based on divisional performance. Some plans measure group or company performance, calculate the bonus based on divisional performance. Some plans measure group or company performance, calculate the bonus pool generated by the performance of a group, and then divide it among group members on the basis of individual performance. By rewarding workers for both individual and group performance, the organization tries to motivate individuals to perform all needed behaviors (see, for example, Lincoln 1951; Fox 1979).

A common error in the design of many pay-for-performance systems is the tendency to focus on measurable short-term operating results because they are quantifiable and regularly obtained in any case. In particular, many organizations reward their top managers on the basis of quarterly or annual profitability (Fox 1979). Such a scheme can make managers very short-sighted in their behavior and encourage them to ignore strategic objectives important to the long-term profitability of the organization. A similar error is the tendency to depend on completely subjective performance appraisals for the allocation of pay rewards. There is considerable evidence that these performance appraisals are often biased and invalid, and instead of contributing to positive motivation and a good work climate that improves superior-subordinate relationships, they do just the opposite (see, for example, DeVries et al. 1981; Latham and Wexley 1981). Other common errors include the giving of too small rewards, failure to explain systems clearly, and poor administrative practices.

In summary, decision of whether to relate pay to performance is a crucial one in any organization. It can be a serious error to assume automatically that they should be related. A sound linkage can contribute greatly to organizational effectiveness. But a poor job can be harmful. Specifically, if performance is difficult to measure and/or rewards are difficult to distribute on the basis of performance, a pay-for-performance system can motivate counterproductive behaviors, invite lawsuits charging discrimination, and create a climate of mistrust, low credibility, and managerial incompetence. On the other hand, to declare that pay is unrelated to performance would be to give up a potentially important motivational tool and perhaps condemn the organization to a lower level of performance. The ideal, of course, is to foster conditions in which pay can be effectively related to performance and as a result contribute to the effectiveness of the organization.

Promotion, training opportunities, fringe benefits, and status symbols are important extrinsic rewards that, like pay, can be linked to performance. When they are linked to pay and are important, they, like pay, can motivate performance. The issues involved in relating them to performance are very similar to those involved in relating pay to performance, thus they will not be discussed in detail. As a general rule they are not usually tied to performance in organizations to the degree that pay is. They also are less flexible than is pay. This is, they are harder to give in varying amounts and to take away once they have been given.

Market Position

The reward structure of an organization influences behavior partially as a function of how the size of its rewards compares to what other organizations give. Organizations frequently have well-developed policies about how their pay levels should compare with the pay levels in other companies. For example, some companies (e.g., IBM) feel it is important to be a leader and consciously pay more than any of the companies with which they compete. Other companies are content to set their pay levels at or below the market for the people they hire. This structural issue in the design of reward systems is a critical one because it can strongly influence the kind of people that are attracted and retained by an organization as well as the turnover rate and the number of job applicants. Simply stated, organizations that pay above market end up attracting and retaining more people. From a business point of view this policy may pay off for them, particularly if turnover is a costly factor in the organization and if the business strategy requires a stable, highly talented staff.

On the other hand, if many of the jobs in the organization are low skilled and people are readily available in the labor market to do them, then a corporate strategy of high pay may not be effective. It can increase labor costs without offsetting benefits. Of course, organizations need not pay above market for all their jobs. Indeed, some organizations identify certain key skills that they need and pay generously for them, while offering average or below-average pay for other skills. This approach has some obvious business advantages, because it allows the organization to attract critically needed skills and at the same time to control costs.

Although it is not often recognized, the market position that a company adopts with respect to its reward systems can also affect organization climate. For example, a policy of paying above market can make people feel that they are members of an elite organization that employs only competent people and that they are indeed fortunate to be there. A policy that awards extra pay to certain skilled employees but leaves the rest of the organization at a lower pay level can cause divisive social pressures within the organization.

Finally, some organizations try to offer more noncash compensation than the average as a way of competing for the talent they need. They talk in terms of producing an above-average quality of work life, and stress not only hygiene factors but interesting and challenging work. This stance potentially can be a very effective one and could give the organization a competitive edge, at least in attracting people who value these things. Still other organizations stress such noncash rewards as status symbols and perquisites. This approach also can be effective in attracting certain kinds of people.

In summary, the market position and mix of an organization's total reward package has a critical effect on both the behavior of members and the climate of the organization. This decision needs to be carefully related to the general business strategy of the organization, in particular, to the kind of human resources needed and the organization climate desired.

Internal/External-Pay-Comparison Oriented

Organizations differ in the degree to which they strive toward internal equity in their pay and reward systems. An internal-equity-oriented company tries to see that individuals doing similar work will be paid the same even though they are in very different parts of the country and/or in different businesses. Some corporations (e.g., IBM) base their national pay structure on the highest pay that a job receives anywhere in the country. Organizations that do not stress internal equity typically focus on the external labor market as the key determinant of what somebody should be paid. Although this approach does not necessarily produce different pay for people doing the same job, it may. For example, two industries—say, electronics and automobiles—may differ significantly in what they pay for the same job.

The internal-equity approach has both advantages and disadvantages. It can facilitate the transfer of people from one location to another, because there will be no pay difference to contend with. Similarly, it avoids the problems of rivalry and dissatisfaction that can develop within the organization if one location or division pays more than another. In addition, it can produce an organizational climate of homogeneity and the feeling that all work for the same company and all are treated fairly.

On the other hand, a focus on internal equity can be very expensive, particularly if pay rates across a diversified corporation are set at the highest level that the market demands anywhere in the corporation (Salscheider 1981). If it pays much more than is necessary to attract and retain good people, the organization may become noncompetitive in certain businesses and find that it has to limit itself to businesses in which its pay structures permit competitive labor costs. Overly high labor costs have, for example, often made it difficult for auto and oil and gas companies to compete in new business areas.

In summary, the difference between focusing on external equity and internal equity is a crucial one in the design of pay systems. It can influence the organization's cost structure as well as its climate and behavior. The general rule is that highly diversified companies are pulled more strongly toward an external market orientation, while organizations that are based on a single industry or single technology typically find themselves more comfortable with an internal-equity emphasis.

Centralized/Decentralized Reward Strategy

Closely related to the issue of internal versus external equity is the question of centralization. Organizations that adopt a centralized-reward-system strategy typically make the corporate staff responsible for seeing that such things as pay practices are similar throughout the organization. They ordinarily develop standard pay grades and pay ranges, standardized job-evaluation systems, and perhaps standardized promotion systems. In decentralized organizations, decisions about pay, promotion, and other rewards are left to local option. Sometimes the corporations suggest broad guidelines or principles to follow, but the day-to-day administration and design of the system is left up to the local entity.

The advantages of a centralized structure rest primarily in the expertise that can be accumulated at the central level and the homogeneity that is produced in the organization. This homogeneity can lead to a clear image of the corporate climate, feelings of internal equity, and the belief that the organization stands for something. It also eases the job of communicating and understanding what is going on in different parts of the organization. The decentralized strategy allows for local innovation and for closely fitting reward practices to the particular business.

There is no one right choice between the centralized and decentralized approaches to reward system design and administration. Overall, the decentralized system tends to make the most sense when the organization is involved in businesses that face different markets and perhaps are at different points in their life cycles (Greiner 1972; Galbraith and Nathanson 1978). It allows variation in practices that can give a competitive advantage to one part of the business but may prove to be a real hindrance in another. For example, such perquisites as cars are often standard operating procedure in one business but not in another. Similarly, extensive bonuses may be needed to attract one group of people, for example, oil-exploration engineers, but not others, for example, research scientists. Over-all, then, an organization needs to look carefully at its mix of businesses and the degree to which it wants a single set of principles or policies to prevail across all its operating divisions, and then decide whether a centralized or decentralized reward strategy is likely to be more effective.

Degree of Hierarchy

Closely related to the issue of job-based versus competence-based pay is the strategic decision concerning the hierarchical nature of the organization's reward systems. Often no formal decision is ever made to have a relatively hierarchical or relatively egalitarian approach to rewards. A hierarchical approach simply happens because it is so consistent with the general way organizations are run. Hierarchical systems usually pay people more money and give them greater perquisites and symbols of office as they move higher up the organization ladder. This approach strongly reinforces the traditional hierarchical power relationships in the organization and fosters a climate of different status and power levels. In some cases, a hierarchical reward system may include more levels than the formal organization chart, creating additional status differences in the organization.

The alternative to a hierarchical system is one that downplays differences in rewards and perquisites based only on hierarchical level. For example, in large corporations that adopt an egalitarian stance to rewards (e.g., Digital Equipment Corporation), such privileges as private parking spaces, executive restrooms, and special entrances are eliminated. People from all levels in the organization eat together, work together, and travel together. Further, high levels of pay are not restricted to managers but can be earned by those who have worked their way up a technical ladder. This approach to rewards produces a distinctive climate in an organization, encouraging decision making by expertise rather than by hierarchy position, and minimizing status differentials in the organization.

In general, a steeply hierarchical system makes the most sense when an organization needs relatively rigid bureaucratic behavior, strong top-down authority, and a strong motivation for people to move up the organizational hierarchy. A more egalitarian approach fits with a more participative management style and the desire to retain technical specialists and experts in nonmanagement or lower-level-management roles. It is not surprising, therefore, that many of the organizations that emphasize egalitarian perquisites are in high-technology and knowledge-based industries.

Reward Mix

The kind of rewards that organizations give to individuals can vary widely. Monetary rewards, for example, can take many forms, from stock to medical insurance. When cash rewards are translated into fringe benefits, perquisites, or other trappings of office, they may lose their value for some people and as a result may be a poor investment for the employer (see, for example, Nealy 1963; Lawler 1971). On the other hand, certain benefits can best be obtained through mass purchase, and therefore many individuals want the organization to provide them. In addition, certain status symbols or perquisites may be valued by some individuals beyond their actual dollar cost to the organization and thus represent good buys. Finally, as was mentioned earlier there often are some climate and organizational structure reasons for paying people in the form of perquisites and status symbols.

One interesting development in the area of compensation is the flexible or cafeteria-style benefit program (Fragner 1975; Lawler 1981). The theory is that if individuals are allowed to tailor their own reward packages to fit their particular needs, the organization will get the best value for its money, because it will give people only those things that they desire. Such an approach also has the advantage of treating individuals as mature adults rather than as dependent people who need their welfare looked after in a structured way. While flexible benefit programs have not yet been widely implemented, the results of experiments to date have been favorable, and there is reason to believe that other organizations may adopt this approach in the near future, because it can offer a strategic cost-benefit advantage in attracting and retaining certain types of employees.

Overall, the forms in which the organization rewards its members should be consistent with the climate it hopes to foster. For example, a flexible compensation package is highly congruent with a participative open organization climate that treats individuals as mature adults and wants to attract talented mature people. A highly status-symbol-oriented approach, on the other hand, may appeal to people who value position power and need a high level of visible reinforcement for their position. This would seem to fit best in a relatively bureaucratic organization that relies on position power and authority to carry out its actions.

PROCESS ISSUES AND REWARD ADMINISTRATION

Reward system design and administration raise numerous process issues. Indeed, process issues are confronted more frequently than structure and content issues, because organizations must constantly make reward-system management, implementation, and communication decisions while structures tend to be relatively firmly fixed in place. Rather than discussing specific process issues here, the focus will be on broad process themes that can be used to characterize the way reward systems are designed and administered.

Communication Policy

Organizations differ widely in how much information they communicate about their reward systems. At one extreme, some organizations are extremely secretive, particularly in the area of pay. They forbid people to talk about their individual rewards, give minimal information to individuals about how rewards are decided upon and allocated, and have no publicly disseminated policies about such things as market position, the approach to gathering market data, and potential increases and rewards for individuals. At the other extreme, some organizations are so open that everyone's pay is a matter of public record, as is the overall organization pay philosophy (many new high-involvement plants operate this way; see, for example, Lawler 1978; Walton 1980). In addition, all promotions are subject to open job postings, and in some instances peer groups discuss the individual's eligibility for promotion.

The difference between an open and a closed communication policy in the area of rewards is enormous. There is no clear right or wrong approach. The issue is rather to choose a position on the continuum from open to secretive that is supportive of the overall climate and types of behavior needed for organizational effectiveness. An open system tends to encourage people to ask questions, share data, and ultimately be involved in decisions. A secretive system tends to put people in a more dependent position, to keep power concentrated at the top, and to allow an organization to keep its options open with respect to commitments to individuals. Secrecy can lead to considerable distortion in people's beliefs about the rewards given to other organization members, and can create a low-trust environment in which the relationship between pay and performance is not clear (see, for example, Lawler 1971; Steele 1975). Thus, a structurally sound pay system may end up being rather ineffective because its strong secrecy policies open it to misperceptions.

Open systems put considerable pressure on organizations to do an effective job of administering rewards. Thus, if such difficult-to-defend policies as merit pay are to be implemented, considerable time and effort needs to be invested in pay administration. If such policies are poorly administered, strong pressures usually develop to eliminate discrimination and pay everyone the same (see, for example, Burroughs 1982). Ironically, therefore, if an organization wants to spend little time administering rewards but still wants to base pay on merit, secrecy may be the best policy, although secrecy in turn may limit the effectiveness of the merit pay plan.

Decision-Making Practices

Closely related to the issue of communication is the matter of how decisions about compensation are to be made. If individuals are to be actively involved in decisions concerning reward systems, they need to have information about policy and actual practice. Open communication makes it possible to involve a wide range of people in the decision-making process. Secrecy by its very nature limits the number of people who can be involved in pay decisions.

It is important to distinguish between decisions concerning the design and ongoing administration of reward systems. Traditionally, of course, organizations have made both design and administration decisions in a top-down manner. But it is possible to adopt a different decision-making style for each type of decision.

Systems typically have been designed by top management with the aid of staff support and administered by strict reliance on the chain of command. The assumption has been that this approach provides the proper checks and balances in the system and locates decision making where the expertise rests. In many cases this is a valid assumption and certainly fits well with an organizational management style that emphasizes hierarchy, bureaucracy, and control through the use of extrinsic rewards. It does not fit, however, with an organization that believes in more open communication, higher levels of employee involvement, and control through individual commitment to policies. Nor does it fit when expertise is broadly spread throughout the organization, as is often true in companies that rely heavily on knowledge workers or spend a great deal of effort training their people to become expert in technical functions.

Some organizations have experimented with involving employees in the design of pay systems (Lawler 1981). Favorable results have generally been achieved when employees help design their own bonus system. They tend to raise important issues and provide expertise not normally available to the designers of the system. And perhaps more importantly, once the system is designed, it is well accepted and understood. Employee involvement often makes possible a rapid start-up of the system and creates a commitment to see it survive long-term. In other cases systems have been designed by line managers, because they are the ones that need to maintain it. Unless they have had an opportunity for design input, it often is unrealistic to expect line people to have the same level of commitment to the pay system as the staff people have.

Some organizations have also experimented with having peer groups and low-level supervisory people handling the day-to-day decision making about who should receive pay increases and how jobs should be evaluated and placed in pay structures. The best examples are the new participative plants that use skill-based pay (see, for example, Walton 1980). In these plants, the work group typically reviews an individual's performance and decides whether he or she has acquired the new skills. This approach appears to work well. Peers often have the best information about performance and thus are in a good position to make a performance assessment. In traditional organizations their expertise is of no use, because they lack the motivation to give valid feedback and to respond responsibly. In more participative open systems, this motivational problem seems to be less severe, and as a result involvement in decision making is more effective.

In a few cases, executives have been asked to assess each other in a peer-group reward system (e.g., in Graphic Controls Corporation). Again, this approach can apparently work well in an organization that has a history of open and effective communication. Deciding on rewards is clearly not an easy task, and thus should not be assigned to a group unless members have good confrontation skills and can talk openly and directly about each other's performance.

Overall, there is evidence that some participative approaches to reward systems can be effective because of their congruence with the overall style and because the skills and norms needed to make them work are already in place. In more traditional organizations, the typical top-down approach to reward-system design and administration probably remains the best. From a strategic point of view, then, the decision about how much participation is desirable in reward-system design and administration depends on whether a participative, high-involvement type of organization is best suited to accomplish the strategic objectives of the business. If so, then participation in pay decisions and reward-system decisions should be considered.

REWARD SYSTEMS AND ORGANIZATIONAL CHANGE

In many major organizational changes, it is difficult to alter all the relevant systems in the organization simultaneously. Typically one change leads to another. Modification of the reward systems may either lead or lag in the overall change process.

Reward as a Lead

Perhaps the most widely discussed example of pay as a lead change is the use of a gain-sharing plan to improve plant productivity (Moore and Ross 1978; Lawler 1981). In these situations the initial change effort is the installation of a system of bonuses based on improvements in productivity. In the case of the Scanlon Plan, attempts are also made to build participative problem-solving groups into the organization, but the clear emphasis is on the gain-sharing formula and the financial benefits of improved productivity. The participative management structure is intended to facilitate productivity improvement, which in turn will result in gains to be shared. Not surprisingly, once gain-sharing starts and factors inhibiting productivity are identified, other changes follow. Typical of these are improvements in the organization structures, the design of jobs and work, and additional training programs. The gain-sharing plan itself provides a strong motivation to swiftly and effectively deal with those issues.

Other reward system changes can also lead to broader organizational change efforts. For example, the introduction of skill-based pay can potentially prompt a broad movement to participation because it gives people the skills and knowledge they need to participate. The movement to a more flexible fringe-benefit program can change organizational climate by creating one of innovation in the area of human-resource management.

In a somewhat different vein, a dramatic change in the pay-for-performance system can be very effective in shaping an organization's strategic directions. For example, installing bonus systems that reward previously neglected performance indicators can dramatically shift the directions of an organization. Similarly, a long-term bonus plan for executives can lead them to change their time horizons and their decision-making practices in important ways.

Rewards as a Lag

In most major organization change efforts, pay is a lag factor. As an organization moves toward participative management, for example, the initial thrust often comes in such areas as team building, job redesign, and quality circles. It is only after these practices have been in place for some time that the organization makes the associated changes in the reward system. Often, the organization does not originally anticipate a need to revise the reward system. But because all organizational systems are interconnected, it is almost inevitable that major changes in strategic direction or management style and practices will require that changes be made in the reward system as well.

New participative plants represent an interesting example of the simultaneous installation of participative reward systems and other participative practices (Lawler 1981). The success of these plants is probably due in part to the fact that all their systems have operated in a participative manner from the outset.

Rewards as a Motivator of Change

Major strategic changes are often difficult to accomplish even though they don't involve a change in management style. The forces of equilibrium have the effect of canceling out many changes. To the extent that changing one component of an organizational system reduces its congruence with other components, energy will develop to limit, encapsulate, or reverse the change. In addition, attention may be diverted from other important tasks by the need to direct a change, deal with resistance, and cope with the problems created by change.

Management is therefore faced with two key tasks if change is to be brought about. The first is *motivating change*—overcoming natural resistance and encouraging individuals to behave in ways that are consistent with both the immediate change goals and long-range corporate strategy. The second major task is *managing change*.

It is useful to think of organizational changes in terms of transitions (Beckhard and Harris 1977). The organization exists in a current state (C). An image has been developed of a future state of the organization (F). The period between C and F can be thought of as the transition period (T). The question is how to manage the transition. Too often, however, managers overlook the transition state, assuming that all that is needed is to design that best possible future. They think of change as simply a mechanical or procedural detail.

In most situations, the management systems and structures developed to manage either C or F are simply not appropriate for the management of T. They are steady-state management systems, designed to run organizations already in place rather than transitional management systems. During the transition period, different systems, and specifically different reward systems, may be needed temporarily. Many change efforts are resisted because organization members see them as a threat to their pay level. Particularly when the present system is highly standardized and tied to objective measures, such as the number of subordinates, people may resist a reorganization or other type of change whose impact on their pay is unclear but potentially negative. There is no magic formula for overcoming this resistance, but two approaches can help.

First, a floor should be put under individual pay rates throughout the transition period. That is, no one should have to fear losing pay during the change process. This point is critical in the case of a major reorganization, which may require some people to give up some subordinates and responsibilities, and to accept a lower salary if their jobs were reevaluated. If this problem is likely to be severe, the organization may want to assure individuals that their pay will not be cut, even after the change is in place.

A second important step is to appoint a group of high-level managers to develop an approach to compensation that will fit the new organization. This group should articulate a corporate rewards philosophy that includes the following:

1 The goals of the pay system
2 How the pay system will fit the new organizational structure
3 The fit between the management style of the organization and the process used to administer the pay system
4 How the pay system will be managed once it is developed

There are several reasons for developing a compensation system in this way. First, a philosophical base is needed for an effective pay system. More and more evidence is accumulating that, unless supported by some sort of widely accepted philosophy, corporate pay administration ends up being haphazard and a source of internal conflict. A philosophy cannot answer all the problems associated with rewards, but it can at least provide a touchstone against which new practices, policies, and decisions can be tested.

A second advantage of the group approach is that it will give key individuals a chance to influence how they will be paid in the future. A big unknown in the new organization thus becomes something under their control, rather than a potentially threatening factor about the reorganized structure. Moreover, by seriously considering how the pay system will have to change to fit other changes, the group can prevent "surprise" pay-system problems from occurring once the other changes have been implemented. Finally, as discussed further below, by assuring that an acceptable supporting pay system will exist, the group can promote institutionalization of the new organization structure.

Putting a floor under existing salaries helps reduce resistance, but it does nothing to encourage good implementation of change. It is possible, however, to use the reward system to support implementation of the reorganization. First of all, the organization needs to make it clear that the jobs and associated rewards given to managers after the transition will depend on their contribution to an effective transition process. One-time bonuses and payments may also ease the transition. In most cases, it makes sense to award these one-time financial payments on a group basis rather than on an individual basis.

It is important that transition goals specify, as precisely as possible, both the rate at which change is introduced and the process used to introduce it. One-time bonuses should be tied to meeting these goals, which can be a critical ingredient in the effective motivation of change. The organization should specify target dates for particular implementation events, such as having a new unit operating or completing the relocation of personnel. In addition, measures should be defined for the process used to implement change; examples might include people's understanding of the new system, the degree to which it was explained to them, the level of turnover among people that the organization wished to retain, signs of stress among people involved in the transition, and the willingness of managers to give up people to other parts of the organization where they can make a greater contribution.

Rewards, goals, and performance measures are critical tools in managing the transition process. They can help to assure that the change strategy is implemented rapidly and in a way that minimizes the dysfunctional consequences for both the organization and the people who work in it.

REWARD SYSTEM CONGRUENCE

For simplicity, we have so far treated each reward-system design feature as an independent factor. Overall system congruence is an important consideration, however. There is considerable evidence that reward-system design features affect each other and thus should be supportive of the same types of behavior, the same business strategy, and reflect the same overall managerial philosophy.

Table 2 illustrates one effort to define congruent sets of reward-system practices (Lawler 1977). The two management philosophies portrayed here are the traditional bureaucratic management style and a participative employee-involvement strategy. Their reward-system practices are different in every respect. The practices associated with traditional bureaucratic models tend to be more secretive, top-down, and oriented toward producing regularity in behavior. The participative practices, in contrast, encourage self-development, openness, employee involvement in reward-system allocation decisions, and ultimately more innovation and commitment to the organization.

Greiner (1972) and Galbraith and Nathanson (1978) have pointed out that reward-system practices need to be congruent with the maturity of the organization and the market in which the business operates. For example, rapidly developing businesses need to stress skill development, attraction, high-potential individuals, and incentives tied to business growth, while declining businesses need

TABLE 2
APPROPRIATE REWARD-SYSTEM PRACTICES

Reward system	Traditional or theory X	Participative or theory Y
Fringe benefits	Vary according to organizational level	Cafeteria—same for all levels
Promotion	All decisions made by top management	Open posting for all jobs; peer-group involvement in decision process
Status symbols	A great many carefully allocated on the basis of job position	Few present, low emphasis on organization level
Pay		
Type of system	Hourly and salary	All salary
Base rate	Based on job performed; high enough to attract job applicants	Based on skills; high enough to provide security and attract applicants
Incentive plan	Piece rate	Group and organization-wide bonus; lump sum increase
Communication policy	Very restricted distribution of information	Individual rates, salary-survey data, and all other information made public
Decision-making locus	Top management	Close to location of person whose pay is being set

to reward expense reduction and to have a formalized job-evaluation system that closely tracks the market.

The reward system also needs to fit other features of the organization to ensure congruence in the total human-resource-management system. The reward system should be consistent with the way jobs are designed, the leadership style of the supervisors, and the types of career tracks available in the organization, to mention just a few examples. Unless this kind of fit exists, the organization will be riddled with conflicts, and the reward system practices may be canceled out by practices in other areas. For example, even the best performance-appraisal system will be ineffective unless accompanied by interpersonally competent supervisory behavior and jobs designed to allow for good performance measure (see DeVries et al. 1981).

CONCLUSION

An effective reward system should be designed to fit well with the other design features of the organization as well as with its business strategy. Thus there is no one best set of reward practices; indeed, it is impossible to design an effective reward system without knowing how other features of the organization are arrayed. Decisions about the reward system should be made in an interactive fashion: shaped by the business strategy, tentative reward-system design choices would then be tested against how other features of the organization are being designed. The ultimate goal is to develop an integrated human-resource-management strategy that is consistent in the ways it encourages people to behave, attracts the kind of people that can support the business strategy, and encourages them to behave appropriately.

REFERENCES

Beckhard, R., and R. Harris. 1977. *Organizational Transitions: Managing Complex Change*. Reading, Mass.: Addison-Wesley.

Burroughs, J. D. 1982. "Pay Secrecy and Performance: The Psychological Research." *Compensation Review* 14, no. 3:44–54.

Crystal, G. S. 1978. *Executive Compensation*. 2d ed. New York: AMACOM.

DeVries, D. L., A. M. Morrison, S. L. Shullman, and M. L. Gerlach. 1981. *Performance Appraisal on the Line*. New York: Wiley, Interscience.

Ellig, B. R. 1982. *Executive Compensation—A Total Pay Perspective*. New York: McGraw-Hill.

Fox, H. 1979. *Top Executive Bonus Plans*. New York: Conference Board.

Fragner, B. N. 1975. "Employees' 'Cafeteria' Offers Insurance Options." *Harvard Business Review* 53:2–4.

Galbraith, J. R., and D. A. Nathanson. 1978. *Strategy Implementation: The Role of Structure and Process*. St. Paul, Minn.: West.

Greiner, L. 1972. "Evolution and Revolution as Organizations Grow." *Harvard Business Review* 50, no. 4:37–46.

Goldberg, M. H. 1977. "Another Look at Merit Pay Programs." *Compensation Review* 3:20–28.

Henderson, R. I. 1979. *Compensation Management: Rewarding Performance*. 2d ed. Reston, Va.: Reston.

Hills, F. S. 1979. "The Pay-for-Performance Dilemma." *Personnel*, no. 5:23–31.

Kerr, S. 1975. "On the Folly of Rewarding A, While Hoping for B." *Academy of Management Journal* 18:769–783.

Latham, G. P., and K. N. Wexley. 1981. *Increasing Productivity Through Performance Appraisal.* Reading, Mass.: Addison-Wesley.

Lawler, E. E. 1971. *Pay and Organizational Effectiveness: A Psychological View.* New York: McGraw-Hill.

———. 1973. *Motivation in Work Organizations.* Monterey, Calif.: Brooks/Cole.

———. "Reward Systems." In *Improving Life at Work,* ed. J. R. Hackman and J. L. Suttle, pp. 163–226. Santa Monica, Calif.: Goodyear.

———. 1978. "The New Plant Revolution." *Organizational Dynamics* 6, no. 3:2–12.

———. 1981. *Pay and Organization Development.* Reading, Mass.: Addison-Wesley.

Lincoln, J. F. 1951. *Incentive Management.* Lincoln Electric Co., Cleveland, Ohio.

Macy, B. A., and P. H. Mirvis. 1976. "A Methodology for Assessment of Quality of Work Life and Organizational Effectiveness in Behavior-Economic Terms." *Administrative Service Quarterly* 21:217–26.

Mobley, W. H. 1982. *Employee Turnover: Causes, Consequences, and Control.* Reading, Mass.: Addison-Wesley.

Moore, B. E., and T. L. Ross. 1978. *The Scanlon Way to Improved Productivity.* New York: Wiley, Interscience.

Nealy, S. 1963. "Pay and Benefit Preferences." *Industrial Relations* 3:17–28.

Patten, T. H. 1977. "Pay: Employee Compensation and Incentive Plans." New York: Free Press.

Salscheider, J. 1981. "Devising Pay Strategies for Diversified Companies." *Compensation Review* 58, no. 6:15–24.

Stata, R., and M. A. Maidique. 1980. "Bonus System for Balanced Strategy." *Harvard Business Review* 58, no. 6:156–63.

Steele, F. 1975. *The Open Organization.* Reading, Mass.: Addison-Wesley.

Vroom, V. H. 1964. *Work and Motivation.* New York: Wiley.

Walton, R. E. 1980. "Establishing and Maintaining High Commitment Work Systems." In *The Organization Life Cycle,* ed. J. R. Kimberly, R. N. Miles, and associates. San Francisco: Jossey-Bass.

Whyte, W. F., ed. 1955. *Money and Motivation: An Analysis of Incentives in Industry.* New York: Harper.

Gainsharing

Tove Hammer

Of the different gainsharing plans, the Scanlon Plan is the best known and the one to have received the most research attention. Other programs, such as the Rucker and Improshare Plans, have not been studied extensively. However, a fair amount of descriptive material is available to allow a comparison of the different plans' features.

From J. P. Campbell & R. J. Campbell (Eds.), *Productivity in Organizations.* 1989. Reprinted by permission.

It should be noted that gainsharing plans bearing the same name take on many forms, because the plans are tailored to meet the needs of the organizations in which they are installed (see Cummings and Molloy, 1977; Frost, Wakeley, and Ruh, 1974; Schuster, 1984b; Lawler, 1986). The common features of gainsharing plans are a management philosophy of worker participation in decision making and two structural characteristics: a bonus payment formula and a committee system established to facilitate worker participation and adopt productivity improvement suggestions when worker involvement is part of the plan design.

The Scanlon Plan

The Scanlon Plan was developed in the 1930s by Joseph Scanlon, a union leader in the steel industry, as a mechanism to turn around financially threatened plants. It gained widespread attention several years later when data showed that it could also make financially healthy companies healthier. (The history of the plan can be found in Davenport, 1950; Frost, Wakeley, and Ruh, 1974; Goodman, Wakeley, and Ruh, 1972; White, 1979.)

The philosophical foundation given to the plan is the premise that all people have needs for psychological growth and development and are capable of and willing to fulfill those needs in their employer's service if they are allowed the opportunity to participate in organizational decision making and if they are equitably compensated for the participation (see Frost, Wakeley, and Ruh, 1974; Lesieur, 1958; McGregor, 1960). This philosophy follows the basic unitarist line, with the exception of the caveat stipulating a financial return to the employee for the effort and intelligence generated through need fulfillment.

From the plan's philosophy comes the structure that allows participation to take place: a series of shop-floor (and office) level *production committees* with rank-and-file representation that meet periodically to evaulate and act on suggestions contributed from individual employees on methods to improve productivity and eliminate waste, and plantwide *screening committees* with joint union-management representation that act on suggestions exceeding certain cost limits, adjudicate work-group boundary disputes caused by suggestions, review current business problems and formulate general long-range plans for improving productivity, and administer the bonus plan.

The bonus component is designed to reward cooperation and to create a unified interest group working toward common goals. Bonuses are therefore paid on a plantwide basis, monthly or quarterly. The common Scanlon Plan formula uses the ratio of labor costs to the sales value of production to calculate deviations from a base or norm period. Productivity will have increased if the sales value of production has increased at a faster rate (or decreased at a slower rate) than labor costs. (For details on the use of the formula, see Geare, 1976; Nightingale and Long, 1984; Puckett, 1958; Schuster, 1984b.) It is not unusual to find expanded formulas in operation that include other factors over which workers have control, such as materials and energy (see Frost, Wakeley, and Ruh, 1974). Usually, the bonus pool generated through labor cost savings is split twenty-five–seventy-five between the company and its work force (which includes *all* employees). From the employee portion, a percentage is kept in reserve to offset time periods without productivity gains. At the end of the fiscal year, the remainder of the reserves is distributed to the work force.

Implicit in the Scanlon Plan is a recognition of organized labor. The plan is used primarily in unionized firms to build and strengthen labor-management cooperation, and it functions best with a strong local union and a management that accepts collective bargaining as a legitimate mechanism for controlling labor-management conflicts and solving interest-group disputes (Driscoll, 1979).

The Rucker Plan

The Rucker Plan, designed by Allen Rucker in the 1930s, covers hourly employees and involves a more sophisticated measure of productivity improvement but a less developed participative philosophy and structure. The bonus formula is a ratio that expresses the amount of production required for each dollar of the company's total payroll. Production value is calculated as the difference between the selling price of products and the costs of materials, supplies, and services (again, see Geare, 1976; Nightingale and Long, 1984; Schuster, 1984b, for more details and calculation examples). Of the labor cost savings, 75 percent is distributed to the workers while 25 percent is kept in a reserve pool to offset poor months. The remainder of this pool is then released to the workers at the end of the year.

The Rucker Plan has a similar structure for participation to the Scanlon Plan, but it emphasizes participation less. Some plans may have both production and screening committees; other plans have just the screening committee.

Improshare

A more recent addition to gainsharing plans, Improshare was developed by an industrial engineer, Mitchell Fein. Like the Scanlon Plan, it measures only labor costs, but it uses engineered time standards to calculate a base productivity factor. Its bonus formula is a ratio that includes the number of units produced to number of hours worked; thus it is a straight labor productivity measure (see Nightingale and Long, 1984; Schuster, 1984a, for examples). The formula can be applied to whole organizational units or groups within them. Productivity gains are split fifty-fifty between the company and its employees. Distributions are usually made on a weekly basis, which makes connections between performance and rewards more immediate than under the Scanlon and Rucker Plans.

There is no philosophy of participation inherent in the Improshare Plan. However, it is possible for organizations to add participative structures to their tailor-made version of it, and some do so (Schuster, 1984b; Lawler, 1986). Information about the exact number of companies that have tried Improshare is not available, but a recent estimate of at least 150 is given by Lawler (1986).

ON THEORIES ABOUT GAINSHARING

Gainsharing is a practice in search of profits and in need of theory. The literature has ample descriptions of various plans, prescriptions for what to do to make them succeed, and what not to do to avoid failure. The question of why they work (or do not work), or how they work, has been raised only infrequently. It is possible that theory on gainsharing is hard to come by because knowledge about the effects of contingent rewards is well developed in learning theory and in cognitive models incorporating learning theory principles. Thus it may seem obvious how the programs work. However, the gainsharing philosophy, at least in Scanlon Plans, goes far beyond individual workers' subjective expected utility calculations. A brief review of the available models, all of which come from the Scanlon Plan literature, follows.

Theoretical explanations for Scanlon Plan success in the 1970s centered on the relative importance of worker participation and bonus payments. Frost, Wakeley, and Ruh (1974) gave most of the weight to the presumed intrinsic value of participation, which was reinforced by bonus payments and workers' perceptions of being equitably rewarded for extra effort. Geare (1976) argued to the contrary: employees exert extra effort to improve organizational productivity because they get paid for it. For Geare, participation had an auxiliary effect because it focuses on the day-to-day activities of immediate concern to workers. Cummings and Molloy (1977) listed a number of motivational features of the plan that emphasize benefits made available by participation (skill utilization, fulfillment of higher-order needs, worker control over the labor process). In addition, they argued, gainsharing works because it increases labor-management trust and two-way communication, improves work-group cohesion and group pressure on individuals to perform, and reinforces worker effort by bonus payments. The extrinsic rewards help to strengthen worker perceptions of effort-reward contingencies and beliefs about labor-management equity.

Goodman and Moore (1976) moved beyond lists of general motivators and global worker responses to them to focus on a subset of psychological processes believed to operate in gainsharing. They used expectancy theory to explain workers' beliefs about the personal utility of the Scanlon Plan, assuming that subjective expected utilities would determine the extent of active participation in gainsharing programs. They were not able to predict perceptions of effort-performance (in their case, *effort* meant *participation*) and performance-outcome contingencies from a series of individual, interpersonal, and organizational-level variables. There are no further published accounts of expectancy theory as a model of how gainsharing works.

Theory development has not advanced much beyond the vague and elementary causal statements when we move into the 1980s. Bullock and Lawler (1984) developed a rudimentary model to analyze information from case studies of Scanlon Plans, which predicts plan success from the separate effects of structural variables (what is done in implementing the plan), implementation factors (how it is done), and situational variables (where it is done). However, their model is more a heuristic device for cataloging existing information and is not intended as an explanation of why the plans work or not.

The most extensive and well-designed evaluation research on the effectiveness of gainsharing plans is the recent work of Schuster (1983b, 1984a, 1984b, 1985). Unfortunately, he brings us no closer to a theoretical understanding, because his research is designed primarily to test models of labor-management collaboration. Gainsharing programs are a subset of such programs. In fact, Schuster admits to the frustration of not knowing what it is that makes the plans successful and believes that it cannot be determined from present research data. He suggests, tentatively, that an organizational commitment model may be a better fit to the data than an expectancy mode, but such a model has not yet been developed (Schuster, conversation with the author, February 13, 1986).

RESEARCH ON THE OUTCOMES OF GAINSHARING

Early Research

Empirical research on gainsharing plans is focused on Scanlon Plans. Quite detailed reviews of the early research, which is primarily case studies, are available in Schuster (1983a), Bullock and Lawler (1984), and Geare (1976) and will not be summarized here. In general, the findings are positive, showing that gainsharing is accompanied by improvements in productivity and labor relations. However, these studies are poorly designed and lack detailed statistical analyses of data used in the evaluation.

Schuster (1983b) also reviews attitude studies conducted by Ruh and his colleagues (Goodman, Wakeley, and Ruh, 1972; Ruh, Wallace, and Frost, 1973; White and Ruh, 1973) to explain how the Scanlon Plan works to increase worker effort. The results strengthen a central finding from the case studies: participation is an important feature in Scanlon Plan success. Otherwise, the data shed little light on the process questions. Neither the attitude surveys nor the case studies contain information to support the hypothesis that participation influences gainsharing plan effectiveness by releasing an untapped reservoir of worker talent and energy.

Recent Research

Recent studies move gainsharing research beyond evaluations of single cases. White (1979) used a sample of twenty-three firms to examine the importance to Scanlon Plan success of worker participation, top management support for worker participation in a gainsharing program, and company size. He found positive correlations between plan success, which was measured by judges' ratings and by whether gainsharing was still used or had been discontinued, and employees' reports of the extent of participation, as well as managerial attitudes toward worker participation.

Bullock and Lawler (1984) used thirty-three published and unpublished cases as the basis for a study describing characteristics of Scanlon Plans (unpublished cases included eleven doctoral dissertations and master's theses and one senior honor thesis completed at MIT, the academic "home" of the Scanlon Plan, from 1950 to 1961). They focused on the identification of three sets of variables hypothesized to influence Scanlon Plan success: structural factors (financial formulas, bonus shares distributed to employees, participative mechanisms used), implementation factors (presence and roles of external consultants and internal change agents, degree of worker involvement in implementation planning), and situational factors (company size, union status, technology, management style).

The results showed that two-thirds of the programs were reported as successful, with improvements in productivity, quality, cost reduction or customer service, worker attitudes, and quality of worklife. Improvements in labor-management relations and communications and cooperation between workers and managers were reported in over half the cases. In all but three cases, bonus payments and pay increases were granted based on performance improvements. The majority of plans (73 percent) used formal participative structures.

Of the situational factors believed to facilitate or hamper gainsharing plans, organization size was not important, corroborating data from White's (1979) study, but technology mattered; all but two plans were installed in manufacturing operations. Data on management style, available in eleven cases, showed that most managements were participative rather than autocratic.

More than half of the plans in the Bullock and Lawler (1984) study produced some tangible benefits to the employer, but the researchers were unable to discover what kinds of structures and processes worked best to create the results. They hypothesize that gainsharing works because it transforms individual workers, engaged in separate tasks and unaware of their interrelationships to the rest of the organization, into groups of workers with a much broader understanding of and commitment to the organization. It is the sense of a community of people and purpose that encourages employees to work smarter, even harder. This interpretation follows the original propositions about the Scanlon Plan set forth in Frost, Wakeley, and Ruh (1974).

Schuster (1983b, 1984a, 1984b) examined the effectiveness of gainsharing plans as part of a larger study of labor-management cooperation programs. Included in his sample were nine Scanlon, seven Rucker, and eight Improshare Plans, on which monthly productivity data, employment levels, and absenteeism and turnover data were collected for a period of from five to six years (Schuster, 1984b). In addition to the effectiveness measures, information was collected on methods of bonus payments, company strategies to build employee acceptance of the plans, and worker participation structures. Schuster's studies contain the best published evaluation data available on gainsharing plans on a case basis.

In the research sample, twenty-eight firms had some form of financial sharing provision (gainsharing plans and one profit-sharing plan). Of the firms for which productivity data were available, about half showed significant improvements in productivity (measured as employee output) after the introduction of the plan. In the rest, productivity was either unchanged or it declined.

Two-thirds of the firms used a plantwide distribution of bonuses, while the rest distributed bonuses to work groups. The productivity improvements occurred more often in firms with plantwide bonus systems, and Schuster (1984b) concludes that plantwide distribution is preferable to group-based distribution, in part because feelings of inequality are created when work groups receive different bonus payments.

The effects of participation are less clear. Of the seventeen sites with both employee involvement in decision making and productivity data, eight had positive changes in productivity levels after plan implementation, seven had no change, and two showed declines.

Detailed, plan-specific data are available on six Scanlon Plans, five Rucker Plans, and one Improshare Plan (Schuster, 1983b, 1984b) that allow some comparisons across plan type. They show that the Scanlon Plan appears to do the best, and keeps on doing well the longest. It is not clear whether this is due to the bonus formula, the high level of worker participation, or some unknown other factor(s). Schuster concludes that the Scanlon Plan differs from other gainsharing plans in the organizations' commitment to and institutionalization of a high level of worker involvement.

The analysis of cases in which gainsharing failed in Schuster's study demonstrates the importance of preserving labor and management equity in gainsharing. When there are very few bonus payments, programs are not successful. When management "adjusts" or "manipulates" the bonus formula without consulting (and obtaining the agreement of) labor, cooperation ceases. When management does not demonstrate its commitment to worker involvement, and—where the work force is unionized—does not work honestly with the union leadership, programs do poorly.

A Comment on Gainsharing Research

Because methodologically adequate research on gainsharing is scant and not theory-driven, it is difficult to draw confident conclusions from the empirical literature. Nevertheless, two features stand out in the empirical evaluations of gainsharing plans (in particular, of Scanlon Plans): the presence of worker participation as an almost necessary condition for success, and the absence of the wage and effort bargain as a variable of importance in explaining both successes and failures.

Given the integral part that bonus payments play in the design of these programs, and the fact that the Scanlon Plan originated in the trade union movement, where the wage and effort bargain is the crux of labor-management relations, the very secondary role ascribed to the distribution of gains in the explanations offered for productivity improvement data seems more like a decision to neglect it (Bachrach and Baratz, 1970) than a reflection of its actual power. This is probably due to the strong philosophical commitment that early Scanlon Plan followers had to participation as a solution to interest-group conflict (see Frost, Wakeley, and Ruh, 1974; McGregor, 1960). Unfortunately, the belief that worker participation is highly desirable in itself and has very high utility as a work motivator has put a disproportionate amount of research attention on it as a primary cause of productivity improvement (the exception to this is Geare, 1976), and may have served to restrict the field of alternative hypotheses.

A THEORETICAL MODEL OF THE ROLES OF PARTICIPATION AND PRODUCTIVITY BONUSES IN GAINSHARING

The research findings suggest that both bonus payments and participation have been important factors in successful gainsharing programs. It is unlikely, how-

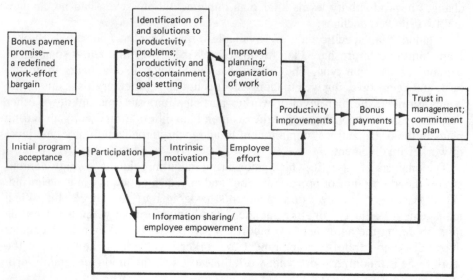

FIGURE 1
The roles of worker participation and productivity bonuses in gainsharing programs.

ever, that the documented productivity improvements have resulted solely from increases in intrinsic motivation and employee perceptions of labor-management equity. Figure 1 presents a model that describes how the bonus and participation components of gainsharing plans may operate to influence productivity levels.

The productivity bonus appears twice in the model: first as a promised outcome in a redefined labor exchange; second, as payments to employees following productivity gains. The bonus serves to secure employee acceptance of an organizational change that will, by definition, require more worker effort—physical, mental, or both. It is the promise of equity in the contractual relationship between employer and employee (the wage and effort bargain) that creates the initial acceptance of gainsharing programs.

The functions served by worker participation depend in part on the nature of the participation—on whether it is direct or indirect, restricted to short-range decisions about the immediate work situation or encompassing long-range decisions about the organization's goals and policies, the degree of control (from none to self-management) employees have over decision making, and the level at which participation takes place (from the shop floor to the board room) (Bernstein, 1976; Dachler and Wilpert, 1978). It is difficult to state exactly where the participation found in gainsharing programs falls on these four dimensions, because the nature of the participation appears to vary considerably, both between formal gainsharing plans and within plans. The large number of tailor-made plans adds to the variety of ways employees are involved in managerial decision making (Lawler, 1986; Schuster, 1984b). The only element common to the participation in the different plans is the area of decision making; workers are involved in short-range decisions about the labor process and the factors immediately surrounding it—the "nuts and bolts" of work performance.

In the traditional Scanlon Plan, participation is both direct, through the suggestion system open to all plan participants, and indirect, through representatives on production and screening committees. The degree of control that employees exercise in the decision-making process differs between the direct and indirect participation, however. Participation by suggestion making is involvement, not influence—what Bernstein (1976) calls "consultation." In contrast, worker representatives on the committees that evaluate and decide on implementation of the suggestions have both involvement and influence. They operate at the level of "coinfluence," where managers may veto decisions made by workers, but seldom do so (Bernstein, 1976). Of course, if there is a large number of production committees in an organization, a larger percentage of the work force experiences direct participation with both involvement and influence—a situation that should generate more satisfaction and a sense of empowerment in the participatory program than in a program that involves only indirect participation (IDE International Research Group, 1981). While it is difficult to be certain from the research literature, it appears that a substantial amount of worker participation in gainsharing programs is direct (see, for example, Rosenberg and Rosenstein, 1980), and at the coinfluence level. The model shown in Figure 1 is based on the assumption that the employees covered by a gainsharing plan with participation experience the direct form.

From the model, we see that participation—direct worker involvement in and influence over work process and productivity issues—leads to three outcomes. The first is the identification of obstacles to improved productivity, the solution to performance problems, and agreement on work-related actions and behavior to overcome the obstacles. The participation process results in a set of accepted, specific work performance goals.

This argument is supported by Rosenberg and Rosenstein's (1980) research, which showed that productivity improvements in a shop-floor-level participation program were related to the amount of "managing" activity the workers engaged in together with management. In particular, the more often participants met, the more their discussion focused on production-related issues, and the higher the ratio of rank-and-file workers to supervisory personnel present in the meetings, the more productivity increased. Rosenberg and Rosenstein (1980) argue that it is the output of participation activity that raises productivity, not how employees experience the participation psychologically. (By *output*, they mean the organized problem identification, problem solving, and joint labor-management decision making that takes place in productivity-focused shop-floor-level participation programs.)

From the problem-solving and goal-setting activities follow (1) improvements in the planning and organization of the work, including the removal of bottlenecks and other sources of inefficiency from the production process, and (2) increased worker effort toward the attainment of the productivity and cost-containment goals. Worker effort to perform and a more efficient organization of work lead to improvements in productivity.

Intrinsic motivation as an outcome of participation contributing to worker productivity has a more nebulous status in a gainsharing model. Intrinsically motivated behavior is the set of activities for which there is no apparent reward other than the behavior itself. Actions are motivated by people's need to feel competent and self-directed in dealing with their environment (Deci, 1975). If we accept the hypothesis that involvement in and influence over organizational decision making is intrinsically motivating, workers will be motivated to participate, but they will not necessarily be more motivated to do the work they are supposed to do at the point of production. The model therefore has a feedback loop from the experienced intrinsic motivation back to participation, but not a direct causal arrow from participation to an intrinsic motivation to engage in other forms of work.

Two arguments can be raised against this line of reasoning. The first is that participation can be viewed as an integral part of the job—a form of vertical job loading (Herzberg, 1966). The intrinsic motivation experienced as workers participate influences the work people do at the point of production. Thus intrinsic motivation belongs in a model that explains how gainsharing with participation operates to improve productivity.

It is true that in a formal participation program, worker involvement in decision making is part of the job and requires effort for which employees are compensated. But if we want to explain the processes that link participation to productivity, we need more precise descriptions of the psychological properties of our variables. In the present case, we need to separate the components of the job—that is, the *work* people are paid to do—into those directly related to, and necessary for, the production process, and those auxiliary to it. Participation is an important auxiliary function. The primary job can be done without it, but the job may be done better with it. As long as the basic work process remains the same, with participation only added to it, intrinsic motivation will not be a direct cause of work performance.

The second argument is based on the assumption that the basic jobs people do will be changed where there is gainsharing. From the evidence presented on the emergence and adoption of a new industrial relations model by Kochan, Katz, and McKersie (1986), Lawler (1986), and McKersie (1986), it appears that gainsharing is accompanied by, or accompanies, changes in job design. If the basic work process changes to include broader job scopes, longer work cycle times, decision making, and worker autonomy (the hallmarks of sociotechnical systems theory [Hackman and Oldham, 1980; Trist, 1981]), participation will be a fully integrated part of the labor process. It can then be argued that the whole job, of which participation is a part, is intrinsically motivating. That will mean that intrinsic motivation can be a direct cause of worker performance. Of course, when participation is a component of "high-involvement management," it will be difficult to separate its effects on the intrinsic motivation to work from the effects of other job components.

A third outcome of worker participation is the empowerment of nonmanagerial employees through their access to management-level information. Effective worker participation creates pressure on management to open communication and share information with labor. Information is power in organizations (Bacharach and Lawler, 1980), and extensive information sharing decreases traditional labor-management power gaps. It is easier to build mutual trust and commitment to common economic interests between labor and management when power is more evenly distributed. This is consistent with the pluralist view of labor-management collaboration.

Trust in management and commitment to gainsharing are further strengthened by the payment of bonuses. The monetary gains, and employee trust and commitment, reinforce participation. Over time, a new culture may emerge, as Lawler (1986) suggests and Schuster (1984b) implies.

The model shows how participation and productivity bonuses work together to facilitate and improve worker performance. It is also possible to have the same positive outcomes from participation without gainsharing, as long as employees can be induced to participate and convinced to adjust their expectations about the ratio of wages to effort. Rosenberg and Rosenstein (1980) demonstrated empirically that the addition of productivity bonuses to a shop-floor participation program led only to a modest increment in productivity beyond that provided by participation. Similarly, gainsharing by itself can influence performance levels if the promise of bonus payments leads to worker acceptance of higher work performance goals and management takes action to improve the planning and organization of work. The actual bonus payments balance the wage and effort bargain and reinforce the increased effort levels.

SUMMARY

Research has demonstrated that gainsharing can have positive effects on economic outcomes for both employees and employers. The use of more sophisticated research designs and statistical analyses of criterion data in the evaluation research contributes considerably to the confidence one can have in these plans.

A number of research questions are still unanswered. Some are primarily practical: for example, What kinds of plans, or combination of plan components, work best under what circumstances (see Bullock and Lawler, 1984)? The most important empirical question is still how gainsharing works to improve labor productivity. It is better to ask how than why, because the why seems to lead to studies that pit predictors against one another. Instead of investigating whether participation is more important than bonus payments, research should examine how they interact to jointly create labor productivity. The model presented here can perhaps guide such endeavors. There is no longer a need for more exploratory research on gainsharing.

A useful research design can be the longitudinal case study with repeated quantitative measures of both predictors and criteria over several years. Recent research on models of union-management collaboration demonstrates both the utility and the necessity of long-term observation and assessment (Hammer and

Stern, 1986). Schuster's (1983b; 1984a) analyses of productivity trend data support this argument.

REFERENCES

Bacharach, S. B., and Lawler, E. J. *Power and Politics in Organizations: The Social Psychology of Conflict, Coalitions, and Bargaining*. San Francisco: Jossey-Bass, 1980.

Bachrach, P., and Baratz, M. S. *Power and Poverty, Theory and Practice*. London: Oxford University Press, 1970.

Bernstein, P. *Workplace Democratization: Its Internal Dynamic*. Kent, Ohio: Kent State University Press, 1976.

Bullock, R. J., and Lawler, E. E., III. "Gainsharing: A Few Questions, and Fewer Answers." *Human Resource Management*, 1984, *23*, 23–40.

Cummings, T. G., and Molloy, E. S. *Improving Productivity and the Quality of Work Life*. New York: Praeger, 1977.

Dachler, H. P., and Wilpert, B. "Conceptual Dimensions and Boundaries of Participation in Organizations: A Critical Evaluation." *Administrative Science Quarterly*, 1978, *23* (1) 1–39.

Davenport, R. "Enterprise for Every Man." *Fortune*, 1950, *41* (1), 51–58.

Deci, E. L. *Intrinsic Motivation*. New York: Plenum Press, 1975.

Doyle, R. J. *Gainsharing and Productivity*. New York: AMACOM, 1983.

Driscoll, J. W. "Working Creatively with a Union: Lessons from the Scanlon Plan." *Organizational Dynamics*, 1979, *8*, 61–80.

Frost, C. F., Wakeley, J. H., and Ruh, R. A. *The Scanlon Plan for Organization Development: Identity, Participation, and Equity*. East Lansing: Michigan State University Press, 1974.

Geare, A. J. Productivity from Scanlon-Type Plans. *Academy of Management Review*, 1976, *1* (3), 99–108.

Goodman, P. S., and Moore, B. E. "Factors Affecting Acquisition of Beliefs About a New Reward System." *Human Relations*, 1976, *29* (6), 571–588.

Goodman, R., Wakeley, J., and Ruh, R. "What Employees Think of the Scanlon Plan." *Personnel*, 1972, *49* (5), 22–29.

Hackman, J. R., and Oldham, G. R. *Work Redesign*. Reading, Mass.: Addison-Wesley, 1980.

Hammer, T. H., and Stern, R. N. "A Yo-Yo Model of Cooperation: Union Participation in Management at the Rath Packing Company." *Industrial and Labor Relations Review*, 1986, *39* (3), 337–349.

Herzberg, F. *Work and the Nature of Man*. New York: New American Library, 1966.

IDE International Research Group. *Industrial Democracy in Europe*. Oxford, England: Clarendon Press, 1981.

Kochan, T. A., Katz, H. C., and McKersie, R. B. *The Transformation of American Industrial Relations*. New York: Basic Books, 1986.

Lawler, E. E., III. *High-Involvement Management: Participative Strategies for Improving Organizational Performance*. San Francisco, Calif.: Jossey-Bass, 1986.

Lesieur, F. G. (ed.). *The Scanlon Plan: A Frontier in Labor-Management Cooperation*. Cambridge, Mass.: MIT Press, 1958.

McGregor, D. *The Human Side of Enterprise*. New York: McGraw-Hill, 1960.

McKersie, R. B. "The Promise of Gainsharing." *ILR Report*, 1986, *24* (1), 7–11.

Nightingale, D. V., and Long, R. J. *Gain and Equity Sharing*. Ottawa, Canada, Ministry of Labour, 1984.

Puckett, E. S. "Measuring Performance Under the Scanlon Plan." In F. G. Lesieur (ed.), *The Scanlon Plan: A Frontier in Labor-Management Cooperation*. Cambridge, Mass.: MIT Press, 1958.

Rosenberg, R. D., and Rosenstein, E. "Participation and Productivity: An Empirical Study." *Industrial and Labor Relations Review*, 1980, *33*, 355–367.

Ruh, R. A., Wallace, R. L., and Frost, C. F. "Management Attitudes and the Scanlon Plan." *Industrial Relations*, 1973, *12*, 282–288.

Schuster, M. H. "The Impact of Union-Management Cooperation on Productivity and Employment." *Industrial and Labor Relations Review*, 1983a, *36*, 415–430.

Schuster, M. H. "Forty Years of Scanlon Plan Research: A Review of the Descriptive and Empirical Literature." In C. Crouch and F. Heller (eds.), *International Yearbook of Organizational Democracy*. 1983b, *1*, 53–71.

Schuster, M. H. "The Scanlon Plan: A Longitudinal Analysis." *Journal of Applied Behavioral Science*, 1984a, *20* (1), 23–28.

Schuster, M. H. *Union-Management Cooperation: Structure, Process, and Impact*. Kalamazoo, Mich.: Upjohn Institute, 1984b.

Schuster, M. H. "Gainsharing Issues for Senior Managers." Unpublished manuscript, School of Management, Syracuse University, 1985.

Trist, E. "The Evolution of Sociotechnical Systems." In A. Van de Ven and W. Joyce (eds.), *Perspectives on Organizational Design and Behavior*. New York: Wiley-Interscience, 1981.

White, J. K. "The Scanlon Plan: Causes and Correlates of Success." *Academy of Management Journal*, 1979, *22* (2), 292–312.

White, J. K., and Ruh, R. A. "Effects of Personal Values on the Relationship Between Participation and Job Attitudes," *Administrative Science Quarterly*, 1973, *18* (4), 506–514.

QUESTIONS FOR DISCUSSION

1 As a manager, how would you use a knowledge of the factors affecting reward allocation to distribute organizational rewards more effectively?

2 Given the causes of reward displacement discussed by Kerr, what problems might you anticipate in trying to remedy the situation by altering the reward system?

3 How do Kerr's remedies specifically deal with the causes of rewarding A while hoping for B? What other remedies might be suggested?

4 If you were the top executive of a newly formed organization deciding on compensation policies, on what criteria would you base a choice between the compensation design options presented by Lawler? Why?

5 What implications do Kerr's observations suggest for each of the approaches to compensation discussed by Lawler?

6 Discuss the managerial implications of the Pearce article. How would you adapt your management practices to be consistent with both reinforcement theory and Pearce's recommendations?

7 What organizational factors would impose obstacles which inhibited the effective functioning of gainsharing programs in organizations?

8 How would you go about introducing a gainsharing plan into an organization? Discuss the steps you would take and the timing of each step?

9 What criteria would you use to evaluate the success of a gainsharing program?

12

COMMUNICATION, FEEDBACK, AND MOTIVATION

For the final chapter in this section we look at a topic that is inextricably linked to motivation: communication. It is difficult to think about affecting another person's motivation without considering communication, and likewise it is hard to imagine how communication can take place without considering its motivational bases. For our purposes in this chapter, however, we are primarily focusing on the former rather than the latter situation; that is, we are examining how communication impacts motivation. Thus, communication can be thought of as an action that either facilitates and increases motivation or, conversely, that interferes with and decreases motivation. In work settings we seldom find that communication has a neutral effect on motivation.

In the first selection, by Sullivan, the author discussed several different roles that language used by managers can play in influencing the motivation of employees. Utilizing speech act theory, Sullivan classifies the functions of language as those communication acts that reduce uncertainty, those that facilitate the making of meaning or sense, and those that establish and develop human bonding. It is his thesis that most motivational approaches relating to the work situation typically overemphasize the first of these functions—communication that reduces uncertainty—while tending to ignore the other two functions. He contends that if managers' communication acts are to be maximally successful in motivating employees, all three functions must be combined in an integrated manner.

In almost any analysis of communication in organizational settings, increased feedback is stressed as a method to improve communication because it supplies useful information and reduces ambiguities. Seldom, though, do we consider the issue of whether explicit feedback—even if ostensibly "positive"—sometimes might have negative consequences for the motivation of those who receive it.

This, essentially, is the question examined in the second article, by Pearce and Porter. They describe the results of a study that investigated the effects of a newly installed performance appraisal system designed to provide more precise and systematic—and, therefore, supposedly more useful—feedback to employees than had been the case with the prior system. The findings showed that the subsequent attitudes of those employees receiving explicit "satisfactory" ratings were, in fact, negatively affected. Under the old "looser" and informal rating system, they could convince themselves that they were probably above average in their performance since they were not confronted with formal "hard" evidence to the contrary. The study therefore raises some interesting points regarding the possible unintended motivation effects of supposedly "good" communication practices.

Three Roles of Language in Motivation Theory

Jeremiah J. Sullivan

Motivation theories describe an employee's mental state and the external influences on it of such things as job characteristics, incentives, organizational culture, and so forth. This paper presents a theory of motivational language usage by managers that extends and broadens current theory. Motivational language theory is based on several important presuppositions. First, what a manager says to an employee affects employee motivation. Second, managerial communication can be categorized in terms of three kinds of speech acts: (a) those that reduce employee uncertainty and increase his or her knowledge; (b) those that implicitly reaffirm the employee's sense of self worth as a human being; (c) and those that facilitate the employee's construction of cognitive schemas and scripts, which will be used to guide the employee in his or her work. Third, current motivation theories focus almost solely on uncertainty-reducing managerial speech acts. Fourth, managerial influence on employee motivation through communication is a function of the variety of speech acts that are employed. The more varied the speech acts, the greater the likelihood that the manager will influence employee motivation. If multiple language tools are available, the manager should use them to attain the maximum control of the motivational communications process.

The focus of current theory on motivation as informing—the reduction of employee uncertainty—is described. Next, managerial communication as meaning making and schema fostering is described. Then the third kind of motivational language, which reaffirms human bonds and self-worth, is introduced. The three types of speech acts are linked to psycholinguistics and speech act theory by their labels as perlocutionary, locutionary, and illocutionary. Motivational language theory is then reviewed in terms of current research findings. A model is presented, hypotheses are generated, and testing of the theory is discussed.

MOTIVATING AS INFORMING

Information (defined as message content that reduces uncertainty) is believed to be crucial in the motivation process. Arousal theories of motivation focus on need-deficiencies in workers and the information that managers supply to the worker to reduce uncertainty regarding the correction of the deficiencies or imbalances. In addition, research has emphasized the perceived expectations of co-workers and supervisors as the causes of arousal. This approach looks at the connotations embedded in communication and at how managers can inform workers so that evaluation apprehension can be reduced or social acceptance facilitated with a corresponding increase in motivation (Salancik & Pfeffer, 1977, 1978).

From *Academy of Management Review*, 1988, **13**(1), 104–115. Reprinted by permission.

Other work concentrates on uncertainty reduction communications of managers used to inform employees about a self-esteem-task match (Korman, 1976) or a growth need-job characteristics match (Hackman & Oldham, 1980).

Choice theories of motivation stress goal setting, expectancies, operant conditioning, and equity theory. If workers' knowledge of specific, difficult goals is developed, they tend to do better than if they are given either no goal information or vague information (Locke, 1978; Yukl & Latham, 1978). Apparently, workers seek knowledge to reduce uncertainty, and they perform better if they are informed by supervisors. Expectancy theory and operant conditioning focus on information to reduce reward uncertainty instead of process and goal uncertainty (Mitchell, 1982). Finally, equity theory presumes a demand on the worker's part for information about fairness (Carrell & Dittrich, 1978).

Assume that a manager has studied current motivation theories in an effort to motivate a worker. Depending on the situation and the worker, the manager's objective might be:

To communicate with the worker in order to learn his or her needs and then to tell the worker how those needs can be satisfied. Job enrichment, for example, involves changing the nature of the job. Managerial communication of the change provides information to the employee that reduces his or her uncertainty about whether a need for challenging creative work will be met.

To inform the employee about mismatches in his or her cognitions and behaviors and point out how the worker can establish balance and consistency.

To inform the worker of the goals and data that facilitate the accomplishment of goals (e.g., feedback).

To provide information on the costs and benefits of work behavior.

All of these communications are required by motivation theories, and all of these theories involve the process of providing information to reduce worker uncertainty. All theories presume, first, that the worker is uncertain about how to satisfy needs, restore imbalances, accomplish goals, act in accordance with values, or maximize utility, and, second, that the worker will seek or accept uncertainty-reducing information.

THE LANGUAGE OF MOTIVATION

The underlying presupposition of current motivation theories is that language can transmit information to reduce uncertainty, that is, to increase a worker's knowledge that his or her view of the world corresponds to the way the world really is. A worker who has only a general notion of his or her job responsibilities is eager to establish specific goals to increase his or her understanding of what is expected. Goal-setting theory, for example, views workers—and all humans—as creatures trying endlessly to turned flawed beliefs into perfect knowledge. Just as philosophers have wanted to define themselves as truth seekers, so theorists in the social sciences have sought to define people as knowledge acquirers. Theories of motivation have this definition built into them, and they presume that the function of language is to facilitate the belief-toward-knowledge process. The theories assume that uncertainty-reducing language is the primary form of communication in organizational settings where workers are motivated.

In addition to reducing uncertainty, however, language has other motivational functions that theories ignore. By examining the other functions of language, one can see how narrow motivation theories are and how they can be expanded. One can also see new theories emerge.

MEANING-MAKING LANGUAGE

One use of language that is almost ignored by motivation theorists is the establishment of meaning. Language as a meaning-making tool helps workers construct mental models of reality. Workers do seek information to develop a better understanding of how their needs can be met, how their expectations can be developed and fulfilled, how their values can be carried out, and how their purposes can be made more specific. But they also want to construct an interpretation of their world that makes sense. Managers must foster, allow, and even endure, the meaning making that all humans do. To motivate is to facilitate the communication that leads to meaning making: the informal small talk, gossip, narratives, myth making, and account giving that generally are considered *down time*. These forms of communication may be just as important as the uncertainty-reducing performance appraisal session or the structured feedback program.

Meaningfulness

The idea of work as meaningful is not new, but motivation theorists look at the meaning work gives workers in a special way. Steers and Porter (1975) asserted that work is meaningful to workers:

As a tool to obtain extrinsic and intrinsic rewards.
As an exercise in social interaction and integration.
As a mechanism for symbolically identifying status or rank.
As a means to establish an identity in terms of societal purpose, role, or value commitment.

All of these approaches treat work as a tool for accomplishing some end. Work, however, can be an end in itself, the behavioral counterpart to an internal sense the worker has of his or her place in the world. In this latter view, work is not an instrumental act, but what one does as part of the ongoing process of constructing a specific sense of one's place in the world. This approach emphasizes the nonutilitarian presentness of work, not its futureness, as does Steers and Porter's.

The other extensive discussion of meaningfulness in the literature is Hackman and Lawler's (1971; Hackman and Oldham, 1980; Hackman, Oldham, Janson, & Purdy, 1974). They define a meaningful job as one that tests a variety of skills, that results in some significant and noticeable change, and that is considered by the worker as worthwhile. This implies that workers view work as an action that should be characterized by involvement and important behavior. This is not the same approach discussed here, in which the meaning a worker constructs about work cannot be defined and prescribed ahead of time by theorists. The *meaningfulness* construct developed and tested by Hackman and Oldham (1975) may, in fact, be that of some American workers, but this occurrence does not justify the presumption that *all* workers make sense of their lot in similar ways. Theorists who hold the Hackman and Oldham perspective describe motivational communication as the information that increases a worker's beliefs that the job will be involving and important. This approach is appropriate for some workers, but managerial language of this kind will not work well with workers who have constructed different meanings. For these workers, communication that facilitates different meaning making is in order.

Managerial Influence on the Construction of Meaning

What employees perceive in organizations is colored not only by what they see and hear, but also by the mental guidelines they have constructed over time in order to help them interpret their situations (Downey & Brief, 1986; Staw, 1975). In a study of CEO's, for example, executive decisions were based in large part on strongly held beliefs concerning the appropriateness of certain organizational structures (Donaldson & Lorsch, 1984). In effect, the CEOs were acting in response to sets of meanings they had constructed. Workers often do the same thing, using sets of meanings developed mainly through informal communications with supervisors and coworkers.

Both CEO's and workers use communication to acquire uncertainty-reducing information about their environments and their place in it, but they also use interactions as a source of meaning-making raw material for constructing their mental models or schemas. Work behavior depends on both the information that is acquired and the meanings that are constructed. CEOs and workers are impelled by the real environment and by their own constructed vision of that environment. Sometimes one set of knowledge or beliefs dominates, sometimes the other, and sometimes both sets are important.

A *schema* can be described as a mental map or network in which concepts are organized into a systematic pattern (Park, Sims, & Motowidlo, 1986). A self-constructed body of beliefs is used to impose structure and meaningfulness on social situations and encounters. As such, mental models serve as a basis for interpretation of information, events, and people, and for subsequent behavior (Gioia & Poole, 1984). A *script* is a kind of a schema. It provides step-by-step guidelines for action. For supervisors, the major function of meaning-making language is to facilitate the construction of schemas and scripts in subordinates so that these models guide work behavior in ways that are useful to the organization. Rarely do supervisors consciously direct their communications along these lines; instead, they foster schema construction unintentionally through countless informal interactions in which they simply play the role the organization has asked them to adopt, as upholders of the values embodied in the organizational culture.

Job Satisfaction Schemas

Job satisfaction is the result of the positive feelings and beliefs regarding job characteristics and job-related experiences held by employees (Locke, 1976). It is developed by mentally challenging work, good work conditions, high and equitable rewards, and good opportunities for promotion. Job satisfaction reduces absenteeism and turnover, although it does not necessarily increase performance (Landy & Trumbo, 1976; Locke, 1976). Job satisfaction can be viewed as part of a work schema that is constructed by employees, a schema that might involve, for example, regular attendance. Other schemas that are not focused on job satisfaction would be associated with greater work effort and better performance.

Rewards contingent on performance may increase job satisfaction (Cherrington, Reitz, & Scott, 1971), although the simple presence of the reward may be enough (Gupta, 1980). It may be, however, that neither performance actions nor reward information is the source of job satisfaction. An alternative view based on motivational language theory is that workers who see themselves as well-rewarded, high performers tend to develop job satisfaction schemas. Managers who employ meaning-making communication that stresses a view of the organization as one in which all employees are hard workers and good performers could facilitate worker construction of a satisfaction schema.

If this is the case, then the satisfaction schema legitimizes regular attendance, but not necessarily harder work. Indeed, the performance schema on which the satisfaction schema is based would make harder work seem meaningless. Satisfaction may be the result of a positive performance/reward schema, a mental construction developed in informal, meaning-making communications with managers, rather than (or as well as) the direct outcome of real rewards or real performance.

Motivational language theory (MLT) helps to explain the nature of satisfaction in an organization by focusing on communications between supervisors and workers. Managers who try to get employees to feel good about their jobs by giving them information about rewards, some of which are tied to performance, are using uncertainty-reducing language to establish an association in the employees' minds between satisfaction, rewards, and performance. A correlation between satisfaction and performance will exist. But managers who, through communication, facilitate employee schemas in which workers become convinced that they are inherently praiseworthy will see an improvement in employee satisfaction, but not necessarily improved performance. MLT directs attention to the nature of managerial communication as an explanation of the complex relationship between job satisfaction and performance.

Uncertainty Reducing vs. Meaning Making

A motivational communication that reduces uncertainty, the kind implicitly called for in current theories of motivation, is very much like a formal interview in which the worker questions the manager to obtain information about the relationship between work and his or her attainment of goals. In meaning-making communication, the worker and manager interact as a matter of routine, informal role play. The manager does not intentionally try to reduce the worker's uncertainty; instead, he or she develops his or her role as a representative of the organization's beliefs, values, and goals over time. When interacting with workers, he or she shares the meaning attached to the role, and they in turn develop appropriate (from the organization's point of view) schemas and scripts to guide work behavior. Notice that the manager does not consciously use meaning-making language to inspire workers; what he or she has consciously developed is role-playing ability. This role playing, when performed without conscious effort, leads to managerial language usage that may foster suitable meaning making by workers. The successful motivator not only purveys the correct uncertainty-reducing information to workers at the right moment, he or she also plays the correct role in an organization that has set roles for its managers. This correct role inspires worker construction of appropriate schemas and scripts.

Research on managers' motivational communication has focused on desire to interact; communicative initiative; receptiveness to communication; and information formality, direction, overload, and accuracy (Penley & Hawkins, 1985; Schuler, 1979). Little work has related communication to mental models and performance. One attempt by Schuler (1979) focused on role perceptions as mediators between supervisory communication and performance. He found that low role conflict and low role ambiguity led to improved performance. In terms of the theory of language usage proposed here, supervisory communication that facilitates the construction of a strongly delineated, dominant work schema and script leads to improved performance. This schema dampens the employee's sense of role conflict and ambiguity. In Schuler's formulation, workers construct schemas in response to the employees-reducing information provided by managers about tasks, about the integration of tasks, and about rules governing behavior at work and reporting to work. Here, however, the role play work schemas generally are developed in association with meaning-making interactions between supervisors and employees. Schemas, of course, can come from both uncertainty-reducing *and* meaning-making language. The claim here is that dominant schemas, the ones that guide role formation, and in turn much of work behavior, are constructed in association with the informal meaning-making talk of supervisors rather than their uncertainty-reducing communication.

SPEECH ACTS

The differing functions of language can be described in terms of speech act theory (Austen, 1962), which classifies the uses of utterance in terms of *locutionary* acts, focused on the meaning of the words; *illocutionary* acts, focused on what the speaker is doing while talking; and *perlocutionary* acts, what the speaker hopes to accomplish. Current motivation theory emphasizes the perlocutionary use of language. Meaning-making language focuses on its locutionary nature. The third use of language, as a human communion, emphasizes its illocutionary dimension.

If a manager says to a subordinate, "Ed, I'm just so happy to tell you that your chances of promotion will be good if you do well on this project," what is being said and done in terms of motivating? As perlocutionary communication, the words reduce the worker's uncertainty about the relationship between an action and the attainment of a need, value, or goal, and they trigger a mental calculation that presumably results in an intention to expend a specific level of effort. Most motivation theories treat utterance in this way.

However, this communication also can serve to facilitate meaning. In the meaning-making perspective on motivation, the emphasis shifts to the sentence's locutionary nature. The worker can use the information in the sentence to construct a view of himself within the work context. With this building material, he may create a schema of himself as a specific part within a specific whole, possibly as a *reasoning machine* that acts on and is aided by a rational environment (Berger, Berger, & Kellner, 1974). To a person guided by a vision of himself as a reasoning machine, work becomes an appropriate link between internal reasoning and the external rational context. This kind of understanding is congenial to the manager. Notice, however, that the manager's focus in this case was not perlocutionary. It was not directed toward an outcome. Instead, his speech was primarily locutionary, stressing in an informal, nonpurposeful way, the way the world might be. The locutionary use of motivational language can be as effective as the perlocutionary use.

The third dimension of motivational language as human communion is illocutionary. Illocutionary communication says nothing meaningful about the world, nor is it instrumental. It is an end in itself, an act of sharing unique to human beings. In the sentence above, the manager could be expressing joy in a way that allows the worker to share it with him or her. The manager has learned that simply by sharing his or her humanness with workers, they often will perform well. It's not a case of a manager saying, "Today, I'll be human." He or she simply behaves in a natural, empathetic manner.

Perlocutionary communication by managers helps employees answer the question, "What is or will be the nature of my work environment, given my work behavior and the management's behavior?" Locutionary speech helps the employee construct a set of meanings to answer the question, "What should I think, feel, and do?" Illocutionary language between managers and employees makes work a part of the employee's human bonding. It does not reduce uncertainty or foster meaning-making: It simply affirms human existence.

MOTIVATIONAL COMMUNICATIONS RESEARCH

Research on managers' and leaders' communications with employees has focused, first, on providing uncertainty-reducing information regarding tasks, production, performance, goals, innovations, policies, rules, and careers (Penley & Hawkins, 1985). A second focus is on communications that offer encouragement, show concern, and so forth. These are sometimes labeled *consideration* communications (Stogdill, 1970). Together task-oriented and consideration-oriented messages form the universe of types of utterance in managerial, motivational, and leadership research. Often, these types are broken down into finer categories, such as in Penley and Hawkins' five dimensions, or Roberts and O'Reilly's multidimensional list (Roberts & O'Reilly, 1974). In research on leader-follower communications, however, only the two categories are examined. Consideration messages in themselves reduce uncertainty, and thus they really may not be a separate type (Penley & Hawkins, 1985; Weiss, 1978).

Motivational language theory, which emerges out of speech act theory in linguistics and its three categories of utterance, describes three types of supervisor-subordinate communications. The first, perlocutionary, corresponds to task-oriented and uncertainty-reducing communications. Illocutionary communications correspond to consideration messages in their bonding function. Locutionary utterances are new to the managerial communications literature.

Research has noted the tendency of employees to construct their own version of work, and to respond to their version as if it were true (Feldman & Brett, 1983; Louis, 1980; Van Maanen, 1978). This sense making establishes meaning, and although it can be the result of both the perlocutionary and illocutionary utterances of supervisors, it is mainly the result of the meaning-making interactions of employees with their supervisors (Palermo, 1983). Supervisors' language usage in these interactions is locutionary; it facilitates cognitive schema and script construction rather than uncertainty reduction or bonding. Thus, motivational language theory adds a third conceptualization to the model of managerial communications, thereby making research paradigms consistent with the speech act model of linguistic theory.

THEORETICAL MODEL AND HYPOTHESES

Figure 1 illustrates the process through which managerial speech acts can lead to motivated work and improved performance. The dotted lines linking schemas to other mental entities show how these constructions can occur in response to both perlocutionary and illocutionary speech actions. However, most worker schema building occurs in the informal communications of managers with employees; these communications will be laden with the small talk, managerial role playing, account giving, folklore, myth making, and use of metaphoric language which constitute locutionary language usage.

A number of hypotheses emerge from the theoretical model.

Hypothesis 1. When the three kinds of speech acts are mutually supportive, motivation will be greater.

Japanese management studies suggest that the use of different kinds of language tend to have a strong influence on employee motivation (Nakane, 1973; Pascale & Athos, 1981). Japanese managers spend enormous amounts of time in informal communication with workers and are expected to be genuinely interested in them as people. If speech act usage is expanded in non-Japanese organizations, similar results could be expected.

Hypothesis 2. The use of perlocutionary language alone will not have the impact on motivation that coordinated use of three speech acts will.

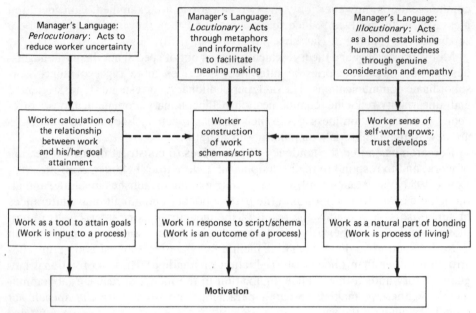

FIGURE 1
The impact of managerial language usage on work.

The effect for perlocutionary language will not be as great as the effect of all three speech acts in interaction. A manager who reduces a worker's uncertainty about goals, tasks, needs, and so forth will not influence motivation as much as he or she can within a context of managerial meaning making and bonding. This same hypothesis also could be made for the other two speech acts.

> *Hypothesis 3.* An organization in which managerial role conflict and ambiguity are low also will be characterized by a high ratio of informal to total communications. The result will be strong work schemas and scripts and improved motivation.

An organization with a clear sense of its mission and how to attain its goals develops managers who know what roles they are expected to play and who will play their expected roles all the time. They will seek out information opportunities to "talk company" with employees, and their language will help the employee to make sense of his or her place in the organization. This will "turn off" a number of workers, and they will quit their jobs, leaving those who have accepted their supervisors' meaning-making "raw material" as meaningful.

> *Hypothesis 4.* Illocutionary speech acts that display consideration and empathy will inspire a manager-worker bonding based on trust and a sense of worker self-worth. Motivation will improve.

A manager who treats his or her communication with workers as an end in itself also will show an interest in the workers as people worthy of consideration and empathy. Therefore, employees will develop a sense of self-worth, trust, and a bonding with the manager. Work motivation will be a natural part of the bond.

IMPLICATIONS AND TESTING

Goal-Setting Theory

Goal-setting theory has been the best predictor of motivated effort and performance (Miner, 1984; Pinder, 1984). According to one of its developers, the theory is successful because goals are the most important factor in an employee's intent to work hard and long—it is more important than needs, values, situations, or tasks (Locke & Henne, 1986). The impact of goals comes from the rational nature of people, who generally are calculative and utilitarian (Locke, 1983). Motivational language theory sees humans in a broader perspective—as creatures focused not only on *utility,* but also on *meaning* and *bonding* (Sullivan, 1986). From this perspective, goal-setting theory implicitly and explicitly calls for managerial communications with employees to foster all three results. When employees encounter utility, meaning, and bonding through hard work, they are likely to keep working hard.

Goal-setting theory involves more than setting goals; it also requires acceptance and implementation (Locke & Latham, 1984). Although managers' uncertainty-reducing communications fulfill the goal-setting requirement, additional meaning-making and bonding communications lead to acceptance and implementation. The few studies conducted along these lines support this assertion. Supportive (bonding) communications during goal implementation lead to better performance (Latham & Saari, 1979). As for meaning-making communications, Erez and Zidon (1984) found that *goal acceptance* mediates between goal difficulty and performance. Employees' goal acceptance could depend on their supervisors' meaning-making communications. In sum, the success of goal-setting theory may be due to its tendency to encourage multiple speech acts by managers during the goal setting, goal acceptance, and goal implementation process.

Job Characteristics and Social Information Processing

Glick, Jenkins, and Gupta (1986) found a relationship between actual job characteristics and employee effort, which implies that uncertainty-reducing information unmediated by cognitive reconstruction has a direct impact on work behavior. They also found evidence for the social information processing model, in which acquired job information is cognitively transformed to fit in a social context. Such transformation is facilitated by locutionary discourse on the part of supervisors. Guidance from the schemas and scripts that result from the transformation also influences motivated effort and performance. Motivational language theory supports the dual findings of Glick et al. (1986), and it offers a description of the communications process that uses both facts *and* reconstructed reality. Different speech acts by managers influence the differential use of information by employees. Perlocutionary utterance fosters the acquisition of job characteristics data and its impact on effort. Locutionary utterance promotes cognitive transformation of the data to make it meaningful.

Commitment and Performance Appraisal

Committed employees remain in an organizational role and fulfill role requirements (Cummings, 1983). According to motivational language theory, commitment can be the result of a supervisor's uncertainty-reducing information on such things as tenure and long-term rewards. It also can result from bonding communications or from managerial facilitation of employee schemas. Thus, commitment can be a rational, calculative, instrumental behavior; an emotion-laden behavior; or a cognitively constructed meaningful action. Cummings (1983) noted that commitment is a substitute for performance appraisal systems as directive and control mechanisms. According to motivational language theory, commitment that results from schemas fostered by managerial locutionary or illocutionary utterance will direct and control. This process is followed in Japanese companies, in which formal control mechanisms are weak. However, commitment that results from uncertainty-reducing communications (perlocutionary) is a rational, calculated, instrumental act requiring ongoing uncertainty reduction from every possible source, including supervisors and performance appraisal systems. Committed employees and managers who generally use perlocutionary discourse will require more uncertainty reduction and, thus, will need the information from appraisal and control systems. Managers who encourage employees to be instrumental will find that their workers' need for uncertainty reduction is almost infinite. Motivational language theory hypothesizes that the nature and strength of performance appraisal and control systems are, in part, a function of the dominant speech act of the supervisor's discourse and its impact on employee commitment.

Using Multiple Language Functions

MLT proposes that all the functions of language are likely to have a greater positive impact on work behavior than the use of one function alone. It questions the effectiveness of management theories that implicitly call for one kind of utterance from managers. Theory Z, for example, prescribes managerial locutionary discourse that focuses on helping employees construct loyalty schemas. Social learning theories set up managers as models who nonverbally communicate, in a perlocutionary manner, information to reduce an employee's uncertainty on how to act. Other theories require only supportive, illocutionary communications from managers to motivate workers. All of these theories require supervisors to use language in a restrictive manner. Motivational language theory calls for the opposite; all functions of language must be combined in a coherent discourse in order to have the greatest impact on employee motivation.

Testing the Theory

Are speech acts independent of each other? How does a researcher determine the nature of the act? A predominantly *emic* (rather than an *etic*) approach is required (Pike, 1967). Emic research focuses on the identification of the concepts and theories held by subjects rather than on those developed by the researcher. In the case of MLT, employees must tell whether a given communication or set of communications with a supervisor reduced uncertainty, helped the employee make sense of his or her lot, or developed bonding. Indicators of perlocutionary speech acts—those that increase the employee's knowledge—are employees' perceptions that they have provided information on tasks, goals, policies, rewards, performance, and so forth. Locutionary speech acts—those that help the employee construct a coherent, meaning-laden vision of work—are indicated by employee perceptions that a supervisor "made a lot of sense." Specifically, the supervisor represented and upheld organizational values, made the complex and the confusing appear simple and clear, showed that a job made sense in terms of the unit's and the organization's functioning, and sought out informal opportunities to exchange ideas and attitudes. Illocutionary speech acts—those that are an act of sharing rather than a tool for representing—are indicated by employee perceptions that a supervisor tended to establish a bond with them by revealing inner feelings, showing consideration for others, relieving feelings of isolation and alienation, and sharing a common vision.

Indicators of each speech act can be collected in field settings, and speech acts can be related to effort, persistence of effort, and performance. This research will require a strategy of confirmatory factor analysis and modeling with structural equations (Bagozzi & Phillips, 1982). The approach estimates the strength of relationships among independent latent variables (the three speech acts) and between independent and dependent latent variables (effort, etc.). Three models can be developed. The first follows the conventional approach and divides speech acts into information and consideration. The second model, based on Penley and Hawkins' (1985) finding that consideration communications may be only a form of information, specifies one latent independent variable. The third, based on motivational language theory, specifies three latent variables. The structural equations method can show the viability of the model proposed by MLT. Additional analysis through multiple regression can test the hypotheses.

Motivational language theory describes the communications of managers who are successful in motivating employees. Not only do these managers supply the information and feedback needed by workers, but they also do more. They make themselves advocates of the organization's values and goals and develop the habit of engaging in frequent informal communications with workers. They exhibit a genuine interest in communicating, with employees as people. These mutually supportive speech acts will lead to improved employee motivations. In terms of the theory, managerial motivating behavior is communicative, but it is not solely the purposeful communication of uncertainty-reducing information. It is also the existence of nonpurposeful habits of communicating in the down time that makes up most of the work day. Thus, motivating is seen as an all-day, every-day managerial task. Motivated work by employees, can be the result of the individual needs and values of workers as well as the nature of the situation. But that element of motivation that comes from the actions of managers is described by MLT as a result or characteristic of the perlocutionary, locutionary, and illocutionary speech acts by supervisors. These managers have learned three things: (a) what employees need to know, (b) the importance of role play and informal communicating, and (c) the importance of viewing workers as people rather than as instrumentalities.

REFERENCES

Austen, J. L. (1962) *How to do thing with words*. Oxford: Oxford University Press.

Bagozzi, R. P., & Phillips, L. W. (1982) Representing and testing organizational theories: A holistic construal. *Administrative Science Quarterly, 27*, 459–489.

Berger, P., Berger, B., & Kellner, H. (1974) *The homeless mind*. New York: Vintage House.

Carrell, M. R., & Dittrich, J. E. (1978) Equity theory: The recent literature, methodological considerations, and new directions. *Academy of Management Review, 3*, 202–210.

Cherrington, D., Reitz, H., & Scott, W. (1971) Effects of contingent and noncontingent reward on the relationship between satisfaction and task performance. *Journal of Applied Psychology, 55*, 531–536.

Cummings, L. L. (1983) Performance-evaluation systems in the context of individual trust and commitment. In F. Landy, S. Zedeck, & J. Cleveland (Eds.), *Performance measurement and theory* (pp. 89–93). Hillsdale, NJ: Erlbaum.

Donaldson, G., & Lorsch, J. W. (1984) *Decision making at the top*. New York: Basic Books.

Downey, H. K., & Brief, A. P. (1986) How cognitive structures affect organizational design: Implicit theories of organizing. In H. P. Sims, Jr., D. A. Gioia, & Associates (Eds.), *The thinking organization* (pp. 165–190). San Francisco: Jossey-Bass.

Erez, M., & Zidon, I. (1984) Effect of goal acceptance on the relationship of goal difficulty to performance. *Journal of Applied Psychology, 69*, 69–78.

Feldman, D. C., & Brett, J. M. (1983) Coping with new jobs: A comparative study of new hires and job changers. *Academy of Management Journal, 26*, 258–272.

Gioia, D. A., & Poole, P. P. (1984) Scripts in organizational behavior. *Academy of Management Review, 9*, 449–459.

Glick, W. H., Jenkins, G. D., Jr., & Gupta, N. (1986) Method versus substance: How strong are underlying relationships between job characteristics and attitudinal outcomes? *Academy of Management Journal, 29*, 441–464.

Gupta, N. (1980) Performance contingent rewards and satisfaction: An initial analysis. *Human Relations, 33*, 813–829.

Hackman, J. R., & Lawler, E. E. (1971) Employee reactions to job characteristics. *Journal of Applied Psychology, 55*, 259–286.

Hackman, J. R., & Oldham, G. (1975) Development of the job diagnostic survey. *Journal of Applied Psychology, 60*, 151–170.

Hackman, J. R., & Oldham, G. R. (1980) *Work redesign*. Reading, MA: Addison-Wesley.

Hackman, J.R., Oldham, G., Janson, R., & Purdy, K. (1974) A new strategy for job enrichment. [NTIS No. AD–779827]. Arlington, VA: Office of Naval Research.

Korman, A. K. (1976) Hypothesis of work behavior revisited and an extension. *Academy of Management Review,* 1, 50–63.

Landy, F., & Trumbo, D. (1976) *Psychology of work behavior.* Homewood, IL: Dorsey Press.

Latham, G. P., & Saari, L. M. (1979) Importance of supportive relationships in goal setting. *Journal of Applied Psychology,* 64, 151–156.

Locke, E. A. (1976) The nature and causes of job satisfaction. In M. D. Dunnete (Ed.), *Handbook of industrial and organizational psychology* (pp. 1297–1350). Chicago: Rand McNally.

Locke, E. A. (1978) The ubiquity of the techniques of goal setting in theories and approaches to employee motivation. *Academy of Management Review,* 3, 594–601.

Locke, E. A. (1983) Performance appraisal under capitalism, socialism, and the mixed economy. In F. Landy, S. Zedeck, & J. Cleveland (Eds.), *Performance measurement and theory,* (pp. 309–326). Hillsdale, NJ: Erlbaum.

Locke, E. A., & Henne, D. (1986) Work motivation theories. In C. L. Cooper & I. Robertson (Eds.), *International review of industrial and organizational psychology* (pp. 1–36). Chichester, England: Wiley Ltd.

Locke, E. A., & Latham, G. P. (1984) *Goal setting: A motivational technique that works!* Englewood Cliffs, NJ: Prentice-Hall.

Louis, M. R. (1980) Surprise and sense making: What newcomers experience in entering unfamiliar organizational settings. *Administrative Science Quarterly,* 25, 226–251.

Miner, J. B. (1984) The validity and usefulness of theories in an emerging organizational science. *Academy of Management Review,* 9, 296–306.

Mitchell, T. R. (1982) Motivation: New directions for theory, research, and practice. *Academy of Management Review,* 7, 80–88.

Nakane, C. (1973) *Japanese society.* Middlesex, England: Penguin Books.

Palermo, D. S. (1983) Cognition, concepts, and an employee's theory of the world. In F. Landy, S. Zedeck, and J. Cleveland (Eds.), *Performance measurement and theory* (pp. 97–115). Hillsdale, NJ: Erlbaum.

Park, O. S., Sims, H. P., Jr., & Motowidlo, S. J. (1986) Affect in organizations: How feelings and emotions influence managerial judgment. In H. P. Sims, Jr., D. A. Gioia, and Associates (Eds.), *The thinking organization* (pp. 215–237). San Francisco: Jossey-Bass.

Pascale, R. T., & Athos, A. G. (1981) *The art of Japanese management: Applications for American executives.* New York: Simon & Schuster.

Penley, L. E., & Hawkins, B. (1985) Studying interpersonal communication in organizations: A leadership application. *Academy of Management Journal,* 28, 309–326.

Pike, K. L. (1967) *Language in relation to a unified theory of the structure of human behavior.* The Hague: Mouton.

Pinder, C. C. (1984) *Work motivation.* Glenview, IL: Scott, Foresman.

Roberts, K. H., & O'Reilly, C. A. (1974) Failure in upward communications in organizations: Three possible culprits. *Academy of Management Journal,* 17, 205–215.

Salancik, G. R., & Pfeffer, J. (1977) An examination of need satisfaction models of job attitudes. *Administrative Science Quarterly,* 22, 427–456.

Salancik, G. R. & Pfeffer, J. (1978) A social information processing approach to job attitudes and task design. *Administrative Science Quarterly, 23,* 224–253.

Schuler, R. S. (1979) A role perception transactional process model for organizational communication-outcome relationships. *Organizational Behavior and Human Performance,* 23, 268–291.

Staw, B. M. (1975) Attributions of the 'cause' of performance: A general alternative of interpretation of cross-sectional research on organizations. *Organizational Behavior and Human Performance,* 13, 414–432.

Steers, R. M., & Porter, L. W. (1975) *Motivation and work behavior.* New York: McGraw-Hill.

Stogdill, R. (1970) *Handbook of leadership: A survey of theory and research.* New York: Free Press.

Sullivan, J. J. (1986) Human nature, organizations, and management theory. *Academy of Management Review,* 11, 534–549.

Van Maanen, J. (1978) People processing: Strategies of organizational socialization. *Organizational Dynamics,* 7(1), 18–36.

Weiss, H. M. (1978) Social learning of work values in organizations. *Journal of Applied Psychology,* 63, 711–718.

Yukl, G. A., & Latham, G. P. (1978) Interrelationships among employee participation, individual differences, goal difficulty, goal acceptance, instrumentality, and performance. *Personnel Psychology,* 31, 305–324.

Employee Responses to Formal Performance Appraisal Feedback

Jone L. Pearce
Lyman W. Porter

Performance appraisal is one of the most widely researched topics in all of personnel psychology. In recent years attention has been even greater because of important potential implications relating to fair employment practices and because of increasing concerns about employee productivity in organizations. Much of this rather voluminous literature on appraisals has focused on improving the accuracy of ratings by means of better instrumentation and more effective rater training. However, the present study is concerned with the effects of received appraisals on those being evaluated.

Formal performance appraisals can be viewed as a particular kind of feedback. One of the primary purposes of formal appraisals is the provision of clear, performance-based feedback to employees (Carroll & Schneier, 1982). There has been a substantial body of research on the effects of feedback, with Ilgen, Fisher, and Taylor (1979) providing a comprehensive review of the research literature. They identify the *sign* of the feedback—whether it is seen as positive or negative—as one of the key variables in message perception. In fact, Landy and Farr (1983) view the sign of the message as "the most important message characteristic in terms of its impact on the acceptance of feedback" (p. 168).

Despite the availability of prior research concerning the "acceptability" of positive/negative feedback, no empirical studies were located that have directly

From *Journal of Applied Psychology,* 1986, **71**(2), 211–218. Copyright © 1986 by the American Psychological Association. Adapted by permission of the publisher.

investigated the impact of the sign of the feedback on the subsequent attitudes and behavior of employees in the work situation. Although rigorously developed research on perceptions of feedback suggests that the sign of the feedback message is critical in perception of message content, it provides no data concerning the effects of feedback perceptions on subsequent attitudes and behaviors. There have been suggestions that performance appraisal feedback can have negative impacts on recipients' attitudes and subsequent behaviors, but these observations have not been subjected to empirical test.

Several theorists have, however, described "defensive" responses to negative feedback. De Nisi, Randolph, and Blencoe (1980) suggest that employees may attempt to retaliate when they receive low ratings from peers. Taylor, Fisher, and Ilgen (1984) argue that, even when a feedback system is perceived as fair, negative feedback may threaten employees' perceived freedom of choice and could result in defiant opposition or reaction to the supervisor.

Thompson and Dalton (1970) and Meyer (1975) have written on the dysfunctional effects of appraisal ratings feedback. Thompson and Dalton (1970) analyzed the experiences of several engineering firms with the introduction of formal appraisals for their technical employees. They found widespread dissatisfaction and reported generally lowered individual self-confidence and job performance. The authors noted:

> Performance appraisal touches on one of the most emotionally charged activities in business life—the assessment of a man's contribution and ability. The signals he receives about this assessment have a strong impact on his self-esteem *and* on his subsequent performance. (Thompson & Dalton, 1970, p. 150)

Similarly, Meyer (1975) suggested that employees given "below average" merit ratings become alienated and demoralized. This is because most employees consider their own work performance to be "above average." For example, Meyer, (1975) reported the results of four samples of employees rating their own performance. He found that from 70%–80% of the employees in these samples rated their own performance as "in the top 25%." Meyer, Kay, and French (1965) found that criticism had a negative effect on the achievement of goals, whereas praise had little effect one way or the other. There is, however, a virtual absence of research evidence to support these or any other conjectures concerning the possible reactions of employees to their appraisal ratings, and therefore the present study is concerned with testing these arguments.

This study was part of a large-scale research effort to evaluate the effects of the 1978 Civil Service Reform Act (Perry & Porter, 1981). One of the primary areas of the Act involved the initiation of formal objective-based performance appraisal procedures in all Federal agencies. Although appraisal systems had previously been put into operation in some agencies prior to the Act, they were not conducted systematically and universally throughout the government. The Act mandated that formal performance-based procedures be developed and implemented in all agencies. In the larger investigation of which this study was one component, five diverse federal agencies formed the sample of organizations. For two of these five agencies it was possible to obtain a sufficient sample of employee attitude data before and after the imposition of the new performance appraisal systems. In each agency attitude data were collected from separate samples of managers and nonmanagement employees, because each group received the new appraisal ratings at different times—managers 12 months before nonmanagement employees. This allowed limited control of the "history effects," with the lower level employees acting as a control group during the first 12 months of the managers' appraisal period.

Although actual performance appraisal ratings are available in only one of the agencies, self-reported ratings are available in both. However, because the present study is concerned with reactions to appraisal feedback, *perceived* rating would be expected to be a better predictor of recipient reactions and to represent the primary focus of this investigation. Nevertheless, both actual (where available) and self-reported ratings results are reported. Thus, one by-product of the present study is the opportunity to examine the accuracy of self-reported ratings in the one agency in which both are available.

The present sample—two federal agencies, each composed of managers receiving feedback on the new performance-based appraisal system 12 months before nonmanagement employees in the same agency—provides a unique opportunity to test the effects of performance appraisal feedback. It is rare in field settings to find the introduction of a new form of appraisal feedback for some groups but with other groups not receiving such feedback. For the first time in these organizations individuals were given a formal performance rating, based on objectives for their specific jobs, that was (by law) to be used for all promotions, pay increases, and reductions-in-force (layoffs). Furthermore, the data were available for all respondents over a 30-month period, before and after appraisal feedback, to both management and nonmanagement employees. Finally, the two agencies serve as independent tests (each can be seen as a replication of the test in the other) of the hypotheses.

It is suggested that performance feedback that one is "satisfactory" or "meeting standards" will be experienced as negative by many of these appraisal feedback recipients, not just by those receiving objectively poor performance ratings. This follows from Meyer (1975) among others, who indicated that most employees consider themselves to be above-average performers. Additional support is provided by Parker, Taylor, Barrett, and Martens (1959), Ilgen, Peterson, Martin, and Boeschen (1981), and Smircich and Chesser (1981), who found that subordinates rate their own performance more highly than their supervisors do. This discrepancy in the perceptions of supervisors and subordinates has also been noted by Mowday (1983) and Feldman (1981). Thus, it might be expected that many average performers would experience such feedback as negative.

If subordinates experience disconfirmation of their self-perceptions of "above average" performance, it could be expected to result in experienced cognitive dissonance. Such individuals should, therefore, be motivated to reduce the dissonance (Festinger, 1961). However, there is little evidence from employment situations to suggest how they might attempt to reduce it. Limited direction is provided by Mowday (1983), who suggests that ego-defensive bias would lead employees receiving perceived poor ratings to blame their failure on external factors rather than on their own personal characteristics.

One way to reduce dissonance is to minimize the importance of the information received. However, this is particularly difficult with appraisals that represent the organization's formal assessment of one's performance. As Thompson and Dalton (1970) noted above, appraisals become emotionally important to many in organizations. Furthermore, when appraisals will be used to administer organizational rewards such as promotions and pay (as in the present agencies), it is even more difficult to devalue them. Alternatively, blame can be placed on such external factors as task difficulty, the source of the rating, that is, the supervisor, or the organization that sponsored such a (poorly run) appraisal system. This follows from Meyer (1975), who suggested that employees given below-average merit raises often become disenchanted with their employers, and Thompson and Dalton (1970), who argued that any system that includes either explicit or implicit peer-comparisons results in self-blame (lowered employee self-confidence and reduced individual performance) and employer blame (increased turnover).

The present hypotheses follow from this attribution theory framework. Following Mowday (1983) and others, we expect the ego defense mechanisms for such important feedback as work performance will lead those receiving (merely) satisfactory ratings to blame external factors rather than themselves. We would expect the most likely targets of such blame to be the supervisor (who made the judgment), the performance appraisal system (inappropriate measures), and the organization (it developed the policy), with no *a priori* predictions concerning which target will be preferred. There is some evidence that characteristics of the appraisal system (and other features of the feedback process) may influence which target is chosen. Landy, Barnes-Farrell, and Cleveland (1980) found that characteristics of the performance appraisal system (e.g., frequency of evaluation, supervisor's knowledge of performance) were better predictors of the perceived "fairness" of the evaluation than was the actual rating received by the employee. That is, when the appraisal system was perceived as fair and accurate, it was not blamed for the low rating. In the present study, those receiving relatively high ratings would be expected to experience "confirmation" of their positive self-perception, and thus we would expect no change in their attitudes toward these objects (Meyer et al., 1965). Data are available on two of these external targets. (Because the present test is taken from a larger evaluation of the impact of personnel changes on these organizations rather than a direct assessment of employee attributional processes, no reliable scale for "blaming the supervisor" was used during the entire 30-month study period.) Therefore, the present study addresses two hypotheses:

Hypothesis 1. Attitudes toward the performance appraisal system will decrease and remain lower after the introduction of the appraisal system for those receiving relatively low ratings on it, whereas the attitudes of those receiving relatively high ratings will be unchanged.

Hypothesis 2. Those receiving a relatively low rating on the appraisal system will have more negative attitudes toward the organization after its introduction and the attitudes will remain significantly lower, whereas the attitudes of those with relatively high ratings will remain unchanged.

METHOD

Context and Sample

Data were obtained from a random sample of federal civil service employees from a National Aeronautic and Space Administration research center and a Department of Defense engineering station. The research center is responsible for research in the storing of lightweight flight structures, fluid mechanics, and fundamental aerodynamics. The engineering station provides inservice engineering support for the surface warfare systems of the United States Fleet and the ships of friendly nations. Engineers and scientists are the dominant employee groups in both organizations (engineers, scientists, and professional administrators comprise 64% of the respondents; technicians, 23%, and clerical and trades, 13%). Seventy-eight percent of the sample is male and 78% are non-Hispanic whites. The present study reports data from these two organizations for managers—managers and supervisors in federal civil service Grades 13 to 15—and nonmanagement employees (hereafter called "employees")—nonsupervisors in Grades 13 to 15 and all employees in Grades 12 and below. The data are analyzed separately, because the managers received their first ratings on the new performance appraisal system a year before the employees. Several other research sites that were part of the larger evaluation of the effects of the Reform Act could not be used in the present study because the number of managers in these agencies was prohibitively small for the analytic techniques employed.

Prior to the implementation of the Act's mandated objectives-based performance appraisal system, both agencies used more informal and subjective means to appraise performance. Appraisal practices at the research center varied widely. Many supervisors preferred informal face-to-face sessions with subordinates. One center respondent referred to them as "blank paper reviews," since the subordinate and supervisor would sit down to discuss performance, "each with a blank piece of paper." At the engineering station there was a more formal system, but it was "trait-based," in which supervisors rated their subordinates on characteristics such as "leadership."

Title II of the Civil Service Reform Act of 1978 mandated at least yearly evaluation on an appraisal system: "establishing performance standards which will, to the maximum extent feasible, permit the accurate evaluation of job performance on the basis of objective criteria (4302 (b)(1))." Both sample organizations met their statutory requirements. The sample managers received ratings and performance feedback in October 1981 and again in October 1982; the sample employees received their first performance ratings in October 1982. Managers and employees were rated on objectives, and these ratings were summarized as an overall rating through approved formulae. For managers these ratings directly determined merit pay awards, but for employees standard pay increases were given to all those with satisfactory or better performance. The new system required performance-based objectives, a summary rating, and face-to-face feedback with the subordinate signing the appraisal form and required that these ratings be the basis for personnel decisions.

Procedure

The study used a time-series, repeated measures quasi-experimental design (Cook & Campbell, 1979). The present sample is composed of a panel of respondents who completed attitude questionnaires at the following series of time periods across a total of 30 months.

Time 1—Pre-ratings period. Attitude questionnaires were distributed to respondents by members of the research team at three points in time before either managers or employees received formal ratings. If a respondent provided complete attitude data in June 1980, December 1980, and June 1981, or any two of these, the mean of the responses is used as the Time 1 value. Whenever more than one Time 1 response was available the responses were averaged rather than the random selection of one questionnaire administration, so that all available data could be used to provide a more stable measure of pre-ratings attitudes. If the respondent completed the questionnaire only once during this period, the single value is used.

Time 2—First ratings feedback for managers and pre-ratings for employees. The fourth survey was conducted in December 1981, 2 months after the first ratings feedback was received by managers in October 1981, but ten months before the employees received their ratings.

Time 3—Second ratings feedback for managers and first ratings feedback for employees. The final survey was conducted in December 1982, 2 months after the second year-end ratings feedback to managers and the first ratings feedback to employees.

Respondents were fully informed that this was an Office of Personnel Management funded evaluation of the act, that their responses would be completely anonymous, and they were given brief "letter format" feedback after each questionnaire session. Respondents were randomly selected, and the average response rate was 81%. . . .

DISCUSSION

The results only partially support Hypothesis 1 but are consistent with the predictions of Hypothesis 2. Hypothesis 1 proposed that the receipt of a below-average satisfactory rating would lead to increased negative views of the operation of the appraisal system and its effects on the organization. This prediction was not supported for the nonmanagement employees. In fact, all research center employees showed significant improvements in attitudes toward how well the appraisal system operates between Times 2 and 3. One reason for the failure of Hypothesis 1 to be confirmed for this group of nonmanagement employees could be simply the fact that perceptions of how well the system operates and its effects on the organization are relatively "distant" in a psychological sense and not very important one way or the other to those who are neither supervisors nor personnel specialists. A related reason may be the fact that the employees' ratings were *not* to be used for pay increases, but a portion of the managers' pay increases were based on their performance ratings. Under these circumstances, it would probably be easier for employees to reduce experienced dissonance by minimizing the importance of their performance ratings. However, because Hypothesis 1 *was* generally confirmed for the managers, the salience of attributes of the performance appraisal system may be greater for those with supervisory responsibilities and under merit pay systems, and hence their attitudes toward the appraisal system would be more likely to be affected by the receipt of "unexpected" satisfactory ratings.

The other trend in the findings that did not consistently support the predictions of Hypothesis 1 concerned the research center subsample. For those who worked in this agency, attitudes toward the appraisal system and towards its perceived impact on the organization *increased* between Time 2 and Time 3 regardless of whether the individuals received relatively high or satisfactory ratings. Although the reasons for this are not entirely clear, it should be noted that the management of the research center devoted intensive personal effort between Time 2 and Time 3 to improving the operation of the appraisal system. This appears to have had the effect of making most individuals, managers and nonmanagers, more positive about the appraisal system regardless of the rating they received (see Landy et al., 1980). It may be that, in effect, the organization's actions to improve the appraisal system inoculated individuals from disparaging the system, even if they received a rating lower than they expected or felt they deserved. It should be noted, however, as will be discussed below, that efforts to improve and perfect the appraisal system did not prevent a subsequent drop in organizational commitment on the part of those who received satisfactory ratings. It may be that the extensive organizational attention to improving the research center's appraisal system simply removed it as a likely target for blame by those who received feedback that they were satisfactory but did not have an impact on experienced dissonance or on resultant blame of another target, namely, the organization.

The major finding of the present study, consistent with the predictions of Hypothesis 2, is that receipt of relatively low ratings caused a distinct and significant drop in attitudes toward the organization within 2 months of feedback of the appraisal results. This occurred in both sites and for both management and nonmanagement employees and persisted a year later. Whether this type of impact should be of concern to organizations, assuming it would be replicated in other types of samples, would depend on how particular organizations view those who are performing adequately but are not superior or clearly above average. In certain organizations (e.g., major public accounting firms), where only the most outstanding performers are retained after a few trial years, the drop in positive attitudes toward the organization probably would not be a cause for concern. For other organizations, however, where turnover of adequate performers is costly or where (as in a research and development type of organization) all such members are considered important contributors, such reactions from those who receive relatively—but not necessarily absolute—low ratings may be a greater problem.

Before concluding, several limitations of the study should be noted. First, the data on individual performance at the engineering station (which provided results most consistent with the hypotheses) consisted of self-reports of ratings received from supervisors, rather than the actual records of those ratings. The comparative data from the research center indicates that, although respondents are substantially correct in their reports, there is a small upward bias in self-reports. However, as noted above, it is the respondent's perceived feedback that should best predict their reactions.

A second limitation of the design was the fact that no items were included in the questionnaire regarding a major factor in the performance ratings environment, namely, the supervisor. The reason for this is simply that the chief aim of the larger project, of which the present study is only a small segment, was to assess the organizational impacts of the Act. Hence, at the time the questionnaires were designed prior to the start of the overall investigation, items were not included that focused on the individual's reaction to the supervisor. Obviously, such data would have been useful and pertinent to the question of the impact of received ratings had items of this type been included as part of an already-lengthy questionnaire.

The third limitation related to the nature of the particular sample of respondents. In this sample, a rating of "satisfactory" may be more psychologically negative than would perhaps be the case with some other types of samples. The dominant employee groups in both samples were highly educated scientists and engineers. Many of these individuals reported working for the federal government, rather than in private organizations, because they were able to do "state of the art" work in these agencies. Clearly, these employees, as would be the case for other high status professionals, found the feedback that they were merely satisfactory to be negative feedback, indeed. Yet, this reaction may not be as severe among members of other kinds of occupations.

Fourth, the study was restricted to attitudinal variables, and there were no tests of their direct effects on behaviors. We know that lowered organizational commitment is associated with reduced attendance and increased turnover in other samples (Mowday, Porter, and Steers, 1982) but have no evidence of its impact on these research center and engineering station employees. Thompson and Dalton (1970) argued that the "demoralization" resulting from such feedback would reduce individuals' performance because they would see little likelihood that increased effort would result in a major movement in their relative ranking. However, Mowday et al. (1982) found no significant association between commitment and individual performance in their extensive review.

Finally, the present study is limited in its focus only on the first few months (for nonmanagement employees) and first 14 months (for managers) after the implementation of a new formal appraisal system. The feedback that one is "merely average" no doubt loses its shock value upon repetition year after year. The present study did provide evidence that the decrement in attitudes toward the appraisal system can be temporary (for research center employees) and it may be that other nonperformance feedback issues become a more salient factor in one's organizational commitment over time.

Nevertheless, it appears that Thompson and Dalton's (1970) and Meyer's (1975) concerns about the possible unintended negative consequences of "overly precise," implicitly comparative, appraisal systems may be well founded, given the results found in this study regarding the sharp and immediate drop in organizational commitment on the part of those receiving satisfactory ratings. It seems clear that for many people self-perceptions of their organizational or work performance are closely aligned with their feelings of self-esteem, and thus they want to believe that they are making important contributions. Any appraisal system, then, that provides data, whether explicit or implicit, on how one ranks compared to one's peers is likely to generate some loss in positive feelings on the part of those who are not (as is the case in any ranking system) in the upper part of the distribution. Furthermore, this study demonstrates that such reactions are not confined only to those with clearly unsatisfactory performance but may extend to most of those below the upper rankings. This would suggest that organizations need to consider carefully how their appraisal systems affect not only the attitudes and performance of those ranked at the top, but also those "solid citizens" who are performing at acceptable, but not outstanding levels.

This is not intended to imply that formal performance appraisals should be abandoned. This problem is primarily one of perception and interpretation, and there are several practical steps that personnel specialists can take to minimize these negative attitudinal effects. For example, performance appraisal systems can be examined for any unintended or unnecessary (for the uses of the system) ranking of employees. If the rating will not be used for any comparative purposes (e.g., pay allocation from a fixed pool, layoff decisions), the potential attitudinal costs of implicit or explicit employee performance rankings would suggest that the system be modified. Furthermore, personnel specialists can do much to anticipate the potential negative attitudinal consequences through training supervisors. Supervisors can be helped to anticipate and more effectively manage the possible negative reactions of employees to such feedback.

In conclusion, the results of the present study suggest that perhaps less attention should be paid to refinements of the psychometric details of ratin instruments and relatively more attention paid to the organizational behav . impacts of performance ratings feedback. Performance appraisal takes place in a complex social system, and feedback concerning relative performance is an important signal to employees about how their organizations value them. Thus, any system that drifts into a pattern (and an associated way of thinking) of separating and identifying the "stars" from the "also rans" is likely to have effects that may not be intended or organizationally desired, regardless of the technical quality of the measurement system.

REFERENCES

Cook, T. D., & Campbell, D. T. (1979). *Quasi-experimentation: Design and analysis issues for field settings.* Boston: Houghton Mifflin.

Carroll, S. J., & Schneier, C. E. (1982). *Performance appraisal and review systems.* Glenview, IL: Scott, Foresman.

Feldman, J. (1981). Beyond attribution theory: Cognitive processes in performance appraisal. *Journal of Applied Psychology, 66,* 127–148.

Festinger, L. (1961). The psychological effects of insufficient rewards. *American Psychologist, 16,* 1–11.

Ilgen, D. R., Fisher, C. D., & Taylor, M. S. (1979). Consequences of individual feedback on behavior in organizations. *Journal of Applied Psychology, 64,* 349–371.

Ilgen, D. R., Peterson, R. B., Martin, B. A., & Boeschen, D. A. (1981). Supervisor and subordinate reactions to performance appraisal sessions. *Organizational Behavior and Human Performance, 28,* 311–330.

Landy, F. J., Barnes-Farrell, J., & Cleveland, J. N. (1980). Perceived fairness and accuracy of performance evaluation: A follow-up. *Journal of Applied Psychology, 65,* 355–356.

Landy, F. J., & Farr, J. L. (1983). *The measurement of work performance.* New York: Academic Press.

Meyer, H. H. (1975). The pay-for-performance dilemma. *Organizational Dynamics, 3,* 39–50.

Meyer, H. H., Kay, E., & French, J. R. P. (1965). Split roles in performance appraisal. *Harvard Business Review, 43*(1), 123–129.

Mowday, R. T. (1983). Beliefs about the causes of behavior. The motivational implications of attribution processes. In R. M. Steers & L. W. Porter (Eds.), *Motivation and work behavior* (3rd ed.). New York: McGraw-Hill.

De Nisi, A. S., Randolph, W. A., & Blencoe, A. (1980, November). Peer evaluations: Causes and consequences. *Proceedings of the 12th Annual Meeting of the American Institute of Decision Sciences* (pp. 420–431). Las Vegas, NV.

Parker, J. W., Taylor, E. K., Barrett, R. S., & Martens, L. (1959). Rating scale content III: Relationship between supervisory- and self-ratings. *Personnel Psychology, 12,* 49–63.

Perry, J. L., & Porter, L. W. (1981). *Organizational assessments of the Civil Service Reform Act of 1978.* Washington, D.C.: U.S. Office of Personnel Management.

Smircich, L., & Chesser, R. J. (1981). Superiors' and subordinates' perceptions of performance: Beyond disagreement. *Academy of Management Journal, 24,* 198–205.

Taylor, M. S., Fisher, C. D., & Ilgen, D. R. (1984). Individuals' reactions to performance feedback in organizations: A control theory perspective. In K. M. Rowland & G. R. Ferris (Eds.), *Research in personnel and human resources management* (pp. 81–124). Greenwich, CN: JAI Press.

Thompson, P. H., & Dalton, G. W. (1970). Performance appraisal: Managers beware. *Harvard Business Review, 48,* 149–157.

QUESTIONS FOR DISCUSSION

1 Based on the two communication and feedback articles, what kind of feedback would you offer to an employee whose performance you considered "satisfactory." How would you communicate your feedback?

2 How does "meaning-making" increase motivation and facilitate the performance of individuals?

3 Compare Sullivan's categories of speech acts with the major tenets of social learning theory. Can similar managerial implications be derived from both perspectives?

4 Sullivan categorizes managerial communication into three types of speech acts. Can you think of additional categories of speech acts that may be important in the motivational process?

5 What advice would you offer a manager who wanted to know several methods for determining employees' reactions to feedback?

6 What is the role of feedback in equity theory? Goal-setting theory? Expectancy theory?

7 Why would feedback that your performance is "satisfactory" have a negative impact on your work motivation? Base your answer on the motivation theories presented in this book.

MOTIVATION THEORY IN PERSPECTIVE

13

WORK AND MOTIVATION: SOME CONCLUDING OBSERVATIONS

The concept of the organization has long symbolized the efficient, effective, and rational allocation of resources for task accomplishment. Thus, many attempts have been made by managers and researchers to define the optimal balance of financial, physical, and human resources as they help determine the growth and development of business, governmental, and educational institutions. The present volume has focused on the human aspects associated with such concerns. Specifically, we have reviewed in a systematic fashion the current level of knowledge concerning motivational processes as they affect work behavior.

Before attempting to summarize the current status of motivation theory and research, however, we should review briefly what we know about the nature of work itself. After all, if one objective of an increased knowledge of motivational processes is to improve both work attitudes and work performance, then we must be aware of the functions served by work activities in a modern society.

THE MEANING OF WORK

Work is important in the lives of individuals for several reasons. First, there is the notion of reciprocity, or exchange. Whether we are talking about a corporate executive, an assembly-line worker, or a Red Cross volunteer, each worker receives some form of reward in exchange for his or her services. These rewards may be primarily extrinsic, such as money, or they may be purely intrinsic, such as the personal satisfaction that comes from providing the service. In either case, a worker has certain personal expectations concerning the type and amount of reward he or she should receive for services rendered. The extent to which such expectations are met would presumably affect in large measure the inclination of

573

the worker to continue at the current level of performance and, indeed, might even ultimately affect the decision concerning whether to remain with the organization.

Second, work generally serves several social functions. The workplace provides opportunities for meeting new people and developing friendships. In fact, many employees appear to spend more time interacting with their coworkers than they do with their own families!

Third, a person's job is often a source of status, or rank, in society at large. For example, a carpenter who is trained in a specific craft is generally considered to be on a higher social plane than an unskilled ditchdigger. And a bank president would generally be accorded higher status than a carpenter. A point not to be overlooked here is the fact that work, or more precisely what one does at work, often transcends the boundaries of the work organization. The bank president in our example can have status in the *community* because of his or her position within the organization. Thus, work can be simultaneously a source of social differentiation as well as a source of social integration.

Fourth, and an aspect of work of special concern to the study of motivation, is the personal meaning that work has for the individual. From a psychological standpoint, it can be an important source of identity, self-esteem, and self-actualization. It can provide a sense of fulfillment by giving an employee a sense of purpose and by clarifying his or her value to society. Conversely, however, it can also be a source of frustration, boredom, and feelings of meaninglessness, depending on the characteristics of the individual and on the nature of the task. People tend to evaluate themselves according to what they have been able to accomplish. If they see their job as hampering the achievement of their full potential, it often becomes difficult for them to maintain a sense of purpose at work. Such feelings can then lead to a reduced level of job involvement, decreased job satisfaction, and a lowered desire to perform. Hence, the nature of the job—and the meaning it has for the employee—can have a profound impact on employee attitudes and work behavior.

As our society has increased in both complexity and affluence, so, too, have the problems associated with such developments. Alcoholism and drug abuse at work are prevalent, as are problems of turnover and absenteeism. Moreover, by several indications, worker productivity appears to be declining in many areas. Managers have often tried to explain away such problems by reverting to the old scientific management, or Theory X, assumptions about human nature—namely, that people are basically lazy and have little desire to perform well on a job. However, a more realistic explanation for such problems may be found by looking at the type of work most employees are asked to perform.

Consider, for example, the case of younger workers just entering the job market. With higher educational levels as well as greater expectations concerning their work, many young workers have shown a strong aversion toward many of the more traditional (and well-paying) jobs at both the blue- and the white-collar levels. However, these same workers are largely in agreement with the notion that one should "work hard" on a job. How are these two points reconciled? Perhaps the answer lies in the nature of the tasks. That is, rather than simply rebelling against the traditional (hard) work ethic, many younger workers appear to be demanding greater substance in the *nature* of their job activities. In this sense, it is qualitative revolt, not a quantitative one. What they object to, it seems, is being placed on jobs which are essentially devoid of intrinsic worth.

Other examples could be cited (minority-group workers, women employees, and even corporate executives). In all cases, a common denominator appears to be a reduced level of employee motivation to perform a job or even to remain with an organization. If we are to understand more clearly the nature and extent of such work-related problems and, better still, if we are to be able to find appropriate solutions to these problems, we must begin by understanding the very basic role played by motivation as it affects job behavior.

THE IMPORTANCE OF MOTIVATION IN WORK BEHAVIOR

Review of Major Variables

Perhaps the most striking aspect of the study of work motivation is the all-encompassing nature of the topic itself. Consider again our definition of motivation: that which energizes, directs, and sustains behavior. Following such a definition, it becomes readily apparent how many divergent factors can affect in some way the desire of an employee to perform. In Chapter 1, a conceptual framework, or model, was proposed to assist us in organizing these factors for detailed study and analysis throughout this book (see Exhibit 3 in Chapter 1).

By way of review, the model suggested that variables affecting motivation can be found on three levels in organizational settings. First, some variables are unique to the individual himself or herself (such as attitudes, interests, and specific needs). Second, other variables arise from the nature of the job (such as degree of control over the particular job and level of responsibility). Third, still other variables are found in the larger work situation, or organizational environment. Factors falling into this third category would include such things as peer group relations, supervisory practices, systematic rewards, and organizational climate. In addition, it was emphasized in the model that a systems perspective is necessary. That is, instead of viewing these variables as three static lists of items, consideration has to be given to how they affect one another and change over time in response to circumstances. The individual is thus seen as potentially being in a constant state of flux vis-à-vis his or her motivational level, depending on the nature, strength, and interactive effects of these three groups of variables.

Let us consider briefly how some of the more important findings reviewed in this book relate to this conceptual framework, beginning with those variables unique to the individual. Only highlights of the major findings will be mentioned here. An analysis of the data presented throughout this volume reveals that several *individual* characteristics can represent a significant influence on employee performance. For instance, there is fairly consistent evidence that individuals who have higher needs for achievement generally perform better than those who have lower needs for achievement (as shown, for example, in Chapter 2). Moreover, other evidence indicates that individuals who have strong negative attitudes toward an organization are less inclined to continue their involvement in organizational activities. Locke and Latham review field evidence indicating that personal aspiration level on a task (the level of performance for which an individual is actually trying) can be an accurate predictor of subsequent performance (see Chapter 9). Finally, investigations by Adams and others (see Chapter 4) found that *perceived* inequity in an organizational exchange situation is associated with changes (up or down) in performance levels. While many other examples could be cited, these kinds of findings generally support the proposition that personal characteristics unique to an individual can have an important impact on his or her work behavior.

A similar pattern emerges when we consider *job-related* characteristics. Numerous studies indicate that variations in the nature of the task itself can influence performance and satisfaction (see Chapter 10). For example, several studies have found that "enriching" an employee's job by allowing him or her more variety, autonomy, and responsibility can result in somewhat improved performance. However, many of these findings are not overly strong. Stronger evidence concerning the impact of job- or task-related variables emerges when we simultaneously consider the role of individual differences in such a relationship. That is, when variations across individuals are also taken into account, evidence indicates that certain task attributes are more strongly related to performance only for specific "types" of people, such as those with a high need for achievement. For other persons, such attributes appear to have diminished effects. In other words, it appears that not everyone wants *to the same degree* to have an enriched job, nor does everyone necessarily perform better when assigned to one. Recognition must be given, therefore, to the background characteristics of individual employees when considering job design changes.

Finally, let us review *work environment* effects on motivation and performance. Articles presented in Chapter 5 focused on these effects and reviewed much of the research on environmental impact, and they noted the importance of such variables as group influences, leadership styles, and organizational climate in the determination of employee performance. Again, however, we must consider the interactive dynamics between such factors and other individuals and job-related factors. Thus, it is possible that high group cohesion (a work environment characteristic) may be a much more potent influence on behavior for a person with a high need for affiliation (an individual characteristic) than for a person with a low need for affiliation. Persons with high needs for achievement may be less influenced by the degree of group cohesion and more interested in potential economic rewards. Moreover, a job that lacks enrichment (a job-related characteristic) may be eased somewhat by a supervisor who shows a good deal of consideration toward his or her subordinates (another work environment characteristic).

The important point, then, is that when we consider the variables involved in work motivation, we must take a strong, integrative approach. We must study *relationships* between variables rather than focus on one specific topic. Only then can we achieve a greater understanding of the complexities of the motivational process.

REVIEW OF MAJOR THEORIES

A central purpose of any theory is to organize in a meaningful fashion the major sets of variables associated with the topic under study. In fact, one test of the usefulness of a theory or model is the degree to which it can account for a wide diversity of variables while simultaneously integrating them into a cohesive—and succinct—unifying framework. Such a theory of work motivation would ideally account for variables from the three major areas discussed above (individual, job, and work environment), as well as consider the implications of interactive effects among these areas. Unfortunately, such a totally unifying theory does not appear to exist at this time. What does exist is a set of different theories that address themselves to one or more of these sets of variables, none of which, however, is completely and thoroughly comprehensive (both in terms of hypothesized inter-action effects among the variables and in terms of accounting for a diverse array of evidence).

In the absence of a "master" theory, it may be well to review briefly the several major theories that were discussed in the early chapters of this book. In this way, we can see to what extent they do deal with different sets of variables and thus compare their relative explanatory power. As was stated at the end of Chapter 1, however, many of the theoretical approaches are complementary rather than contradictory. Thus it is often not just a matter of choosing which is the "best" theory, but rather one of deciding which approaches are, *relatively speaking,* the most helpful for understanding particular aspects of employee work behavior.

The need theories of Maslow, McClelland, and others and Deci's focus on intrinsic motivation are primarily individual theories of motivation. Strong emphasis is placed on the characteristics of the individual, and these models represent highly developed statements concerning the role played by personal need strengths in the determination of work behavior. While the influences of the job and work environment are not central themes, it is easy to see how such factors could play a major role in these models. For example, for employees with a strong need for self-actualization, providing a work environment that would promote fulfillment of this need should increase their propensity to remain with the organization and respond positively to organizational objectives. A similar argument could be advanced for creating an achievement-oriented work environment under McClelland's learned needs model for individuals who develop high need for achievement. Even so, although a good deal of speculation is possible concerning how such a job and environmental variables might affect personal need satisfaction and performance, it should be recognized that such considerations are dealt with relatively lightly in these models.

Next, reinforcement approaches were discussed and analyzed. It is clear that of all the theoretical approaches considered in this book, reinforcement theory is the one that places by far the heaviest emphasis on the work environment cluster of variables. For those who advocate this approach, the response of the work environment—including its various elements such as the work group, the supervisor, and company reward practices—is *the* controlling factor in affecting employee behavior (assuming a given level of ability). The notion of individual differences, and particularly the notion of individual needs and attitudes, is virtually ignored by this approach. Rather, as stressed earlier in the book, the reinforcement approach to explaining behavior is epitomized by the aphorism, "Behavior is a function of its consequences." Thus, this kind of orientation to understanding motivated behavior in the organizational setting deliberately focuses on, basically, only one set of variables—the reaction of the environment to specific behaviors.

The next category of theories were essentially cognitive-based models (Chapter 4) that emphasized person-environment interactions. Here we examined several related theories, including equity theory, expectancy/valence theory, and social learning theory. It was noted that equity theory centers on the relationship between individual characteristics—attitudes toward inputs and outcomes, tolerance for feelings of inequity, and the like—and work environment characteristics (especially systemwide reward practices). This process-oriented approach does place considerable stress on the individual's *perceptual* reactions to environmental variables, and in that sense the theory considers interactive effects. The approach does not, however, provide a comprehensive framework for integrating the major sets of variables affecting motivation at work, and in particular it fails to consider many of the other impacts of these variables (besides producing feelings of equity or inequity).

Expectancy/valence theory can be examined in terms of how it deals with the three major sets of variables—individual, job, and work environment. To begin with, the theory is specific in dealing with the role of individual differences. It recognizes individual variations in need strengths by acknowledging that not everyone values the same rewards equally; people attach different valences to potential outcomes. People also differ in their perceptions of how equitable a given level of rewards is (in relation to their own standards of comparison). Moreover, the model particularly emphasizes that individuals have differing beliefs, or expectancies, that certain actions on their part will ultimately lead to desired rewards. Expectancy/valence theory also encompasses job-related variables by pointing to how these factors can affect future expectancies and by arguing that job attributes can at times serve as sources of intrinsically valued rewards. The more sophisticated versions of the model have also included the notion of role clarity; that is, performance can often be improved by specifying more carefully the direction of behavior. Finally, expectancy/valance theory focuses fairly explicitly on several work environment influences on performance, particularly those relating to reward structures. Throughout, this model stresses the necessity of analyzing relationships between variables as a prerequisite to an understanding of the motivation *process*. It does, however, place heavy (some would say too heavy) emphasis on individuals' cognitions about how their own behavior will or will not lead to particular outcomes potentially available in the work situation. Whether individuals actually engage in the kinds of thought processes implied by the theory is the major issue to be raised with the conceptual approach.

Similar conclusions can be drawn about social learning theory. This type of model emphasizes the important role of self-efficacy in the motivational process. Social learning theory recognizes that there are individual differences in self-efficacy—but does not give those differences major attention. Rather, important job and work environment determinants of self-efficacy are highlighted. In addition, this approach focuses on the influence of role modeling and goal-setting in directing the behavior of individuals in organizations. It should be noted that all three of the cognitive-based models (social learning, expectancy/valence, and equity) attach considerable importance to individual thought processes as employees attempt to make sense out of their work environment and decide how they will perform in work activities. The unique contribution of the social learning approach is its explicit focus on the *reciprocal* relationships between the person, his or her behavior, and the environment.

In summary, each of these theories has something to offer in the attempt to explain motivation in the work situation. Also, as we have emphasized several times, various parts of the theories are, in many ways, complementary. For example, individuals who have particularly strong needs, (e.g., for achievement) may also be inclined to make equity comparisons with regard to how their peers are being rewarded in relation to the types and amounts of rewards that they themselves are receiving. In addition, they are also likely to be sensitive to what it is that they do that results in "good" responses (from supervisors, peers, the organization, etc.) and thus are likely to form ideas (i.e., "expectancies") that a certain action (behavior) on their part will, or will not, result in a "good response" (i.e., a reward) next time. In other words, it seems clear that each of the major approaches to motivation provides an important *perspective* from which to view motivation, and—and this is *crucial*—these perspectives are not necessarily contradictory but rather provide a comprehensive viewpoint that permits an increased and (it is hoped) sophisticated understanding. If there is any utility to studying motivational theories, it is exactly this fact: One can obtain more meaning about the events and situations that one observes or takes part in if one knows something about the theories than if one is not familiar with them. In this sense, improved knowledge about motivational processes is requisite not only for management but also for the employees themselves if all members are to contribute more effectively to the goals of the organization and simultaneously receive greater personal satisfaction.

IMPLICATIONS FOR MANAGEMENT

As we have found, the level of understanding concerning work motivation has increased considerably in the past several decades. However, when we survey current practice in this area, we soon discover that there is a sizable discrepancy in a number of organizations between such practice and many of the more advanced theories of motivations. Why does such a discrepancy exist? There are several possible explanations.

First, many managers still hold conservative beliefs about how much employees really want to contribute on a job. They still tend to view motivation as largely a "carrot-and-stick" process, despite the fact that current research has demonstrated that employees by and large want active involvement in organizational activities.

Second, owing primarily to increased automation and machine-placed technology, some managers apparently feel that motivation is no longer a critical issue, since production control is often largely out of the employee's hands. Such a position ignores, however, the impact that turnover, absenteeism, strikes, output restrictions, and the like have on productivity, even with machine-paced technology. And, of course, the potential effects of motivation levels on performance are greatly increased as we move toward a more service-oriented economy (and, indeed, as one considers the *management* sector of organizations; if motivation differences have an impact anywhere, it is among *managers* themselves).

Third, considering the attitudes of some labor union leaders, we find that a few such leaders apparently still feel that increasing motivational and performance levels might ultimately lead to fewer jobs. Such attitudes in the past have led to the strengthening of the status quo insofar as potential changes in the performance environment were concerned.

It is our contention that such reasoning is somewhat superficial and is, to a large extent, unfounded. The creation of a stimulating, productive, and satisfying work environment can be beneficial for both management and workers if honest concern is shown for all parties involved. If everyone is to derive some benefit from such an environment, however, the problems of the *employee* must be clearly recognized and taken into account. The pivotal role in this process belongs to managers (and, particularly, to upper-level managers) because of their influence in determining the characteristics of the performance environment. If improvements are to be made, management must take the first step. Assuming such an orientation, several implications for managerial practices can be drawn from the material presented here. While this list is not intended to be all-inclusive, we do feel that it points to several of the more important conclusions to be drawn:

1 Perhaps one of the most important lessons to be learned from the data reviewed here is that if managers truly want to improve performance and work attitudes, they must take an active role in *managing* motivational processes at work. Managing motivation is conscious, intentional behavior; it is not something that just happens. Any organization desiring to improve attitudes or work behavior must therefore accept responsibility for active involvement and participation if such changes are to be successful.

2 Any attempt by managers to improve the motivational levels of their subordinates should be prefaced by a self-examination on the part of the managers themselves. Are they aware of their major strengths *and* their major limitations? Do they have a clear notion of their own wants, desires, and expectations from their jobs? Are their perceptions of themselves consistent with the perceptions others have of them? In short, before managers attempt to deal with others, they should have a clear picture of their own role in the organizational milieu.

3 The importance of recognizing individual differences across employees has been pointed to time and again throughout the studies reviewed here. Managers should be sensitive to variations in employees' needs, abilities, and traits. Similarly, they should recognize that different employees have different preferences (valences) for the rewards available for good performance. Research has shown, for example, that money as a reward is much more important to some than to others. A greater awareness of such variations allows managers to utilize most efficiently the diversity of talents among their subordinates and, within policy limitations, to reward good performance with those things most desirable to the employees.

4 Somewhat relatedly, it is important that employees (i.e., anyone in the organization) see a clear relation between successful performance on their part and the receipt of their desired rewards. It therefore becomes incumbent upon management to be able to identify superior performers and reward them accordingly. When this is done, employee expectations generally increase, and this in turn should lead to greater effort toward goal attainment. Such an implication raises questions about the use of non-merit-based compensation systems and of seniority as a major factor in promotions. Where rewards are not based upon performance, we would expect motivational levels to be markedly reduced.

5 A further factor to consider is the nature of the tasks which employees are asked to perform. Questions should be raised by management concerning the feasibility of providing employees with jobs that offer greater challenge, diversity, and opportunities for personal need satisfaction. Managers might begin by putting themselves in the place of their subordinates and asking themselves what they would get out of doing such a job. Similarly, questions should be raised as to whether employees understand exactly what is expected of them. Research has shown that increasing role clarity on a job generally increases the likelihood of improving task performance.

6 In a broader sense, managers could give increased attention to the quality of the overall work environment. How are group dynamics affecting performance? Are the current styles of leadership effective, or would other styles be preferable? In short, is the "climate" within the work group such that it would facilitate task accomplishment or do obvious barriers exist that can be remedied?

7 In many cases greater efforts could be made to assess worker attitudes on a continual basis. In the past, attitude surveys have received little attention outside of personnel departments, or sometimes they have been used as a tool of last resort when managers noted a decline in performance. A more effective strategy might be to monitor job attitudes and use such information as a motivational barometer to identify potential trouble spots. It is essential for managers to become intelligent consumers of behavioral data so that they can act more from a position of knowledge and understanding than from one of uncertainty or ignorance.

8 Finally, if employee motivational levels—and consequently performance— are to be increased, it becomes especially important to involve the employees themselves in a cooperative venture aimed at improving output, for after all they too have a stake in what happens to the organization. Thus, one key factor in motivating employees is to engage them more fully in the processes aimed at attaining organizational effectiveness. Without employee cooperation and support, a great deal of managerial energy can be wasted.

In summary, it is our belief that theories of motivation, like research in the behavioral sciences in general, are useful for practicing managers and employees and are not solely for academicians. Their value lies primarily in their capacity to sensitize managers and researchers to specific factors and processes that can have an important bearing on the behavior of people at work. In this sense, theories and research data in the area of motivation are one more tool available to managers—and to employees—in the performance of their jobs.

NAME INDEX